Jolly Sailors Bold: Ballads and Songs *of* the American Sailor

excavated from whalemen's shipboard manuscripts in the
Kendall Collection of the New Bedford Whaling Museum

Stuart M. Frank

CAMSCO MUSIC
East Windsor, New Jersey
2010

© 2010 by Stuart M. Frank. All rights reserved.

Published by CAMSCO Music
145 Hickory Corner Road, East Windsor, NJ 08520

ISBN 978-1-935243-91-5 (Cloth)
ISBN 978-1-935243-90-8 (Paper)

Second Printing

COVER ILLUSTRATION: *Hornpipe.* Anonymous whaleman's scrimshaw on a sperm whale tooth, circa the 1840s. Loosely after an illustration entitled "Improvidence if Sailors," in *Tales of the Ocean* by Hawser Martingale [John Sherburne Sleeper], New York, 1840. Kendall Collection, New Bedford Whaling Museum.

TITLE PAGE ILLUSTRATION: *Dans la Grand'hune.* Sheet music illustration by the French artist Jules David (1808-1892), lithographed by Guillet (of Paris) for lyrics by Félix Mouttet and music by Paul Henrion, Paris, 1849. Author's Collection.

TO THE MEMORY OF

Bob Frank
Mark Herman
and
Bruce Rosenberg

Table of Contents

Acknowledgements	vii
Introduction	ix
A Few Words about Chanteys	xix

Chapter One — Classical Songs of the Sea: An Eighteenth-Century Garland — 1
1. Black-Eyed Susan [Dark-Eyed Susan] — 2
2. Tom Bowling [Poor Tom] (Dibdin) — 5
3. Bay of Biscay O — 7
4. The Storm [Cease, Rude Boreas] — 8
5. Henry Martin [Salt Sea] (Child #250) — 10
6. The *Bold Trinity* (Child #286) — 13
7. High Barbary (Child #285; Laws #K-33) — 16
8. Spanish Ladies [Farewell and Adieu] — 18

Chapter Two — The Girl I Left Behind Me: Songs About Women — 21
9. The Girl I Left Behind Me — 23
10. The Lily of Lake Champlain — 25
11. The Norfolk Girls — 28
12. My Dream — 30
13. My Wife—A Song — 31
14. Lines to Mary — 33
15. The Carpenter and the Maid — 34
16. The Milking Maid — 36
17. Frozen Limb — 37
18. Can Ladies Be Compared to Man ? — 38

Chapter Three — The Sailors' Farewell: Songs of Parting — 39
19. The Lowlands of Holland — 40
20. The Nantucket Mother and Daughter — 43
21. The Banks of the Schuylkill — 45
22. West's Farewell — 47
23. The British Man-of-War [The Yankee Man-of-War] — 48
24. The Captain Calls All Hands — 51
25. Farewell, Charming Nancy (Laws #K-14) — 53
26. Adieu, Sweet Lovely Nancy — 55
27. My Mary Ann [Mary Ann] — 57
28. Outward Bound — 59
29. The Sailor Boy's Farewell — 60
30. The Ship Is Ready — 62
31. Caledonia [Jamie Raeburn's Farewell] — 64

Chapter Four — Jolly Sailors Bold: Deepwater Songs and Ballads — 66
32. Jolly Sailors Bold [Sailors' Come-All-Ye] — 67
33. Boston ['Twas on the Twenty-First of May] — 71
34. Captain Avery — 74
35. The *Brooklyn* — 75
36. The *Dreadnought* (Laws #D-13) — 77
37. Eighteen Hundred Forty-Nine — 80
38. Unmooring [The Boatswain's Call] — 81
39. The Loss of the *Ramillies* (Laws #K-1) — 84
40. Prince Edward's Isle — 86
41. Homeward Bound — 88
42. We'll Soon Be There — 89
43. Sweet America — 90

Chapter Five — Heave Away, My Hearties: Deepwater Chanteys — 91
44. The Sailor's Alphabet — 92
45. Goodbye, Fare Ye Well — 95
46. Heave Away [We're All Bound to Go] — 97
47. Reuben Ranzo — 99
48. Old Horse — 101
49. Homeward Bound and Outward Bound — 104
50. Homeward Bound (II) — 107

Chapter Six — Battle Pieces: Naval, Military, and Patriotic Ballads — 109
51. Paul Jones's Victory (Laws #A-4) — 110
52. *Constitution* and *Guerriere* (Laws #A-6) — 113
53. Columbia's Ships — 115
54. The Sinking of the *Commodore* — 117
55. The Hills of Chilia — 118
56. The *Somers* — 119
57. The *Monitor* and the *Merrimac* — 122
58. Lee's Invasion of Maryland — 125
59. *Florida*'s Crew [The *Florida*'s Cruise] — 127
60. Navy Song [We Ride Head to Wind] — 130

Chapter Seven — A Bonny Bunch of Roses: Napoleonic Songs and Ballads — 131
61. Bonaparte Crossing the Alps — 132
62. Bonaparte on the Isle of St. Helena — 133
63. Bonny Bunch of Roses O (Laws #J-5) — 135
64. The Drummer Boy of Waterloo (Laws #J-1) — 137
65. Napoleon's Dream [Bonaparte's Dream] — 139
66. The Green Linnet (O'Neill #1262) — 142

Chapter Eight — Tarry Trousers: Ballads of Lovers Lost and Lovers Spurned — 145
67. Lady Franklin's Lament (Laws #K-9) — 146
68. The Sailor Bride's Lament (Laws #K-10) — 151
69. The Sailor Boy (Laws #K-12) — 153
70. Mary's Dream (Laws #K-20) — 156
71. The Maid on the Shore (Laws #K-27) — 158
72. Green Beds [Young Johnny] (Laws #K-36) — 160
73. The Sailor and the Country Girl (Laws #K-38) — 162
74. The Maiden's Pride Punished — 164
75. Bright Phoebe — 165
76. Tarry Trousers [The Mother and Daughter] — 166

Chapter Nine — Love Impeded: Ballads of Family Opposition to Lovers — 169
77. Early, Early in the Spring (Laws #M-1) — 170
78. William and Harriet (Laws #M-7) — 171
79. The Banks of Sweet Dundee (Laws #M-25) — 173
80. The Bold Soldier (Laws #M-27) — 177
81. Vilikins and His Dinah (Laws #M-31b) — 179
82. The Constant Farmer's Son (Laws #M-33) — 181
83. Edwin in the Lowlands Low (Laws #M-34) — 183

Chapter Ten — Love Entangled: Ballads of Lovers' Disguises and Tricks — 185
84. Jack Munroe (Laws #N-7) — 185
85. The Silk Merchant's Daughter (Laws #N-10) — 188

86.	The Handsome Cabin Boy (Laws #N-13)	193
87.	The Noble Duke (Laws #N-15)	195
88.	The Prince of Morocco [The Sailor Boy's Trick] (Laws #N-18)	197
89.	The Dark-Eyed Sailor (Laws #N-35)	200
90.	The Mantle So Green (Laws #N-38)	203
91.	The Pride of Glencoe (Laws #N-39)	205

**Chapter Eleven — The Jolly Roving Tar:
Ballads of Faithful and Unfaithful Lovers** 209

92.	Cuper's Garden [Cobit's Garden]	212
93.	The Lass of Mohee (Laws #H-8)	213
94.	The Jacket of Blue	217
95.	Ellen the Fair (Laws #O-5)	219
96.	The Sailor and the Shepherdess (Laws #O-8)	220
97.	The Jolly Sailor	222
98.	The Sailor's Return	223
99.	Green Mossy Banks of the Lea (Laws #O-15)	224
100.	The Bold Fisherman (Laws #O-24)	226
101.	The Jolly Roving Tar (Laws #O-27)	227
102.	The Bold Privateer (Laws #O-32)	228
103.	William Riley	229
104.	Jemmy on the Sea	231
105.	The Sailor and the Tailor (Laws #P-4)	233
106.	The Pride of Kildare (Laws #P-6)	234
107.	The Rakish Young Fellow	236
108.	Mary of the Wild Moor (Laws #P-21)	238
109.	Caroline of Edinburgh Town (Laws #P-27)	239
110.	Oxford City (Laws #P-30)	241
111.	Jack Robinson	242

**Chapter Twelve — Terra Incognita:
Comic and Convivial Songs** 244

112.	All Around The Room [Ellen Taylor]	245
113.	Charming Jane Louisa	248
114.	The Cove Wot Spouts	250
115.	I Am One of the Boys [One of the Boys]	251
116.	Sailors Ashore	253
117.	He Is Only Gone Home with a Friend	254
118.	Jayne's Hair Tonic [Dr. Jayne's Hair Tonic]	255
119.	Come Landlord Fill the Flowing Bowl	256
120.	Lannigan's Ball [Lanigan's Ball]	257
121.	The Wild Rover	259

**Chapter Thirteen — Lubbers and Swabs:
Miscellaneous Songs and Curiosities** 260

122.	The Cobbler	261
123.	Dick Turpin's Bonny Black Bess (Laws #L-9)	263
124.	Dick Turpin and the Lawyer (Laws #L-10)	265
125.	Johnny Sands (Laws #Q-3)	266
126.	The Farmer's Boy (Laws #Q-30)	268
127.	Doran's Ass	270
128.	Limerick Races	272
129.	The Pearl of the Sea	274
130.	Et Tu Bruce	275
131.	There's Changes in the Mill	277
132.	Go Down Moses [Let My People Go]	278
133.	The Parson's Narrative	280

**Chapter Fourteen — There She Blows:
Classic Whaling Songs** 283

134.	The Greenland Whale Fishery (Laws #K-21)	284
135.	Arctic Whaling Song	287
136.	The Coast of Peru (Laws #D-26)	289
137.	Diego's Bold Shores	293
138.	There She Blows [The Wounded Whale]	295
139.	Blow Ye Winds ['Tis Advertised In Boston]	298
140.	The Bold Harpooner [Captain Bunker]	302
141.	The Wonderful Whale [Jack and the Whale]	304
142.	How to Catch a Whale	306
143.	Rolling Down to Old Mohee	308
144.	No Ke Ano Ahiahi [Hawaiian Song]	313

**Chapter Fifteen — The Whaleman's Lament:
Original Whaling Songs** 317

145.	One Year in a Blubber Hunter	318
146.	The *Aurora*'s Whaling Song	320
147.	The Schooner *Varnum Hill*	321
148.	Stanzas from the *Mermaid*	324
149.	On a Passage to the Crozet Islands	325
150.	Cape Horn	327
151.	Address to Young Sailors	328
152.	The Lay System	329
153.	Landsmen One and All	330
154.	The Whaleman's Lament	331
155.	I and Betty Martin	333
156.	Indian Ocean Whaling Song	335
157.	Bowhead Whaling Song	337
158.	All the Whales Are Wild and Ugly	340
159.	A Song of the Hatteras Whale	341
160.	I Was Once a Sailor Lad	342

**Chapter Sixteen — "Plenty of Music":
Two Voyages of the Bark *Kathleen*** 344

161.	A Voyage on New Holland	346
162.	Song Composed aboard the Bark *Kathleen*	355

**Chapter Seventeen — "Musick on the Brain":
Frederick Howland Smith's Tune List** 359

163.	Fisher's Hornpipe (O'Neill #1575, 1576)	361
164.	The White Cockade (O'Neill #1803)	362
165.	Zip Coon [Turkey in the Straw]	363
166.	Rory O'More (O'Neill #856)	363
167.	Oh, Dear, What Can the Matter Be?	364
168.	Harvest Home Waltz	365
169.	Soldier's Joy (O'Neill #1642)	365
170.	Pop! Goes the Weasel	366
171.	Yankee Doodle	367
172.	Russian Waltz	369
173.	The Poor Old Slave	369
174.	Nelly Gray [Darling Nelly Gray]	371
175.	Nelly Bly (Foster)	374
176.	Augusta's Favorite	375
177.	Oh! Susanna [Susanna] (Foster)	375
178.	Fanny Elssler Leaving New Orleans	376
179.	Off She Goes (O'Neill #914)	378
180.	The Old Leather Breeches (O'Neill #167, 763)	379
181.	Home, Sweet Home	380
182.	Old Folks at Home [Swanee River] (Foster)	381

Chapter Eighteen — Hurrah For the Sea: Parlor Songs of Ships and Seafaring		382
183.	The Heart that Can Feel for Another	385
184.	Bounding Billows, Cease Your Motion	386
185.	Lashed to the Helm	387
186.	Saturday Night at Sea [The Sailor Boy]	388
187.	The Minute Gun at Sea	389
188.	Steady She Goes	391
189.	True Yankee Sailor [True British Sailor]	392
190.	The White Squall	393
191.	The Sailor's Consolation [Barney Buntline]	395
192.	A Wet Sheet and a Flowing Sea	397
193.	The Sea [The Sea, the Sea, the Open Sea]	399
194.	The Sailor Boy's Last Dream	401
195.	Over the Mountain Wave	403
196.	Poor Bessy [The Parting]	404
197.	The Fisher's Wife [The Fisherman]	405
198.	A Life on the Ocean Wave	407
199.	The Sailor Boy's Carol	408
200.	The Soldier's Tear	409
201.	The Sailor's Tear	411
202.	Hurrah for the Sea [A Home on the Mountain Wave]	412
203.	Away, Away o'er the Boundless Deep [The Buccaneer's Bride]	415
204.	I'm Afloat, I'm Afloat [The Rover of the Sea]	417
205.	The Pirate of the Isles	419
206.	The Robbers of the Glen	421
207.	Pirates' Chorus (Balfe)	423
208.	The Life of a Tar	423
209.	Our Way Across the Sea	424
210.	Jamie's on the Stormy Sea	425
211.	Willie's on the Dark Blue Sea	427
212.	Good News from Home	428

Appendix 1 Nature and Nancy: Dibdin's Songs		431
213.	The Signal to Engage	432
214.	Poor Jack	433
215.	Saturday Night at Sea	435
216.	Who Cares?	436
217.	Nature and Nancy	438
218.	The Lass that Loves A Sailor	439

Appendix 2 How Cheery Are the Mariners: Sailors' Parlor Songs of Seafaring		441
219.	The Sailor	442
220.	How Cheery Are the Mariners	443
221.	On New Year's Day	444
222.	The Sailor Is a Wanderer Free	444
223.	O Think of the Sailor	444
224.	We're Bounding o'er the Dark Blue Sea	445
225.	The Sailor on the Ocean Wide	445
226.	The Mariner's Song [Gaily We Go]	446
227.	A Seaman's Life	446
228.	Farewell to the Arctic	447

Appendix 3 The King of the Boundless Sea: Selected Whaling Poems		448
229.	The King of the Southern Sea	449
230.	The Sailor Boy's Dream	450
231.	Wood and Black-Skin	453

Appendix 4 The Homebound Whaleman	456

Appendix 5 John Martin's Musical Programme	458

Appendix 6 Biographical Notes on the Diarists and Journal-Keepers	462

Appendix 7 Inventory of Additional Song Texts	477

References	498

Bibliography	509
Primary Sources	509
Secondary Sources	511
Informants	521

Glossary of Technical Terms	522

Index of Lyricists and Composers	524

Index of Titles, Alternate Titles, First Lines, and Tunes	524

Masthead lookout with bare poles, from J. Ross Browne, *Etchings of a Whaling Cruise* (1846).

Acknowledgements

So many people contributed generously and substantially to so many aspects of this book that I can do little more than simply list them here as a token of my profound and enduring gratitude, along with a disclaimer that any errors, shortfalls, or misinterpretations are surely my own.

Some of those to whom the greatest debt is owed are several whom I was privileged to count among my most cherished friends and closest mentors, and are now among the dear departed. They deserve special mention here: Bill Doerflinger, Mark Herman, David Hirsch, Stan Hugill, Henry Kendall, Bob Kotta, Louis Mink, Buck Ramsey, Duke Schirmer, and Stuart Sherman. Also gone from our midst are several who provided useful citations, biographical details, and textual insights during the past thirty years: Dorothy Brewington, Alan Lomax, Sam Morrill, Charles Nichols, U. Utah Phillips, and Arthur Schrader.

In standpoint of inspiration and guidance, the contributions and wise counsel of Raymond Bliss, Ellen Cohn, David Krause, Patrick Malone, Thomas Philbrick, Bruce Rosenberg, and Barton St. Armand were of singular importance and inestimable value to me. They set very high standards, and I earnestly hope that this result vindicates their investment of time and effort in my behalf, and in some measure meets with their expectations and approval.

I am deeply indebted to Steve Gardham, who generously guided me to ballad sources that eluded the first iterations of the manuscript; to Dick Greenhaus, whom I am grateful and proud to call my publisher, for his patience and wisdom; and to Catherine Reynolds, for her heroic efforts at the grinding labor of proofreading.

I could not have hoped to track down all of the materials required for the research without the gracious help of knowledgeable and supportive friends and colleagues: Virginia Adams, Douglas Allen, Eline Anders, Tony Barrand, Joshua Basseches, Edmund Berkeley, Jr., Lee Carle, Bertha Chandler, David Cruthers, Paul Cyr, Michael Dyer, Sharon Elliot, Rob Ellis, Paul Fees, James A. Frazier, Sunnee Gallup, Greg Gibson, Bill and Kerstin Gilkerson, Ken Gloss, Glenn Gordinier, Tom Goux, Jacqueline Haring, Hisayasu Hatanaka, Rev. Stephen Holmes, the late Mrs. William B. Holmes, Henry Hornblower III, Llewellyn Howland III, Gregory Johnson, Tetsuo Kawasumi, David Kleiman, Edward Lefkowitz, Stanley Lemons, Judy Lund, Alan MacLeod, Sandy Marrone, Ken Martin, Rheta Martin, Valerie Murphy, Paul O'Pecko, Laura Pereira, Bill Peterson, Nancy Elizabeth Pick, Caroline Preston, Roberto Ramacciotti, Gare Reid, John Roberts, Doug Stein, Amy Stillman, Michael Stone, Jacek Sulanowski, Dick Swain, Elizabeth Tatar, Bob Walser, Jeff Warner, Bob Webb, and Andy Wilkinson. I am also grateful for many wonderful bits of help provided by twenty years worth of valiant volunteers and Curatorial Interns at the Kendall Whaling Museum and ten years at the New Bedford Whaling Museum; by the fine folks in the Music Department at the Boston Pubic Library, the John Hay Library at Brown University, the Olin Library at Wesleyan University, the Trinity College Library and Irish Traditional Music Archive in Dublin, and the Lester Levy Music Collection at Johns Hopkins University. The New Bedford Whaling Museum graciously extended permission for many of the illustrations (as noted in the text), for which I am indebted to James Russell, Michael Lapides, and Kate Mello.

And of course I am indebted to my dear parents, Pearl Frank and the late Bob Frank, for their unfailing support, persistent goading, and enthusiastic encouragement; and Mary Malloy, without whom there would be little music in my life.

Stuart Frank
Foxborough, Massachusetts
16 December 2010

Introduction

> In the afternoon music with dancing, cheering and all sorts of nonsense…
> in the evening singing music & deviltry.
> — John Martin's journal, ship *Lucy Ann*, 1842.

On 28 November 1841, a 21-year-old native Pennsylvanian and third-time whaleman, John F. Martin, pen and brush in hand, set sail from Wilmington, Delaware, as Able Bodied Seaman in the ship *Lucy Ann*. She would carry him once again halfway round the world, past the stormy Capes to the baking oppression of the tropic sun and the dark incognita of the rocky Siberian coast, on what would turn out to be a voyage of 31 months. Like generations of whalemen before, and three generations of whalemen after, he would bend his back at a long oar in an eggshell craft in pursuit of the terrible leviathan; would bask dogwatches in the gentle tropic breezes, stave off tedium through lonely hours at the masthead aloft, freeze his fingers and his toes in the howling, eternal winter of the Arctic; and from day to day, week upon week, year upon year, would frolic mischievously on liberty ashore in far flung out-ports and exotic South Sea islands, supping indifferently at sea on ugly salt-beef and hardtack. He would converse with bronze aboriginals on islands not-so-enchanted, would cut blubber and render oil on the storm-tossed North Pacific, tipple in the rowdy taverns of Peru, holystone a heaving deck to the incongruous strains of fiddle music, survey scrimshandering shipmates with a scurvy eye, play his bugle in the ship's band, and, like any sailor in any ship in any age, would complain about just about everything, wishing the whole time to be back home among friends and sleep through the night in a comfortable bed.

Like Richard Henry Dana, Jr., Francis Allyn Olmsted, and Herman Melville,[1] John Martin was attentive to the cheering effects of music on shipboard and took even greater pains than they to describe musical affairs on his own vessel. As whaleships go, the *Lucy Ann*'s was rather a musical company. While Martin transcribed no song texts, nor wrote any original lyrics of his own, he provides insights into the several contexts in which songs and music were an integral feature of day-to-day life at sea.

In the *Lucy Ann*, at least, from the very first day, "All hands were in high spirits at the time having a band of Music on board, composed of a Drum, Fife, Bugle & giving three hearty cheers was responded to on shore…." (28 Nov. 1841). Naturally, the "band" was called forth by popular acclamation on holidays and special occasions. As a bugler and occasional impresario, Martin took care to note the particulars:

Friday January 1st 1842… in the evening roused out the Old year with songs and merriment.

Monday July 4th [1842] The anniversary of the declaration of our Independence. The day opened with a young gale of wind from the E[astwar]d. Ship heading to the S[outwar]d. we had nothing to do all day after sail was made — in the forenoon the Captain & officers practiced firing at a mark. Mr. Dunott [one of the mates] knocked a junk bottle from the fore yard arm with a ball from his fowling piece. the Captain was the best shot with the Ships pistols — at noon we had a first rate sea pie for dinner made of fresh pork — in the afternoon music with dancing, cheering and all sorts of nonsense. towards evening a sail in sight, she proved to be the Dutch East Indiaman bound home. Hen & Jim amused themselves all day by cleaning out the try pots & coolers. in the evening singing music and deviltry.

---

[1] Dana's *Two Years Before the Mast* (New York, 1840) was the first realistic narrative of sailing "before the mast" as a common sailor in a merchantman; analogously, Olmsted's *Incidents of a Whaling Voyage* (New York, 1841) was the first one rooted in the whaling trade; and Melville's *Moby Dick* (New York, 1851) is now recognized as a towering work of serious literature. These are among the reigning classics of firsthand American seafaring narratives, the latter of course highly fictionalized. The ship *Lucy Ann* of Wilmington, the American whaler in which Martin sailed, is not to be confused with the whaleship *Lucy Ann* of Sydney, Australia, in which Melville's contemporaneous temporary stint provided some of the materials for *Omoo* (New York, 1848).

A *gam,* or intermural social visit among whaling crews at sea, could also provide an occasion for music, as Martin relates about his own shipmates gamming with the captain and crew of the New Bedford bark *Canton Packet* aboard the *Lucy Ann* in January 1843:

> Wednesday Janry 26th [1843] of course we done our best to please the crew who were a decent set of chaps. we made them a present from the forecastle of Turkey, Oranges, Bannanas, Cocoanuts, Sugar cane &c. the boat steerers treated them to some wine that they had saved for such occasions. we also exchanged books & newspapers after which we had singing & dancing. some excellent songs were sung, such as One eyed riley, Morgan Ratler, Oh, if I had her, Dingi i otten dotten & other fashionable airs (I mean among sailors).[2] when they left they promised to see us again on New Holland.[3]

The crew celebrated the eighteen-month anniversary of their voyage with a "foo-foo" band made up of kitchen implements, which must have made quite a hit with the officers:

> 28th May [1843] To day is $1\frac{1}{2}$ years since we left the mouth of the Brandywine. We had a grand concert of Instrumental & vocal music on the strength of it on combs (Fine tooth), Triangle, pet pig, Tin pots, pans, & spoons, Cat & divers other musical instruments.

There are also many references to music on ordinary days. One fellow is punished for dancing instead of working, "on account of his feigning sickness in the day time" (10 Dec. 1841); the mate procured a new fiddle for use only in scraping-down the deck, a practice borrowed from the Royal Navy and in this case sanctioned by the "aftercabin" (the captain and officers); and many evenings were filled with band practice and extemporaneous singing and dancing:

> [Dec. 13, 1841] in the evening... spinning yarns with flute and violin acompaniment.... [Dec. 14, 1841] in the evening music and singing as usual.... [Jan. 3, 1842:] At night had a grand musical soiree on the forward deck with Bugle, Fife, Drum, Violin &c. The sounds were truly heart rending & would [have] astonished the natives had there been any of them near [enough] to have heard it.... [June 15, 1842] we have fine warm weather & beautiful moonlit evenings. after sail is taken in we generally commence with a dozen or two tunes by the whole band then practice Reels, Jigs, Cotillions, top off with singing.... [July 10, 1842:] in the evening singing hymns.... [Apr. 20, 1843] at night took in sail as usual. we still have jollifications at night after sail is taken in, some singing and dancing, some scrimshawing, others reading or writing, but far the greatest number patching [clothing]. some of us are a complete mass of patches of all colours.... [May 21, 1843] in the evening singing hymns and talking about home... .

The shipboard journals of John Martin in the 1840s; Lizzie Marble, whaling on New Holland in the '50s; New London whaleman Charles Durgin, wintering-over at Hudson's Bay in the '60s; Captain George Comer, at Hudson Bay a generation later; and Fanny Weeks, wife of the master of the auxiliary-steam bark *Beluga,* wintering with the Western Arctic fleet at Herschel Island off Alaska, in 1895—among many others—reveal that not only were many ad hoc evenings passed in extemporaneous singing and dancing, but more than a few shipboard musical and theatrical soirees were ceremoniously planned and carefully organized. Lizzie Marble, a captain's wife, fabricated costumes, encouraged the performers, and helped direct music productions in the Indian Ocean aboard the bark *Kathleen* of New Bedford. At Herschel Island, performances were usually initiated and the arrangements made by the wives of the captains, without whose morale-building ministrations the long Arctic winter might have proven truly miserable. Handwritten invitations and programs, listing the performers and the skits and musical pieces to be presented,

---

[2] For identification and a brief discussion of these songs, see Appendix 7.

[3] The so-called New Holland whaling grounds, in the Indian Ocean off Western Australia.

were circulated among the crew or around the entire fleet for all hands to scrutinize. In the Arctic, where months of icebound inactivity kept the fleet together and the inmates ever on the lookout for diversions of any kind, such evening performances were repeated regularly and often. Aboard the *Monticello* of New London at Hudson Bay, whaleman-diarist Charles Durgin was a mainstay of both a shipboard musical troupe and an amateur theatrical company, both of which gave regular evening performances throughout the long winter. He relates that during the day—frozen into the ice, as they were, until the spring thaw—he had little to do beyond minor chores, and so he passed the time enthusiastically making scrimshaw (which he produced in prodigious quantities) and building a banjo.[4]

The same was the case, but to a lesser degree, in the merchant services, where crews were characteristically shorthanded and leisure time less abundant, but where hands were nevertheless often idle. In the North Atlantic packets, plying the routes between Europe and North America, as well as aboard the Cape Horn clippers on the China and California run, the crew would often amuse themselves with music, dance, and song. Occasions are known where the crew mounted performances for the entertainment of passengers. On some vessels, the passengers themselves put on shows for their own diversion. However, as characterized by a participant in the 1850s, most sailors' music on shipboard was spontaneous and extemporaneous, to fill the idle hours:

> During the first part of our voyage great regret was expressed that there were no musical instruments on board, but music like murder will out. An old fiddle was discovered…. In the meantime a jack had begged an old flour sieve from the steward, over which he fastened the dried stomach of a blackfish, and with some bits of tin and copper to make a jangle he had constructed a bona fide tambourine. This brought out a flute from its hiding place, and soon the forecastle resounded to the merry notes of a fiddle, two flutes, the tambourine, bones and a triangle.[5]

Informal singing and dancing were largely free of the oppressive profit- and discipline-motivated scrutiny of the owners, master, and officers; and music was one of the few pastimes accorded to seamen. Thus, musicians and singers were often highly valued on shipboard; in some vessels they were the mainstays of deckside social life in the off hours; many sailors and not a few captains mourned their absence if there did not happen to be any musicians on board. As the presence of songs in mariners' journals readily attests, there was among some sailors (presumably the most musically inclined) a keen interest in swapping and collecting songs. The singing, dancing, and skylarking of sailors in the off hours has invariably figured into firsthand sea-narratives and fictional accounts of the Age of Sail from Dana and Melville onward, and are deeply embedded in popular notions and stereotypes of the sailor as Jolly Jack Tar. Oddly, such images seem to be at loggerheads with the darker and more threatening popular notions about sailors that marginalized them as a labor class and discriminated against them ashore.

Leisure-time songs were of all types; and while they were not customarily used (as chanteys were) in the performance of shipboard duties, they were nonetheless integrally related to life and labor at sea, furnishing a ready outlet for creative self-expression and topical improvisation, providing structure for social interaction, occasionally smoothing the turgid waters of shipboard tension with a camaraderie unavailable elsewhere. This appears to have been the case in just about every service and trade, including the inland canal barges and Great Lakes schooners, and certainly in all the deepwater trades. At core was the sailors' own special repertoire with its own stylistic features and fashions. Dana alludes to most of this in his description of a gam between his own ship, the *Alert,* and the ship *California* at San Diego:

---

[4] Manuscript sources mentioned are in the Kendall Collection at the New Bedford Whaling Museum. "John Martin's Musical Programme," performed aboard the *Lucy Ann* on 16 February 1842, is reproduced as Appendix 7. Charles H. Durgin's analogous playbills and concert programs from the *Monticello* of New London in the 1860s, appear as an appendix in Frank 1998b.

[5] N.W. Taylor 1927, 35.

> Among her crew were two English man-of-war's men, so that, of course, we had music. They sung in the true sailors' style, and the rest of the crew, which was a remarkably musical one, joined in the choruses. They had many of the latest sailor songs, which had not yet got about our merchantmen, and which they were very choice of.
> They began soon after we came on board, and kept it up until after two bells, when the second mate came forward and called "The Alert's away!" Battle-songs, drinking-songs, boat-songs, love songs and everything else, they seemed to have a complete assortment of, and I was glad to find that "All in the Downs," "Poor Tom Bowline," "The Bay of Biscay," "List ye landsmen!" and all those classical songs of the sea, still held their places.

Dana goes on specifically to point out that "genteel" shore songs were also popular at sea, and to draw a distinction between these and the folk songs, ballads, and vernacular pieces alluded to earlier. Most tellingly of all, he is keenly aware (if somewhat disdainful) of the salubrious effect that a good performance has on the crew, and on himself:

> In addition to these, they picked up at the theatres and other places a few songs of a little more genteel cast, which they were very proud of; and I shall never forget hearing an old salt, who had broken his voice by hard drinking on shore, and bellowing from the mast-head in an hundred northwesters, with all manner of ungovernable trills and quavers—in the high notes breaking into falsetto — and in the low ones, growling along like the dying away of the boatswain's "all hands ahoy!" down the hatchway, singing "Oh no, we never mention him." ... This was very popular, and Jack was called upon every night to give them [the ship's companies] his "sentimental song." No one called for it more loudly than I, for the complete absurdity of the execution, and the sailors' perfect satisfaction in it, were ludicrous beyond measure.

* * *

In *Redburn, His First Voyage* (1849), Herman Melville provides a rather more rhapsodic view of sailors' songs and ballads which provides a thematic prologue to this anthology:

> Now music is a holy thing, and its instruments, however humble, are to be loved and revered. Whatever has made, or does make, or may make music, should be held sacred as the golden bridle-bit of the Shah of Persia's horse, and the golden hammer, with which his hoofs are shod. Musical instruments should be like the silver tongs, with which the high-priests tended the Jewish altars— never to be touched by a hand profane. Who would bruise the poorest reed of Pan, though plucked from a beggar's hedge, would insult the melodious god himself.
> And there is no humble thing with music in it, not a fife, not a negro-fiddle, that is not to be reverenced as much as the grandest architectural organ that ever rolled its flood-tide of harmony down a cathedral nave. For even a Jew's harp may be so played, as to awaken all the fairies that are in us, and make them dance in our souls, as on a moon-lit sward of violets.

This anthology is not so much intended as a book *of* songs as a book *about* songs, and more than that, a book about songs in the particular context of seafaring life aboard American ships in the nineteenth century. It is thus equally a book about sailoring and about the men — and a few women—who picked up bag and baggage and ventured out on the great oceans for years on end, hunting whales, transporting cargoes, and trying to punctuate the spartan gloom of sea labor and to ease protracted periods of crushing boredom, with a few modest pastimes and pleasures that could preserve sanity and render life bearable. In the absence of parents, clergy, or teachers to counsel the crew or minister to their psychological, spiritual, intellectual, and sexual condition, and in the absence of any widespread humanitarian regard for the shipboard laboring classes, sailors were left to amuse themselves in whatever leisure hours they were allotted by the often harsh, dictatorial forces that generally controlled almost every aspect of their lives.

In fact, sailors worked for scanty pay under deplorable living conditions, with few rights and privileges.[6] They were perpetually cut off from the pleasures and ordinary comforts of ordinary life ashore. At sea for weeks or months or even years at a time, they had few opportunities to develop and sustain normal relationships of family, church, labor unions, or society at large. In ports-of-call the world round, "respectable" folks ashore characteristically segregated sailors into a separate and distinct class, consigned them to specific locales along the waterfront, denied them the company of their daughters, and at best contributed to the Sunday collection plate from a safe distance.[7] The Sailortowns and waterfront precincts of the major seaports became disreputable avenues of illicit traffic, catering to a vulnerable transient clientele, pandering merchandise suited to the sailors' pent-up needs and prolonged deprivation.[8] A few well-meaning missionaries found their way to the harborfront to improve the spiritual and fiscal lot of the downtrodden, but their efforts could have little effect upon a class of men whose society had relegated them to the shadowy periphery.

Deprived of participation in the mainstream when away from home (by nature of their trade, sailors tend to be away from home most of the time), and associating almost exclusively with one another and with the denizens of the harbor who traded on their needs, sailors established their own mores and improvised their own culture. With a tradition of defensive pride in their trade and perpetual scorn of landlubbers ("land-lovers"), they developed their own ship-bred language,[9] arcane customs and protocols, and peculiar hierarchy of social values.[10]

This was especially the case aboard whaleships, where the voyages were typically longer—sometimes lasting two, three, or even for years—and leisure more abundant. In the whale fishery the labor-intensive technology of the hunt required larger crews than would have been necessary merely to handle the ship; thus, while merchant vessels in the nineteenth century were chronically shorthanded, whaleships had the opposite problem. Except when actually on the grounds hunting and processing whales, at which times the full complement of officers and crew were busily engaged—that is, on the long outward and homeward passages around Cape Horn and the Cape of Good Hope, and in transit between and among widely-separated whaling grounds—there were usually more men than needed for ship's work, and the crew generally had evenings off, as the hunt and the hazardous process of cutting-in whales could transpire only in daylight hours. This translated into a surplus of discretionary time, which whalemen, far more than other classes of American mariners, could utilize for their own pursuits, and which, for the purposes of shipboard order and discipline, they were often encouraged to utilize constructively. When whale's teeth and baleen ("whalebone") were abundant, they originated the delicate scrimshaw art. Others did fancy ropework. Of the many literate enough to consider it recreation rather than tedium, some kept daily journals of their experiences at sea, many of them elaborately illustrated or punctuated with verse. They spun yarns about actual or imagined events, part fact and part fancy, voiced with the syntax and embellishments of deepwater sailor lingo; and some learned the waterfront *patois* of Sailortowns on several continents—ports of call that shaped their world view into a random mixture of cosmopolitan sophistication and pitiable naivete.

Among the richest and most consistently fascinating cultural legacies of deepwater sail is the tradition of shipboard song, which achieved its greatest prosperity and extension in the middle decades of the nineteenth century. This was a period of dramatic growth in the shipping industry and in the whaling trade, with significant increases in the sizes and numbers of ships and crews, and of internationalization of the seafaring labor force.

---

[6] See Hohman 1928; Hohman 1952; Healey 1952.

[7] See Campbell 1977; Frank 1977; H.M. Davis 1979; Langley 1967.

[8] See Hugill 1969; Sanger 1899; Frank 1995.

[9] See Colcord 1945.

[10] The literature here is very extensive. See Hugill, 1969; Healey 1952; Harlow 1928; Langley 1967; Melville, *White-Jacket.*

In American and British vessels especially, rhythmic work songs called *chanteys* or *shanties* enjoyed a particular florescence. With larger sails, spars, anchors, and cargoes, and with larger (if chronically shorthanded) crews to handle them, chanteys were used to coordinate heaving and hauling, regulate tempos, allay boredom, and vent frustration among the crew. Each deckside task had its own rhythms and requirements, hence each had its own repertoire of chanteys. These were made up by the sailors themselves, they were passed along from ship to ship, and they were ordinarily sung on no other occasion than the chores for which each had been intended. They are authentic folk creations, having to do intrinsically and inseparably with the work performed on shipboard.

Such leisure time as sailors had on shipboard was also often filled with music. Songs made up by the sailors themselves or borrowed from oral tradition, hymn-singing, dance halls, minstrel shows, saloons, and bawdyhouses ashore were sung *a capella* or were accompanied on various musical instruments, including ones that might have been brought from home as well as the cheap ones that ship chandlers and marine outfitters sometimes kept in stock: fiddles, tin whistles and fifes, accordions, concertinas, banjos, guitars, and an assortment of homemade (or, rather, ship-made) percussors crafted from steak bones, tins, and common kitchen implements. Like the chanteys, a large number of these leisure songs are of anonymous origin and were transmitted orally, passing from hand to hand and from ship to ship. As Dana notes, songs from the parlor and music hall—the productions of professional songwriters produced for commercial or artistic purposes—were also numerous and were sung "as is" or were freely adapted, often evolving into chanteys or entering oral tradition. Old versions could be tailored to suit any particular place or occasion, new components were improvised to suit any mood or circumstance, and some sailors prided themselves as songwriters, immortalizing their ships and shipmates in original ballads and ditties, some of which survive today in oral tradition and in manuscript. Like the chanteys, these leisure-time songs reflect the cultural, aesthetic, and attitudinal diversity of the sailor caste and the mind and spirit of the men and women who sang them.

The nature of song on shipboard is thus fundamentally dualistic, straddling the two spheres of sea and shore, at once the heir and product of shoreside culture, at the same time sequestered and insulated from it. Songs acquired on shore were adopted, adapted, enhanced, expanded upon, and the repertoire added to far from shore, in ways uniquely and distinctively rooted in the sailors' occupation. Which is to say that seafaring culture in the Age of Sail was something of a culture apart, intimately rooted in but temporally and geographically so far removed from the general culture ashore as to have its own self-perpetuating protocols and esoteric occupational outlook.

Historians, sociologists, and labor organizers have attentively characterized the peculiar circumstances and restrictions that distinguished and circumscribed the mariner classes, which isolated them at sea and marginalized them on shore:[11] "their distinctive way of life cuts them off from… services usually available to other groups" (Straus 1950, 4). Ever since the time of their occupational antecedents, the galley slaves of classical antiquity — a status that from the very dawn of the profession intrinsically alienated sailors from polite society — sailors' work exiled them to long absences, enabling only intermittent contact with the nurturing institutions of home, family, community, and church, from which they typically became estranged and with respect to which, as a class, they were naive and largely dysfunctional. Meanwhile, partly in consequence of this estrangement and partly because of the very early and impressionable age at which seafaring apprenticeships normally commenced, mariners continued to be relegated to almost the lowest rung on the ladder of social respectability. This isolated and estranged them even further, exiling them to specific neighborhoods and social circles ashore, hamstringing their efforts to unionize, inhibiting their development as individuals. Thus, while they may have been typical American

---

[11] Hohman 1928; Straus 1950; Hohman 1952; J.C. Healey 1952; Hohman 1954; J.H. WIlliams 1959; Hugill 1969a; Weibust 1969; Frank 1985; Frank 1995; Bolster 1998.

lads drawn from across the entire spectrum of urban, rural, racial, ethnic, and religious diversity of American and immigrant society, as a class they were at the same time effectively stultified, stunted, and in some instances virtually cast out as social pariahs. Importantly — as many of the whalemen's original ballad compositions disclose — sailors characteristically saw themselves as the perpetual victims of their own employers, chronically ill-used by the owners on shore and by the owners' surrogates at sea (the officers), perpetually struggling for fair pay, respect, sailors' rights, and personal dignity.

Whalemen were an extreme case, as their situation removed them even further from normal life on shore. Amongst the general population they were perhaps no more discriminated against than other sailors — on Nantucket, whalers were downright heroes, to hear Nantucketers talk about it: the greatest of all seafarers. And because their work transpired on the far-flung whaling grounds of distant seas, whalemen seldom came ashore in the great urban seaports of Europe, North America, and the Orient that were frequented by merchantmen, so they rarely had to suffer the indignities and prohibitions heaped upon their merchant-sailor brethren. However, whalemen typically drew the disdain of other sailors, who — unjustifiably it seems — considered them rubes and less-than-competent seamen. This alleged deficiency has been roundly disputed by credible authorities [see, for example, Royal Navy and clipper-ship veteran E.C. Sear's comments in the headnotes to song #139]; but whatever their comparative skills, several features of the whaling trade facilitated whalers being the most energetic practitioners of, and the most comprehensive informants about, shipboard song.

First of all, their removal from shore was of much greater duration, thus their privation was all the more extreme — hence the advent of an independent shipboard culture. The extraordinary length of whaling voyages, in the middle nineteenth century customarily extending well beyond two years and often approaching four years, combined with a distinctive pattern in the work itself — episodes of frenzied, dangerous, arduous labor alternating irregularly and unpredictably with debilitating periods of unrelieved inactivity and crushing boredom — resulted in excessive leisure time and a level of artistic and literary productivity that is remarkable by any standard. Journal-keeping, scrimshaw-carving, picture-making, and even poetizing and songwriting were common. This was increasingly the case at mid century when whaling reached its apogee, as Yankee ships ventured out farther and longer than ever before to the remotest corners of the "terraqueous globe" (as Melville calls it), to regions of relentless, howling wind, baking tropical sun, and death-dealing Arctic cold. Peopled by a polyglot ship's company gathered from four or five continents and countless islands between, calling at exotic outports half a world from home, in frequent contact with a colorful assortment of humanity for which no previous anticipation or experience back home could have been adequate preparation, and ceaselessly in pursuit of bloody hand-to-flukes combat with the Leviathan, the whaleship was an eccentric and provocative laboratory which was more than occasionally surprising, revealing, stimulating to the creative imagination, yet with time aplenty to mull it over and set it down on paper. There are even a precious few lyrical relics of contemporaneous African American, Native American, and Native Hawaiian interest in songs [note for example "Fanny Elssler Leaving New Orleans," #178; "No Ke Ano Ahiahi, #144; and the songs and biographical notes concerning Sylvanus Fulmoon, #333 and 340].

The eccentricities and excesses of the whalers' plight and the high drama of the hunt for the Leviathan distorted the whalers' experience beyond microcosm into an esoteric micro-world that suggested, perhaps demanded that an ocean of experience be recorded, interpreted, translated into art, and fashioned into souvenirs for loved ones (or, in some cases, for an incredulous public) back home. In the bargain, the accouterments of a genuine mini culture emerged. Journal-keeping took on certain characteristic formalistic dimensions, fomulaic in organization and structure, learned on shipboard, passed from one whaleman to another. Scrimshaw developed conventions, style, even a reiterative iconographic vocabulary. Likewise whalemen's songs — in addition to those adopted from general culture, and especially those crafted by whalemen and other sailors at sea — tended to be of a sort, profoundly influenced by popular fashion but also independent, occupationally rooted, and often distinctly heroic or tragic in tone (though almost as often comic or ironic). Collectively they are much focused on the genuine, perhaps predictable concerns of an almost wholly male society of self-proclaimed adventurers, often at serious odds with one another within a rigid and unyielding hierarchy of authority, tightly confined for months at a time under harrowing conditions, their work gruesome with little respite and little hope of escape. It is seafaring amplified and elaborated to the heroic mode. More so than other sailors, whalers had time and the opportunity to commit their thoughts, meditations, literary aspirations, and musical impulses to paper; more so than other sailors, they also had a dramatic impetus to do so.

Heretofore, sailors' own transcriptions of their songs—most voluminous in the whale fishery but by no means exclusive to whaling—have received little serious attention. This seems odd, as music has great popular appeal in any case, and these particular materials fit handsomely into already established and flourishing scholarly interests in folklore and the history of popular music. Most of these whalemen's transcriptions were made decades, even generations before the first pioneer folklorists took to the field; hence, by virtue of sheer chronology, being the earliest or among the earliest manifestations ever encountered in tradition (or anywhere else), they are of enormous value in tracing the evolution of particular texts, tracing the distribution of particular ballads and songs, and discerning the process of transmission.

It is our great good fortune that a substantial record of this phenomenon remains, to provide a clear and evocative picture of songs and music on American sailing vessels. Among multitudes of manuscript archives wherein myriad particles of American cultural heritage are housed, none can have greater potential as fountains of literary, musical, and visual occupational art than the collections of whaling logbooks and journals housed in a few maritime museums and archives in southeastern New England. Written, compiled, and illustrated by practitioners at every level and station of the whale fishery throughout its heyday in the nineteenth century, and occasionally by the wives and children who accompanied whaling captains on long sea voyages, these shipboard diaries and copybooks reflect every feature and facet of life at sea and ashore in a most peculiar industry. As such, they represent the mores and popular culture of the entire seafaring labor class, serve as fairly reliable barometers of contemporaneous taste, and constitute as complete a first hand record of the technology, sociology, and aesthetic of a particular occupational group as exists anywhere. At the very least, by virtue of sheer critical mass they outweigh any other body of evidence revealing of American shipboard music and song.

Many whaling men and women transcribed song texts into their journals; apparently most did not. Some merely scratched a few unidentified lines here and there in odd corners or on blank pages. A few kept voluminous copy books, or reserved pages at the backs of their bound journal volumes, in which they wrote down lyrics of wide variety and eclectic origin. Some authored their own original ballads and songs, or collected the original compositions of shipmates. But only rarely did a sailor or whaling wife take the time, as part of a daily entry in the main part of a journal, to describe the musical activities that took place during the voyage—thereby establishing a context in which the ballads and songs were sung at sea. Fortunately, there are enough of these to provide a fairly comprehensive notion of the significance of songs and ballads on shipboard.

This anthology has been largely an exercise in literary and musical archaeology. The lyrics were excavated directly from the sailors' own shipboard manuscripts in their own hand, and the tunes—none of which was transcribed in any of the whalemen's journals—were recovered from the original sheet music or from field collections of oral tradition, as dictated by circumstances attaching to each individual song or ballad. The survey field was the enormous inventory of some 1100 manuscript logbooks, journals, and copybooks in the Kendall Collection, constituting above 20% of the approximately 5300 American whaling logbooks and journals known at the time. Song texts were encountered in only 88 of the volumes, not quite nine percent of the total sample. These mostly span the era from 1825 to 1895 (with but one earlier and one later journal), and comprise transcriptions made by about 100 individual journal-keepers and secondary contributors, the latter mostly being shipmates who collaborated in varying degrees by reciting or writing down the words. Some journals contained only one or two songs; the largest number found in any one volume is 156. In all, approximately 800 song texts and variants (in addition to as many poems and literary fragments) were recovered and identified, yielding 452 discrete ballads and songs, with variants (often multiple variants) of perhaps half. From a cursory survey of a majority of the whalemen's manuscripts in other major repositories,[12] and a systematic close comparison of the yield with such other inventories of song texts as have hitherto been compiled,[13] the sample was adjudged not only to be statistically significant but also comprehensively representative. For the purposes of completeness, to this core were added three transcriptions of "literary pieces" found in the journals — sets of lyrics that have been regarded (by Frederick Marryatt, J. Ross Browne, and Herman Melville, among others) as songs intended to be sung, but which were evidently not originally so intended and may never actually have been sung [Appendix 3]; a parlor song that has a whaling theme and a comically landlubberly text, included for comparative purposes [Appendix 4]; and two or three significant whaling songs from journals in other collections, to round out the ensemble of sailors' original compositions.

On the basis of internal evidence and existing literature in the fields of folklore, musicology, poetry, and whaling history, each song text was identified and separated out from among myriad poetic texts of other species. In turn, analogously to the slivers of clay pottery excavated from a formal archaeological dig that may be pieced together to form a whole amphora—or to mastodon bones which, when assembled, form the complete fleshless skeleton of the original pachyderm—that is, by means as familiar to the field archaeologist as to the literary historian, these chards from shipboard manuscripts were identified, classified as to species and type, and, wherever possible, realigned with their original components—their skeletons "fleshed out" and the missing chards "filled in," as it were, wherever the texts could be reunited with their original tunes and related to kindred species and types.

Once the excavation and restoration were complete, some fundamental taxonomic distinctions could be made. It came as no surprise that a slight majority of the songs encountered in sailors' journals (257 of 454) are of the types known as parlor songs, music hall pieces, minstrel ditties, sacred hymns, and other "composed" songs of professional or commercial origin from the Tin Pan Alleys of their day. These are generally regarded (by Dana as much as by folklorists and musicologists) as distinct in kind from the folk songs and ballads, which latter are presumed to have arisen from "the people" as part of a living culture and to have enjoyed significant grassroots and occupational popularity. As many "composed" songs also entered shipboard tradition their presence in the journals is significant; so, too, any textual transformations that resulted from transmission on shipboard (unfortunately, musical transformations that may have occurred simply cannot be definitively documented, as no shipboard scores exist for comparison). Clearly, these songs are too numerous for inclusion in a study of this magnitude. Happily, unlike the folk songs and ballads, by definition virtually all of the "composed" songs have been published, and though some appear to be lost, most can be fairly readily located in popular anthologies. However, the most significant transformations in sailor hands can be presumed to concern songs with nautical themes. Thus, for the purposes of this work, the "nautical" parlor songs and music hall pieces — thirty popular "sea songs"—make up Chapter 18 ("Parlor Songs"), while six of Charles Dibdin's compositions form Appendix 1. The remaining 257 professional pieces were consigned to an annotated inventory (Appendix 8) with taxonomic and bibliographic documentation.

---

[12] Notably, the 1100 volumes in the original New Bedford Whaling Museum/Old Dartmouth Historical Society collection, and hundreds of others in the New Bedford Free Public Library, the Nicholson Collection at the Providence [Rhode Island] Public Library, and the Nantucket [Massachusetts] Historical Association—in the aggregate comprising an additional 50% of the known resources.

[13] Notably Huntington 1964 and Huntington MS; also Frank 1985; and Mead 1973.

It also came as no surprise that among folk songs in the journals, the prevailing type turned out to be the so-called broadside ballads of Industrial Revolution vintage, a genre definitively surveyed, described, and catalogued by G. Malcolm Laws in *Native American Balladry* (1950) and *American Balladry from British Broadsides* (1957).[14] Accordingly, the useful guidelines and categories established in Laws's compendia were recruited to impart organizational rationale and structural integrity to the present anthology, especially respecting Chapters 7-14. For much of the remainder there simply was no transferable precedent, but the topical organization of the songs is intended to remain harmonious with the sense and intention of Laws's example.

The results address not only the locus of song types and musical entertainments on shipboard in nineteenth-century America, but also the process of transmission and its documentation. The majority of songs and ballads are familiar and may be readily identified as examples of materials known to Child, Laws, and generations of collectors, though the sailors' versions or variants may be unusual or unique. In many cases the texts are the earliest manifestations of particular ballads and songs ever encountered, which has intrinsic value to tracing the evolution of the later forms. Some, though they may have been recovered previously in the British Isles or Australia, were hitherto unknown in North America, or were known in Maritime Canada but not in the United States. A few are entirely new discoveries, unknown to Laws or to William Chappell, which nonetheless can be assigned to their relative places in the Laws taxonomy as fundamentally familiar "types," the specific manifestations of which must have passed out of tradition by the time folklorists actually started collecting in the field. Others are mariners' original compositions that may never previously have seen light of day outside the maritime trades; still others appear to be folk songs the existence of which was not previously known or suspected. Most are worthy additions to an already rich heritage. In a few cases, they add immeasurably to the body of seafaring lore and to our knowledge of singing tradition.

Whatever the subject matter of this anthology may from its methodological synthesis and catholicity of contents seem to be, it is more than anything else a book about American seafaring and the social history of song at sea. The conditions, concerns, syntax, sociology, ideology, and tragic-heroic notions of the American sailor—and of the American whaleman in particular, and more than a few whaling wives—are encompassed and epitomized in the songs themselves, and in the mariners' choices of songs. Together with the meditations of journal prose, they articulate from the brutal interior a human perspective on a sometimes inhumane industry, in a manner that transcends and enlightens the customary statistical-economic-technological purview of history, and provides an intrinsically meaningful sidelight on American literature, folklore, and song.

---

[14] The ballad genre is defined and foundation taxonomic guidelines provided in several works that have become indispensable to any responsible study of folk songs: Francis James Child, *The English and Scottish Popular Ballads* (5 vols., 1883-98), which established the canon of traditional ballads; B.H. Bronson, *The Traditional Tunes of the Child Ballads* (4 vols., 1959-72), based on the Child canon, which anthologizes and analyzes literally thousands of surviving ballad melodies; Claude M. Simpson, *The British Broadside Ballad and Its Music* (1966), which presents a comprehensive spectrum of contemporaneous tunes, drawn from a variety of printed sources, including academic compositions and stage productions that were often the sources of materials recovered from oral tradition but which are often neglected by folklorist; and especially, for the purposes of the present work, G. Malcolm Laws, whose *Native American Balladry* and *American Balladry from British Broadsides* establish a classification system for latter-day ballads that entered tradition from the late eighteenth-century and nineteenth-century press.

A Few Words about Chanteys[15]

> Double hawsers ran through the great blocks to the windlass on the topgallant fo'c'sle, and there, under the eye of the Old Man himself, the greater part of the crew rocked the windlass and hoisted the strip of blubber as it was loosened from the whale. This was the least cheery part of the business, work that could not be done without a song, and, to the accompaniment of squeaking bearings and click-ing pawls, the husky chorus rang out…(Murphy, 53).

The florescence of sailors' chanteys in the nineteenth century is closely tied to the influence of black stevedores in Southern cotton ports, with whom deepwater sailors came into increasingly frequent contact in the expansionary post-Napoleonic era. Age-old call-and-response work song traditions transplanted from Africa, transmuted through generations of singing at hard labor in the cotton fields and cane brakes, tempered by a sacred tradition of Negro Spirituals cherished as cultural touchstones through the anguish of slavery, emerged as work-rhythms for handling cargo on the wharves of New Orleans and Mobile, inspiring sailors to adopt analogous heaving-and-hauling songs for their work at sea. Mixed and blended with the songs the sailors brought with them — Irish tunes, English music-hall pieces, American stage-minstrelsy, and miscellaneous singing traditions of a remarkably polyglot class of sea-laborers — the result was a piquant soup of shipboard work songs, respecting which the only rule was that they serve the utilitarian functions of providing workable rhythms and some slight diversion from the labor at hand.

A large number of chanteys survive; probably as many have been lost since steam propulsion supplanted them. But comparatively few original cotton-steeving songs survive. "Fanny Elssler Leaving New Orleans" [#178] is a rare specimen of known vintage. By contrast, "Sing Sally O" is a hybridized work song recruited for triple duty loading cargo, hoisting sail, and working the capstan. In introducing her version Joanna Colcord writes, "Sometimes an earlier shanty of non-Negro origin was taken by the cotton stevedores and made over into a song to suit themselves… 'Sing Sally O' is one of these." With reference to his two versions, Stan Hugill adds: "These I had from Harding ['the Barbadian Barbarian,' a chanteyman], who declared they were both used *ashore* in the West Indies for any job where a work-sing was needed. [Frank] Bullen gives the capstan version, Miss Colcord and [Cecil] Sharp give it as a halyard song." The cargo-loading song "Hurrah! Hurrah, My Bullies!" mentioned by Dana may be a form of the same chantey.[16] Unfortunately, whaleman John Jones only quotes a snippet of the chorus — "hura hura for old marm dinah"—as he does for a number of chanteys of which no full text have been encountered

---

[15] The etymology of *chantey* (also rendered *shanty* or *chanty,* and variously pluralized, but always pronounced with an *sh* or a soft *ch*, as in *chandelier*) is obscure and the orthography controversial. Advocates of the *ch* spelling—including Cecil Sharp, John Masefield, Rudyard Kipling, Ferris & Tozer, Charles Frothingham, Captain Frederick Pease Harlow, Captain John Robinson, P.A. Hutchinson, Charles Finger, and Frank Shay—generally agree that it has French-Latin roots, either from the French *chanter* ("to sing") and *chanson* ("song"), or directly from the English *chant.* Joanna Colcord and William Main Doerflinger, among the most meticulous scholars to have addressed the issue, agree that the derivation is from *chant,* but prefer the phonetic convenience of *sh* to the etymological propriety of *ch*. Other advocates of *sh* are divided between two theories of its derivation: (a) from the "shanties" (shacks) and "shanty-town" logging camps of North America, from which seafaring men are alleged to have brought the word with them; and (b) from the "shanties" (shacks) built on stilts by black West Indians, who periodically hauled their cabins (*shanties*) along the beach, singing *shanty*-songs led by *shanty*-men; but as attractive as these hypotheses may seem, there is little historical evidence to connect the phenomena with the terminology for shipboard work songs. Here, as in many instances of specific nautical terminology, the *Oxford English Dictionary* is of little help mediating the dispute, as it lists *shanty* and claims derivation from the French, but fails to mention the *ch* spelling even as a variant, despite that by the time the OED was published in 1928 *chantey* and *chanty* had been in continuous use in print for at least fifty years, including by such literati as Sharp, Kipling, and Masefield, the Poet Laureate of England. By then, both spellings had attained wide currency among writers and folklorists, but field collecting and scholarly analysis had evidently not yet raised the etymological issue for scrutiny among historical lexicographers. Mystic Seaport Museum, the Kendall Whaling Museum, South Street Seaport Museum, and several other institutions adopted *chantey* as their standard, in deference to its historical precedence, the preference of early folklore authorities (beginning with the great Cecil Sharp), its prevalence among in American literature, and to avoid confusion with other English nouns spelled *shanty*. See Frank 1985, pp. 7-12; and Frank 2000a.

[16] Colcord 60; Frank 1985 #154; Hugill 388 (2 versions); Sharp 1914, n.p.; Bullen & Arnold; Dana, *Two Years…*, Ch. 29.

in the whalemen's journals. But even Jones's fragments are significant in demonstrating the comparative antiquity of the chanteys and to document that they were known to whalemen.[17] All of this, of course, runs counter to the groundless rumor that chanteying—singing rhythmic work songs while setting sail, weighing anchor, or loading cargo—was rare or nonexistent in the whale fishery. In point of fact, the special purposes of a whaler frequently called for chanteyable work, notably at the windlass when cutting-in whales. Spurious claims to the contrary notwithstanding, there was plenty of chanteying aboard nineteenth-century Yankee whalers.

Few of the sea-chantey anthologists have said anything specific about whaling at all,[18] and so leave the reader with the probably accurate impression that chanteying on whaleships transpired much as it did in other deepwater trades. Hugill, whose knowledge of whaling is flawed,[19] nevertheless makes several cogent connections between whalemen's chanteys and the evolution and dissemination of the chantey repertoire.[20] Harlow mentions the importance of windlass chanteys on whalers; Huntington observes that "the only songs that were not recorded in the journals are the chanties. And that is because the whalemen, like all seamen, did not think of the chanties as songs at all. They were a part of the routine of working ship and everyone knew them." If there has been an error of reporting, it has been made on the other side—not by chantey anthologists commenting about whaling, but by whaling historians commenting about chanteys.[21]

---

[17] John Jones, steward, ship *Eliza Adams* of New Bedford, 1852. His rendition of "Sing Sally O" coincides with Sharp 1914, #31. In addition, he quotes, paraphrases, or refers to several other chanteys: "Around the Corner Sally," "Cheer'ly, Man" ("Sally Racket"), "The Girls Around Cape Horn" ("Spanish Gals"; "The Girls of Chile"), "Haul on the Bowline," "Hieland Laddie," and "The Sailor Loves His Bottle O"; also a wide variety of other folk songs, parlor songs, minstrel songs, popular songs, sacred songs, and tunes—in many cases alluding to them more than once—including: "De Boatman's Dance," "Bonaparte Crossing the Alps," "Clare de Kitchen," "The Fourth of July," "The Girl I Left Behind Me," "The Great Sea Snake," "John's Ale" ("Jones's Ale"; "Joan's Ale"), "Juba," "Miss Lucy Neal," "My Eye and Betty Martin," "My Old Aunt Sally," "Oh Susanna," "Old Dan Tucker," "Poor Jack," "Saturday Night at Sea," "Sweethearts and Wives," "Tally Ho," "A Voice from the Tomb," "Whar Yu Kum From?," "When I Can Read My Title Clear," "Who Dat [... Knocking at the Door]?," and "Yankee Doodle." For particulars, see Frank 1991b, where the journal has been printed in its entirety and annotated, pp. 14-30.

[18] E.g., Bone, Colcord, Doerflinger, Masefield, Meloney, C. Fox Smith, and Whall.

[19] In *Sailortown* (1967, 52) Hugill claims that at Maui, Hawaiian Islands, in 1846, "395 ships, mostly whalers, lay abreast of the port" of Lahaina *simultaneously*, a ludicrously inflated figure. In *Songs of the Sea* (1977) he claims that the same number of ships anchored at Lahaina "during the year 1846," a more credible statistic that nevertheless remains unascribed and undocumented. In his miscellaneous lectures and concerts Hugill often claimed that Yankee whaleships carried crews averaging 100 men, a figure about *three times the maximum* for the largest American whalers of the nineteenth century. When Hugil's claim of "around 400 whaleships" at Lahaina is combined with his notion of 100 men per ship, the yield is an incredible 40,000 whalemen at Lahaina at one time. His remarks to this effect delivered at the *Dogwatch and the Liberty Days* Symposium at the Peabody Museum of Salem, Mass., in October 1982, may or may not be preserved in an audiovisual record of the proceedings; but these and similar remarks have been institutionalized in the audiovisual and oral history archives of the San Francisco Maritime National Historical Park (Sea Music Festival Papers, September 1979) and Mystic Seaport Museum (Sea Music Symposium Papers, June 1980, May 1981, June 1982, etc.).. Hugill also erroneously denies the existence of pay advances in the American whale fishery (*Sailortown*, 170; for refutation, see Hohman, 255) and has some bizarre interpretations of the American Revolution (q.v., in *Sailortown*). For an authoritative treatment of the economics of American whaling, including pertinent statistics regarding crew size, estimated total labor force, scale of the fishery, distribution in the Pacific Ocean, etc., see Hohman 1928, passim.

[20] Hugill 1969, pp 37, 49, 69, 70, etc.; Hugill 1961, 242-244; Hugill 1981.

[21] It is worth pointing out that occasional references to Clifford W. Ashley's *The Yankee Whaler* as authority for the mistaken notion that chanteys were an infrequent occurrence aboard whaleships are misdirected. In the first place, Ashley's experience and opinions as a nominal member of the crew of the New Bedford bark *Sunbeam* in 1903, during a period of precipitous decline in the industry, do not necessarily render him omniscient concerning the classic era of American whaling two and three generations earlier. And as Robert Cushman Murphy, Frederick Pease Harlow, and Captain W.B. Whall observe from their own firsthand experience, chanteying had degenerated by the first decade of the twentieth century, and was not what it had been even in the merchant service. Nevertheless, when pressed to discuss chanteys, Ashley clearly corroborates that even in his latter-day fishery, chanteying had not disappeared from windlass work and was still associated with cutting-in whales. In the widely circulated first edition of *The Yankee Whaler* (1926) he, like Bullen, is silent on the subject of chanteying; and this in itself evidently created something of a stir among his readership, in response to whose inquiries he appended the following statement in his preface to the second edition, specifically listing the various occasions when chanteys were appropriate and were sung on his latter-day voyage:

> The sea shanty developed spontaneously in the merchant service, where it served a very definite purpose on ships of many nations until donkey engines superseded man-power on deck. On the whaler, however, its employment was intermittent and

Frank Bullen's famous whaling narrative *Cruise of the Cachalot* (1898) mentions shipboard song only rarely and chanteys not at all. Anglo-centrism and jingoism aside, Bullen's authority and reliability in straightforward matters of fact suggest that his silence on the chantey issue is probably a fair reflection of the state of affairs aboard the unidentified New Bedford whaler of which he purportedly served as mate in the 1870s (his actual presence on such a voyage and the identity of the pseudonymous vessel have never been corroborated). It is justifiable to suppose that had chanteys been a significant feature of the whaling life as Bullen knew it or supposed it to be, he would have reported it. From the time the book appeared at least until *Moby Dick* (1851) was rescued from obscurity in the 1920s, *Cruise of the Cachalot* was probably the best known of the few whaling "classics," ranking just below Richard Henry Dana and Robert Louis Stevenson on the shelf of Approved Sea Stories for Boys. Bullen's narrative contributed mightily to British and American notions of whaling and may have been partly responsible for the widespread impression that chanteys simply were not sung by whaleship crews. However, a cursory examination of firsthand Yankee narratives from the Palmy Days of whaling in the middle nineteenth century reveals that chanteying was more the rule than the exception on American whaleships.[22]

One explanation for the supposed absence of chanteying aboard whaleships is the correlation frequently made between the size of a deepwater vessel and the relative numerical strength of the crew expected to man it. This argues that chanteys are most useful when a vessel and its fixtures are disproportionately large in proportion to the size of the crew, and thus that singing at work is especially useful in vessels that are under-manned or short-handed. Whall and Hugill both note that exceptions to the Royal Navy taboo on chanteying tended to occur on smaller vessels: chanteys were superfluous on ships-of-the-line, which were overmanned for the purposes of heaving and hauling, and which in any case would normally have had a generous complement of official musicians to beat the necessary rhythms, as stipulated in Navy Board regulations. Similarly, the claim is made that the relative decrease in the number of crew per ton on merchant ships during the expansionary post-Napoleonic age, resulting in harder work for all hands, was a contributing factor in the rise of chanteying at that time, the so-called Golden Age of merchant sail.

There is no denying a significant correlation between crew size and chanteying. Generally, the more men per ton, the less need for chanteys. And if this formula be carried to its logical extension and applied to whaling, the conclusion is that there was not—or need not have been—chanteying in whaleships. Like naval ships of the line, whalers were grossly overmanned from a navigational point of view. In the carrying trades the complement of crew was determined by whatever minimum number of hands might be required to man the vessel efficiently; the object was essentially just to get a cargo from one place to another. In the whale fishery, however, as in the navy, getting the vessel from point to point was a necessary but ancillary feature of a vessel's purpose. Crew size was determined by what was required when the ship was actually engaged in the work for which it was intended. In the Navy, this was waging war, preserving the peace, and performing ceremonial and diplomatic functions. In the whale fishery it was hunting whales and

---

generally incidental. It never became an important part of daily life on the whaleman. Once on the whaling ground, during daytime, all unnecessary noise was discouraged. Even orders were given in lowered voices so that whales might not be frightened off. Usually in the dog-watches all hands were permitted to dance, sing, and play whatever musical instruments they had. But there was no occasion for shantying after the lookout had once left the masthead, for ships were then under shortened sail until sun-up. The one purpose of the sea shanty was to lend rhythm to heavy hauling.

Sometimes when getting up anchor, or when cutting in a whale, there would be a burst of a shanty. When homeward bound with a full ship a cre/w often shantied, but it was then more an expression of their gladness of heart than it was an adjunct to their work. Whalers were small and watches disproportionately large. About forty hands [sic], all told, made up the crew of an average vessel. In consequence working ship was mere child's play beside the heavy grind aboard a more short-handed merchantman. There every pound a man possessed had to be brought to bear on his task.

[22] For example, Olmsted 1841, Davis [1927], Taylor 1929, Haley 1947, Ely 1971. There is also in *Omoo* and *Moby-Dick* abundant evidence of the significance that Melville attached to chanteying, based, in part, on his own experiences in the whale fishery (see Frank 1985a).

processing blubber into oil. In the nineteenth century this meant a formula of six men for each of the whaleboats (excluding spares), plus the captain and a few "idlers" to look after the ship when all the boats were launched on the grounds. Thus, a three-whaleboat ship or bark would ordinarily carry 20 to 23 men, a four-boat vessel 27 or 28, a five-boat vessel some 33 to 35. In the merchant service, any of these vessels might have been manned effectively and safely with half these numbers, and in actual practice might be sent across the Atlantic or along the coast even shorter-handed than that. By carrying-trade standards, and from the point of view of navigation, whaling vessels were grossly over manned.

However, the situation was not so simple. In the whale fishery, it was not only in actually manning the boats during the hunt that the full ship's complement was required. In *cutting-in* a whale — stripping the carcass and preparing the blubber for rendering into oil — a third to half the crew might be employed hauling on lines and at the brake windlass hoisting aboard the heavy "blanket pieces" of blubber and (in the case of sperm and right whales) the head and jaws for processing on deck. This had to be accomplished with relative speed and efficiency, especially in warm climates, before rapid deterioration of the carcass adulterated the oil and reduced its value, or, finally, rendered the carcass unfit for processing. Likewise, in *trying-out* — rendering or boiling-down the blubber — a similar proportion of the crew was engaged at the windlass, hauling up barrel *shooks* for assembly on deck, and lowering full barrels of oil into the hold. Both processes often transpired on deck simultaneously or in close succession, and, if the ship were lucky in the hunt, there might be several whale carcasses to be cut-in and tried-out in sequence. This back-breaking windlass work was the same heavy labor entailed in weighing anchor or loading cargo, except that, despite occasional pauses for the windlass crew while the cutting-in squad caught up with their work on the blanket pieces, windlass work for cutting-in was likely to be more frequent and of longer duration than analogous work with anchor or cargo. In any case, Melville is unequivocal about the cheering effect of a chantey at the windlass on the whaling grounds — a result no less salubrious than Dana's report of recreational singing among American crews on the coast of California.[23]

---

[23] Sailors' perception, and notably Melville's and Dana's renditions of the beneficial effects of chanteying, are treated in greater depth in my article "'Cheer'ly Man': Chanteying in *Omoo* and *Moby-Dick*" (Frank 1985a).

CHAPTER ONE
Classical Songs of the Sea
An Eighteenth-Century Garland

In *Two Years Before the Mast* (1840), Richard Henry Dana, Jr., identifies a select group of what he calls "classical songs of the sea." Likewise, whether through Dana's influence or as the result of his own seafaring experience—probably a combination of both—Herman Melville presents much the same list. In their day these songs were presumably known on just about every ship, were heard at one time or another by just about every deepwater sailor, and, according to Dana and Melville, were characteristically sung by experienced navy tars—"man-of-war's men"— just as Dana heard them performed during a *gam* (visit) between his vessel and the *California*:

> Among the crew were two English man-of-war's men, so that, of course, we soon had music. They sang in the true sailor's style, and the rest of the crew, which was a remarkably musical one, joined in the choruses. They had many of the latest sailor songs, which had not yet got about along our merchantmen, and which they were very choice of. They began soon after we came on board, and kept it up until after two bells... Battle-songs, drinking-songs, boat-songs, love songs and everything else, they seemed to have a complete assortment of, and I was glad to find that "All in the Downs," "Poor Tom Bowline," "The Bay of Biscay," List ye Landsmen!" and all those classical songs of the sea, still held their places.

Though Dana identifies the songs in sailor lingo rather than by the official titles, they are readily and unequivocally recognizable. "All in the Downs" is "Black-Eyed Susan," which Dana cites by its universally-familiar first line. "Poor Tom Boline" is "Tom Bowling" or "Poor Tom"—by any standard the greatest and longest-lived composition of Charles Dibdin. "The Bay of Biscay" is certainly "The Bay of Biscay O"; and "List Ye Landsmen" is actually the second line of a song more often identified by its opening phrase, "Cease, rude Boreas," but which the original lyricist entitled "The Storm." All of these songs came into the shipboard repertoire from the English popular stage, all of them remained familiar to mariners through the late 19th century, and transcriptions of all of them have been found in whalemen's shipboard journals and copy books.

Melville's list in his narrative of the Navy, *White-Jacket* (1850), varies from Dana's only in omitting "Black-Eyed Susan." He cites the other three songs as typifying a certain cadre of navy deepwater men, about whom Melville is not entirely complimentary:

> Besides these topmen, who are always made up of active sailors, there are Sheet-Anchor-men—old veterans all—whose place is on the forecastle; the fore-yard, anchors, and all the sails on the bowsprit being under their care.
> They are an old weather-beaten set, culled from the most experienced seamen on board. These are the fellows that sing you "The Bay of Biscay Oh!" and "Here a sheer hulk lies poor Tom Bowling!" "Cease, rude Boreas, blustering railer!" who, when ashore, at an eating-house, call for a bowl of tar and a biscuit. These are the fellows, who spin interminable yarns about Decatur, Hull, and Bainbridge; and carry about their persons bits of "Old Ironsides," as Catholics do the wood of the true cross. These are the fellows, that some officers pretend never to damn, however much they may anathematize others. These are the fellows, that it does your heart good to look at;—hearty old members of the Old Guard; grim sea grenadiers, who, in tempest time, have lost many a tarpaulin overboard. These are the fellows, whose society some of the midshipmen much affect; from whom they learn their best seamanship; and to whom they look up as veterans; if it be so that they have any reverence in their souls, which is not the case with all mid-shipmen.

To Dana's and Melville's canon can be added the few classic "English and Scottish Popular Ballads" that were known on shipboard in the 19th century; and in Appendix 1 are a few of Dibdin's other songs left over from the popular stage of the Napoleonic Era, which were perhaps less universally performed by 19th-century sailors than might qualify them as true classics.

1. Black-Eyed Susan
[Dark-Eyed Susan; Sweet William's Farewell to His Black-Eyed Susan]
(Laws #O-28)

Anonymous woodcut in the popular, pocket-sized *Forget Me Not Songster* (New York, circa 1829). There were also contemporaneous Boston and Philadelphia editions.

The lyrics were written by John Gay (1685-1732), best known for his contributions to *The Beggar's Opera* and his occasional collaborations with Alexander Pope; and the standard melody was composed by Richard Leveridge (1670?-1758) circa 1720-30. However, as is often the case with songs of 18th-century vintage, Leveridge's tune is widely believed to be merely an adaptation of an earlier air borrowed from Irish tradition.

The text is related to the "Broken Token" and "Lovers Parted / Lovers Reunited" families of folk songs and broadside ballads, among which chards of Gay's phrasing are frequently intermingled. *The Amateur's Song Book* (Boston, 1843) presents the usual eight stanzas (erroneously numbered, so as to appear to include only seven), with minor variations throughout, and appends a two-stanza "Sequel" of unascribed authorship. *Miller's New British Songster* (Edinburgh, 1853) erroneously attributes both the words and music to "the gifted pen of [Charles] Dibdin," to whom many romantic and patriotic nautical songs were often mistakenly credited (see song #2 and Appendix 1). Perhaps because of the enormous popularity of the song at sea and ashore, both text and tune have been remarkably stable over the centuries. The first line, "All in the Downs the fleet was moored," refers to a section of the Thames estuary that was a customary mustering place of the Royal Navy. Other musical settings by Henry Carey (1685-1743), Pietro Giuseppe Sandoni (circa 1720), and John Frederick Lampe (1703-1751) never achieved the popularity of the Leveridge melody and are scarcely remembered today. There are also at least two Irish fiddle tunes of the same name (O'Neill #53 and #54), of which one (#54) is closely related to the Leveridge melody, from which the fiddle tune may derive.

TUNE from John Hullah, *The Song Book,* Philadelphia and London, 1866, #43. Compare *Calliope,* 1788, p. 408; *English Musical Repository,* 1811, p. 199; H.K.Johnson 1881, 125; *Naval Songs,* 1883, 60; Luce 1889, 160; etc.

A.

"BLACK EYED SUSAN." Copybook of Lydia and John Marble, Warren, Rhode Island, 1846-47, written into Stephen O. Hopkins's whaling journal of the ship *Rosalie* of Warren, 1843-44, later taken to California by Hopkins and Lemuel C. Richmond, Jr., on a Gold Rush voyage in the *Perseverance* of Providence, 1849. A fragment comprising only the first three stanzas. Interestingly, while most of the published texts exhibit minor variations from other printed versions, none has been found that matches the Marble fragment precisely.

1. All in the Downs[1] the fleet was moored
   The streamers waving to the wind
   When black eyed Susan came on board
   Oh where shall I my true love find
   Tell me jovial sailors tell me true
   If my sweet William sails among your crew

2. William who high upon the yard
   Rocked with the billows to and fro
   Soon as her well known voice was heard
   He sighed and cast his eyes below
   The cords glides swiftly through his glowing hands
   And quick as lightning on the deck he stands

3. So the lark high poised in the air
   Shuts close his pinions to his breast
   If chance his mates shrill call to hear
   And drops at once into her nest
   The noblest Captain in the British fleet
   Might envy William's lips those kisses sweet

B.

"BLACK EYED SUSAN." George Wilbur Piper, seaman, ship *Europa* of Edgartown, 1868-70. Typically of the prolific Piper (who transcribed the lyrics of nearly 200 songs during two years on the *Europa*), this is a standard and substantially complete text, quite similar to A, likely copied from one of many possible printed sources and retaining the elegant poetic sensibilities as well as the Royal Navy regalia of the original.

1. All in the Downs 1 the fleet lay moored
   With streamers waving in the wind
   When black eyed Susan came on board
   O where shall I my true love find
   Tell me ye jovial sailors tell me true
   Does my sweet William, does my sweet William
       Sail among your crew

2. William who high upon the yards
   Tossed by the billows to and fro
   As soon as her well known voice he heard
   He sighed and cast his eyes below
   The rope slides swiftly through his glowing hands
   And quick as lightning, and quick as lightning
       On the deck he stands

3. So the sweet lark high poised in the air
   Shuts close his pinions to his breast
   If chance his mate's shrill notes to hear
   And sinks at once into her nest
   The noblest Captain in the British Fleet
   Might envy William's, might envy William's
       Lips those kisses sweet

4. O Susan Susan lovely dear
   My vows shall ever true remain
   Let me kiss off that falling tear
   We only part to meet again
   Change as ye list ye winds my hope shall ever be
   The faithful compass   the faithful compass
       That still points to thee

5. O heed not what the landsmen say
   Who tempt with doubts thy constant mind
   They tell tee sailors when away
   In every port a mistress find
   Yes yes believe them when they tell thee so
   For thou art present, for thou art present
       Where so e'er I go

6. If to fair India's coast we sail
   Thine eyes are seen in diamonds bright
   Thy breath in Africa's spicy gale
   Thy skin in ivory so white
   Thus every beauteous object that I view
   Brings to my mind   brings to my mind
       Some charms of lovely Sue

7. Though battles call me from thy arms
   Let not my pretty Susan mourn
   Though cannons roar yet safe from harm
   William shall to his dear return
   Love turns aside the balls that around me fly
   Lest precious tears   lest precious tears
       Should drop from Susan's eye

8. The boatswain gave the dreadful word
   The sails then swelling bosoms spread
   No longer must she stay on board
   They kissed she sighed and bowed her head
   [And] as the boat unwilling rows to the land
   Adieu she cries adieu she cries
       And waived her lily hand

May the pleasure of return ever bear up the spirits of the absent

2. Tom Bowling
[Poor Tom, or The Sailor's Epitaph; Tom Bowline]

> In looking among the mounds by which the whole cemetery [at Port Louis] was broken, I came upon a rude wooden cross, worm-eaten and weather-beaten, fast mingling its dust with his who lay below. Upon the horizontal piece were cut in rude letters, probably done with a sailor's jack-knife, the words,
>
> "Here, a Sheer hulk, lies poor Tom Bowling."
>
> It was the last resting-place of some poor weatherbeaten sailor who had found here, far away from home and friends, the peace he had sought in vain during a hard and perilous life.
>
> — Charles Nordhoff,
> *The Boys Own Sea Stories* (1857)

One is tempted to say of "Tom Bowling" that it was the greatest "composed" sea-song of the 18th and 19th centuries. Written by Charles Dibdin (1745-1814), it has usually been regarded as a eulogy on the death of his elder brother Thomas, who died at sea, "but more recent scholarship has pointed out that Dibdin would have been familiar with the singing and conviviality Edward (Tom) Bowling, a naval rating popular in the Portsmouth taverns for his singing prowess, who then died."[1] The song was featured in *The Oddities,* a ballad opera first produced in 1789. Universally accorded Dibdin's masterpiece, it came into its own in Nelson's navy and in the merchant service thereafter, where it was still being sung in the middle part of the 19th century, withstanding the test of time better than any of Dibdin's myriad other compositions. That Dana and Melville both include it in their lists of "classical songs of the sea"— among the songs that, in Melville's words, "breathe the very poetry of the ocean"—corroborates the general notion that it was a perennial favorite wherever square-rig sailors gathered. But it seems to have faded out of use before sail had been entirely supplanted by steam: none of the latter-day deepwater field collectors or professional folklorists reported it in tradition or accorded it much importance.[2] Hugill even says of it, "Such popular nautical ballads as Dibdin's *Tom Bowling* and *Anchor's Weighed,* cannot compare with the tough and often coarse fore-bitters... true sea songs from unknown sailor authors" (Hugill 1969, 21). And speaking from his own experience in square-riggers in the 1920s, he adds, "Many shore-composed sea-songs had no place in the fo'c'sle 'banyans',[3] at least not in the merchant ships of the 19th century. *Tom Bowling,* for example, was banned on superstitious grounds; it was considered a harbinger of death if sung, most certainly someone would fall from aloft or be killed in some strange way, or so sailors believed" (Hugill 1969, 44). These attitudes are difficult to reconcile with Dana's and Melville's contemporaneous account of the song's former glory; moreover, apart from the occasional allusion here and there in the lesser literature there is little evidence to suggest that Yankee tars ever paid the Dibdin song much heed. Thus, while the two whalemen's texts of "Tom Bow-ling" presented here do not constitute proof that the song was ever sung on shipboard with "a hearty good will"—Dana, Melville, and Nordhoff are more convincing on this score—they are evidence that "Tom Bowling" was familiar to and appreciated at by some American mariners, perhaps as much as it had been by British navy seamen a generation or two before.

TUNE - "Poor Tom Bowling," from John Hullah, *The Song Book,* Philadelphia and London, 1866, #81. See also *American Musical Miscellany,* 31; Hogarth I:245f (variations in tune and setting); *Naval Songs,* 18; Luce 1889, 79.

---

[1] Steve Gardham, private communication, November 2010.

[2] e.g., Whall, Colcord, Harlow, Bone, Doerflinger, Hugill.

[3] Banyan: "This expression for a 'party' probably dates back to the days of the East Indiamen. In India, in early times, religious festivals were held under the branches of the great banyan trees" (Hugill's note, 1969, 44).

A.

"TOM BOWLING." Daniel K. Ritchie, second mate, ships *Israel* and *Herald* of New Bedford, 1843-47. A complete and literate text, roughly contemporaneous with Dana and Melville, virtually identical to Hogarth I:245f and Luce 79. Minor variations in B are noted in italics in brackets. Printed versions indicate that the last line of each stanza is to be repeated when sung, which the melody requires but which neither of the whalemen's transcriptions disclose.

1. Here, a sheer hulk, lies poor Tom Bowling,
   The darling of our crew;
   No more he'll hear the tempest howling,
   For death has broach'd [*brought*] him to.
   His form was of the manliest beauty
   His heart was kind and soft,
   Faithful below, he did his duty,
   But now he's gone aloft.

2. Tom never from his word departed,
   His virtues were so rare,
   His friends were many and true-hearted
   His Poll was kind & fair;
   And then he'd sing [*he sung*] so blithe & jolly
   Ah! many's the time and oft;
   But mirth is turn'd to melancholy
   For Tom is gone aloft.

3. Yet shall poor Tom find pleasant weather,
   When He, who all commands,
   Shall give to call life's crew together
   The word to pipe all hands.
   Thus Death who kings and tars dispatches
   In vain Tom's life has doff'd
   For though his body's under hatches
   His soul is [*has*] gone aloft.

B.

"TOM BOWLING." George W. Piper, ship *Europa* of Edgartown, 1868-70. Variations as noted in italics in A. As was Piper's habit, some lines are doubled, contractions are often re-divided into whole words, punctuation is largely omitted, and spelling is variable.

3. The Bay of Biscay O
[Ye Gentlemen of England]
(Laws #K-3)

With words by Irish lyricist Andrew Cherry (1762-1812) and music by Englishman John Davy (1765-1824), "The Bay of Biscay O" made its debut in the ballad opera *Spanish Dollars,* first produced in London in 1805. It was frequently anthologized thereafter, the melody has been adapted as the setting for other naval and patriotic songs, and it has occasionally been collected from oral tradition.

TUNE from John Hullah, *The Song Book,* Philadelphia & London, 1866, #88 (transposed from B$^\flat$); also Adm. S.B. Luce, *Naval Songs,* 1889, p. 174.

"THE BAY OF BISCAY." George W. Piper, ship *Europa* of Edgartown, 1868-70.

1. Loud roared the dreadful thunder
   The rain a deluge showered
   The clouds were rent asunder
   By the lightning's vivid powers
   The night both drear and dark
   Our poor devoted bark
   As she lay till next day
   In the Bay of Biscay O
   As she lay till next day
   In the Bay of Biscay O

2. Now dashed upon the billow
   Her opening timbers creak
   Each fears a watery pillow
   None stops the dreadful leak
   For to cling [to] the slippery shrouds
   Each breathless seaman crowds
   As she lay till the day
   In the Bay of Biscay O
   As she lay till the day
   In the Bay of Biscay O

3. At length the wished for morrow
   Broke through the azure sky
   Absorbed in silent sorrow
   Each heaved a bitter sigh
   A dismal sight to view
   Struck horror in the crew
   As she lay till that day
   In the Bay of Biscay O
   As she lay till that day
   In the Bay of Biscay O

4. Her yielding timbers ever
   Her pithy seams are rent
   But Heaven all bounteous ever
   Its boundless mercy sent
   A sail in sight appears
   We hail it with three cheers
   Now we sail with the gale
   From the Bay of Biscay O
   Now we sail with the gale
   From the Bay of Biscay O

Note: The alternate title, "Ye Gentlemen of England," is a misnomer and seems to originate with G. Malcolm Laws. He lists the song (Laws #K-3) as "Bay of Biscay, Oh (Ye Gentlemen of England II) (The Stormy Winds Did Blow)" and cites as his source a broadside entitled, "New Version of the Bay of Biscay, or The Stormy Winds Did Blow," of which the first line is "Ye gentlemen of England who live at home at your ease...." Laws does not mention or identify Cherry's lyrics as the original of which the broadside purports to be a "new version"; and while this "new version" might properly be called "Bay of Biscay II" or "The Stormy Winds Did Blow," or even "Ye Gentlemen of England II" (see Laws #K-2), it is not "Bay of Biscay O." The versions of "Bay of Biscay O" that appear in the early songsters and whaling manuscripts are clearly derived from and closely akin to Cherry's original poem, and have no evident connection with "Ye Gentlemen of England."

4. The Storm
[Cease, Rude Boreas; List Ye Landsmen]

A great part of this song's appeal among sailors must have been its authentic nautical flavor. George Alexander Stevens (1710/20-1784), the English lecturer responsible for the lyrics (1754), evidently knew more than the average songwriter about sailing-ship terminology and technical aspects of weathering a heavy gale at sea. The circumstances he narrates are, in one way or another, familiar to anyone who has ventured out on the stormy ocean in a frail ship, while the third stanza typifies the seaman's professional pride and a sailor's disdain for the landlubber's life of relative ease. That farmers and tradesmen spend their lives lounging about while the mariner toils in hardship and perpetual jeopardy at sea is a recurring theme in authentic sailor-made songs, and the sentiment is quintessentially expressed in the contemporaneous deepwater song "Jolly Sailors Bold" [#32]. The tune is an adaptation of the traditional English air "Welcome, brother debtor" or "Come and listen to my ditty," which was originally published in 1729 or 1730 and which Stevens himself expropriated for his lyrics. Like "Tom Bowling" [#2], there is little evidence that "The Storm" survived in oral tradition at sea much beyond the 1830s.

"THE STORM": Text and tune from broadside sheet music "Printed for J[ohn] Bland. N° 45. Holborn" (London, n.d., circa 1775-94) which attributes neither words nor music [Kendall Collection, New Bedford Whaling Museum]. Instructions regarding the relative speed with which each stanza is to be sung are reproduced here as given in the printed lyrics, as they are in Luce, 70.

Lively. (1)
    Cease, rude Boreas, blustering railer,
        List ye landsmen all to me,
    Mess-mates hear a brother sailor
        Sing the dangers of the sea.
    From the bounding billows first in motion
        When the distant whirlwinds rise
    To the tempest-troubled ocean,
        Where the seas contend with skies

Slow. (2)
    Hark! the Boatswain hoarsely bawling - - -
        By topsail-sheets and haulyard stand - -
    Down top-gallants quick be hauling - - -
        Down your stay-sails; hand, boys, hand;
    Now it freshens set the braces - - -
        The topsail-sheets now let go.
    Luff, boys, luff, don't make wry faces - - -
        Up your topsails nimbly clew.

Slow. (3)
    Now all you on down-beds sporting,
        Fondly lock'd in Beauty's arms;
    Fresh enjoyments, wanton courting;
        Safe from all but Love's alarms;
    Round us roars the tempest louder,
        Think what seas our minds enthral;
    Harder yet it blows harder. - - -
        Now again the Bo'sun calls!

Quick. (4)
    The topsail-yards point to the wind, boys ---
        See all clear to reef each course - - -
    Let the fore-sheet go; don't mind, boys,
        Though the weather should be worse.
    Fore and aft the spritsail-yard get - - -
        Reef the mizen - - See all clear.
    Hands up each preventer-brace set - - -
        Man the fore-yard   Cheer, lads, cheer.

Slow.   (5)

    Now the dreadful thunder roaring,
        Peal on peal contending clash,
    On our heads fierce rain falls pouring,
        In our eyes blue lightnings flash.
    One wide water all around us,
        All above us one black sky.
    Different deaths at once surround us - - -
        Hark! - - - What means that dreadful cry

Quick.   (6)

    The fore-mast's gone! cries every tongue out;
        O'er the lee twelve feet 'bove deck;
    A leak beneath the chest-tree's sprung out - -
        Call all hands to clear the wreck.
    Quick the lanyards cut to pieces - - -
        Come, my hearts, be stout & bold!
    Plumb the well — the leak increases - - - -
        Four feet water in the hold!

Slow.   (7)

    While o'er the ship wild waves are beating,
        We for wives and children mourn;
    Alas! from hence there's no retreating;
        Alas! from hence there's no return.
    Still the leak is gaining on us,
        Both chain pumps are choak'd below;
    Heav'n have mercy here upon us!
        For only that can save us now.

Quick.   (8)

    O'er the lee beam is the land, boys.
        Let the guns o'erboard be thrown -
    To the pump come ev'ry hand, boys - - -
        See our mizen-mast is gone.
    The leak we've found it can't pour fast
        We've lighten'd her a foot or more;
    Up and rigging a jury-foremast - - -
        She rights! she rights! boys, wear of[f]
            shore

Slow.   (9)

    Now once more on joys we've [we're] thinking,
        Since kind Fortune sav'd our lives.
    Come, the cann boys, let's be drinking,
        To our sweet-hearts and wives.
    Fill it up about ship wheel it
        Close to th'lips a brimmer join
    Where's the tempest now who feels it!
        None. - - - Our danger's drown'd in wine.

Notes: Celebrated folk-musicologist Frank Kidson says of this: "As a purely nautical song, perhaps the above is the finest in the English Language. I think it would be impossible to convey in so small a space a more lucid and spirit-moving description of one of the old wooden men-of-war in a terrible storm with a lee shore in sight" (Kidson 1890 #14). The air was first published in 1730 in *The British Musical Miscellany*, vol. IV (Duncan I: 257). Stevens's poem was first published in 1754 in "a Marine medley" entitled *The Muses' Delight* (Duncan, op. cit.; Kidson, op. cit.) and again in *Apollo's Cabinet* (1757). Words and melody together were issued as sheet music soon after, and were anthologized as "The Storm" in 1788 in the collection entitled *Calliope* (London, 1788, 30; the "Welcome, welcome, brother debtor" text also appears, p. 441, with the designation "Tune, Cease, rude Boreas, page 30"); they were anthologized again in 1800 in the *Yorkshire Musical Miscellany* (Kidson, op. cit.). Huntington (1964, 70) gives an orthodox text of "The Storm" from a whaling journal of the 1820s, but, for reasons unexplained, entitles it "The Tempest" and confuses it with Colcord's rendition of "The Sailor's Come-All-Ye" ("Jolly Sailors Bold"). However, Huntington's choice of the "Welcome, brother debtor" air for the text he calls "Hearts of Gold"—which is actually a version of "The Sailor's Complaint" or "Jolly Sailors Bold" [#32]—is quite a good one, despite that he does not try to explain it: according to Chappell, though "Cease, Rude Boreas" is "the most famous" of the various texts set to permutations of this tune in the 18th century, others include: "How happy are the young lovers" ("On some rock, by seas surrounded"), which appeared in the ballad operas *Robin Hood* (1730) and *Silvia; or, The Country Burial* (1731); "Hosier's Ghost" (circa 1740), a poem by Richard Glover (1712-1785); and a companion piece, "Admiral Vernon's Answer to Admiral Hosier's Ghost," which was printed with "Hosier's Ghost" in J.O. Halliwell's *Early Naval Ballads of England* (1851). Even with so many alternatives, the melody that Chappell actually prints accompanies a text of "The Sailor's Complaint," identified as having come from John Walsh's *British Musical Miscellany* (1730) (Chappell 1893, II:165-166).

5. Henry Martin
[Henry Martyn; Salt Sea; The Three Brothers; Andrew Bardeen]
(Child #250)

This classic Anglo-Scottish ballad of piracy and sea-battle is based on an actual historical event at the turn of the 16th century, involving two kings of Scotland and Henry VIII of England. With an extensive provenance in tradition and in print dating back to the 17th century, it is known in virtually every corner of the English-speaking world and has been collected from oral tradition throughout the British Isles and North America. Thus, it seems significant that neither Dana nor Melville mentions it among the "classical songs of the sea" and that it was evidently rare on shipboard in the 19th century. The journals and memoirs of deepwater sailors seldom mention having encountered it, and only one mariner's text has been located, transcribed by William Keith in his journal of whaling and merchant voyages out of Boston and Wellfleet, Massachusetts, in the late 1860s and early 1870s.

There are several possible explanations for the evident failure of "Henry Martin" to make the mariners' hit parade. First of all, just because it may not have been a favorite in the whaling trade does not necessarily mean it was not popular on merchantmen. However, as merchant sailors rarely transcribed songs in their journals—in fact, compared with whalemen, merchant seamen rarely kept personal journals—there is little statistical evidence on either side of the question of the ballad's popularity in the merchant service. Or perhaps deepwater sailors just did not care for this ballad, which, unlike "Dark-Eyed Sailor" [#89], for example, has no love interest and, unlike "Boston" [#33], evidences little nautical sophistication (though the whaleman's text is more technologically specific than most). But the real reason may be that "Henry Martin" was not picked up by the 19th-century ballad and songster printers, who evidently provided seamen a surprisingly large proportion of their shipboard repertoire. Keith's manuscript text is strangely, naively Americanized in a few instances, beginning with the very first line: in orthodox versions the first line is commonly rendered, "There were three brothers in merry Scotland," but here the first line ("In Scotland city there lived three brothers") seems to lose track of the song's allusion to Bonnie Caledonia, as though it referred, say, to Scotland, Connecticut.

"Henry Martin" is descended from the English ballad "Sir Andrew Barton" (Child #167) which has an historical basis. A text entitled "Andrew Bardeen," collected in Oklahoma (Moore 1964, 115), preserves a vestige of the original name. In 1476 a "richly loaded" Scottish ship under the command of Andrew Barton's father was captured under questionable circumstances by a Portuguese squadron, and the Scottish king issued letters-of-reprisal authorizing the Bartons to plunder Portuguese shipping. Thirty years later, Andrew and his two brothers—all three of them "men of note in the naval history of Scotland"—were still seeking redress. The customary excesses occurred, in which Andrew "took the Englishmen's goods" under pretext of their being Portuguese; and this is the source of his fearsome reputation as "a pirate of the sea." The English story is that despite protests from England and Portugal, King James VI of Scotland reissued the Bartons's letters-of-reprisal in 1506; thus, in 1511, the Earl of Surrey and his sons, sailing as privateers under authority granted by young King Henry VIII, went after Andrew and vanquished him at sea (Child III:334-338). The Scottish story, in the words of Scots historian Andrew Lang, is that "in 1507 the pope failed to draw James into the league formed to check French aggression in Italy… [thus] the Holy League of 1511 against France found James committed to the cause of the old French alliance." Thus, far from being a pirate, in Scotland Andrew Barton is considered to be the legitimate "admiral" of King James, in whose service Barton died of wounds sustained in a patriotic engagement arising from Scotland's de facto alliance with France against England and the Holy League (*Enc.Brit.* 24:442).

As a ballad "Sir Andrew Barton" may subscribe to the English point of view, but whether or not Andrew Barton the historical personage was a proper pirate is strictly a matter of perspective:

to an Englishman he was a brigand; to a Scot or a Frenchman, perhaps, a hero. However, in the case of "Henry Martin" piracy is not a function of viewpoint but a demonstrable certainty, about which the narrative is unequivocally specific: there is neither politics nor patriotism here, only Henry's desire to raise money "to maintain his two brothers and he." And the ballad implies that he does this quite successfully, though it does not state categorically that he actually boards the English merchantman or removes any booty before sinking it.

TUNE: "Henry Martin" from Cecil J. Sharp, *One Hundred English Folk Songs,* 1916, #1, p.1: a minor-modal melody well suited to the text, but requiring adaptation to accommodate the whaleman's refrain. Compare the two versions in Kidson 1891 (and 1893), pp. 30f; and the 50 versions gathered by Bronson IV:24-46.

"SALT SEA": William H. Keith, whaling schooner *William Martin* of Boston, merchant schooners *Edith May* of Wellfleet, *Cora Nash* of Boston, etc., circa 1865-72.

1. In Scotland city there lived three brothers,
   Three brothers of late, brothers three.
   And they did cast lots to see which of them
   Should go robbing on the salt sea.
   Chorus: Salt sea.
              And they did cast &c. &c.

2. The lot it fell to Henry Martin,
   The youngest of these brothers three,
   That he should go robbing all on the salt sea
   To maintain his two brothers and he.
   Cho.—   And he
              (Repeat last two lines)

3. They sailed all night until the morning
   Until the morning sailed he
   Then they espied a tall lofty ship
   Come sailing down under their lee.
   Chorus: Their lee.
              (Repeat last two lines)

4. Who's there, whoes there cries Henry Martin
   Who's there comes sailing so nigh.
   T'is a rich merchant ship to London she's bound
   If you please you may let her pass by.
   Cho.—   Pass by. &c. &c.

5. Back your main topsail and heave your ship to
   Come drift down under my lee,

And I will take from you your rich flowing gold,
and your bodies I'll sink in the sea.
Cho.—   Salt sea   &c. &c.

6. I'll not back my main topsail nor heave my ship to
Nor come down under your lee.
But we will save from you our rich flowing gold
And our bodies we'll save from the sea.
Cho.—   Salt sea   &c. &c.

7. Broadsides, broadsides they gave to each other
Broadsides they gave two or three.
When Henry Martin gave them their death wound
And their bodies he sank in the sea.
Cho.—   Salt sea   &c. &c.

8. Bad news bad news go tell to old England
Bad news I tell unto thee.
For a rich merchant ship has been robbed, set adrift
And her mariners sunk in the sea
Cho.—   Salt sea   &c. &c.   (Finis)

Notes: Child maintains that this ballad "must have sprung from the ashes of 'Andrew Barton', of which name Henry Martyn would be no extraordinary corruption" (IV:393). Laboring over Child's syntax, Bronson respectfully argues for a closer relationship: "…The life history of ['Sir Andrew Barton'] cannot justly be separated from that of its avatar, 'Henry Martyn' (N° 250). The present division is made only out of deference to Child's example and for the sake of consistency of method" (III:133). However, while "Andrew Barton" is historically and politically based, and in as many as 82 stanzas goes into some specific detail about the royal intrigue surrounding Barton's "piracy," "Henry Martin" is a far shorter and less complex affair: its form, syntax, meter, narrative structure, and plot distinguish it as a separate, though certainly derivative ballad about pure, mercenary piracy, without a political or patriotic subtext. "A True Relation of the life and death of Sir Andrew Barton, a Pyrate and Rover on the Seas" (as it is titled in some broadsides) may be the oldest surviving ballad in English on the theme of swashbuckling freebootery under sail; at least it concerns the earliest scenario of any extant pirate song (on the other hand, the earliest known broadsides of it were not printed until circa 1648-80; several other pirate ballads thus predate it in print). Based on historical events spanning the end of the 15th and beginning of the 16th centuries, according to Bronson it was popular in the 16th century and remained so well into the 18th. While it did not enjoy the subsequent staying-power at sea or ashore that other pirate ballads have enjoyed—even the original air may be lost—it remains a hoary cornerstone of the sea-rover repertoire and the direct ancestor of "Henry Martin." In Tudor times and long after, there was a formal distinction between true piracy on the high seas—the pelagic preying upon seagoing ships of any nationality for pure adventure and pecuniary gain—and privateering, which is often called merely a legalized form of piracy. Privateers (the word refers both to the vessels and the human participants) were granted so-called letters-of-marque—licenses issued by the crown or by Parliament authorizing specified privately-operated vessels to harass and plunder hostile shipping, a practice widely regarded as a necessary adjunct in wartime as navies were not yet sufficiently developed to disrupt enemy shipping and supply-lines to a comparable degree. The prime incentives were adventure and profit. Licensed privateers were not subject to the whims and dictates of the Admiralty, thus could operate virtually without restriction; the proceeds of plunder were commonly retained by the captors as booty (though in some circumstances it was divided with government authority according to formula, which increasingly became the practice in later centuries). Naturally enough, as candidates for sea-roving adventure were not necessarily the most deferential and self-effacing subjects of the Crown, errors and excesses were many. In the Tudor and Stuart eras especially, the distinction between piracy and letter-of-marque privateering was not so finely drawn. Buccaneers tended to interpret their licenses liberally, navigating around the legal niceties. In "Andrew Barton," the effect is epitomized in the merchant's reluctance to send his ships and cargo to sea because "Sir Andrew Barton makes us quail" (stanza 4). In "Henry Martin," one puzzles why the sea-rover broadcasts his piratical intentions in time for his intended prey to stage a resistance, thereby perhapshaps sinking the cargo along with ship and crew.

6. The Bold Trinity
[The Golden Vanity; The Sweet Trinity; The Golden Willow Tree; The Green Willow Tree]
(Child #286)

> The Captain... was all excitement, saying, 'He stands up! Only strike that whale and I will give you anything I have, anything except my wife'; and as my iron struck the whale he threw off his hat, saying, "He is fast! Take my wife and all I have!"
> I guess he forgot about his offer after we got on board, for I got nothing but the proud satisfaction that I had struck my first whale and proved that a boy only seventeen years old could fill a man's place on a whaleman's deck.
> — Nelson Cole Haley, *Whale Hunt*

As "Henry Martin" [#5] is an evolved form of "Sir Andrew Barton," this heroic old ballad, concerning a cabin boy who rescues his ship from a piratical enemy and is then betrayed by his own captain's treachery, is descended from "Sir Walter Raleigh Sailing in the Lowlands" (Child #286), a ballad of circa 1635. An anonymous broadside published in London gives the original title in full: "Sir Walter Raleigh Sailing in the Low-lands. Shewing how the famous Ship called the SWEET TRINITY was taken by a false Gally, and how it was again restored by the craft of a little Sea-boy, who sunk the Gally; as the following song will declare. To the Tune of, The Sailing in the Low-Lands. Printed for J. CONYERS, at the BLACK-RAVEN the first shop in FETTER-LANE next HOLBORN" (Euing #334; Frank 1998 #7). The later "Bold Trinity"/"Golden Vanity"/"Sweet Trinity" form is extremely widely distributed in the British Isles and North America; it seems also to have been fairly popular among English and American sailors, but less so among whalemen, in whose journals only this one, foreshortened text of circa 1829 has been located. Lyrics recovered from tradition on both sides of the Atlantic are of two essential formats, having stanzas of either two or three lines, customarily followed by a slightly variable refrain of one line that is repeated. The two-line stanza seems to have prevailed in the southern highlands of North America, while deepwater ballad and chantey manifestations are generally of the three-line type, including a manifestation from New York State of which Cazden (1982, #67) claims the text and tune to be unique. Surprisingly, the Yankee whaleman's fragmentary text belongs to the two-line species, of which few examples have hitherto been encountered at sea or ashore in New England (and which Bronson's taxonomy identifies as tune group C). There are tunes and variants in major, minor, and modal keys, but of the many extant, a haunting modal melody collected in Vermont is the only compatible specimen to have been recovered from New England tradition.

TUNE: "The Green Willow Tree," from Helen Hartness Flanders and Marguerite Olney, *Ballads Migrant in New England,* 1953, IV:195: collected in Vermont. Compare: Bronson IV:346, #80 [Hammond Coll., Cecil Sharp House, London]; and Bronson IV:354, #96 [Library of Congress Archive of American Folk Song #11,435(B5)].

A.

[UNTITLED.] A very foreshortened version transcribed by Edward W. Collins, 1829, in a journal formerly belonging to his brother, Silas Collins, seaman aboard the brig *By Chance* of Dartmouth, Massachusetts, 1826-27.

1.   I have a ship in the North Countries
    And she goes by the name of the Bold Trinity
    And she sails in the lowlands, lowlands low
    And she sails in the lowlands low

2.   She had not sailed past glasses two or three
    Before she espied a French gallee
    As she sailed in the lowlands...

3.   Then up steps the little cabin boy
    Saying, What will you give the ship to destroy
    And to sink her in the lowlands...

4.   'Tis I will give you gold, 'tis I will give you fee
    And my eldest daughter your wedded wife shall be
    If you'll sink her in the lowlands...

5.   In his hand he carried an auger fitter for his work
    Of which he bored four-and-twenty holes all in a quick
    And he sank her in the lowlands...

B.

"THE CRUISE IN THE LOWLANDS LOW." A more complete text from a deepwater source: "'This sea ballad I heard in Black Forest [Pennsylvania] in 1874, sung by John A. Watts, a deep sea sailor before the mast, and I now write it from memory for the first time, and there might be slight errors in the words used to express the tale of poetic justice and gusto of the men 'who went down to the sea in ships!'—John C. French, Roulette [Pennsylvania], 1918" (Shoemaker, *Mountain Minstrelsy of Pennsylvania*, 133). *Mary Golden Tree* is an unlikely name for a Turkish vessel, and in the many texts in which it appears it is almost always the name of the protagonist's ship. Retribution on the captain is not ordinarily a part of the "*Sweet Trinity*" cycle.

1   Our good ship sailed from the north countree—
    She went by the name of the "Green Willow Tree."

    Chorus— As she sailed in the lowlands, lowlands—
              As she sailed in the lowlands low.

2   We had been out but two days or three,
    When we espied a Turk's ship a-lee.

3   Up jumped the cabin boy: "What will you give me
    If I sink that pirate a-lee?"

4   "Oh," said our captain, "I'll give you golden store,
    And my only daughter you shall wed, soon as we reach the shore,
    If you'll sink her in the low lands low."

5   The boy had an instrument, made for the use,
    Four and twenty holes, to make at one push.

6   He bent upon his breast and away swam he,
Swam to the "Merry Golden Tree."

7   Some were playing cards and some throwing dice,
When he let in the water and put out their lights.

8   Some took their hats and some took their caps,
To shut out the salt water caps.

9   The boy bent his breast and away swam he,
Swam till he came to the "Green Willow Tree."

10   "Captain, oh captain, take me aboard,
And be unto me as good as your word,
For I sunk her in the lowlands low."

11   "No," said the captain, "I'll not take you aboard,
Nor be unto you as good as my word;
You may sink with them in the lowlands low."

12   The boy bent his breast and down sank he,
Sank by the side of the "Green Willow Tree."

13   We took that captain to the starboard side,
And threw him overboard in the lowland tide.

14   He sank by the side of the "Green Willow Tree,"
And he drowned like the Turk's revelry.

15   We weighed the anchor on our starboard side,
And sailed away with a fair wind and tide.

16   Away and away our good ship did plough,
As we sailed from the lowlands low.

Note: The names of the principal vessels vary widely in the numerous versions of the ballad that survive; so too the nationality of the enemy warship—French, Turkish, Spanish—which seems to mirror fluctuations in international politics from one era to the next. As ship-names, "Golden Vanity" and "Sweet Trinity" (less so "Bold Trinity" or "Mary Golden Tree") imply symbolic significances, now lost but perhaps open to theological interpretation. The "lowlands" refrain, where lowlands refers to the sea rather than to any "low land," is an epithet originally alluding to the Dutch Provinces, the so called Pay-Bas or Low Countries—as in "The Lowlands of Holland" [#19], a Scots-Irish ballad of 17th-century origin about impressment into the royal service to fight a European enemy overseas. In oral tradition, some "Golden Vanity" and "Bold Trinity" texts have understandably been corrupted with the infusion of phrases from the mid 19th-century minstrel song "Louisiana Lowlands" ("In the Old Virginia Lowlands"), which phrases "Bold Trinity" may have inspired.

7. High Barbary
[The Coast of Barbary; High Barbaree]
(Child #285; Laws #K-33)

This venerable ballad has roots in an ancestral Elizabethan and Jacobean form, "The Sailor's onely Delight, Shewing the brave Fight between the George-Aloe, the Sweepstake, and certain Frenchmen at Sea" (Child #285), originally published in London around 1595 and issued in an enlarged edition in 1611. A portion of it appears in *The Noble Kinsman,* a play published in 1634 that was at one time spuriously attributed to the collaboration of William Shakespeare and John Fletcher. Firth suggests that the original ballad may have an historical basis in the issuance of official letters of marque for an English privateer named *Sweepstakes* in 1596, and Child cites a tune called "The Sailor's Joy," registered in 1595 but now evidently extinct, to which air "The George Aloe and the Sweepstake" is said to have been sung. "High Barbary" or "The Coast of Barbary" is the incarnation in which the ballad was known to sailors in the 19th century (unaccountably, Laws erroneously attributes it to Charles Dibdin). The two whalemen's texts here are manifestations of the ballad situated chronologically midway between Melville's mention of it in *Omoo* (1847) and efforts to collect songs from oral tradition "in the field" in the late 19th century. It was sung in navy wardrooms, and, probably thanks to a hearty double refrain, it was occasionally used before the mast as a chantey. The names of the vessels and specific details of the text vary widely, but the hallmark theme is consistently that two English ships engage and vanquish the "bold pirate" in a vigorous sea battle.

TUNE from *Naval Songs,* New York, 1883, p. 16; also Luce, *Naval Songs,* 1889, p. 77. Transposed from G minor. Second ending variant supplied from tradition (see numerous specimens in Bronson III:306-311).

A.

"COAST OF BARBARY." Horace Wood, bark *Andrews* of New Bedford, 1866-67. Here the phrase "yard arm to yard arm" replaces the usual "broadside to broadside" and is clearly intended to indicate the relative positions of the ships, rather than volleys of cannon fire.

1   There was two lofty ships I would have you understand
        Blow you high, blow you low, and so sailed we
    The one the Princess Charlotte and the other the Prince of Wales
        Cruising down on the coast of Barbary

2   Go aloft, go aloft our noble Captain cries
    Look ahead, look astern, look to windward and to lee

3   There is nothing ahead, there is nothing astern
      But a loft[y] ship to wind'ard and a loft[y] ship is she

4   O hail the lofty ship our noble Captain cries
      Are you a Man of War or a Privateer said he

5   I am neither a Man of War nor a Privateer said he
      But I am a jolly Pirate as ever you did see

6   Yard arm and yard arm the gallant ships did lay
      Until the Princess Charlotte shot the Pirate's mast away

7   For quarters for quarters this jolly Pirate cried
      But the quarters that we gave them we sank them in the sea

B.

"COAST OF BARBARY." Holmes C. Fisher, written in the journal of George W. Piper, ship *Europa* of Edgartown, Martha's Vineyard, 1868-70; signed "Your friend & Shipmate / Holmes C. Fisher. Edgartown, Mass."

1.   Two fine ships from England did sail
      Blow high, blow low, and so sailed we
      One was the Prince Rupert and the other Prince of Wales
          Cruising down the coast of high Barbary

2.   Oh then hail her! then hail her! the Captain he did cry
      Are you a man-of-war or a privateer? says he

3.   Oh I am neither man-of-war nor privateer, says he
      But I am a bold pirate and am seeking for a prey

4.   Then to broadsides, to broadsides these noble ships did come
      Till at last the English ship the pirates' mast away had blown

5.   For more than two long hours this battle lasted as you see
      The ship it was their coffin, their grave it was the sea

8. Spanish Ladies
[Farewell and Adieu]

The day passed away; the sun sank behind the blue mountains of Mexico, and night flung her spangled curtains over and around the scene... and the crew were assembled on the forecastle whiling away the time with the good old songs and stories that still constitute the chief shipboard pastime of poor Jack. Old songs and old stories, because your thorough-bred tar despises everything like innovation in either; and the ditties and ballads that resounded through the decks of old England's oaken castles, perhaps fifty years before were now chanted from the forecastle in the "Sparrow Hawk," with all their original beauty and pathos, not deteriorating one iota from their frequency of repetition, and awakening as much feeling and interest in the weather-beaten breast of the worn-out mariners as when they first broke upon his ear. As many of our readers may not have had the good fortune to have heard what is called a sea-song, we subjoin a verse extracted from one which their universal suffrage has rendered the most popular.

"It's farewell and adieu to ye, Spanish ladies,
It's farewell and adieu to ye, ladies of Spain,
For we've received orders to set sail from Cadiz,
In hopes that short time we may see you again."

— Captain Frederick Marryatt,
The Sea King (circa 1840).

This homeward-bound song rehearses stanza-by-stanza the geography and ship-handling operations of a passage through the English Channel to the Downs, culminating in a convivial toast at voyage's end. It originated with the Grand Fleet of the Royal Navy stationed at Cádiz in 1695, in anticipation of the return to England later that year; and it persisted virtually intact into the 20th century, with two principal variants of the melody emerging, the older one in a minor key, a more modern one, perhaps no earlier than the 1890s, in a major key. As Captain Marryatt and Herman Melville indicate, it was universally popular in the Royal Navy and the British and American merchant services, where it was sometimes used as a chantey at the capstan or windlass. In *Moby Dick*, the chapter entitled "Midnight Forecastle" opens with "the watch...all singing in chorus, 'Farewell and adieu to you, Spanish Ladies'" (Ch. 40); and in *White-Jacket* not only does Melville refer to it as "a favorite thing with British man-of-war's men," but the text can be interpreted as a coded key to revealing ulterior meanings in the novel. It is also featured in the film version of Patrick O'Brian's *Master and Commander* (2003). On shipboard and in numerous local adaptations ranging from sailors' and fishers' ditties in New England to a drovers' song in Queensland, the second stanza typically functions as a chorus that is repeated after each verse. Oddly, whaleman George Piper's text appears to have been influenced by Liverpool, which has nothing historically to do with the Grand Fleet of the 1690s; yet, despite mention of the Mersey, the other geographical allusions, though slightly corrupted, nevertheless unequivocally refer to the passage through the English Channel to London. Piper's essentially orthodox text is thus an additional indication that, for all its minor variations, "Spanish Ladies" has been remarkably stable on three continents, with a little galaxy of descendants on dusty Australian sheep stations, on blue water, and in the North Atlantic outports.

TUNE A. "Farewell and Adieu," from Captain W.B. Whall, *Sea Songs and Shanties, Glasgow,* 1910, n.p.: "This here given is the original one: there is a modern substitute in a major key, with none of the character of this one." The chorus is sung by repeating the principal air. Transposed from G minor. Compare Sharp 1916, #97; and Perrin, 318 and 352, which are in the true Æolian mode while this one is in the harmonic minor, i.e., with sharp seventh.

TUNE B. "Farewell and Adieu to You," from Davis & Tozer, *Sailors' Songs or Chanties,* London: Boosey, 1887, #50. Perhaps uniquely, the chorus is a variation of the principal melody rather than merely a repeat of it.

"FAREWELL AND ADIEU." George W. Piper, ship *Europa* of Edgartown, 1868-70. The whaleman's text is corrupt with respect to geographical details and place-names, but is otherwise intact and by no means Americanized. Though no chorus is indicated in the MS, the second stanza is customarily repeated as a refrain. The orthography indicates that it may have been transcribed directly from singing or recitation.

1. Fare you well and adieu to ye Spanish Ladies
   Fare you well and adieu to ye Ladies of Spain
   For I have received orders for to sail for Old England
   But I hope in a short time for to see you again

2. We will rant and we will roar like true British sailors
   We will rant and we will roar all o'er the salt sea
   Until we strike soundings in the channel of Old England
   From Uceant[4] to Mersey[5] is thirty five leagues[6]

3. Then we hauled back our main yard all for to get soundings
   Then we hauled back our main yard and soundings got we
   It was thirty five fathoms with a white sandy bottom
   We squared in our fore yard up the channel steered we

4. O the first land we made it was called the Dead Man[7]
   Next Ram's Head off Plymouth, Start, Portland and the Wight
   We sailed by Beachy the Fairly and the Dunehenes
   And the[n] bore away for the South Foreland Light

---

[4] *Ushant:* a standard British corruption for *Ile d'Oussant,* an island off the Norman coast of France, the significance of which to sailors is that it is the first landfall on the homeward passage through the English Channel to Southampton, Portsmouth, London, and lesser ports along the south coast of England.

[5] The nearly universal phrase is "from Ushant to Scilly…," the two gateways on either side of the English Channel: Ushant, on the French side; and Scilly, off Land's End, Cornwall, on the English side. The Mersey is, of course, the river estuary on which the ports of Liverpool and Birkenhead are situated, and was thus perhaps the best known and most frequently visited English river in the 19th century; its presence here is a naive corruption. Later allusions, per orthodox versions of the song, are to landfalls and place-names on the south coast of England, along the eastward route through the English Channel toward London.

[6] See Hugill 1969, 386, for a discussion of variations in the song's representation of the distance between Ushant and Scilly, none of which have geographical or historical relevance to the distance between Ushant and the Mersey.

[7] *Dead Man:* A corruption of *Dodman,* in reference to Dodman's Point, Cornwall.

5. The signal it was given for the grand fleet to anchor
   All in the Dow[n]s that night for to meet
   Then it is stand by your stoppers see clear your shank painters
   Haul in your clew garnets stick out tacks and sheets

6. Now let every seaman toss off a full bumper
   Now let every bold seaman toss off a full bowl
   For we will drink and be merry and drown melancholy
   With a health to each jovial and true hearted soul

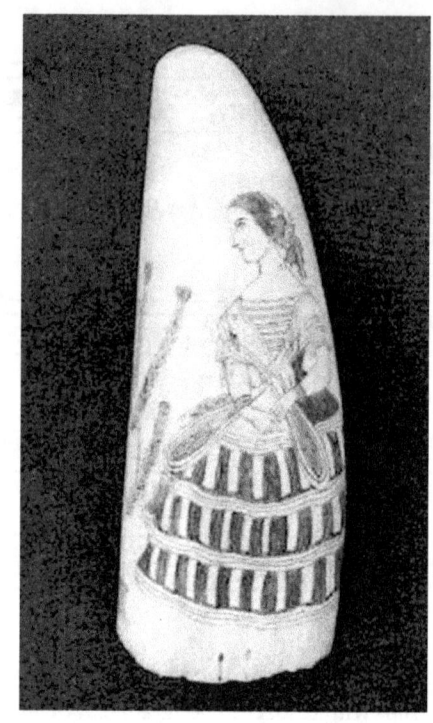

Anonymous whaleman's scrimshaw on a sperm whale tooth, American, mid 19th century. New Bedford Whaling Museum

Notes: Baring-Gould corrects textual errors, notably in the broadside literature. The origins and provenance were convincingly established by L.G. Carr Laughton and others in an exchange of letters in the "Queries and Answers" column of *The Mariners' Mirror* during 1919-21 (q.v.; also Frank 1985, 746-731). With regard to the tune, in the same series of exchanges W.G. Perrin cites P.W. Joyce as authority for his contention that the "standard" (minor-key) tune is derived from a traditional Irish air, appropriately entitled "Farewell to Spain"; however, given the age of the "Spanish Ladies" text, and that a mere coincidence in the titles is highly improbable, the direction of influence is not certain (which presents much the same quandary as that of Prince Hoare's "The Saucy Arethusa" versus its Irish twin, "The Princess Royal," attributed to Turloch O'Carolan—a classic Hobson's Choice between plagiarism of an English composer or the assimilative folk-memory of the Irish bards. "Farewell to Spain" versus "Spanish Ladies" is equally enigmatic, but there can be no doubt that they inhabit the very same tune). Apart from bringing to light a few texts and tunes hitherto forgotten, the upshot of the discussion is essentially what Sharp had said of the song a few years earlier: "The tune is in the Æolian mode and, in my opinion, it is one of the grandest of our folk-tunes and one of which a seafaring nation may well be proud. Nowadays, alas! sailors sing a modernized and far less beautiful form of the air in a major mode" (Sharp 1916, xi). Hugill, who favors the "major mode" tune and who was at the time unaware of Baring-Gould or the *Mariners' Mirror* discussion, restated this same position from the opposite point of view: "It has two tunes—the more livelier [sic] and faster one being preferred by the later generation of sailing-ship men" (Hugill 1969, 384); however, Hugill's minor-key tune is quite different from the ones collected elsewhere. It has not been noted in the published literature that "The Countersigns" (Colcord, 134; reprinted from Trident, 14), an obscure American naval song about John Paul Jones (Revolutionary War), James Lawrence (War of 1812), and David Farragut (Civil War), is also sung to the major-key melody of "Spanish Ladies." Nothing much seems to be known about that song, but it is certainly of comparatively recent vintage—probably not much earlier than the Spanish-American War; and it may have influenced the major-key tune. Finally, as Perrin observes from the minor-key melody given by Joyce, "the second section of the air is marked to repeat"; however, he is mistaken that "this would seem to indicate that there was a refrain to each verse, now lost." Irish tunes tend *pro forma* to repeat, whether or not the texts to which they are connected—or to which they become connected—mirror such repeats, and whether or not repeats are indicated in a latter-day musical score. Also, just because an English navy song on a 17th-century theme may sound like or be related to a traditional air of unknown vintage, it does not necessarily follow after years—centuries—of separate evolution, until the text and tune are finally anthologized, that the parallel phrases and repeats of each will remain identical, if they ever were identical. "Spanish Ladies" was customarily sung with a chorus, the text of which is well known to have been what Mackenzie calls "the second stanza repeated"; and the chorus is in most instances sung to the regular air, repeated. Uniquely among principal versions, Davis & Tozer's, published in 1887, has a chorus tune that is not so much a repeat of the melody as a development or true variant of it. Even so, the chorus text is the same as elsewhere, "We'll rant and we'll roar…," and could not be less "lost."

CHAPTER TWO
The Girl I Left Behind Me
Songs About Women

> [February 1857] ... The Capt[ain] spoke to me that we might possibly have a female visitor in the after-cabin as the Capt of the brig had a wife on board... At first the very thought astonished me, but I mustered up all of my energy and endeavored to make the best of it.... I was somewhat pleased with the boy's yarn that he had to spin after he was released from the stateroom where circumstances placed him for a short time. Says he, "I had a fair sight at her. I peeked through the keyhole and viewed her from top to toe, &c." As for myself I did not call her very handsome although being deprived from the society of them for so long a time. She looked more angelical than any thing else, and I earnestly believe that it is for the want of good female society among seamen that causes them to be degraded below any other class of people. There would be less drinking, carousing, gambling &c when they return to port and many other things that tend to corrupt the morals of the seafaring men.
>
> — Benjamin Franklin Gallup, seaman, bark *South America* of New Bedford.

Many of the sailors' songs about women were sentimental parlor pieces lifted from the popular repertoire [see Appendix 8]; others were songs of parting, understandably a dominant theme when it comes to seafaring, often of the sailors' own manufacture [Chapter 3]. Still others were ballads telling stories of love and courtship, borrowed from oral tradition and printed broadsides and carried to sea in large numbers [Chapters 8-11]. Some were yarns about entanglements ashore, many of them comic and self-deprecating [Chapter 12]. But the songs in this section are neither the tearful songs of farewell, nor the narrative ballads of lovers parted, nor the heroic epics of winning a bride in the face of adversity; rather, they are the songs about the women left behind—reveries and amorous fancies about wives and sweethearts back home, from the sailors' perspective of being perpetually away at sea.

For centuries, much has been made in the popular imagination of sailors' bawdy language and lewd behavior. And while the sailor has ever been more the victim than perpetrator in such matters, there are substantial historical reasons for his unsavory reputation in the culture at large. In classical antiquity, common sailors were mostly galley slaves, and ship's crews were typically comprised of convicted criminals and captured prisoners-of-war — expendable pariahs, in steady supply, who were of no sentimental consequence to the ruling elite and posed a potential threat to the hierarchical society if allowed to intermingle. Galley oarsmen were sequestered, literally caged and shackled, to keep them separate, submissive, and under control. From this beginning, and down through the centuries, the legacy of mariners is as an underclass, as the pawns of complex political, mercantile, and naval interests, in comparison with which the sailors' welfare and well being stacked up as inconsequential. Even the labor-conscious advances of the late 19th century left sailors struggling and their unionization movement retarded: in order to work, sailors had constantly to be going away to sea, at best attending union meetings only intermittently; so continuity among leadership and membership tended to be sporadic at best. Meanwhile, the sailors' accustomed confinement for long periods on shipboard without women or freedom or drink—lacking family stability, adequate recreation, and the moral counseling of the church — added to the perceived social and biological consequences of his presumptive fraternizing with unsavory elements in filthy sailortowns abroad, could only contribute to the stereotype. This fueled polite society's jaundiced prejudices and created a self-fulfilling prophesy that sailors will get into trouble when let loose ashore. In European cultures, and hence our own, sailors have always been segregated as an unseemly element and quarantined from the nicer parts of town.

Sailors' chanteys—the seamen's own sailor-made shipboard work songs—loom large in the popular imagination as monstrously lewd, unsuitable for singing when any landlubber or woman might be present. This is true only to a degree: social improprieties have indeed been committed in the conceptual fabric and rude language of some sailors' chanteys, few of which have ever been documented in print or sung in the raw state in public to general audiences. Part of the reason that the "dirty versions" of sea songs remain mostly unknown is that mariners themselves have been shy about singing them: too polite, too embarrassed, and too reluctant to offend. After all, it was sailors, not folklorists, who censored and expurgated the texts, refusing to sing the dirty ones, in order to protect society from an ugly (and perhaps not all that significant) aspect of shipboard culture. If Stan Hugill's 20th-century experiences can be interpolated to reflect at least partly upon the larger, earlier context of sea-labor in square-rig, there certainly were a lot of unprintable texts of chanteys, but they were sung only occasionally and with the impolite content mostly taking the form of crude expletives—as opposed to, say, high allegory or clever double entendre; so they tended not to be very interesting or memorable.

In the 19th century the reality was that most whalemen were not hardened reprobates, but callow, fumbling boys. They mostly came from ordinary families in the whaling towns, from the farms and villages of the American hinterland, or were among the happy few able to escape from sharecropping or urban ghettos and factories. Anecdotal data indicates that even the many foreigners, far from being the dregs of Dickensian London, revolutionary anarchists, or fugitives from criminal prosecution, were mostly hopeful immigrants—English, Scottish, Irish, Portuguese, Continental European, African, Polynesian, even the occasional Asian, mostly young and inexperienced. Which is to say that while whaling did transpire as an all-male society, it was not an all-male society of angry criminals and vicious womanizers. There must have been plenty of hard language even aboard the many whalers where pietistic captains forbade swearing (and, of course, according to whalemen's firsthand testimony, some whaling masters were guilty of the hardest language and worst abuse imaginable); and there certainly must have been lewd and foul-mouthed chanteys. The point is that crudity and coarseness were demonstrably not the prevalent impulses at sea any more than they were on shore; that the literary compositions and private meditations of whalemen in their journals indicate quite the opposite; that, if anything, as a group these lads tended more towards being sentimental, predominantly pious (even when iconoclastic), enthusiastically patriotic, sometimes stridently, even self-righteously temperate and, when it came to women—much more often than not—reverential, even fawning. The passage quoted above from Franklin Gallup's journal typifies the gawky adolescence that frequently characterizes the whalemen's ruminations on women and sex. Even in a lascivious state of mind, few whalemen would likely have had anything of real prurience to say, owing, if nothing else, to inexperience.

Even were lewd pictures and verse in wide circulation, a whaleman's journal is one of the last places one would expect to find them immortalized. Journals were not only personal records of voyages, but were often explicitly intended—or implicitly expected to function—as souvenirs for mothers, sweethearts, and wives back home. Nevertheless, a few bawdy and suggestive songs have come to light. One of the finest is "The Young Virgin," a progressive "song of occupations" that cleverly manipulates the double-entendre significances of the tools and practices of various trades and professions without resorting to crude or explicit language (collected by Huntington from Thomas Delano's journal of the *Herald* of Fairhaven, 1817-18; Huntington 1964, 100). Three others, each equally good in its way, appear below, at least two of them evidently original songs written by the whalemen who transcribed them: "The Carpenter and the Maid" [#15], in which nothing racier occurs than that the girlfriend loses her virginity; "The Milking Maid" [#16], a classic-type roll-in-the-hay narrative with a few surprisingly graphic remarks; and the *piece de resistance,* "Frozen Limb" [#17], which is the most explicitly sexual literary art yet discovered in the whalemen's journals.

9. The Girl I Left Behind Me

The two whalemen's texts, which begin "I'm lonesome since I crossed the hills," are variants of what appears to be the original form of this ubiquitous Anglo-Irish folk song, which over more than a century-and-a-half in active circulation accumulated several quite different sets of lyrics and evolved into an entire family of songs, all sung to a traditional air called "Brighton Camp." Most of the texts incorporate some form of the refrain "the girl I left behind me," and most have been recovered from tradition at one time or another. The name and nationality of the tune are disputed between England and Ireland, but whatever its genesis and original name (and Fitz-Gerald may be right that it was known in Ireland in the seventeenth century), perhaps because early in its life in the eighteenth century "Brighton Camp" was recruited by military file-and-drum corps for regular ceremonial use in the British Isles and the colonies, the tune has been comparatively constant and stable, as much in North America as in England and Ireland. It was certainly a standard in the marching tune repertoire on both sides of the American Revolution.

There are several divergent manifestations of the lyrics. Admiral Luce's rendition in *Navy Songs* and both of the whalemen's texts are traditional, beginning "I'm lonesome since I crossed the hill(s)" (form 1 of the lyrics). Chappell presents a convincing argument that this form "may be dated with great probability in 1758" (Chappell 1893, 189), making it contemporaneous with the French and Indian War. Shay's version in *Iron Men and Wooden Ships* (form 2), beginning "The dames of France are wild and free," has later lyrics written by the Irish poet Thomas Davis (AKA Davies) (1814-1845), intended for the same air (O'Reilly 520). These are the two forms of the words that were most frequently encountered at sea and which have been anthologized in various "national" songbooks in England and Ireland as well as in dozens of folksong collections bearing such epithetical titles as "fifty best," "world's finest," and "best loved." Other versions, variants, adaptations, and parodies, most notably including Irish lyrics by Thomas Moore and Samuel Lover, enjoyed varying degrees of more fleeting popularity ashore. In introducing his rendition in *The Songs of Ireland* (1873), J.L. Molloy states categorically, "This melody, although claimed by the English, is indisputably of Irish origin, and has been sung, with the words here published, for many centuries in Ireland"; however, the words he actually prints are not the traditional ones, but the latter-day lyrics by Thomas Davis, which could not have been even forty years old when *The Songs of Ireland* was published. If Molloy can be so mistaken about the words, he also can be in error about the tune.

TUNE - "Brighton Camp, or The Girl I Left Behind Me," from William Chappell, *Old English Popular Music*, [1840] 1893, II:187f; transposed from E^b Major. Compare *Davidson's Universal Melodist* (1848), II: 407; Hullah, 76; etc., where minor differences are in evidence primarily in the gracenote-like slurs.

A.

"THE GIRL I LEFT BEHIND ME." William Gillaspia, ship *Atlantic* of Nantucket, 1846-49 (4/4). Slightly corrupted and incomplete. No chorus indicated.

1. im lonesome since i crossd the hills
   and or the mor that sedges
   with heavy thoughts my mind is filed
   since i have parted nagy

2. when ere i turn to view the place
   the tears doth fall and blind me
   when i think on the charming grace
   of the girl i left behind me

3. the hours i [do] r[e]member well
   when nex to sea doth move me
   the burning flames my heart doth feel
   [*line missing in the MS*]

4. in serch of some one fair and gay
   sevrel doth [re]mind me
   i no my darling loves me well
   though i left her behind me

B.

"THE GIRL I LEFT BEHIND ME." Henry Tripp Pettey, bark *Mary Ann* of New Bedford, 1853-55; and bark *Chili* of New Bedford, 1856-59.

1. I am lonesome since I crossed the hills
   And o'er the moor that's sedgy
   With heavy thoughts my mind is filled
   Since I have parted peggy

2. Where e'er I turn to view the place
   The tears do fill and blind me
   When I think on the charming scene
   Of the girl I left behind me

3. The hours I remember well
   When next to see doth move me
   The burning flame my heart doth fill
   Since first she owned she loved me

4. In search of some one fair and gay
   Several doth remind me
   I know my darling loves me well
   Though I left her behind me

5. The bees shall lavish make no share
   And the dove becomes a ranger
   The fallen water cease to roar
   Before I'll ever change her

6. Each mutual promise faithfully made
   By her whom tears do blind me
   And bless the hours I passed away
   With the girl I left behind me

7. My mind her image full retains
   Whether asleep or awakened
   I hope to se[e] my jewel again
   For her my heart is breaking

8. And if e'er I chance to go that way
   And that she has not resigned me
   I will recoil my mind to stay
   With the girl I left behind me.

10. The Lily of Lake Champlain
[The Lily of the Lake; The Lady of Lake Champlain]

This anonymous ballad-like song, which has been encountered in three whaling journals of 1860s vintage, survives in two distinct forms. One is conventional and predictable; the other has a bizarre twist. At core in both is a pleasantly formulaic celebration of the charms of "my lovely Mary, the Lily of the Lake," whom the narrator has left behind and whom he could never forget, whether he "be in America or in some foreign land." The setup and syntax of the descriptions are reminiscent of "The Lily of the West" (Laws #P-29), with which "Lily of Lake Champlain" has several phrases in common, including a similar refrain ("She is my lovely Mary, the Lily of the West" and "O she is my lovely Mary and the Lily of the Lake"). However, in "Lily of the West" the protagonist feels himself jilted by the woman, and out of jealousy murders his rival. In "Lily of Lake Champlain," un-jilted, he merely goes off to sea, expressing his intention to return. This is as far as the conventional form of the song goes, a kind of "ballad of faithful lovers," as in the lyrics transcribed at sea in the late 1860s by Nantucketer George P. Worth (text A, below) and the one that appears in the Wm. A. Firth & Co. anthology of *Naval Songs*, published in 1883.

The second form of the song begins much the same way, but carries the story further: in case the Lily has forgotten the sailor-narrator, "there is a rose in New York town" named Catherine, who *also* has many charms, which he accordingly enumerates. The Lily can be exchanged for the Rose—and ultimately is. This second form is thus a kind of "ballad of unfaithful lovers," but without any specified consequences or ill effects: any resulting unhappiness on the part of the forsaken Lily, callously discarded by the narrator, is left to speculation. This is the sense of two earlier transcriptions, one made by whaleman Albert F. Handy of Binghamton, N.Y., in 1862 (text B), and the other a similar text in the journal of George H. Gooding aboard the bark *John Dawson* of New Bedford in 1863 (Houghton Library, Harvard University).

The questions of precedence and derivation remain: which form of the song is indebted to the other? Is the "faithful lovers" the "original," and the other a later configuration? or do text B and its cognate, the "unfaithful" form, represent the original intention of the song, later "cleaned up"? Clearly, while the chronological sequence of transcription is no reliable indication in such cases, the two "unfaithful" texts, dated 1862 and 1863, are several years earlier than the "faithful" ones, and, in the absence of a clear publication history, the "unfaithful" form would have the edge.

In a larger sense, the song may be derived from some undiscovered broadside or published poem, or it may be traditional, but in any case, in its catch-phrases and meter (and in the dualism of B), it is related to "The Lake of Pontchartrain" (Laws #H-9) as well as "Lily of the West," to either of the tunes of which it may be sung. It may also be related to "The Banks of the Dee" and "The Banks of Lake Champlain," as Huntington suggests, though it has little in common with the latter apart from locale and cannot be sung to the same tune.

TUNE - "Lily of the Lake," unattributed, from *Naval Songs,* New York, 1883, p. 77.

A.

"LILY OF THE LAKE." George P. Worth, in the journal of William Keith, whaling schooners *William Martin* of Boston and *Edith May* of Wellfleet, 1865-69; and merchant schooner *Cora Nash* of Boston, circa 1869-71.

1. There is as pretty a landscape as ever you did see,
   Its located between O Canada and the Atlantic seas,
   Its covered all over with flowers & clad with virgin green,
   O it is to one the fairest land that lies on Lake Champlain.

2. One evening as she sat on my knee I told her my design
   I clasped her to my bosom & asked her to be mine
   She answered me with a glowing blush & said she's be my maid
   O she is my lovely Mary and the Lily of the Lake.

3. Her eyes they are like diamonds bright her cheeks were rosy red
   Her hair was dark and glossy hung in ringlets round her head
   O the most recesses of her [sic] heart her eyes would penetrate
   O she is my lovely Mary & the Lily of the Lake.

4. Perhaps she has forgotten me but her I never can,
   May I be in America or in some foreign land
   O may I be rolling far oer the deep what else may be my fate,
   O she is my lovely Mary and the Lily of the Lake.

End,
George P. Worth,
Nantucket
Siasconset Co.
Mass.

B.

"THE LADY OF LAKE CHAMPLAIN." Albert F. Handy, bark *Waverly* of New Bedford, 1862.

1. Thair is a pleasant Landscape as ever you did see
   It lies between the Canardies[1] and the Atlantic sea
   Tis covered all o'er with flowers and hangs in [bunting?] green
   It is the fairest land to me that on Lake Champlain

2. Its on this Lakes fair bosom ships may securely ride
   Beneath its sparkling waters the playful Fishes glide
   The birds are singing in the air with a delightful hue
   Whilst the notes are so full of melody directed unto you

3. Thair rests a lovely Maiden she is fairer than the Rose
   Or ainy other flower that in Natures Garden groes
   She caused me to love her whitch makes my hart to ache
   Oh she is my lovely Mary the Lily of the Lake

---

[1] *Canardies:* that is, "the Canadas," i.e., Upper Canada (Ontario) and Lower Canada (Quebec).

4. Her eyes are bright as diamonds they are as black as gets [jets]
   Her hair is dark and glosey and hangs in ringlets down her neck
   The inmost reseses of my hart her eyes do penitret
   She is my lovely Mary the Lily of the Lake

5. Her waist is neat and slender her cheeks are rosy red
   Upon her snow white bosom ive oftimes laid my head
   And felt the beatings of her hart my pure celestial mate
   Oh she is my lovely Maiden the Lily of the Lake

6. One evning she sat on my knee I told her my design
   I clasped her to my bosom and asked her to be mine
   She answered me with a glowing cheeks and said she'd be my mate
   Oh she's my lovely Mary the Lilly of the Lake

7. But now Ive gon and left her ive biden her adue
   In New York there does dwell a maid boath butiful and true
   She has posesion of my hart sweet Catheran[2] is her naim
   So I ll wed the rose and bid adue to the Lilly of Lake Champlain

8. Fair well my dearest Mary fair well my blushing rose
   Your love is on the ocian whair stormy winds do blow
   Land serges dash o're our galant Barque which causes our harts to ache
   May god protect the roses and the Lilly of the Lake

9. God speed the Barque Waverly to her own dear native shore
   God grant us a few days of liberty with those we most adore
   God grant us a few days of liberty the seas we will forsake
   And I will wed the rose and bid adue to the Lilly of the Lake

10. Perhaps she has forgoten me but her I never can
    Whither I am in America or in som foreign land
    If I chance to meet with shipwreck or whatever be my fate
    I hope to return saf home agan to Mary the Lilly of the Lake

*Pened down by Albert F. Handy on bord
the Barque Waverly May 4th 1862.*

---

[2] The Dawson MS (Houghton Library, Harvard; quoted in the Huntington MS 533) also has Catherine here, but presents the stanza in a different context that appears to make more sense:

> But if she has forgotten, soon I'll bid her adieu
> There is a rose in New York town that is both kind and true
> She claims possession of my heart sweet Catherine is her name
> I'll marry the rose and bid adieu to the Lily of Lake Champlain.

11. The Norfolk Girls
[Our Topsail's Reefed]

This is a wardroom song—the navy equivalent of a parlor song—written and composed circa 1840 by Midshipman (later Commodore) William F. Spicer, the most accomplished songwriter to emerge in the American sailing navy and one of the few sailor-songwriters whose name has been preserved in connection with his songs. Of Spicer's several compositions anthologized by Admiral Luce, this is probably the best and is undoubtedly the best known. The Norfolk and Portsmouth referred to in the text are, of course, adjacent Virginia seaports on Chesapeake Bay that served as seats of U.S. Navy operations on the mid Atlantic coast. The song was collected by Samuel T. Braley, first mate of the whaleship *Arab* of Fairhaven (1845-49), in the form of a clipping reprinted from the *New York Mirror* pasted into his journal. Braley, who was captain of the *Arab* on her next voyage (1849-52), is known to have been an accomplished accordion player, but for some reason he never wrote much in his diaries about music on shipboard.

TUNE - "The Norfolk Girls" by William F. Spicer, from *Naval Songs,* 1883, p. 13; see also Luce 1889, p. 184.

"OUR TOPSAIL'S REEF'D." Samuel T. Braley, first mate, ship *Arab* of Fairhaven, 1845-49: a clipping (reprinted from the *New York Mirror,* in an unidentified, undated periodical) pasted into his shipboard journal. Reorganized into stanzas from the undifferentiated printed text. The repeats required by the melody as a chorus (the two last lines of each stanza to be repeated twice) are not indicated in the MS.

1. Our topsail's reefed and filled away,
    All snug aloft we know;
   Despite the storm we'll still be gay,
    Among our friends below:
   Come mingle round and listen boys,
    With spirits warm and true;
   Here's a health to all the Norfolk girls
    And Portsmouth maidens too.

2. May the darksome eye of loveliness,
    And that of azure ray,
   Shed only tears of happiness
    Forever, and for aye;

Fill up though far away from home,
   And our native hills of blue;
We cherish still the Norfolk girls
   And Portsmouth maidens too.

3. May the cheek whereon reposes
   Emotion young and dear,
Still wear the hue of roses
   Through each succeeding year.
We'll drink to by-past scenes, and hope
   Some day again to view
The beauteous girls of Norfolk,
   And the Portsmouth maidens too.

4. And if perchance we ne'er return,
   O'er ocean's fickle wave,
But find amid the caves below
   A sailor's changeful grave,
Yet ere we close our eyes and pass
   Beneath the depths of blue,
We'll think of all the Norfolk girls,
   And Portsmouth maidens too.

5. Should the foe appear before us,
   To our guns we'll fondly cling,
While our stars are gleaming o'er us,
   Shall their notes of freedom ring;
While life's warm stream is glowing,
   Our eager pulses through,
We'll fight for home, the Norfolk girls,
   And Portsmouth maidens too.

6. Fill up, fill up, yet once again,
   Before we say Good night;
From every glass in sweetness drain,
   To friendship's hallowed light;
May peace around our kindred dwell,
   All beings loved and true,
The beauteous girls of Norfolk,
   And the Portsmouth maidens too.

7. Good night, good night, our pillows no[w]
   With pleasant thoughts we'll press.
And dreams, perchance may linger ne[ar]
   Our slumbering to bless;
Amid delightful reveries
   That fancy brings to view,
Perhaps we'll meet the Norfolk girls,
   And Portsmouth maidens too.

12. My Dream

    These original lyrics by whaleman Charles Swain are clearly based on "Napoleon's Dream" [#65], an Irish broadside ballad that, despite that it was published in the *American Songster* circa 1835, and despite its evident popularity in the whale fishery (which Swain's parody additionally substantiates), has become extremely obscure. Though the whaleman-poet's subject matter is quite different, the opening lines are borrowed directly from the Napoleonic prototype, and the parallel treatment is carried through to the end—an awakening from the dream with a somewhat surprising denouement. Most of the whaleman's song is comprised of somnambulistic reflections on a beloved woman back home, with the result that it becomes a kind of tender reverie akin to "Lines to Mary" [#14] and "My Wife" [#13]. But the fifth and last stanza packs a payoff that makes it as much about seafaring and life on board as about love or homesickness, and imparts a comic character analogous to that of a whaleman's gothic poem, "The Sailor Boy's Dream" [#230]. The tune is not identified, and as the whaleman's lyrics and meter are based on the A part of "Napoleon's Dream" only, they cannot be sung to the same air.

"MY DREAM. BY C.B. SWAIN."   Charles B. Swain, bark *Cachalot* of New Bedford, 1857-59.   Compare #65.

1.   I dreamed on[c]e a dream a dream of home
    Whilst away oer the heaving billows
    And the forms that I loved e'er any feet did roam
    Come clustering round my pillow

2.   Whilst that gentle voice I love so well
    On my name seemed softly calling
    Like the distant chimes of a silver bell
    On my ear that sound seemed falling

3.   And a soft white hand was linked in mine
    Sweet lips to my own close pressing
    Round the loved ones firm my arms entwined
    As I breathed on her name a blessing

4.   A balmy kiss sank soft on my brow
    And strengthened the spell that bound me
    Whilst that dear sweet voice so soft and low
    Kept breathing still around me

5.   Twas a witching dream to my heart most dear
    But it fled with a rough awaking
    For <u>the watch is called,</u> bawled a voice in my ear
    And a messmate my arm was shaking.

13. My Wife—A Song

Oh Could I but see my sweet lady so fair
I'd care not for ellen nor lillys so rare
but at home I would stop & always be true
to dwell with my sweet ones in that cottage so fair.

this verse is to my wife
Irena Dexter
oh you charmer

At sea in 1846, Captain Rodolphus W. Dexter transcribed into his journal the words to "Ellen the Fair" [#95] and "The Banks of the Schuylkill" [#21], sentimental songs that set him thinking about his wife and inspired him to compose the few lines of awkward verse quoted above. There he alludes to "Ellen the Fair" and perhaps to "The Lily of Lake Champlain" [#10].

In a similar mood, another lonely husband on the Pacific in the 1850s, whaleman Charles B. Swain, wrote the lyrics of his own original love song, which he signed "By C.B. Swain. Air: The land of the West."

In naming the melody as "The Land of the West," Swain is almost certainly referring to "The Indian's Prayer" [#333], of which the first line is given variously as "Let me go to my home in the far distant West" (evidently the original), "Let me go to my home that is far distant West," and "Let me go to my home in the land of the West."[3] This song has been recovered from oral tradition in Maritime Canada and in Australia, in both of which places it is called "White Man, Let Me Go" and is widely regarded—erroneously—as a Canadian folk song (Fowke & Johnston, 32; Meredith & Anderson, I:228). It is actually a parlor song of circa 1846 that only later entered tradition. It was originally written and composed by American songsmith Isaac Baker Woodbury (1819-1858), who dedicated it to his friend and sometime collaborator L.O. Emerson of Salem, Massachusetts. Though it has rarely if ever been anthologized, there are contemporaneous editions of sheet music by four Boston publishers in which the melody, accompaniment, attribution to Woodbury, and copyright (Charles Bradlee & Co., 1846) are identical.[4] The text also appears in several shipboard journals and copybooks from the 1840s through the 1870s, indicating that it was fairly well known among seafaring folk, lasted for quite a long time, and was thus fair game for parody and adaptation.[5] However, to sing the whaleman's lyrics to the melody of "The Indian's Prayer" will itself require some adaptation, such as repeating part of the tune to accommodate the sixth line in each stanza of the text.

TUNE - "The Indian's Prayer" by I.B. Woodbury, from identical settings in sheet music editions by several Boston publishers, all bearing the copyright of C. Bradlee & Co., Boston, 1846. Compare the much-transformed variants collected from tradition and entitled "White Man, Let Me Go," in Fowke & Johnston, 32f (Newfoundland); and Meredith & Anderson, I:228 (Australia).

---

[3] Not to be confused with "The Indian Hunter" [#331], a popular English parlor song with words by Eliza Cook (first line: "Oh why does the white man follow my Path… "). Huntington (1964, 180f) correctly intuits that "The Indian's Lament" is not a folk song, but it is Henry Russell's music for Eliza Cook's "The Indian Hunter" that he erroneously provides for his whaleman's transcription of the Isaac Baker Woodbury lyrics.

[4] All are undated except for the Bradlee copyright on all editions—successively, C. Bradlee & Co., 1846; E.H. Wade, 197 Washington Street, circa 1847-60; A. & J.P. Ordway, 399 Washington Street, circa 1848-51; and Oliver Ditson & Co., — Washington Street, after 1858. According to Dichter & Shapiro (175), "E.H. Wade took over C. Bradlee & Co. business [circa 1847]. [Oliver] Ditson, Boston, took over Wade business. J.P. Ordway used Bradlee plates."

[5] Five transcriptions were encountered in the Kendall Collection: [A] George D. Marble, ship *Le Baron* of Rochester, 1837-39 (probably transcribed sometime after the voyage); [B] John Marble, ship *America* of Hudson, N.Y., 1839-41 (also probably transcribed somewhat later); [C] Sylvanus C. Fullmoon (a Native American whaleman from Long Island, N.Y.), ship *Nimrod* of New Bedford, 1842-45; [D] Eleanor Braley and Jason L. Braley, family copybook, New Bedford, undated; and [E] William H. Keith, several voyages, circa 1865-71. Additionally, Huntington (1964, 180f) cites two texts, from the *Marcus* of Fairhaven, 1844, and the *Cortes* of New Bedford, 1847, but assigns them the wrong title and tune.

"MY WIFE—A SONG."   Charles B. Swain, bark *Cachalot* of New Bedford, 1857-59.

1. A wish to thee dearest from over the sea,
   And the burthen it bearest is my love unto thee;
   When the sea breeze is sighing with soft plaintive wail
   Oh! list, to its notes love it bears thee the tale,
   And the light breaking waves, with their murmuring strain
   Hark! they whisper thee softly of one o'er the main

2. On the waves falling lightly, is the moons silver light,
   And the stars twinkle brightly, thru the long silent night;
   And the swift gentle breezes sweep light o'er my brow,
   But my heart, is not here love, it heeds them not now;
   O'er this wide waste of waters, bright crested with foam,
   It hath wandered to thee love, its own native home.

3. How my spirit is yearning forever and aye
   To thee ever turning throughout the long day
   Whilst the hours passeth weary and heavy to me
   And I'm alway[s] [*weeping*?] whilst away o'er the sea
   But yet mid my sorrow comes hopes beaming ray
   Tis the sunlight that turns love, my night into day

4. How our burthens are lightened by hopes gentle beam
   Each sombre cloud brightened that hung o'er lifes stream
   Now glimmering faintly, then glowing distinct,
   Yet never quite vanished till life is extinct:
   Tis this Love, that brightens the gloom of my life
   The hope soon to meet thee, my own darling wife.

14. Lines to Mary
[Believe Me, Dearest Susan]

This is a variant of the beautiful shipboard reverie known to Joanna Colcord as "Believe Me, Dearest Susan," expressing a sailor's loneliness and anticipation with respect to a woman ashore: both are distinguished by an unusual format, having three six-line stanzas in which the final couplet of each expresses a lyrical, homeward-wishing fidelity. "Lines to Mary" is specifically localized to the Okhotsk whaling grounds, evoking powerful images of sea, sky, and ice. The whalemen almost certainly took it down from memory or recitation, and may be an original adaptation by one of the journal collaborators aboard the *Waverly*.

TUNE - "Believe Me, Dearest Susan," after Joanna Colcord, *Songs of American Sailormen*, [1924] 1938, p. 163: collected from Joseph McGinnis, who learned it while a sailor on the Great Lakes from an ex man-of-war's man, who claimed it was popular in the Navy in his day.

"LINES TO MARY." George M. Jones and Albert F. Handy, bark *Waverly* of New Bedford, 1859-63. The meter is uneven, especially in stanza 1, which requires considerable adaptation to be sung. If stanza 2, which is more regular, be taken as the standard, the text is easily adapted to Colcord's melody.

1. It is night and o'er the dark expanse
   The twinkling stars doth seem to dance
   Round the pale moon whose silver light
   Reflects the rays o'er the waters bright
   As homeward we dash o'er the dark blue sea
   A thinking of home your friends love and thee

2. And oft dearest Mary as I walk the lone deck
   A hopeing that heaven thy fair form protect
   And guard the[e] in safety until thou shalt be
   Fondly pressed to the bossom that loves only thee
   As homeward we steer through the waters so blue
   A thinking of home your friends love and you

3. But soon dearest Mary we shall reach that bright clime
   Where souls brightest rays in their lusture do shine
   Cheering each heart as homeward we go
   And leave far astern those cold regions of snow
   From the shores of Ochotsk o god let me flee
   To my home my companions and Mary to thee

15. [The Carpenter and the Maid]
[The Maid of Warren]

When an anonymous diarist aboard the ship *Warren* of Warren, Rhode Island, committed this untitled ballad to paper in 1832, he subtitled it "A most shocking story about two lovers without any murder and blood shed written by Bob Short Esqr." The attributed lyricist appears to have have been the Robert Short who was born in Boston in 1805 and received a Seaman's Protection Paper (passport) at New Haven in 1831, but the song is in any case an original composition in the broadside-ballad genre, employing imitative conventions to weave a new plot with slightly blue results. Specifically set in the diarist's home port, it almost becomes a "ballad of unfaithful lovers," but everything turns out all right in the end. A Warren woman is courted by a carpenter, who leaves her pregnant and runs off to sea; she recites some formulaic, prophetic stanzas about what may become of her unborn child ("And should it prove to be a boy / A sailor he shall be…," etc.), and speculates hopefully that her man may yet return; at which point she discovers she has been dreaming all along, that her carpenter never left her, and that she is still a maiden—which latter circumstances prove to be merely temporary. The unspoken (and perhaps unintentional) implication is that, given the outcome of the ballad, her prophetic dream could still come true: with her maidenhead lost for real, her carpenter could still run off to sea. The air is not specified.

[UNTITLED]. From an anonymous copybook entitled "Scraps, Odd-thoughts & Tag-ends Of a Rope Hauler," ship *Warren* of Warren, 1832.

1. There was a girl in Warren town
      A very pretty maid
   Courted she was by a young man
      A Carpenter by trade

2. Her name was Angelina Brown
      Her features they were fair
   She had a very pretty form
      And flaxen was her hair

3. One sundy night the winds blew hard
      In torrents fell the rain
   When Angelina sighed and said
      My heart is racked with pain

4. For my true love is doomed to roam
      Upon the watery main
   And I'm afraid he'll never return
      To bless my sight again

5. Last night he pressed me in his arms
      And kissed me oer and oer
   But now the gale is wafting him
      Far from his native shore

6. And he perhaps will soon forget
      The promises he made
   And I by trusting in his faith
      Be shamefully betrayed

7. But if [he] does not come again
    And leaves me to my shame
The little baby when tis born
    Shall bear its fathers name

8. And should it prove to be a boy
    A sailor he shall be
And have the tempests and the breeze
    Upon the raging sea

9. And he perhaps around Cape horn
    May one day take a trip
And be a Captain stout and bold
    On board a Bungtown ship

10. And should he then his father find
    Upon the Spanish main
Oh let him tell his mother's woe
    Her misery and pain

11. Perhaps the story then may cause
    Some bitter tears to fall
And wring from out his heart of steel
    Its wormwood and its gall

12. And then again these arms may press
    The form of him I love
And he be glad to stay at home
    And never from me roam

13. Around she turned to clasp the form
    Her fancy now complete
When slap! the tea kettle one turn
    And scalded both her feet

14. She quickly started with surprise
    And gave a dreadful scream
And wiped the tears from out her eyes
    And found she'd dreampt a dream

15 And scarcely had she looked around
    Before there did appear
Her own true love the Carpenter
    The man to her so dear

16. And all for grief and woe and pain
    By kisses were repaired
That very night, oh! shame to tell
    She ceased to be a maid.

16. [The Milking Maid]
[Nelly the Milking Maid; Coming Home from the Wake]

This is a rare example of a mild but nevertheless explicitly bawdy song, one of very few such songs encountered in whaling journals. John Martin's Musical Program [Appendix 7] mentions a song called "The Milking Maid" performed in a shipboard gala at sea in 1842; and while this may not be the same song, it is probably the same kind of thing, a classic roll in the hay, with the woman paying the price in the end. The air has not been identified; on the other hand, there are dozens of contemporaneous tunes that will do.

[UNTITLED.] James Donahue, ship *Atlantic* of Nantucket, 1850-53. Stanza 5 is overlong in the MS. The chorus is repeated after each verse.

1. Oh she was A milking maid So gay
   And all she delight in was dancing and play
   A jig she did have and another she did take
   When she asked her mothers leaf if she might go to the dance [*wake*]

   Chorus: Tala du tala du dle dle tal a da

2. Oh Nelly oh nelly Id have you beware
   of meeting young roger for he will be there
   for he will delude you and he will laugh at the fun
   and he will slip it into you As he did Sally Ann

3. Nelly put on her fix and Away to the wake
   wishing all the way that young roger might be there
   Oh the wake being over and the[y] all came Away
   young roger he went home with his milking maid so gay

4. going along through the meadows the maiden So gay
   young Rogers laid her down on a green cock of hay
   Saying Oh nelly oh nelly I will do it for your Sake
   and I will play you up A jigging coming home from the wake

5. Next morning the old woman to nelly did say
   What usage did you have last night to the play
   The best of good wine and best of good cake
   and the [best] of good usage did I have at the wake
   then nelly she did laugh till her two sides did ache
   when She thought upon the jigging coming home from the wake

6. Six months being over and the seventh being past
   her red rosy cheeks the[y] grew pale at the last
   her two sides did swell and her head began to ache
   when she thought upon the jigging coming home from the wake

7. Oh roger oh roger Id have you prepare
   And b[u]y me some ribbons to ty up my hair
   And if it is boy I will name him for your sake
   And if it is A girl I will keep her from the wake

17. Frozen Limb
[Lubin and Mary]

This broadside ballad is distinctive both for being an explicitly bawdy type rarely encountered in whaling journals, and for being the result of sharing between two shipmates. Frederick H. Russell, second mate, and George W. Howland, seaman, were cousins who grew up in Dartmouth, Mass. They kept parallel journals of a voyage made together in the New Bedford bark *Pioneer* during 1875-77. Portions of the text appear in Russell's journal (Houghton Library, Harvard University) and a complete text in Howland's (Kendall Collection). The whalemen do not specify the melody but it is elsewhere associated with the traditional English air of "The Banks of Claudy," while textual evidence suggests "Early One Morning" (which Chappell calls one of the "most popular songs among the serving maids" of his generation) and the traditional Irish tune "Old Leather Breeches" [#180].

TUNE - "Early One Morning," from John Hullah, *The Song Book,* Philadelphia and London, 1866, #65. Compare J.L. Hatton and Eton Faning, *The Songs of England,* London, n.d., I:132.

"FROZEN LIMB." George W. Howland, second mate, bark *Pioneer* of New Bedford, 1875-77.

1. one cold and frosty eav[n]ing
   as her father lay sleeping
   I tap[p]ed on the window
   where Mary did lay
   by the light of the taper
   I saw her come creeping
   and whose at my window
   she softly did say

2. it is of my Dear mary
   Benighted and weary
   My Limbs are all Frozen
   I am wet to the skin
   I prey you take pity
   And kindly admit me
   At last She concented
   I climbed and got it [in]

3. She scarce had perceived me
   Before I enroled her
   Hugging and kissing
   her every charm
   She says you deceived me
   you have falsely tole me
   That your limbs were all frozen
   But I find them quite warm

4. Oh Mary dear mary
   This bosom I am presing
   Possesses more beauty
   More whiteness than snow
   And this little white hand
   I am so tenderly squeezing
   Might well freeze the limb
   that we melted just now

5. She eagerly grasped it
   And tenderly clasped it
   Crying Leubin dear Leubin
   The truth is quite plain
   For the more I am Squeesing
   The harder Its freezing
   And now Its quite stiff
   Let us melt it again

6. O Leubin dear Leubin
   Its now you must leave me
   Heed not the cold the hail or the rain
   But if it is freezing
   Your limbs should
   Keep teasing
   Come back to me quickly
   And we will melt them again

18. Can Ladies Be Compared to Man?

    Third Mate George Edgar Mills of Nashua, New Hampshire, was in love and had just recently shipped on a whaling voyage when he wrote down this song in January 1857. In fact, his entire journal is contrived as a series of love letters, original poems, homemade songs, and copy texts addressed to his beloved, Mary Frances Hopkins of Milford, New Hampshire. He shows all the symptoms, including obsessive rhapsodizing about their love and experimenting with various permutations of his name on the many pieces he signed for her—"G.E. Mills," "G. Edgar Mills," "George E. Mills," "George Edgar Mills"—as well as different ways of addressing his beloved, writing her name as "Mary," "Frances," etc., on page after page. Did he have the lady specifically in mind in the lyrics of "Can Ladies Be Compared to Man?"—a song that in some antiquated, pre–feminist way anticipates Harry Belafonte's calypso hit of the 1950s, "Man Smart, Woman Smarter," which has a remarkably compatible chorus, "That's Right! The woman is smarter! That's right!" Unfortunately, no tune is indicated here.

"CAN LADIES BE COMPARED TO MAN." George Edgar Mills, third mate, bark *Aurora* of Westport, 1857.

1.   The world gets wiser every day
        That's so that's so
    And woman's bound to have her way
        That's so too
    To contradict will raise a spree
        That's so that's so
    But man with her should still agree
        That's so too

Chorus: Yes that is so my Boys
        That is so my Boys
        That is so my Boys
        That's so too
        That's so too

2.   She carries hoops beneath her skirts
        That's so that's so
    They show her off whenever she flirts
        That's so too
    She measures her bonnets very small
        That's so that's so
    And flounces if she's very tall
        That's so that's so too

3.   The woman now will let them pass
        That's so that's so
    For men are greater fools, alas—
        That's so that's so too
    Tis of the gents with shawls I sing
        That's so that's so
    With large Moustache and all such thing
        That's so too

CHAPTER THREE
The Sailor's Farewell
Songs of Parting

Welcome ever smiles,
And farewell goes out sighing.
—*Troilus and Cressida*

The Sailor's Adieu. Colored lithograph published by J. Baillie & Co., New York; and J. Sowle, New Bedford, circa 1845. New Bedford Whaling Museum.

19. The Lowlands of Holland
[A Dream; The Maid's Lamentation for the Loss of Her True Love]

This venerable ballad, known in some early incarnations as "The Maid's Lamentation for the Loss of Her True Love" and "The Sorrowful Lover's Regret, or, The Low-Lands of Holland," has deep roots in the 17th-century, emanating from the hostilities between England and Holland that preceded the unification of the Dutch and English crowns in the person of William of Orange (William III) in 1689. Child observes that the text in the *Roxburgh Ballads* (IV:73; Ebsworth VI: 444) must have been printed between 1684 and 1695 (Child V:229);[1] but the song is almost certainly older than that, and probably dates back at least to the three Anglo-Dutch wars of 1652-74. Palmer (1973, #9) convincingly argues that it dates from the 1620s. Tradition and internal evidence suggest that it is Scottish in origin;[2] and it flourished in Scotland and Ireland, taking firm root in tradition.[3] Several interesting adaptations and localizations have resulted—such as the reference to *Galloway,* in Scotland, which becomes *Galway* in Ireland, and even *Galilee* in the degraded New England text that New Bedford whaleman Edward W. Collins transcribed in 1829. Collins's version, probably the earliest text of "Lowlands of Holland" yet recovered in North America, exhibits some remarkable folkloric features, by virtue of which it is a delightful departure from the many later versions too much affected by the leveling influence of broadside publication. Another splendid American adaptation is "The Nantucket Mother and Daughter" [#20], transcribed by George Wilbur Piper of New Hampshire aboard an Edgartown ship on the Pacific Ocean whaling grounds forty years later. There are many forms of the air, most of which are permutations of one or the other of two principal subspecies of tunes identified in Bronson's taxonomy (II:418-427). These, in turn, have provided the melodies for literally dozens of other Scots ballads (e.g., see Mackay's *The Songs of Scotland,* passim). The samples here are selected from representative English, Irish, and American renditions.

---

[1] Initially, Child (II:317) quotes William Stenhouse (editor of the 1852 edition of *The Scots Museum*) as authority that the ballad was composed in the 18th century, in which case the allusion to Holland would be anachronistic. But in his "Additions and Corrections" (V:229), he remarks that the *Roxburgh* version "was printed for J. Deacon, in Guilt-spur-street [London], and the date, according to Chappell, would be 1684-95," fully a century prior to some of Child's other citations—e.g., a text dated "Newcastle 1778"; "The Sorrowful Lover's Regrate, or, The Low-Lands of Holland," dated 1776; and the *Roxburgh* text (IV:73; Ebsworth VI:444) which "begins with two stanzas which resemble" the latter (Child V:229). If there be a distinction between "Lowlands of Holland" and "Maid's Lamentation," it is that the latter commonly lacks the press-gang setting mentioned by Bronson (II:418) as a late feature also lacking in the Collins manuscript. "Lowlands" often lacks the "goodly (bonny) ship" reference and any mention of a sea-storm, the implication in those texts being that the young man died in battle rather than in a natural catastrophe at sea.

[2] "'This ballad,' Stenhouse was informed, 'was composed ... by a young widow in Galloway, whose husband was drowned on a voyage to Holland'" (Child II:237). It has a hoary heritage of publication among Scottish songs (see Child II:317 and V:229); the Galloway locale is preserved in many versions and is recognizably altered in others. Child suggests a thematic kinship between "Lowlands of Holland" and the Scots ballad "Bonny Bee Hom" (Child #92), with which "Lowlands" shares a few phrases pertaining to the widow's vow (II:239); in fact, the relationship between the two accounts for Child's interest in "Lowlands," which is not itself part of his canon. Bronson suggests that "Lowlands" actually supplanted "Bonny Bee Hom" in the 18th century and "in its later form it has the makings of a more gripping story." "Lowlands" has certainly been by far the stronger of the two in active tradition in England, Ireland, and North America. "Bonny Bee Hom" (the sense of which seems to signify "lover come back," i.e., "darling, be home") appears to be one of those almost purely literary ballads that persists more by reason of having been calcified on paper than by virtue of some magical folk process that kept it alive in tradition among "the people." There is little evidence of its presence of in the singing tradition anywhere, while "Lowlands of Holland" is sung even today by English-speaking people on at least three continents. Belden makes much the same point on his remarks on "Lowlands of Holland," but presents no evidence that "Bonny Bee Hom" was ever sung in the past, as he implies it was:

> "It is on the whole a relief to turn to the 'modern' ballad of the impressed sailor which has supplanted ['Bonny Bee Hom'] in popular favor, and which, going back at least to the middle of the eighteenth century, is still sung widely in England, in Ireland, and occasionally in America. Even though we may readily allow that the song is likely to have had its rise in Sydney's day—and in its press-gang form long after—there is perhaps as good reason for regarding it as a traditional ballad as there is for so regarding 'Bonny Bee Hom.' It has been revamped and modernized more than once by the broadside press; but all the while, for at least 200 years, it has gone on its way as a piece transmitted by *singing,* and the singing has been independent of print. During that time the hero, as is usual in songs that continue to live, has notably descended in the social scale, from the commander accompanied by 'seven good mariners' to the bridegroom impressed by a common seaman. In its later form it has the makings of a more gripping story" (Bronson II:418; Bronson 1976, 237).

[3] Bronson II:418-427; Bronson 1976, 237ff; Sharp 1916 #23; Healy 1967 #42; O Lochlainn 1965 #7a; Joyce (Bronson II:423).

TUNE A - "The Lowlands of Holland": composite, after Joyce 1905, 69; Joyce 1909, 214; Molloy 1873, 150 ("At eve I wandered by the shore"); Bronson II:423, #11: "As sung in Limerick." The tune is also traditional in Scotland and Ireland in association with various other texts; compare Bronson II:423, #10 (County Derry); O Lochlainn 1965, #7a (variant "Reilly the Fisherman"); Sharp 1932, #26; Palmer 1973, #9.

TUNE B - "The Lowlands of Holland", from B.H. Bronson, *The Traditional Tunes of the Child Ballads,* 1962, II: 420, Appendix, #3: "Sung by Mrs. Carrie Grover, Gorham, Me., 1941.... Collected by Alan Lomax."

TUNE C - "The Low, Low Lands of Holland" from Cecil J. Sharp, *100 English Folksongs,* 1916, #23, p. 54; reprinted with adjustments in Karpeles 1987, p. 7: "Sung by Robert Dibble, Bridgewater, Somerset"; collected by Sharp, 1905.

A.

"A DREAM." Edward W. Collins, on the eve of his departure on a whaling voyage in 1829, written into a journal formerly belonging to his brother, Silas Collins, seaman aboard the brig *By Chance* of Dartmouth, Mass., 1826-27.

1. I dreamed that my love was sailing down by a river side
   It was enough to pierce a fair maids heart When so late had been his bride
   Who d been his bride brave boys so terrible [wonderful] to behold
   May the Gods above love and protect All jolly seamen bold

2. I built my love a goodly ship a goodly ship of fame
   With four and twenty mariners to box about the main
   The winds began to blow brave boys the sea began to toss
   Twas then my true loves goodly ship was like to meet a loss

3. I'd scarcely got into my bed I'd scarcely got to sleep
   Before this noble Captain stood smiling at my feet
   Saying aris[e] you worthy noble and go along with me
   To the lowlands of holland to fight for germany

4. No chain of gold about my neck no combing to my hair
   No candle light nor fire bright can tell what beauties are
   For its never married I will be until the day I die
   Since stormy winds and raging seas has parted my love and I[4]

5. My mother cried oh daughter what makes you so alarmed
   You know there is a Lord in Gallilee To ease you hearts complaint
   I know there is a Lord in Gallilee but alass there is none for me
   For I never had but one true love he is drownded in the sea
   He is drownded in the salt salt sea so terrible to behold
   May the Gods above protect and love all jolly seamen bold

Edward W Collins
Fairhaven 1829

B.

"THE LOWLANDS OF HOLLAND." Composite: compare 1905, 69; Joyce 1909, 214; Molloy 1873, 150 ("At eve I wandered by the shore"); 1916, #23, p. 54; Sharp 1932, #26; Bronson II:423, #11 (Limerick); Palmer 1973, #9.

1. Last night as I lay married all on my wedding bed
   Up came a bold sea captain and stood at my bedstead
   Saying, Arise, arise, you married man, and come an go with me
   To the Lowlands of Holland to fight the enemy

2. I held my love all in my arms, thinking he still might stay
   But up spake this bold commander, saying, It's time we were away:
   There's many a blithe young married man this night must go with me
   To the Lowlands of Holland to fight the enemy

3. Says the mother to the daughter, Why do you so lament?
   Is there nay a man in Galloway who can ease your discontent?
   There's many a man in Galloway, but nary a one for me
   For the Lowlands of Holland lie between my love and me

4. No fancy clothing will I put on, no comb shall touch my hair
   No firelight nor candle bright shall show my beauty rare
   Nor will I wed with any man until the day I die
   For the Lowlands of Holland lie between my love and me

5. Oh Holland is a wild place and in it grows much green
   It's a wild habitation that my true love does lie in
   The flow'rs they grow in every field, there's birds on every tree
   But the Lowlands of Holland lie far across the sea

---

[4] Stanza 4 corresponds to the one intended by Child (II:317) with reference to his observation that "Bonny Bee Hom" and "Lowlands of Holland" have the lamenting widow adopt "like vows" of chastity. He gives as the fourth stanza of "Bonny Bee Hom" (#92A, II:318): There shall be neither a shoe gang on my feet, / Nor a kaim [comb] gang in my hair, / Nor eer a coal nor candle-light / Shine in my bower nae mair. Where the Collins MS gives "can tell where beauties are," some texts have "shall show my beauties rare" (e.g., Healy 1967 #42); but most preserve the sense of "bower": "shine in my bower mair" (Child II:318); "shine in my bower fair" (Flanders 1953 #114); "shine in my chamber mair" (Masefield 260); "shine in my chamber bare" (O Lochlainn 1965 #71); "shall in my chamber be" (Sharp 1932 #26); etc.

20. The Nantucket Mother and Daughter
[*adaptation of* The Lowlands of Holland]

This ballad of idealistic fidelity is a kind of Nantucket parody of "The Lowlands of Holland" [#19], complete with the mother coaxing her daughter to make a good marriage, while the young woman obstinately refuses to accept any other man than her sailor-boy who went off to sea. The salient distinction is that "Lowlands of Holland" is a lament, with the mother hoping to remedy the daughter's grief over the tragic loss of a husband, while "Nantucket Mother and Daughter" is more in the comic vein, with the mother disparaging sailors altogether and trying to convince her rebellious daughter to listen to reason and wed a farmer. In both cases the daughter's tenacity is characterized as an admirable trait betokening true love and nobility of purpose. From the whalemen's point of view, it is also a kind of patriotic testimony to the innate superiority of sailors over landlubbers [see "Jolly Sailors Bold," #32]. In standpoint of structure and syntax, the legacy from "Lowlands of Holland" is evident. Some phrases are borrowed directly ("Says the mother to the daughter / What makes you talk so strange?"); some are adaptive (the line "There is many a fine young married man / This night must go with me" in the original, becomes "There is many a pretty fair maid / That cries out filly lu"); while other features are cleverly made over (what in the original is the daughter's threat to confine herself in mourning, is in the whaling text transformed into the mother's threat to confine the daughter "for seven long years" as punishment for her obstinacy). "Nantucket Mother and Daughter" can be sung to any of the airs for "Lowlands of Holland," but which one may have been known to George W. Piper is probably impossible to determine.

TUNE: There being no other air specifically collected in New England (unfortunately, Flanders gives no music with her text), of the many variant tunes available the best choice is probably the one collected by Alan Lomax in Maine and published in B.H. Bronson, *The Traditional Tunes of the Child Ballads,* II:420, #3 [see #19-B]. The closely related variant here, recalled from childhood memory, is likely of Scottish origin:

"THE NANTUCKET MOTHER AND DAUGHTER." George W. Piper, ship *Europa* of Edgartown, 1868-70.

1. Our orders came this morning
    And we will sail to morrow
    And there is many a pretty fair maid
    That cries with grief and sorrow
    For there is many a pretty fair maid
    That cries out filly lu[5]
    For when those sailor boys do leave
    Dear girls what shall we do

---

[5] *Fillaloo:* "A din, an uproar… A perversion of *hullabaloo*. In dialect as *filliloo* or *fillyloo*" (Partridge 1961, 275).

2. Says the mother to the daughter
   What makes you talk so strange
   You never shall be a sailor's wife
   This wide world for to range
   For the whaling boys are roving blades
   They will travel far and near
   And when they do come back again
   It is not for you they will care

3. Says the daughter to the mother
   What makes you run them down
   For there is many a rich farmer's son
   On board of a Sperm Whaleman
   For they are so neat and handy
   They will make such a dubious noise
   They will make the girls of Talcahuano Town[6]
   Run after the whaling boys

4. Says the mother to the daughter
   I will confine you in your room
   Until these whaling boys do leave
   Nantucket Town all through
   If you lock me up for seven long years,
   And the eighth one set me free
   I will away to Talcahuano Town
   For to court his company

5. O my love is tall and handsome
   His limbs are all complete
   With his blue jacket and white pantaloons
   He looks so trim and neat
   With his rosy cheeks and ruby lips
   Likewise his sparkling eyes
   All for my life I will be his wife
   And love him till he dies

---

[6] Talcahuano, in Chile, was one of the principal outports of the Pacific whaling fleet in the 19th century and is often mentioned in whaling songs and lore, where it has been described as a place "where a man can buy a whorehouse for a barrel of flour" [see "Blow Ye Winds," #139, version A, stanza 18). Scarcely a deepwater haven of any intrinsic promise, it rose to prominence as a provisioning station by virtue of the services it could provide to sailors on liberty. The mariners were so disruptive and their influence locally judged to be so destructive, that for several years in the early part of the 19th century the Chileans closed their ports to whaler traffic, giving a boost to the Peruvian ports of Callao, Paita, and Tumbez farther north. While they all developed rowdy reputations, Talcahuano and Tumbez were the most notorious; Callao and Paita were somewhat quieter, probably owing, in part, to the presence there of British and American consulates.

21. The Banks of the Schuylkill

This uncommon but effective ballad is set in Pennsylvania, where the Schuylkill River joins the Delaware at Philadelphia, which facts have little to do with whaling or with the exposition or known history of the ballad. It is sufficiently rare to have been unfamiliar to Malcolm Laws and does not appear in his venerable taxonomy, even though it is a classic broadside ballad of just the sort he was seeking. In fact, apart from three texts in whalemen's journals (the one below; and two that are consolidated without any tune by Huntington), the only other version located that has this form or this title is a corrupt text with a first-rate tune collected by Vance Randolph in Missouri in 1941. The shipboard texts are at least sixty years earlier and far more complete; they are also virtually identical, suggesting a published source, possibly *The Forget Me Not Songster,* in which the text was printed, sans tune, circa 1840. The central theme is common enough in balladry, a tender love affair interrupted by army conscription [see "The Lowlands of Holland," #19; and "The Noble Duke," #87], however in this instance without any aftermath beyond the woman's hope for a reunion and her resolve that the lovers not be separated again. Randolph's melody is a form of "Johnny Must Fight," which, in turn, is a manifestation of the ballad type that Laws calls "The Girl Volunteer" (Laws #O-33). "Johnny Must Fight" has seldom been encountered in tradition but was popularized by Peter, Paul & Mary in the 1960s under the title "Cruel War," and was widely anthologized as such in the commercial hootenanny-and-coffee-house-type folksong books of that era. According to Randolph (1982, 94), "Although Laws … classifies ["The Girl Volunteer"/"Johnny Must Fight"] as a 'ballad of faithful lovers,' its story is similar to several classified as 'ballads of lovers' disguises and tricks.'" Randolph's implication is clearly that the taxonomy of this ballad might better be premised upon the woman's proposal to dress herself up as a man and follow her beau to war, rather than upon the idea of her faithfulness; but in fairness to Laws it should be pointed out that in most versions of the ballad the "girl volunteer" does not *actually* play any tricks or adopt any disguises, she merely *proposes* to do so. Whatever the merits of Randolph's position on "The Girl Volunteer," by contrast "Banks of the Schuylkill" is *not* a "ballad of lovers disguises" but *is* a "ballad of faithful lovers" as both Laws and Randolph would define the category: neither text of "Schuylkill" makes any mention of the woman even thinking about dressing up like a man or going to war; she simply pledges her trow and hopes her man will return soon. Moreover, far from being a foreshortening, condensation, or adulteration of some larger story, "Banks of the Schuylkill" is complete in itself, making its point poignantly without melodramatic complications of plot. Whether the soldier ever returns to his beloved the ballad does not disclose, but perhaps the lovers would be gratified to know that, even today, on the banks of the Schuylkill, adjacent to downtown Philadelphia, are some of the finest urban parklands in America.

TUNE from Vance Randolph, *Ozark Folk Songs,* IV:281, #769, collected in 1941 from Charles Ingenthron of Walnut Shade, Missouri, who "learned the song near Walnut Shade in the early 1900s." Transposed from D Major.

"THE BANKS OF THE SCHUYLKILL." Rodolphus W. Dexter, master, ship *Israel* of New Bedford, 1846-47. Similar to a Randolph's text, which has only 5 stanzas of 4 lines each, wherein two lines of the second stanza are absent and several anomalies occur (Randolph #769).

1. On the banks of the Schuylkill so pleasant and gay
   There blessed with my true love I spend the short day
   Where the sun shed his rays thro' the mulberry tree
   And the streams form'd a mirror for my true love and me

2. On the spot of clover we set ourselves down
   not envying the greatest of monarchs thats crown'd
   My name in the sand with his finger he drew
   and he swore by the stream he would ever prove true

3. to which I beheld the gay pride of my fair
   I gazed on his face while he played with my hair
   he need not have told me his love with a sigh
   for the schuylkill secures my dear fellow to me

4. Oft times he told me stories of love
   he would sing me a song my affections to move
   My lips were solicited my hand gently press'd
   on the banks of the schuylkill where Jessie was blessed

5. Whenever we leave this enchanting retreat
   With blushes she says when next we shall meet
   Next Sunday he says if the weather proves Clear
   On the banks of the schhuylkill I'll meet you My dear

6. Now all these innocent pleasures are o'er
   the murmuring river can please me no more
   since the banks of the schuylkill have lost all thair Charms
   and the soldiers have torn my dear boy from my arms

7. but should ever I clasp him again to my heart
   no more shall my true love and I ever part
   no more shall the wars take my true love away
   and the banks of the schuylkill shall ever be gay

Rodolphus W. Dexter onboard ship Israel
November Saturday 14th 1846 one ship in sight
oh if I could but [be with] my dear little wife and children
See how pleasant the banks of the schuylkill wo[u]ld be RWD

Note: Captain Dexter's full transcription vindicates Randolph's commentary on his informant's imperfect and incomplete text, where the second line of the second stanza reads "Not an enemy in the greatest of monarchs that crown": Randolph remarks in a footnote, "The words *enemy in* should certainly be *envying,* but Mr. Ingenthron insists on *enemy in*—'It means they didn't have no important enemies, like kings,' he says" (Randolph IV:281).

22. West's Farewell

The title and context of this song, implying the speaker's imminent departure to join the army of General Zachary Taylor in the Mexican War (1846-48), suggest that the lyrics may have been whaleman Benjamin West's own original composition. This is perhaps reinforced by the original orthography. The chronology indicates that he must have written it—or written it down—at the very end of or shortly after his whaling voyage in the Fairhaven ship *Leonidas* (1843-46), and the "onion heap" allusion in the first stanza implies that by that time may already have been farming. The song is actually a parody of "The Bride's Farewell" (Boston, circa 1830), with lyrics by a Miss M.L. Beevor and music by Thomas Williams.[7] There is also a Christian parody, untitled in Caroline Howard Gilman's *Tales and Ballads* (New York, 1839), where the "touching verses of a southern poetess," identified as Miss Mary Palmer, are to be sung "to the tune of the 'Bride's Farewell.'" However, in *The Southern Harp* (Boston, 1841), Mary S.B. Dana calls the piece "The Missionary's Farewell" and credits the words to "Mrs. Dana" and the music to T. Williams.[8] It is not known whether it was the secular original or the religious spin-off that inspired the Mexican War lyrics.

TUNE – "The Bride's Farewell," from an edition of the sheet music (New York: Otto Torp, undated, circa 1835-37).

"WEST'S FAREWELL." Benjamin L. West, ship *Leonidas* of Fairhaven, 1843-46.

1. Farewell Mother—Taylor calles me
   Far away from home and the[e].
   The Onion heap no more enthralls me
   When a lofty ship i see
   Farewell mother do not pain me
   By thine agonizeing woe
   Those fond arms cannot detain me
   Dearest mother i must go

2. Farewell farther [father] O how tender
   Are the cords that bind me here
   Jesus helps me to surrender
   All I love without a tear

   No my Savior wert thou te[a]rless
   Leaning oer the burried dead
   At this hour so sad and cherrless
   Shall not burning tears be Shed

3. Farewell sister do not press me
   To thy young and throbing heart
   Oh no longer now distress me
   Sister Sister we must part
   Farewell pale and silent brother
   How i grieve to pain the[e] so
   Farther—Mother—Sister—Brother—
   Taylor calls.—O let me go!

---

[7] The first of three stanzas in the sheet music is: "Farewell Mother: tears are streaming, / Down thy pale and tender cheek, / I in gems and roses gleaming, / Scarce this sad Farewell may speak, / Farewell Mother: now I leave thee, / (Hopes and fear my bosom swell) / One to trust who may deceive me / Farewell mother: Fare thee well!" The second stanza begins, "Farewell Father"; and the third, "Farewell Sister."

[8] "Farewell, mother! Jesus calls me / Far away from home and thee; / Earthly love no more enthralls me, / When a bleeding cross I see. / Farewell, mother do not pain me / By thine agonizing woe, / Those fond arms cannot detain me / Dearest mother, I must go." Like the prototype, the second stanza begins, "Farewell Father"; and the third, "Farewell Sister."

23. The British Man-of-War
[On Board of a Man-of-War; The Yankee Man-of-War]

> Last night I walked up-on the Top Gallant Forecastle for two hours in the First Watch, listening to the Blue Jackets' Songs: it was grand. Some fellows were very pathetic, singing about "Tom Bowling," "Ben Bolt," "Poor little Nelly, the drunkards lost child," "Polly and Joe the Marine," and so on: but the grand one was, "Fare well an Adieu, Ye fair Spanish Maidens, Fare well and adieu, Ye Maidens of Spain;—for we've received orders to sail for old Eng—land, but we hope very soon we shall see you again—This with "Homeward Bound" and its rousing chorus of "When we get in to Plymouth docks, the pretty little girls come down in flocks, to see Jack Homeward Bound, my lads, to see him Homeward Bound"; and "Haul, lads haul, Our Home is on the Sea, Haul, lads haul and cheerily Oh, Haul, lads haul, the Ship's going free; and the white waves are washing at the Bows, I—Oh"!
> Then comes the "Shannon" and the "Chesapeake," with Brave Brook. He waves his sword, and says Now my lads aboard, and we'll stop their playing Yankee–doodle, Yankee doodle, dandy Oh, Yankee doodle, Yankee doodle dandy Oh; the people of the port, they came out to see the Sport, and their band it played us Yankee doodle dandy Oh! This was finished up with "Homeward Bound" once more, with the last chorus sung over three times, and then the singers went back to Pipes, & Hammocks, the former for the watch on Deck, the latter for the Watch Below: the ditties of the British Blue Jacket being ended...
>
> — HMS *Agincourt*, at sea, 7 August 1880

This nautical ballad, with traditional elements of the Sailors' Farewell and love-token genres, came out of the era of the Opium Wars in China (1840-42). Originally known as "The British Man-of-War," with reference to the Royal Navy (texts A and B), it was later made over into an Americanized adaptation entitled "The Yankee Man-of-War" (C). Belden's contention that this was to accommodate the American Civil War is born out by chronology, as no version of the Yankee remake has been located that is earlier than the 1860s. In fact, while "The British Man-of-War" has been found in a few whaling journals of the 1840s and '50s, George W. Piper's rendition, transcribed circa 1868-70, is the earliest text of "The Yankee Man-of-War" that has yet come to hand. However, any actual mention of the war itself—the ostensible occasion for the young man embarking in a man-of-war of whatever nationality—is absent from the whaleman's text of "The Yankee Man-of-War." The American revision is a song of parting only, lacking the war passages that characterize the last two stanzas of the British prototype; however, jingoistic allusions to the Chinese and Portuguese, present in the original, are anachronistically preserved in the copy. Unaccountably, "Yankee Man-of-War" is not recorded by Laws, though it seems to be a classic instance of what he meant by "American balladry from British broadsides."

TUNE from Frank Kidson, *Traditional Tunes,* 1891, 102f. Transposed from B♭ Major.

A.

"THE BRITISH MAN OF WAR." Theodore D. Bartley, ship *California* of N.B., 1851-54.

1. Down by yonder ocean so carelessly I did stray
   Tis there I saw a lady with her sailor gay
   Oh Susan lovely Susan I soon must leave this shore
   To cross the Briney Ocean on a british Man of War

2. Susan fell a weeping oh sailor she did say
   How can you be so venturesome to throw your life away
   For when my age is twenty one I will receive my store
   So sailor do not venture on a British Man of War

3. Oh Susan lovely Susan the truth to you I'll tell
   Our flag has been insulted old England knows it well
   With my name crowned with laurels and like a jolly tar
   I'll cross the briney ocean in a British Man of War

4. Oh sailor to not venture to face the proud Chinese
   For they will prove more treacherous than any Portuguese
   And by some deadly dagger you may receive a scar
   So sailor do not venture on a British Man of War

5. Oh Susan lovely Susan the time will quickly pass
   Come down to yonder ferry house and take the parting kiss
   My comrades are awaiting to row me from the shore
   For old Englands glory in a British Man of War

6. The sailor took his handkerchief and tore it fair in two
   Saying keep one half for me and I will do as much for you
   While bullets are flying round me and cannons loudly roar
   I'll fight for fame and Susan on a British Man of War

7. A few more words together and her love let go her hand
   The jovial crew now launched their boats and sailed away from the land
   The sailor wove [waived] his handkerchief while parting from the shore
   And Susan Blessed her Sailor on a British Man of War

8. We arrived at China with a fair and pleasant breeze
   Our minds in full intention to face the proud Chinese
   They did attempt to board us as we lay of[f] the shore
   But we fire[d] a broadside in too them from the British Man of War

9. We had one hundred wounded and many more were slain
   They did attempt to fire our ship but it was all in vain
   We drove them in confusion as we lay o[f] the shore
   I returned home safe from [sic] Susan in a British Man of War

B.

UNTITLED. Jonathan Whalon, master, ship *Henry Kneeland* of New Bedford, 1854-56. Similar to A but a lesser text, including such differences as: the first line is, "It was down in yonder *meadow* where *fearlessly* did stray"; in stanza 3, lines 3-4 read, "*I may be* crowned with laurels and like a *gallant* tar / I *face the walls of China* in a British man of war"; stanza 5, line 2 has "parting *glass*"; the last couplets of stanzas 5 and 6 are lacking and the remaining couplets are united to form a single stanza (resulting in a total of 8 rather than 9 stanzas); the consolidated stanza is flawed, as it does not end with the "British Man of War" refrain ; and in stanza 8 (corresponding to stanza 9 in A), the order of lines 1 and 2 is reversed, and the remaining couplet conveys a motivation quite different than A (see below). Stanzas 4 and 8 are sufficiently different from A and C as to warrant including them in their entirety:

4. How can you be so adventuresome to face those proud Chinese
   They will prove as fatal against you as any Portuguese
   And by some deadly dag[g]er you may receive a scar
   So turn your inclinations love from a british man of war

8. They undertook to fire our ship but they proved it all in vane
   Their was five hundred wounded and as many more was slain
   When the bullets they fly round me and the cannons loudly roar
   And I'll fight for lovely Susan in a British man of war

C.

"THE YANKEE MAN OF WAR." George W. Piper, ship *Europa* of Edgartown, 1868-70. Standard Americanized rendition of "The British Man of War," lacking the final two stanzas, which in "British Man of War" (texts A and B) briefly narrate a war sequence in China. For a variant melody and text that has Civil War adaptations, collected in New York State, see Cazden 1982, #13.

1. As down by yonder valley I happened for to stray
   I espied a pretty fair maid along with a sailor gay
   O Susan lovely Susan I soon must leave this shore
   For to cross the briny Ocean in a Yankee Man of War

2. O Willie dearest Willie how can you cross the seas
   How can you be so venturesome for to throw yourself away [1]
   For when I am twenty one I shall receive my store
   O Willie dont you venture in a Yankee Man of War

3. Oh Susan lovely Susan the truth to you I'll tell
   The American flag is insulted and America knows it well
   I may be crowned with laurels just like some jolly tar
   I will face the walls of China in a Yankee Man of War

4. O Willie dearest Willie dont face the proud Chinese
   For they may prove as treacherous as any Portuguese
   And by some secret dagger you may receive a scar
   O Willie dont you venture in a Yankee Man of War

5. O Susan lovely Susan the time will quickly pass
   Come down to yonder ferry house and take the parting glass
   My shipmates are a waiting for to row me from the shore
   I will fight for America's glory in a Yankee Man of War

6. The sailor took his handkerchief and tore it half in two
   Saying Susan you keep half for me and I will do the same for you
   When battles do surround me and the cannons loudly roar
   I will fight for fame and Susan in a Yankee Man of War

7. A few more word[s] of parting her love let go her hand
   The sailors pushed their boat so merrily from the strand
   The sailor waived his handkerchief when far away from shore
   Pretty Susan blessed her sailor in a Yankee Man of War

24. The Captain Calls All Hands
[A Song Concerning Love; Our Captain Cried]

The customary title of this sailors' farewell song comes from the customary first line, "The captain calls all hands and away tomorrow." Remarking on a text from an 1832-35 journal of the Salem whaleship *Bengal,* Huntington cites Frank Kidson's observation in *Traditional Tunes* "that the song must go back to the time of the Napoleonic wars at least." But Huntington's speculation that "Personally I have a feeling that it is older than that" (Huntington 1964, 100) is vindicated in whaleman Stephen Cahoon's 1794 journal of the whaleship *Polly* of Gloucester, Massachusetts. There the lyrics take a somewhat different form with a variant opening line, establishing an 18th-century provenance for the song. Apparently on metrical, musical, and textual grounds, Vaughan Williams maintains that it is related to the great ballad "The Brave Wolfe" of circa 1759; and the *Bengal* text verifies that "The Captain Calls All Hands" was still in circulation among mariners in the middle of the nineteenth century. It is interesting and likely significant that the two manifestations in whalemen's journals are virtually the only vestiges of the song that have been found in North America, and that both transcriptions are from adjacent ports on the so-called North Shore of Boston. Kennedy notes that the song is a kind of corollary of "The Blacksmith" ("The Blacksmith Courted Me"),[9] of which the evident antiquity of the fine modal melody collected by Vaughan Williams[2][10] makes it a suitable alternative to the major-key air that is also associated with "The Captain Calls All Hands."

TUNE A - "The Captain Calls All Hands": composite; meter regularized. Compare Kennedy 1975, #146 ("A Blacksmith Courted Me"); Frank Purslow, *The Constant Lovers,* London, 1972, #8; Huntington 1964, 99.

---

[9] Huntington arbitrarily contends that "The Captain Calls All Hands" is related to "The Bold Privateer" [#102]. While the two share an analogous farewell theme, in that the woman in each resists her lover's imminent departure to sea (a very conventional feature, shared with dozens of parting songs and farewell ballads), the stories are entirely different. "Bold Privateer" is a broken-token ballad most of the distinctive elements of which are absent in "The Captain Calls All Hands," as is readily apparent from Laws's succinct summary of "Bold Privateer": "Molly begs Johnny to stay at home with her instead of risking his life at sea. He replies that *her friends dislike him and her brothers would take his life. He offers to exchange rings with her,* and, if his life is spared in the war, *to return and marry her*" (Laws #O-32; italics added). Peter Kennedy's comparison with "The Blacksmith," which he astutely regards as merely a form of the same song, is far more compelling, though his notion that the two songs may once have been paired as a duet is only speculative:

"['The Blacksmith Courted Me' is] an interesting song, in that there are really two forms: *The Blacksmith,* from the girl's point of view, and *Our Captain Calls,* from the man's viewpoint:

> Our captain calls all hands on board tomorrow
> Leaving my dear to mourn in grief and sorrow
> Dry up those briny tears and leave off weeping
> So happy we may be at our next meeting

"... Because of the existence of men's verses and women's verses in the various collected versions, it can be surmised that at one time the song existed in an extended form as a duet-type love song. In our four-verse version [of 'The Blacksmith'] we have only the point of view of the girl who has been left behind while her blacksmith goes off 'fighting for strangers'; other versions supply the man's viewpoint" (Kennedy 1975, #146, p. 370).

[10] "The faithful 'hero' of this song ['The Blacksmith'] is just as often a shoemaker as a blacksmith. Both meter and tune are rather unusual, recalling the well-known *Brisk Young Widow* in SFS III [C.J. Sharp & C.L. Marson, *Folk Songs from Somerset,* London, 5 vols., 1904-09), and *Brave Wolfe,* a song celebrating the hero of Quebec, often found in America though not reported in Britain (*Brave Wolfe* is not to be confused with *Bold General Wolfe,* which is fairly common in England). The opening of the 'strange news' verse also appears in some sets of *Brave Wolfe*" (Vaughan Williams 1959, 111).

TUNE B - "The Blacksmith," from Ralph Vaughan Williams, *The Penguin Book of English Folk Songs,* 1959, p. 22: "Sung by Mrs Powell, nr Weobley, Herefordshire," collected by Vaughan Williams in 1909.

"A SONG CONCERNING LOVE." Stephen Cahoon, ship *Polly* of Gloucester, 1794. Corrective additions for the sake of meter and continuity are indicated in italics in brackets. Characteristic phrases appear in stanza 4 (often the opening stanza), the first couplet of 5, and stanza 6 (of which the syntax is characteristic though the meaning be obscure).

1. Fair you well my dearest dear Since I must leave you
   I Can no Longer Stay I must go from you
   O I Shall Pine and dye if you go from me
   So stay at home my Dear and do not Leave me

2. Why would you go to Sea to Fight for Strangers
   When you [*could stay*] at home free from all dangers
   I will infold you in my arms my dearest juel [jewell]
   and i will keep you from all harmes Love dont be Cruel

3. down By one River[*side*] as I was a walking
   a man and a maid I Espied as they were a talking
   theire hands were joinded together as they were a going
   twas a Black and a Rowling Ere that Proved my Ruin

4. our Captain Calls us Now with haist and hurry
   I Can no Longer Stay I must go from you
   So dry up your watry tears and Leave off weaping
   For happy we Shall Be at our Next meeting

5. then on her [k]neas she fell like one a dying
   and Spreading her arms a Broad and this Replying
   awake you Rocks and Stones that is now relenting
   all for the Sake of one I dye Lamenting

6. Fair well you Parents dear father and mother
   you have Lost your darter dear I have no other
   It is in vain to weap for me for I am going
   whare joys forever Be and fountains a flowing

25. Farewell, Charming Nancy
[Adieu, Lovely Nancy; Adieu, Lovely Mary; Jimmy and Nancy]
(Laws #K-14)

Several virtually interchangeable titles tie this song closely to "Adieu, Sweet Lovely Nancy" [#26]. Both are certainly sailors' farewell songs of great elegance and charm, with similarities of sentiment and phrasing. But the meter and tunes are wholly different. The other, which is English by descent if not in origin, is sung to a fine, lilting melody in a major key, while this one, has an equally fine minor-modal air, indisputably Irish, and neither can be readily sung to the tune of the other. The underlying themes are also quite different. "Adieu, Sweet Lovely Nancy" is naval in character with an explicitly patriotic element; in it the sailor-lover catalogues the hardships and perils of the voyage and proclaims his intention to return. In "Farewell, Charming Nancy," as in so many ballads of sailors' parting and "lovers' tricks," the woman proposes to follow her beau to sea. Like "Jack Munroe" [#84], she is told that she is too delicate to face the rigors of a sailor's life; however, unlike "Jack Munroe," here she seems to heed the warning and does not make the attempt. Though "Farewell, Charming Nancy" has been collected from tradition in England and America, the theme descends from a 1685 printing by J. Deacon of London, entitled "The Seaman's Doleful Farewel, or the Greenwich Lovers Mournful departure" (Pepys, IV:186; Roxburghe, 8:780) and in this form is closely associated with Ireland and intimately related to, and may actually be the ancestor of "The Holy Ground," a Welsh song that was adopted in Ireland and made over into a convivial song localized to Cobh (formerly Queenstown), in County Cork.[11] Examples of the distressed condition of the whaleman's manuscript are failure to differentiate the lines and the presence of an extra line in stanza 3, which reads in its entirety:

> I will cut off my yellow locks and go along
> with you in the midst of all dangers your
> friend i will prove true in the midst of all
> dangers your friend i not fail
> when the cold stormy winds are continually blowing
> my love i be ready to reefe your top sails.

[*Sea Battle.*] Scrimshaw sperm whale tooth engraved by the anonymous whaleman-artist known only as the Naval Engagement Engraver, circa 1840-55. Kendall Collection, New Bedford Whaling Museum.

---

[11] See Healy 1967, #8; and O Lochlainn 1965, #22. Palmer (1985, #93 and #125) presents the plausible theory that "The Holy Ground" is descended from "Adieu, Sweet Lovely Nancy" [q.v., fn 1] and not the other way round.

TUNE - "Farewell, Nancy," from Cecil J. Sharp, *One Hundred English Folksongs,* Boston, 1916, #30, p. 70: "The tune, a remarkably fine one, is in the Æolian mode, and was sung to me by a woman seventy-four years of age."

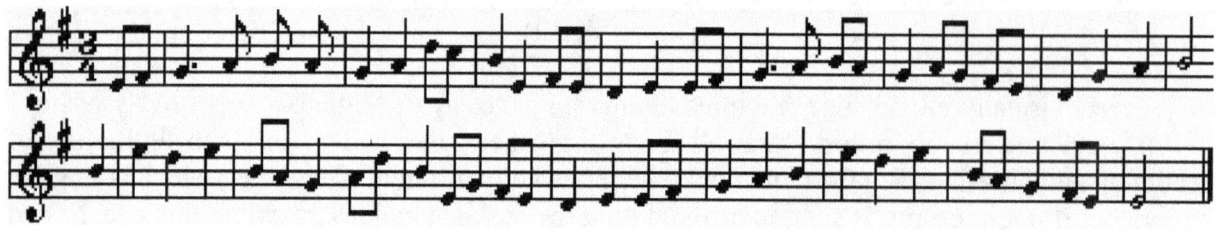

"JIMMY AND NANCY." William Gillaspia, ship *Atlantic* of Nantucket, 1846-49. The syntax and phonetic spelling suggest an oral source. Stanza 6 is a generic convention ("take warning by me") not indigenous to the "Nancy" cycle, not in Laws, not present in other specimens of the ballad. Division into stanzas is clear in the MS, but the un-differentiated lines are here reconfigured. Editorial additions for the sake of meter are indicated in italics in brackets.

1. Adieu Lovely Nancy Its Now I Must Leave You
   Unto the East Indies My Corse I Must Steer
   I Know Verry Well My Long Absents Will greave you
   But My Jewel I will Return In the Spring Of the Year

2. Talk Not of leaving Me [*my*] Dearest Jimmy
   talk Not of Leaving Me Here All Alone
   For Tis your fine company [*that*] i doe admire[, *love*]
   i shal sy [sigh] til i die if i neare [never] see you more

3. I will cut off my yellow locks and go along with you
   in the midst of all dangers your friend i['ll] not fail
   when the cold stormy winds are continually blowing
   my love i['ll] be ready to reefe your top sails

4. Your neat little fingers strong cables cant handle
   nor your neat little foot to the round top cant go
   your delicate boddy strong winds cant endure[, *love*]
   so stay at home nancy to the seas do not goe

5. Now jimmy is sailing and nancy bewailing
   the tears from her eyes down in fountains doth flow
   her gold yellow locks she continualy tearing
   saying i shall sy [sigh] til i dy [die] if i nare see you more

6. Come all you pretty fair maidens whare ever you be
   never give your love to enny one that crosses the sea
   for first they will like you and then they will slite you
   they will leave you broken harted as my love left me

26. Adieu, Sweet Lovely Nancy
[Farewell, My Dearest Nancy; Parting Moments; The Sailor's Farewell]

Though this ballad is excerpted in J. Ross Browne's *Etchings of a Whaling Cruise* (1846), where it is entitled "Parting Moments," and though it has been collected in the British Isles and elsewhere, it has evidently not hitherto been encountered in tradition in the United States, and is not separately catalogued by Laws nor noted by him in connection with "Farewell, Charming Nancy" [#25]. The whaleman's transcription, which he entitles merely "Song," is an uncorrupted text of a song now in circulation in revival as "Adieu, Sweet Lovely Nancy," popularized in the 'States by Louis Killen and tracing to the Copper Family of rural Rottingdean, Sussex (England). The ubiquitousness of that manifestation requires that the title "Adieu, Sweet Lovely Nancy" be adopted here in preference to the whaleman's actual first line, "Farewell, My Dearest Nancy," or Baring-Gould's title, "The Sailor's Farewell." "Adieu, Sweet Lovely Nancy" provides the textual link to "The Holy Ground," which was evidently originally a Welsh song that was appropriated by the Irish and made into a convivial song localized to Cobh (formerly Queenstown), a seaport in County Cork, where it became the "anthem of Cobh" (Healy 1967 #8).[12] The Copper Family rendition boasts a noble air in a major key (the primary tune in revival), while the Copper text is poetic but adulterated, containing nautical incongruities and mixed metaphors adopted willy-nilly from the naval and merchant services and a handful of other songs and genres, with a result that is a fine song but could hardly be pure sailors' work. J. Ross Browne's text, whereof the source may also have been the original source for the Copper version, excises the questionable and incongruous passages. The whaleman's text is the purer ancestor of the Copper Family lyrics: it is more seaworthy and less self-consciously literary, preserving intact the technical proficiency and nautical sophistication characteristic of deepwater songs. As such, the whaleman's version is a more "authentic" sea song (though not necessarily more authentic as a folk song or as an example of the process of oral transmission).

TUNE A - "Adieu, Sweet Lovely Nancy," from the singing of Morrigan (Seattle, 1980); and Louis Killen (New York City, 1980), originally after Bob Copper, *A Song for Every Season*, London, [1971] 1972, 244. It seems to be a variant of the Irish air given by J.L. Molloy for "Weep not for me" (Molloy 1873, 147).

---

[12] The opening stanza of "Adieu..." (Copper 245) is:

> Here's adieu, sweet lovely Nancy, ten thousand times adieu,
> I'm a-going around the ocean, love, to seek for something new.
> Come change your ring with me, dear girl / Come change your ring with me
> For it might be a token of true love while I am on the sea

Compare this with the first stanza of "The Holy Ground" (Healy 1962 #8):

> Adieu, my fair young maidens, a thousand times adieu,
> We must bid good-bye to the Holy Ground, the place that we love true;
> We will sail the salt seas over, and return again for sure,
> To seek the girls that wait for us—In the Holy Ground once more.

Could the original "Farewell, Nancy" [#25], per Sharp and O Lochlainn, have come under the influence of "The Holy Ground" and resulted in "Adieu, Sweet Lovely Nancy"? or the other way round, as Palmer has suggests (1985, #93 and #125)?

TUNE B - "The Sailor's Farewell," from S. Baring-Gould et al., *Songs of the West,* 1905, #38, where the first stanza is: "Farewell, my Polly dear! A thousand times adieu / 'Tis sad to part; but never fear, Your sailor will be true. / And must I go, and leave you so, While thund'ring billows roar? / I am afraid, my own sweet maid, Your face I'll see no more."

"SONG." George W. Piper, ship *Europa* of Edgartown, 1868-70. The MS repeats the last line of each stanza. To reconcile the text with either tune requires that each stanza be treated as a half-stanza and the repeats be eliminated, per Copper Family and J. Ross Browne texts, or that the last line of each stanza be repeated. Minor textual additions for the sake of meter are in italics in brackets.

1. Farewell, my dearest Nancy
   Ten thousand times adieu
   I am bound across the ocean
   In search of something new [*repeat line*]

2. Come change the ring with me dear girl
   Come change the ring with me
   That it might be a token [*of our*] love
   While I am on the sea [*repeat line*]

3. And when I am on the sea, my love
   You know not where I am
   Kind letters I will write to you
   From every foreign land [*repeat line*]

4. And now the ship is out to sea
   Where the winds begin to blow
   When some of us we do feel sick
   And have to go below [*repeat line*]

5. See now the storm arises
   See how it is coming on
   While we poor jolly sailor boys
   Are fighting for the crown

6. Our officers command us
   With orders to obey
   Expecting every moment
   For to be cast away

7. Now see the storm is over
   We merrily go on shore
   We will drink to the health of those we love
   And the girls we do adore

8. We will call for liquor plenty
   And spend our money free
   And when our money is all gone
   We will boldly go to sea

Above: Scrimshaw sperm whale tooth engraved with Royal Navy motifs by William Hill or Edward Hill, circa 1825-35. Kendall Collection, New Bedford Whaling Museum.

27. My Mary Ann
[Mary Ann; Fare You Well, My Own True Love]

Especially in Canada, "Mary Ann" is popularly regarded as a maritime folk song of Canadian origin, in conformity with the precedent set by Fowke & Johnston, who so categorized a version collected by Marius Barbeau from the singing of a Canadian sailor in 1920.[13] However, Fowke & Johnston's version (evidently the only one to have been recovered from tradition[14] and the one upon which the song's extensive subsequent reputation and publishing history as a folk song is premised) is actually a not-much-changed rendition of the text and tune of a mid 19th-century parlor song. While the specific date of its original publication has not been ascertained, the music for "My Mary Ann" is attributed to one M. Tyte and the lyrics are ascribed to Barney Williams, a blackface minstrel performer more familiar to American audiences under his stage name, Dandy Jim from Caroline.[15] The song was originally performed by Mrs. Barney Williams, who actually posed for the picture of "the Yankee Girl" on the sheet music (of which an 1856 Baltimore edition listed by Dichter & Larrabee is likely not the first printing). This, in turn, has quite a long ancestry, tracing back through Robert Burns and James Johnson's *Scots Musical Museum* (1796) to a British broadside of 1688, "The Two Unfortunate Lovers," which appears in the *Roxburgh Ballads* as "The Unkind Parents, or the Unfortunate Lovers," sung to the tune of "My Life and Death" (Cazden 1982, 172ff).

Unfortunately, the transcription by whaleman Richard Reynolds, which appears to have been made in the early 1840s, is only a fragment; but the song is nevertheless unequivocally identifiable from its distinctive first line and characteristic refrain, "And I am bound for the sea Mary Ann." Regarding the discrepancy in the dates, the logical alternatives are: that the song by Williams and Tyte is substantially earlier than the Baltimore edition of the sheet-music would indicate (i.e., was published prior to the 1840s, when Reynolds is presumed to have written down the lyrics), which is the likely scenario; or that it was originally a folk song (or a parlor song by somebody else), extant prior to the 1840s, that was later worked up for Mrs. Williams to sing and published under the borrowers' names—for which scenario there is no evidence; or that the Reynolds transcription was made sometime after his voyage, which from the context of the many songs in his shipboard copybook is not entirely unlikely. In any case, Reynolds's transcription is significant not only in adding to the evidence (cf. Cazden) that there is little justification for the belief that the origins of "Mary Ann" are Canadian, but for its apparent vindication of Fowke & Johnston's hypothesis that the song was in circulation by circa 1850. To compensate the absence of a complete shipboard transcription, the entire text is also provided from one of the several songbooks in which "My Mary Ann" was anthologized in the early twentieth century.

---

[13] "Dr. Marius Barbeau heard this unusual [sic] sailor's song in 1920 at Tadoussac, Quebec. The singer, Edouard Hovington, who was then ninety, had been for many years a *coureur-de-bois* employed by the Hudson's Bay Company. He said he had learned 'Mary Ann' from an Irish sailor some seventy years earlier, which would carry it back at least to 1850. ¶ 'Mary Ann' is obviously [sic] descended from the old English song, 'The True Lover's Farewell' (which is also the ancestor of 'The Turtle Dove' and Burns' 'My Luve's Like a Red, Red Rose'), but it is one of the most unusual of the many variants. The nautical references give it a salty flavour quite appropriate to the Tadoussac region, which abounds in tiny fishing villages" (Fowke & Johnston, 142). Elsewhere, the song has been claimed for Nova Scotia, also on grounds of "suitability." Experience teaches that one should not too readily embrace the arcane extrapolations for which Barbeau is notorious, nor entirely trust the chronological recollections of Ancient Mariners. In any case, the subjective verdict of "suitability" to the Tadoussac region is no guarantee of Canadian or folkloric origin; and any superficial thematic relationship to "True Lover's Farewell," "Turtle Dove" and "Red, Red Rose" is easily accounted for in "Mary Ann" being derivative and substantially later. To the great credit of the folk process, Hovington's orally-transmitted text and tune, while they differ only slightly from the original parlor song, they are in virtually every respect superior.

[14] Except "Fare You Well, My Own True Love," a New York State variant (Cazden 1982, #44); and possibly Rosenberg #882 (not examined)

[15] "J.K. 'Fritz' Emmet, a famous Dutch comedian, also started under the blanket of burnt cork, as did Barney Williams, originally known as 'Dandy Jim from Caroline' and later a specialist in Irish melody" (Paskman, 20). "*Dandy Jim from Carolina. A Popular Negro Melody. As Sung by B. Williams.* Lith: Endicott. Firth & Hall. New York. 1843" (Dichter & Shapiro, 51).

TUNE A - "My Mary Anne," by M. Tyte, from *Heart Songs Dear to the American People,* 1909, p. 246.

TUNE B - "Mary Anne": traditional, primarily in Canada (e.g., singing of John Parry; Ian & Sylvia; etc.).

A.

"MY MARY ANN." Richard C. Reynolds, boatsteerer, ship *Janus* of New Bedford, 1842-44. A fragment, providing just enough for the unequivocal identification of the song.

1. Fare well my own Mary Ann
   Fare you well for a while
   For the ship is ready and the wind is fair[16]
   And I am bound for the sea my Mary Ann
   And I am bound for the sea my Mary Ann

2. Dont you see that turtle dove
   A sit… [*end of transcription*]

B.

"MY MARY ANNE." From *Heart Songs Dear to the American People,* p. 246. Compare Wier 1918, p. 315, who gives only the first two stanzas; and Fowke & Johnston, pp. 143f, an orally-transmitted text which in standpoint of meter and poetic quality is a decided improvement.

1. Fare-you-well, my own Mary Anne,
   Fare-you-well a while,
   For the ship is ready, And the wind it is fair,
   And I am bound for the sea, Mary Anne,
   I am bound for the sea.

2. Don't you see that turtle dove,
   Sitting on yon pine,
   Lamenting the loss of its own true love?
   And so am I for mine, Mary Anne,
   So am I for mine.

3. A lobster in the lobster pot,
   A blue fish wriggling on a hook,
   May suffer some, but oh, no, not
   What I do feel for my Mary Anne!
   What I feel for Mary Anne.

4. The pride of all the produce rare,
   That in the kitchen grow'd,
   Was pumpkins, but none could compare,
   In angel form to my Mary Anne!
   Could compare with Mary Anne.

---

[16] In the MS, *fair* appears to be crossed out and *free* substituted.

28. **Outward Bound**

[Bark *Ohio* Outward Bound; Bark *Roscius* Outward Bound]

The first version of this original outward-bound song expresses affection for the New Bedford bark *Ohio* and wishing her Godspeed on a voyage undertaken in 1850. Eight years later Frederick Howland Smith, an eighteen-year-old boatsteerer outward-bound in the New Bedford bark *Roscius* on his second whaling voyage, obtained the lyrics—almost certainly from fellow boatsteerer Matthew A. Chadwick the only one aboard the *Roscius* who had also been in the *Ohio* in 1850, shipping when *he* was eighteen. Chadwick is presumed to be the author of the lyrics. Later, still outward-bound in the *Roscius,* Smith produced a second version of the song localized to his own vessel. Apart from having intrinsic value as an expression of whalemen's optimism, "Outward Bound" is significant as an instance in which two transcriptions from a single diarist's collection illustrate local adaptation of otherwise identical texts, demonstrating the continuity of traditions by which whalemen shaped their occupational experience. Smith probably recorded the "original" lyrics simply because he liked the song, and later intuitively made the simple adaptation himself he as came to know and appreciate the *Roscius*. Coincidentally, years later, during 1874-78, Smith was master of another New Bedford whaling bark named *Ohio,* which may have provided him the occasion to resurrect the *Ohio* version of the song he had transcribed about a namesake vessel in his youth. The air has not been discovered.

A.

"BARQUE OHIO OUTWARD BOUND 1850." Frederick H. Smith, boatsteerer, bark *Roscius*, 1858. It evidently refers to the first voyage of the bark *Ohio,* Captain Isaac F. Sawtelle, sailed 1 October 1850; attributed to Matthew A. Chadwick, age 18, passed along to Smith 8 years later when they were shipmates on the *Roscius.* Identical to B except that the lines are differently configured into stanzas and "Ohio" occurs in place of "Roscius" throughout.

B.

"BARQUE ROSCIUS OUTWARD BOUND 1858." From the same source as A, to which it is identical except as noted in A. This voyage of the *Roscius* was commanded by Frederick S. Howland.

1. Brightly the morning sun
   Lit the horizon ore
   When the bark Roscius
   Sailed from the shore
   She was a gallant bark
   Noble and free
       Roscius Roscius success to thee

2. Proudly she waived her sails
   High in the air
   Many a manly heart
   Brushed away a tear
   God speed her on her voyage
   ore the dark blue sea
       Roscius Roscius success to thee

3. Six ships for a whaling voyage
   Left that same day
   How many anxious hearts
   They bore away
   Though we wish them all good luck
   Our best we shall be
       Roscius Roscius success to thee

4. Three years must roll arround
   Ere we can return
   How the time will pass away
   We have yet to learn
   But our best our brightest wish
   Always shall be
       Roscius Roscius success to thee

5. Three years have rolled around
   Soon they will return
   How many anxious hearts
   Now with ardor burn
   For sailors love their homes
   Though doomed to roam
       Roscius Roscius welcome ye home

6. Now we are homeward bound
   Soon we shall be there [4]
   May every cheerful heart
   Share the welcome dear
   God speed us on our way
   Onward we come
       Roscius Roscius welcome ye home

29. The Sailor Boy's Farewell

This wardroom song is filled with nautical metaphors that must have appealed to sailors of all kinds. Admiral Luce attributes the words to U.S. Navy Midshipman Richard W. Meade, Sr.,[17] in 1834, but does not acknowledge the composer. The William Firth & Company anthology *Naval Songs* (1883), which was evidently Luce's principal source for this and many other songs, does not credit the words but attributes the music to D.P. Horton, who was also a sometime editor of naval songs for Firth and who may only have been the arranger [Tune B]. However, an earlier sheet music edition (Boston, 1857), which likewise does not name the lyricist, has an entirely different melody [Tune A] and gives H.W.D. Hayward credit as composer. In all three cases, the printed texts have essentially the same six stanzas, with only minor differences, but the sheet music version also has a chorus with a melody of its own, while the two Naval anthology texts have none:

> O a life give me on the rolling sea,
> Far away from the land and shore
> Where hared blows the gale on the swelling sail,
> And the tempests loudly roar.
> Where hard blows the gale on the swelling sail,
> And the tempests loudly roar.

Two whalemen's transcriptions have been located, each with only five stanzas, Both lack the stanza that appears as the opening stanza in the printed texts, thus the whalemen's opening stanza in their journals is the one that appears as the second stanza in the three printed texts. The whalemen's versions also hold in common other textual differences, such as "Farewell to father, *blessed* hulk," instead of what some printed versions give as "Farewell to father, *rev'rend* hulk." In most later reprints of Old Time lyrics — such as in *Ballou's Monthly Magazine,* published in Boston in 1890 — the song customarily opens with the whalemen's opening stanza, while stanza 4 is generally lacking

TUNE A - Sheet music, Boston: Oliver Ditson, 1857. Music by H.W.D. Hayward.

TUNE B - from *Naval Songs,* New York, 1883, p. 47; and Luce, *Naval Songs,* 1889, p. 189. Music by D.P. Horton. This tune is not much for solo singing, but it makes a noble, hymn-like production when sung in three-part harmony.

---

[17] "Richard W. Meade anonymously wrote a remarkable series of 18 articles on a proposed naval reorganization for the United States which ran in the *Army and Navy Journal* from October 1875 to May 1876. Its title was 'Thoughts on Naval Administration—the Nation that Controls the Sea Controls the World'" (Hayes & Hattendorf, 179f).

A.

"THE SAILOR BOY'S FAREWELL." Daniel L. Tinkham, bark *Samuel and Thomas* of Mattapoisett, 1852; and brig *March* of Mattapoisett, 1855-56. Almost certainly a copy text, likely from a different source than B (q.v.).

1. Farewell to father, blessed hulk
   In spite of metal spite of bulk,
      his cable soon may slip;
   While yet the parting tear is moist,
   The flag of gratitude I'll hoist
      In duty to my ship

2. Farewell to mother, first class she,
   Who launched me on life's stormy sea,
      And rigged me fore and aft.
   May Providence her timber[s] spare,
   And keep her hull in good repair;
      To tow the smallest craft.

3. Farewell to sister, lovely yacht,
   But whether she'll be manned or not
      I cannot now foresee;
   May some good ship a tender prove,
   Well found in stores of truth and love,
      And take her under lee.

4. Farewell to George the jolly-boat,
   And all the little craft afloat
      In home's delightful bay.
   Whe[n] they arrive at sailing age,
   May wisdom prove the weather gauge,
      And guide them on their way.

5. Farewell to all on life's rude main
   And though we ne'er may meet again,
      Through stress of stormy weather;
   Yet, summoned by the board above
   We'll harbor in the port of love,
      And all be moored together.

                                                Daniel

B.

"THE SAILOR BOY'S FAREWELL." William H. Keith, schooners *William Martin* of Boston, *Edith May* of Well fleet, Massachusetts, *Cora Nash* of Boston, and others, circa 1865-71. A somewhat flawed copy text, similar to A but differing in minor respects. Both have five stanzas identically configured, both have *I,ll* instead of *I'll*, and both have *guage* instead of *gauge* in stanza 4; but in stanza 1, A has *"While yet* the parting tear" where B has *"Yet while* the parting tear"; the name *George,* present in stanza 4 of A (and in the printed versions that include this stanza), is absent in B; in stanza 4, where A has *delightful,* B erroneously substitutes *delighted;* in stanza 5, A has the American spelling *harbor* and B has the British *harbour,* where A has "the *board* above," B correctly gives "the *bard* above"; and punctuation differs throughout.

30. The Ship Is Ready

In July 1846, nineteen-year-old Henrietta Halstead (1827-1871) of Newburgh, N.Y., inscribed these outward-bound lyrics into the journal of her older brother, Israel T. Halstead (1819-1884), on the eve of his departure for New Bedford to join the ship *Mount Vernon* as fourth mate on a three-year whaling voyage. The words by Vermont hymnist Hannah Flagg Gould (1792-1865) inspired at least two musical settings. The first is by Oliver Shaw (1779-1848), a church organist and composer of sacred music in Providence, R.I., who had been a sailor in his youth; it was published by the author at Providence in 1833, with a fine lithographic cover by Pendleton's of Boston after a drawing attributed to Fitz Henry Lane (previously known as Fitz Hugh Lane). The second setting, published in New York five years later, is a rather odd composition credited to a Moritz Richter (who was evidently a music teacher in Cooperstown, N.Y., not the 17th-century German composer of that name). It is not known which of the melodies the Halsteads may have known. Brother and sister, eight years apart in age, were evidently quite close, and also inscribed into the journal is a sentimental poem entitled "To My Sister," which (uncharacteristically for a deepwater sailor) he appears to have written there as a remembrance of her, though it is not clear when.[18]

TUNE A - "THE SHIP IS READY," music by Oliver Shaw, "Composed & Inscribed to his Friend / Miss Sarah Bradford," from the sheet music published "by the Author" at Providence in 1833.

---

[18] Though it may have been published somewhere prior to Halsead's sailing in 1846, the only publication that has been discovered so far was in the anonymously edited anthology, *Ladies' Gems, Or, Poems on the Love of Flowers, Kindness to Animals, and the Domestic Affections* (New York, 1849):

Sister! dear I am getting old:
My hair is thinner and the cheerful light
That glistened in mine eyes is not as bright,
Though while on thee I look tis never cold.
My hand is not so steady while I pen
These simple words to tell how warm and clear
Flows my heart's fountain toward thee sister dear!

For years I've lived among my fellow-men –
Shared their deep passions known their griefs and joys,
And found Pride, Power, and Fame but gilded toys;
And sailing far upon Ambitions waves,
Beheld brave mariners on a troubled sea,
Meets what they feared not—shipwreck and their graves.
My spirit seeks its haven dear with thee.

TUNE B - "THE SHIP IS READY," music by Moritz Richter, "Dedicated to his / Music Pupils / in Coopers Town / On the occasion of their first Exhibition Concert, / April 18, 1838"; from the sheet music published New York by Samuel Ackerman [for Charles Holt, Jr.?] in 1838.

"THE SHIP IS READY." Henrietta Halstead, Newburgh, N.Y., 1846: inscribed between voyages in the journal of her brother, Israel T. Halstead, ship *Mount Vernon* of New Bedford, 1843-46 and 1846-49.

1. Fare thee well! the ship is ready,
   And the breeze is fresh and steady.
   Hands are fast the anchor weighing;
   High in air the streamer's playing.
   Spread the sails—the waves are swelling
   Proudly round the buoy and dwelling.
   Fare thee well! and when at sea,
   Think of those who sigh for thee.

2. When from land and home receding
   And from that ache to bleeding
   Think of those behind, who love thee,
   While the sun is bright above thee!
   Then, as down to ocean glancing,
   In the waves his rays are dancing,
   Think how long the night will be
   To the eyes that weep for thee.

3. When the lonely night watch keeping
   All below those still and sleeping,—
   As the needle points the quarter
   On the wide and trackless water,
   Let thy vigils ever find thee
   Mindful of the friends behind thee!
   Let thy bosom's magnet be
   Turned to those who wake for thee!

4. When, with slow and gentle motion,
   Heaves the bosom of the Ocean,—
   While in peace thy bark is riding,
   And the silver moon is gliding
   O'er the sky with tranquil splendor,
   When the shining hosts attend her,
   Let the brightest visions be
   Country, Home, and friends to thee!

5. When the tempest hovers o'er thee,
   Danger, wreck, and death before thee,
   While the sword of fire is gleaming,
   Wild the winds, the torrent screaming.
   Then, a pious suppliant bending,
   Let thy thoughts, to heaven ascending,
   Reach the mercy-seat, to be
   Met by prayers that rise for thee!

Henrietta Halstead.
New Burgh, Sunday 4. 1/4. P.M.
July 12th 1846

31. Caledonia
[Jamie Raeburn's Farewell]

In the early decades of the 19th century Australia was a British penal colony to which convicts, debtors, and political prisoners were transported in large numbers. The so-called "convict" or "transport" or "transportation" ballads that resulted, among the best known of which are "Botany Bay" and "Jim Jones," constitute a substantial heritage in Australia and the British Isles but tend to be rare in North America. With the Australian Gold Rush of the 1850s, Pacific Ocean traffic escalated and American sailors came into increasing contact with Australians; meanwhile, Yankee whaleships, which had been calling at Sydney and Hobart all along, were cruising the New Holland grounds at the Australian end of the Indian Ocean, and were visiting Australian ports with greater frequency, especially Fremantle [see Chapter 16; and "A Voyage on New Holland," #161]—any or all of which may account for how this transportation ballad got into the hands of whaleman William Keith in the 1860s. It concerns a Glaswegian who sadly bids farewell to his homeland when he is exiled for robbery and assault, based on an actual incident of 1814. Keith records it as "Caledonia," the title by which it is known in Australia. The Scots call it "Jamie Raeburn's Farewell" or simply "Jamie Raeburn." It is not mentioned by Laws and is unrecorded in American tradition—surprisingly, perhaps, as Gavin Greig calls it "one of the most popular folk songs we have." In all manifestations the locale is identified as Glasgow and the refrain is a lament for the leaving of Caledonia, the Latin name for Scotland. Scottish texts invariably name the protagonist as Jamie Raeburn, hence the consistent title there; in Australia he is often Jimmy Randall, a corruption that is nevertheless essentially Scottish; and the whaleman gives the name David Williams, which is typically Welsh. The rhyme scheme is based on conventional pronunciation in a Scots lowland dialect; the sailor's text requires that it be sung with a long final *a* (i.e., Caledoni*yay*: rhymes with *far away*), which is consistent with other typical sailor pronunciations (e.g. *Ry-o Grandee* for *Rio Grande;* and *wynd* for *wind*). According to Greig, the proper melody is "a variant of 'The Brier Bush'" [Tune A], which the late great cowboy singer Buck Ramsey believed to be the original for the outlaw ballad "Sam Bass."[19] But the lyrics have also been joined to the air of "John Anderson My Jo," and "the tune given by Ford is 'The Plains of Waterloo'" [Tune B], in a minor mode; a northern variant is associated with "When Fortune Turns the Wheel." Other tunes, including the one given by Kidson, are simple corollaries in a major key. Commenting on two Australian manifestations, Meredith & Anderson maintain that the tunes are different; and so they are, but each is merely a degraded variant of "Plains of Waterloo."

TUNE A - "Jamie Raeburn's Farewell," said to be a form of an air entitled "The Brier Bush" (Greig 1914, XXXVI); learned from Buck Ramsey. Most transcriptions are in 4/4 time. Compare Ord 1930, 356; Bikel 1960, 132.

---

[19] Private communication at Cowboy Songs & Range Ballads, Buffalo Bill Historical Center, Cody, Wyoming, April 1995.

TUNE B - "The Plains of Waterloo," from Robert Ford, *Vagabond Songs and Ballads of Scotland,* 1904, p. 61.

"CALEDONIA." William H. Keith, schooners *William Martin* of Boston and *Edith May* of Wellfleet, etc. 1865 -71.

1. My name is David Williams in Glasgow I was born
   The place of my nativity I now must leave in scorn
   The place of my nativity I now go far away
   Farewell—Ye bonny hills & dales of Caledonia.

2. The crime that I must suffer for is robbery and assault[20]
   I leave the blame upon no one although I'm not in fault
   I leave the blame upon no one although with comrades trained
   Farewell—Ye bonny hills and dales of Caledonia.

3. The turnkey came next morning & unto us did say
   Arise, arise, ye convicts I want you on this day
   Arise, arise, ye convicts I want ye one and all.
   Farewell—Ye bonny hills & dales of Caledonia.

4. They mounted us upon coaches our hearts being full of grief
   Our friends they gathered around us could grant us no relief
   Our friends they gathered around us likewise our comrades train
   Farewell—Ye bonny hills & dales of Caledonia.

5. Farewell to my forefathers they were the best of men
   Likewise to my own sweetheart & Catherine was her name
   No more will roam round Clydes own shore around Montgomery's walls
   Since the seas must roll between us and Caledonia

6. Farewell to my poor Mother, I'm sorry for what I've done
   I hope no one will call up to her the race that I have run
   I hope the Lord will protect her when I am far away
   Farewell—Ye bonny hills & dales of Caledonia.

---

[20] The factual basis for the ballad has been controversial but the consensus is that Raeburn was wrongly convicted and unjustly transported. Ford identifies him as "a baker... who was sentenced to banishment for theft.... His sweetheart, Catherine Chandlier ... told the story of his misfortunes:—'We parted at ten o'clock and Jamie was in the police office at twenty minutes past ten. Going home, he met an acquaintance of his boyhood, who took him in to treat him for auld langsyne. Scarcely had they entered when the detectives appeared and apprehended them. Searched, the stolen property was found [on the person of the acquaintance]. They were tried and banished for life to Botany Bay. Jamie was innocent as the unborn babe, but his heartless companion spoke not a word of his innocence'" (Ford, 244). Greig disputes Ford's account and reports that John Ord, Superintendent of Glasgow Police (who later included "Jamie Raeburn" in his own anthology, *Bothy Songs*), "had all the criminal records from 1833 to the present time searched, and failed to find any person of the name of James Raeburn who had been banished from Glasgow for theft or any other crime during the period"; Greig prefers the story of "a neighbor who sang the song to me said that she learned it more than 30 years ago [i.e., before 1880] from a young man whose grandfather knew Jamie, and that forgery was the crime for which he was banished" (Greig 1914, XXXVI). However, testimony indicates that Superintendent Ord's research could not have yielded the desired result because the incident happened much earlier than the compass of his inquiry, in 1814 (Bikel 1960, 127).

CHAPTER FOUR
Jolly Sailors Bold
Deepwater Songs and Ballads

It is said that music hath the power to sooth the savage breast and it is eaven so... my ears is charmed with music at this time and it is with great difficulty that I can keep my thoughts upon writing. I never was so lucky as to get on board a ship before that had any musician before but now the <u>Capt</u> plays the fiddle and the 2nd mate plays an accordion which is much better than a fiddle. It all helps to pass away the time.

> — William H. Chappell, whaleship
> *Saratoga* of New Bedford, 1852-56*

During the first part of our voyage great regret was expressed that there were no musical instruments on board, but music, like murder will out. An old fiddle was discovered... In the meantime a jack had begged an old flour sieve from the steward, over which he fastened the dried stomach of a blackfish, and with some bits of tin and copper to make a jingle he had constructed a *bona fide* tambourine. This brought out a flute from its hiding place, and soon the forecastle resounded to the merry notes of a fiddle, two flutes, the tambourine, bones and a triangle.

> — Nathaniel W. Taylor, M.D.,
> *Life on a Whaler*, 1858

Whalemen playing music on deck in the Acushnet River estuary on sailing day. They are outward bound on a whaling voyage from New Bedford and all dressed up because some of their families are seeing them off, and the owners are probably on board for the departure. Photograph by Pardon B. Gifford, circa 1910. Kendall Collection, New Bedford Whaling Museum.

* Nicholson Collection, Providence Public Library; quoted in Cohn 1982, 187; and Frank 1985 I:80.

32. Jolly Sailors Bold
[Sailors' Come-All-Ye; Hearts of Gold; Nantucket Whaling Song]

This is either two divergent forms of one American deepwater song or two separate songs on similar thematic lines, known in New England as early as the 1760s, with roots in 17th- and 18th-century English broadsides and widely distributed among sailors in various 19th-century forms. Characteristically (as in B), it recounts in heroic terms the generic hardships and dangers of the sailors' plight at sea, in contrast with the comparatively safe-and-easy life of the farmer, culminating with the anticipation of a joyful return to the women and comforts of home. Texts also often include the sailors' customary allusion to voyages yet to come. However, one of the whalemen's versions (text A) represents another, more distinctively American text group, which also describes quite specifically an actual whale hunt in the boats, omits the homecoming, and results instead in a successful capture, with "hearts quite free of care."[1] Mackenzie identifies as "the source of this song and a great many similar ones" a broadside of circa 1635, "Ye Gentlemen of England, or When the stormy Winds Do Blow," written by Martin Parker; "The Joviall Cobbler" is indicated as the air.[2] Another is "To All You Ladies Now on Land," printed in London in 1686.[3]

TUNE A - "The Joviall Cobbler," given for "Neptune's Raging Fury, or You Gentlemen of England" in E. Duncan, *Minstrelsy of England,* 1905, I:54f: "An early version of the air is in *Loyal Songs* (1686)." Essentially the same tune as Colcord's (p. 138). Transposed from B♭. The chorus is a repeat of the last line in each stanza.

TUNE B - "The Whalemen's Wives," a variant of "Jolly Sailors Bold," from Frederick Pease Harlow, *Chanteying Aboard American Ships,* 1962, p. 231f: obtained from Captain Nye. As in Tune A, the chorus is a repeat of the last line. Tune also known as "Rocks of Scillia." Variants are from the playing of Jeff Davis and singing of Ellen Cohn.

---

[1] Compare, for example, "Old Nantucket Whaling Song" and "Edgartown Whaling Song" (Harlow, 216ff, 219ff, and 231ff).

[2] "It is thus described: 'The Praise of Saylors here set forth, with the hard Fortunes that do befall them on the seas, when Landsmen sleep safe in their beds. To a pleasant new tune—*The Jovial Cobler.* Printed at London for C. Wright' (see Ebsworth, *The Roxburghe Ballads,* VI, 431). A later seventeenth-century broadside, altered from this one, is entitled 'Neptune's Raging Fury; or The Gallant Seaman's Sufferings. Being a Relation of their Perils and Dangers, and of the extraordinary Hazards they undergo in their noble adventures. Together with their undaunted Valour and rare Constancy in all their Extremities, and the manner of their Rejoycing on Shore, at their return home' (Ebsworth, VI, 432-433). Still another version from the latter part of the seventeenth century is 'The Jovial Mariner; or, The Sea-man's Renown' (Ebsworth, VI, 369-370)" (Mackenzie #95). Simpson (768f) provides further particulars about the air and its hoary provenance in the ballad tradition.

[3] Baring-Gould 1895, Vol. VIII, 26. See also "You Gentlemen of England," Vol. II, 62.

TUNE C - from the singing of Tom Goux & Jacek Sulanowski, per Huntington 1964, 68: the tune (which Huntington arbitrarily used for his text "Hearts of Gold") is actually an adaptation of the traditional English air "Come and listen to my ditty" or "Welcome, brother debtor," which was originally published in 1730 and by 1754 had been adapted by George Alexander Stevens for his poem "The Storm" ("Cease, Rude Boreas") [q.v., #4].

TUNE D - "The Wreck Off Scilly," from S. Baring-Gould at al., *Songs of the West*, 1905, #52. Textual similarities strongly suggest that this is a variant of the same ballad.

A.

"NANTUCKET WHALING SONG." Thomas Bennett, ship *Condor* of New Bedford, 1839-40; and second mate, ship *William Baker* of Warren, 1840-41. Consolidated from 8-line stanzas. Unfortunately, the transcription is not complete, and leaves off before the kill, the victory celebration, the carousing on shore, and the reflections on the whale fishery that are sometimes found in other texts.

1. Come all you jovial mariner men that ploughs the raging main
   that goes to sea in merchant ships and safe returns again
   Come listen to my story Which I to you relate
   Concerning our bold Whaling men and their most dismall fate

2. It is first they work a month or two their ships to fit away
   Its then they'll cross Nantucket Bar[4] and there in prison lay[5]
   Its when they get all ready Oh then they will set sail
   Bound to the Southern Seas, My boys and there to cruise for whales

3. Its first they cross the atlantick Six thousand miles or so
   Until they arrive at that dread point where S[outh]W[est] gales do blow
   Its their they beat[7] a month or two Just as the gales agree
   Left to the mercy of the wind And of the raging sea

4. And if they do but weather it in spite of gales and wind
   then on the Coast of Chili Cold squalls of hail they find
   which makes them band their jacket[6] and blow their fingers sore
   and wish full of times when theyd been that they could be once more

5. Its now the whalemens troubles is fairly but begun
   and what they have to Encounter is shortly for to come
   for their they cruise whole months or so and never see a whale
   their water all stagnated grows And their provisions fail

---

[4] The sandbar at the entrance to Nantucket Harbor was infamous for the difficulties of access and egress it created, and was a factor in the gradual decline of Nantucket as a whaling port. Nantucket ships and barks often fitted out at Edgartown or New Bedford rather than cross the bar laden. In the mid 19th century, with varying success, a so-called *camel* was employed to float whalers over the bar.

[5] That is, remained on shipboard preparing for sea, without means of escape or liberty ashore.

[6] To *bend a sail* is to install a sail on a yard or spar; thus, *bend a jacket* here is seamen's lingo for *put on a jacket*.

6. Dull prospects all around us and families behind
   it will make the hartiest whaleman to curse his fate and kind
   it will make them all Rejected And spirits sunk quite low
   the joyful news from our mast head its their the sperm whale blow

7. Oh, then they jump full joyful their boats to clear away
   take up that bright and glittering craft[7] all fitted for the fray
   See how our buckeling oars do bend before the sea she flies
   their is a Noble sperm whale boys A spouting towards the skies

8. Now having pull[ed] up to him the craft is left his hand
   its back astern my lively boys is Now the loud command
   you see she fights most dreadfully She will stave our boat so small
   So back astern my lively boys So back astern boys all

9. At last he stops his fighting and turns his flooks to sound
   some hundred fathoms of our line the log[g]erhead goes round[8]
   at last he stops his sounding to seek his up[p]er air
   our line wee quickly haul onboard and hearts quite free from care

10. [*stanza numbered but not present in the MS*]

B.

"SAILORS SONG." George W. Piper, ship *Europa* of Edgartown, 1868-70. Compare Huntington 1964, 68 (ship *Bengal* of Salem, circa 1832-35), to which this much later text is very similar.

1. Come all you nice young girls
   O if you did but know
   The hardships and the dangers
   Poor sailors undergo
   You would have a better regard for them
   Than you ever had before
   And you would scorn to marry a land lubber
   Who always stops on shore

2. They are always among the pretty girls
   A telling them fine tales
   Of the hardships and the dangers
   They find in their cornfields
   In a cutting of the grass so green
   Is all that they can do
   While we like jovial sailor boys
   Go plough the Oceans through

---

[7] *Craft:* here in the sense of *whalecraft,* meaning ironware and edge tools of the various special types used in whaling, including harpoons, lances, cutting spades, blubber knives, etc. The shoreside blacksmith or "shipsmith" who made such implements was referred to as a *whalecraft manufacturer,* and shipsmiths specializing in this trade commonly advertised themselves as such.

[8] The line (rope) attached to the harpoon (which is, in turn, attached "fast onto" the whale) is wound around the *loggerhead* post in the whaleboat, but not tied down; in this way the whalemen can *play* the whale, and the line cane be cut if necessary.

3. By the time that the sun goes down my girls
   They will not work any more
   They lay aside their ploughs and hoes
   And home they do go now
   At eight O clock at eight O clock
   it is unto bed they will crawl
   While we like jovial sailor boys
   Stand many a bitter squall

4. At twelve O clock at twelve O clock
   The wind begins to blow
   The Captain on the quarter deck
   Calls out the watch below
   Lay aloft lay aloft my brisk young tars
   Your lives and ship to guard
   Lay aloft lay aloft my brisk young tars
   Send down you top gallant yards

5. Top gallant yards they being sent down
   And safely stowed away
   All hands All hands our Captain cries
   Unto the companion way
   Here is a bottle of good brandy
   Let it merrily go around
   Now go below the starboard watch
   And sleep both safe and sound

6. O don't you be fait hearted boys
   You will see your girls again
   In spite of all the universe
   We will plough the raging main
   We will sail to all parts of the world
   That ever before was known
   And we will bring home gold and silver too
   Whenever we do return

7. Thanks to kind Providence
   We are safely moored on shore
   The ale house it will flourish
   And the taverns they will roar
   We will make the ale house flourish
   And we will spend our money free
   And when our money is all gone
   We will boldly go to sea

33. Boston
['Twas On the Twenty-First of May; There She Goes]

This powerful deepwater ballad of sea storms and vituperation is a Sailors' Complaint song hitherto known in only one deepwater text, from Captain W.B. Whall, whose unique lyrics and tune were reprinted by Colcord, Harlow, and in the Trident Society anthology; and it is to the opening line of that version, "From Boston Harbor We Sail," that the title "Boston" refers. Otherwise, the song has nothing to do with Boston. MacEdward Leach gives another manifestation entitled "There She Goes." Captain Whall, who does not reveal his source, says that while he never actually encountered the song at sea himself, it was "very popular between the years 1860 and 1870"; and Captain Harlow's testimony, allegedly based on Whall, is that it was used as a capstan chantey, a point on which Whall himself is equivocal. The two superior whalemen's texts given here corroborate not only the songs' probable American origins but also the circa 1860s vintage that Whall claims for its popularity at sea. Whall's chorus and tune — still the only deepwater melody that has come to light — are related to "Bow, wow, wow," a British song to which various texts and parodies were adapted in the 19th century.[9] A compelling feature of Text A (less so Text B) is its New Englandese pronunciation, suggesting that the whalemen's transcriptions may have been made from oral sources. Another is the prevalence of technical terminology that only a sailor could have written. In Text A there is also a charming use of uninhibited language and vituperative curses, including expletives rarely encountered in shipboard journals but here particularly appropriate to the nautical context of a gale at sea.

TUNE - "Boston," from Captain W. B. Whall, *Sea Songs and Shanties,* Glasgow [1910] 1963, pp. 148f.

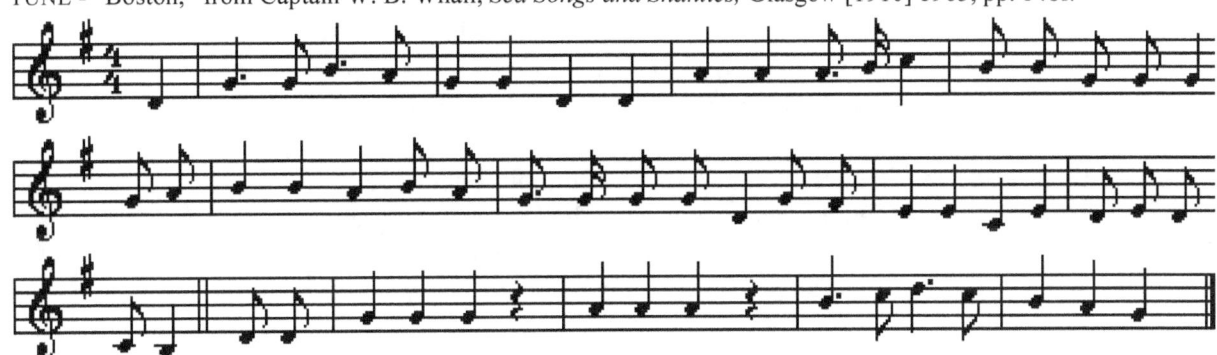

A.

"TWAS ON THE 21 OF MAY." George M. Jones and Albert F. Handy, bark *Waverly* of New Bedford, 1859-63. In this version the sailors' vituperation is directed at a bucko captain. Compare the milder text given by Whall, 148.

1.   'Twas on the twenty first of May
       We crossed our royal yards all three
       Withe our coulors flying at the main peak
       For a rattling breeze makes the old ship squeak

   Chorus: To my rite foddle rol To my fol de rol
               ri diddle lol de day

2.   But soon a squall came rising on
       And struck us in our quarter

---

[9] Whall's "tow, row, row" chorus, not present in the whalemen's texts, is apparently derived from the British song "Bow, wow, wow"; the whalemen's versions substitute chruses of nonsense syllables of the "fal-de-dal-day" / "ri-didle-tol-de-day" type.

>
> Hand down your stunsails alow and aloft
> Clew up your top[g]alent and rialls for and aft[10]

3. Hawl down your jibs and ease them in
   And see all clear for a gale of wind
   Hawl down your jibs and ease them in
   And now for to pissle[11] us the buger does begin

4. Brace Square in your yard and brace your spanker
   Place an abel seaman on the poop
   Clap on your roling tacles too
   That your yards shall not zigzag to and fro

5. Its down in the cabin the old buger goes
   And on his belley he lays low
   Come Steward mix me brandy hot
   Its far better weather below than aloft

6. While we poor sailors walk the deck
   With the wind and rain a beating down our necks
   Not a drop of grog can the old buger aford
   But curse and dam our eyes with every word

7. May god almighty god dam such a hog
   He looks upon a sailor as he would upon a dog
   God dam such a man with a generation curse
   The humbug son of a bitch that make him sciper firs[t][12]

8. Thairs one more thing of the old buger I say
   That he may never have the [h]oner of a grave
   May he never have the honor the bells for to toll
   May the Sharks take his body and the devil take his soul

---

[10] Technical terms in these storm preparations reflect sailor lingo pronounced with a decided New England drawl: *Studding sails,* pronounced by sailors *stuns'ls,* are light-weather sails mounted on expandable extensions of the yard-arms and can be trouble-some, particularly in heavy weather. *Alow and aloft,* a catch-phrase referring to the deck (*below*) and overhead (*aloft*) among the rigging and spars—the two places where the sailor's work principally transpires; usually rendered *aloft and alow.* (In another context, in stanza 5, *below* signifies *belowdecks;* and that perspective, *aloft* can mean *on deck,* as it does in stanza 5). *Topalent* [sic] refers to the *topgallant sails,* also pronounced *t'gan's'ls,* sails high aloft that are normally taken in in heavy weather. Above these are the *royal sails,* or *royals,* here pronounced *rialls* (also *ryalls*), which also must be furled in anticipation of a gale.

[11] *Pizzle:* In general slang, the penis, especially of an animal; hence its vulgar application to the human male member (see OED; Partridge, 637). In whalemen's usage, specifically the penis of a whale, especially the sperm whale, from which a durable skin is obtained that was used to patch clothing, make sheaths for knives, and muffle oars—per the comments of the Brown University-trained future ornithologist Robert Cushman Murphy, collecting specimens for the American Museum of Natural History on a whaling voyage of 1912-13: "Before the largest bull whale carcass was cut adrift, its pizzle was severed at the base and hoisted onto the deck, where it became the object of much noisy and ribald admiration. The purpose was quite serious, however, for Victor skinned it and immediately frapped and laced strips of the black, shiny hide onto several oarlocks. Whaleboat oarlocks always need muffling. The usual method is to braid thole mats from cordage, but black rawhide of the sort mentioned shrinks on the steel as it dries, making a smooth and long-enduring silencer for the loom of an oar" (Murphy, 270).

[12] That is, "the unwise individual who appointed him skipper in the first place."

B.

"SAILOR'S SONG." George W. Piper, ship *Europa* of Edgartown, 1868-70. In many ways closer than A to the text reported by Whall, and contemporaneous with the 1860-70 period that Whall claims for the popularity of "Boston." In this text the sailors' vituperation is directed at the anonymous inventor of the studding-sail boom (see footnote 2).

1. O the very first voyage I went to sea
    Top gallant yards I crossed all three
    With the colors flying at our mizen peak
    And a rattling breeze made the old ship creak

Chorus: Singing Fal de dal de di do
    Fal de dal de day

2. Now our breakfast has come down
    There are empty kids a lying all around
    One kicks them here and another kicks them there
    Saying blame the old cook for a leaving of them there

3. Now our breakfast is all done
    Turn to your duty boys every one
    Some to the gaskets others to the points
    While it is curse the old ship for limbs and joints

4. A squall, a squall is now coming on
    Along the weather quarter boys all along
    Take in your studding sails below and aloft
    Clew up your top gallant sails fore and aft [6]

5. Now our Captain came on deck
    And loudly calls for his boy Jack
    Saying fill us a bumper [7] with a full and hearty glass
    For it is far better weather below than aloft

6. Now it is cursed and hanged be the great old fool
    That first invented studding sail booms
    May he be hanged and his generation cursed
    O the hum bugging rascal that invented of them first

7. There is one more thing that I do crave
    That he may meet with a watery grave
    No bells for to ring no bells for to toll
    May the sharks take his body and the devil take his soul

34. Captain Avery

James Donahue's inscription in his whaling journal unequivocally attributes this ballad to his own authorship, but it is actually a muddled recasting of lyrics printed contemporaneously with the career of the notorious English pirate Henry Avery (1665 - circa 1728), alias Henry Every, John Avery, John Every, Long Ben, and Captain Bridgeman. Even the whaleman's subtitle—"A Copy of Verses, Composed by Captain Henry Every, Lately Gone to Sea to Seek His Fortune"—appears on the printed ballad sheet (Firth, 131ff). The prescribed tune is "The Two English Travelers," of which Simpson says, "Its popularity can be judged from the existence of more than twenty broadsides naming the tune for singing, but unhappily the music has not been preserved" (Simpson, 782f). Whatever the whaleman may have had in mind in reworking the lyrics, his phrases never quite gel into lines, nor the lines into stanzas, the stanzas into a rhyme-scheme, or the aggregate into a metric whole with an intelligible storyline. One interesting thing about it is that it incorporates the naturalistic assertion common in traditional ballads that the narrator's foul deeds can be partly explained by a bad upbringing and lack of affection at home ("my parents have forsaken me"). Of course, many ballad narrators about to be executed or transported for crimes take the opposite tack, explaining that "my parents raised me tenderly," as if to exonerate the parents from complicity in the prodigal's individual wrongdoing.

"CAPTAIN AVERY." James Donahue, ship *Atlantic* of Nantucket, 1851. Reconstituted into lines and stanzas from the undifferentiated text. There is obviously an extra line in stanza 2, and the final couplet is not a full stanza.

Come all you young Seamen with Courage So bold
and enter with avery and he will cloth you in gold
Captain Avery commands her and he calls Her his own
and he will bose her About boys before he comes home

every thing is in readiness all to your gaine
lord prosper the nancy for she is bound to the main
their is three sheaves in the field likewise one to spare
and that refuses to fight he shall die
for under my mizen black Colours do fly

be sure you cry quarters before that you See
that the black flag is flying on board the nancy
king george i ll honor no nation i ll Spare
king george i ll honor his colors not wear

theirs French portugeese and Spaniards and english likewise
For I have declared war against them to the day that I die
their is the isle of Plymouth cut Waters be damned
for I once I was owner of part of that land.

But as my parents has forsaken me its from them ill fly
and the sword shall maintain me to the day that I die

Author James Donahue
Thursday 25th 1851

35. The *Brooklyn*

An application for a Union Navy pension made by William Edward Johnson in 1910 traces the possible genesis of this original, if substantially derivative pirate ballad[13] to William Densmore, Chief Coxswain's Mate of the steam sloop-of-war *Brooklyn* circa 1862-63. Johnson's father was a slave and his mother a free black. Born in Virginia in 1842, he was raised in Pennsylvania and the Midwest, and was employed on Mississippi River steamboats before enlisting under the alias Edward Cendyrlin. From August 1862 to September 1863 he was cabin cook on the *Brooklyn*, commanded by Henry Haywood Bell, and in his deposition (generously provided by W. Jeffrey Bolster) he reports, "William Densmore was Chief coxswains mate, he was kind of a poet and he wrote quite a piece in regard to the 'Brooklyn' and the Civil War, I will repeat a few lines of it.

> It was in December 1861, As you shall understand
> Seceshes gloom had overcast Columbia's happy land
> Craven was our Capt.s name, as you shall understand
> As brave a naval officer as any in the land
> Down through the Gulf of Mexico, 'the Brooklyn' she did steer
> ----- in search of privateer

"Capt. [Thomas] Craven took the vessel out from Phila[delphia] before I joined her, and was relieved by Commodore Bell" (W.E. Johnson, Deposition, 7-8). If this is indeed a fragment of the same ballad, it certainly underwent significant changes (including the loss of the captain's name) by the time, more than a decade later, it reached seaman Frederick Merrill, who inscribed it in his shipboard journal and signed it "F.M." No particular tune is specified and no other transcription or text has been encountered, but textual resonances indicate that it is a parody of "The Girls Around Cape Horn" ("Rounding the Horn"; "The Gallant Frigate *Amphitrite*"), which seems to have been firmly established in British and American shipboard tradition by the mid nineteenth century.[14] Other textual sources appear to be "Kelly the Pirate" (Frank 1998, #22 and #23) and "The Bold Trinity" [#6], perhaps also "Captain Ward and the *Rainbow*" (Frank 1998, #11).

The 1878 Arctic voyage on which the ballad was transcribed had an unusual purpose. After a conventional Atlantic Ocean whaling voyage as a green hand in the New Bedford bark *Janus* (1875-76), the diarist was serving in the crew of the schooner *Eothan* of New York, commanded by Thomas Barry—former mate of the New Bedford whaler *Glacier*—to transport the American Army officer and Arctic explorer Frederick Schwatka and his party to Hudson Bay to conduct a search for the lost Franklin expedition of 1845 [see #67]. Lt. Schwatka not only distinguished himself by traversing large tracts of hitherto unexplored territory and by making the longest sledge journey up to that time, but was at last able to discover tangible evidence of the fate of Franklin.

TUNE A -"Rounding the Horn", from R. Vaughan Williams and A.L. Lloyd, *The Penguin Book of English Folk Songs,* 1959, 90: collected in Lancashire, 1907.

---

[13] According to Steve Gardham it is "a pretty regular but localized version of 'The Nottingham/ The Dolphin/ London Man-o-War/ Bold Wasp' etc.," and he mentions "Shakings" in Whall.

[14] Compare especially the first stanza given by Vaughan Williams & Lloyd (1959, p. 90) (below, left) and the first stanza of what appears to be a much later text given by Colcord (1938, pp. 77f) (below, right), about which she astutely observes that "the wording of [the] song indicates that it has been re-written by a modern shantyman":

The gallant frigate *Amphitrite,* she lay in Plymouth Sound,	The famed ship *California*, a ship of high renown,
Blue Peter at the foremast head, for she was outward bound.	She lay in Boston harbor 'longside of that pretty town,
We were waiting there for orders to send us far from home.	Awaiting for our orders to sail far from home,
Our orders came for Rio, and thence around Cape Horn.	And our orders came for Rio, boys, and then around Cape Horn.

TUNE B -"The Girls Around Cape Horn": composite. Compare Colcord 1938, 177.

TUNE C - "Shakings," from W.B. Whall, p. 113xx.

"THE BROOKLYNN." Frederick Merrill, green hand, bark *Janus* of New Bedford, 1875-76; and schooner *Eothen* of New York, 1878. In the journal the text lacks division into lines or stanzas, and has minimal capitalization and inconsistent punctuation; it is here divided into lines and stanzas, but with capitalization and punctuation verbatim.

1. There is a bark, a gallant bark, which lies in Boston Bay,
   awaiting there for orders, her anchor for to weight,
   she is bound for the coast of Cuba, boys, our gallant ship shall sail,
   we are bound to sink and to destroy, where ever we may roam

2. we has not sailed but 30 leag[ue]s or 40 leag[ue]s or more,
   when we aspied a large ship, and down upon us bore,
   shes hailed us in Spanish voice, and asked her whence she came,
   we just set sail from Charlestown, and the Brooklynn is our name,

3. Are you a man of war sir pray tell you unto me,
   I am no man of war sir, but private as you see,
   then brace away your fore yards, and let your ship come to
   then hoist your tackles and lower your boats, or else i will sink you

4. up speak our Capt[ain] bold, unto his men did say,
   cheer up, my lively lads, we are sure to gain the day
   if it had not been for my own brother, this battle would never been tried,
   let every brave man, stand to his gun, and we give to them a broadside,

5. the broadside was given, w[h]ich coursed them all to wonder,
   to see there fore the gallant mast come rolling down like thunder,
   we showered them our quarter boys, they could no longer stay
   when we gave ha[r]d and the red has stoo[d] and showed them american play

6. now we bid this pirate a dew [adieu], to america we will steer,
   and when we arrive on american shores, those girls they will us cheer
   they will call us there bold hero[e]s and prais[e] our officers, to[o],
   they will drink succes to the Brooklynn and all her jolly crew. F.M.

36. The *Dreadnought*
[The Dreadnaught; The Flash Packet; The Banks of Newfoundland]
(Laws #D-13)

This American ballad of middle 19th-century vintage is the greatest song to emerge from the North Atlantic packet trade. By calling it "the chronicle of an uneventful trip," Laws misses the point, which is to celebrate the exploits of a famous vessel on the prestigious route between New York and Liverpool. Strictly speaking, *Dreadnought* (not *Dreadnaught*), at 1414 tons about four or five times the size of the average whaleship, was not actually a packet—that is, not a scheduled liner—but was operated by the Red Cross Line as an irregular trader, commanded by the celebrated Captain Samuel Samuels (1823-1908), for whom the ship was built by Currier & Townsend of Newburyport, Massachusetts in 1853. In a career spanning 16 years, until, under the command of P.N. Mayhew, she was wrecked off Cape Horn on the Fourth of July 1869, the *Dreadnought* was renowned for making fast Atlantic crossings, and Captain Samuels's name was well known wherever English-language newspapers circulated. The text is more stable than the tunes, which are several. As Hugill notes, "The *Dreadnought*" is probably based on "The Flash Frigate" ("The Fancy Frigate"; "La *Pique*"), a ballad about navy life of which his version is sung to the popular air "Vilikins and His Dinah [see #81 and #161], a tune influential in at least some of the major-key variants of "*Dreadnought*." The air in *Naval Songs* (1883), which appears to be indigenous to the ballad, is in many respects similar to the tune given by Colcord. Hugill himself popularized yet another tune, which is consequently the most popular in revival—an orthodox form of a much older air in a minor-modal key, "Derry Down," circa 1630. All of the tunes seem to have been used at one time or another in instances when the ballad was employed as a capstan or windlass chantey. The two whalemen's texts here were transcribed on voyages already two or three years in progress at the time the *Dreadnought* was wrecked; they are the earliest yet to come to light, suggesting that the song was contemporaneous with the life of the ship and emanated from her fame among sailorfolk at the time, rather than from some posthumous sentiment about the wreck.

TUNE A -"The Dreadnought", from *Naval Songs,* New York, 1883, p. 68; and Luce, *Naval Songs,* 1889, p. 67. Transposed from E^b. Compare: Colcord 1938, 170; and "King John and the Abbot of Canterbury," in *Davidson's Universal Melodist,* London, 1848, II:206.

TUNE B -"The Dreadnaught [sic]," from Hugill 1961, p. 466, who says it comprises "The tune of *The Dom Pedro* joined to the words of *The Dreadnaught,*" however the air is actually an orthodox form of "Derry Down," circa 1730 (see "The Sailor's Alphabet," #44). Transposed from C minor. Compare "A Jolly Jack Tar" in *The English Musical Repository,* 1811, p. 235.

TUNE C -"The Flash Frigate", from Hugill 1961, p. 462; "The Liverpool Packet (b)," from Hugill 1961, p. 469: both "closely allied to the shore-song *Vilikins and His Dinah*." See songs #81 and #161.

A.

"THE DREADNAUGHT." George W. Piper, ship *Europa* of Edgartown, 1868-70. Like most of Piper's song texts, a solid, conventional, well-ordered transcription, superior to B. Like B, no chorus is indicated, which suggests that the "Derry Down" air (Tune B) is not the tune by which Piper knew the song, as his other transcriptions are quite faithful and consistent in replicating refrains, line repeats, and other singing-related aspects of the songs.

1. There is a flash packet a packet of fame
   She belongs to New York and the Dreadnaught is her name
   Bound away to the westward where the strong winds do blow
   Bound away to the westward in the Dreadnaught we go

2. Now the Dreadnaught she is a lying off the Waterloo Docks
   Where the boys and the girls down the pier they do flock
   They will give us three cheers while the tears down do flow
   Bound away to the westward in the Dreadnaught we go

3. Now the Dreadnaught she is a howling down the Irish Sea
   Where the passengers and crew are so merry and free
   Where the birds of the ocean fly around to and fro
   Bound away to the westward in the Dreadnaught we go

4. Now the Dreadnaught she is a howling over the ocean so wide
   Where the dark angry waves dash against her broad sides
   Where the tars of the ocean pace her decks to and fro
   Bound away to the westward in the Dreadnaught we go

5. Now the Dreadnaught she is a lying becalmed of the Banks of Newfoundland
   Where the waters so blue and the bottom all sand
   Where the fish of the ocean play around to and fro
   Bound away to the westward in the Dreadnaught we go

6. Now the Dreadnaught she is a howling down Long Island shore
   Where the pilot he boards us as he has oft times done before
   Fill away your main topsail board your fore tack also
   Bound away to the westward in the Dreadnaught we go

7. Now we are safely landed in New York once more
   I will go see Sally White boys she is the girl I adore
   I will call for good liquors so merry and free
   Bound away to the westward in the Dreadnaught we go

8. Here is success to Captain Samuels and to his officers too
   Here is health to the Dreadnaught and to that ship's crew
   Talk about your flash packets your swallow tails and black balls
   But the Dreadnaught she's a clipper and she excels them all[15]

---

[15] The Swallow Tail Line and Black Ball Line were other prominent North Atlantic carriers on the same run (see Albion 1938). The *Dreadnought* was a "clipper" only in the generic sense of being fast, but not in the formal naval-architectural sense of having an extreme hull and rig (see Cutler 1930 and Cutler 1961).

B.

"THE DREADNOUGHT." John S. Coquin, bark *Pacific* of New Bedford, 1867-68. Inferior to A in meter, syntax, nautical content, and geography (for example, note the migration the adjectives "howling," which can only refer to a stormy passage at sea (as opposed to slipping down the Mersey), the mangled geography, the corruption of Captain Samuels's name in stanza 8, etc.). Like A, no chorus is indicated. Realigned from 8-line stanzas in the MS.

1. There is a flashy packet ship, and a ship of great fame
   She belongs to New York, and the dreadnoughts her name
   She sails to the westard where the storm winds do blow,
   Bound away in the Dreadnought to the westward we go.

2. The time of our sailing is fast drawing nigh
   I will go down to Maggie and bid her good bye,
   Farewell to old liverpool and the girls we adore
   Bound away in the Dreadnought to the westward we go

3. It is now we are howling out of the waterloo docks
   The boys and the girls to the pier heads do flock
   They will give us three cheers while the tears down do flow
   Bound away in the Dreadnought to the westard we go

4. It is now we are sailing off the wild Irish shore
   Where the passengers are many and all for love of joy
   At their passage so fair where the sailors walk the decks to and fro
   Bound away in the Dreadnought to the westward we go.

5. Its now we are sailing off the banks of Newfoundland
   Where the water is blue and the bottom is sand
   Where the fish they do swim back, to and fro
   Bound away in the Dreadnought to the westward we go.

6. Its now we are sailing on the ocean so wide
   Where the deep and blue waters roll along our dark side,
   With our sails all set neatly and the stars we'll show,
   Bound away to the westward in the Dreadnought we go.

7. Its now we are sailing off the wild Yankee shore
   Where the Pilot boards us as he oft did before,
   Fill away your maintopsail and your main tack also
   Bound away in the Dreadnought to the westward we go.

8. Its now we are landing in New York once more
   Here's a health to the Dreadnought she's the boat brought us oer,
   Here's a health to capt[ain] Sanders and all his ships crew,
   And this song was made up in the watch down below.

END

37. Eighteen Hundred Forty-Nine
[Gold Rush Voyage Song]

These original lyrics were written by George H. Ashley on the California coast during a Gold Rush voyage in the ship *Olive Branch* of Boston, 1850-52, and were transcribed by Nicholas Kirby, Jr., First Mate. The text appears to be based on "The New York Trader" (Laws #K-22 B), a widely-published broadside ballad, of which composer-musicologist Ralph Vaughan Williams published the principal surviving melody.

TUNE A - "The New York Trader," from Ralph Vaughan Williams and A.L. Lloyd, *The Penguin Book of English Folk Songs*, 1959, p. 72: sung by Ted Goffin, Catfield, Norfolk (England), 1921; collected by E.J. Moeran. The 5/4 time is quite unusual and has been controversial.

TUNE B - "The New York Trader," tempo regularized.

UNTITLED. Lyrics by George H. Ashley, ship *Olive Branch* of Boston,, 1850-52; in the journal of Nicholas Kirby Jr., First Mate. Compare syntax (especially stanza 2) with "The New York Trader" (Vaughan Williams, 72).

1. In eighteen hundred forty nine
   We left our native land behind
   We left our friends that was so dear
   And to the Southward we did steer

2. Our little brig was good and strong
   And to New Bedford did belong
   We had on board some lively soles
   Bound away in search of gold

3. Hope told to us a flattering tale
   Of oceans mild and pleasant gales
   There was some lads that with us went
   Who thought it a life of merriment

4. When gales did rage and seas did roar
   They wished themselves upon the shore
   They wished themselves at home again
   Delivered from their seasick pains

George H Ashley

38. Unmooring
[The Boatswain's Call; Homeward Bound]

> With sails we will wing the masts...
> Unmoor the fleet, and rush into the sea.
> —*The Odyssey*

According to Captain Whall, "This is an example of the purely professional song, dear to the old-time sailor, and full of seamanship. It was a favourite with the prime old shellback, and was all the more successful in that it had a chorus about the girls." Evidently it was also well known in the whale fishery. Two of the whalemen's texts here are orthodox outward-bound versions entitled "The Boatswain's Call" (A and B); the others (C and D) are homeward-bound remakes not in strict conformity with the structure and meter of the original.

TUNE A - "Unmooring," from *Naval Songs,* 1883, p. 70; and Luce, *Naval Songs,* 1889, p. 64.

TUNE B - "Unmooring," from Captain W.B. Whall, *Songs an Shanties,* Glasgow, 1910 et seq., n.p.

A.

"THE BOATSWAIN'S CALL." George W. Piper, ship *Europa* of Edgartown, 1868-70.

1. All hands on deck the boatswain he cries
   With a voice like thunder roaring
   All hands on deck the boatswain he cries
   Make signals for unmooring
   Come my messmates to and fro
   Heave your anchor to your bow
   And we will think on our love
   When far away
   And we will think on our love
   When far away

2. Our anchor is apeak the boatswain he cries
   Vast heaving boys vast heaving
   You cat and fish and next overhaul
   Your handspikes nimbly heaving
   For to obey the boatswain's call
   Walk away with your catfall[16]
   And we will think on our love
   When far away
   And we will think on our love
   When far away

---

[16] *Avast heaving* (*'vast heaving*) is the order to discontinue work at the windlass, here for weighing anchor. The remainder are orders to secure the anchor for sea, for which the men must leave their *handspikes,* winch-handles used in working the windlass

3. Cast loose your topsails next he cries
   Top gallant sails and courses
   Your jibs and stay sails see all clear
   Haul home your sheets my hearties
   With a swell and a pleasant gale
   We will crowd on all our sail[17]
   And we will think on our love
   When far away
   And we will think on our love
   When far away

4. It was on the 21st of March
   When storm winds they were blowing
   When Kate and Sue two lovely girls
   Tears down their cheeks were flowing
   As the[y] watched our gallant bark
   As she ploughed the water dark
   And we will think on our love
   When far away
   And we will think on our love
   When far away

5. Adieu to friends adieu to foes
   Adieu to all kind relatives
   For I am bound across the seas
   To the East India station[18]
   And while cruising over the main
   The stars and stripes I will maintain[19]
   And we will think on our love
   When far away
   And we will think on our love
   When far away

B.

"THE BOATSWAIN'S CALL." Horace Wood, bark *Andrews* of New Bedford, 1866-67. Here the order of stanzas 2 and 3 is reversed, the syntax is lightly more vernacular (though no less technical) than George Piper's in A, the usual line "Tis the signal for *unmooring*" becomes "Tis the signal for *our mooring*," and the refrain is different. Even so, in substance B is otherwise a direct parallel of A, with interesting minor differences.

1. All hands on deck the boatswain cries
   In a voice like thunder roaring
   All hands on deck the boatswain cries
   Tis the signal for our mooring
   With your messenger bring to
   Heave our anchor to the Bow

   Chorus: And we will think on our love
   When far away
   And we'll think of the girls
   When we are far far away

2. Cast loose your top sails next he cries
   Top Gallant sails and Courses
   Then see your Gibs and Stay sails clear
   Haul home your sheets my Hearties
   With a strong and pleasant Gail
   We'll crowd on the lofty sail
   And we'll think of the loved ones &c.

3. Our anchors apeak the next he cries
   Vast heaving Boys Vast heaving
   Our anchors apeak the next he cries
   Your hand spikes nimbly heaving
   To obey the Boatswain's call
   Walk away with your cat fall…

4. It was on the 21st of June
   The stormy winds were blowing
   When Poll & Sue those pretty girls
   Tears down their cheeks were flowing
   For to see the our gallant ship
   Goes plowing oer the main

5. Adieu to friends adieu to foes,
   Adieu to all relation
   Our anchors apeak our sails unfurled
   We are bound for the East India station
   As we go plouwghing [sic] on the main
   Our lands color[s] to maintain

---

[16] "We will crowd on all our sail" is the key to this stanza about setting sail. *Courses* are large square sails, athwartships on each mast, those lowest-down and closest to the deck; then, in ascending order, are *topsails, topgallants, royals,* and *skysails*. *Jibs* are the *headsails*, triangular-shaped fore-and-aft sails in the bow, forward of the foremost mast, from which they are suspended on cables over the *boom*. *Staysails* are triangular fore-and-aft sails rigged on *stays* (cables) between the masts. *Sheets* and *tacks* are lines (ropes) attached to the loose-footed lower corners of each sail, for maneuvering them into position.

[18] Whall and Luce both have "a *foreign* station."

[19] Luce also has "the stars and stripes I will sustain," but the English Captain Wall gives "the *Union Jack* we will maintain."

C.

"HOMEWARD BOUND." George E. Mills, fourth mate, ship *Java* of New Bedford, 1854. The text is signed "G. E. Mills / Ship Java, New Bedford—John R. Lawrence / Master, North Pacific Ocean / Sunday December 17th 1854." Technical terms abound. The *spanker* is a fore-and-aft sail on the *mizzen* or aftmost mast of a ship or bark, rigged to a wooden spar called a *gaff*. *So heave and pall my hearties all:* The men here weigh anchor using a *capstan*, a kind of *windlass* that requires them to walk around heaving on *capstan bars* or *pawls: Heave and pawl* or *heave a pawl* is both a command and a form of encouragement. *Let fall... avast, hold on your courses:* Here they are setting sail; the *halyards* (*haul-yards*) are the lines (ropes) for hauling up the sails into position. *Walk her up so cheerily:* Instead of hauling up the sails by hand, the crew are here *walking* them up and using the capstan as a winch. *Board tacks and sheets:* Sheets, braces, and tacks are ropes (lines) operated from the deck for positioning sails and yards to catch the wind. See also notes to Text A.

1. Hurah my lads get underweigh
    Right welcome comes the warning
  Up—up on Decks all hands obey
    We're homeward bound this morning

Cho: You John and Dick, and Joe and Jack
    Stand by and get your Anchor
  Here Boy Lay aft to the Mizzen Gaff
    And loose away the spanker.

2. Heave, heave my souls and forge ahead
    The Breeze is gently Blowing
  And whilst the morn is tinged with red
    We're off with sheets aflowing.

  The[n] walk him round

    Each moment brings us nearer
  So heave and pall my hearties all
    For friends at home that's deare

3. Ho, short apeak loud comes the hail
    Avast boys 'vast your heaving
  Jump up aloft loose every sail
    Your handspikes nimbly leaving

  Let fall, let fall comes loud the call
    Hall home your sheets like horses
  Now halyards away and sheets belay
    <u>Avast</u>, hold on your courses

4. Once more your windlass man my boys
    And walk her up so cheerily
  Heave round and break her there she starts
    Your anchor's up or nearly

  Now overhaul cat tackle fall
    And with your fish be handy
  Up with your Jibb and staysail Glibb
    So well there thats the dandy

5. Let fall your courses next the cry
    Round in your weather braces
  Board Tacks and Sheets my lads be spry
    See all things in their places

  And along we swim in gallant trim
  we're homeward bound
    With thoughts that roam
    towards far off home
  To which we're fast returning

6. Homeward bound ah, magic word
    How sweet the hearts emotion
  As memory strikes the magic chord
    Afar upon the ocean

  The[n] Ho, for home we come
    All dangers nobly braving
  Look out, Look out for our welcome shout
    And Banners Proudly waving

D.

"HOMEWARD BOUND." George W. Piper, ship *Europa* of Edgartown, 1868-70. Differs from C principally in that D has a bona fide chorus of nonsense syllables, tune unknown; and the stanzas are doubled (thus, what appears in C as a stanza and chorus, are in C the first and second halves of the same stanza, to be followed by the chorus).

Chorus: fal da doodle dadle day
    right fal se dadle fal dal de dadle do
    We are homeward bound

39. The Loss of the Ramillies
(Laws #K-1)

This ballad commemorates the tragic loss by shipwreck of a British man-of-war in February 1760. The *Ramillies,* 1679 tons, rated 90 guns, launched in 1749, was named for a village in the Brabant, in what is now part of Belgium, where the Duke of Marlborough defeated the French and Bavarians under Villeroi in 1706. The disaster, in which 734 men were lost, occurred on the South Devon coast, where "Ramillies Cove, near the scene of the wreck, is named after the ship" (Palmer 1973, 38). The ballad is only rarely encountered ashore in Great Britain and Canada, and has not hitherto been collected from any American source (Doerflinger's version was obtained in Nova Scotia from an informant of Scots ancestry). The two quite different Yankee whalemen's texts here strongly suggest transcription from oral sources, and constitute compelling testimony that the ballad was circulating among American mariners for at least a hundred years after the event. By that time, oral transmission had corrupted the name of the ship, which is variously given as *Ramillee, Ramalee, Rambolee,* and even *Rambler,* and, no doubt, obliterated any recollection of its original patriotic significance in Britain. Interestingly, text B narrates the entire event and its aftermath, with much attention to the storm itself, while A is foreshortened, giving the disaster short shrift and almost wholly concerned with survival in the boats and the effect of the news in Portsmouth. Both versions are guilty of hyperbole in reporting the death toll ("There were only three to tell the tale"; "There was not but I to tell the sad tale"): there were evidently 26 survivors (Mackenzie, 225). Yet the salty parlance of both whalemen's texts indicates that, like "Lady Franklin's Lament" [#67], "The *Ramillies*" enjoyed a certain currency in the whale fishery—and perhaps among sailors generally—because of the poignant sentiments it expresses about the dangers to which all seamen are perpetually exposed.

TUNE A - "The Old Ramillies," a representative British rendition learned from Stan Hugill in Connecticut, June 1984. Compare Palmer 1973, #17: "Sung by Mr. Peter Pratt (aged 92), Toab, Orkney [Scotland]" (Palmer 1973, 63).

TUNE B - "The Ship *Rambolee,*" from William Main Doerflinger, *Songs of the Sailor and Lumberman,* 1972, p. 144: obtained "from the singing of Guy Morehouse, Nova Scotia... [who] got the song from his father, a deepwater captain" (p. 354). Variant includes a redundant latter-day chorus not present in other versions and omitted here.

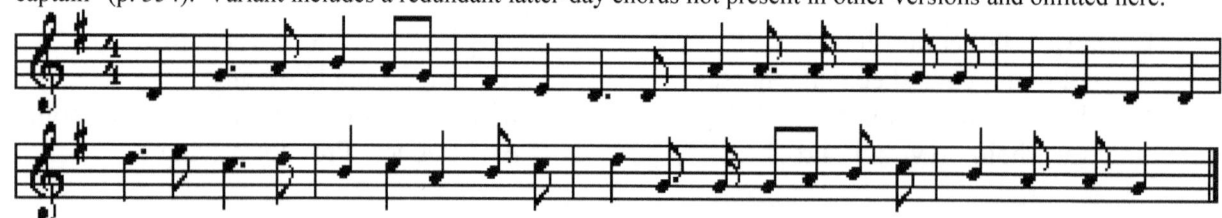

A.

"THE LOSS OF THE RAMERLEE." Theodore D. Bartley, ship *California* of New Bedford, 1851-54.

1. Come now my good fellows all
   And listen to the boatswain while he pipes his call
   Launch out your boats your lives to save
   For the Seas this night will be your grave

2. Now our boats over board were tossed
   Some got saved and some were lost
   Some in our boat and some in another
   Whilst the watch down below all got smothered

3. When this dreadful news to Plymouth came
   The loss of the Ramerlee with most of her men
   Old Plymouth streets did flow with tears
   When these dreadful news did reach their ears

4. Now ye young maidens all listen untoo me
   Who lost your true lovers in the Ramerlee
   There were only three to tell the tale
   How the goo[d]ly ship behaved in that dreadful gale

B.

"THE LOSS OF THE RAMALEE." George M. Jones and Albert F. Handy, bark *Waverly* of New Bedford, 1859-63. Notations in the MS indicate that the last two lines of each stanza are to be repeated throughout.

1. Twas on a certain day
   As the Ramalee at her anchor she lay
   With her yards all down an[d] topgallants struck
   And all on board was complete and snug

2. That very night a gale came on
   And the Ramalee from her anchors swung
   With her close reefed topsails so neatly spread
   All thinking to weather the old rams head

3. The rain poured down in dreadful drops
   The sea broke over our fore top
   She would neither stay nor neither would she wear[6]
   Nor yet gather headway enough for to steer

4. Out boatswain pipes come my good fellows all
   Come listen unto me while I pipes my last call
   Tis launch our boats our lives to save
   Or the sea this night will be our grave

5. The boats were soon overboard tossed
   Some got in but they were lost
   There was some in our place and some in another
   But those down below they all were smothered

6. When the news to Plimouth came
   Of the lossing of the Ramalee with all her men
   Twas Plimouth town that was shed with tears
   For the lossing of husbands and sweethearts dear

7. When the news to Plimouth came
   Of the loss of the Ramalee with all her men
   There was none but I to tell the sad tale
   Of how she behaved in that dreadful gale

40. Prince Edward's Isle

This appears to be an original sailor-made ballad about a shipwreck on a lee shore. Its many substantial flaws of rhythm and syntax notwithstanding, it has the form of a classic come-all-ye ballad but has not been encountered elsewhere than in the journal of Nathan B. Fisher, first mate of the Cape Cod bark *Ocean* on a whaling cruise to the Crozet Islands in the Indian Ocean during 1856-57. In the manuscript the lyrics are inscribed, "Composed and sung by W.T.," who may have been a shipmate. Despite specific names and dates mentioned in the text, the actual event that inspired the ballad is elusive. According to the narrative, the shipwreck occurred on "Prince Edward's Isle" on the night of 25-26 August 1848; the ships *General Taylor* and *Oak Grove* are mentioned but, tragically, the name of the principal vessel is absent. Whatever the identity and nationality of the *Oak Grove* and the anonymous principal ship, the *General Taylor* could only be American and contemporaneous—named for Zachary Taylor, the hero of the Mexican War (1846-48) who was elected the twelfth President of the United States in 1848.[20] "Bay of Whales" is an inconclusive allusion, as it could refer to any of several sites around the world that were so called by whalemen.[21] For "Prince Edward's Isle" the most obvious reference would seem to be the island-province of Maritime Canada, a region rich in shipwreck balladry in its own right. But this would have been a very unlikely venue for an American ship like the *General Taylor,* and there is nothing in the text to indicate Maritime Canada in preference to two other possibilities. Prince Edward's Isles is also an old name, obsolete by the 1840s, for what were once known as Washington's Isles (Rees, Vol. 29, "Prince Edward"), which officially came to be called the Queen Charlotte Islands, now known as Haida-gwaii, in British Columbia. There "Boston" ships called from time to time as participants in the flourishing Northwest Coast leg of the China Trade (see Malloy 1998); in fact, there is still a Prince Edward Island just over the American border on that same coast, in what is now Alaska. Even so, the place-name in the ballad more likely refers to Prince Edward's Islands, a smallish archipelago at 46° 35′ South, 37° 56′ East, in the Indian Ocean between Madagascar and the Crozet Islands. This was the very area where the *Ocean* was hunting whales on the voyage on which Nathan Fisher wrote down the lyrics, characterizing it as a "dismal shore." However, shipwrecks in any of these places tended to be well documented: a disaster on the scale of "about a hundred sail ... cast and wasted" could hardly have escaped the notice of journalists and chroniclers, especially if the *Oak Grove* and *General Taylor* were there to witness it. Yet none of the newspapers or sailors' magazines appears to have carried reports of such a disaster, and none of the recorded shipwrecks correspond to the "facts" as narrated in the lyrics.[22] Perhaps the terrible incident is fictional after all. No tune is specified.

---

[20] There were many vessels named after Zachary Taylor (1784-1850): Cutler (1961) lists five in the coastwise and deepwater packet lines alone during 1848-53; Holdcamp (I:271) records 13, all built 1846-48 and registered or enrolled at New York. No *Oak Grove* has been located in *Lloyd's Register of Ships* or the various American ship registries for the relevant years.

[21] Several places were officially known as Bay of Whales, in addition to Walvis Bay, Southwest Africa, which is simply "Whale Bay" in Dutch; but none is in the vicinity of any Prince Edward (or Prince Edward's) Island. The places *unofficially* so called are legion. Sailors often employed such place names locally, regardless of common usage. For example, in northwest Greenland is a Bay of Whales in which whales were present when first discovered by Europeans, but (despite that whalers frequently visited the spot en route to other grounds in the Davis Strait) no whales have been seen there since. Were the region more heavily traveled, the name might have been changed on maps, but it would likely have remained Bay of Whales to whalemen (Vaughan 1984).

[22] On 25 Aug. 1848 there was a storm on the central and south Atlantic in which many vessels suffered (*Boston Shipping List,* 10 Oct. 1848, 3), but not adjacent to any place called Prince Edward (or Prince Edward's) Island. The same day, the whaler *Maine* of Fairhaven, Mass., Captain Netcher, was wrecked entering the Columbia River in Oregon, but not as the result of any storm: having struck the infamous sandbar without a pilot on board, "She dragged her anchors all night, the sea making a break over her. In the morning the officers and crew left her in their boats and reached the shore in safety. The ship soon after went to pieces and nothing was saved. She had 1400 bbls. of oil" (*Whalemen's Shipping List,* 5 Dec. 1848, 160). But there was no Prince Edward Island nearby, and no report of a vessel named *General Taylor* or *Oak Grove* at the scene. A the major shipping disaster had taken place the day before, when 178 lives were lost in the wreck of the transatlantic packet *Ocean Monarch;* but this was caused by a fire and took place in the Mersey River, near Liverpool (Barnaby, 229; Rushbook, 32; *Sailor's Magazine,* 21:3 [Nov. 1848], 69-74). The annals of shipping simply do not record such an event as W.T. describes having taken place on the day indicated.

"PRINCE EDWARDS ISLE." Nathan B. Fisher, first mate, bark *Ocean* of Sandwich, 1856-57. "Composed and sung by W.T." (not identified). To fit the flawed meter, the first line should be sung, "'Twas in the year eighteen-hundred and forty-eight."

1. Twas in the year 1848
   Down in the bay of whales it was a dismal fate
   Twas about a hundred sails and of a number more
   That was cast and wasted all on that dismal shore

2. Twas on the 25 of August the winds began to blo
   And the clouds began to darken and the seas began to roal
   Whitch caus all hands on board for to lament and crie
   For to think of the danger We was in for the land it was clost bye

3. At three O clock that night the rain began to pore
   and so dark and dismal was the winds and heavy billows roar
   The sea it run most mountains high and not a sail in sight
   whitch cossed our hart to tremble for the land it was clost bye

4. The [   ] lay at her ankors not far off the shore
   Whitch she struck from her morings where foaming billows roar
   She dashed upon the rocks my boys whitch all of you must [k]now
   And tis many a noble harted lad twas thear they had to go

5. About ten miles off shore the general taylor lay
   with the oak grove clost by her Till early the next day
   And when our captain came on deck and to his great surprise
   O look look thear my boys the sea runs mountains high

6. Now tis come all you seamen young and old that to the seas belong
   it is when you are shaping Coa[r]ses unto some foreign land
   if when you shaping Coa[r]ses steer Cloast of land and tide
   for tis many a noble harted lad lies on Prince Edwards ile

41. Homeward Bound
[Now We Steer Our Course for Home]

> Many of the losses which must be experienced [on shipboard] are obvious; such as that of society of every old friend, and of the sight of those places with which every dearest remembrance is so intimately connected. These losses, however, are at the same time partly relieved by the exhaustive delight of anticipating the long wished-for day of return. —Charles Darwin, *Voyage of the Beagle*

Elijah Chase recorded this song in his journal of the Nantucket ship *Navigator* during 1845-49.[23] Laurence Conway quotes a similar text in its entirety and identifies the source as Captain George Palmer, Nantucket ship *Navigator,* 1839-41 (p. 20). That text is undoubtedly authentic, but Conway is certainly mistaken about the dates of the voyage, and therefore the dates of the text:[24] *Navigator* was not built until 1841 (thus could not have been the venue of a transcription of 1839-41), and on her maiden voyage (1841-45) was commanded by Elihu Fisher, not George Palmer (meantime, Palmer was master of the ship *Marion,* 1840-44). But Palmer did command the *Navigator* on her next voyage (1845-49), when Elijah Chase was in the crew; and the two of them probably acquired the song from the same source at that time (Palmer also skippered the *Navigator* on her next outing, 1849-54). The existence of a third text, transcribed aboard the New Bedford ship *Uncas* around 1843 (Huntington 1964, 321), suggests that the song probably did not originate with either Palmer or Chase, or even with the unidentified third party aboard the *Navigator,* but rather that it was circulating around the whaling fleet in the 1840s. The lyrics are distinctly parlor-song-like, florid, labored in places, showing little evidence of the technical proficiency or seamanship that might indicate sailor origins; but each of the three variant texts is clearly localized to its respective vessel. The "dear native Isle in the midst of the sea" in the two *Navigator* texts is also a localization, referring to Nantucket; the *Uncas* text has instead the innocuous "Blow thou good wind and speed us on / The way that leads to our sweet home." No reference to the lyrics has been found in the published literature, nor any air identified.

"HOMEWARD BOUND." Elijah P. Chase, ship *Navigator* of Nantucket, 1845-49.

1. The wished for day at last has come
   And now we turn our course for home
   Blow then good breezes and speed us away
   To our dear native Isle in the midst of the sea

2. Our ship seems conscious of the hour
   That proves her strength and sailing power
   She swiftly ploughs the parting tide
   Her Captain's and her Seamen's pride

3. Our anxious friends methinks I hear
   Repeat the day the month the year
   Which tore us from their arms of love
   Ore oceans wide expanse to rove

4. With watchful eyes the spot they scan
   Where stands the ready signall man
   Who telegraphs each comeing sail
   Borne outwards by the favoring gale

5. Our hearts so long opprest with care
   Haste on before to meet them there
   While nightly in our dreams we trace
   Each well known scene each loved ones face

6. We know that many a fervent prayer
   They raise to ask our fathers care
   Dash on Navigator through the foam
   And bear thy Sons and Brothers home

---

[23] Manuscript notation from Chase's journal, on the back of a watercolor portrait of the *Navigator* by shipmate George H. Clark (Kendall Collection, New Bedford Whaling Museum, #O-262; Martin 1983, 98).

[24] Conway specifically identifies his source as Palmer's journal of the *Navigator,* 1839-41 (p. 54) and gives the date of the text as 1840 (p. 21). An exhaustive search of the manuscript collection of the Nantucket Historical Association, conducted in 1984 with the expert assistance of Jacqueline Haring, Chief Archivist, failed to unearth the original in any of the journals, logbooks, or other papers attributed to George Palmer, Elihu Fisher, Elijah Chase, or the Navigator.

42. We'll Soon Be There

This original homeward-bound song was written by Joseph R. Gorham of Nantucket, ship's cooper, during the final days of a 39-month whaling voyage in the Nantucket ship *Columbia,* and was recorded in the journal of shipmate George Gould, who inscribed it, "Dec. 4, 1845, off Gay Head [Marthas Vineyard] under storm sails," half a day's sail from home port (Starbuck's arrival date of December 2, 1844 is off by a few days.) The tune is not indicated. A charming feature is the nautical jargon metaphorically applied to the "Yankee girls" in the second stanza.

"WE'LL SOON BE THERE." George Gould, ship *Columbia* of Nantucket, 1845; acquired from shipmate Joseph R. Gorham, ship's cooper.

1. Hurrah! Hurrah! we're homeward bound
   Hurrah the wind blows fair
   With joy let every bosom bound
   We'll soon, we'll soon be there

2. Haul line Haul line ye Yankee girls
   And coil it clean and fair
   Then rig ye out with rings and curls
   We'll soon, we'll soon be there

3. O mind ye not what landsmen say
   The storm they fear to dare
   They'll skulk like beaten dogs away
   We'll soon, we'll soon be there

4. Hurrah! we smell the Yankee sod
   Haul line nor slack a hair
   Though rain pours down like Noahs flood
   We'll soon, we'll soon be there

5. And ye who wish to take a bride
   If ye are passing fair
   Haul line and with the wind and tide
   We'll soon, we'll soon be there

6. Hurrah! Hurrah a few leagues more
   We'll throw aside all care
   Then with the handsome girls on shore
   We'll soon, we'll soon be there

"Bo'sun's Dance." Photograph taken aboard the bark *Charles W. Morgan* on a whaling voyage from New Bedford in 1906. Pardon B. Gifford photo, Kendall Collection, New Bedford Whaling Museum.

43. Sweet America

This is a whalemen's homeward-bound song anticipating the return "from distant climes" to "Sweet America." Unfortunately, both of George Cleveland's transcriptions, made circa 1837-39, are fragmentary. Oddly, they were transcribed in five different hands—perhaps by five different whalemen, but more likely as an experiment in penmanship by Cleveland himself. However, at least one other, much later and more complete text survives in Benjamin Coffin's journal of the New Bedford bark *Catalpa,* 1856-57 (text C). The tune is not identified.

A.

"SWEET AMERICA." George S. Cleveland, second mate and first mate, ship *Charles* of New Bedford, 1837-39.

1. Come all you jovial Whalemen that leave your native home
   Through rustling winds and stormy seas to distant climes you roam
   your echoing voices join with ours to cheer us on our way
   Our Ship is full and homeward bound to Sweet America

2. It is you that on the briny sea your toilsome voyage pursue
   We'll spread our Canvass to the breeze and bid you all adieu
   Our swelling sails will catch the breeze our Ship she gathers way
   To bear us to that lovely place Called Sweet America

B.

"SWEET AMERICA." Fragment of two lines from the same source as A (see footnote 1).

C.

"SWEET AMERICA." Benjamin Coffin, bark *Catalpa* of New Bedford, 1856-57 (Nicholson Collection, Providence Public Library); Huntington MS 35. Reconstituted from four 8-line stanzas.

1. Come all you jovial sailors
   That love your native home
   Among strong winds and rushing seas
   Some foreign climes to roam
   Your echoing voices raised with ours
   To cheer us on our way
   Our ship is full and homeward bound
   To sweet America

2. It is eight and ten so tedious months
   Our voyage we did pursue
   From north to south we scoured the coast
   Of Chile and Peru
   At length those happy days arrived
   No longer we will delay
   Our ship is full and homeward bound
   To sweet America

3. It's you and I on the briny deep
   Our voyage we did pursue
   And we'll spread our canvas to the gale
   And bid you all adieu
   Our swelling sails will catch the breeze
   Our ship she gathers way
   So cheer us to that happy place
   Called sweet America

4. And when we are safe landed
   All on our native shore
   We'll bid adieu to troubles past
   And think of them no more
   We'll roam about with pretty girls
   Each happy night and day
   Enjoying love and sweet liberty
   In sweet America

CHAPTER FIVE
With a Heave and a Song
Deepwater Chanteys

> Heigh, my hearts; cheerly, cheerly,
> my hearts; yare, yare: take in the top-sail;
> 'Tend to the master's whistle.—Blow till thou
> burst thy wind, if room enough! — *The Tempest*

A song is as necessary to sailors as the drum and fife to a soldier. They can't pull in time, or *pull with a will*, without it. Many a time, when a thing goes heavy, with one fellow, yo-ho-ing, a lively song... has put strength in every arm.

— Richard Henry Dana, Jr.,
Two Years Before the Mast, 1840.

Was spoken to the other day about whistling by the Mate. he told me that the wind whistled enough for sailors, and though I had not noticed it before, I have since noticed that sailors hardly ever whistle though they sing a great deal. They never pull a rope without singing.

— Seaman Burr S. Kellogg's journal
of a China trade voyage, 1844.

At the cutting in of this whale I had my first experience at the windlass. The heaviest labor falls to the sailors who man the windlass and hoist in the great blanket pieces of blubber and the "old head." Gabriel, the happiest-spirited old soul aboard, bossed the job, as he always did, and cheered the sailors and made the hard work seem like play by his constant chanteys—those catchy, tuneful, working songs of the sea. All the old sailors on the brig knew these songs by heart and often sang them on the topsail halyard or while reefing on the topsail yard. The green hands soon picked up the words and airs of the choruses and joined in. The day laborer on land has no idea how work at sea is lightened by these songs.

— Walter Noble Burns,
A Year With a Whaler, 1913.

"Heave and Bust 'er." Working the brake windlass aboard the whaling schooner *John R. Manta* of New Bedford. Etching by George Albert Gale (1893-1951). New Bedford Whaling Museum.

44. The Sailor's Alphabet
[The Bosun's Alphabet; Alphabet Song]

> Sailors when heaving at a windlass, in order that they may heave together, always have one to sing out; which is done in a peculiar, high and long-drawn note, varying with the motion of the wind lass. This requires a high voice, strong lungs, and much practice, to be done well.
>
> — Richard Henry Dana, Jr., *Two Years Before the Mast.*

This progressive chantey, used for work at the capstan and windlass, mnemonically identifies in alphabetical order the parts of a ship and related nautical lore—ostensibly for the green hand, but in reality also, with respect to the sailors' occupational pride, a joke suitable for the seasoned tar. It is a straightforward parody of a similarly configured British song of the late 18th century, "The Soldier's (or Sergeant's) Alphabet," which is analogously associated with green recruits in the army;[1] and, in turn, "The Sailor's (or Bosun's) Alphabet" gave rise to "The Lumberman's (or Shantyboy's) Alphabet," a 19th-century adaptation from the logging camps of Maine and New Brunswick. Palmer mentions an even earlier progenitor, beginning "A was an archer and shot at a frog," published during the reign of Queen Anne, likely the true ancestor of this entire alphabet-song family. The several variant airs fall into two principal tune groups, in major and minor keys respectively. Hugill identifies the patriotic allusion to the *Union* present in most texts as referring to the Act of Union between England and Scotland in 1706, signifying a British origin of the chantey; however, the evidence actually seems to point to an American genesis with the *Union* allusion referring to the American union of 1776. (To George Wilbur Piper, who transcribed his text aboard a Marthas Vineyard whaler just after the American Civil War, *Union* could hardly have escaped implying an additional, more timely association with the Northern cause.) In fact, Hugill and Palmer, who give texts with murky provenance collected in the mid 20th century, are the only British sources for "The Sailor's Alphabet," whereas the chantey has appeared regularly in American use, *with* the Union allusion, at least since the third quarter of the 19th century (note Piper's whaleship version of 1868-70; and Captain Harlow's, learned from a Brooklyn, New York chantey-man named Brooks aboard the Boston ship *Akbar* in the early 1870s).

TUNE A - "The Sailor's Alphabet," from Frederick Pease Harlow, *Chanteying Aboard American Ships,* 1962, 52; credited to Brooks, a chanteyman from Brooklyn, New York, who "distinguished himself by singing the most vulgar words I ever heard to *The Sailor's Alphabet.* I will not attempt to give them."

---

[1] "The Soldier's Alphabet" ("The Sergeant's Alphabet"). per *The Universal Songster,* London, circa 1825 (first stanza of 6):

> A stands for attention, the first word he knows,
> And B stands for bullet to tickle his foes;
> C stands for a Charge, which the enemies all dread,
> And D stands for Discharge, which soon lays them all dead.
> [*Chorus:*] Derry down, etc.

TUNE B - "The Sailor's Alphabet," composite, after Bob Webb, San Francisco, Sept. 1979; Robert Kotta and Howlin' Gael, Portland, Oregon, May 1980; etc. (San Francisco Maritime National Historical Park archive, Sept. 1979; Mystic Seaport Sea Music Festival archive, June 1982 et seq.; Kendall Whaling Museum Symposium, Oct. 1983).

A.

"THE SAILOR'S ALPHABET." George W. Piper, ship *Europa* of Edgartown, 1868-70.

1.   A is our anchor you very well know
       B is the bowsprit shipped over the bow
       C is the capstan which we walk around
       D is the derrick we are taking aground[2]

Chorus: So merry so merry so merry are we
             No mortals so merry as sailors at sea
             Then its hay derry Ho derry Hi derry down
             Give sailors their grog there will nothing go wrong

2.   E is the ensign[3] which at our mast hung
       F is the forecastle[4] where we lived so long
       G is the guns[5] at which our men stand
       H is the hawser[6] which never will strand

3.   I is the irons our studding booms[7] shipped
       J is the jib[8] which so very well set
       K is the keel on which our ship sailed
       L is the lanyards[9] which never have failed

---

[2] Some versions have "... *Davits* to lower boats down"; these gallows-shaped cranes were common appliances on whaleships.

[3] *Ensign:* a flag, usually the national flag, flown over the taffrail at the stern, from the mizzen or aft-most mast.

[4] *Forecastle* ("fo'c'sle"): wedge-shaped compartment in the bow belowdecks, customarily serving as the seamen's quarters.

[5] *Guns* suggests an allusion to the navy, as most merchantmen were unarmed.

[6] *Hawser:* large-diameter line (rope) used for anchors and mooring.

[7] *Studding sail booms:* see "Boston," #33, version B and footnotes.

[8] *Jib:* a "headsail" or fore-and-aft sail in the bow, suspended between the foremast and jibboom (an extension of the bowsprit). There can be several jibs rigged in tandem, including inner jib, outer jib, flying jib, etc.

[9] *Lanyard:* "A piece of line to sling or hold anything by. A small rope used to set up rigging with" (L. Clark Russell, *Sailors' Language,* London, 1833, 78); typically attached to sailors' hand-tools to prevent their falling from aloft or overboard.

4. M is the main mast both stiff stout and strong
   N is the needle[10] which never goes wrong
   O is the oars of or jolly boat[11]
   P is the pennant which always does float

5. Q is the quarters at which we men stand
   R is the rigging which never does strand
   S is the studding sails which help us along
   T is the tiller both stiff stout and strong

6. U is the union which we all adore
   V is the vane which does fly at the fore
   W is the wheel where we all stand our turn
   There are three more letters which I cannot rhyme

B.

"ALPHA BET SONG." Frederick Merrill, green hand, bark *Janus* of New Bedford, 1875-76; and schooner *Eothen* of New York, 1878. In the journal the text is written without division into lines, and with minimal capitalization and eccentric punctuation; here divided into lines and stanzas, with capitalization and punctuation verbatim.

1. A is the anchor of our gallant ship,
   and B is the bowsprit so neatly, does fit,
   C is the captons [capstan] we all heave upon,
   D is the derrick that hoists in our grog.

Chorus: So merry, so merry, so merry are we
   no mortals on earth, is like sailor at sea,
   so high deary, low deary, high deary down,
   give sailors the grog and there is nothing goes wrong.

2. E is the ensign at our peak flew,
   F is the forecastle that held all our crue,
   G is the grog that seldom came round,
   H is the halyards we all waid upon.

3. I is the iron on stansail-boom fit,
   J is the jib so neatly did set,
   K is the kelson that lies in the hole,
   L is the lanyards that take a good hold.

4. [no stanza]

---

[10] *Needle:* the compass needle.

[11] *Jolly-boat:* a ship's boat or captain's gig, usually slung on davits at the stern.

45. Goodbye, Fare Ye Well
[Homeward Bound; Goodbye, Fare Thee Well]

> The sailors' songs for capstans and falls are of a peculiar kind, having a chorus at the end of each line. The burden is usually sung by one alone, and, at the chorus, all hands join in—and the louder the noise, the better. With us, the chorus seemed almost to raise the decks of the ship, and might be heard a great distance, ashore.
>
> — Richard Henry Dana, Jr., *Two Years Before the Mast.*

This homeward-bound chantey and the other songs found among Captain Charles Robbins's papers were evidently taken down from his dictation and later printed in his memoirs, *The Gam* (published in 1899, reissued in 1913). As his notes explain, "This is a song that is sung by sailors when they are working on the windlass. The first line is sung by one man, and then all hands sing the line following." Captain Whall calls it "one of the regulation songs when getting up anchor abroad," and Doerflinger refers to it as "an old-time sailor song ... the general favorite" among homeward-bound chanteys. According to C. Fox Smith, it "occupied a high place in [sailors'] affections until in later years it became to a considerable extent supplanted by 'Rolling Home.'" Taking his cue from Smith, Hugill calls it "the most popular homeward-bound shanty of them all—with the possible exception of *Rolling Home*," which was not originally a proper chantey at all.[12] Colcord quotes adaptations by clipper-ship sailors and East Indiamen, as well as an unlikely sentiment expressed in a whaler's version, undoubtedly intended as ironic: "the whalemen, when the hold was full of oil and bone, and the course set for New Bedford or Nantucket, sang: 'The *whales* we are leaving we'll leave with regret.'" The chantey was also widely adopted and adapted abroad, notably by French and Norwegian sailors in their own languages. Compared to these, Captain Robbins's Yankee text is rather simple and naive, lacking both poetic distinction and the raucous edge that authentic sailor lingo often imparts. Virtually all of the extant versions are sung to variants of what is essentially the same cheerful tune in a major key—even Captain Harlow's rendition, which he collected at sea in the 1870s and which uniquely adds to the chorus a compellingly musical refrain not encountered elsewhere, "Your hair of nut brown is the talk of the town."

TUNE - "Good-Bye, Fare You Well!" from Joanna C. Colcord, *Songs of American Sailormen,* [1924] 1938, p. 113.

---

[12] However, "Rolling Home" is of later vintage, and while it may have held sway in Hugill's days in square rig (the 1920s) and even in Captain Whall's (the 1870s), it would have been no match for "Goodbye, Fare Ye Well" in the palmy days of Yankee whaling (the 1840s and '50s). Whall says of "Rolling Home" that it is "a rather more modern type of sea song" known only since the 1870s. C. Fox Smith adds, "I suppose some people would say that 'Rolling Home' is not a shanty at all, but a popular song converted into a shanty" that was "universally known among the later generation of sailormen ... right up to the end of the windjammer period." But it is nevertheless of somewhat mysterious origin. The words have been attributed to Scottish poet Charles Mackay (1814-1889), based on his lyrics known as "Rolling Home to Bonnie Scotland," which may be the original or merely an adaptation; and also to a Captain "Hurricane" Brown of the American clipper-ship *Flying Cloud,* whose very existence Smith questions in connection with the *Flying Cloud* and respecting whose authorship she accordingly regards as "far from probable" (Smith, 79). De Charms & Breed identify "Rolling Home" as lyrics by one L. Hansen, sung to the Irish traditional tune "Kevin Barry" (SIC #5947).

"A SHANTY." Captain Charles H. Robbins, Cape Cod, Massachusetts, manuscripts papers circa 1837-97: "This is a song that is sung by sailors when they are working on the windlass. The first line is sung by one man, and then all hands sing the line following."

1. We are home ward bound, we cannot stay.
   Good bye, fare you well, Good bye fare you well.
   We will come again some other day,
   Hurrah my boys we're home ward bound

2. Home ward bound, oh isn't it grand.
   Good bye fare you well, Good bye fare you well.
   We will soon be at home in that distant land
   Hurrah my boys we're home ward bound.

3. To that land we are going across the sea.
   Good bye fare you well, Good bye fare you well.
   You know it well, its America.
   Hurrah my boys we are home ward bound.

4. We will heave up our anchor and set all our sail
   Good bye fare you well; Good bye fare you well,
   And speed our way before the gale,
   Hurrah my boys we are home ward bound.

5. It's little we care how hard it does blow.
   Good bye fare you well, Good bye fare you well.
   For the stronger the wind the faster we go.
   Hurrah my boys we are home ward bound.

6. And when we arrive on America's shore.
   Good bye fare you well Good bye fare you well.
   It's to sea that we never will any more go.
   Hurrah my boys we are home ward bound.

46. Heave Away
[Heave Away, My Johnnies; We're All Bound to Go]

In most incarnations this is a North Atlantic packet chantey, usually with a chorus that begins "Heave away, my Johnnies" or "Heave away, my bullies," attached to lyrics set on the Liverpool docks, concerning Liverpool shipping agent William Tapscott and an American ship — either the *Henry Clay* or the *Joseph Walker,* which plied the New York-to-Liverpool run in the 1840s and '50s.[13] The tune has been fairly stable, with variations occurring primarily in the solo line; but of numerous textual variants and localizations, only the one recorded by whaling captain Charles H. Robbins is closely adapted to the whale fishery, recounting the outlines of a whaling voyage, the hunt in the boats, and an optimistic vision of a victorious homecoming. It also ends with the resolution frequently reiterated in sailor songs, especially whaling songs, to "go to sea no more" [see "The Whaleman's Lament," #154]. Unaccountably, Captain Robbins's version also lacks the second refrain "We're all bound to go," which seems otherwise ubiquitous in manifestations of "Heave Away."[14] He titles the text simply "A Shanty for the windlass."

TUNE - "Heave Away," from Frederick Pease Harlow, *Chanteying Aboard American Ships,* 1962, p. 14: capstan chantey. Transposed from B♭ Major. Compare Colcord, 93 (windlass ro capstan chantey).

---

[13] Versions given by Colcord, Shay, and Whall name the *Henry Clay.* Harlow's text has *Josie Walker,* one of Hugill's has *Jinny Walker,* and Doerflinger has *Joshuay Walker*—all of which Doerflinger explains as corruptions of *Joseph Walker.* The original so-called packet-ship *Henry Clay,* 435 tons, was primarily in the coastwise trade out of Boston from 1837 (Cutler 1961, 447), and is not the vessel referred to in the chantey. The Liverpool packet-ship *Henry Clay,* 1207 tons, launched by Brown & Bell in 1845 for Grinnell, Minturn & Co., was "the largest packet at the time," noted for speed (Albion 1938, 170, 198). She worked the Blue Swallowtail Line on the New York-Liverpool run under Captain Ezra Nye from 1845 to 1848, "was gutted by fire as she lay at her East River dock" in September 1849, was bought and rebuilt by Spofford, Tileston & Co., and returned to the New York-Liverpool run in the Dramatic Line (1850-52; Captain Francis M. French) and Patriotic Line (1852-65; Captain David Caulkins) (Albion 1938, 170, 198, 225, 278; Cutler 1961, 258, 320, 378, 380, 389). The *Joseph Walker,* 1326 tons, was built in 1850 by Isaac Webb to the order of Thomas & Nephew for service in the Black Star Line between New York and Liverpool, in which she was commanded by William E. Hoxie until she was destroyed by fire at dockside in December 1853 (Cutler 1961, 320, 382). Doerflinger discloses an interesting play on words in the original text of "We're All Bound to Go" and a related chantey, "Yellow Meal," adding that the *Joseph Walker* was "not a very fast vessel, and not really a packet, though she was doubtless so described by the emigrant houses, with their loosely organized 'lines'"; the *Kangaroo,* often mentioned in conjunction with the *Walker,* was "a crack British steamship of the Inman Line also running between Liverpool and New York" (Doerflinger, 62).

[14] E.g., from Colcord: Some say we're bound for Liverpool, some say we're bound for France,
Heave away, my Johnny, heave away!
I think we're bound for 'Frisco, boys to give the girls a chance,
And away, my Johnny boy, we're all bound to go!

A common variant is: Some say we're bound for Liverpool, some say we're bound for France,
Heave away, my bullies, heave away!
I think we're bound for 'Frisco, boys to give the girls a chance,
Heave away, my bully boys, we're all bound to go!

"A SHANTY FOR THE WINDLASS." Captain Charles H. Robbins, Cape Cod, Massachusetts, manuscripts papers circa 1837-97 (Kendall Collection). The text was subsequently published with some emendations in his memoirs, *The Gam* (1899), 155. The text is here reorganized into stanzas from undifferentiated lines and requires some editing if it is to fit any of the standard variants of the tune. To adapt the text to the tune, replace the second refrain with the customary lines "And away, my Johnny boy, we're all bound to go!"

1. My boy he was a sailor, he sailed away to sea.
   Heave away my hearties, heave away my boys.
   But when he went he promised he would soon come back to me.
   Heave away my hearties, heave away my boys.

2. He sailed upon a vessel, a whaling for to go
   Heave away my hearties, heave away my boys.
   It was a tedious journey, but he was bound to go.
   Heave away my hearties, heave away my boys.

3. The captain was a good man, a sailor to the core.
   Heave away my hearties, heave away my boys.
   He had sailed upon the ocean for twenty years or more.
   Heave away my hearties, heave away my boys.

4. It was early in the morning the watch was down below.
   Heave away my hearties, heave away my boys.
   A sailor on the lookout sang out "There she blows."
   Heave away my hearties, heave away my boys.

5. They lowered the boats and struck him and soon the monster died
   Heave away my hearties, heave away my boys.
   They tied a rope upon him and towed him alongside.
   Heave away my hearties, heave away my boys.

6. We cut him in and try him out, and stow him down below.
   Heave away my hearties, heave away my boys.
   And set all sail, and head her straight, and homeward we will go.
   Heave away my hearties, heave away my boys.

7. And soon we will be home again, our friends we soon will see.
   Heave away my hearties, heave away my boys.
   For when we see New Bedford, we will no more go to sea.
   Heave away my hearties, heave away my boys.

8. And when we go longside the wharf, and put our feet on shore,
   Heave away my hearties, heave away my boys.
   You can gamble that we wont go whaling any more
   Heave away my hearties, heave away my boys.

47. Reuben Ranzo

> When they took the falls to the windlass and manned the bars it was a joy to hear them sing. Sailor-songs are not metrically faultless, any more than Whitman's poems; but they have the Jack Tar spirit of the forecastle breathing all through them, and here and there a touch of easy humor. This particular song ran, as I remember it, something after this fashion:—
>
> "O, Johnny was no sailor,
>   (Renso, boys, Renso.)
> Still he shipped on a Yankee whaler,
>   (Renso, boys, Renso.) … etc.
>
> — Charles H. Robbins, *The Gam* (1899).

"Reuben Ranzo" is usually classified as a long-drag halyard chantey used for setting the large topsails and topgallants of a deepwater square-rigger. On whalers it was also used at the brake windlass for cutting-in blubber, as it was aboard the *Clara Bell* of Mattapoisett, Massachusetts, when Captain Robbins commanded her in the 1850s. It is one of few chanteys with a narrative explicitly set in the whale fishery. According to Colcord, there are "many variants in the words and air." There are also divergent theories endeavoring to explain the origin and significance of the name Reuben Ranzo, all of them speculative and none supported by empirical evidence.[15] A comparatively early British version (anthologized by Davis & Tozer in 1887) places Ranzo in the crew of a Greenland whaler bound for the Arctic. Other texts are less specific about the grounds but follow the general outlines of the characteristic storyline: Reuben Ranzo (whose name some have interpreted to be Azorean Portuguese) is described as "no sailor" and often "just a tailor" or "just a New York tailor" (which some have interpreted to mean "immigrant Jew"); he ships on a whaling voyage and proves to be a bumbler, one of the least promising green hands ever to plough the salt wave. Refusing duty, he is brought to the gangway for punishment by flogging, when, Pocahontas-like, the captain's daughter intercedes in his behalf. Relenting, "The captain, being a good man / took Ranzo to his cabin"; "he taught him navigation / to fit him for a station," and, in some versions, "gave him wine and water / and he married the captain's daughter," with the final result that "He sails upon the water / Captain Ranzo gives the orders." It is thus a kind of ballad that lends itself to a variety of interpretations: the optimistic hope of Everyman to find a niche and succeed; the victory of brains over brawn; the unwarranted success of a manipulative opportunist who cheats his way to the top; or the ironic injustice of a shipboard bureaucracy that, on the basis of sycophancy, nepotism, and a bit of book-learning would elevate a nincompoop to command. Robbins's version is a departure from the norm: the name Reuben Ranzo has been lost and the phonetic "Renso" become merely a meaningless refrain; the "plot" simply concerns attempted desertion, recapture, and accommodation; and the *denouement* is the whaleman's oft-repeated resolve never to go whaling again.

TUNE A - "Reuben Ranzo," from Davis & Tozer, *Sailors' Songs or "Chanties,"* [1887], #20, p. 38.

TUNE B - "Reuben Ranzo," from Joanna C. Colcord, *Songs of American Sailormen*, [1924] 1938, p. 70.

---

[15] See endnote.

[REUBEN RANZO]. Captain Charles Henry Robbins, *The Gam, Being a Group of Whaling Stories* (New Bedford, 1899; revised ed., 1913), p. 180. The manuscript of this one chantey was unaccountably absent when the Kendall Whaling Museum acquired the papers of this Cape Cod whaling master [see "Goodbye, Fare Ye Well," #45; and "Heave Away," #46]. The text is here reorganized into stanzas from undifferentiated lines.

1. O Johnny was no sailor,
      (Renso, boys, Renso.)
   Still he shipped on a Yankee whaler,
      (Renso, boys, Renso.)

2. He could not do his duty,
      (Renso, boys, Renso.)
   And he tried to run away then,
      (Renso, boys, Renso.)

3. They caught him and brought him back again,
      (Renso, boys, Renso.)
   And he said he never would go again,
      (Renso, boys, Renso.)

4. They put him pounding cable,
      (Renso, boys, Renso.)
   And found him very able,
      (Renso, boys, Renso.)

5. He said he'd run away no more,
      (Renso, boys, Renso.)
   He only waited to get on shore,
      (Renso, boys, Renso.)

6. So when he put his feet on shore,
      (Renso, boys, Renso.)
   A-whaling he would go no more,
      (Renso, boys, Renso.)

Note: Anthologists have speculated widely on the origins and significance of the name Reuben Ranzo. Captain Whall remarks: "Either Bret Harte or Mark Twain—I forget which —has a character, an old skipper who is fond of singing about the trials of a certain 'Lorenzo.' Whether this was the original name I do not know. But as far back as fifty years ago [circa 1860] it was plain 'Ranzo.' Lorenzo it might have been, for Yankee whalers took a large number of their men from the Azores, men of Portuguese descent, among whom 'Lorenzo' would have been a common name enough. In the days I speak of, the shanty was always sung to the regulation words, and, when the story was finished, there was no attempt at improvisation; the text was, I suppose, considered sacred. I never heard any variation from the words here given" (Whall, 63). Doerflinger appears to concur in Whall's Portuguese hypothesis: "The name 'Ranzo' was probably suggested by 'Portugees' who shipped in American whalers, and it is no accident that Ranzo's first name suggests the farmer" (Doerflinger, 23). Here Doerflinger is referring to a definition best articulated by slang lexicographer Eric Partridge: "*rube; reub, reub, reuben* or *Reuben*. A country bumpkin: US (middle 1890s)" (however, if the significance of the name Reuben in the chantey be *bumpkin* or *joskin*, Partridge's chronology is be flawed and the slang term is certainly much older than the 1890s). Meanwhile, a lesser authority, responding to Whall, appears to regard Ranzo as more of a manipulative opportunist, and incidentally remarks on improvisational textual variants and implies an American dissemination: "This long-drag chantey starts off on a note of disarming sympathy for poor Reuben, supposedly one Reuben Lorenzo, who was anything but a sailor. But that sympathy is short-lived and the chantey becomes a caustic comment on all foremast hands who curry favor with the captain to claim a place on the quarter-deck. Captain Whall insists he never heard any improvisations, but there are so many versions we must credit his lack of information traceable to the fact that he never served on an American vessel" (Shay 1948, 50). Meanwhile, speaking from his own vast experience in American vessels, Captain Harlow confidently posits an entirely different theory, based upon meanings rooted in racial prejudices of which his predecessors were evidently not aware: "Ranzo is purely a Southern negro term used in the cotton ships at Mobile and New Orleans, and also sung by 'Badian negro[e]s at the fall…. Reuben Ranzo was depicted as a joskin; a man that was not very bright. Such sailors the officers called 'joskins' or gave them the name of 'Reuben.' When a man was once called Reuben the crew were not slow in following up, and the name stuck throughout the voyage" (Harlow, 89). Another interpretation comes from C. Fox Smith, who descends to ugly, jingoistic stereotypes. Rejecting a notion that links Ranzo to "a Danish national hero of the sixteenth century named Daniel Rantzau," she goes on to say: "My own private idea is that Ranzo was one of the small and select band, of which the Marques of Reading is the most eminent representative, of Jews afloat. He may have been a Russian or Polish Jew named Ronzoff or something of the kind, *in which case he would very likely be a tailor* [!], and the fact of his presence in the whaler would be sufficiently remarkable to be worth making a shanty about. It may also be observed that he *displays the characteristic national tendency to get on in the world.* ¶ Whalers, of course, were particularly giving [sic] to shipping lubbers of all sorts, and the point is worth noting that Reuben (or Rube, especially in conjunction with the patronymic Hayseed) is an American generic term for greenhorn or new chum" (Smith, 46). Hugill's commentary on the issue is scarcely more enlightened. However, though the wording of such remarks be essentially racist and anti-Semitic, the claims they make about Reuben Ranzo's Portuguese, African-American, or Jewish origins—and the pejorative characterization such origins are said to imply—could nevertheless be accurate on their own terms: that is, a century and a half ago Reuben Ranzo may have been created as the product of a bigotry analogous to that embedded in the terminology in which the claims were more recently expressed.

48. Old Horse
[The Sailor's Grace; Salt Horse; Poor Old Horse]

Most of the sea-song anthologists include in their collections some form of "Poor Old Man," a chantey that concerns a dead horse. Some have assumed, perhaps because there are few other evident differences between 19th-century British and American chantey traditions, that the ritual it accompanied on British merchant vessels was also practiced on American square-riggers. But on this point, Colcord's commentary is illuminating:

> ["Poor Old Man,"] used on American ships for halliards and sometimes for capstan, was used on British ships in connection with a celebration...held on board ship when one month at sea. Sailors received one month's pay in advance before leaving port; and, of course, duly spent it. After one month at sea, it was considered that this "dead horse" had been worked off, and a rough effigy of canvas and straw remotely resembling a horse was solemnly carried about the deck as the song was being chanted, and was then hoisted to the yardarm, cut away, and allowed to float off astern. I have never heard of the ceremony taking place aboard an American ship. (Colcord, 63)

Doerflinger also places the ceremony exclusively on British vessels, adding, "This custom was shelved in most vessels after about 1890, but both lime-juicers and Yankees continued to sing the shanty." He also reiterates Colcord's astute observation, which she attributes to "an anonymous newspaper correspondent," that the "Dead Horse" words derive from the American minstrel song "Clare de Kitchen"[16] and "may go back ultimately to shore folk song" (Doerflinger, 13).[17]

Evidently common on American vessels was a related practice more in the character of sailor shenanigans than the "solemn" ceremony Colcord describes: the radically different "Dead Horse" ritual recorded by Captain Harlow in *The Making of a Sailor* (113):

> It was customary...when a cask of salt beef was opened, to let the steward first pick out the choice pieces, for the cabin, and leave the lean pieces for the crew. These were called by the sailors "old horse," and were thrown into the "harness cask" only as the cook needed them. The name of "old horse" is ancient history. Richard H. Dana in his "Two Years Before the Mast" says, "There is a story current among seamen that a beef-dealer was convicted, at Boston, of having sold an old horse for ships' stores, instead of beef, and had been sentenced to be confined in jail until he should eat the whole of it, and that he is now lying in Boston jail." He also quotes the rhyme all sailors knew in my time [1870s], "Old horse! Old horse! what brought you here?" This would seem to show that the name is purely American.
>
> Another writer claims the words to be of Welsh extraction of years ago. The fact that Dana mentions the "harness cask" would indicate that it was used years before he went to sea and he sailed from Boston, around the Horn to California in the brig *Pilgrim* in the year 1834.
>
> The "harness cask" no doubt obtained its name from throwing scraps of old salt beef to be soaked out in a tub and it is easily understood how these scraps could have been called the horse's harness. Even in my day I have heard some old sailor with a grouch, when the evening meal was brought in, stab at a particularly uninvitingly dry piece of salt beef, with his fork or his sheath-knife, in a vicious manner and with an oath that would arrest the attention of us all, hold it above the pan and reverently proceed to recite the well-known rhyme:

---

[16] *Clare de Kitchen:* words and music by Thomas Dartmouth Rice (1808-1860), a New York musical entrepreneur who originated "Jim Crow" (1830) and thus pioneered the blackface minstrel genre, which he exported to Britain in 1836. *Minstrel Songs Old and New* (Boston, 1882, 153) contains the definitive original form of the words and music.

[17] Hugill's response to Colcord and Doerflinger —"Some authorities seem to think that [the chantey] was developed from the... minstrel ditty *Clear the kitchen, young folks, O' Virginny never tire,* but I fail to see any connection" (Hugill, 553)—misses the point. The proof is not the burden, which Hugill misquotes in any case (it should be "Clare de kitchen, old folks, young folks, Virginny never tire"), but, rather, the second and third stanzas: "I went to de creek, I couldn't get across, / I'd nobody wid me but an old blind horse; / But old Jim Crow came riding by, / Says he, 'old feller, your horse will die.' / My horse fell down upon the spot, / Says he, 'don't you see his eyes is sot;' So I took out my knife and off wid his skin, / And when he comes to life I'll ride him agin'" (*Minstrel Songs Old and New,* 153).

> Old horse! old horse! what brought you here?
> From Sacarap' to Portland pier
> I carted stone for many a year.
> I labored long and well, alack,
> 'Till I fell down and broke my back.
> They picked me up with sore abuse
> And salted me down for sailor's use.
> The sailors they do me despise,
> The pick me up an damn my eyes,
> They eat my flesh and gnaw my bones
> And throw the rest to Davy Jones.

Another instance comes from George William Smith, who was later a whaling captain. Speaking about his maiden voyage as a sixteen-year-old green hand in the whaling bark *Abraham Barker* during 1871-75, he makes the point that, in his experience at least, the shipboard grub was not nearly so terrible as is usually reported; but they evidently squawked about it nevertheless:

> How was the food on the voyage, you ask, with no refrigeration or fresh meat obtainable from nearby stores? Why it was exceptionally good! It consisted of Lob Scousecracker hash, salt horse, swanky, etc. "Salt Horse" was salted beef and the sailors soonb made up a rhyme. The first verse of which went as follows:
>
> > Old Horse, Old Horse, How came you here?
> > You carted stone for many a year
> > Until at last from bad abuse
> > You were salted down for Sailors use.
> >
> > The Sailors You they do despise
> > They eat your meat but leave your eyes
> > But make a Soup out of your bones
> > And throw the rest to Davey Jones.[18]

As its structure immediately reveals, this recitation is not a proper chantey, and even when sung is quite different from the "Dead Horse" chantey given by Colcord and Hugill:

> *Solo:* I say, old man, your horse will die
> *Crew:* And I say so, and I know so
> *Solo:* I say, old man, your horse will die
> *Crew:* Oh. poor old man!   (Colcord, 63)

Of this, Hugill says that "many lines and couplets" derive from "a 'chant' commonly known as 'The Sailor's Grace,' as it was recited or sung when the first barrel of 'salt horse' (salt beef or salt pork) was opened on the outward passage"; like a proper chantey, the form was *communal,* not *individual,* that is, "all hands would come in on the dirge-like" refrain. Hugill's versions of the salt-horse chant are quite similar to Harlow's and Smith's recitations; he also notes that the names Portland Bay and Saccarapp were used in American ships as substitutes for the British Bantry Bay and Ballywhack (however, if Doerflinger is right about the etymology from the American minstrel song "Clare de Kitchen," the derivation may have been the other way round). Whall (136) gives something similar and combines it with the "Dead Horse" ceremony, in which it was evidently sometimes recited as an epilogue on British ships. Davis & Tozer give another version: two complete stanzas entitled "Salt Horse," incorporating an unfortunate racial epithet:

---

[18] *The Autobiography George William Smith, Whaler,* transcribed and edited by Robert Sherman. Unpublished typescript, written by Captain Smith at age 85, circa 1940.

Salt Horse, Salt Horse, both near and far,
You're food for ev'ry hard work'd tar;
In strongest brine you have been sunk,
Until as hard an coarse as "Junk;"
To eat such tough and wretched fare,
Would whiten e'en a n——'s [sic] hair,
Salt Horse, Salt Horse, What brought you here?

Salt horse, salt horse, we'd have you know
That to the "Galley" you must go;
The cook without a sign of grief
Will boil you down, and call you beef;
And, we poor sailors standing near,
Must eat you, though you look so queer;
Salt Horse, Salt Horse, What brought you here? (Davis & Tozer, 86f)

Clearly, B.J. Gilman's vintage text from a New Bedford whaleship in the 1840s is a form of what Davis & Tozer call "Salt Horse," though his version is closer to what Hugill gives as "The Sailor's Grace" and what Whall gives as an epilogue in his British "Dead Horse" ceremony. From Colcord and Doerflinger we may presume that in the Yankee whaleship context "Old Horse" may have served as part of a "Salt Horse" ritual, though neither Gilman nor Davis & Tozer gives any evidence of a chorus. Interestingly and perhaps uniquely, Gilman's text adopts the first-person voice of the ill-used horse. The only authentic tunes for it seem to be the two given by Hugill, one of which he evidently got from Davis & Tozer.

"SALT HORSE." - from Frederick J. Davis and Ferris Tozer, *Sailors' Songs or "Chanties,"* [1887], #46, pp. 86f: "Salt beef is called by this name, the song is sung when opening a cask of salt beef." Compare "The Sailor's Grace (b)" (Hugill, 557), for which Davis & Tozer was evidently the source.

[UNTITLED.] B.J. Gilman, ship *Mary* of New Bedford, 1844-47.

Old horse Old horse, what brought you Here
From Sacarap to portland Pier
I have Carted Stone this many a year
Till killed by Blows and Sore abuse
they Salted me down for Sailors use
The Sailors they do me despise
The[y] turn me Over and dam[n] my Eyes
Cut off my meat and pick my bones,
And pitch the rest to Davy Jones.

49. Homeward Bound and Outward Bound
[Get Up Jack, Let John Sit Down]

Not a few wished that they could stay ashore, to escape the frozen fingers and toes, the ice and snow, and the keen northwesters which chill the very marrow in one's bones, on a winter passage, that most terrible ordeal the sailor passes through. But there is no escape. Ship you must, for they are already beginning to sing:

> "So get up Jack, let John sit down,
> For you know you're outward bound—
> You know you're outward bound.

— Charles Nordhoff, *The Merchant Vessel* (1855).[1]

This deceptively jovial windlass chantey is one of the best known of many that describe the sailor's anticipation of homecoming and his plight at the hands of landsharks ashore. Whall calls it "a prime favorite … all the world over"; it was sung at the capstan, at the windlass (Harlow 136; Hugill 540), at the pumps (Hugill), and in the forecastle (Hugill; Whall 5), and its popularity was no doubt enhanced by several broadside printings. The text and tune are uncommonly stable and lend themselves especially well to a greater-than-usual degree of localization. However, despite liberal substitutions of names, places, and destinations, the structure and general flow of the story are unvarying in virtually all texts reported (however, see the separately-classified variant, #50). At least one adaptation to the whale fishery is known;[19] but in the whalemen's texts here, a vestige of the song's origins in the deepwater merchant service is that the ships depart from Saint Catherine's Dock or the West Indies Dock, which are both in London. The point of arrival in George W. Piper's transcription (text A) is the "Yankee docks," which is rather more generic than the usual "New York Town," "Boston Town," "Baltimore," etc., found in American versions; and John Coquin's transcription has thundering guns suggesting a provenance in the Navy. Yet both versions retain some elements of what must have been the original form from the British East India trade, such as a call at Malabar (in India) and, of course, the "get up, Jack, let John sit down" outcome of the obligatory spree ashore.

TUNE - "Outward and Homeward Bound," from Stan Hugill, *Shanties from the Seven Seas,* 1961, pp. 540-541: "A favorite forebitter occasionally used as a capstan or pumps shanty… ."

A.

"HOMEWARD BOUND AND OUTWARD BOUND." George W. Piper, ship *Europa* of Edgartown, 1868-70: entitled both "Homeward bound and Outward bound" and "Outward bound and homeward bound" in the MS. Most texts differentiate between the general chorus and a special chorus for the final stanza; Piper specifies three choruses, as noted, which vary only slightly to accommodate the sense of the narrative.

1.   To St. Catherine's Docks we will bid adieu
    Likewise to Paul[20] and lovely Sue

---

[19] Ephraim Flanders, journal of a whaling voyage in the bark *Minerva Smyth* of New Bedford, 1852-53 (collection of the Dukes County Historical Society, Edgartown, Marthas Vineyard; reported in Huntington MS, 101).

[20] *St. Catherine's Dock,* on the Thames, east of the Tower of London, was originally built for the East India trade. In American

For our anchor is weighed our sails are unfurled
And we are bound for to cross this watery world

Chorus for the first four verses:

For we know we are outward bound
For we know we are outward bound

2. Our orders we have just received
To foreign ports we will proceed
For our anchor is weighed our sails unfurled
And we are bound to cross this watery world

3. Our ship will sail twelve knots at ease
With a pleasant breeze to cross the seas
For the Captain will our wants supply
And whilst we have life we ill never say die

4. And when we arrive at Malabar
Or top some foreign port afar
Our purser recorded our wants supplied
And while we have rum we will never say die

5. And it is when we arrive at the Yankee Docks
The pretty girls come around in flocks
They will come alongside and this they will say
You are welcome Jack with your three years pay[21]

Chorus for the 5th and 6th verses:

For we know you are homeward bound
For we know you are homeward bound

6. And it is now we are in sight of the Dawning bell
Where they keep good liquors for to sell
In comes the landlady with a smile
Saying drink my boys for I know it is worth while

7. Now it is when Jack['s] money is all gone and spent
There is none to be borrowed and none to be lent
In comes the landlady with a frown
Saying rise up Jack let John sit down

Chorus for the last verse:

For I know you are outward bound
For I know he is outward bound

---

manifestations of the chantey this is usually Pensacola Town or Surabaya Town. *Paul* here is certainly a corruption of *St. Paul's,* the great London cathedral: in most versions this usually another woman's name—e.g., "Likewise to Kate and pretty Sue."

[21] "Three years' pay" is atypical of any seafaring trade but the whale fishery, and may be a whaling adaptation. "Three months' pay" would be closer to the norm in the transatlantic trade.

B.

"HOMEWARD BOUND." John S. Coquin, bark *Pacific* of New Bedford, 1867-68; merchant voyages out of Boston, 1869-73. The single chorus repeats throughout.

    1.   From the West Indie[s] docks I bid adieu
          To lovely Sal, and charming sue,
          Our ships unmoored, our sails unfurled
          We are bound to plough the watery world.

Chorus: For we are outward bound;
                " " " " " "

    2.   The wind blew a gale from the S[outh] S[outh] E[ast]
          Our ship did send nine knots at least,
          Our purser well our wants supplied
          And whilst we have grub we will never say die

    3.   When we arrive at Mallebar
          Or any port that is twice as far
          Our thundering great guns we'll let fly
          And whilst we have shot we will never say die

    4.   Then for America we will steer,
          To see our wives and familys dear
          When every man can take his glass
          And drink success to his favorite lass.

    5.   In hauling into the West Indie docks
          The girls of the town come down by flocks,
          And if you will listen you will hear them say
          Here is my flash man[22] from America.

    6.   When we arrived at the west Indie docks
          The girls of the town come down by flocks,
          And if you listen you will hear them say
          You are welcome jack with your three years pay

    7.   When we arrive at the Dog and bell
          Where the best of the liquors they do sell,
          I twigged the landlord with a smile
          Come drink my boys, it is worth your while.

    8.   Now my money is all gone and spent,
          There is none to be borrowed, none to be lent
          I twigged the landlord with a frown
          Its rise up jack let john sit down

                        END

---

[22] *Flash man:* contemporaneous slang for *beau* or *boyfriend* ("My flash man he's a Yankee / With his hair cut short behind / He wears a pair of tall sea boots / And he sails in the Black Ball Line"—from the North Atlantic packet service chantey "New York Girls" ("Can't You Dance the Polka").

50. Homeward Bound (II)

As soon as they were aboard the anchor was hove up, probably for the last time, to the tune of "Homeward Bound" and "The bottle oh," and we stood of[f] right before the wind in fine style.

— Burr R.S. Kellogg, ship *Horatio* of New Bedford, homeward bound from Canton to New York, 1844.[23]

This variant of the preceding, with a storyline and tune of its own, is separately classified by Hugill, who calls it simply "Homeward Bound" and maintains that this was the form most often employed as "a proper capstan shanty—a homeward-bound song." As the text, tune, and chorus are little more than adaptations of "Homeward Bound and Outward Bound" [#49], the separate "Homeward Bound" form has seldom been collected or identified elsewhere. As Hugill notes, "The only other writer who gives it, and he gives only one verse, is Captain Robinson (in *The Bellman*)." Hugill's version is British, with a Liverpool setting analogous to "Homeward Bound and Outward Bound," while whaleman George Wilbur Piper's text is equally distinctive as an adaptation casually localized to the whale fishery and his to own ship, the *Europa* of Edgartown.

TUNE - "Homeward Bound," from Stan Hugill, *Shanties from the Seven Seas,* 1961, 542: obtained from "Old Paddy Griffiths, with whom I once sailed… It was connected to Liverpool and sung aboard ships in the Saltpetre trade to Chili [sic] and aboard Guano Traders to Peru…." The simple melody must be repeated to accommodate the whaleman's double-length stanzas (per "Homeward Bound and Outward Bound," #49). Transposed from C minor.

"HOMEWARD BOUND." George W. Piper, ship *Europa* of Edgartown, 1868-70. Related to the text given by Hugill (542) but more complete and less like "Homeward Bound and Outward Bound," lacking the characteristic line, "Get up, Jack, let John sit down."

1. Hurrah my boys do you hear the news
   the ship Europa is bound home
   Cheer up my lads in a few days more
   we will all be safe on the Yankee shore

Chorus: Hurrah we are homeward bound my boys
   Hurrah we are homeward bound

2. And as we are sailing over the sea
   how short to us the time will be
   How cheerful everything appears
   to what it has these last three years

3. And when the man from the lookout
   Proclaims the land with a joyful shout
   How ready every heart does bound
   to echo back the joyful sound

---

[23] Quoted courtesy of Edward J. Lefkowicz, Fairhaven, Massachusetts and Kingston, Rhode Island.

4. The wind is free Gay Head we see
A pilot boat is on our lee
We back our sail unto the west
and the pilot comes on board at last

5. Our anchor is gone the cable veers
All hands furl sails next greets our ears
And as our ship swings to the tide
friends to receive us mount the side

6. The landlords to[o] from Water Street
do flock around you in a fleet
For to skin some they have skinned before
Likewise a few young greenhorns more

7. The landlady she is the best of all
she says she wants a brand new shawl
The daughter too does want a gown
and you cannot refuse for you are homeward bound

8. The children too do want some cakes
and that another dollar takes
Good hearted Jack cannot say no
but laughs at them all and the children too

9. And now my friends take my advice
they will talk to you so stand smooth and nice
For they will [rob] you of your money ease
and ship you off just when they please

10. And now we are safely moored on shore
it is how we will make those taverns roar
We will drink to the girl who loves as she ought
and not forget the ship that home us brought

Note: Water Street is mentioned in Stanza 6, and as might be expected, there are many such in seaports and coastal towns throughout New England, including Edgartown, Marthas Vineyard, the *Europa*'s port-of-registry; and New Bedford, home port for the largest portion of the American whaling fleet. Even vessels from the outports sometimes outfitted at and returned their cargoes to New Bedford, the hub of the industry, commodiously equipped with the appropriate facilities, infrastructure, and commercial resources. Though the whaleman's text mentions a three-year cruise (about average for a Pacific Ocean whaling voyage at the time), the *Europa,* commanded by Captain Thomas Mellen, was actually out six years, from 29 August 1866 to 17 August 1872, during the latter portion of which (in 1871) the vessel participated in the rescue of some 1200 survivors of an Arctic whaling fleet disaster involving 33 American whaling vessels in the Beaufort Sea, off the Arctic Ocean coast of Alaska. On a voyage so long, the roster of officers and crew turned over several times, and Piper was not on board for the duration; only Captain Mellen made the whole circuit. The chantey text, which Piper transcribed sometime during 1868-70, must thus be regarded as a generic and speculative adaptation, rather than a true account of his actual experiences on board. (For a classic instance of such homeward-bound speculation, see "Spanish Ladies" [#8]; and L.G.C. Laughton 1919, 160.)

CHAPTER SIX
Battle Pieces
Naval, Military, and Patriotic Ballads[1]

"… So, Four-decker,[2] give us a broadside! Can't you bellow the 'Commodore', or have you clean forgot it, so long since you was a blue jacket?"[3]

"The 'Commodore' — give us the 'Commodore,'" the sailors shouted, "give us the 'Commodore' or we'll scuttle your old hulk and send you plumb to Jimmy Squarefoot."[4]

The blue-jacket — or, as some would say, the jolly[5] — was proud of his former service in the navy, so proud, in fact, that he thought he had stepped down a ratline[6] or two in reducing himself to a mere mercenary blubber-hunter. He had been waiting all the evening for somebody to call for a line-of-battle-ship yarn, but this invitation to sing was the nearest approach to such solicitation. He therefore jumped at the chance. He assumed for the moment an air of aggrieved timidity, but when the crowd insisted, he reluctantly, but firmly, submitted.

Four-decker was a stout, deep-chested, beef-laden seaman with a cavernous mouth and a ponderous bass voice. He sang with the gusto of a music-hall soloist and an occasional tragic gesture enlivened his ballad:—

> "It was on a dark and stormy night,
> The wind nor'west did blow;
> And from the ship's high, lofty bows,
> That were pitching to and fro,
> Could be heard loud, rattling peals of thunder,
> And fierce, wild lightnings fly.
> Hail, rain and sleet and thunders meet,
> And dismal was the sky… "

The singer wound up his song with a lusty cadenza that made the forecastle[7] fairly shiver with its vibrant, tragic resonance. It was easy to see that Four-decker considered himself entirely responsible for the sinking of the *Commodore*.[8] You would have thought it his habit, had you heard him sing, to engage a foreign corvette or sloop-of-war every ten or fifteen minutes.

There was a hearty round of applause, much kicking of heels against sea-chests and a prodigious clapping of hardened hands, but no verbal suggestion of an encore. A whaleman never dips his colors to man-of-war service.

— Captain Charles H. Robbins, *The Gam* (1899), pp 189-191.

---

[1] The title is after Herman Melville's *Battle-Pieces and Aspects of the War,* a volume of Civil War poetry published in 1866.

[2] *Four-decker:* nautical slang for a larger-than-life line-of-battle warship, of which the largest type was usually a *three*-decker, referring to the number of gun-decks on which the broadside armament was mounted.

[3] *Bluejacket:* nautical slang for a navy sailor, from the traditional color of the uniform tunic in the British and American naval services. Accordingly, the *Bluejacket's Manual* is a handbook for seamen.

[4] *Jimmy Squarefoot* is evidently a later American corruption of *Jemmy Squaretoe,* a nautical slang term for the Devil.

[5] *Jolly:* originally, nautical slang for a Royal Marine, hence for an American marine; though usually the marine uniform jacket was red, not blue (see footnote 3), hence the nautical slang terms *redcoat* and *lobsterback,* referring to a *soldier* or a *marine,* and the (usually pejorative) slang term *soldier* or *so'jer* used in reference to a marine on shipboard.

[6] *Ratline:* a part of a sailing ship's standing rigging: the *ratlines* are the footropes of the ladder-like shrouds (stays running outboard of the rail, roughly from deck level up to the mastheads), which enable sailors to climb aloft into the rigging, into the tops, and out onto the yards to set, reef, and furl sail, maintain a lookout, and render any necessary repairs.

[7] *Forecastle* (fo'c'sle): at the prow, the forward-most part of a ship, where the sailors typically gathered on deck during the late-afternoon dog-watch, on some evenings and Sundays, for a *gam* (a shipboard social meeting between crews at sea), and at other leisure times. Belowdecks, the forecastle was traditionally the space reserved for the crew's quarters.

[8] See #54 for the complete text of "The Sinking of the Commodore" from Captain Robbins's manuscript papers.

51. Paul Jones's Victory
(Laws #A-4)

This patriotic ballad about America's great Revolutionary War naval hero, John Paul Jones (1747-1792), dates from the War of 1812 era and recounts his celebrated encounter in the *Bon Homme Richard* against the British frigate *Serapis*.

While cruising around the British Isles with a small squadron, Commodore Jones sighted a fleet of forty sail off Flamborough Head on September 23, 1779. They were merchantmen from the Baltic, under convoy of the 44-gun ship *Serapis*, Captain Richard Pearson, and the *Countess of Scarborough,* 20 guns. Commodore Jones ordered his consorts to form in line of battle, but only the *Pallas* obeyed the signal, engaging the *Countess of Scarborough*, while the *Bon Homme Richard* attacked the *Serapis* single-handed. ¶ Captain Pearson was knighted as a reward for his gallant action with Jones. The latter, upon hearing of it, remarked: "Should I fall in with him again, I'll make a lord of him." (Neeser, 26f)

The whaleman's text is a mere fragment of two lines, significant here as evidence that the ballad was known and was presumably sung on whalers and merchantmen as well as in the Navy. Text and tune have remained comparatively stable in tradition (but compare Cazden 1982, #8).

TUNE - "Paul Jones," from the singing of Jeff Warner and Jeff Davis; per Anne Warner, *Traditional American Folk Songs from the Anne & Frank Warner Collection,* 1984, p. 349. Compare Luce, 44; *Naval Songs,* 48; L.W. Chappell, *Folk Songs of the Roanoke and the Albemarle* (Morgantown, W.V.: Ballad Press, 1939), #24.

A.

"PAUL JONES." Richard C. Reynolds, boatsteerer, ship *Janus* of New Bedford, 1842-44. The Baltimore allusion also occurs in New York State versions in Warner (349) and Cazden (1982, #8).

> An american frigate from baltimore came
> her guns mounted forty the richard by name

B.

"PAUL JONES' VICTORY." Full text, per *Naval Songs,* New York, 1883, p. 48 (also Luce, 44). Firth (358) cites *Roxburghe Ballads,* viii, 332, and a "more correct version" in a broadside printed in London by Such, Forth, and others. Compare Firth 259; Cazden 1982 #8; Warner, 349. Note that Warner's chorus differs slightly from in Neeser's text (see notes, below): "Hurrah! Our country forever, Hurrah!"

1. An American Frigate: a frigate of fame,
   With guns mounted forty, "The Richard" by name,
   Sailed to cruise in the channels of old England,
   With a valiant commander, Paul Jones was his name.

Chorus: Hurrah! Hurrah! Our country forever, Hurrah!

2. We had not cruised long, before he espies
   A large fourty-four, and a twenty likewise;
   Well manned with bold seamen, well laid in with stores,
   In consort to drive us to from England's shores.

3. About twelve at noon, Pearson came alongside,
   With a loud speaking trumpet, "whence came you?" he cried:
   Return to me answer—I hailed you before,
   Or if you do not, a broadside I'll pour.

4. Paul Jones then said to his men, every one,
   "Let every true Seaman stand firm to his gun!
   We'll receive a broadside from this bold English man,
   And like true Yankee sailors, return it again."

5. The contest was bloody, both decks ran with gore,
   And the sea seem to blaze, while the cannon did roar,
   "Fight on, my brave boys," then Paul Jones he cried,
   "And soon we will humble this bold Englishman's pride."

6. "Stand firm to your quarters—your duty don't shun,
   The first one that shrinks, through the body I'll run,
   Though their force is superior, yet they shall know,
   What true, brave American seamen can do."

7. The battle rolled on, till bold Pearson cried:
   "Have you yet struck your colors? then come alongside!"
   But so far from thinking that the battle was won,
   Brave Paul Jones replied, "I've not yet begun."

8. We fought them eight glasses, eight glasses so hot,
   Till seventy bold seamen lay dead on the spot.
   And ninety brave seamen lay stretched in their gore,
   While the pieces of cannon most fiercely did roar.

9. Our gunner, in great fright to Captain Jones came,
   "We gain water quite fast and our side's in a flame,
   Then Paul Jones said in the height of his pride,
   "If we cannot do better, boys, sink alongside."

10. The Alliance bore down, and the Richard did rake,
    Which caused the bold hearts of our seamen to ache:
    Our shot few so hot that they could not stand us long,
    And the undaunted Union-of-Britain came down,

11. To us they did strike and their colors hauled down;
    The fame of Paul Jones to the world shall be known,
    His name shall rank with the gallant and brave,
    Who fought like a hero—Our Freedom to Save.

12. Now all valiant seamen where'er you may be,
    Who hear of this combat that's fought on the sea,
    May you all do like them, when called to do the same,
    And your names be enrolled on the pages of fame.

13. Your country will boast of her sons that are brave,
    And to you she will look from all dangers to save,
    She'll call you dear sons, in her annals you'll shine,
    And the brows of the brave shall green laurels entwine.

14. So now, my brave boys, have we taken a prize—
    A large 44 and a 20 likewise!
    Then God bless the mother whose doom is to weep
    The loss of her sons in the ocean so deep.

The Constitution and the Guerriere. Scrimshaw on a sperm whale tooth by the anonymous so-called Banknote Engraver, circa 1835, copied after a wood engraving entitled "The Constitution in Close Action with the Guerriere" by Abel Bowen (1790-1850), published in Bowen's *Naval Monument* (Boston, 1816, 1830, 1836). Bowen's illustration is based in turn upon an oil painting by Michele Felice Corne (1752-1845)The engagement took place at 41.42 North and 55.48 West on 19 August 1812. The victor was the American Commodore Isaac Hull; the British captain, James R. Dacres, was wounded in the battle.

52. The *Constitution* and the *Guerrière*
(Laws #A-6)

Commodore Isaac Hull's celebrated triumph in "Old Ironsides"—the USS *Constitution*—over the Royal Navy frigate *Guerrière* on 12 August 1812 was immediately commemorated in broadside poetry and in the otherwise unrelated fiddle tune "Hull's Victory." The American patriotic ballad is sung to the traditional air "Drops of Brandy" ("The Landlady of France"). The subsequent capture of the Yankee frigate *Chesapeake* by the British *Shannon* in June 1813 off Halifax, Nova Scotia, was witnessed by spectators on shore and gave rise to parallel a British countersong, "The *Shannon* and the *Chesapeake*," sung to the same air. The chronological precedence of the American ballad over the British one—that the British song is a parody created in response to the American prototype—is usually taken for granted, even by Captain Whall, but Firth weakly disputes the evidence. However, there can be no doubt that both ballads addressed matters of national honor and were much sung on land and sea, as William Davis relates in his narrative of a Pacific Ocean whaling voyage in the ship *Chelsea* of New London during 1834-38:

> We spoke the ship *Caroline*, of London, England, with whom we exchanged courtesies.... We boys went into the forecastle to discuss a jorum of grog, which, English style, was set before us. Good fellowship prevailed. The joke and yarn in their turn amused us. Of course the song must come in, and we took pride in the voice and exultation of the Nightingale, "Blue-Eyed Mary," "Cease Rude Boreas," etc., etc., wiled the fleeting hours. In an unfortunate moment, however, the Dibdin of the *Caroline* gave us the naval ditty, "When Gallant Jarvis Sailed." Now the difficulty of our position was just this: Dibdin might sing all night of the rows between Johnnies Crapaud and Bull,[9] without touching our corns; but we had no musical reminiscences of naval warfare which might not breed a sudden storm in our peaceful circle. Song for song had been the order of the exercises, and theme for theme. Expecting a row, we gathered about Hinton, as he trolled our modest "Constitution and Guerrière."
>
> Our hosts looked glum, but bore it right manfully. Soon as Hinton ceased singing, however, Dibdin struck up with "Chesapeake and the Shannon," the words of which I do not take to heart, as no true American takes any interest in that fight. But the song was an unnecessary affront, as they could have sung all night of the glories of English prowess on the sea, and we would have shared in their just pride. There was no help for it now... " (*Nimrod of the Sea*, 1874, 336f).

TUNE - "Drops of Brandy" ("The Landlady of France"), composite. The tune varies little in important details, but note that the C in measure 13 is often given as a D, resulting in a somewhat different harmonic structure (e.g., compare *Naval Songs*, 50; Luce, 42; Molloy 1873, 8 ["Eveleen's bower"]).

---

[9] *John Bull* is, of course, England. *Johnny Crapaud* (spelling varies; sometimes "John Crapose") is low, 19th-century slang for France: "The singular is *Crapo* or *Crappo*—but not very frequent... Ex Fr. *crapaud*, a toad (not a frog)" (Partridge, 443).

"THE CONSTITUTION AND THE GURRIERE [sic]." George W. Piper, ship *Europa* of Edgartown, 1868-70: A standard text, the first four stanzas of which are virtually identical with the text given by Luce.

1. It oft times has been told that the British seamen bold
   Could whip the tars of France so neat and handy O
   But they never found their match
   Till the Yankees they did catch
   O the Yankee boys for fighting are the dandy O

2. The Gurriere a frigate bold over the foaming ocean rolled
   Commanded by proud Dacres the Grandee O
   With as choice a British crew
   As a trigger ever drew
   They could lick the Frenchmen two to one so handy O

3. When this frigate bore in view says Hull unto his crew
   Come clear the decks for action and be handy O
   To the weather boys get her
   And to make his men fight better
   Give them to drink gunpowder mixed with brandy O

4. The Dacres loudly cries make the Yankee ship your prize
   You can in thirty minutes neat and handy O
   And that is enough I am sure but if you do it in a score
   I will treat you to a double score of brandy O

5. O the British shot flew hot which the Yankees answered not
   Until they got within the distance they called handy O
   Then says Hull unto his men O give it to them then
   And we will give them Yankee doodle dandy O

6. The first broadside was poured carried their mainmast by the board
   Which made the British feel quite ready O
   Captain Dacres shook his head and to his men he said
   Lord I didn't think that the Yankees were so handy O

7. Our second told so well that their fore and mizen fell
   Which made this lofty frigate look abandoned O
   By George says he we are done and he fired a lee gun
   While the Yankees struck up Yankee doodle dandy O

8. Captain Dacres came on board for to deliver up his sword
   Loth was he to part with it was so handy O
   O keep your sword says Captain Hull
   for it only makes you dull
   Come cheer up and we will take a glass of brandy O

9. Come fill your glasses full and we will drink to Captain Hull
   And so merrily we will push about the brandy O
   John Bull may toast his fill let the world say what it will
   But the Yankee boys for fighting are the dandy O

53. Columbia's Ships

This rousing patriotic song celebrating American naval and merchant prowess is undated and unascribed in Stephen O. Hopkins's journal of the 1840s. He may have copied it out of a printed source, but no other text has been found. The murder ballad "Fuller and Warren"—which begins, "Ye sons of Columbia, your attention I do crave"—is based on an incident in Indiana in 1820 but is frequently anthologized among cowboy songs in Texas and the southwest (e.g., Lomax 1938, 295). The two evidently descend from a common ancestor, suggesting that the melody most often used for "Fuller and Warren" is the one intended for "Columbia's Ships." The tune is quite old, appears in tradition in the British Isles in both march time and waltz time, and is known by the names of various texts associated with it: in England, "Dives and Lazarus" (Child #56; a later melody for a Yuletide ballad first published in 1558) and "The Thresher and the Squire"; in Ireland, "My Love Nell" and "The Star of the County Down"; in liturgical music, "Kingsfold" and an Anglican Rogation hymn selected and arranged by Ralph Vaughan Williams.

TUNE A - "Lazarus," from Broadwood & Maitland, *English County Songs,* 1893, pp. 102f.

TUNE B - "The Thresher and the Squire," from Broadwood & Maitland, *English County Songs,* 1893, pp. 68f.

TUNE C - "The Star of the County Down," from Herbert Hughes, *Irish Country Songs,* n.d. (circa 1909), IV:8f.

"COLUMBIA'S SHIPS." Stephen O. Hopkins, ship *Rosalie* of Warren, R.I.; and bark *Perseverance* of Providence and Newport, 1843-49.

1. The ships from young Columbia's shore
   As fleet they are and free
   As those from haughtier realms that boast
   Dominion over the sea
   As gallantly their banners float
   As keen their lightnings fly
   And braver hearts than there are found
   Beat not beneath the sky

2. White as the glancing sea bird's wing
   Their swelling sails expand
   Beside the bright Egean [Aegean] isles
   Or green Formosa strand
   Or where the sparse Norwegian pine
   A sudden summer shares
   Or Terra del Fuegos torch
   Amid the tempest glares

3. Unmoved their trackless course they hold
   Though vengeful Boreas roars
   And make their port on stranger coasts
   Or undiscovered shores
   Rude people of a forreign speech
   Have learned their cheering cry
   Land ho — aloft and bear a hand
   And the ready tars reply

4. From zone to zone — from pole to pole
   Wherever in swift career
   The ventrious keel a path explores
   Our Yankee sailors steer
   The white bear on his field of ice
   Hath seen their signals tossed
   And the great whale old Ocean's king
   Doth know them to his cost

5. The spices from the Indian isles
   The plant of China's care[10]
   The sweet blood from tropic climes[11]
   Their merchant vessels bear
   Wherever Commerce points his wand
   They mount the restless waves
   And link together every sea
   The rolling globe that laves

6. Still nearest to the Antarctic gale
   Our daring seamen press
   Where storm wrapped Nature thought to dwell
   In hermit loneliness
   Whose masts are those so white with frost
   Where fearful icebergs shine
   My country from her watch tower looked
   And answered These are mine

7. Columbia's [ships] with dauntless prow
   The tossing deep they tread
   The pirates of the Libyan sands
   Have felt their prowess dread
   And the British lion's lordly mane
   Their victor — might confessed
   For well their nation's faith and pride
   They guard an Oceans breast

8. When strong oppression fiercely frowns
   Her eagle rears its crest
   And means no bird of air shall pluck
   His pinions or his breast
   And brighter on the threatening cloud
   Gleam out her stars of gold
   Hurrah — for young Columbia's ships
   And for her seamen bold!

---

[10] It is not clear whether this is an allusion to *tea,* which was a staple return cargo from China; or to *sandalwood,* a tropical plant of great value to the Mandarins and hence a regular cargo of the American Pacific "triangle" trade from Polynesia and the East Indies to the Chinese treaty ports. Great quantities of tea were carried in American and British bottoms, but sandalwood was a characteristically Yankee cargo because various territorial monopolies and trade restrictions largely inhibited British vessels from competitive viability in this respectable and lucrative trade.

[11] Evidently an allusion to wine, and in particular the Port and Madeira wines of Portugal and her "tropical" island dependencies.

54. The Sinking of the *Commodore*

This naval ballad is evidently unknown apart from two foreshortened texts provided without a tune by Captain Charles H. Robbins, according to whom it was sung by an ex Navy man aboard the whaling bark *Clara Bell* of Mattapoisett, Massachusetts in the 1850s. The version published in 1899 in Robbins's memoir, *The Gam,* is based on a text later found among the Captain's manuscript papers in the Kendall Collection, from which the printed version differs only slightly. He introduces it in *The Gam* as though the crew were already familiar with the song and were clamoring for it (quoted here in the chapter headnotes), but there is no other evidence that it was ever in general circulation aboard British or American ships.

"THE SINKING OF THE COMMODORE." Papers of Captain Charles H. Robbins, Cape Cod, Mass., circa 1837-97. Except for ambivalent punctuation in the MS, it is virtually identical to the text published in Robbins's memoir, *The Gam* (New Bedford, 1899), pp. 190f, as sung aboard the *Clara Bell* of Mattapoisett in the 1850s by "Four-decker," an ex Navy man, with minor differences as indicated in italics in brackets; also, in stanza 2, the word *royal* is added in the manuscript in the original hand, but is not present in the published text.

1. It was on a dark and stormy night,
   The wind Nor'west did blow,
   And from the ship's high and lofty bows,
   That were pitching to and fro,
   Could be heard loud rattling peals of thunder
   And fierce wild light-nings fly.
   Hail, rain, and sleet, and thunders meet
   And dismal was the sky.

2. It was early on next morning,
   Our brave commander said,
   Who ever has the lookout,
   go up to the masthead
   And keep a good look out my boy,
   And try what you can see.
   And he soon cried out from the royal masthead
   Two large ships under our lee.

3. Now one was of[f] our quarter,
   The other off our cathead
   We cleared away for action
   As our brave commander said.
   The job being done it counted one,
   And last [*lasted*] from twelve to four.
   And what was fearful to relate,
   We sank the French Commodore.

4. Now five sailors we picked up were Frenchman [*Frenchmen*],
   And six [*were from*] from haughty Spain.
   We picked them up from off the wreck,
   That had floated from the main.
   Soon we'll send them to proud France,
   Where they had been before,
   To tell the proud French Admiral,
   We sank his Commodore.

55. The Hills of Chilia

Whaleman George Piper's transcription of this American ballad is incomplete but evidently unique: no other text has been found nor any melody,[12] and it may not have survived elsewhere. The narrative combines the rough-and-tumble of the Chilean Sailortown outports, with American patriotism for Chile's war of independence from Spain, prosecuted during 1810-18 under the leadership of national heroes José de San Martín and Bernardo O'Higgins. American sympathies were always favorably disposed towards independence and democracy.

"THE HILLS [OF] CHILIA." George W. Piper, ship *Europa* of Edgartown, 1868-70. MS lacks stanzas 4 and 5.

1. I was born in a city, which I left with a free good will
   I left New York city for to cross the Chilian hills.
   Where some thousands did assemble and so mutually did agree,
   For to stand by [one] another, and to fight for Liberty.

   Chorus: Then keep up your spirits my brave boys
   While we fight for Liberty

2. Valparoes[13] is our headquarters that place of high renown
   The standard that we bear, is a star without a crown.[14]
   For there's Englishmen, there's Irishmen, and Americans likewise
   They will cause our guns to rattle like thunder in the skies

3. Up steps a young Chilian boy so nimble and so spry
   Saying I've wounded a Spanish Officer as he was riding by
   With his musket on his shoulder and his field pike in his hand
   Saying fight in fight in! Brave patriots for Chilia is the land

   [*stanzas 4 and 5 are omitted in the manuscript*]

6. Up steps a young Chilian girl and sets down upon my knee
   Saying my dear American sailor boy I want you to marry me?
   Some thousands shall be your portion beside the land you see
   And I'll dress myself in men's attire and fight for Liberty

7. Oh daughter dearest daughter how dare you talk so free
   For if the Spanish fleet come in an we'll all be masacreed
   And if Calliao[15] be taken the whole coast shall go free
   And we'll cross the hills of Chilia and fight for Liberty

---

[12] The Chilean locale, several phrases, and a marginally compatible meter suggest that the words may have been intended to be sung to one of the airs for "The Girls Around Cape Horn" (e.g., Colcord, 177; and Vaughan Williams, 90). Other phrases appear to have been borrowed directly from "The Girls of Dublin Town" ("The Harp Without the Crown") (Hugill, 141; 2 versions): this is sung to the Irish tune "The Wearing of the Green," which in George Piper's era was better known as the Union Army marching song "The Bonny Blue Flag." However, the chorus in Piper's text is not compatible with any of these.

[13] Valparaiso, the port for Santiago and the principal Chilean port, was commonly known to sailors as *Valipo* (*Vallipo*).

[14] "Hurrah for the bonnie green flag and the Harp without the Crown" is the refrain of "Girls of Dublin Town" (see footnote 1).

[15] *Callao*, on the coast of Peru, is the port for Lima.

56. The *Somers*

This ballad about a controversial and divisive mutiny in the U.S. Navy in 1842 is immediately contemporaneous with the event. Homeward bound on an unruly training mission in the brig *Somers,* the commander, Alexander Slidell Mackenzie, suspected a midshipmen and two ratings of mutinous conspiracy. Assisted by his officers he confined the accused mutineers in irons and convened a court martial, with the result that the presumptive ringleader—a son of the Secretary of War—and the two alleged co-conspirators were hanged at sea. When the *Somers* returned to Brooklyn shortly after, questions were raised about whether Mackenzie's action was justified, given that no mutiny was actually attempted, the three "boys" were convicted on suspicion alone, and the *Somers* was close enough to an American port that the prisoners might have been held in irons until they could be tried ashore. The Secretary of War was understandably outraged, many literary, political, and naval luminaries took sides, and a tumultuous public sensation ensued. In varying degrees, James Fenimore Cooper, Washington Irving, Richard Henry Dana, Jr., and the Perry family, together with the entire Cabinet and the whole naval establishment, were embroiled in a bitter, acrimonious exchange, which was not mitigated by the circumstance that Matthew C. Perry, the commandant who had dispatched the *Somers* and assigned Mackenzie as captain in the first place, was also Mackenzie's brother-in-law and a bitter, implacable enemy of Cooper. The *Somers* Affair remains controversial today, likewise the spectrum of critical opinion about *Billy Budd,* the literary masterpiece that the *Somers* partly inspired. Written decades later by Herman Melville, whose cousin had been executive officer of the *Somers* and presided over the court martial, *Billy Budd* was left unfinished and unpublished at the time of Melville's death in 1891. Though it is set in the Royal Navy in the 1790s, allusions to the *Somers* are clear; yet, there being no consensus among critics, Melville's take on the *Somers* affair has been hotly disputed.

On the other hand, like Melville's own *White-Jacket* (concerning navy life on a Yankee man-of-war, published in 1849), the *Somers* ballad is unequivocally sympathetic to the common sailor and critical of the dehumanizing tyranny of officers and naval procedure. It was published in the *New York Herald* on 11 May 1843; the whaleman's transcription was made shortly after. The authorship is uncertain: in both the newspaper and the whaling journal it appears as "A Ballad—By Horser Clenling, Esqr., Quarter Master in the United States Navy," but the name is pseudonymous, the attribution remains uncorroborated, and the tune is not identified—if, indeed, it was ever intended to be sung at all. The narrative voice is precisely coeval with the event, as though the poem were written on shipboard immediately afterwards. However, if written by an actual naval rating such lyrics would constitute a degree of sedition that the Navy would hardly have tolerated: if the author was a navy quartermaster (and whomever it was certainly familiar at first hand with navy technical lingo and procedure), perhaps he mustered out before his poem was published. Or perhaps it was merely a bit of well-informed journalistic propaganda. Of the principals, only the three alleged mutineers are specifically mentioned by name: Samuel Cromwell, boatswain's mate; Elisha Small, originally a quartermaster but demoted to seaman during the voyage; and Acting Midshipman Philip Spencer, the son of John Canfield Spencer (1788-1855), Secretary of War in Tyler's cabinet, and the grandson of Ambrose Spencer (1765-1848), a former member of Congress and retired Chief Justice of the New York Supreme Court. Philip Spencer was himself a founder of the Chi Psi fraternity while an undergraduate at Union College. Alexander Slidell Mackenzie (1803-1848), Matthew Perry's brother-in-law, is referred to in the ballad only as the Captain; and Herman Melville's cousin, Guert Gansevoort (1812-1868), who served as executive officer in the *Somers* and president of the Court Martial, is not mentioned at all.

"A BALLAD — by Horser Clenling, Esqr., Quartermaster in the United States Navy." Dean C. Wright, boatsteerer, ship *Benjamin Rush* of Warren, 1841-45. For contemporaneous testimony and historical accounts of the *Somers* affair, see: Cooper 1844; Hayford 1959 (who prints the ballad, pp. 164-168); Leyda 1969; McFarland 1985; A.S. Mackenzie 1843; Sturgis 1844; Sumner 1844; Van de Water 1954; and the respective bibliographies in each.

1. Come listen all ye sailors bold,
    Come listen unto me,
  I'll sing you of a cruel deed;
    A bloody tragedy

2. Come listen landsmen, one & all,
    Come listen unto me,
  I'll make you bless your lucky stars
    You've never gone to sea.

3. It was the Somers, graceful, swift,
    As trim a little brig
  As ere was moddled by shipwright,
    Or sailor helped to rig—

4. That right before the steady trades,
    Was cleaving her swift way,
  And dashing from her glancing bows
    The sparkling, snowy spray.

5. Like unto some live ocean bird,
    Swiftly and light she breasts
  The up-curled, watery rolling hills,
    And skims along their crests.

6. Like unto some live ocean bird
    She spreads her wings of snow,
  And piles the canvass, gleaming white,
    On spars aloft, alow.

7. On, on she fleetly rushes,
    Her wake a stack of foam,
  Outstreatching far, attests the speed
    With which she flies for home

8. Home! Home! ah! what a joyful word
    For every seaman's ear,
  But ah! vain word! vain word! to some
    Of that brig's crew I fear.

9. Stern sounds of import, dark & dread,
    Rise from her peoples deck;
  They're not the thrilling battle cheers
    Or shrieking of the wreck

10. They're not the friendly trumpets hail,
    Far o'er the waters cast;
  Nor boom of cannon belching forth
    The fierce & deadly blast.

11. They're not the orders, loud & hoarse,
    High rising o'er the Gale,
  "Clew up! clew down! lay out & pass
    The gaskets round the sail!"

12. They're sounds of anguish & despair
    Low, mournfull dread & drear,
  Sighs, prayers, & inward curses
    The mutterings of fear.

13. They're sounds that ne'er were heard before
    Among a Yankee crew;
  That ne'er before disgraced a ship
    O'er which our bright flag flew.

14. The grating's rigged—the hangman's whip
    Dangles from main yard arm,
  The wondering crew gaze on the sight
    With terror & alarm.

15. In doubt & fear they whispered low,
    Scarcely above their breath,
  "What mean these novel sights & signs,
    These signs of crime and death?"

16. Alas! the meaning's soon to clear;
    The noose is round the neck
  Of three poor men, but men as brave,
    As walked the Somers' deck.

17. But what's the cause, & what's the crime,
    That thus, in manhood's bloom,
  And without form of law, these men,
    To such a death, can doom?

18. Alas! suspicion, hate, & fear,
    And vanity are rife;
  And a poor pride that will not count
    The worst of human life.

19. A lubber's heard a wild boy's yarn,
    That makes his cheek turn pale,
  And straightway to the Quarter deck,
    He tells the wond'rous tale.

20. Tis taken up, & for this cause
    These men are doomed to die;
  A tale which most men would have called,
    A weak & silly lie.

21. On one side Small & Cromwell stand
    Bold men and sailors true,
  They quail not, though the boldest might,
    With such a death in view.

22. The meanest Yankee tar that lives,
    Will dare the ghastly foe,
  Where bullets fly, where cutlass, pike,
    Gives fiercely, blow for blow

23. Amid the flashing cannon's roar,
    Where hand to hand we board,
    But, ah! Tis different far to face
    The Hangman's cruel cord

24. Starboard, young, foolish Spencer stands;
    The tears are in his eye;
    What feeling of a deep agony
    Must through his bosom fly.

25. He thinks of home, his father, friends
    His mother's fond caress;
    He thinks of all the hopes & fears
    That promised life to bless

26. He thinks, too, of his comrades bold
    Doomed by his idle tales,
    And their dread fate more than his own
    He bitterly bewails.

27. The whips are manned with pistol raised
    The first Luff bravely stands
    To guard that on the murd'rous ropes
    Are laid unwilling hands.

28. Now, doomed men, look your last on life
    Look on the gathered crew;
    Look on the bounding joyous brig;
    Look o'er the waters blue.

29. Look on the fleecy floating clouds;
    Look on the suns calm light;
    Look on that banner waving free,
    Emblem of law & right.

30. Look! look your last! for hark! a gun
    Sends forth its smoky breath,
    "Whip!"—instantly upon the word
    Their eyes are sealed in death.

31. The deed is done! that cruel deed—
    "Three cheers" the captain cries,
    "Three cheers" for that dark blood striped flag
    That o'er us mocking flies.

32. Pipe down! pipe down! The Captain cries
    Tis dinner time o' day.
    That over in their ocean tombs
    These corpses we will lay

33. And sad and slow our messmates dead
    We lowered into the waves,
    And watched them sink, mid ocean's moans
    Deep in their watery graves

34. O'er them the winds a requiem sing;
    Deep mournful sounds the blast;
    And shriller kiss the curling waves
    As homeward we speed fast

35. Our brig flies like some guilty thing
    Faster, more fast she flies,
    From where the blood of murdered men
    From thee deep ocean cries

36. In vain! in vain! Thou can'st not escape,
    Fatal, perfidious bark!
    The stains of blood are on thy deck,
    Thy freight is curses dark

37. And other hands than flesh & blood
    Thou numberest 'mongst the crew;
    And a ghostly "mess" thou'lt always bear
    Across the ocean blue

38. And not alone by mortal hands,
    Will be, when howls night's blasts,
    The reefpoints knotted, ear[r]ings hauled,
    Or main yard gaskets passed.

39. No! often on that gallows spar,
    The yardsman brave will quail,
    In the midnight watch all figures three
    Unearthly—fleshless—pale.

40. Strange sounds will float upon the air,
    And in the blast will speak;
    And round the mainyard arms three ghosts
    Will play, & dance, & shriek!

41. And ill luck, & misfortune dire
    Will follow in thy wake,
    Till the ghostly three, where lie their bones,
    Thy last dark haven make.

42. O! better far to yield her then
    At once unto the dead,
    Than keep the bloody, cursed craft,
    An honest seaman's dread!

43. Take, take her far away from land,
    And rudder lash midships;
    From all the yard arms, fore & main,
    Let hang the murderous whip.

44. Sheet home on every cursed spar,
    Let every rag of sail,
    And leave her to the ocean ghouls,
    And demons of the gale!

57. The *Monitor* and the *Merrimac*

This Yankee ballad commemorates the most celebrated naval engagement of the Civil War. At Hampton Roads, Virginia, on 9 March 1862, the Confederate ironclad *Virginia*—consisting of a heavily armored superstructure and battering ram built onto the reclaimed hulk of a conventional Yankee steam-frigate named *Merrimac*—routed a Union Navy squadron comprised of the sailing ships *Cumberland, St. Lawrence,* and *Congress* and the steam-frigates *Minnesota* and *Roanoke.* The *Cumberland* was sunk, the *Minnesota* was run aground, and the others were dispersed, occasioning a ballad called "The *Cumberland* and the *Merrimac*" (Warner #11) or "The *Cumberland* Crew" (Cazden 1982, #15). That ballad forms a kind of Confederate prologue to the main event. Late that same evening the newly-built Union ironclad *Monitor*—an ingenious floating gun-turret devised by the Swedish-born engineer John Ericsson—steamed in from New York, and the next day successfully defended the Yankee fleet and restored the Union blockade but without actually vanquishing the *Virginia* (ex *Merrimac*). The two ballads are historically and thematically connected but metrically and textually distinct. The whaleman's transcription of *"Monitor* and *Merrimac"* may be unique: no other version quite like it has been reported. The chorus combines elements of "Maggie Mac," "Larry Marr" (a version of "The Five-Gallon Jar"), and the chantey "Virginia Lowlands," all of which are related; but "The *Monitor* and the *Merrimac*" is primarily a parody of the popular minstrel song "In the Louisiana Lowlands," which provides both the melody and the chorus. ("In the Louisiana Lowlands" also furnished the tune for some southern variants of "The Bold Trinity/Golden Vanity" [#6].)

TUNE - "In the Louisiana Lowlands," from *Minstrel Songs Old and New,* Boston, 1882, p. 72: neither the words nor music is attributed but it has an 1859 copyright of Oliver Ditson & Co. Boston. Compare the very different melody Cazden 1982, #16.

"THE MONITOR AND MERRIMAC." George W. Piper, ship *Europa* of Edgartown, 1868-70. Somewhat regularized from the unevenly versified transcription in the MS.

1. Ye tars of Columbia come listen to my song
   It is of a Union Battery I will not detain you long
   She was built by Captain Ecrisson [sic] a Union man is he
   And she has proved to all the traitors the terror of the sea

   Chorus: In the old Virginia Lowlands, lowlands lowlands
   In the old Virginia Lowlands low

2. It was on the eighth of March my boys
      I remember well the day
   The Rebel steamer Merrimac
      From, Norfolk came straightway
   For to burn and sink our Union ships
      At Newport News they lay
   And for to strike the hearts of Union men
      With terror and dismay

3. She first attacked the Cumberland
      Whose guns did not avail
   Against her iron plated hull
      And storm of iron hail
   She struck her about amidships
      Which parted her in two
   And to the awful bottom went
      This frigate's gallant crew

4. She next attacked the Congress
      A cowardly act you will say
   And fired at her both shot and shell
      While she at anchor lay
   Her guns they being disabled
      Her men a scanty few
   And prisoners they were taken all
      Both officers and crew

Scrimshaw sperm whale tooth, anonymous, 1860s.

5. She next came down to Hampton Roads
      For to destroy our fleet
   But on her way the Monitor / She happened for to meet
   Which poured at her a galling fire / Which made them wink their eye
   While from the Rebel Monster / The splinters they did fly

6. This little battery fought her well / For five long hours or more
   The monster was disabled / And retreated for the shore
   Show was towed into Norfolk City / In a sinking state they say
   Which proves to all the traitors / That the Yankees gained the day

7. Here is success to Captain Ericsson[16]
    A Union man is he
And to the little Monitor
    She is champion of the sea
And to the gallant blue jackets
    Wherever that they be
But death to all the traitors
    By either land or sea

8. Here is success to Captain Worden[17]
    For he is true as steel
And to his officers and crew
    For fear they never feel
And if the Rebel Commodore
    Sends out a match to him
He will quickly show him how the Yankee boys
    Can quickly douce the glim.[18]

Note: The "plot," meter, and chorus of *"Monitor and Merrimac"* suggest a provenance entirely separate from "The *Cumberland* and the *Merrimac*"; however, comparison with a corrupt text entitled "Maggie Mac," collected by Creighton in Nova Scotia (a text she correctly identifies as a corruption of "Merrimac"), illustrates the remarkable affinity between these two Civil War ballads, where the most striking difference is in the choruses, which are so dissimilar as at first to seem unrelated. The chorus for "Maggie Mac" is:

    And we'll hoist up our flag and long may it wave / Over the Union so noble and brave,
    We'll hoist up our flag and long may it wave / Over the station as she slumbers in the grave (Creighton 1933 #131)

And this is closely related to the chorus of the capstan-and-pumps chantey "Larry Mar," which Hugill insists (on good evidence) is actually a version of "The Five-Gallon Jar" (of which his latter-day British rendition is blighted by an unfortunate racial slur):

    Then hoist up your flag, long may it wave, / Long may it lead us to the glory of the grave,
    Steady, boys, steady, we'll sound this Jubilee, / For Babylon's a-fallen an' the n——s [sic] are set free! (Hugill 59)

"Larry Mar" / "Five Gallon Jar" also has in common with "Maggie Mac" both the emancipation theme and explicit, unequivocal Union sympathies; and the chorus of Hugill's second version of "Five Gallon Jar" is the same as in "*Monitor* and *Merrimac*" ("In the Old Virginia Lowlands..."). The compelling implication is that both "Maggie Mac" and "*Monitor* and *Merrimac*" are related to "Five-Gallon Jar"—an hypothesis further corroborated by "The Big Five-Gallon Jar," which Doerflinger collected from Captain Harry E. Burke (of Toronto, Ontario; formerly of Lunenburg, Nova Scotia) and which has the same "Virginia Lowlands" chorus. Doerflinger presents convincing evidence for his contention that "the refrain is no doubt from the Civil War song 'The Seven Days' Fight' ('Air — "Louisiana Lowlands"')." The textual circle indicates that all of these songs (including "Seven Days' Fight" and "Louisiana Lowlands") constitute a single, interrelated network of songs that take a variety of forms, not the least of which are the chanteys and the *"Monitor and Merrimac"* ballad (in a superb state of preservation). Hugill correctly takes the "Virginia Lowlands" chantey to be American, though it may be indirectly descended from "The Golden Vanity" / "Sweet Trinity" cycle (Child #286) [#6]. However, far from being British the forecastle version "Larry Marr" can be nothing but American: "Babylon" and "Jubilee" were standard Union epithets referring, respectively, to the Confederate slavehold and (inevitable) Union victory, both terms having unmistakable scriptural overtones. In fact, "Babylon is Fallen" is the adoptive title of an emancipation song written in dialect by northern lyricist Henry Clay Work, who was also the author of "Marching Through Georgia," the chorus of which begins, "Hurrah, hurrah! we bring the jubilee!"

---

[16] John Ericsson (1803-1889) was well known, even among many sailors, as the Swedish-born engineer who designed and supervised the construction of the *Monitor.*

[17] John Lorimer Worden (1818-1897): U.S. Naval officer, commander of the *Monitor,* later promoted to Read Admiral (1872).

[18] *Dowse the glim*: put the light[s] out, as in the slang expression "put their lights out," i.e., extinguish them.

58. Lee's Invasion of Maryland

This anonymous Civil War adaptation of "Maryland, My Maryland" is highly sympathetic to the Union cause. The original words were written in 1861 by James Ryder Randall (1839-1908), a native of Maryland and graduate of Georgetown College who was employed as a journalist and professor of classics and literature at Poydras College in New Orleans. Miss Hattie Carey (or Carrie) of Baltimore is credited with suggesting that the lyrics be set to the familiar German air "O Tannenbaum" ("Oh Christmas Tree").[19] The words and melody were accordingly published together in sheet music later the same year.[20] Thus constituted, "Maryland" was taken up by the Confederacy, enjoyed universal popularity, North and South, throughout the war, and inspired numerous parodies and adaptations, including battle songs on both sides. The British sea captain W.B. Whall observes: "Never was there a war so prolific of song. 'Dixie,' 'Maryland,' 'Tramp, Tramp, Tramp,' and a score of others were sung, not in the States alone, but all over the world. The two chiefly used as shanties were, I think, 'Dixie' and 'Maryland.' The latter was sung both by Confederates and Federals, with, of course, different words to suit either side, for Maryland was 'on the fence,' and both sides wooed her." The source of this particular Yankee parody is not known; Union Infantry veteran Frederick H. Smith's 1866 shipboard transcription is the only text located. Oddly, General Robert E. Lee is specifically named in the title only,[21] though Jefferson Davis ("Jeff") and Union generals Meade and Hooker are alluded to in the text.[22]

TUNE - " Maryland, My Maryland," from sheet music published at Baltimore by Miller & Beacham, 1861.

---

[19] The seemingly trivial point—who suggested what—is controversial. In his description of an association copy of the book *The Women of the South in War Times,* edited by Matthew Page Andrews (Baltimore, 1920), antiquarian bookseller William Reese declares, "One of the most striking literary efusions of the beginning of the Civil War was the poem 'Maryland, My Maryland,' by James R. Randall. Set to music, it became one of the South's most striking tunes, and is still the state anthem of Maryland. This book… gives credit for setting the poem to music and arranging for its publication to the Misses Jenny and Hetty Carrie of Baltimore. The owner of the present copy, Rebecca Lloyd Nicholson Shippen, has written an angry refutation of this on the front fly, claiming that she was responsible for this, and has excised the page containing the offending information. An interesting tempest in a teapot, and hitherto unknown light on the origin of "Maryland, My Maryland'" (W. Reese 1995 #7).

[20] Baltimore: Miller & Beacham, 1861 (repr. in R. Jackson 1976, 130; Crawford 1977, 21); also 1862 (Dichter #1525).

[21] As commander of the Army of Northern Virginia, Lee commenced his campaign into Maryland in the summer of 1862, was halted at Antietam (17 September), repulsed Union offensives at Fredericksburg (13 December) and Chancellorsville (1 May 1863), but met with decisive defeat at Gettysburg, Pennsylvania (1-4 July 1863).

[22] Among the specific allusions are: in stanza 2, "Jeff" is, Jefferson Davis (1808-1889), President of the Confederacy. In stanza 4, the "Keystone State" is Pennsylvania, an allusion to Gettysburg and other battles and skirmishes fought on the North side of the Mason-Dixon line, which forms the northern border of Maryland. In stanza 5, General Joseph Hooker (1814-1879) succeeded Ambrose E. Burnside as commander of the Union's Army of the Potomac (January 1863) and "failed to defeat Lee at Chancellorsville (May 2-4, 1863); at his own request, on June 28, 1863 he was relieved of command and succeeded by General George Gordon Meade (1815-1872), a veteran of Antietam and Chancellorsville; he "repulsed [the] confederate army under Lee at Gettysburg (July 1-4, 1863), but was criticized for lack of aggressiveness in following up repulse to obtain decisive victory" (*Webster's Biog. Dict.,* 1974, 727 and 998). In stanza 8, the Potomac is both the river that forms part of the border between Maryland and Virginia (and hence, technically, between the Union and the Confederacy) and the name of the principal Union force participating in the military engagements alluded to in the song. In stanza 9, the *Rapidan* River: "Streams in Virginia are sometimes said to be [named] for Queen Anne or some other Anna, but the name seems more likely to be a rendering of the Algonquian *hanne,* 'stream,' or *hanough,* 'people.' Cf. such nearby streams as *Rappahannock, Rapidan,* the last even explained as rapid Ann" (Stewart, *American Place-Names,* 1970, 16).

"LEE'S INVASION OF MARYLAND." Frederick H. Smith, third mate, ship *Herald* of New Bedford, 1866.

1. The Rebel hordes by Thousands came
    To Maryland, My Maryland;
They hoped to gather wealth and fame
    In Maryland, My Maryland,
Through fertile val[l]eys in freedoms pride,
The traitors scattered, far and wide,
To plunder all the eyes espied,
    In Maryland, My Maryland.

2. They thought our Veterans far away
    From Maryland, My Maryland;
Where Rappahanock's riplets play,
    Oh, Maryland, My Maryland.
This cruel war would soon be done,
The North out fought, and <u>treason</u> won,
And <u>Jeff</u>. would reign in Washington,
    Oh, Maryland, My Maryland.

3. The Hills are green, wild Breezes blow,
    In Maryland, My Maryland;
Through valleys fair the streamlets flow,
    In Maryland, My Maryland;
Each Rebel heart was light and gay,
To fight Malitia [militia] would be play
And Love would crown their holiday
    In Maryland, My Maryland.

4. No arms were near, to bar their path
    In Maryland, My Maryland;
The Rebel hordes flew on in wrath,
    Through Maryland, My Maryland;
Emboldened by their trick of [*fate*]
They ravished at a winter rate
Mills & Hamlets in the Keystone State,
    Oh, Maryland, My Maryland.

5. But as their Joy was at its fill,
    In Maryland, My Maryland;
They saw a sight that bode them ill,
    In Maryland, My Maryland.
For all the hosts that Hooker led
Far over Hills and Valleys spread
While gallant Meade was at their head,
    In Maryland, My Maryland.

6. At Gettysburgh they are made to fight
    For Maryland, My Maryland,
While courage rules oer plain and height
    Oh, Maryland, My Maryland.
No green Malitia to met their dash,
But Veteran Steel, in warlike clash,
Crossed Veteran Steel, amidst cannons flash
    For Maryland, My Maryland.

7. The Yankee band they's met of yore,
    In Maryland, My Maryland,
Now whipped them worse than ere before
    For Maryland, My Maryland.
And their [sic] were hundreds Rebel dead,
And tens of hundreds, who but bled,
Were left behind while Thousands fled,
    From Maryland, My Maryland.

8. They wildly pushed to cross the tide,
    By Maryland, My Maryland;
Where old Patomuc's waters glide,
    Oh Maryland, My Maryland.
But cannot cross, till in their rear,
The fearless Bands of Meade appears,
To drive them on with frantic fears,
    From Maryland, My Maryland.

9. The Rebel hordes pursued their Van,
    From Maryland, My Maryland,
Again to reach the Rapid Ann,[9]
    Oh Maryland, My Maryland.
They halt again, <u>again</u> to run,
For 'neath the shade of our nations sun
We'll guard the Flags of <u>Washington</u>
    And Maryland, My Maryland.

Ship Herald, April 24th [18]66
Fredk. H. Smith

59. *Florida's* Crew
[The *Florida's* Cruise]

This Civil War ballad is the only Confederate piece encountered among hundreds of song transcriptions in whaling journals: after all, the overwhelming majority of whalemen were from New England and New York, in the solidly Union Northeast. The ballad recounts the exploits of the auxiliary-steam commerce-raider *Florida,* commanded by James Newland Maffitt (1819-1886), who has been called "one of the most dashing and daredevil captains of the Confederate States Navy" (Townley 1989). Born at sea, Maffitt was a career naval officer who accumulated over twenty years of sea duty before the outbreak of hostilities in 1861. Like so many military men of Southern origin, he resigned his commission to enter the Confederate service. "He was promoted (1863) to commander in recognition of his successful running of the blockade at Mobile in the insufficiently equipped *Florida,* and also performed notable feats of blockade running (1865) in the *Owl*" (Barnhart, II:2572).

It is with the *Florida's* running of the blockade at Mobile and subsequent ravages of Yankee shipping that the ballad is concerned. The Southern objective in these raids was more economic and psychological than military or political: to deprive the North of revenue and supplies, inflate insurance premiums, and erode morale. Confederate corsairs were of particular interest to whalemen, as their depredations were directed largely against the defenseless blubber-hunters. Called pirates by the Yankees, they were the scourge of the fleet. Robert Lloyd Webb summarizes the situation handily: "Armed cruisers built in British shipyards served the Confederate States Navy, and three of these, *Alabama, Florida,* and *Shenandoah* among them captured and destroyed more than fifty whaleships operated by merchants in Union states" (Webb 1988, 120). New England whalers were diverted in droves from their routes and grounds in tropical and temperate waters—where they became easy targets—to the comparative security of Hudson Bay in the Canadian Arctic. There they were less comfortable and less productive (and could not hunt sperm whales), but the grounds themselves and most of the route lay outside the range of the Confederacy. In the Atlantic and Pacific, on the many occasions when the raiders did capture Northern vessels, the gentlemanly conduct of the Confederate officers was exemplary: ships were burned, provisions commandeered, cargoes destroyed, and liquid assets confiscated; vessels and property were lost, but whaleship officers, crews, and any incidental passengers were normally courteously treated and put ashore in safety.

The ballad is attributed to an anonymous foretopman in the *Florida's* crew. According to John Townley and contrary to Frank Moore's indication, it is not set to the old patriotic song "The Red, White and Blue" (parody of "Columbia, the Gem of the Ocean" to which the *Florida* lyrics do not fit comfortably), but rather to "the tune of the also very popular *Red, White and Red*"—the chorus of which nevertheless sometimes refers to "the red, white and *blue."* The shipboard text entitled *"Florida's* Crew" is less complete than the text of twenty stanzas entitled *"Florida's* Cruise" that was printed two decades later in Moore's *The Civil War in Song and Story* (1889).[1]

The "Red, White and Red" tune derives its title from a text printed in at least three broadside editions published at Baltimore and possibly elsewhere in the South during the Civil War ("red, white and red" refers to a tricolor badge of the Confederacy). The melody was evidently adopted for several Confederate ballads, including "On the Plains of Manassas" (Brown III:444 and V: 252). According to one "Red, White and Red" broadside, the lyrics "by Y.P Prevette, Co. E, 6th Georgia Regiment," were intended to be sung to "Gum Tree Canoe" (Brown III:445). This was a minstrel song officially entitled "Tom-Big-Bee River," lyrics by S.S. Steele, composer unknown, published in 1847 [Tune C]. But the tune is not the same as any of the ones usually given for "The Red, White and Red." Whaleman William Keith, who transcribed the lyrics of *"Florida's* Crew" in his journal, also transcribed "Tom-Big-Bee River" [Appendix 8, #312]. It is not certain which of the tunes he may have had in mind for the *Florida* ballad.

128

TUNE A - "Red, White and Red," from *The Frank C. Brown Collection of North Carolina Folklore,* Vol. 5, #375, p. 252: "Sung by Miss Jewell Robbins, Perkin, Montgomery county [N.C.], July 1922."

TUNE B - "The Red, White and Red," from Anne Warner, *Traditional American Folk Songs,* 1984, p. 90: A "fine Confederate song" sung by John Galkusha, learned from his brother in Maryland.

TUNE C -"Tom-Big-Bee River, or Gum Tree Canoe," minstrel song, lyrics by S.S. Steele, composer unknown, from Chamberlain & Harrington, *Minstrel Songs,* 1882, 208.

"FLORIDA'S CREW." William H. Keith, schooners *William Martin* of Boston and *Edith May* of Wellfleet, etc., circa 1865-71. The lyrics may be related to a Florida version of the chantey "Blow, Bullies, Blow," which begins, "One night off Cape Horn I remember quite well": textual and metrical similarities are readily apparent and the "Red, White and Red" tune is compatible with both. However, the specimen given by Morris in *Folksongs of Florida* (p. 55) is evidently a corruption, sung to the ubiquitous air of "Vilikins and His Dinah" [#81].

1. One night off Mobile the Yanks thought they knew
   And the wind from the N[orth] W[est] most bitterly blew
   They thought they knew and was so sure
   That the Florida was blocked in so snug and secure

   Chorus: Huzza Huzza for the Florida's crew
   We'll roam with bold Maffitt this world through & through

2. Nine cruises they had as they laid off the bar
   And their lines to the seaward extended so far

And old Preble[23] did say as he closed his eyes tight
I'm sure they are hammocked this cold bitter night

3. Bold Maffitt commanded a man of good name
When he cruised in the Dolphin you've all heard the same
He called his men aft and to them did say
I am bound to run out boys heave your anchor away.

4. Our hull it was whitewashed our sails were well stowed
Our steam it was up and the fresh winds did blow
Oh! when we ran by them the Yanks gave a shout.
We dropped all our canvas then opened her out.

5. Oh! the R.R. Cuyler a boat unrivalled for speed
She quick slipped her anchor very quickly indeed
She thought to overhaul us and keep us in play,
Till her larger companions would get underway.

6. Our coals being poor and our fuse being unclean
The Cuyler was gaining Twas plain to be seen
So a long eleven inch, boys, we got ready for the chase
With two sixty eights boys, beside her we placed

7. Those two sixty eight bull dogs to bear her company
And very sharp teeth have those dogs of the sea.
But there's something to me which seems very strange—
That the Cuyler broke down when she got within range

8. Oh! the first prize we took was a Brig I don't know her name
Well loaded with stores and from New York she came.
We burned her and sank her so quickly you'll hear
Then straight for Havana steered the bold privateer

9. The next prize we took was a sch[oone]r well loaded with bread
What in the devil got into the President's head,
For to send us such biscuits, its a might fine thing
We have a good laugh, boys, then sit down and sing

10. The next prize we took was the Lapwing[24] as I will unfold
With a hold full of black diamonds which people call coal
With those in our bunkers we can tell Uncle Sam,
That we don't think his gunboats they are worth a d—n

—Finis—

---

[23] George Henry Preble (1816-1885), born in Portland, Maine, was a nephew of Commodore Edward Preble, "entered the Navy as a midshipman in 1835, commanded the *Katahdin* and the *St. Louis* during the Civil War, was promoted captain in 1867, commodore in 1871, and rear admiral in 1876, and was retired in 1878" (Barnhart, III:3247). Both James Maffitt and George Preble were moderately successful authors in later life. Preble devoted himself to history, including a book about the American flag entitled *Our Flag* (1871). Maffitt, on the other hand, produced the novel *Nautilus, or Cruising under Canvas* (1871).

[24] This *Lapwing* was evidently a common collier and not the New Bedford whaleship *Lapwing*, 432 tons, which was built in 1853 at Mattapoisett, Mass. On her wartime voyage she had sailed for the Indian Ocean on 14 June 1860 under Captain George H. Soule, was "sold at Mauritius in 1863" with no report of mishap at the hands of the Confederacy, and, "Renamed W.A. Farnsworth returned to whaling under the Hawaiian flag, 1876" (Starbuck, 577).

60. [Navy Song]
[We Ride Head to Wind…]

Beginning in the 1870s, Canadian mariner E. C. Sears served in the Royal Navy, the British, American, and Canadian merchant services, the New Bedford whaling schooner *Franklin,* and various coastal trades. His memoirs are full of schematic drawings and technical descriptions of naval architecture and ship's gear, and his original navy ballad is full of salty technical lingo about weighing anchor, setting sail, and clearing for action. The intended melody is unknown, but the meter is compatible with "The Coast of Peru" [#136], "The Dreadnought" [#36], and numerous other deepwater ballads.

[UNTITLED.] Memoirs and sketchbook of E.C. Sears, whaleman and mariner of Montreal, 3 vols., circa 1890-1930.

1. We ride head to wind, and the breeze whistles free
   The land is to windward, the sea's on our lee
   Man the bars, and heave short, of stoppers, heave round
   Clear the Jib, port your helm; now the anchor breaks ground

2. Lay aloft, you sail loosers! Man halliards and sheet!
   There's nothing can catch our fair lady so f[l]eet,
   We're bound for the uttermost rim of the day
   Lay down from aloft! Now sheet home, hoist away!

3. We are running off sounding, the wind hauls abeam;
   Along the horizon there comes a white gleam
   We'll take off the stu'nsails and still onward spin;
   So lower away now! Haul down and rig in

4. The wind comes ahead and the Jib falls aback;
   Now ready about! Tis the order to tack
   Hard-a-Lee! From the quarter deck echoes the call;
   It's raise tacks and sheets! Haul tight mainsail haul!

5. Up yonder to windward the clouds darkly frown
   Man clewlines and buntlines! Look lively! Clew down
   The gale is upon us with riot and route;
   'Loft topmen come cheer'ly! trice up and lay out

6. At last to the southward the swift gale has whirled.
   Once more to fair breezes our sails are unfurled;
   At the masthead the lookout swings wide to and fro
   Till the silence is rent with the warning, "sail ho!"

7. Then hark! The sharp beat of the hollow voiced drum;
   To Quarters! See yonder, the enemy's come
   Our colors break out, Oh the foe woe betide!
   To Quarters! Now silence! Cast loose and provide!

8. Run in, Serve and sponge! Load run out and Prime
   Now point ready, fire! There are smoke blood and Grime,
   But down comes her colors; she yields to our pluck;
   Raise cheer upon cheer! she is ours! She has struck

CHAPTER SEVEN
A Bonny Bunch of Roses
Napoleonic Ballads and Songs

Mardi 17 [July 1860]. *Brume é paisse. le Capitaine du Genet est venu à bord après dé juner et est resté à bord toute la journé e. un de ses hommes sachant jouer du violon, notre é quipage a dancé comme une bande de dé mons toute la Sainte Journé e.*

Tuesday 17 [July 1860]. Thick fog. The Captain of the Genet came aboard after lunch and stayed aboard all day. One of his men knew him to play the violin, [and] our crew danced like a bunch of demons the whole day long.

—Eugene A. Lepetit, ship *Josephine* of New Bedford, 1859-62.[1]

British and American sailors had mixed feelings about Bonaparte. The tragic-heroic Napoleonic paradigm remains intact in the many folksongs and even the traditional tunes associated with his name. Much of his career, including his downfall and exile, was commemorated in music—most notably by Beethoven (*Eroica Symphony*) and, much later, by Tchaikovsky (*1812 Overture*)—by those who despised him as a monstrous despot, venerated him as the military savior of France, feared him as the iron conqueror of Europe, or, like Beethoven, had cause to revise their assessment in midstream. The Irish musicians created dozens of songs and tunes on Napoleonic themes must have had equivocal views of Bonaparte that were as enigmatic as the Emperor himself. As Gaelic patriots they had cause to admire Bonaparte's challenge to British supremacy in Europe; yet, perhaps on romantic grounds, they were sympathetic to Josephine and Maria Louisa, who is cast as a grieving widow [e.g., "The Green Linnet," #66]. Certainly, ties of honor and blood required a sincere, if ironic, respect for the thousands of Irish foot soldiers, sailors, and marines in the Crown's service who took to field and sea against France, and the many who died heroes' deaths in the crusade to contain the Gallic Caesar.

American perceptions of Napoleon were no less ambivalent. The Anglo-Scottish linguistic, social, cultural, and institutional heritage of America strained under political rupture with Britain, yet as a de facto ally of France in the War of 1812, we Americans effectively sided with an imperialistic tyrant. He supplanted a populist Revolution we commonly regarded as the spiritual godchild of our own American Revolution (which, in turn, looked to France and Rousseau for its inspiration), and was the grand destroyer of its most meaningful achievements, obliterating the electoral franchise, judicial presumption of innocence, and other prerogatives of citizenship that "we hold to be self-evident" and on which our Constitution and Bill of Rights are explicitly predicated. In point of fact, before the United States actually declared war on England in 1812, France was no better to our merchant fleet on the high seas than Britain had been.

It may be this intriguingly equivocal quality of Napoleon-as-tragic-hero—as Champion and Destroyer—that accounts for the manufacture and popularity of these Napoleonic songs in the divided worlds of Ireland and America, where individualism and pluck are greatly admired, where despotism and tyranny are despised, and where political loyalties regarding King George and the Empire of the French were never clearly drawn.

---

[1] The "Genet" is actually the whaleship *Jeaennette* of New Bedford, Captain Hudson Winslow. The passage was translated from the French by Nancy Elizabeth Pick.

61. Bonaparte Crossing the Alps

Napoleon's arduous crossing of the Alps with a well-equipped army in a bold strike against Italy in 1800—for which Hannibal's invasion of Rome in 218 B.C.E. is the type—is the subject of countless artistic and literary interpretations commemorating the resourcefulness and military genius usually attributed to the Emperor. Napoleon's crossing of the Rhine—for which the type is Caesar's famed crossing of the Rubicon against Pompey in 49 B.C.E.—signifies his daring campaign against Prussia, Austria, and the German states during 1805-06, notable also for having precipitated Beethoven's change of views on Bonaparte. The hornpipe and march "Bonaparte Crossing the Alps" is mentioned by John Jones, steward, as having been played on the fiddle by seaman John J. Goss of Port Byron, New York, during off-duty hours aboard the whaleship *Eliza Adams* of New Bedford in 1852. A related tune called "Bonaparte Crossing the Rhine" (O'Neill #1824), with which "Bonaparte Crossing the Alps" has often been combined and with which it has understandably often been confused, is also known as "Listowel," after a town in County Kerry that in 1600 was the last Irish stronghold against Queen Elizabeth (Rees, v. 22, "Listowhill"). The Irish title is symbolic of the hopeless Irish stand opposing Tudor subjugation.

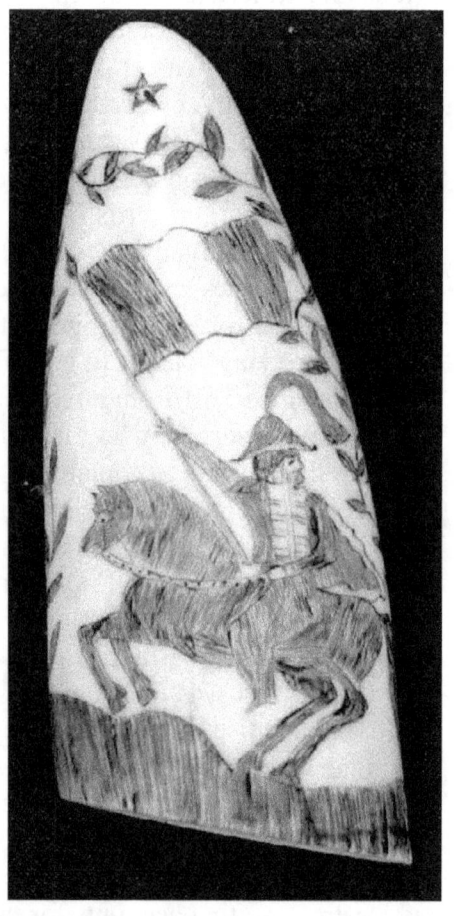

"NAPOLEON CROSSING THE ALPS," from American editions of the sheet music, where it was customarily printed with "Leander Crossing the Hellespont" (Baltimore: F.D. Benteen, circa 1839-51; Boston: Oliver Ditson, circa 1844-57; New York: William Hall & Son, circa 1848-58; also *The Singer's Companion,* New York, [1854] 1855, p. 187). See also "Napoleon [or Boney] Crossing the Alps" in Kennedy 1954, p. 7.

"BONAPARTE CROSSING THE RHINE [BONAPARTE'S MARCH CROSSING THE RHINE]," from undated American sheet music (New York: E. Riley, circa 1819-31; Firth & Hall, circa 1832-48; William Hall & Son, circa 1848-58; Philadelphia: Geo. Willig, circa 1819-53; Boston: C.H. Keith, circa 1834-46; Boston: G.P. Reed, circa 1839-49). Compare "Bonaparte Crossing the Rhine (Listowell)," O'Neill #1824.

62. Bonaparte on the Isle of St. Helena
[Boney's Defeat; Napoleon in Exile; The Island of St. Helena]

> When I descended the steps, and stood upon the spot where, for nineteen years, Napoleon had slept, I felt for a moment utterly lost in the confusion of thoughts and emotions occasioned by the novelty of my situation. I had pictures in my own mind all that I now saw; I had lingered with rapture over the pages of description; I had from early boyhood ardently cherished the hope of seeing what I had so long thought an read of; now, all my desires and aspirations were realized. It was no dream of fancy; no vision conjured up by youthful enthusiasm. I was in the grave of NAPOLEON! To be on ground thus famed in the world's history; to stand in the grave over which a nation had wept; to have the most ardent wish of my heart gratified beyond expectation, was an epoch in my life too novel and impressive ever to be erased from my memory.
>
> — J. Ross Browne, *Etchings of a Whaling Cruise* (1846).[2]

St. Helena, with its steep mountains, operatic landscape, and narrow harbor, far out in the South Atlantic, is the site of Napoleon's final exile and original burial. The desolate island was well known to whalers. Yankee whaleships, homeward bound, were among the few that had occasion to call there with any regularity, and the Emperor's tomb was still a popular attraction with whalemen long after his remains had been removed to the Invalides Palace in Paris in 1840. His last, humble residence, various scenes associated with his exile, and, most of all, his tomb were the frequent subjects of whalemen's drawings and scrimshaw; and this song about his final, solitary days was widely circulated at sea and on shore—appreciated perhaps because it embraces the moral weather-gage and seems to capture the ironic mystique of the Emperor's humiliation, reduced from his former glory as the scourge of Europe, mounted on splendid horseflesh at the head of vast armies (alternate images of Bonaparte that also appear on whalers' scrimshaw). The anonymous text, which, like many Napoleonic songs and tunes, may be of Irish origin, was often printed in English broadsides and songsters, sometimes with the title "The Island of St. Helena." It must have appeared shortly after Bonaparte's death in 1821, as Huntington locates two texts in journals of the whaleships *Galaxy* and *George* of Salem, circa 1827-29. The core melody has been fairly stable through oral transmission; however, minor variations are so ubiquitous that no two transcriptions exactly alike in the details. Whaleman Thomas Bennett's copy text of 1840 (below) has the distinction of having been made on the very spot, in the very year the Emperor's bones were ceremoniously transported back to France.

TUNE - Composite. Compare "Bony on the Isle of St Helena" in Warner, #143, p. 332; and "Napoleon Song," in Flanders & Brown, p. 111, which differ markedly in cadence.

---

[2] pp 462f. Somewhat naively, Browne is outraged that Bonaparte also had detractors: In the guest registers of Napoleon's tomb, "I found some good pieces of poetry, and a great deal of execrable doggerel. Of the latter description there were some verses that could not but excite indignation in any man of feeling, containing jests and jeers on the dead body of the illustrious emperor. One in particular, written by an officer in the British navy, had something actually fiendish in it. The utter heartlessness and moral depravity of a wretch who could profane the memory of the dead by a burlesque description in verse of his removal from the tomb, and a satire on his *fallen* nose, should brand him with infamy" (Ibid., 461).

"BONAPART ON THE ISLE OF ST HELENA." Thomas Bennett, second mate, ship *William Baker* of Warren, 1840: the text was evidently transcribed in conjunction with a visit to St. Helena while homeward bound, and is virtually identical with the version printed in the *Forget Me Not Songster*.

1. [Oh] Boney he is gone from the wars of all fighting
   He has gone to a place that he never took delight in
   Oh there he may sit down and tell the scenes he has seen, ah
   While forlorn he doth morn on the isle of St Helena

2. Louisa does morn for her husband departed
   She dreams when she sleeps and wakes broken hearted
   Not a friend to console her even there that might be with her
   But she mourns when she thinks of [the] isle of St Helena

3. Come all ye that have got your wealth and pray beware of ambition
   For it is a degree in faith that might change your condition
   But ye steadfast in time for what is to come ye know not
   For fear that you may be hanged Like he on the isle of St Helena

4. The rude rushing waves all around the shores are washing
   And the great billows heave and the wild rocks are dashing
   He may look to the moon of the great Mount Diana
   With his eyes over the waves that are around St Helena

5. No more in St Clouds he will be seen in such splendour
   Or go on with his crowds with the great Alexander
   For the young king of Rome and the prince of ganah
   Says he will bring his father home from the isle of St Helena

6. The parliaments of England
        and the holy alliance
   To a prisoner of war
        you may now bid defiance
   For your base intreagues
        and your base misdemeanors
   Have caused him to die
        on the isle of St. Helena.

   St. Helena Latt. 16. Long. 5.

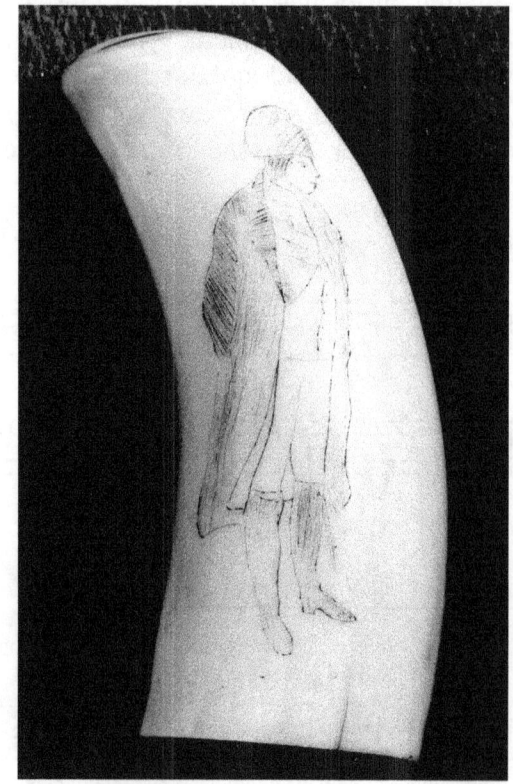

Illustration: Anonymous engraved scrimshaw on a sperm-whale tooth, 19th century. Kendall Collection, New Bedford Whaling Museum.

63. Bonny Bunch of Roses O
(Laws #J-5)

One interpretation is that "bunch of roses" refers to the British infantry and Royal Marines—"redcoats," whose exploits in the era of Trafalgar and Waterloo were among the proudest in their history and among the most costly in lives. "Bunch of roses" is also the title and forms part of the chorus of a Cape Horn halyard chantey that Hugill reports was current on sailing ships even in his time, with reference to which he subscribes to the "redcoats" theory. Another explanation consistent with Laws's description of the "Bonny Bunch of Roses" ballad is given by Huntington in connection with a complete text he collected from William Histed's copybook of the ship *Cortes* of New Bedford, circa 1847: "The bonny bunch of roses-o is England. The young Napoleon in the song is the Emperor's son by Marie Louise [Maria Louisa] of Austria about whom not very much is known except that he did not live very long, and most certainly did not follow in his father's footsteps to sting the bonny bunch of roses-o. Like 'The Green Linnet' [#66] this song is Irish and a lament for a lost cause" (Huntington 1964, 364f). Like so many Napoleonic songs, and despite its long publishing history in English broadsides and songsters, it does indeed appear to be of Irish origin and was, at least, cherished and preserved in Ireland—another example of Celtic equivocation about Bonaparte at a time when the British Empire was hardest pressed.

Inasmuch as the "Bonny Bunch of Roses" chantey (which has little but the title and a snippet of refrain in common with the ballad) has been collected only from British and Irish sources, Hugill was probably correct in insisting that it was probably more popular in British vessels than American. Likewise, not unexpectedly, the ballad has been encountered in tradition in Canada, but, though it was published in several editions of *The Forget Me Not Songster*, it has been found less often in the United States. That the text is relatively stable but the tune is not suggests that it may have been introduced into oral tradition from printed texts at various times in various places. The melody has certainly enjoyed its greatest popularity as a fiddle tune in Irish, Irish-Canadian, and Irish-American tradition, though it is scarce in anthologies of traditional Irish tunes.

It is not clear in the whaleman's corrupt American transcription of circa 1868-70 whether any sense of either meaning of "bunch of roses" is consciously retained. There is no warning about "England, Ireland, and Scotland" here, as there is in the fifth stanzas of the versions in the Histed manuscript and the *Forget Me Not Songster*. In Piper's text, Moscow is lost without reference to the threat of the British army; any reference to the Emperor himself—"On the isle of St. Helena, his body lies low / And you must soon follow after him / So beware of the bonny bunch of roses, O"—is absent; and there is no indication that the lyrics are about the Emperor's *son* and not about the Emperor himself. Thus, oddly, this text could be construed as narrating a childhood vision or portent of an ambitious would-be emperor doomed to failure, Napoleon Bonaparte himself.

TUNE - from S. Baring-Gould et al., *Songs of the West,* 1905, #27, where Baring-Gould says that despite "a great number of versions… the melody is always the same," and adds, "This was a favorite fo'castle song in the middle nineteenth century" (notes, p.9). Compare Huntington 1964, p.207, who cites "The Island of St. Helena" (*Journal of the Folk-Song Society,* 2:88-90) and "Bonaparte on St. Helena" (*Journal of American Folklore,* 35:358f).

"THE BONNY BUNCH OF ROSES O." George W. Piper, ship *Europa* of Edgartown, 1868-70. Regularized from unevenly transcribed stanzas.

1. By the border of the Ocean
   one morning in the month of June
   For to hear those warlike songsters
   their cheerful notes and dreadful tune
   I overheard a female talking
   Who seemed to be in grief and woe
   Conversing with young Bonaparte
   Concerning the bonny bunch of roses O

2. Then up steps Young Napoleon
   and takes his mother by the hand
   Saying Mother dear have patience
   until I am able to command
   Then I will take an army and
   through tremendous dangers
   Then I will conquer the universe I will go
   And return for the bonny bunch of roses O

3. When first I saw young Bonaparte
   down on his bended knees
   He asked the pardon of his father
   Who granted it to him most mournfully [mournful he][1]
   Dear father I will take an army
   and all over Europe I will go
   Then I will conquer Moscow
   Or die by the bonny bunch of roses O

4. He took five hundred thousand men
   and kings likewise to bear his train
   He was so well provided for that
   he could sweep this world all over again
   But when he came to Moscow
   He was overpowered by the driven snow
   When Moscow was a blazing he lost the bonny bunch of roses O

5. Now do believe my dearest mother
   now I lie on my dying bed
   If I had lived I would have been clever
   But now I droop my youthful head
   But when our bodies lie mouldering
   And over our bodies the weeping willows grow
   The deeds of great Napoleon
   Shall sing the bonny bunch of roses O

64. The Drummer Boy of Waterloo
(Laws #J-1)

The ambivalent Irish ballads of Napoleon stress the tragic-heroic fate of the Emperor himself, but, for obvious reasons of patriotism and fealty to the Crown, Napoleonic ballads and parlor songs from the English perspective tend to be unequivocal in vilifying Bonaparte and elevating British martyrs as symbols of the epic national effort to defeat the French tyrant. For example, General Sir John Moore (1761-1809), mortally wounded at his moment of triumph at La Coruña, was venerated as a hero long after Wellington's apotheosis at Waterloo and Napoleon's final days on St. Helena. A eulogy entitled "The Death of Moore" by an obscure poet named Frome was printed in the *Universal Songster* in the 1820s. Another, "The Burial of Sir John Moore," based on a prose piece that appeared in the *Edinburgh Annual Register* shortly after Moore's death, was written by an Irish-born Anglican priest, Charles Wolfe (1791-1823), and published anonymously in an Irish newspaper in 1817. Ten years later it was set to music by Thomas Williams (1761-1844) and issued as sheet music with the title "The Soldier's Grave: Monody on the Death of Sir John Moore"; another setting was composed for it by John Barnett (1802-1890). While this song has evidently not been collected from oral tradition, two similar copy texts of it were found in American whaling journals, one transcribed in 1846 by Rhode Islander John G. Marble in a volume that whalemen Stephen O. Hopkins and shipmate L.C. Richmond, Jr., took on a Gold Rush voyage to California in 1849; and the other by New Hampshireman George Wilbur Piper on a whaling voyage in the ship *Europa* of Edgartown, Marthas Vineyard, circa 1868-70.

Similarly, "The Orphan Boy," an English song with lyrics by Amelia [née Alderson] Opie (1769-1853), relates the sad tale of a young boy orphaned by his father's death in the Battle of the Nile, typifying in flowery profusion the heart-rending consequences of war as they affect an innocent youth, and enshrining the incident as the tragic-ironic counterpoint of Nelson's brilliant naval victory. This song, too, was written down by George Piper in his *Europa* copybook.

"Drummer Boy of Waterloo," an English broadside ballad concerning a lad killed in action at the moment of Britain's greatest victory over Napoleon, analogously styles the patriot's death as a symbol of all the young lives sacrificed in the service of king and country. This, and the bereavement of relatives safe at home in the England so nobly defended, constitute the wages of war and the price of victory. Neither song focuses upon valor in the field. But where "Orphan Boy" descends to bathos in maudlin pursuit of the orphan's fate (partly accounting for the song's obscurity and eventual demise), "Drummer Boy" becomes a kind of *memento mori*: sentimental, perhaps, but like Benjamin West's pieta of General Wolfe on the Plains of Abraham, a haunting reminder of the human cost that success in the field entails, and an elegy for all the young heroes whose lives were thusly spent. The same whaleman-scribe, George Piper, copied this ballad into his journal; so, too, did William Keith, a former whaleman serving in the crews of merchant schooners out of Boston around the same time. *The Singer's Gem* (1845) identifies the air as "Woodland Mary."

TUNE A - "Drummer Boy," from Helen Creighton, *Songs and Ballads from Nova Scotia,* 1932, #70, p. 145. Transposed from E♭ Major.

TUNE B - "The Drummer Boy of Waterloo," from Mary O. Eddy, *Ballads and Songs from Ohio,* 1939, #58, p. 163.

A.

"THE DRUMMER BOY OF WATERLOO." George W. Piper, ship *Europa* of Edgartown, 1868-70. Unlike text B, there are no repetitions indicated in the MS; A is otherwise identical to B and virtually identical to the lyrics in *The Forget Me Not Songster* except for the omission of punctuation, and minor variations as noted in italics in brackets.

1. When battle roused each warlike band
   And carnage loud her trumpets blew
   Young Edwin left his native land
   A drummer boy for Waterloo

2. His mother when his lips she pressed
   And bad her noble boy adieu
   With ring[ing] [*wringing*] hands and aching breast
   Beheld him march for Waterloo

3. But he who [*that*] knew no infant fears
   His knapsack o'er his shoulder threw
   And cried dear mother dry those tears
   Untill [*'Til*] I return from Waterloo

4. He went and e er the set of sun
   Beheld our arms the foe subdue
   The flash of death and[*the*] murderous gun
   Has laid him low at Waterloo

5. O comrades, comrades Edwin cried
   And proudly beamed his eye of blue
   Go tell my mother Edwin died
   A soldier's death at Waterloo

6. They laid [*placed*] his head upon his drum
   Beneath [*And 'neath*] the moonlight's mournful hue
   When night had stilled the battle's hum
   The dug his grave at Waterloo

B.

"THE DRUMMER BOY OF WATERLOO." George W. Piper, ship *Europa* of Edgartown, 1868-70. A second transcription by the same whaleman-scribe, identical to A except for minor variations in punctuation. The MS indicates that the second couplet of each quatrain is to be repeated when sung.

C.

"THE DRUMMER BOY OF WATERLOO." William Keith, whaling schooners *William Martin* of Boston and *Edith May* of Wellfleet, 1865-69; and merchant schooner *Cora Nash* of Boston, circa 1869-71. Similar to A and B.

65. Napoleon's Dream
[A Dream of Napoleon; Bonaparte's Dream]

The lyrics of this Irish ballad were printed on English broadsides and reprinted without music in the *American Songster* circa 1835, but while the song has been collected from tradition in the British Isles it has not survived in American tradition and this form of the melody has evidently never before been printed. In connection with "Bonaparte on the Isle of St. Helena" [#62] it was noted that whalemen were among the few outsiders to visit St. Helena, the remote volcanic island where Napoleon was exiled and buried. It is therefore not surprising that Napoleonic songs flourished with greater resiliency in the whale fishery than elsewhere. Several texts have emerged are in Yankee whaling manuscripts: one in William Histed's copybook of the ship *Cortes* of New Bedford, circa 1847, which Huntington calls "One Night Sad and Languid"; four in journals in the Kendall Collection, cited below; and "My Dream" [#12], a serious parody by whaleman Charles B. Swain, written circa 1857-59. An interesting feature in this one is, in the final stanza, the bitter calumny that Bonaparte heaps on the world in the name of freedom.

Tune: "Napoleon's Dream." Collected in Norfolk (England) by Sam Larner; recorded by Sam Larner and Parson's Hat (citations provided by Joan McDermott, Irish Traditional Music Archive, Dublin); transcribed by Mary Malloy.

A.

"NEAPOLONS DREAM." James S. Colton, bark *Tenedos* of New London, 1840-43. Substantively much like the other texts, but if this be a copy text from some printed source, it is extremely badly copied: the faulty orthography includes even the Emperor's name, and stanza 4 is severely flawed. Apostrophes have been added here to clarify the whaleman's unpunctuated past-participial contractions, otherwise transcribed as found.

1. One night sad & languish'd I went to my bed
   I scarce had reclin'd on my pillow
   When a vision supprizing came into my head
   I thought I was crossing the billows
   I thought as my vessel was dashed ore the Deepe
   I beheld the rude roocks that grew craggy & steepe
   Oh the rock where the willows are now seen to weepe
   Ore the grave of the once famed neapolon

2. I thought as my vessel she drew into the land
   Clad [   ] in Green I beheld his bold figure
   With a sword famed of war he grasped firm in his hand
   On his brow there sat valour & vigour
   Oh stranger he cried hast though ventured to me
   From the land of thy fathers who [boasts] we are free
   And If so a true story they tell unto me
   Concerning the once famed neapolon

3. Remember the year so immortal he cried
   When I crossed the wide alps fam'd in story
   With the legions of france for her sons were my pride
   And I led them to honor & glory
   On the plaines of merengo her tyrany I hurl'd
   And where on my banners their eagles unfurl'd
   It was the standard of freedom all over the world
   And the signal of fame cried neapolon

4. As a soldier I have borne both the heat & the cold
   And have marcht through the dreary
   By dark deeds of treachery I have been sold
   Though monarchs before me did tremble
   You rulers & princes your stations demean
   And like scorpions spit forth there venamous spleen
   But liberty all over the world will be seen
   As I woke from my dream cried neapolon

B.

"NAPOLEONS DREAM." Benjamin A. Freeman, bark *Sea Queen* of Westport, Mass., 1851-55. Similar to A, except: in stanza 1, the first line is the more standard "One night sad and *languid...*" and the rock *"hangs* craggy and steep." In stanza 2, "a *trumpet* of fame he held firm in his hand" and "thy forefathers boast *thou* art free." In stanza 3, "honour" is spelled in the British fashion. Stanza 4 opens with *"Like* a soldier...," standard in most texts (as in C and D) and (unlike A) is metrically resolved; but "stations you been" in B is undoubtedly a corruption.

4. Like a soldier I have borne both the heat & the cold
   And I've marched to the trumpet and symbol [cymbal]
   But by dark deeds of treachery I have been sold
   While Monarchs before me did tremble
   You rulers and princes your stations you been
   And like scorpions spit forth there venom and spleen
   But liberty all over the world shall remain
   As I woke from my dream cried Napoleon

C.

"BONAPARTES DREAM." Robert Nathaniel Hughson, bark *Java* of New Bedford, 1857-60. Quite different from the other texts in that C has a chorus and only three stanzas. Stanza 1 is similar to A, B, and D, but has "When a vision *surpressed* Came into my head / and *methought* I was crossing the billow"; and the rocks "*grows* craggy and steep." This is followed by a chorus comprised of a fragments of stanza 2 (see below). The remaining two stanzas, similar to texts A, B, and D, follow in sequence, unnumbered, with indications that the chorus is to be repeated after each. The Emperor's name is not spelled correctly here, either.

Chorus: ah Stranger he cries hast thou ventured to me
From the land of thy Fathers who boast they are free
If so a true story I will tell unto thee
Concerning that once Famed Napolean.

D.

"A DREAM OF NAPOLEON." George W. Piper, ship *Europa* of Edgartown, 1868-70. Of the four texts, this is the most nearly correctly rendered into English (though punctuation is almost entirely lacking), the most singable, and (by reason of spelling, syntax, versification, and rhyme scheme) the one most likely a straightforward copy from a printed source. Note "surprising" in stanza 2 (compare A, B, and C) but "symbol" (instead of *cymbal*) in stanza 4. Uniquely, the names *Napoleon* and *Marengo* are correctly spelled throughout; *honor, vigor,* and *valor* are spelled in the American fashion; and the transcription is rendered as 4 stanzas of 10 lines each, i.e., with the last two lines of each 8-line stanza being repeated as a refrain.

1. One night sad and languid I went to my bed
   I scarce had reclined on my pillow
   When a vision surprising came into my head
   Methought I was crossing a billows
   Methought as my vessel dashed over the deep
   I beheld that rude rock that grew craggy and steep
   The rock where the willow is seen now to weep
   Over the grave of that once famed Napoleon
   The rock where the willow is seen now to weep
   Over the grave of that once famed Napoleon

2. Methought as my vessel drew near to the land
   I beheld clad in green his bold figure
   A trumpet of fame he clasped firm in his hand
   On his brow there shown valor and vigor
   O stranger he cried hast though ventured to me
   From the land of thy fathers who boast they are free
   If so a true story I will tell unto thee
   Concerning that once famed Napoleon
   If so a true story I will tell unto thee
   Concerning that once famed Napoleon

3. Remember the year so immortal he cried
   When I crossed the rude Alps famed in story
   With the legions of France for her sons were my pride
   And I led them to honor and glory
   On the Plains of Marengo I tyranny hurled
   Where ever my banner it's eagle unfurl'd
   It was the standard of freedom all over the world
   And the signal of fame cried Napoleon
   It was the standard of freedom all over the world
   And the signal of fame cried Napoleon

4. Like a soldier I have suffered both the heat and the cold
   And have marched to the trumpet and symbol
   But by dark deeds of treachery I have been sold
   Though Monarchs I have caused for to tremble
   Now rulers and princes their stations demean
   Like scorpions they spit forth their venom and spleen
   But liberty all over the world shall be seen
   As I awoke from my dream of Napoleon
   But liberty all over the world shall be seen
   As I awoke from my dream of Napoleon

Note: The last two lines of the text in *The American Songster,* which was published with punctuation, reads "'But liberty soon o'er the world will be seen,' / As I woke from my dream, cried Napoleon," indicating that it was the Emperor's remark and (it seems) his own dream. Most of the unpunctuated manuscript texts, however, lacking the double quotation marks, are ambiguous and it is not clear who is doing the dreaming and who is waking. Version D, even without punctuation, is clear only up to a point: the awakening is from a dream *of* (that is, *about*) Napoleon, not *by* him (i.e., the narrator's dream, not Napoleon's); but what remains unclear in D is who has the vision of "liberty over this world," Napoleon or the narrator?

66. The Green Linnet
[Josephine's Lament]

A linnet is a songbird, generally gray or gray-brown in color, but scarlet in some seasons; the green linnet is posited here, somewhat enigmatically, as a kind of symbol of Bonaparte himself. The comparatively rare Napoleonic song, which has been collected from tradition in England and Ireland, survives in at least two texts in whaling manuscripts and, evidently, almost nowhere else in the United States. While it is cited by Barry in Maine, it is not reported by Laws or in any of the other American field collections; nor is it included in the O Lochlainn or Healy anthologies of Irish folk ballads. A popular reel of the same name (O'Neill #1262) is apparently unrelated.

William Histed's text from the whaler *Cortes* of New Bedford, circa 1847 (Huntington 1964, 211) offers an interesting comparison with the Rhode Island transcription here, which is of similar vintage. Lacking the sixth of Histed's seven verses,[3] there are textual variations in the remaining six, which are arranged in a different order and are not divided into stanzas. Histed's text also has an incongruous allusion to Napoleon in Virginia, absent in the version here. Both texts are clearly related to "Napoleon's Dream" [#65], not only with respect to snippets of phrasing imported from one to the other (the direction of influence is not known), but with images and larger themes in common.

"THE GREEN LINNET." Air transcribed by Mary Malloy from the singing of Joe Heaney (per the LP recording *Joe Heany*, Philo #2004, 1975), who learned it from Willie Clancy of Miltown Malbay, County Clare, Ireland.

"JOSEPHINE'S LAMENT." John G. and Lydia Marble, Warren, Rhode Island, circa 1846-47: inscribed in the journal of Stephen O. Hopkins, ship *Rosalie* of Warren, 1843, and (with L.C. Richmond, Jr.) bark *Perseverance* of Providence, 1849. Undifferentiated text here arranged into stanzas.

> 1. Curiosity bore a young native of Erin
>   To view the gay banks of the rijhn[4]
>   When an Emphress he saw and the robe she was wearing
>   All over with diamonds did shine
>   No goddess in splendor that ever yet was seen
>   Could equal this fair one so mild and so serene
>   In soft murmer she cried my sweet linet so green
>   Are you gon shall I never see you more

---

[3] "In great Waterloo where numbers lay sprawling / In every field high and low / Fame on her trumpets the Frenchmen were calling / Fresh laurels to place on her brow / Usurpers did tremble to hear that loud call / The third babe's fine new buildings did fall / Spaniards their fleet in the harbor did call / Are you gone will I never see you more"

[4] While the spelling of *Rhine* is inconsistent in the MS, this approximates the Dutch *Rijn*.

2. The crowned heads of Europe when you were in splendor
   They swore they'd have you submit
   But the Goddess of Freedom soon made them surrender
   And yield up their standard to your might
   Old Fredericks colors into France you did bring
   His offspring found shelter all underneath your wing
   My dearest Napolaen she sweetly did sing
   Are you gone shall I neve[r] see you more

3. The cold loft alps that so freely you passed oer
   That nature had placed in your way
   Maringo and Boliyo[5] around you did hover
   And Parris rejoiced on that day
   It grieves me the hardships that you did undergo
   Oer hills and loft mountains all covered with snow
   You[r] ballance of power and your courage laid low
   Are you gone that I shall ner see you more

4. The trumpet of war its loud blasts are a blowing
   We will march to the north with good will
   To set free the captives that are chained down in fetters
   We will use our exertions and skill
   We will travel on the wings of bright envied fame
   Transgressers then we will set all in a flame
   Because that their subjects do eat herbs on the plain
   Are you gone shall I ner see you more

5. What numbers of men they were eager to slay you
   But their malice you bore with a smile
   England and all Europe were sworn to betray you
   And the Mameluke sustained on the Nile
   Like Ravens for blood their fierce bosoms did burn
   The Orphans they slew and caused widows to mourn
   Oh Napoleon she cried will you never return
   Are you gone shall I ner see you more

6. I would travel all over the wild deserts of Arabia
   In hope to find some cure for my pain
   It is I would away to the isle of St Helena
   But reason teaches me tis in vain
   Ye critics come tell me come tell in time
   What nation I shall roam Napoleon to find
   Was he slain at Waterloo on the Elbe or the righe [Rhine]
   Are you gone shall I ner see you more

---

[5] The Histed MS has "That Marengo Saloney...."

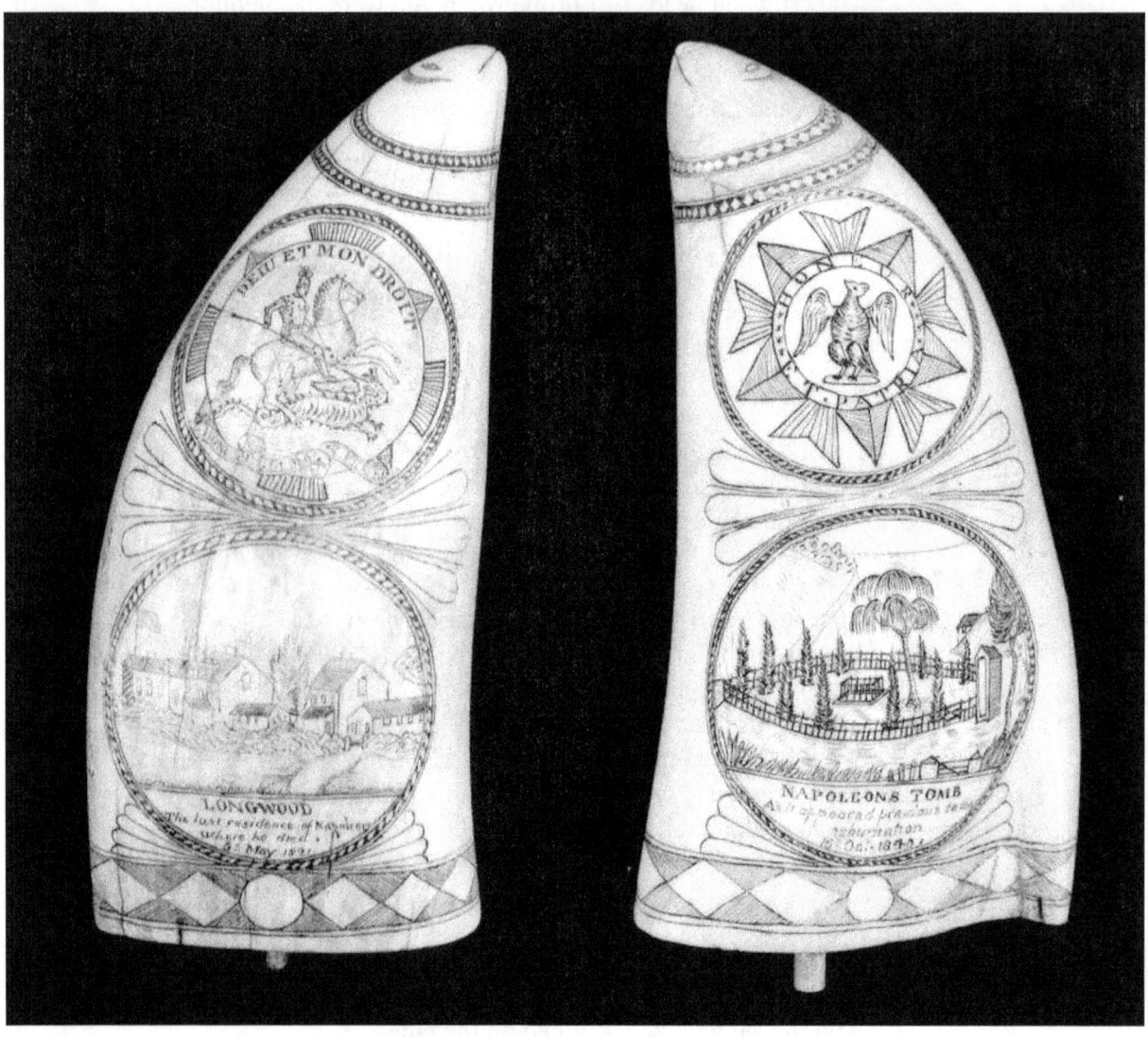

[*Napoleonic sites on St. Helena.*] Anonymous whalemen's scrimshaw on a pair of sperm-whale teeth, circa 1850. St. Helena, a remote island in the South Atlantic, was the site of Napoleon Bonaparte's final exile from 1815 until his death in 1821. Almost the only visitors in the 19th century were homeward-bound English and American whalers, Royal Navy warships, and British garrison troops returning from India and the Pacific. Even after the deposed Emperor's remains were moved to Paris in 1840, his tomb on St. Helena remained a popular attraction for mariners, no matter what their political opinions.

The tooth on the left is engraved with a landscape scene labeled "LONGWOOD / The last residence of Napoleon / Where he died / 5th May 1821," surmounted by a device of St. George, inscribed in Old French, "DIEU ET MON DROIT" ("God and My Right," the motto of the monarch of England, who was Queen Victoria at the time that the scrimshaw was made); and "HONI SOIT QUI MAL Y PENSE" ("shamed be he who thinks evil upon it," the motto of the English Order of the Garter). The other has a vignette labeled, "NAPOLEON'S TOMB / As it appeared previous to the exhumation 15th Oct. 1840," surmounted by an eagle device with the motto "HONOR ET PATRIA" ("Honor and Country"). The backs are elaborately inscribed, including "The cypress & willow / waves over his Tomb; By no tablet his name is exprest: / This unletter'd stone it points out / alone / The place where his ashes rest. / And the howling tempests angry voice / As it swells o'er the rolling wave Is the requiem song that sweeps / Along; / O'er the EMPEROR'S lonely / grave." Kendall Collection, New Bedford Whaling Museum. Photo by Eric Muller.

CHAPTER EIGHT
Tarry Trousers
Ballads of Lovers Lost and Lovers Spurned

O spirit of love, how quick and fresh art thou!
That notwithstanding thy capacity
Receiveth as the sea, nought enters there,
Of what validity and pitch soever,
But falls into abatement at low price,
Even in a minute!

— *Twelfth Night*

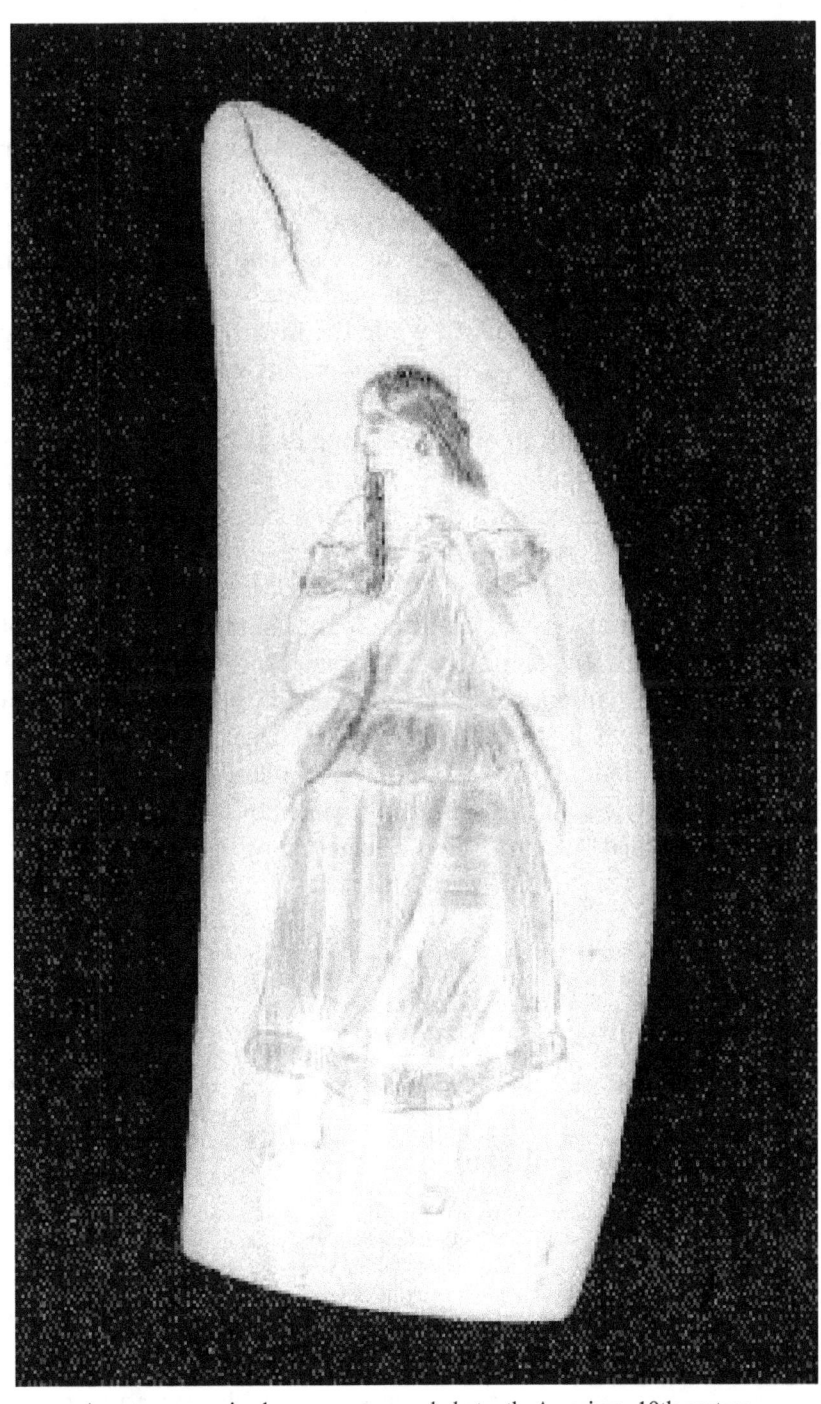

Anonymous scrimshaw on a sperm whale tooth, American, 19th century.
Kendall Collection, New Bedford Whaling Museum.

67. Lady Franklin's Lament
[Franklin's Crew; Sir John Franklin; A Sailor's Dream]
(Laws #K-9)

This ballad elegy concerns the lost Arctic expedition of Sir John Franklin and the prolonged search to discover its fate. His party of 129 sailed on 18 May 1845 in HMS *Erebus* and HMS *Terror* to search for a Northwest Passage, the discovery of which had been a British fixation since the era of Sir Martin Frobisher in the 1570s. Apart from one sighting in 1847, *Erebus* and *Terror* were not seen or heard from again. Their fate was confirmed in 1859 by a search party in the yacht *Fox,* commanded by Leopold M'Clintock, the *thirty-ninth* relief expedition dispatched from England and the United States in the intervening years. An expedition under Lieutenant Francis Schwatka of the U.S. Army, embarking from New York in the schooner *Eothan* in 1878, greatly expanded for M'Clintock's findings and provided artifactual corroboration [see #35].

When he sailed in 1845 Franklin was already a celebrated Arctic veteran.[1] His disappearance was one of the most sensational and persistent mysteries of the century, and when his death was finally discovered he was mourned as a national hero. The romantic dimensions of his quest, the gothic circumstances of his ordeal in the ice, the years of uncertainty, and finally the ballad, which canonized both his own suffering and his widow's back home, assured him epic stature in the popular imagination, in America no less than in England.

The ballad was created during the interval, while the mystery was as yet unsolved and when the explorer's wife, Lady Jane Franklin, had already won universal sympathy and respect for her tenacious encouragement and sponsorship of relief parties (it was she who later underwrote the M'Clintock expedition). The ballad first emerged around 1852 or '53,[2] and for several decades thereafter remained enormously popular among sailors, American whalemen in particular. Its obvious appeal was not only that it is narrated in the first person by a common seaman (whose station is indicated by his sleeping in a hammock, rather than a bunk, bed, berth, or cabin), but especially that it articulates keenly and powerfully the all-too-real and pertinent dangers to which mariners are perpetually subjected. It was an American whaleship that last spotted Franklin at the entrance to Lancaster Sound; it was mostly whalemen who had been to those regions before or who would ever go again. In an era when the ice floes of the Arctic Ocean and Beaufort Sea were the burgeoning bowhead whaling grounds for the Yankee fleet, Arctic whalemen no doubt felt an heroic kinship with the doughty explorer and the hapless sailors who accompanied him to the Frozen North. Accordingly, from the statistical frequency of its appearance in whalemen's journals, "Lady Franklin's Lament" seems to have been one of the most popular songs of all time

---

[1] Franklin (1786-1847) was a veteran of the campaigns at Trafalgar (1805) and New Orleans (1814), he commanded one of the vessels in an expedition to Spitsbergen (1818), and was appointed to lead subsequent explorations to the North American Arctic (1819-22, 1825-27). Rewarded with a knighthood (1829) and the governorship of Van Dieman's Land Colony (1838-43), he lobbied successfully to be appointed, under Crown auspices, to command a new expedition to seek a sea route across the Canadian Arctic to the Pacific. "M'Clintock found traces of the missing expedition in 1859, which confirmed previous rumors of its total destruction. From a paper containing an entry by Captain Fitzjames of the missing expedition, it was learned that Franklin died June 11, 1847, having the previous year penetrated to within 12 miles of the northern extremity of King William Land" (B. Smith 1889, 408). Colcord adds: "The last entry [in the journal] was made in April 1848; an Eskimo woman told Captain M'Clintock that after that 'the men fell down and died as they walked'" (Colcord 158).

[2] The evidence for a circa 1852 date is compelling. Most texts specifically mention some of the would-be rescuers by name, but none who rose to prominence after 1852, suggesting that the original authorship likely occurred around that time—that is, before subsequent developments could be incorporated. The reference to "three years ago" in text A seems to imply that the ballad may originally have been written as early as 1848; however, this is nullified by the phrase "seven long years have gone and past" in stanza 6 of the same text. Frequent mention of Franklin-search luminaries who had risen to prominence by 1852, combined with the conspicuous absence any whose involvement commenced *after* 1852-53, and the frequent reference to "seven years" in many texts, lends credence to 1852 as the probable date of authorship. This is consistent Colcord's remarks about her text, one of few that actually lacks the "seven years" component: "It is possible to fix with considerable accuracy the dates between which the… version must have been composed; it was after Captain Osborne [sic]… in 1852, and before Captain McClintock's [sic] discovery in 1859" (Colcord, 158).

onboard Yankee whaleships: in addition to the seven whalemen's texts reported here, Huntington reports another in a journal of the New Bedford bark *Morning Light,* circa 1861;[3] a ninth is found in Joseph P. Faulkner's narrative, *Eighteen Months in a Greenland Whaler* (1879). The melody is almost always some form of the traditional Irish air best known as "The Croppy Boy," after one of the most familiar texts to which it attaches; the same tune has also been used for many other ballads, including versions of "The Sailor Boy" ("My Love Willie") [#69] and "Oxford City" [#110].[4]

TUNE A - "Franklin's Crew," from Joanna C. Colcord, *Songs of American Sailormen,* 1938, p. 157. Compare B; O Lochlainn 1939 #56 (Ireland); "Sweet William," in Broadwood & Maitland, 74 (Worcestershire); "All on Spurn Point," in Broadwood & Maitland, 180 (Whitby, Yorkshire); and Doerflinger, 145 (tune from Greenleaf #145).

TUNE B - "The Sailor Boy," source unknown, learned at Yale University circa 1972: an ornamented form of tune A.

A.

"LADY FRANKLIN'S LAMENT." Robert N. Hughson, bark *Java* of New Bedford, 1857-60.

1. Come all you young and seamen bold / Thats Stood the storms of the briney flood,
   Give ear to these few lines I name / T'will put you in mind of a Sailors dream.

2. Twas homeward bound oer the briny deep / Slung in my hammock while fast asleep
   I dreamed a dream which I thought was true / Concerning Franklin and his bold crew.

3. And as we neared old Englands shore / I saw a Lady that did deplore
   She wept aloud and those words did say / Alas my Franklin is long away

4. Three years ago two ships of fame / Had bore my Franklin far oer the main
   With one hundred seamen with courage stout / To find the Northwestern passage out.

5. He sailed East and he sailed West, / On Greenlands coast where he thought best
   Till by gales of wind and driven snow / On mountains of ice their ships were drove.

---

[3] Collection of the Dukes County Historical Society, Edgartown, Marthas Vineyard (Huntington MS 271).

[4] The air has also been adopted for pieces of a more local nature, including a shipwreck ballad of indeterminate vintage from Whitby, the Yorkshire whaling port that was home to two famous seafarers, explorer James Cook and Arctic whaleman William Scoresby. While the ballad is widely distributed and versions of it have been collected from tradition in the British Isles and North America, it is mentioned only disparagingly by Firth, is not included in the Ashton anthology, and is not mentioned by Broadwood, Sabine-Gould, or O Lochlainn.

6. But seven long years have gone and past / And many a keen and bitter blast
   Blew oer the graves w[h]ere poor seamen fell / What the[y] endured no tongue can tell.

7. Those sad forebodings doth my heart pain / Since my long lost Husband crossed oer the main
   Ten thousand pounds would I freely give / On earth to know that my Franklin lives.

8. There was Captain Ross[5] of high renown / There is Grenell[6] Pursey[7] of Edgartown
   There was Captain Ingram[8] and as many more / Has long been cruising those Arctic shores.

9. Where lightnings flash and loud thunders roll / To find a passage around the North pole
   Its more than any man can do / With hearts undaunted and courage true.

10. In Baffins Bay where the whale fish blows / The fate of Franklin no farther goes
    Alas he's gone like as many more / Who has left their homes to return no more.

B.

"LADY FRANKLIN'S LAMENT." George M. Jones and Albert F. Handy, bark *Waverly* of New Bedford, 1859-63.

1. You seamen bold that have withstood / The storms that rage o're the briney flood
   Attend these liens that I will Name / It will put you in mind of a sailors dream

2. It was homeward bound whilst on the deep / Slung in my hammock I fell asleep
   I deamt a dream which I thought was true / Concerning Franklin and his bold crew

3. It was as we neared old englands shore / I saw a lady she did implore
   She wept aloud and they did say / Alas my Franklin is long away

4. Its three long years since two ships of fame / Did guide my Franklin across the main
   With one hundred seamen both bold and stout / To find a Northwestern passage out

---

[5] The allusion refers to either or both of two Arctic explorers of this name. Admiral Sir John Ross (1777-1856) commanded expeditions in search of the Northwest Passage in 1818 and 1829-33, the results of which were published and widely distributed. He conducted a search for Franklin during 1851-52, but was preceded in the field by his nephew, Sir James Clark Ross (1800-1862). The latter had served on earlier expeditions commanded by his uncle and by Parry (see footnote 11 below), commanded an Arctic expedition in HMS *Erebus* and HMS *Terror* during 1839-43 (results published 1847; credited with the discovery of the magnetic pole), and led a relief expedition for Franklin during 1848-49.

[6] Henry Grinnell (1797-1874) was a New York shipping magnate who sponsored two Franklin-search expeditions during 1850-51 and 1853-55. According to Pierre Berton, "at Lady Franklin's behest" Grinnell purchased two small vessels and "turned them over to the U.S. government so that they might be placed under navy discipline." Edwin De Haven commanded the first Grinnell Expedition in the *Advance,* with S.P. Griffin commanding the *Rescue;* but the expedition "is notable not so much for its commander ... (who discovered Grinnell Land), but for its chief medical officer... Elisha Kent Kane. This was the expedition that launched Kane into an orgy of Arctic exploration, that made him the best-known explorer of his day, and provided, through his own colorful accounts, the stimulus for future expeditions" (Berton, 175). The second Grinnell Expedition was organized privately without navy participation; Kane led it himself aboard the *Advance.* The names *Grenell* and *Granville* appearing in a few versions of the ballad—also probably *Randall* and *Cromwell*—are corruptions of *Grennell*.

[7] *Perey, Perry,* and *Pursey*: corruptions of William Penny, a Scottish whaling captain who participated in Franklin search expeditions from 1847 and commanded the brigs *Lady Franklin* and *Sophia* during 1850-51. Between voyages he was among the gray eminences who discussed, planned, argued about, and deployed various rescue attempts. Variant texts of the ballad represent him as *Perey, Perry,* and *Pursey,* in evident confusion with the greater fame of Sir William Edward *Parry* (1790-1855), who was much connected with Arctic exploration, was a member of the Sir John Ross expedition in 1818, and afterwards commanded several Arctic forays, but did not undertake a Franklin search of his own.

[8] *Ingram* must be a corruption of *Inglefield*, referring to Cdr. Edward A. Inglefield, R.N., inventor of the Inglefield anchor. On leave from the navy he made a foray into the Arctic in the *Isabel:* "Though he found no trace of Franklin, his discoveries on that brief summer voyage in 1852 were among the most significant made during the great search" (Pierre Berton, 235).

5. To find a passage round the north Pole / Where lightning flash and loud thunders role
   Tis more than any man can do / With hearts undaunted and courage true

6. This sad foreboding does give me pain / My long lost Franklin across the Main
   Ten thousand pounds I would freely give / To know if on earth that my Franklin lives

7. There's Captain Kelley[9] of cragburg town / And Randall[10] Perey[7] of high renown
   There's Captain Ross[5] and many more / Have long been cruising the Arctic shore

8. They sailed East and they sailed West / On Greenlands coast where they thought best
   Midst toil and danger they vainly strove / Till on Mountains of ice these two ships strove

9. In baffin bay where the whale does blow / The fate of Franklin no one does know
   Alass he's gone like many more / And left his friends to return no more

C.

"LADY FRANKLIN'S LAMENT." G.H. Prescott, ship *Ocean* of New Haven, 1860-61; and bark *Belle* of Fairhaven, 1861-62. The only song text transcribed in this journal (they were bound to the Arctic at the time), consisting of 10 stanzas: like D somewhat corrupt ("*four* ships"; "*four* hundred seamen") and localized ("one night as we neared the *Yarmouth* shore") ("Yarmouth *town*" in F). Stanza 6 seems to accommodate the knowledge that the entire party perished; nevertheless, stanza 7 reverts to a voice with Franklin's fate yet unknown, referring back to stanza 6 as "forebodings" (compare D, stanza 6). Excerpts epitomize significant departures from A and B. The last line of stanza 10 expresses the universality of Lady Franklin's distress.

6. But since that time many a year has past, / And many a keen & wintry blast,
   Sweeps o'er the graves where poor seamen fell, / Their dreadful suffering no tongue can tell.

7. Such sad forebodings do give me pain, / Because my husband is Across the Main.
   Ten thousand pounds I'd freely give, / To know on earth that my Franklin lives.

8. There's Capt Kane[11] of Seaborough Town / Brave Cromwell,[10] and Perry[11] of high renown,
   There's Capt Ross[5] and many more, / That long have been Crusing the Artic shores

10. In Baffins Bay where the Whalefish blows, / The fate of Franklin no one knows,
    Which causes many a heart to mourn, / And many a maid to weep for her lovers return.

D.

"LADY FRANKLIN'S LAMENT." George W. Piper, ship *Europa* of Edgartown, 1868-70. A text of 10 stanzas that, rather than being localized (as in D), is de-Anglicized ("and as we neared the *humble* shore"). Otherwise, like C, a fairly standard text, somewhat corrupt ("*three* ships of Fame"), with stanza 6 accommodating knowledge that the entire party perished, but without the reversion in stanza 7. Stanzas 8 and 9 reinforce the idea of Franklin's fate as a tragic certainty ("in vain they strove"; "Alas he has gone like many more / Who have left their homes to return no more"). Thus, Lady Franklin's tenacity in stanza 10 becomes ironic.

---

[9] *Kelley* and *Kellsey* likely refer to Captain Henry Kellett, commander of a Franklin search expedition launched by the British government in 1852, in which M'Clintock participated as a subsidiary commander. However, the names could conceivably refer to William Kennedy, commander of an earlier expedition financed by Lady Franklin herself during 1851-52.

[10] *Randall* and *Cromwell* are almost certainly corruptions of Grinnell (see footnote 6); however, *Cromwell* could possibly refer to Samuel G. Cresswell, a lieutenant in the *Investigator* on McClure's Franklin-search expedition of 1850-54. Cresswell's watercolors were published after his return to England in 1853, and his name might therefore have been familiar.

[11] Elisha Kent Kane (1820-1857) was a physician from Philadelphia who accompanied the first Grinnell Expedition (1850-53) as ship's surgeon and commanded the second Grinnell Expedition (1853-55) (see footnote 6).

7. There is Captain Osborne[12] of Scarboro Town / There is Granville[6] Park[13] of high renown
There is Captain Ross[5] and many more / Who have long been cruising the Arctic shore

10. And all along from day to day / Lady Franklin weeps and these words did say
Ten thousand pounds would I freely give / To know on Earth if my dear Franklin lives

E.

"LADY FRANKLIN'S LAMENT." Horace Wood, bark *Andrews* of New Bedford, 1866-67. Undistinguished text of 8 stanzas.

F.

"LADY FRANKLIN LAMENT." Charles D. Atherton, bark *Oak* of Nantucket, 1869. Fragmentary text of five and one half stanzas, quite similar to C and D.

6. There Captain Osbray[13] of Sebray town
Brave Perry[11] & Granville[7] of high renown

G.

"SIR JOHN FRANKLIN." Edward J. Kirwin, cooper, bark *William Gifford* of New Bedford, 1872-73. Standard text of 9 stanzas, similar to C and D; like D localized to Yarmouth and ending with the universal implications of the lady's distress (stanza 9). The transcription indicates that the last two lines of each stanza are to be repeated. Kirwin inscribed the text at the end: "June 2nd 1872 Bk. Wm. Gifford / at anchor in Papeete Tahiti / E.J. Kirwin / Just come from Eng[lish] ship / Golden Horn of London."

7. There is Capt. Kellsey[9] of Selborn town
And Cromwell and Perry[7] of high renown
There is Capt. Osbern[12] and many more
Long time has cruised the Arctic shore

9. In Baffin's bay where the right whale blows
The fate of Franklin no one knows
Caused many a wife to weep and mourn
For her long lost husband till he returns

H.

"LADY FRANKLIN'S LAMENT." Title entered (but no text given) by William H. Keith, schooners *William Martin* of Boston, *Edith May* of Wellfleet, *Cora Nash* of Boston, etc., circa 1865-71.

---

[12] Admiral Sherard Osborn (1822-1875) participated in two expeditions to relieve the Franklin party, his accounts of which were published in 1852 (establishing his fame) and 1856; he also wrote an account of the Franklin tragedy, published in 1859. Colcord errs in the spelling of his name, and mistakes the date of the publication of his book (1852) for his date of embarkation.

[13] Lieutenant M. T. Parkes was a mate in the *Enterprise* on a Franklin-search expedition commanded by Richard Collinson, and in that capacity led a subsidiary detachment to Melville Sound in 1852.

68. The Sailor Bride's Lament
[The Sailor's Bride; The Sailor and His Bride; The Sailor Boy's Bride]
(Laws #K-10)

This broadside ballad, with lyrics attributed to James H. Wooley, involves a wife who mourns her sailor-husband's death at sea. The text is remarkably stable, likely owing to wide dissemination of printed texts. In connection with her version, Flanders indicates that the poetry was first published without music as an undated broadside printed "at some time between 1860 and 1878"; and, in fact, Wolf sites three broadsides published in New York circa the 1860s, two issued by H. DeMarsan and another by Wrigley. However, the comparatively early date of whaleman George Edgar Mills's transcription, made at sea in 1858, indicates that either the ballad's broadside debut was a few years earlier than either Flanders or Wolf suspected, or it had already been published elsewhere by the time the broadsides appeared. Despite the usual titles given by the printers of these slip-ballads ("The Sailor Boy's Bride") and by traditional singers ("The Sailor's Bride"), both whalemen's texts are entitled "The Sailor Bride's Lament," suggesting a possible common source not among the printed versions yet discovered. Both of the young men who copied the lyrics into their whaling journals were New Hampshire men on New Bedford ships: of the known versions of the air, the one Flanders collected in Vermont would seem to be the most appropriate.

TUNE - "The Sailor's Bride," from Helen Hartness Flanders et al., *The New Green Mountain Songster,* 1939, 231f: "Sung by Mr. Horatio Luce, South Pomfret, Vermont, as learned from his father, Mr. Edwin A. Luce, Bridgewater, Vermont." The text has a chorus absent in the whalemen's transcriptions: "Trull, lull, lulla, lull, lull, lull, lullay / Trull, lull, lull, lulla, lull, lull, lullay... ," with the last two lines of the stanza repeated. This is similar to Eddy #34, where the chorus ("Tra, la, la... etc.") also repeats the last two lines of each stanza. Transposed from the key of A^b.

A.

"THE SAILOR BRIDE'S LAMENT." George Edgar Mills, third mate, bark *Aurora* of Westport, 1858. Similar to B, with variations signifying oral sources probably in both cases. Contrary to Flanders Eddy, no chorus is indicated.

B.

"THE SAILOR BRIDE'S LAMENT." George W. Piper, ship *Europa* of Edgartown, 1868-70. As in A, contrary to Flanders's version (5 stanzas) and Eddy's two (7 stanzas each), no chorus is indicated.

1. It was early spring and the year was young
   The flowers they bloomed and the birds they sung
   But not a bird was so happy as I
   For my sailor lad was sailing nigh

2. The morning star was shining still
   And the twilight beamed over the eastern hill
   My sailor lad and his lovely bride
   were walking by the ocean tide

3. It is scarce six months since were wed
   Alas how soon the moments fled
   For we must part at the dawning of the day
   When the proud ship bears my love away

4. Six months have passed and he came no more
   To his weeping bride on the ocean's shore
   the ship went down in a howling storm
   And the waves engulfed my sailors form

5. My sailor sleeps beneath the ocean wave
   And the mermaids sigh over his lonely grave
   His body is in the bottom of the sea
   And he weeps no more sad tears for me

6. O that I was a sleeping too
   Beneath the waves of ocean blue
   My soul to God my body in the sea
   And the white waves rolling over me

7. T'is Autumn now I am left alone
   The flowers have bloomed and the birds have flown
   But not a bird so sad as I
   For my sailor lad no more sails nigh

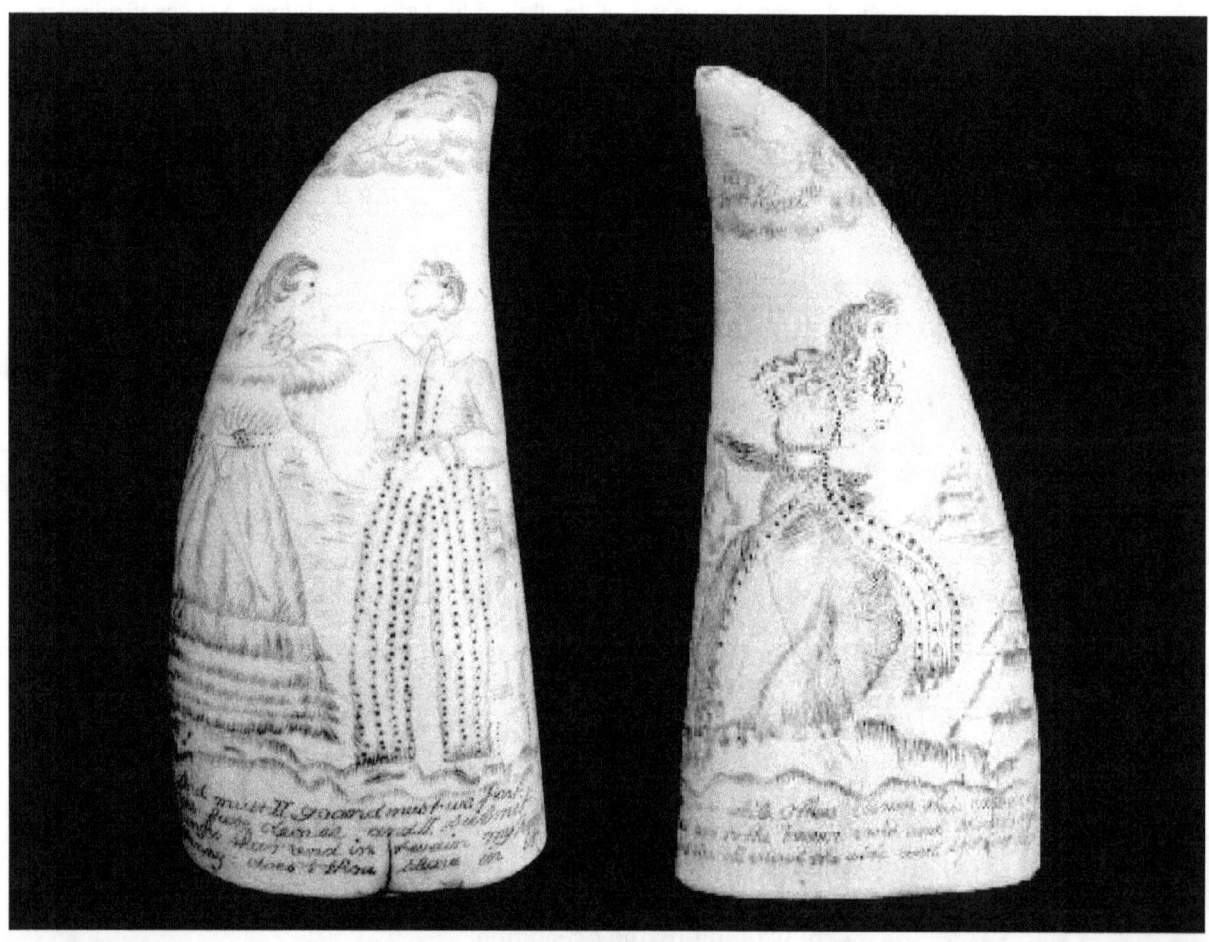

The Sailor's Farewell. Scrimshaw sperm whale tooth. The scene on the left features a loving couple at seaside with a ship in the offing, surmounted by a figure of Cupid in the clouds, inscribed below: "And I must go and we must part./Yes; fate decree that I submit/The pangs that rend in twain my heart. O Fanny; doesn't thou share in it." The other side has the same woman standing by the sea, her bodice rent, breast bared, and hair disheveled, inscribed: "And now while others drown their cares in sleep,/I will run to the barron [sic] roots and shores to weep,/And view all round wide and spacious deep." Signed and dated "Eng[raved] By / Wm. Read M[aster] M[ariner]. Dec. 14, 1834." Kendall Collection, New Bedford Whaling Museum.

69. The Sailor Boy
[My Love Willie; My Boy Willie; A Sailor's Trade; A Sailor's Life; Sweet William; Murmuring Side]
(Laws #K-12)

One of the most frequently encountered sailor ballads, concerning a woman's sea journey in search of her sailor-lover and her eventual discovery of his tragic fate. Its wide dissemination throughout the British Isles and North America was undoubtedly fueled by frequent publication in songsters and broadsides, but it has ever been held strongly in tradition. Among the recurrent narrative features, almost always present together in pure forms of this ballad, are the blue jacket and rosy cheeks, the woman's quest to find her sailor-lover, her interrogation of the sea captain, and her pleas to build a boat, to dig a grave, and to place symbolic markers on her tomb—all elements that are shared with many other ballads.[14] Details of the tunes vary significantly, but most seem at core to be variants of the same "Sweet William" tune that is known in Ireland as "The Croppy Boy" and was also the standard air for "Lady Franklin's Lament" [#67]. Vaughan Williams discusses affinities with "Died for Love" (ancestor of "There is a Tavern in the Town") and "Early, Early in the Spring" [#77], and notes a tune and portion of text shared with "Died for Love," while Creighton's tunes seem influenced by "The Dark-Eyed Sailor" [#89] and "O Waly, Waly" ("The River Is Wide").

TUNE A - "My Boy Willie" ("Sweet William") used for the text of "Franklin's Crew" (Colcord, 157): see "Lady Franklin's Lament" [#67, Tune A].

TUNE B - "The Sailor Boy" ("Sweet William"): see "Lady Franklin's Lament" [#67, Tune B].

TUNE C - "Sweet William," from Cecil J. Sharp, *One Hundred English Folk Songs,* 1916, #72, pp. 162f. Sharp's text, which begins "A sailor's life is a merry [dreary] life... " (compare text B below) is the original source of "The cowboy's [lumberman's] life is a dreary life... " (e.g., see Tinsley, 8-11; Lingenfelter & Dwyer, 347f).

TUNE D - "The Sailor Boy," from the singing of Mary Malloy, Seattle, Washington, 1979 (similar to her recording on *Songs of the Sea: The National Maritime Museum Festival of the Sea,* Folkways #FTS 37315, 1980): "Learned from the singing of Triona ni Dhomhnaill on the Bothy Band recording of *Out of the Wind, Into the Sun.*"

---

[14] If there be a single distinguishing stanza, it is the one that appears in text A as stanza 3, and in text B as stanza 2: "O father come build me a boat / So that on the ocean I may float / To watch the king's ships as they pass by / That I may enquire for my sailor boy."

A.

"MURMERING SIDE." Samuel Bunker, master, ship *Alexander* of Nantucket, 1824-27. Must be read phonetically.[15]

1. Down by one murmering river side / Where purling streams do gently glide
   I herd a fair maid making her moarn / How can I live and my true love gone

2. It was erley erley all in the spring / He went on board for to serve his king
   The rageing seas and the winds blue high / Which parted me and my sailor boy

3. If there be thurtey all in a roe / My love he bairs the gre[a]test show
   The greatest show amongst them all / I'l have my sailor or none at all

4. She built herself a little boat / That on the ocean she might float
   To view all ships as they pass by / Till I find out my young sailor boy

5. She had not sailed long on the deep / Five sail of frenchman she cha[n]ced to meat
   Come tell to me all ye jovi[a]l crew / Whether my love william is on board of you

6. No no fair maiden he is not here / For he is drownded poor soul I fear
   We pas[s]ed yon green Islands as we passed by / It was there we lost our young sailor boy

7. She wrung her hands and she tore her hair / Just like some woman in great dispair
   Her boat against the rocks she run / How can I live and my sailor gone

8. O this fair maid in fashon run / With pen and paper she wrote a song
   At every letter she dropped a tear / At every line she cried O my dear

9. O this fair maid on a sick bed fell / And for a doctor loudly did call
   My pain is great and I cannot live / And she descended unto her grave. *Finis.*

B.

"A SAILORS TRADE IS A ROVING LIFE." Thomas R. Bryant, Jr., ship *Elizabeth* of New Bedford, 1847.

1. A sailors trade is a roving life / Its robbed me of my own hearts delight
   He has gone and left me a while to mour / But I can wait till he does return

2. That short blue jacket he used to wear / His rosy cheeks and coal black hair
   His lips so smooth as the velvet fine / Ten thousand times he has kissed mine

3. Come father build me a little boat / That over the ocean I may float
   And every ship I do pass by / I will enquire for my sailor boy

4. She had no[t] sailed far over the deep / Before a king's ship she then did speak
   Captain Capt. come tell me true / Does my sweet William sail among [your crew]

---

[15] Discussing his garbled rendition of this transcription in *Songs the Whalemen Sang*, Huntington notes that the manuscript is damaged and is difficult to read. He evidently did not recognize the ballad and fails to provide a tune or citations. However, even 35 years later, much more of the text is plainly legible than Huntington was able to decipher, and some "missing" fragments can be interpolated from partially visible writing in the MS and the many close analogues collected elsewhere.

5. Oh no fair lady he is not here / He's lately died [   ] I fear
   On yon green isle as I did pass by / Twas there [that] I lost your sailor boy

6. She wrung her hands and she tore her hair / Like some female in deep despair
   And then her boat to the shore did run / Saying how can I live since my sailors gone

7. Come all ye young women that dress in white / Come all ye young men that take delight
   Come hoist your colours at half mast high / And help me to weep for the sailor boy

8. I will sit down and write a song / I will write it both sweet and long
   At every line I will drop one tear / At every verse where is my dear

9. Come dig me a grave both wide and deep / Place a marble stone at my head and feet
   And on my breast place a turtle dove / To let the world know that I died for love

C.

"A SAILOR'S TRADE." George W. Piper, ship *Europa* of Edgartown, 1868-70. Realigned from haphazard 3-line stanzas in the MS.

1. A sailor's trade is a weary life / So beware young maidens of this life
   They will leave you behind for to sigh and mourn / Not knowing when they will return

2. O father come build me a boat / So that on the ocean I may float
   To watch the king's ships as they pass by / That I may enquire for my sailor boy

3. She had not sailed long on the deep / when a jovial crew she chanced for to meet
   Come tell to me my jovial crew / Does my Willie sail on board of you

4. What kind of lad was your Willie dear / And what kind of clothes did your Willie wear
   A round about jacket of the Royal blue / He is easy known for his hart is true

5. O your love Willie he is not here / for he is drowned we all do fear
   By yon green island as we passed by / There we did loose a sailor boy

6. O she wrung her hands and she tore her hair / just like a maid all in deep despair
   Her little back against a rock she flung / Crying how can I live since my Willie's gone

7. She called for pen ink and paper too / that she might write her last adieu
   And at every word she dropped a tear / And at every line she cried farewell my dear

8. Come all you fair maids all dress in black / and all you sailors for my sake
   And the little cabin boy on the main mast high / For to mourn the loss of my sailor boy

9. Come dig my grave both long and deep / Place a marble slab at both head and feet
   And over my head place a turtle dove / For to show the world that I died for love

70. Mary's Dream
[Mary o' the Dee]
(Laws #K-20)

This was one of the more popular "Scottish lyric gems" and was often published in songsters, broadsides, sheet music, and musical anthologies. It has also been collected from oral tradition. Laws evidently considered it a folk song in the broadside-ballad canon; and Huntington found whalemen's texts in copybooks of the New Bedford ships *Frances Henrietta* (circa 1835) and *Cortes* (circa 1847). However, the lyrics were written circa 1772 by John Lowe (1750-1798), who is reputed to have composed a tune for it himself.[16] Helen Kendrick Johnson maintains that Lowe's melody is extinct and that the music customarily printed with the text (including in her own anthology) is a 19th-century substitute, but she may be mistaken about the extinction. An unattributed tune printed with Lowe's lyrics in *The American Musical Miscellany* in 1798 [A] is likely the original; and the customary air, the one that Johnson calls a substitute, appeared with Lowe's lyrics at least as early as 1802 in Thomson's *Select Collection of Original Scottish Airs* [B]. Creighton's tune (1971, #165), from tradition in New Brunswick, is yet a third manifestation.

TUNE A - "Mary's Dream," unattributed, from *The American Musical Miscellany,* 1798, p. 193.

TUNE B - "Mary's Dream," unattributed in G. Thomson, ed., *Select Collection of Original Scottish Airs,* 1802, Vol. 3, #7; also in *Davidson's Universal Melodist,* London, 1848, pp. 66 and 126 (printed twice). Compare *Lyric Gems of Scotland,* 2nd Series, Glasgow, circa 1875, p. 182.

---

[16] Lowe was the son of the gardener of Kenmore Castle in Galloway. Educated in theology and music at Edinburgh University, he was hired as tutor by the M'Ghie family at Airds, "an estate near the confluence of the Dee and the Ken" (Whitelaw, 151). During his tenure there, circa 1772, a man named Alexander Miller, "the accepted lover of Miss Mary M'Ghie" (*Lyric Gems,* 182), perished at sea, "and this gave occasion to the song which preserves Lowe's name" (loc. cit.). Lowe is supposed to have emigrated to America circa 1773 and taken orders in the Episcopal Church at Fredericksburg, Virginia, where he died in 1798.

"MARY'S DREAM." Benjamin Franklin Gallup, bark *South America* of New Bedford, 1857-59.

1. The moon had climbed the highest hill
     Which rises o'er the source of Dee
   And from the eastern sumit shed
     Her silvery light in tower & tree
   When Mary laid her down to sleep
     Her thoughts on Sandy far at sea
   When soft and low a voice she heard
     Saying, Mary weep no more for me

2. She from her pillow gently raised
     Her head to ask who there might be
   She saw young Sandy shivering stand
     With pallid cheek & hollow eye
   Oh Mary dear cold is my clay
     It lies beneath the stormy sea
   Far, far, from thee I sleep in death
     So, Mary weep no more for me

3. Three stormy nights and stormy days
     We tossed upon the raging main
   And long we strove our bark to save
     But all our striving was in vain
   And then when horror chilled my blood
     My heart was filled with love for thee
   The storm has passed and I'm at rest
     So, Mary weep no more for me

4. Now Mary dear thyself prepare,
     We soon shall meet upon that shore
   Where love is free from doubt & care
     And thou and I shall part no more
   Loud crew the cock, the spirit fled
     No more of Sandy she could see
   When soft the passing spirit said
     Sweet Mary weep no more for me

   Franklin Gallup
   Bark South America
   New Bedford, Mass.

71. The Maid On the Shore
[The Fair Maid by the Sea Shore; The Sea Captain]
(Laws #K-27)

A sea captain lures a woman onto his ship, and to escape his predatory intentions she sings a sweet song that causes the sailors to fall asleep, whereupon she robs the ship and returns safely to shore. The woman's powers of enchantment are reminiscent of the Sirens of Homer's *Odyssey*, and the ballad has been compared to "Lady Isabel and the Elf Knight" (Child #4), from which it is purported to derive, and "The Broomfield Hill" (Child #43), to which it is alleged to be closely related;[17] it has also been seen as incorporating supernatural elements[18] which are not readily apparent in most versions. Cazden traces Irish and Scottish textual and melodic precursors, and skeptically cites Alan Lomax's tenuous conjecture that the text "may have been translated from another language, or at least thought out in one" (Cazden 1982, 279), though opinion appears to be divided whether the original language might have been French or Irish Gaelic (Ibid, 278f), or, as Steve Gardham speculates, may "a remnant of an earlier broadside in the 17th-century style." He also reports a 14-stanza Scottish rendition from the 1820s (Crawford Collection, II:88). The occurrence of the ballad in tradition in the United States has been comparatively uncommon; most North American versions have been collected in the Maritime Provinces of Canada, and one in New York State. Huntington reports a text in Marshall Keith's journal of the bark *Ocean Rover* (1859). Many variants survive of the strangely haunting modal tune.

TUNE A - "The Sea Captain," from W. Roy Mackenzie, *Ballads and Sea Songs from Nova Scotia,* 1928, #19, pp. 74, 394f: "From the singing and recitation of Mrs. James Campbell, River John, Pictou County."

TUNE B - "The Sea Captain," from Helen Creighton, *Maritime Folk Songs,* 1961, p. 41: "Sung by Mrs. Greta Heighton, River John, N.S., Dr. Roy W. [sic] Mackenzie's informant."

TUNE C - "The Maiden Who Dwelt by the Shore," from Elizabeth Bristol Greenleaf and Grace Yarrow Mansfield, *Ballads and Sea Songs of Newfoundland,* 1933, #28, p. 63: "Sung by Annie Walters, Rocky Harbour, 1929."

---

[17] Mackenzie 74; Greenleaf 64; Creighton 1971, 111; Cazden 1982, 276; etc.

[18] Cazden 120f; Karpeles 274f.

"THE MAID ON THE SHORE O." George W. Piper, ship *Europa* of Edgartown, 1868-70. Most of the tunes require several repeats of the last line of each stanza. These repeats are represented in Piper's text as a "chorus," by which he apparently intends a sequence of last-line repeats that is somewhat different than in other versions. In some texts, the line "Let the winds blow high or blow low" (which occurs here in stanza 2) functions as a refrain in each stanza, lengthening the narrative commensurately.

1. There was a young maiden all crossed in love
   All crossed in love and despair O
   And all that she could find, for to ease her sad mind
   Was by walking alone on the shore O

Chorus: Shore, shore O
   And all that she could find
   For to ease her sad mind
   Was by walking alone on the shore O

2. There was a sea captain who followed the sea
   Let the winds blow high or blow low
   I will die, I will die, this sea captain did say
   If I dont get that maid on the shore O

3. Our captain has got jewels, our captain has got gold
   Our captain has got costly ware O
   Oh if you will come on board, we will treat you as well as we can
   And we will give you a sail Around the shore O

4. I will sing you a song, if it is pleasing to all
   Which caused the bold seamen to stare O
   She sung it so sweet, so neat and complete
   That she sung all the bold seamen to sleep O

5. She robbed him of all his jewels and gold
   And all of his costly ware O
   She stole his broad sword for to make her an oar
   And she paddled along to the shore O

6. Were my men all mad, were my men all drunk
   Or were they all deep in despair O
   She has robbed me of all of my jewels and gold
   And still she is a maid on that shore O

72. Green Beds
[Young Johnny; Johnny the Sailor; The Liverpool Landlady]
(Laws #K-36)

This ballad, about a sailor who outwits a golddigging innkeeper and her daughter, is a kind of sailors' wish fulfillment (other examples are "The Sailor and the Country Girl" [#73] and "The Jolly Sailor" [#97]). The whaleman's text is one of two distinct subspecies that differ markedly in meter and form but which Laws lumps together under a single heading. The specimen he actually quotes epitomizes the *other* type:

> Oh Johnny been on the sea,
> An' Johnny been on shore,
> And Johnny come to London,
> To where he's been before,
> Welcome home on shore, Johnny
> Welcome home from sea,
> Last night my daughter Polly
> Lay a-dreaming of thee.[19]

One of Mackenzie's texts, entitled "The Liverpool Landlady," which begins "I'll tell you a story, I'll not keep you long, / Concerning a sailor whose name it was John" (Laws #93A), typifies the more ballad-like form, of which whaleman George W. Piper's text is another example, the earliest yet recovered from manuscript or oral tradition.

TUNE - "Green Beds" ("The Liverpool Landlady"), from W. Roy Mackenzie, *Ballads and Songs from Nova Scotia*, 1928, #93, p.400: from two or more informants in River John, Pictou County, N.S. (see Mackenzie #93A and #93C).

"YOUNG JOHNNY." George W. Piper, ship *Europa* of Edgartown, 1868-70.

1. A story a story a story of one
   it is of a young sailor whose name it was John
   He had been a gallant voyage at sea and just returned on shore
   All ragged and ragged like on[e] that was poor

2. He went unto that place where he used to lay in
   He went to that place where he oftimes had been
   You are welcome home from sea
   Last night my daughter Polly was dreaming of thee

---

[19] Laws #K-36 (II:159). Mackenzie also notes that his text B does not fit the tune intended for his texts A and B. An adaptation or parody entitled "Jackson" relating to the Mexican War is given by Sandburg (430), cited by Laws as a version of his #K-36.

3. I will call down my daughter Polly and set her on your knee
   I will call down my daughter Polly and set her down by thee
   For my green bed[20] it is empty John and has been so this week
   And if you wish young Johnny you may go and take a restful sleep

4. O Johnny dear Johnny come tell unto me
   I hope that you have made a successful voyage at sea
   Young Johnny he then sighed and said by fortunes have been crossed
   All on the stormy ocean my ship and cargo was lost

5. Call down your daughter Polly and set her on my knee
   Call down your daughter Polly and set her down by me
   My daughter she is engaged John and cannot come to you
   Neither can I trust you for one glass or two

6. Young Johnny feeling sleepy he hung down his head
   He called for a candle to light him up to bed
   My green bed is engaged John and has been so this week
   And for some other lodgings poor Johnny you must seek

7. How much then do I owe you tell down it shall be paid
   How much then do I owe you tell down it shall be laid
   It is eight and forty shillings John you owe to me of old
   Young Johnny he pulled out two handfulls of gold

8. The sight of the gold made the old woman stare
   The sight of the gold made the old woman swear
   She cried forgive me Johnny for I was but in jest
   And don't you know young Johnny I love you the best

9. I will call down my daughter Polly and set her on your knee
   I will call down my daughter Polly and set her down by thee
   For my green bed it is empty John and has been so this week
   And if you wish young Johnny can go take a silent sleep

10. Before I would lie there I would lie in some dark cave
    Before I would lie there I would lie in my grave
    When a man has got money in his pockets it is then he can rant and roar
    For without that companion they will kick him out of doors

11. Come all you bold sailors who ploughs the raging main
    Who earns all of your money in thunder hail and rain
    I pray you take good care of it and lay it up in store
    For without that companion they will kick you out of doors

---

[20] There is no special slang significance to green bed as such, and there are many meanings of *green* that could explain the term in this context: inexperienced (as in *green hand* and *greenhorn*), foolish, bankrupt ("greenbonnet"), harlot ("green goose"), sexual sport ("green gown"), and other explicit sexual allusions ("green grocery"; "green grove"; "green meadow")—see Partridge, 352f, 1117f. The vernal sense of *green* implying fecundity and progeny is suggestive; but its sense as currency (from *greenbacks,* first issued by the U.S. government in the 1860s) was introduced chronologically too late for relevance here.

73. The Sailor and the Country Girl
[Jack Tar; The Saucy Sailor Boy; The Tarry Sailor]
(Laws #K-38)

This ballad expresses a kind of wish-fulfillment, where the sailor-protagonist takes revenge on the snobbery and discrimination of which Jack Tar is so often the victim. A seaman whose suit is rejected by because he is ragged, dirty, and poor, reveals to the woman that he is actually wealthy; she promptly declares her love and willingness to marry; but now *he* refuses *her* because she is only a country girl with no fortune [see also "Green Beds," #72]. The ballad was fairly widely distributed among sailors in the 19th and 20th centuries, with variations in format and meter; and it was sometimes pressed into service as a work song: Doerflinger reports it as a forecastle song for the leisure hours at sea, while Davis & Tozer and Hugill categorize their versions as pumping chanteys. Doerflinger's and Hugill's versions establish a sing-along chorus by repeating the last two lines of each stanza. With rare exceptions (e.g., Sharp 1932, #168), most forms of the air seem to be related, though, as Hugill points out, his chantey version is "reminiscent of" and may have been influenced by "My Darling Clementine": this would seem to relate the chantey most closely to Baring-Gould's ballad tune [Tune D].

TUNE A - "The Saucy Sailor," from Cecil J. Sharp, *One Hundred English Folk Songs,* 1916, #45, pp. 102f, xxxii: "The tune is a variant of the air traditionally associated with 'Chevy Chase.'" Compare Baring-Gould 1905, #21.

TUNE B - "The Saucy Sailor Boy," from Frederic J. Davis & Ferris Tozer, *Sailors' Songs and "Chanties,"* [1887], #39, p. 72, among "Songs for Pumping the Ship Out," sans chorus.

TUNE C - "Jack Tar," from William Main Doerflinger, *Songs of the Sailor and Lumberman,* [1951] 1971, p. 294: an English folk song dating from the eighteenth century; "The Nova Scotiaman who sang this version had learned it from his father, a deepwater captain." Here the last two lines of each stanza are repeated as a sing-along chorus.

TUNE D - "The Saucy Sailor," from S. Baring-Gould et al., *Songs of the West,* 1905, #21; transposed from E Major.

"THE SAILOR AND THE COUNTRY GIRL." George W. Piper, ship *Europa* of Edgartown, 1868-70. Two related inscriptions in Piper's hand, below the song text in the manuscript, are also reproduced here.

1. Come ye lovely come ye fair one
   Come ye lovely one to me
   Can you fancy a jolly sailor boy
   Just returned home from sea

2. No I cannot fancy a jolly sailor boy
   No I cannot fancy thee
   So begone you saucy sailor boy
   So begone you from me

3. For you are ragged love for you are dirty love
   For you smell so strong of tar
   So begone you dirty sailor boy
   So begone you Jack tar

4. If I am ragged love if I am dirty love
   If I smell so strong of tar
   I have got silver in my pockets love
   And gold in great store

5. As soon as she had heard these words
   On her bended knees did fall
   Crying forgive me you jolly sailor boy
   For I love you Jack tar

6. Do you think that I am foolish love
   Do you think that I am mad
   For to court a poor country girl
   When her fortune is so hard

7. No I will cross the briny ocean
   where the big fish do swim
   And if I do not find my love
   Some other girl shall wear the ring

The country girl to her father	Oh father father here is a sailor who wants for to stop here for the night
The father to the daughter	All right Sally put him in the barn and give him some hay

Jack's money comes hard and goes away easy

74. The Maiden's Pride Punished

   This countryside pastorale, not encountered elsewhere, draws on the same themes as "Green Beds" (Laws #K-36) [#72], "Will You Wed With a Tarry Sailor?" (Laws #K-37), and "The Sailor and the Country Girl" (Laws #K-38) [#73]. However, as it is not metrically compatible with any of these and cannot be sung to their tunes, it cannot be regarded as a mere variant but stands as a separate ballad, not reported by Laws. Even so, the thematic correspondence is precise: a humble laborer (in this case not a sailor but a rural cottager) courts a young woman, not herself of high station; she refuses him because he is poor and his prospects (and aroma) are unbecoming; he then reveals that he is actually wealthy and his poverty merely a ploy to test her love, whereupon she declares her love for him; to which he replies, "Adieu, proud Edith, you shall not be mine."

"THE MAIDEN'S PRIDE PUNISHED." Theodore D. Bartley, ship *California* of New Bedford, 1851-54.

1. Fair Edith if you will be mine
   You[r] cottage with the wreathing vine
   Shall be our home where love shall stay
   With folded wings the livelong day

2. Dost think I'd leave a city life
   To be a hum-drum cotager's wife
   Love in a cotage may do for thee
   But its wings must glisten with gems for me

3. Of the comforts of life I've enough and to spare
   And thou shalt be shielded from want and care
   Our home may be lowly but content with our lot
   we'll think the earth holds not a loveless spot

4. No more sir Tis useless thus talking to me
   A wealthy mans bride I'm determined to be
   I thought your Rich uncle had made you his heir
   The world said he had — 'tis to[o] bad I declare

5. If you were but rich as I hoped you would prove
   I known no one I could so easily love
   But tis folly thus balancing love against pride
   The latter has conquered I'll not be your bride

6. I go then fair Edith since you'll not be mine
   With joy and forever thy love I resign
   My coffers tis true are o'erflowing with gold
   Yet I covet a heart that cannot be sold

7. The world was right when it said I was heir
   To my uncle's wealth for with fatherly care
   He settled on me all his bank stock and rents
   And enjoined me to marry a woman of sense

8. Adieu proud Edith you shall not be mine
   But there's one that I wot of I know will decide
   To dwell in my cot without prospect of wealth
   Save that and its owner my own humble self

75. Bright Phoebe
[Phoebe; The Down-East Maid]

The narrative here turns tables on the customary tragic sailor-ballad scenario. Most often it is the woman who, left behind when her sailor-lad ships out, is left to mourn when she discovers he has perished. However, in this case the sailor returns from a voyage intending to marry his lady-love only to find that she died during his absence. Huntington gives a text from the New Bedford ship *Cortes* (1847), Creighton collected versions in the Maritime Provinces, and Cazden reports others from Maine and Minnesota; thus, the ballad appears to have been fairly widely distributed in North America and is therefore unaccountably absent from the Laws's taxonomy. One of Creighton's texts (p. 97) is metrically incompatible with the others; her other version (p. 96), is remarkably close to the whaleman's text here, which was transcribed at sea 110 years earlier. Both were clearly copied down from singing, and comparison reveals a classic instance of the kinds of variations in syntax, phrasing, nomenclature, and rationale that one might optimally expect to encounter in a ballad alive in tradition for well over a century. The first two stanzas of each are echoes of one another, the story is essentially the same in each case (with some significantly divergent implications), they share narrative conventions, have phrases in common, and express essentially the same sentiments; yet, stanza by stanza, the two texts really are quite different.[1]

TUNE - "Bright Phoebe," composite (compare Cazden 1958, 87; and Cazden, *Songs of the Catskille,* 1982, 260. At core it is the same melody as (and perhaps the ancestor of) Creighton's bizarre, highly ornamented tunes from Maritime Canada. Some passages are strongly reminiscent of "Greensleeves"; others of "The Days of 'Forty-Nine.".

"BRIGHT PHOEBE." Richard C. Reynolds, boatsteerer, ship *Janus* of New Bedford, 1842-44.

1. Twas erly in the month of May
   Just at the dawning of the day
   I heard a young man sigh and say
   He had lost his onely jewel

2. Bright phoebe was my true lover
   Whose beauty did my heart enflame
   Scarse could you find as fair a dame
   Go search this wide world over

3. My love and i we did agree
   That shurely maried we would be
   And when i did return again
   To bind that solem bargan

4. But when i did return again
   Death had my dear companion slain
   The pride and beauty of her fame
   In deaths cold grave lay mouldering

5. I wish I never had returned on shore
   Nor seen my native land no more
   But died whear bilows loud did roar
   Since fortune proved so cruel

6. I am ondone what shall i do
   I will be like some forsaken hue
   I will reign loves vallies through and through
   And spend my days in mourning

7. I will go unto some lonesome place
   Whear i can see no human face
   I will spend the renent of my days
   In morning for bright phoebe

76. Tarry Trousers
[The Mother and Daughter]

This ballad-like song expresses the familiar theme of a parent's opposition to the daughter's union with a sailor, in this case a lad on his way to fight in a foreign war. Palmer dates it to 1820 or earlier, based on a text appearing in *The New Skylark,* printed in London by J. Evans around that time; but Steve Gardham reports two Evans editions in the Madden Collection that may date from 1800 or earlier. Laws mentions it but did not consider it a proper ballad, probably because it failed to satisfy his criteria for telling a full-scale story. Huntington reports two texts in journals of New Bedford ships, the *Cortes* (circa 1847), where the transcription is similar to whalemen's text B here, and the *Nauticon* (circa 1848), whereof the structure and meter vary significantly.[21]

TUNE A - Learned from the singing of Ellen Cohn, New Haven, Connecticut and Sharon, Massachusetts: virtually identical to a version collected by Ralph Vaughan Williams in 1904 (Palmer 1973, #2, p. 9; JFS II:153) except for the difference of one note (this one is in the Mixolydian mode; the Vaughan Williams tune is in the Dorian mode).

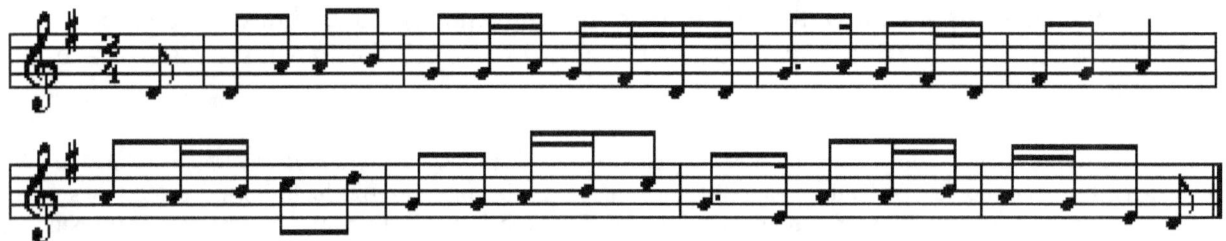

TUNE B - " Tarry Trousers," from Cecil J. Sharp, *English Folk-Songs from the Southern Appalachians,* 1932, #133, II:168: "Sung by Mrs. Lawson Grey at Montvale, Va., June 4, 1918."

A.

"WIDOW'S DAUGHTER." Richard C. Reynolds, boatsteerer, ship *Janus* of New Bedford, 1842-44. A corrupt text nevertheless distinctive for its last stanza having been Americanized.

1. As I walked out one fair days morning
   Down by the river side so dear
   O their I espy'd a tender mother
   Talking to her daughter dear

2. O daughter O daughter I advise you for to marry
   Not to tarry a single life any more
   Tis O my dearest mamy I had a little rather tarry
   Until my Sailor returns on shore

---

[21] While other specimens of the ballad have 4-line stanzas conforming to the meter of texts A and B here, and are accordingly compatible and the tunes virtually interchangeable, the *Nauticon* version (titled in the manuscript "The Mother's Admonition") has 6-line stanzas and is distinctive enough that it might justifiably be regarded as a different song on a similar theme.

3. Sailors you know they are apt for to ramble
   Away to some Foreign Contries they'll go
   First they will court you and then they'll leave you
   And that will prove your overthrow

4. O mamy i suppose you would have me wed a farmer
   Not to enjoy my own hearts delight
   But give to me the lad with his tary hat and trousers
   Shines to me like diamonds so bright

5. O dont you [k]now the war is declared
   And he is the lad that is forced for to go
   All for to cross the cruel ocean
   Whear the storms and winds do blow

6. Polly she loth to be contented
   Tears from her eyes like fountains do flow
   O stay at home my own dearest Billy
   O stay at home and dont you go

7. The anchors are a weighing and the billows are roaring
   And polly i have come to take my leaf [leave]
   And since we have been hear no longer on the seas roaming
   Tis O my charming girl dont you grieve

8. O dont you hear the great guns roar and rattle
   And the small arms do make such a noise
   While Billy he stands in the front of the battle
   Crying fight on my brave yankee boys

B.

"THE MOTHER'S DAUGHTER." George W. Piper, ship *Europa* of Edgartown, 1868-70. A remarkably complete text distinctive for its happy ending, perhaps copied from a broadside or other printed source.

1. As I walked out one fine summer's morning
   For to take the pure and the pleasant air
   There I overheard a tender hearted mother
   Talking to her daughter dear

2. O daughter O daughter I would have you for to marry
   And to lead a single life no more
   O mother dear mother I would much rather tarry
   Until my bold sailor returns on shore

3. I suppose that you would have me to marry some farmer
   And not the man of my heart's delight
   But it is give me the sailor with his tarry tarry trousers
   That shines to me like diamonds bright

4. I suppose that you would have me to marry some farmer
   One who is always digging dirt
   But I will marry my jovial hearted sailor
   Although he wears a ruffled shirt

5. I suppose that you would have me to marry some farmer
   One who is always following the plough
   But I will marry my true hearted sailor
   If I have to wait ten years from now

6. O sailors you know are apt to ramble
   Unto some foreign ports they will go
   And then they will leave you quite broken hearted
   Which will prove your overthrow

7. And while this couple stood together talking
   Up steps a bright young sailor lad
   He cries out Polly O fair you well Polly
   O fare you well for the seas I am bound

8. She laid her hand upon her true lover's bosom
   While the tears from her eyes did flow
   She cries out Willie O stay at home Willie
   O stay at home for the seas dont go

9. O war it is declared against our country
   O I you know for one must go
   For to cross the wide and watery ocean
   Where the stormy winds do blow

10. O the wind it is a blowing and the anchor is a heaving
    And our ship will shortly leave
    And since it is so I can no longer tarry
    O my charming girl dont grieve

11. The war it was a raging and the cannons were rattling
    And the small arms did make noise
    When Polly dreamt she saw her true lover in the heights of the battle
    She cried fight on brave sailor boy

12. Now the war it is over and Polly she is married
    She is married to the man of her own heart's delight
    O see how snug and trim he keeps her
    All dressed in silk like a sailor's wife

CHAPTER NINE
Love Impeded
Ballads of Family Opposition to Lovers

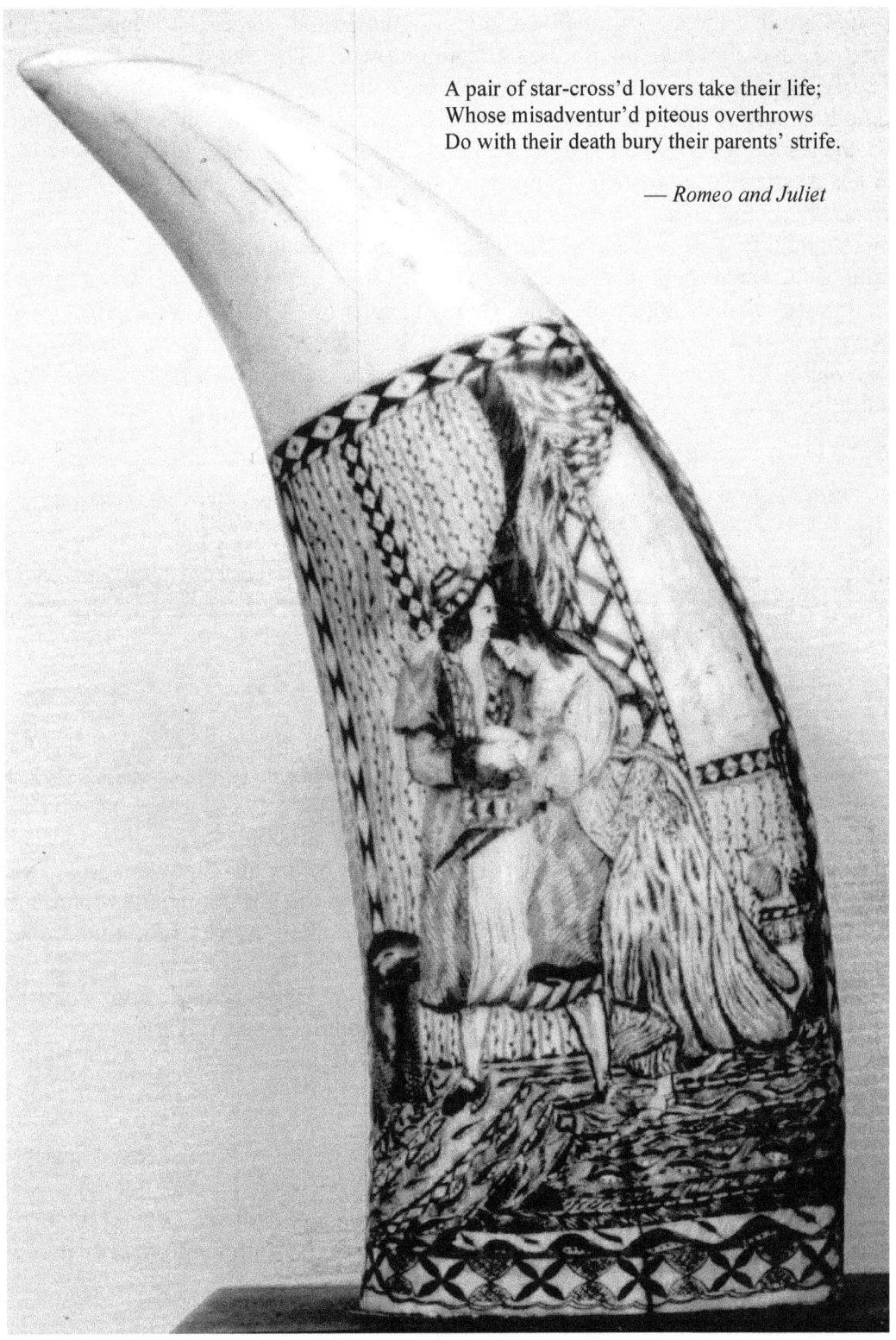

> A pair of star-cross'd lovers take their life;
> Whose misadventur'd piteous overthrows
> Do with their death bury their parents' strife.
>
> — *Romeo and Juliet*

Romeo and Juliet. Scrimshaw on a sperm whale tooth by seaman William A. Gilpin of Wilmington, Delaware, who made voyages in the whaleships *Ceres* of Wilmington (1834-37) and *Jason* of New London, Connecticut (1841-42). New Bedford Whaling Museum; from the estate of Captain Michael Rodgers.

77. Early, Early in the Spring
(Laws #M-1)

This ballad has a mixed ancestry. Belden traces it to a 17th-century blackletter broadside, Sharp points out that the setting of Logan's text is the British siege of Cartagena in 1793, and most versions have elements and phrases in common with "The Sailor Boy" [#69], from which "Early, Early" may also derive and to any of the tunes for which it may be sung. But the whaleman's rendition here is significant for its departure from the usual outcome. Until the last stanza, it follows the standard exposition as described by Malcolm Laws: "The sailor keeps writing to the girl who has promised to marry him, but gets no answer. When he returns, her father announces her marriage to another man. She blames her father for keeping the sailor's letters from her, and disclaims culpability." But then, instead of his giving instructions for his burial and thereby foreordaining the usual tragic conclusion to the deception, here the woman vows to forsake her family and possessions to follow the sailor (in the manner of "The House Carpenter," "Wraggle-Taggle Gypsies," and "Gypsy Davy"). Thus, the Sailor Deceived of mainstream versions here becomes a Sailor Vindicated, resulting in quite a different ballad with a particularly nautical bias [see "The Jolly Sailor," #97]. The tunes vary widely in tradition.

TUNE A - "Early, Early in the Spring," from Cecil J. Sharp, *English Folk-Songs from the Southern Appalachians*, 1932, #125E, II:154: "Sung by Mrs. Fanny Coffey at White Rock, Va., May 8, 1918."

TUNE B - "The Sailor Boy," from the singing of Mary Malloy after Triona ni Dhomhnaill. See song #69.

"SONG." George W. Piper, ship *Europa* of Edgartown, 1868-70. Realigned from seven 2-line stanzas in the MS.

1. It was early, early in the spring
   I shipped on board for to serve my king
   Leaving my dearest dear behind
   who oftimes told me her heart was mine

2. In writing letters to my dear
   Not one word from her could I hear
   Until I arrived at her fathers hall
   And so loud so loudly for her I called

3. My daughter is married you must know
   My daughter is married long time ago
   My daughter is maried for the term of life
   So go go young man seek some other wife

4. Cursed be all gold and all silver too
   Cur[s]ed be the girl that wont prove true
   Cursed be the girl that would promise me
   And foresaken her vows for more richery

5. I will turn back turn back from whence I came
   I will sail those sea_dover again
   I will sail those seas till the day I die
   I will split those waves that run mountains high

6. Turn back turn back my dearest dear
   if you have wrote letters I got none
   It was fathers fault and none of mine
   So dont be hard on the female kind

7. I love my father I love my mother
   I love my sister likewise my brother
   I love my friends and relations too
   I will forsake them all love and follow you

78. William and Harriet
[Harriet and Young William; The Rich Merchant]
(Laws #M-7)

Captain Jonathan Whalon evidently had some trouble transcribing the text of this ballad, as he struggled to resolve the meter and rhyme schemes of stanzas 7 and 8. As his spelling and handwriting indicate, he was no literary paragon in any case, and he never got the lyrics quite right. Nevertheless, the jumble is clear evidence that he could not have copied it from a printed text but seems to have been trying to recall it from memory as he went along, and it emerges a fairly respectable specimen of a broadside rare in tradition and known in only a few texts (most of them printed broadsides). The story concerns lovers who escape her parents' opposition by shipping to sea together—she disguised as a man—only to be shipwrecked and stranded on a barren island, where they perish. There is little actual nautical content that might have appealed to a sailor, and the fate of the lovers is not the sort of thing sailors usually liked to think about, so it comes as no surprise that Whalon's text is the only one that has come to light from a nautical source. Despite its sometime appearance in printed broadsides, the tune remains elusive.

[UNTITLED.] Jonathan Whalon, master, ship *Henry Kneeland* of New Bedford, 1854-56. A labored text in which in a continuous act of transcription the diarist struck stanza 7 in its entirety, rewrote it immediately below, struck two lines out of this second attempt, yet failed to resolve the stanza with a substitute line, which he began but did not complete (the struck passages are given here in italics inside brackets). The "come-all-ye" at the conclusion is down right bizarre, as it invokes "all you young people who may this way pass bye" to memorialize the unfortunate couple by shedding a tear from one "bleeding eye" and pointing to the spot where they died.

1. In the city of London a rich merchant did dwell
   Hh [he] had an only daughter whom a sailor loved well
   Because she was handsome he loved her so true
   Hhr [her] parents gave her orders to bid him adeu

2. O parents cruel parents dont be so unkind
   To banish sweet William far out of my mind
   The unruly daughter confined you shall be
   I ll send your love a sailing far over the sea

3. Its Harriet was a sitting in her bower one day
   As William was a walking he herd her to sing
   She sung like a Linnet and appeared like a dove
   And the song the [she] sung was concerning her love

4. As William was a sitting in his bower one day
   As Harriet was a walking he herd her to say
   Since my cruel parents and yours does agree
   To send you a saling far over the sea

5. And since they have been so cruel as to serve me so
   I will dress myself in some clothes along with I ll go
   I ll inlist as your shipmate and do all I can
   I ll adventure my live as some jovial young man

6. as they wer a sailing unto some fairer shore
   the winds they did whisel and the billows loud did roar
   the ship she sank down to the bottom of the sea
   and upon an island was cast william and she

7. [*They wanderd a land some place for to lived*
   having nothing to eat and no whire to ly down
   and hunger increasing and deth drawing ny
   they foled in each others arms contentedly to dye]

   What more could have been bolder to bid this wourld adeau
   [*They wandered about some place for to find*
   Having nothing to eat nor onwhere to lie down]
   She cride O cruel father how could you be so unkind
   To banish your daughter far and of[f] your…
   … …

8. And hunger increasing and death drawing nigh
   They folded in each others arms contentedly to dye
   What more could have been bolder to bid this world adeu
   They folded in each others arms like lovers so true

9. Come all you young people who may this way pass bye
   Shed one tear of pity from your bleeding eye
   Shed one tear of pity and point to the place
   Where William and Harriet lies mouldering in the dust

79. The Banks of Sweet Dundee
[The Banks of Dundee; Undaunted Mary]
(Laws #M-25)

A rare annotation appended to boatsteerer Richard C. Reynolds's incomplete transcription of this ballad (text A) is of one the most revealing aspects of any text copied down in whalemen's journals, as it provides a clue, in the diarist's own hand, to the methods by which such songs were sometimes gathered on shipboard. The narrative concerns a young woman whose wealthy uncle and guardian opposes her liaison with a ploughboy in preference to the squire he selected for her. The uncle summons a press gang, who haul the lad off to sea or maybe to murder him (it is not definitively clear in texts A or B). But when the squire attempts to press his suit, the woman repudiates him and admonishes him for his role in dispatching her lover. Reynolds's text ends at this point. Comprised of seven stanzas, it was evidently written in at least two sittings: the pen, color of ink, size of the handwriting, and style of penmanship—but not the hand itself—change dramatically after the first two stanzas. However, the story, as far as Reynolds takes it, is obviously unresolved and there is no outcome worthy of the ballad-maker's art. So, in the same style and ink as the preceding five stanzas, and likely at the same sitting, he scrawled on the bottom of the page: "has more verses / call on the writer for the rest / R C Reynolds." He got the ballad from one of his shipmates—or some other acquaintance—and evidently intended to go back for more. Unfortunately, if he ever did obtain the missing stanzas there is no evidence of it in his journal.

Two or three years later, aboard a different ship, fellow-boatsteerer William Gillaspia wrote down a text (B), seemingly complete in ten stanzas with a thrilling climax (absent in A) in which the woman kills the squire *and* the uncle in pitched battle, and, evidently through the good offices of justifiable homicide, inherits her freedom and her uncle's fortune. The ballad was still in circulation almost a generation later when seaman John S. Coquin copied yet another text (C) into his journal: eleven stanzas that make it clear that the ploughboy survives after all and returns to marry the lady and share in the inheritance. Ostensibly Scottish in origin, the ballad dates from the 18th century and was widely distributed in the British Isles and North America. Creighton's is the most interesting of the handful of variant melodies in minor and modal keys, and Belden's the best of the few sung in a major key.

TUNE A - "The Banks of Sweet Dundee," from Helen Creighton, *Maritime Folk Songs,* 1961, p. 38: "Sung by Mr. Isaac Doyle, West Jeddore [N.S.], July, 1953.".

TUNE B - "Blow the Candle Out," a form of "Banks of Sweet Dundee" (compare tune A): original source unknown; also from the singing of Mark Herman, Columbia University, 1967.

TUNE C - "The Banks of Sweet Dundee," from H.M. Belden, *Ballads and Songs Collected by the Missouri Folk-Lore Society,* 1955, p. 138: "Contributed by Mrs. Case in 1916 from her childhood memories in Harrison County."

A.

"THE BANKS OF SWEET DUNDEE." Richard C. Reynolds, boatsteerer, ship *Janus* of New Bedford, 1842-44. A foreshortened text of seven stanzas, excerpted to illustrate syntax and orthography for comparison with the similar but more complete 10-stanza texts that follow.

1. It was of a rich noblemans daughter, beautiful I am told
   Her parents died and left her five hundred pounds of gold
   She lived with her uncle the cause of all her woe
   But you soon shall hear this maiden fair did prove his overthrow

4. O a fig for all your squairs your lords and dukes likewise
   For my ploughboy apears like diamonds in my eyes
   Begone unruly feemaile happy you nevver shall be
   For I mean to banish william from the banks of sweet dundee

7. As young mary was a walking lamenting for her love
   She espied the wealthy Squaire down in her uncles grove
   He clasped his armes around her begone base man said she
   For you have sent the only lad I love from the banks of sweet dundee

(has more verses   call on the writer for the rest   R C Reynolds

B.

"THE BANKS OF SWEET DUNDEE." Lyman Holmes, ship *John Howland* of New Bedford, 1841-43. Almost the same as C but far more literate, with the text better understood by the sailor scribe. The odd phrase in stanza 1, "this maid unfair deprove his over throw," which should be "this maiden fair did prove his overthrow," suggests that the lyrics were transcribed (and misunderstood) from singing or oral recitation.

1. It was of a farmers daughter so Beautiful untold
   Her parents died and left her 500 lbs in gold
   She lived with her uncle the caused all her woe
   You soon shall hear this maid unfair deprove his over throw

2. Her uncle had a plough boy young Mary loved full well
   Down in her uncles garden those tales of love would tell
   There was a wealthy squire came her oft times to see
   But still she loved the plough Boy on the banks of sweet Dundee

3. It was early one summer morn he uncle went straightway
   He knocked at her bedroom door and unto her did say
   Rise up pretty maiden, a Lady you might be
   For the squire is a waiting for you on the banks of sweet Dundee

4. A fig for all your squires, your lords, and Dukes likewise
   For Williams hand in favour is worth di[a]monds in my eyes
   Begon unruly female said he you ne'er shall happy be
   For I mean to banish William from the banks of sweet Dundee

5. Her uncle and the squire rode out one summers day
   It's being William in favour and unto him did say
   Oh, now it is my intentions to tie you to a tree
   Or else to bribe the press gang on the banks of sweet Dundee

6. The pres gang came to William as he was all alone
   He boldly fought for liberty but there was six to one
   The blood did flow in torrents, pray kill me now said he
   For I had rather die for Mary on the banks of sweet Dundee

7. As marry was a walking lamenting for her lover
   It is ther[e] she spied the squire down in her uncles grove
   He clasped his arms around her[1] stand off base man said she
   For you have banished the only lad i loved from the banks of sweet Dundee

8. He put his arms around her and tried to throw her down
   She spied two pistols and a sword beneath his morning gown
   Young Mary took the weapons the sword did use so free
   She then did fire and shot the squire on the banks of sweet Dundee

9. Her uncle overheard the noise and hastened to the ground
   Since you have killed the squire I will give you your death wound
   Stand off bad man said Mary undaunted I will be
   She the trigger drew and her uncle slew on banks of sweet Dundee

10. A doctor now was sent for a man of noted skill
    Now likewise a law[y]er for him to sign his will
    He willed his gold to Mary who fought so manfully
    he closed his eyes no more to rise on the banks of Sweet Dundee

C.

"THE BANKS OF SWWEET [sic] DUNDEE." William Gillaspia, ship *Atlantic* of Nantucket, 1846-49. Stanzas are as given in the MS but lines (undifferentiated in the MS) are here realigned, preserving their original order in the MS. In stanza 4 "a *fib* for all your squires" should be he slang expression "a *fig* for all your squires," as in A, B. and D.

1. thare was a farmers Daughter so beautiful i told
   her parents died and left her 5000 pounds in gold
   she lived with her unkle the caus of all her wo
   you soon shall here this maiden fair she proved her [his] over throw

2. her unkle had a plough boy yong mary loved full well
   and in her unkle garden the tones of love wuld tel
   but thare was a welthy Squire who came her of time to see
   but still she loved her plough boy on the banks of sweet Dundee

3. her unkle rose one morning and cam to her strait way
   and rap[p]ed at her bedroom dore and unto her did say

---

[1] B has "He then stept up towards her…"

com arise up pretty maiden and a lady you may be
for the squire is a waiting for you on the banks of sweet Dundee

4. a fib for all your squires your lords and dukes like wise
for williams hand appears to me like diamonds in my eyes
stop unrooly female you nare shall happy be
for i will banish william from you on the banks of sweet Dundee

5. her unkle and the squire road out one summers day
william is all her favourite her unkle he did say
indeed it my intention to hang him to a tree
or els to bribe the pres gang on the banks of sweet Dundee

6. the pres gang came to william when he was all alone
he boldly fought for liberty but thare was 6 to one
the blood did flow in torrents pray kill me now cride he
for i had rather die for marry on the banks of sweet Dundee

7. next morning as marry was walking lamenting for her loved
she spide the squire all in her unkles grove
he then stept up towards her stand of[f] base man cride she
for you sent the only lad i loved from the banks of sweet Dundee

8. he clasp his armes around her and tride to Shove her down
two pistols and a sword she spide beneath his morning gound
she took the pistol from him and the sword he used so free
she fired and shot the squire on the bank of sweet Dundee

9. her unkle herd the nois and hasten to the ground
and [said] sence you killed the squire i will give you yor deth wound
Stand of[f] then cride young marry undanted i will be
and the tricker drew her unkle slew on banks of sweet Dundee

10. a doctor then was sent for a man of noted skill
likewise thare came a lawer for him to sine his will
he willed his gold to marry [w]ho faught so manfully
he closed his eyes no more to rise on the banks of Sweet Dundee

D.

"ON THE BANKS OF SWEET DUNDEE." John S. Coquin, bark *Pacific* of New Bedford, 1867-68; and merchant voyages out of Boston, circa 1860's-'70s. A complete text of 11 stanzas transcribed as 8 lines each; excerpted for comparison with B and C, respecting the narrative aspects of which only stanza 11 here is additional.

1. Its of a pretty fair maid
As you shall shortly hear.
Her parents died and left her
Five thousand pounds a year
She lived with an uncle
The cause of all her woes
And soon you will hear of this maiden fair
That she proved his overthrow.

11. Young william he was sent for
Who speedily returned
As soon as he came back again
Young mary ceased to mourn
Next morning they were married
And joined their hands so free
And now they live in splendor
On the banks of sweet dundee

80. The Bold Soldier
[The Lady and the Dragoon; The Young Sailor Boy]
(Laws #M-27)

This ballad of a father's opposition to his daughter's liaison with a royal dragoon is said to be related to "Earl Brand" (Child #7) and "Erlinton" (Child #8) — an old story tracing back to 1679 (Cazden 1982, 182) that also has affinities with "The Prince of Morocco" (Laws #N-18) [#88]. It enjoyed new popularity when it was recast in broadside form in the late 18th century,[2] remained in modest vogue through most of the 19th century, and enjoyed a small renown in the folksong revival of the mid 20th century. Unfortunately, the whaleman's transcription is only a fragment; and despite that several melodies are associated with the ballad in modern tradition, according to Bronson all knowledge of what tune may have been used for it in the 18th and 19th centuries has been lost.

TUNE – "The Bold Soldier," from the singing of the late Mark Herman and others: similar to the singing of Burl Ives and likely a latter-day, 20th-century manifestation. To fit the lyrics, the melody is repeated verbatim all the way through. The "original" tune or tunes appear to be lost: various melodies have been collected from tradition in major, minor, and modal keys, but despite Bronson's attempt to discern a systematic taxonomy, they are seemingly unrelated to one another. Several are reminiscent of Appalachian murder ballads and frontier outlaw songs, materials with which, for comparative purposes, Bronson was presumably less familiar than with the Child ballads; but such a comparison nevertheless seems to bear out his conclusion that the extant tunes of "Bold Soldier" are of relatively recent application to the text: "The melodic tradition, as we have it, belongs entirely to the present [20th] century, and appears to be cut out of the same materials, to which effect, no doubt, the jog-trot of the broadside text in long couplet quatrains has largely contributed.... It is impossible to determine the earliest shape of the tune" (Bronson I:128).

A.

"THE BOLD SOLDIER." John G. Marble, Warren, Rhode Island, circa 1846-47: a partial text inscribed in the journal of seaman Stephen O. Hopkins, ship *Rosalie* of Warren, 1843, and bark *Perseverance* of Providence, 1849. There may be a nautical adaptation afoot here, as in most manifestations the first stanza opens with some permutation of "A Soldier, a Soldier, coming from the plain, / He courted a lady through honour and through fame"; but here the soldier comes "from sea," perhaps returning from a foreign posting or foreign war; or perhaps the scribe really had a sailor in mind. It should be noted that in American tradition, there is often also a "fa la la" refrain following each stanza, certainly derived from British precursors but not present in the whaleman's manuscript.

1. I'll tell you of a soldier who lately came from sea
   Who courted a lady of honer rich and free
   Her fortune was so great that it hardly could be told
   But, yet, she loved the soldier because he was so bold

---

[2] "The ballad is plainly of broadside manufacture, and has kept the clear marks of its urban birth throughout its life in tradition. Its age, nevertheless, is impressive enough: the record is much older than anything else we possess in English of ['Earl Brand'], on which it may perhaps have been based. The earliest texts are Restoration broadsides, printed by Thackeray and his confrères, as 'The Master-Piece of Love Songs,' to be sung to the tune of 'The Week Before (or *after,* in later copies) Easter, the Day's long and clear, &c.'... A metrical reworking of this is 'The Seamans renown in winning his fair Lady,' to the same tune—a tune which I have not found" (Bronson I:128). "'The Bold Soldier,' as it is known in the New World, probably dates from after the time of the American Revolution. There is a broadside printed by Nathaniel Coverly of Boston [active 1767-1816]... which, with others like it, is the source for the American tradition of the song. This broadside, according to Greene, was based on an earlier British printer's version. Greene gives an extensive bibliography of 'The Bold Soldier' and songs, such as 'The Seaman's Renown' and 'The Masterpiece of Love Songs,' that are associated with its history. The story, almost always the same in general form, has been popular with the Anglo-American press at least since the early 1600's" (Flanders & Olney, I:131).

2. She said my fairest jewel i fain would be your wife
   But my father is so cruel I fear he'd end my life
   He took his sword and Pistol and hung them by his side
   And swore that he would marry her whatever might betide

3. As they had been to church and returning home again
   Her cruel father met them with seven armed men

B.

"THE BOLD SOLDIER." To complete the narrative, the following is a complete composite text of five stanzas. As in A, to fit the lyrics, the melody is repeated verbatim.

1. A soldier, a soldier, a-coming from the plain,
   He courted a lady through honour and through fame;
   Her beauty shown so brightly that it never could be told;
   She always loved the soldier because he was so bold

2. "O Soldier, O Soldier, well I would be your bride,
   But for fear of my father, some danger might betide."
   So he pulled out sword and pistol and he hung them by his side;
   He swore he would be married, no matter what betide.

3. He took her to the parson and then back home again,
   And there they met her father with seven armed men.
   "Let us fly!" cried the Lady, "I fear we shall be slain!"
   "Hold your hand," said the soldier, "and never fear again."

4. Then he took out sword and pistol and caused them for to rattle;
   The lady held the horses while the soldier fought the battle.
   "Hold your hand," cried the old man, "And do not be so bold.
   You shall have my daughter and seven pounds of gold."

5. "Fight on!" cried the Lady, "The portion is too small!"
   "Hold your hand," said the old man, "and you shall have it all."
   So he took them to his parlor and he called them son and dear,
   Not because he loved them, but only through fear.

81. Vilikins and His Dinah
[Vilikins and Dinah; Villikins and His Dinah]
(Laws #M-31b)

This English comic ballad by John Parry (1776-1851) is a broad parody of such tragic folk ballads as "The Constant Farmer's Son" [#82] and "Edwin in the Lowlands Low" [#83], and Cox calls it "a comic stage version of 'William and Diana.'" American sheet music for "Vilikins and Dinah" was in print by 1855 and the song entered tradition, where text and melody were widely adapted and parodied—most memorably furnishing the air for the American pioneer folk classic "Sweet Betsy from Pike," which, ever after, has been far better known than the original. Spaeth refers to it as "one of the most popular melodies in America, appearing in college song-books and elsewhere, and was often called simply 'the tooraloo tune,'" from its nonsense chorus. Hugill ranks it with the Irish air "Shule Agra" ("Shule Aroon") as one of the great "universal melodies" used for all kinds of improvisational chanteys:

> This is a tune which crops up attached to various types of shore- and sea-songs. It has been called the 'primal tune' and it certainly has been used by folk singers down through the ages as a handy perennial to apply to ballads of all kinds… Shanties and forebitters making use of this tune at times are *Ratcliffe Highway, The Towrope Girls,* and *The Liverpool Packet.* (Hugill, 468)

The tendencies towards adaptation and comedy are certainly consistent with the original spirit of "Vilikins and His Dinah," which is itself a lampoon of "serious" ballads about London merchants, their fortunes, their daughters, and their daughters' suitors. Even the title is backwards, as the ballad is not really about Vilikins and *his* Dinah at all, but about the lady and *her* troubles; and it's not just that she doesn't want to marry "her" Vilikins, she simply doesn't want to marry at all, at the moment. In a reversal of the usual format of "family opposition to lovers," this is a ballad of the lover-designate's opposition to her family. Some original whalemen's ballads, notable among them "A Voyage on New Holland" [#161] and "Song Composed Aboard the Bark Kathleen" [#162], were specifically set to "Vilikins and His Dinah"; and at least a dozen others for which no air is specified, could have been.

The whaleman's text — one of almost two hundred transcriptions of song lyrics made by New Hampshireman George Wilbur Piper aboard the ship *Europa* of Edgartown during 1868-70 — was certainly copied from some unidentified printed source. In addition to the orthodox lyrics, quite carefully rendered, it has a sentimental inscription at the end, the kind of thing one might find incised on a scrimshaw corset busk and something also likely copied directly from a printed prototype: "Community of goods / Unity of hearts / Nobility of sentiment and truth of feeling to all lovers of the fair sex."

TUNE - "Vilikins and His Dinah," after the original sheet music published in Boston by Oliver Ditson, 1855; in Baltimore by George Willig, Jr., 1860; reprinted in Sigmund Spaeth, *Reed 'em and Weep,* 1926, p. 56; and in Henry Randall Waite, *Carmina Collegensia,* [1868] 1876, I:110, where it is used as the air to the Williams College song "Away to the Mountain." Transposed from the key of E^b.

"VILIKENS AND HIS DINAH." George W. Piper, ship *Europa* of Edgartown, 1868-70.

1. There was a rich merchant in London did dwell
   He had a fine daughter an uncommon nice girl
   Her name it was Dinah scarce sixteen years old
   And she had a large fortune in silver and gold

Chorus: Right tu ral ral ru ri right tu ral ral ray
Right tu ral ral ru ri right tu ral ral ray
Right tu ral ral ru ri right tu ral ral ray
Right tu ral ral ru ri right tu ral ral ray

2. As Dinah was walking in the garden one day
   Her father cam to her and this he did say
   Go dress yourself Dinah in gorgeous array
   And choose yourself a husband both gallant and gay

3. O father dear father I have not made up my mind
   For to marry just yet why I dont feel inclined
   To you my large fortune I will gladly turn o'er
   If you will let me live single just a year or two more

4. Go go boldest daughter the parent replied
   If you dont consent for to be this young man's bride
   I will give your large fortune to the nearest of kin
   A[nd] you shan't reap the benefit of one single pin

5. As Vilikens was a walking in the garden around
   He saw his dear Dinah lying dead upon the ground
   With a cup of cold poison lying close by
   And a billet dieux saying twas by poison she died

6. Now all young maidens take warning by her
   And never by any means disobey your governor
   And all you young lovers when the girls you clap eyes on
   Think of Vilikens and his Dinah and the cup of cold poison

Community of goods   Unity of hearts
Nobility of sentiment and truth of feeling
to all lovers of the fair sex.

82. The Constant Farmer's Son
[The Merchant's Daughter]
(Laws #M-33)

This narrative about an aspiring suitor running afoul of his evil would-be brothers-in-law is thematically related to several other ballads of thwarted love, notably "Edwin in the Lowlands Low" [#83]: here it is her brothers, there her father, who murders the suitor to keep him from the young woman and hence from the family fortune. Both are prime examples of the kinds of tragic ballads that are lampooned in "Vilikins and His Dinah" [#81] and "Married to a Mermaid."[3] Of "The Constant Farmer's Son" there appear to be two textual subspecies, differing markedly in syntax and meter. One type is epitomized in Mackenzie's version (collected in Nova Scotia and cited by Laws):

> In London there lived a pretty fair maid.
> She was comely, fair, and handsome, her parents loved her well.
> She was courted by lords and noblemen, but all their love was in vain.
> There was but one, the farmer's son, poor Mary's heart could gain.

The other type is exemplified in versions collected by Broadwood (in England) and Creighton (in New Brunswick and Nova Scotia). As the whaleman's text most resembles this second type in meter, phrasing, and structure, the tunes are accordingly given from Broadwood and Creighton. Neither form has hitherto been recovered from tradition in the United States.

TUNE A - "The Merchant's Daughter, or The Constant Farmer's Son," from Lucy E. Broadwood, *English Traditional Songs and Carols,* 1908, p. 28: "Sussex."

TUNE B - "There Was a Wealthy Farmer," from Helen Creighton, *Folksongs of Southern New Brunswick,* 1971, #38, p. 83: "Sung by Angelo Dornan, Elgin, N.B." Closely related to the air of "The Handsome Cabin Boy" [#86].

---

[3] "Married to a Mermaid," which begins, "There was a rich young farmer / And he lived on Salisbury Plain," and has as its chorus the refrain of "Rule Britannia," appears to be a parody of "The Constant Farmer's Son"; see, e.g., L.A. Smith, 34.

"THE CONSTANT FARMER'S SON." George W. Piper, ship *Europa* of Edgartown, 1868-70.

1. There was a rich old farmer
   Near London town did dwell
   He had a handsome daughter
   And her parents loved her well
   She was admired by lords and squires
   But all their hopes were vain
   For there was one farmer's son
   Young Mary's heart did gain

2. Long time this couple courted
   And fixed the wedding day
   Both their parents gave consent
   But her brothers they did say
   There lives a squire has pledged his word
   And hi[m] you must not shun
   For we will betray and we will slay
   Your constant farmer's son

3. A fair was held not far from home
   Her brothers went straightway
   They asked young William's company
   With them to pass the day
   But Mark returning home again
   He swore his race was run
   And with a stake they the life did take
   Of the constant farmer's son

4. As Mary was a sleeping
   She had a dreadful dream
   She dreamt she saw him murdered
   And the blood ran down in streams
   The[n] up she rose and put on her clothes
   And straightway she did run
   Both dead and cold she did behold
   Her constant farmer's son

5. The soft tears they ran down her cheeks
   And mingled with the gore
   She wept in vain for to ease his pain
   And kissed him ten times o'er
   She gathered leaves from all the trees
   For to shield him from the sun
   Both day and night she wept besides
   Her constant farmer's son

6. But sickness it came creeping on
   Poor girl she wept with woe
   For to try to find the murderers out
   Straight homeward she did go
   O brothers dear you soon shall hear
   The dreadful deed that's done
   Both dead and cold I did behold
   My constant farmer's son

7. Then up steps the younger brother
   And said it was not he
   Up steps the other brothers
   And swore most bitterly
   Oh brothers dear you need not strive
   Nor try the law to shun
   You did the deed and you must bleed
   For my constant farmer's son

8. But soon the villains owned their guilt
   And for the same must die
   The doctors got their bodies
   All for to anatomize
   But Mary's thought both night and day
   On her murdered love does run
   And now she dwells in a mad house cell
   For her constant farmer's son

83. Edwin in the Lowlands Low
[He Ploughed in the Lowlands Low; Young Edwin; Young Edmon Bold]
(Laws #M-34)

This ballad tells the story of a sailor who returns from the formulaic seven years at sea only to be murdered by his lover's family. Of the many manifestations encountered in tradition in the British Isles and America, the one most like the transcription made at sea by whaleman George W. Piper of New Hampshire is the one collected by Flanders & Brown in Vermont, except that the whaleman's text is more elaborate and more complete. Both versions preserve the "come-all-ye" introductory stanza (which is absent in many traditional versions), and the two narratives proceed along much the same sequence. However, intervening stanzas in the Piper text flesh out the story, providing material that had apparently been discarded from tradition in Vermont by the time Flanders & Brown recovered their text. It is as though the whaleman's version were the direct ancestor of the later New England rendition.

TUNE - "Young Edmon Bold," from Helen Hartness Flanders and George Brown, *Vermont Folk Songs and Ballads,* 1932, p.106: "Recorded by Mr. Brown, September 24, 1930, in Manchester, Vermont, from the playing of Mrs. Henrietta Sheldon, who learned it from her great aunt, Sarah Whitcomb."

"HE PLOUGHED IN THE LOWLANDS LOW." George W. Piper, ship *Europa* of Edgartown, 1868-70.

1. Come all you gay young people and listen to my song
   Whilst I unfold concerning gold that leads so many wrong
   Young Emma was a serving maid and she loved a sailor bold
   He ploughed the main some gold to gain for her love we are told

2, Young Emma she did daily mourn when Edwin first did roam
   When seven long years were past and gone young Edwin he came home
   He came one night to Emma's house his gold all for to show
   That he had gained upon the main he ploughed the lowlands low

3. My father keeps a public house down by the river side
   You may go there for lodging and there this night abide
   I will meet you in the morning don't let my parents know
   That your name it is Young Edwin who ploughed the lowlands low

4. Young Edwin he then went away, and went unto the shore
   And little was he thinking that he should see his love no more
   And when he got unto the door her father says who's there
   Says he I am a stranger who wishes shelter here

5. Young Edwin he sat drinking till time to go to bed
   And little was he thinking what sorrows crowned his head
   To Emma's cruel parents his gold all did he show
   That he had gained upon the main he ploughed the lowlands low

6. Young Edwin he retired to bed and scarce had fell asleep
   When Emma's cruel father into the room did creep
   He struck him with a dagger which caused the blood to flow
   And sent his body floating down in the lowlands low

7. As Emma was a-sleeping she had a dreadful dream
   She dreamt she saw him murdered and the blood ran down in streams
   She got up in the morning and Straightway she did go
   For she did love him dearly he ploughed in the lowlands low

8. O mother where is that stranger who here last night did stay
   Your father he has murdered him her cruel mother did say
   O father cruel father to the gallows you must go
   For the murder of my Edwin who ploughed in the lowlands low

9. She went unto the police and the story she made known
   Her father he was taken and his trial soon came on
   The jury found him guilty to the gallows he was forced to go
   For the murder of young Edwin who ploughed in the lowlands low

10. The fishes in the Ocean swim over my true loves breast
    If his body is in motion I hope his soul is at rest
    The waters of the Ocean as they roll to and fro
    Do remind me of my Edwin who ploughed the lowlands low

11. Then many a day she passed away a trying to ease her mind
    But all her fiends were dead and gone and she poor girl behind
    Being mad frantic and broken hearted to the mad house she must go
    And her cries they are for Edwin who ploughed in the lowlands low

CHAPTER TEN
Love Entangled
Ballads of Lovers' Disguises and Tricks

> When we are both accoutered like young men,
> I'll prove the prettier fellow of the two,
> And wear my dagger with the braver grace;
> And speak, between the change of man and boy,
> With a reed voice; and speak of frays,
> Like a fine bragging youth: and tell quaint lies
> How honorable ladies sought my love,
> Which I denying, they fell sick and died;
>   could not do withal; — then I'll repent
> And wish, for all that, that I had not kill'd them:
> And twenty of these puny lies I'll tell,
> That men shall swear I have discontinued school
> Above a twelvemonth: — I have within my mind
> A thousand raw tricks of these bragging Jacks,
> Which I will practise.
>
> — *The Merchant of Venice*

84. Jack Munroe
[Jack Went A-Sailing; The Wealthy Merchant]
(Laws #N-7)

    This is one of the better ballads about a woman who disguises herself as a sailor to follow her lover to war. In most texts she eventually finds him "among the wounded" (or "among the dead and wounded"). In the complete songster versions the couple return safely and celebrate nuptials at a sumptuous feast hosted by her repentant father. However, the whaleman Thomas Bennett's transcription of 17 stanzas is a verbatim portion of a 22-stanza text published circa 1835 in *The American Songster,* including the same nonsense chorus and a reference to *Chatham* (which is *London* or *England* in some American texts; the Canadian versions seem all to omit that stanza entirely). In that particular songster text there is no mention of wedding bells or reconciliation with the father: they go off to battle again together and eventually die side by side. It is interesting and perhaps significant that the five stanzas the whaleman omitted are the unpleasant and contentious ones, even though it leaves the story unresolved (for comparison the five "missing" stanzas are included as text B); and it may be for this reason that, although the ballad has been widely distributed in British, American, and Canadian tradition, it seems to have been scarce in the whale fishery. Most of the many tunes are merely variants of one another.[1]

---

[1] There are literally dozens of melodies extant to which the various renditions of this ballad have been sung. Some are fine, distinctive modal tunes among which it is difficult to choose on any criterion of probable age, geographical proximity to the whale fishery, or aesthetic appeal. Creighton presents two versions; Eddy, four; Gardner, one; Sharp, twenty; etc., all with tunes, some of them related to one another, some of them not, and no two alike. Nor are there adequate textual grounds to match any of the anthologized variants with Bennett's (or *The American Songster*) text.

186

TUNE A - "The Wealthy Merchant," from Emelyn Elizabeth Gardner and Geraldine Jencks Chickering, *Ballads and Songs of Southern Michigan,* 1939, #59, p. 165: "Sung in 1934 by Mr. E.W. Harris, Greenville, who learned the song in Kalamazoo County, Michigan, circa 1858"; thus perhaps the earliest claim for a tune for this ballad.

TUNE B - "Jack Monroe," from Mary O. Eddy, *Ballads and Songs from Ohio,* 1939, #35D, p. 111: "From Charles A. Sneary, Canton, Ohio… learned… from the singing of his parents.…"

TUNE C - "Johnny's Gone a Sailing," from Helen Creighton, *Maritime Folk Songs,* 1961, p. 143: "Sung by Mr. Berton Young, West Petpeswick, N.S., and Mrs. W.J. Johns, Musquodoboit Harbour, N.S., August, 1952."

A.

"JACK MONROE." Thomas Bennett, second mate, ships *Condor* of New Bedford and *William Baker* of Warren, 1839-41. The chorus is an extremely rare form, syllable-for-syllable identical with one contemporaneously printed with the very similar (but more complete) text in *The American Songster* (text B) but not encountered elsewhere. It is therefore reasonable to suppose that A may derive from B (or that the two may descend from a common source). However, from the lack of punctuation, the lack of capitalization of proper nouns, and various grammatical errors in A (e.g., *"trouble* mind" in stanzas 4 and 8 in A, versus *"troubled* mind" in B), A appears not to be a direct copy. One or two words are absent from stanza 16 owing to a part of the page missing in the MS; one word missing from stanza 15 is provided in brackets in italics, from B.

1. In Chatham lived a merchant
   A very wealthy man
   He had an only daughter
   As you shall understand

   Chorus: And sing tire e dum de dee

2. She was courted by lords and dukes
   And many a wealthy knight
   There was none but jack the sailor
   Could gain her hearts delight

3. When her father came to hear of this
   An angry man was he
   Saying I will press young jack the sailor
   All in the wars of germany

4. Now jack he is on board
   With a sword and trouble mind
   Leaving off his own true love
   So closely confined

5. Now jack he is on board
   No more of him i'll see
   Saying i will be at your disposal
   If you will set me free

6. She left her fathers house
   And dressed in mens array
   She is waiting for an officer
   To carry her away

7. We do not list any young man
   Until their names we know
   So boldly she answered him
   They call me Jack Monroe

8. Now jack she is on board
   With a sword and trouble mind
   To land at french flanders
   Is her whole design

9. She fought in many a battle
   She fought courageously
   Privates and colonels
   Down by her side did die

10. An officer's commission
    On you i will bestow
    Saying push and make your fortune
    My darling jack Monroe

11. The drums they did beat
    And the trumpets they did sound
    And for the field of battle
    They all did march around

12. She walked along among the ranks
    And among the wounded men
    And there she saw her own true love
    She thought he had been slain

13. She pulled out her handkerchief
    Some private marks to show
    Saying jacky wont you marry me
    Oh jacky dont you know

14. The priest he was sent for
    The knot for to be tied
    The officers and privates
    Begrudged jack his bride

15. The drums they did beat
    And the trumpets they did sound
    And for Old England
    They [*did*] march around

16. And as they were going down [   ]
    The people they did say
    Heare comes the tars of war
    From the wars in germany
    To land at french flanders

17. As they [*stanza crossed out in the* MS]

18. I do not like your clothing
    I do not like your talk
    I do not like that vagabond
    That by your side does walk

19. Then up steps her mother
    And unto her did say
    You look just like my daughter
    That from us went away

B.

"JACK MONROE," from *The American Songster* (Philadelphia, circa 1835): quite similar to A but a more complete text, incorporating stanzas 17 and 20-22, lacking in A. The "missing" stanzas are accordingly given here.

17. As they were going down Dover Street,
        Her father chanced to meet,
    Saying merchant wont you list,
        In the wars of Germany.

20. I am not your daughter.
        Neither do you I know,
    I am from the Highlands,
        They call me Jack Monroe.

21. She fought in many a battle,
        She fought courageously
    Until young Jack, the Sailor,
        Down by her side did die.

22. She pulled out her broadsword,
        And bid the world adieu,
    Here's an end to Jack, the Sailor,
        Likewise to JACK MONROE.

85. The Silk Merchant's Daughter
[The Constant Lovers; The Test of Love; The Castaways]
(Laws #N-10)

Entitled in his copybook "The Test of Love," whaleman George Piper's transcription [text B, circa 1868-70] is actually a foreshortened text of a well-known broadside ballad usually called "The Silk Merchant's Daughter."[2] But like "The Castaways," Greenleaf's Newfoundland version of the same ballad, the whaleman's rendition omits the opening stanzas that normally provide a rationale for the story. "The Silk Merchant's Daughter" is usually premised upon the merchant's opposition to his daughter's liaison with a sailor: she dons men's clothing to follow her lover to sea, and thus is present on board when a shipwreck occurs and is among the survivors who face starvation in the lifeboat. But without this prelude, "Test of Love" tells quite a different tale: the woman could as well be a passenger as a surreptitious member of the crew, her gender is already known, there is no indication that her lover is one of the crew rather than a passenger himself, and there is no explanation of how (as she claims in stanza 5) her imminent murder could have been precipitated by love. Many years earlier, aboard the Gloucester, Massachusetts ship *Polly* in 1795, whaleman Stephen Cahoon transcribed a much longer and more complete text [A] which has the same title as, and is almost precisely contemporaneous with, the broadside cited by Laws, which latter is dated 1794 and titled "The Constant Lovers; or, The Valiant Young Lady." But the song is even older than that. Palmer mentions a manuscript of 1778; and in the third stanza of Cahoon's text the young porter is sent "to serve the Queen" (rather than the King), indicating that it may trace all the way back to the reign of Queen Anne (1702-14) (or this feature could merely be an adaptation during the 19th-century reign of Queen Victoria). Other ballads employ similar themes of women disguised as sailors (e.g., see "Jack Munro," #84; and "The Handsome Cabin Boy," #86), but the secondary theme of cannibalism in lifeboats is surprisingly rare in old ballads, though it is fairly widely distributed in history, folklore, and formal literature.[3] Several related major- and minor-key tunes survive, of which the four given by Sharp are representative and the one given by Doerflinger (q.v.) is an interesting modal variant from Ontario tradition.

TUNE A - "The Silk Merchant's Daughter," from Cecil J. Sharp, *English Folk Songs from the Southern Appalachians,* 1932, #64A, I:381: "Sung by Mrs. Mary Sands at Allanstand, N.C., July 31, 1931."

TUNE B - "The Silk Merchant's Daughter," from Cecil J. Sharp, *Op.cit.,* 1932, #64C, I:383: "Sung by Mrs. Kate Thomas at St. Helen's, Lee Co., Ky., Sept. 12, 1917." Variations omitted.

---

[2] Private communication from William Main Doerflinger.

[3] E.g, Owen Chase, *Narrative of the...Shipwreck of the Whaleship Essex, of Nantucket...with an account of the unparalleled sufferings of the captain and crew during ninety-three days at sea, in open boats, in the years 1819 & 1820* (New York, 1821), a firsthand account of the survivors of a ship stove by a whale. Eugene O'Neill's "Thirst," in *Thirst and Other One-Act Plays* (Boston, 1914) is a literary treatment of an analogous theme.

A.

"Constant Lovers / 1795 year / Song / Valiant Young Laday / An Excellent New Love Song to a Butiful [Tune]."
Stephen Cahoon, ship *Polly* of Gloucester, 1794. Unfortunately, the final stanza (stanza 29) is incomplete.

1. Both young men and damsels that to love belong
   Come draw near and Listen a while to my Song
   I make no grate Question but that this new ditty
   Unto many People well Pleasing may be

2. This ['Tis] of a rich merchant in London i Rightt
   He had a fair daughter his hearts Chief delight
   She Loved a Porter and to Prevent the day
   Of marriege he forced this young man a way

3. For to Serve the Queen and when gone from the shore
   This forsaken damsel was grieved full Sore
   Then in Mans apparal in a marchants Ship
   She ventured her Life over the raging deep

4. When Come to anchor near Some Sove[r]ign Land
   Where She went on Shore as i do understand
   A Sword of the Captains in her hand She took
   A way She did wander her love for to Look

5. Then going thro a forest Long time before night
   A Couple of indians appearing in her Sight
   When drawing near to them these two heathens they
   Intended to take this fair maids Life away

6. But She haveing a Sword her Life to defend
   From Blood thirsty ones who did murder intend
   Thro marcy She ConQuerd one of them She killd
   And forced the other for to Qit the field

7. She wandered So Long till Some Smoak did appear
   Which made her to think that Some houses were near
   But as She Sought truly in the Evening tide
   She Came to a town that Stood by the Sea Side

8. In this harbour there was a Ship bound to See
   With all expedition to Jamaica
   In Which She did Sail and Came to kingston
   When to her grate Joy unexpected she found

9. Her Love the Young Porter was walking the Street
   She made it her business this young man to meet
   And Said what Ship Brother Pray tell unto me
   He told her and Said Bound unto England we be

10. She Said unto London i am Willing to go
    But how to git thither i do not well know
    I am not a Sailor But if you want a man
    For my Passage home i will do the best i Can

11. Not knowing who is was he Took her on bord
    The Captain Said what do you do with a Sword
    Account of her travels unto him She gave
    And told how that Sword once her Life did save

12. They Set Sail for England and now pray give Ear
    What Sudden destruction to them did appear
    The Ship Sprung a Leak and to Bottom she went
    When out at main Seas to their great discontent

13. Thirty Seven hands ware Confind in a Boat
    In which Small allowance of Room they did float
    Food being all gone death appeared So nigh
    The Captain then made Lots to See who might die

14. They were made of Paper as the Captain thot fit
    To draw for Life fairly on them to be writ
    A Number of figures begining at one
    unto thirty Seven which things was Soon done

15. Then in a Small Bay they together ware Shook
    and So at a venture Each one his Lot took
    This Poor damsels Lot Was to draw the least
    For one must die first for to feed all the Rest

16. They drawd Lots again that they fairly might see
    Who a mong them all her butcher must be
    it was a hard Lot you will Say when you hear
    She was to be Slain by that young man her dear

17. For whose sake So far She had ventured her Life
    For to do his office he came with a knife
    Another with a bowl the blood for to take
    At which action She Sighed and these words She spake

18. Spare me a few minutes i have Something to Say
    Unfortunate Creature this unhappy day
    I might have Escaped if i had ben wise
    Lord have mercy upon me and hear my sad cry

19. Must i who have venturd So many Score miles
    Thro forests and hedges high mountains and Stiles
    Shund So many dangers and Last indeed
    Die a Sacrifice to hunger a man for to feed

20. Round the neck She Caught him and with a kiss Said
    You are going to kill a Poor innocent maid
    A Rich merchants daughter of London i be
    See what i am Come to by Loveing of the[e]

21. She Shewd him a Ring that between them was broke
    He knowing the token then with a Sith [sigh] Spoke
    Alas Poor Lady my heart it will burst
    In hopes of your Long Life my dear i ll die first

22. With tears Runing down Each other Embraced
    To Satisfy hunger the Rest were in haste
    The Captain Said if your loves debt you will pay
    Prepare now for death i Can no Longer Stay

23. Like a noble martyr this Loveing young man
    Said to him that Stood with a knife in his hand
    Be Quick in your office my business is done
    Before the Stroke was given they all heard a gun

24. At which this Poor young man Cryd out hold thine hand
    I did here a gun we are near Some Ship or Land
    Within half an hour then a Ship did appear
    Bound for ireland wich Sight did them Cheer

25. They were teken up and to Dub[l]in Conveyd
    This Captain and Couple as t is now Said
    Thay Came to fair London Powder Treason Day[4]
    And there at a tavern this Couple did Stay

26. While the Captain unto her father did go
    He asked for his Daughter his a[n]swer was So
    This twenty five weeks my dear Child has been Lost
    To be Shure She is dead wich my Life it will Cost

27. My heart it will break for the Lost of my Child
    To hear those Expressions he Said with a Smile
    She had been near Death But now is alive and well
    Now [No] Souls grief on Earth Can her Sorrow Excel

28. Account of her travels unto him he gave
    And told him how Such a young man did her Save
    Well if it Be So then She Shall be his wife
    And i Shall adore him all the days of my life

29. The Captain Sent [   ] [text ends]

---

[4] That is, Guy Fawkes Day, the anniversary of Fawkes's treasonous attempt to blow up King James I and Parliament with gun powder on 5 November 1605.

B.

"THE TEST OF LOVE. / THE LOVE TEST." George W. Piper, ship *Europa* of Edgartown, 1868-70. The transcription bears both titles on different pages.

1. On a Monday took shipping on tuesday set sail
   We were bound to the Eastward with a sweet pleasant gale
   As we were sailing, to our heart's content
   Our ship took to leaking, to the bottom she went

2. There were fourteen pour souls together in a boat
   In want of provisions they were all afloat
   In want of provisions and death drawing nigh
   They all casted lots to see which of them should die

3. The tickets were made and in a box put
   And out of it a number of each of them he took
   A beautiful maiden it is her's was the last
   She was to be murdered to feed all the rest

4. They all casted lots fain fain would they see
   Which out of their number her murderer should be
   And as it turned out you plainly shall hear
   She was to be murdered by the young man her dear

5. Hold you rank butcher this maiden she said
   O how can you murder an innocent maid
   I am a rich merchants daughter from London it is true
   O see what I have come to by a loving of you

6. Then quickly the color flew into his face
   With his heart in his bosom it beat a great pace
   With his heart in his bosom just ready to burst
   In hopes of your long life my love I'll die first

7. They all casted lots fain fain would they see
   Which out of their number his murderer should be
   Be quick in your motions let the business be done
   And while they were waiting they all heard a gun

8. Hold you rank butcher the Captain he said
   I espy a little village down by the sea side
   The bells of the village so merrily shall ring
   The young men shall dance and the maiden shall sing

86. The Handsome Cabin Boy
[The Female Cabin Boy]
(Laws #N-13)

This comical escapade — concerning a young woman who disguises herself as a sailor, ships as a cabin boy, and bears the captain's child on shipboard — makes light of material that could as readily have been rendered as operatic tragedy. There are a few actual historical precedents for a woman disguising herself as a man to go to sea on a whaler. In her article "The Female Sailor on the *Christopher Mitchell:* Fact and Fantasy," Elizabeth Little catalogues the best-documented cases of females disguised as sailors on Yankee ships, including a woman discovered in the crew of the Nantucket whaleship *Lydia* in 1800, who "claimed it was not her first whaling voyage"; and the one aboard the Nantucket whaleship *Christopher Mitchell* in 1848, who "was dramatized by Nelson Cole Haley of the ship *Charles W. Morgan* of New Bedford, after a gam with the *Mitchell*" in the Pacific in 1850. According to Dr. Little, "A number of female sailors passing as men went to sea and their stories are recorded in newspapers and other accounts…. Although hardly commonplace, the discovery of a female sailor on a whaleship would not have been a unique event."[5] Several are well remembered. In 1852 a woman using the name John Amenas was in the crew of the New Bedford whaleship *William and Eliza*. Using the pseudonym George Stewart, Emma Barnes, age 17, from the State of Maine, was aboard the merchant ship *James Rae* of Philadelphia in 1855. A woman known as Charles Baker was in the New Bedford whaleship *Euphrates* in 1862, and that same year Georgiana Leonard shipped as George Wheldon on the bark *America* for a whaling voyage out of Holmes Hole, Martha's Vineyard. By the 1860s, when whaleman William Keith made his shipboard transcription of "The Handsome Cabin Boy," some of these cases had been widely publicized and were fairly well known. In fact, they may have directly inspired an undated broadside of "Handsome Cabin Boy" that was published (without music) by H. de Marsan of New York in the early 1860s. Sailor William Keith's version is an orthodox copy text virtually identical with the broadside.[6]

TUNE - "The Handsome Cabin Boy," from the singing of Stuart Gillespie, professor of music at Mattatuck College, Waterbury, Connecticut; as recorded in *Sea Chanteys and Sailor Songs at Mystic Seaport* (Folkways #37300, New York, 1978); evidently indirectly after the singing of Louis Killen, a native of Gateshead, County Durham. Most of the other tunes are derivative: compare Gardner #163, which seems to incorporate elements of "Paddy West" (e.g., Hugill, 335) and "The Limejuice Ship" or "According to the Act" [see "One Year in a Blubber Hunter," #145].

---

[5] Little 1994, 252. Along with her fine treatment of the *Christopher Mitchell* incident, she has an excellent bibliography.

[6] See Irving Post, "'My God, Captain, he's a… a WOMAN!': Hunting whales as George Weldon during the Civil War, Georgiana Leonard fooled them all," in the *Sunday Standard-Times Magazine,* Providence, R.I., 18 Jan 1987.

194

TUNE B - "The Female Drummer," source unknown.

"THE HANDSOME CABIN BOY." William H. Keith, schooners *William Martin* of Boston and *Edith May* of Wellfleet, etc., 1865-71. Departures from the de Marsan broadside text indicated in italics in brackets.

1. It is of a pretty female, as you shall understand,
   She had a mind for roving into some foreign land;
   Attired in sailor's clothing, this fair maid did appear,
   And engaged with a captain to serve him for a year.

2. She engaged with the captain his cabin boy to be.
   The wind it being favorable they soon put out to sea:
   The captain's lady being on board, who seemed to enjoy
   The favorable appearance of the handsome cabin boy.

3. So nimble was the cabin boy and done his duty well,
   But mark what followed after, the thing itself will tell;
   The captain with this pretty maid would often kiss and toy,
   And he soon found the secret of the handsome cabin boy.

4. Her cheeks were [*just*] like roses, and with her side locks curl'd,
   The sailors often smiled and said, "she looks just like a girl."
   But by eating the captain's biscuit, her color it did destroy,
   And the waist [*it*] did grow larger on this handsome cabin boy.

5. As through the Bay of Biscay our gallant ship did plow
   One night among the sailors there was a pretty row:
   They turned from their hammocks, their sleep it did destroy,
   And swore about the groaning of the handsome cabin boy.

6. Oh! doctor! Oh, doctor the cabin boy did cry —
   The sailors swore by all that's good the cabin boy would die.
   The doctor ran with all his might & laughing at the fun
   To think a cabin boy should have a daughter or a son.

7. The sailors soon found out the joke, and all began to stare
   The child belonged to none of them they solemnly did swear:
   The captain's lady to him said, "My dear, I wish you joy,
   For either you or I've betrayed the handsome cabin boy.

8. Then they all took a bumper and drank success to trade.
   Likewise to the cabin boy that neither man nor maid.
   And if the waves should rise again the sailors to destroy,
   Why, then we'll ship some sailors like the handsome cabin boy.

87. The Noble Duke
(Laws #N-15)

The naval impressment elements here are clearly related to analogous manifestations in "The White Cockade" ("The Summer Morning"; "The Soldier's Farewell"), an English ballad of army recruitment with which "The Noble Duke" has many key phrases in common—notably including the woman's vituperative rhetoric directed at the officer who enlisted her lover, and her specific wish that a foreign enemy might sink the perpetrator in the sea.[7] On the other hand, her disguise and the clever subterfuge by which she rescues her man—characteristic elements of "The Noble Duke"—are absent in "The White Cockade." Versions and variants of "The Noble Duke" have been known in tradition as "The True Lovers' Departure," "The Simple Ploughboy," "The Pretty Ploughboy," and "The Damsel Disguised."

TUNE – "The True Lovers' Departure," from Huntington & Hermann, *Sam Henry's Songs of the People*, p. 331.

[UNTITLED.] Captain Samuel Green, Jr., ships *Flora* and *Neptune* of New London, 1835-44. Reconstituted from stanzas of four half-lines each.

1. Come all you pretty fair maids that sports on Cupid's plain.[8]
   I tell you of a fair maid that was sporting with his chains
   It was with her intended love where she did sport and play
   till a pressgang overtuck them and pressd her love away

2. [It was with her intended love where she did sport and play
   till a pressgang overtuck them and pressd her love away]
   She rung her hands in sorrow and then she tore her hair
   Saying i am ondone forever for the looseing of my dear

3. I wish the french might kill that man that pr[e]ssed my love away[1]
   and heave his body sinking forever in some sea
   She dressd herself like a noble duke with a starplate on her breast
   and swore the Captain she would kill if he did her molest

4. She went down to the raging sea befor the ship had sailed away
   and then she hailed the Captain and boldly bid him stay
   The officers stood with hats in hand this noble duke to see
   all thinking she was comeing on board their commander for to be

---

[7] In "The White Cockade" the foreign enemy is "Hollanders," which Kidson (1891, 113) suggests refers to a British "expedition to repel the French from Flanders and the Netherlands" in 1793. In Captain Green's text the allusion is directly to France, perhaps signifying the 1793 episode or, more likely, the Napoleonic Wars prosecuted during the following decade.

[8] *Cupid's plain:* may actually refer to "Cupid's Garden," so-called after Cuper's Garden, an 18th-century place of amusement in the London Borough of Southwark—see "Cupid's Garden" [#92].

5. But when she saw her own true love she took hold of his hand
Saying this is my servant man and him I do demand
for he has robed me of all my gold that I had laid in store
now I will venter life and fortune that I try him for it over

6. This young man pled for liberty to cross the raging main
Saying I never robed a man my lord no my lord in all my days
So when she had him fettered she could handle him alone
Saying now I will confine you all in some prison strong

7. But when she had him safe on shore she set him in the shade
and then began to ask him if he knew such a maid
The Tears they flow from his eyes at he[a]ring her sweet name
my dear says she dont troubled be for verily I am the same

8. Then with everlasting imbraces he fell into her alms
imbracing all the comforts was renewing to her charms
My dear says she how could you ventur your sweet life
So to a church he took her and soon made her his wife

88. The Prince of Morocco
[The Sailor Boy's Trick; The Young Prince of Spain]
(Laws #N-18)

This is one of several broadside ballads in which a lowly sailor and his lady outwit and outdo his "betters," in this instance by dressing up as royalty to deceive the lady's wealthy father when he opposes her marriage to a sailor. In the end, of course, the sailor wins the woman and the gold. The distinguishing feature is the almost ludicrously implausible disguise, which, in the context of what Laws calls "Ballads of Family Opposition to Lovers," presents an interesting alternative to "The Bold Soldier" [#80] and "The Constant Farmer's Son" [#82].

George Wlbur Piper was an inveterate collector of songs whose copy book, compiled during 1868-70 on a Pacific Ocean whaling voyage in the ship *Europa* of Edgartown, Massachusetts, is by a fair margin the most prodigious extant compilation of whalemen's songs in manuscript. In most cases the direct source of any given song is unrecorded, and it can only be assumed from internal evidence that Piper obtained his songs from shipmates as well as from broadsides, sheet music (perhaps), and various periodicals. Some he undoubtedly transcribed from recitation, from singing, and from memory. However, his text of "The Prince of Morocco" (text B, entitled in the manuscript "The Sailor Boy's Trick") is specifically inscribed as the gift of fellow-whaleman James A Peacock. The slightly earlier transcription by John S. Coquin on the New Bedford ship *Pacific* in 1867 (text A, entitled in the manuscript "The Young Sailor Boy") takes essentially the same form but the differences make an enlightening comparison, including that in A the daughter has a final, grudging reconciliation with the father but in B she does not. Regarding Laws's tacit implication that "Prince of Morocco" is the mainstream form of the ballad, it is worth noting that the Prince of Morocco is one of Portia's suitors in Shakespeare's *Merchant of Venice;* and that both of these whalemen's texts (as well as the one collected in New Hampshire by Anne and Frank Warner) describe the sailor disguised as the Prince of *Spain*.

TUNE - "The Young Prince of Spain," from Anne Warner, *Traditional American Folk Songs,* #61, p. 161: collected from Lena Bourne Fish, New Hampshire, 1940.

A.

"THE YOUNG SAILOR BOY." John S. Coquin, bark *Pacific* of New Bedford, 1867-68; and merchant voyages out of Boston, circa 1860's-'70s. Stanzas 8 and 9, and several of the allusions, appear to have been garbled in transmission: note the word *rocco* in stanza 4, which may be a corrupt holdover of *Morocco* (see B); in stanza 2, *lackey,* evidently also intended as a place-name, has not been identified. An excess of commas has been pared.

1. Then up steps the sailor,
   With courage stout and bold —
   He courted a Lady;
   Worth thousands of gold.
   Oh! Daughter, Oh! Daughter,
   If that is your intent,
   Go wed with a sailor boy,
   I'll never give consent

2. Five thousand pounds —
   Your portion it shall be,
   If this little sailor boy
   You will banish far away.
   The he bought him fine robes,
   Sweet pearls he did wear,
   And straight-way for lackey
   His course he did steer.

3. Then she wrote a long letter,
   To her sailor boy she sent;
   All for to let him know
   Her old father's intent.
   Saying my heart it is sincere,
   My words they will prove true,
   There is none in this wide world
   I fancy but you

4. So she brought him fine robes,
   Sweet pearls he did wear;
   And straight back to rocco
   His course he did steer.
   With a star upon his breast
   For to see his friends again,
   The old man was pleased
   With the young prince of spain.

5. Now he says dearest prince,
   If you will agree
   To marry my daughter,
   Your bride she shall be,
   The up speaks the prince,
   If she will be my bride,
   We will go straight to the church,
   And be married with speed.

6. And away they went together,
   And were married with speed.
   The old man gave up his daughter,
   His daughter, indeed,
   And while that the glasses —
   Were going merrily round,
   The old man paid his daughter
   Down twelve thousand pounds.

7. Then up steps the sailor,
   Saying dont you know me:
   I am that little sailor boy
   You once turned away.
   But since I have outwitted you,
   And crafted but my life,
   I've twelve thousands pounds,
   And your daughter for my wife

8. Then go to the deyvil,
   The old man he cries,
   You have got all my money,
   And my daughter likewise.
   And now they are married,
   And comfort do enjoy,
   She flies to the arms
   Of her jolly Sailor boy.

9. But since you have been so crafty
   As me to deceive
   My blessings I will give to you,
   My estates you shall have.
   And now they are married,
   And comfort do enjoy,
   She flies to the arms
   Of her jolly sailor boy.

B.

"THE SAILOR BOY'S TRICK." James S. Peacock, ship *Europa* of Edgartown, 1868: inscribed in the copybook of George W. Piper, ship *Europa,* 1868-70. Unlike Warner #61, in this text the sailor-protagonist goes to Morocco (not Spain); but, significantly, like the Warner text, he distinguishes himself as a prince of Spain (not Morocco).

1. It is of a young sailor boy of courage stout and bold
   Who courted a lady worth thousands in gold
   Her father said dear daughter if this be your intent
   To marry with a sailor I will never consent

2. She wrote a long line to her sailor boy she sent
   All for to let him know her old father's intent
   She says my dearest Willie I ever will prove true
   There is no one in this world I will marry but you

3. O dearest Mary since you I cant obtain
   I will cross the wild ocean and go unto Spain
   And this crafty prospect he did lay out to try
   To deceive her old father or else he would die

4. He bought him a robe like an earl did appear
   Disguised as a prince from Morocco he did steer
   With a star all on his breast he soon came back again
   The old man was pleased with the young prince of Spain

5. Says he most noble prince if you both can agree
   To marry my daughter your bride she shall be
   O yes with all my heart this young prince did say
   If she will be my wife we will get married to day

6. So off to the church they were hurried with speed
   The old man paid off his daughter his daughter indeed
   And while the full bumpers so merrily went around
   The old man paid off his daughter with ten thousand pounds

7. Up steps this young sailor boy O dont you know me
   I am that young sailor boy you once turned away
   Since you I have outwitted I have gained my life
   Besides ten thousand pounds and a beautiful wife

8. Go to the devil the old man replied
   You have robbed me of my daughter my money likewise
   If I had once mistrusted that this had been your plot
   Not a devil of a cent would you ever have got.

From Your Shipmate
James A Peacock
on board of the whale ship Europa of Edgartown
Captain Mellon [Thomas H. Mellen]
May 29, 1868, up in the North East part of the Okhotsk Sea.

89. The Dark-Eyed Sailor
[Fair Phoebe and Her Dark-Eyed Sailor]
(Laws #N-35)

"The Dark Eyed Sailor" has been described as "one of the most widely known ballads on the 'broken ring' theme" (Fowke 1965, 166), "among the most popular songs on both sides of the Atlantic" (Karpeles, 283), and "one of the most stable songs in folk tradition" (Manny & Wilson, 230). With only rare exceptions it is sung to the same tune as "The Female Smuggler," to which the "Dark Eyed Sailor" text "seems bonded" (Manny & Wilson). As Fowke observes, "Most versions of 'The Dark Eyed Sailor' have the distinctive pattern created by the fourth line… also found in 'The Female Smuggler' which is sung to the same tune." The central premise of the ballad, the woman's loyalty, must have been especially appealing to sailors.

TUNE: "The Female Smuggler," from *Beadle's Dime Melodist,* 1859, p. 23; also in Frank 1998, #26, p. 70 (music corrected from miscounts in measures 9 and 10: compare the change of time signature in Whall and Shay). Compare Healy 1967 #4; O Lochlainn 1939 #5; Karpeles #55; Shay 1948, 190.

A.

"THE DARK EYD SAILOR." John G. Marble, Warren, R.I., circa 1846-47: inscribed in the journal of Stephen O. Hopkins, ship *Rosalie* of Warren, 1843; bark *Perseverance* of Providence, 1849.

1. Tis of a comely young lady fair
   Was a walking out to take the air
   She met a Sailor upon the way
   So I paid attention to hear what they did say

2. Fair maid said he why roam alone
   For the night is coming and the days far gone
   She said while tears from her eyes did fall
   Its my dark eyed sailor that proved my down fall

3. These two long years since he left this land
   A gold ring he took from off my hand
   He broke the token here is half with me
   And the other is roolling at the bottom of the sea

4. Cried William drive him from your care [mind]
   As good a sailor as him you will find
   Love turns aside and cold does grow
   Like a winters morning when the hills are clad with snow

5. These words did Phebes fond heart inflame
   She cried on me you shall play no game
   She drew a dagger and then did cry
   For my dark eyed Sailor a maid I ll live and die

6. Tis coal black eyes and his curly hair
   And flattering tongue did my heart ensnare
   Genteel he was no rake like you
   To advise a maiden to slight the jacket of blue

7. But a tarry sailor I will never disown
   But always I will treat the same
   To drink his health here's a piece of coin
   But my dark eyed sailor still claims this heart of mine

8. When William did the ring unfold
   She seemed distracted midst joy and woe
   Youre welcome William I have lands and gold
   For my dark eyed sailor so manly and bold

9. In a cottage down by the river side
   In unity and love they now reside
   So girls be true while your lovers away
   For a clouday morning oft brings a clouday day

John G. Marble

B.

"THE DARK EYED SAILOR." Theodore D. Bartley, ship *California* of New Bedford, 1851-54.

1. As I walked out one evening
   All along by the Ocean side
   I met a maiden on the way
   And I paid attention to hear what she did say

2. Oh the day is past and the nights come on
   Pray young maid why do you wander alone
   She said whilst the tears from her eye did fall
   Tis my dark eyed sailor has proved my down fall

3. Tis seven long years since he sailed from this land
   He took a gold ring from off my hand
   He broke the token gave one half to me
   While the others rooling to the bottom of the sea

4. Oh drive young William from your mind
   For there is plenty of sailors
   Love turns aside and colder grows
   Like a Winters morning when the hills are covered with snow

5. Oh his coal black eye and his curly hair
   His flattering toung did my heart ensnare
   My William is no rake like you
   To advise a maiden to slight the jacket blue

6. These fond words did her heart inflame
   And on me you shall play no game
   She drew a dagger and then did cry
   For my dark eyed Sailor a maid I'll live and die

7. A tarry sailor I will never disdain
   But always with Respect and kindness breath
   For to drink his health here is half a crown
   But my dark eyed sailor still claims this heart of mine

8. When William did his ring unfold
   She grew distracted with joys untold
   Youre welcome William for I've land and gold
   Tis my dark eyed sailor so manly true and bold

9. I v a cottage down by the River side
   In Unity and love they do both Reside
   So girls be true whilst your lover's away
   For a cloudy morning brings forth a pleasant day

C.

"DARK EYED SAILOR." George M. Jones and Albert F. Handy, bark *Waverly* of New Bedford, 1859-63. Similar to A, including *"two* years" (stanza 3), *"clad* with snow" (4), *"Genteel* he was no rake like you" (6), *"disdain"* (7, line 1), *"piece of coin"* (7, line 3), and "Half distracted with joy and wo[e]" (8); but, in stanza 6, *"cold* black eyes" (see D); and in stanza 8, "manly *true* and bold" (as in B) and "For a cloudy morning oftimes [sic] brings a *pleasant* day" (thus correcting an obvious corruption in A).

D.

"MY DARK EYED SAILOR." William H. Poole, ship *Minnesota* of New York, 1868-72. Orthodox copy text similar to A and C, including "two *long* years" (stanza 3), *"clad* with snow" (4), *"cold* black eyes" and *"genteel"* (6), *"disdain"* and *"piece of coin"* (7), "manly *true* and bold" and "For a cloudy morning *oft* brings a *pleasant* day" (8); but *"She seemed* distracted with joy and woe" (stanza 8).

90. The Mantle So Green
[William O'Reilly; William O'Riley; Fain Waterloo; Famed Waterloo; Erin's Green Shore]
(Laws #N-38)

Up to a point, this is a fairly orthodox text of the ballad described by Laws: a man encounters a woman in a meadow and proposes marriage but she declines, declaring her troth to William O'Riley (or O'Reilly), whose name is embroidered on her "mantle so green." The narrator tells her that William was killed at Waterloo, and describes the circumstances in some considerable detail. Finally, in classic ballad form, he reveals himself to be William O'Riley, but contrary to Laws's description, there is no mention of marriage or further developments, which are here left to the imagination. Its origin is almost certainly Irish and it has frequently been encountered in tradition in Ireland, less often in North America. As the ballad indicates, the final British-allied victory over Napoleon at Waterloo was indeed secured on 18 June 1815.

TUNE - "Mantle So Green," composite, after Helen Creighton, *Songs and Ballads from Nova Scotia*, 1932, #30, p. 60, where the meter (transcribed from singing) is eccentric and is here regularized. Of the several melodies collected in North America, this is by far the most interesting. Compare "Fain Waterloo" (Gardner #57, of which version B is entitled "The Mantle So Green"), where the tune is through-composed for double stanzas and a chorus is added (absent in the whaleman's MS and most other versions): "To the wildwoods I'll wander to shun all men's views, / For the lad I love dearly is in fain Waterloo."

"WILLIAM O'RILEY." William H. Keith, schooners *William Martin* of Boston and *Edith May* of Wellfleet, etc., 1865-71.

1. As I was out walking one morning in May,
   The fields were in blossom & the meadows so gay
   When I espied a fair damsel she appeared like a queen
   With a costly fine robe round her mantle so green.

2. I says my pretty fair maid if you'll but go with me
   We'll both join in wedlock and married will be
   And I will dress you in rich attire you'll appear like a queen
   With a costly fine robe round her mantle so green.

3. She says my pretty young man I must you refuse
   For I will wed with no man so you must excuse
   But through the green fields I will ramble and learn to serve you
   Since the lad that I love is at famed Waterloo.

4. Since you will not marry me pray tell me your lover's name
   For I've been in battle and might know the same
   Draw near to my fair mantle it is there to be seen
   For his name is embroidered on my mantle so green.

5. She threw back her fair mantle
        and there to behold
   His name and her own name
        were in letters of gold
   It is William O Riley
        it appeared in full view
   He was my chief commander
        at famed Waterloo

6. He there fought for victory
        when bullets did fly
   On that field of honor
        your true love did die
   He fought for two days
        till the third afternoon
   He received his death summons
        on the 18th of June.

7. When he was a dying
        these words I heard him say
   If you were here Nancy
        content would I die.
   She then fell in my arms
        with her heart full of woe,
   Rise up lovely Nancy
        your sorrows are oer.

8. O don't you remember
        the last time we met
   It was in your father's garden
        when I first gained your heart
   It was in your father's garden
        where we oftimes have been
   Where I never more will behold you
        in your mantle so green

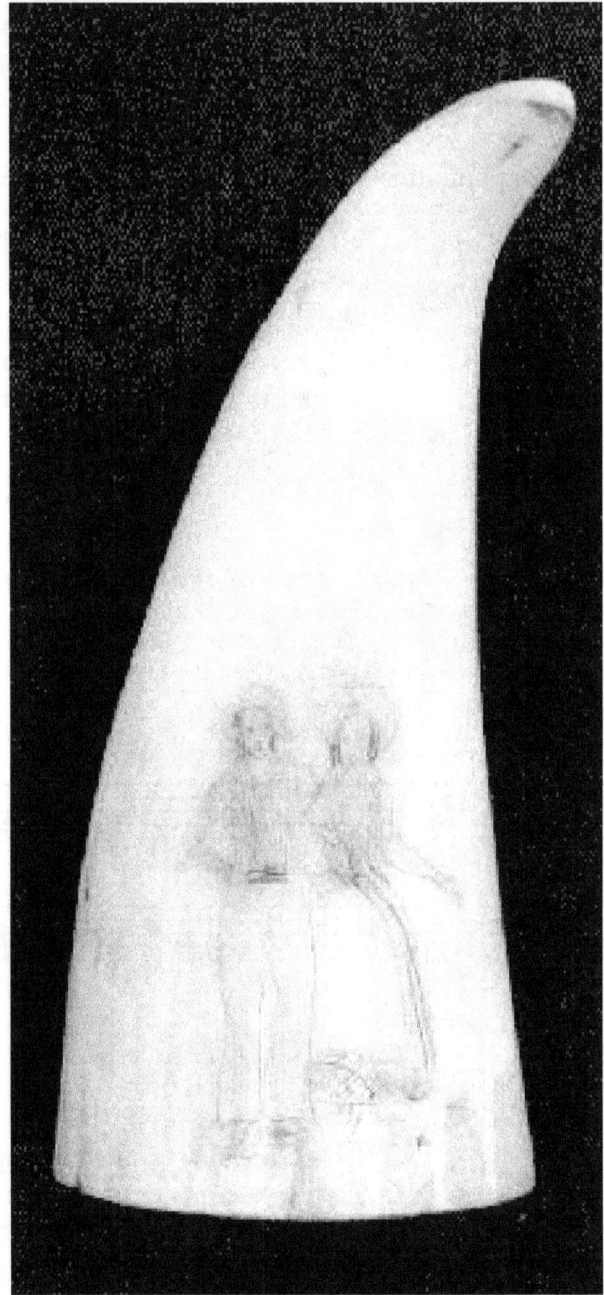

Whaleman's scrimshaw on a sperm whale tooth, depicting a young sailor in nautical togs and his lady, wearing a bonnet. Anonymous, American, mid 19th century. Kendall Collection, New Bedford Whaling Museum.

91. The Pride of Glencoe
[The Banks of Glencoe; MacDonald's Return to Glencoe; etc.]
(Laws #N-39)

On the basis of textual evidence which seems to consist primarily of associations of names and places, most authorities infer that this ballad hearkens back to the Campbell clan's "horrible massacre" of the MacDonalds in the valley of the River Coe in Argyllshire (Scotland) in 1692 and is approximately contemporaneous with the event.[9] "However," claims Edith Fowke to the contrary, "the ballad apparently dates from the early nineteenth century, and the reference to Spaniards suggest that the composer [sic] was thinking of the Peninsular War," that is, Napoleon Bonaparte's conquest of Iberia. The Napoleonic Wars were certainly temporally closer to the broadsides published in the early 19th century, and there is very little in extant texts of the ballad to suggest anything but foreign wars against France and Spain. However, whether these latter-day broadsides represent the original authorship of the ballad or updated revisions of older material has not been definitively ascertained. Presumed to be of West Highland or North Irish origin,[10] it "seems to have had wide currency in both Great Britain and Ireland and was especially popular in Scotland,"[11] which perhaps accounts for wide circulation in Maritime Canada, where it has frequently been recovered from tradition.[12] It is not surprising that a Scots-Irish folk song should also turn up in Australia. In addition to the four texts from whaling journals reported here, Huntington gives two others, which Fowke interprets as an indication of the ballad's particular "appeal for seafaring men." What is remarkable is that despite many sightings in the American whale fishery, the ballad is comparatively rare ashore in the United States, where only a small handful of specimens have been collected.

TUNE A - "Donald's Return to Glencoe," sung to the same air as "The Merchant's Daughter Turned Sailor," from John Ord, *Bothy Songs and Ballads,* 1930: see pp. 63 (tune) and 65 (notes indicating this air).

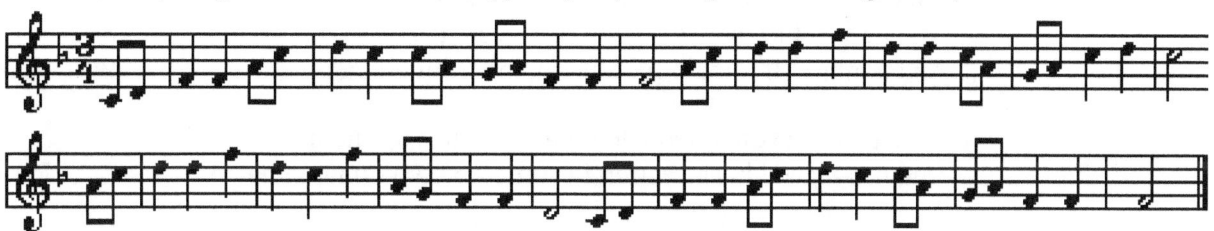

TUNE B - "The Pride of Glencoe," from Helen Creighton, *Maritime Folk Songs,* 1961, p. 60: "Sung by Mr. Tom Gamble, Amherst, August, 1953."

---

[9] Creighton (1971, 78), quoting Kenneth Peacock (1965), erroneously gives the date as 1672. But see Fowke 1981, 68; and *The Columbia Encyclopedia* (New York, [1935] 1950), from which the phrase "horrible massacre" is quoted.

[10] Karpeles 283, quoting Broadwood (JFSS II:171 or V:100).

[11] Mackenzie 180.

[12] According to Edith Fowke, "There are at least four versions from Newfoundland, four from Nova Scotia, two from New Brunswick, and four from Ontario. Another indication of its popularity in [Canada] is the fact that the 'Old Favourites' section of the *Family Herald* printed it nine times between 1917 and 1951, usually by request" (1981, 68f). In addition to the versions from Canadian sources anthologized by Creighton, Fowke, Karpeles, Mackenzie, and Manny & Wilson, even Greenleaf's #87C was collected in Michigan but from an Ontario source.

A.

"MC DONALD RETURN FROM GLENCO." Nathan B, Fisher, first mate, bark *Ocean* of Sandwich, Mass., 1856-57. Initial transcription from the MS by James A. Frazier, Kendall Whaling Museum, 1984. Lines realigned from hap hazard arrangement into stanzas.

1. As I Was a walking one Evening of late
   Where floras green [splendours?] the fields decorate
   I calesly [carelessly] wandered in a place I did not know
   On the banks of a fountain That lyes near Glenco

2. Like her who the pride Of mount ida[13] had won
   She approached me a damsel As bright as the sun
   The ribbons and tartons All around her did flow
   Whitch soon won Mac Donald The pride of Glenco

3. With courage undaunted I unto her drew nigh
   The red rose and lily on Her cheek seemed to vie
   And when I [asked] her her name And how far she had to go
   She answerd cind sir I am bound to Glenco

4. Says I my pretty fair maid Your enchanting smiles
   And your lovly sweet fetures how my hart begu[i]led
   And if your afections Will on me bestow
   You will bless that hapy our we met in Glenco

5. She answerd kind sir Your suit I dislike
   I once had a sweethart young Donald by name
   And he went to the wars about ten years ago
   And a maid I ll remain till he remains from Glenco

6. Perhaps your young Donald regards no to your name
   And has placed his affection in some lovely young dame
   And has quite forgotone for [   ] that you know
   the lovely young lass he lives in Glenco

7. My Donald from his love vowd he can never depart
   For love truth and honer are found in his hart
   And if I never see him I single will go
   and mourn for my Donald the pride of Glenco

8. The french and the spanards are hard to put down
   And many a hero has died of his wounds
   and with your young Donald it may have hapened so
   and the lad you loved dearly perhaps he lies low

9. My Donalds true valor when tried in the field
   Like his gallant ancestors detaining to yield
   the french And the spanards he ll sure Over through
   and in splendor Return to the lasse of Glenco

---

[13] According to Greek mythology and Homeric epic, it was from atop Mount Ida, in Phrygia near Troy, that the gods watched the Trojan War. Mount Ida was also the name of a mountain in Crete, where Zeus is said to have spent his childhood.

10. He finding her constant he drew forth a glove
    whitch she gave Him at parting as a token of love
    She fell into his arms while The tears down her cheeks did flow
    saying are you my Donald returned from Glenco

11. Cheer up my lovely flora [your] trials are oer
    for whilst life Remains we never part more
    And the cruel storms of war At present may blow
    While in pleasant contentment we Reside in Glenco

B.

"MACDONALD." Nellie [Eleanor] Braley, Rochester, Massachusetts, in the journal of her husband, Jason L. Braley, third and second mate, ship *Stephania,* 1847-50; first mate, bark *Louisa,* 1851-53; master, ship *William Badger,* 1853-57, all of New Bedford. Internal evidence in the journal indicates that she transcribed the song shortly after the *William Badger* voyage. The text of 11 stanzas, which begins "As I went out walking one evening of late…" (see Frank 1985 #128B), is similar to A, C, and D: less corrupt and more literate than A, not quite as literate or complete as C and D.

C.

"THE BANKS OF GLENCOE." George W. Piper, ship *Europa* of Edgartown, 1868-70. The first of Piper's two tran scriptions (see D). Note "*seven* years ago" in stanza 5 (A and B have "*ten* years ago").

1. As I walked out one evening of late
   Where Floras gay mantle does the fields decorate
   I carelessly wanderd where I did not know
   On the banks of a Fountain that lies near Glencoe

2. It was there where the pride of Mt Ida[5] was won
   There approached me a damsel as bright as the sun
   With ribbons and tartans around her did flow
   That once gained McDonald the pride of Glencoe

3. With corage undaunted I unto her drew nigh
   The rose and the lily on her cheeks seemed to vie
   I asked her name and where she did go
   She answered me kindly I am bound to Glencoe

4. I said my sweet creature your enchanting smiles
   And your comely fine features has my heart beguiled
   And if your kind affections on me you'll bestow
   You will bless the happy hour we met in Glencoe

5. She answerd me kindly our suit I disdain
   For I once had a true love young Donald by name
   He went to the wars about seven years ago
   And a maid I'll remain till he returns from Glencoe

6. Perhaps your young Donald regards not to your name
   And has placed his affections on some other dame
   And he has quite forgotton for all that you know
   That handsome young lassie he left in Glencoe

7. His true words and vows he never will part
   For love truth and honor I have found in his heart
   And if I never see why it is single I will go
   And I will mourn him he is the pride of Glencoe

8. The French and the Spaniards they are hard to pull down
   They have caused many a hero to die of his wounds
   And with your young Donald it may happen so
   The lad you love dearly perhaps he lies low

9. It is Donalds true valor when tried on the field
   Like his ancestors disdaining to yield
   the French and the Spaniards he will soon overthrow
   And in Splendor he'll return to his maid in Glencoe

10. Now finding her constant he pulled out a glove
    That she gave him at parting as a token of love
    She wept on his breast while the tears down did flow
    Saying are you my Donald returned to Glencoe

11. Now cheer up dearest Flora our sorrows are o'er
    For while life remains we will never part more
    While the rude storms of war at a distance may blow
    In peace and contentment we will live in Glenco

D.

"THE BANKS OF GLENCOE." George W. Piper, ship *Europa* of Edgartown, 1868-70. The second of Piper's two transcriptions, virtually identical to C (q.v.). Note "*seven* years ago" in stanza 5 (A and B have "*ten* years ago").

CHAPTER ELEVEN
The Jolly Roving Tar
Ballads of Faithful and Unfaithful Lovers

> O! swear not by the moon, the inconstant moon,
> That monthly changes in her circled orb,
> Lest thy love prove likewise variable.
>
> —*Romeo and Juliet.*

Jemmy's Farewell. English "Liverpool" creamware pitcher, circa 1790. New Bedford Whaling Museum.

92. Cuper's Garden
[Cupid's Garden; Cobits Garden; Covent Garden; Laurel Wear; The 'Prentice Boy]

This 18th-century ballad is pure English with a beautiful melody. The title of the whaleman's text, *"Cobit's* Garden," is a corruption of *"Cupid's* Garden," which is the title of another 18th-century song reported from the Salem whaleship *Leopart* in 1767 (Huntington 1964, 92); but it is also the corrupt title of the text of "Cobit's Garden" in Chappell's classic *Popular Music of the Olden Time,* which is printed with what is probably the original air. "Cobit's Garden," in turn, is a corruption of *Cuper's* Gardens, which, according to Chappell (II: 727), "were once a place of amusement on the Surrey side [South Bank] of the Thames, exactly opposite to Somerset House," in the London Borough of Southwark. "They derived their name from Boydell Cuper, a gardener in the family of Thomas, Earl of Arundel," who opened the garden in 1678. Facilities for outdoor concerts were added in 1736, and it "subsequently became famous for its displays of fireworks" and "kept up its celebrity for many seasons, but at length yielded to its formidable rival, *Vauxhall,* and was finally closed in 1753. Some accounts say that it was suppressed in consequence of the dissoluteness of its visitors… the company was not always the most select" (Rimbault, *Fly Leaves,* 2nd series, 52, quoted in Chappell II:727). Analogously, *"Covent* Garden" is the title of a text of the same ballad from the ship *Hercules* circa 1828 [text A], an even further corruption in confusion with London's famous coffeehouse district and marketplace since the 17th century.

The confusion certainly did not originate with the whaleman, as one untitled manifestation of "Covent Garden" in a whaleman's journal [text A] is in the form of a printed broadside pasted inside the back cover. In fact, broadsides of "Cupid's Garden" date back at least as far as circa 1785. Like "Cupid's Garden," "Covent Garden" exemplifies evolution in the direction of familiarity: *Cupid* is a natural step from *Cuper,* with implications that are obvious in a love song; and in the 19th century, Covent Garden amusements were a fundamental fixture in the cityscape when Cuper's Garden was long forgotten by most Londoners. While the *"Copit's* Garden" and *"Covent* Garden" titles are each a generation removed from *"Cupid's* Garden," the texts themselves are recognizable variants of the same ballad, with all of the fundamental characteristics fully intact (per Chappell): there are two women in the garden; one is a virgin to whom the narrator becomes betrothed; where her name occurs at all, it is Nancy; he must abandon her temporarily to go to sea, sailing from Portsmouth; but they intend to marry upon his return. On the other hand, while the *Leopart* text of 1767 is chronologically closer to the source and retains the old "Cupid's Garden" title, the ballad itself is quite different, evidently influenced by other ballads, resulting in a text that is fundamentally distinct: there is only one woman in the garden; her name is Sally; there is no mention of a virgin; the woman speaks about following her sailor to Portsmouth and if she does not find him, "it will prove to me severe"; or "if he's buried in the sea, Let me die in his arms." Whatever may be the mixture and corruption of titles and texts, the whalemen's versions here surely resemble closely the original ballad, which could only have arisen in the period 1736-53, when Cuper's Garden was thriving. As such, it is substantially older than most of the kindred broadside ballads in the whalemen's ken. Apart from the three whalemen's texts, it has evidently not been recovered from tradition in North America, and is thus not reported by Laws, though it may be the ancestor or inspiration of "Soldier Boy" (Laws #O-31).

TUNE "'Twas Down In Cupid's Garden," from William Chappell, *Popular Music of the Olden Time,* 1855-59, II:728.

A.

[UNTITLED]. Jephtha Jenney, Jr., ship *Hercules* of New Bedford, 1828-30. From a printed broadside pasted inside the back cover (Huntington 1964, 90). This may be a broadside originally entitled "'Cupid's Garden' or 'The 'Prentice Boy,'" printed in Liverpool by W. Armstrong circa 1820-24. In any case, not only is the text less complete than B, but there are several anomalies and omissions that mark it as a lesser specimen.

1. It was down in Covent Garden
   One day I chanced to rove
   To view the finest flower
   That in the garden grows
   The one it was the [*charming*]
   Pink lily and the rose[1]
   Which was the finest flower
   That in the garden grows
   That in the garden grows

2. The one was lovely Nancy
   Most beautiful and fair
   The other was a virgin
   That still the laurel wear
   In hand and hand together
   This lovely couple went
   Resolved was the sailor
   To know the maid's intent
   To know the maid's intent

3. Altho' that she did slight me
   Because that I was poor
   Oh no my lobe no not my love
   I love a sailor dear
   Down in Portsmouth Harbour
   Our ship lies waiting there
   All fitted out for sea my boys
   When the wind is shall blow fair
   When the wind is shall blow fair

4. If ever I return again
   How happy I shall be
   To have my own true love
   Set dangling on my knee
   And if ever I should return again
   Unto my native shore
   I will marry pretty Nancy
   I'll go to sea no more
   I'll go to sea no more

[*Courting.*] Scrimshaw sperm whale tooth, engraved by an anonymous American whaleman-artist known as the Eagle Portraitist, circa the 1830s. Kendall Collection, New Bedford Whaling Museum.

---

[1] From other texts it appears that the original intent must have been to name four flowers—jasmine, pink, lily, and rose (see text B)—but the implication is that the "fairest flowers" in the garden are the two women.

B.

"COBIT'S GARDEN." Richard C. Reynolds, boatsteerer, ship *Janus* of New Bedford, 1842-44. All of Reynolds's transcriptions are characterized by atrocious spelling, poor capitalization, lack of punctuation, and inconsistent (if any) division of lines into stanzas. However, some of his texts are truly significant. This one appears to be the most substantial, articulate, poetic, and complete rendition of "Cobit's Garden / Cupid's Garden" ever recovered from a traditional source. For singing, though there is no indication in the transcription, the tune requires that the last phrase of the least line of each stanza be repeated (e.g., "These were the fairest flowers that in this garden grow, *that in this garden grow*"; "The other it was a virgin and still the laurels wear, *and still the laurels wear*").

1. A down in cobit's garden with pleasure i did go
   To view the fairest flowers that in this garden grow
   The first it was the jassamine the lily pink and rose
   These wer the fairest flowrs that in this garden grow

2. I had not walked this garden the space of half an hour
   Before i spied tow pretty fair maides setting under the shady bower
   The first it was lovely nancy moste beautifull and fair
   The other it was a virgin and still the laurels ware

3. I boldely steped up to them and u[n]to her did say
   Are you engaged to anny young man tell to me i pray
   I am not engaged to any one i solemnly declare
   I am to live a virgin and still the laurels ware.

4. Then hand in hand togeather this loveing couple went
   Resolved was the sailor to know her full entent
   To know if she would slight him and from his presence go
   No said she a no my dear i love a sailor boy

5. A down in portsmouth harbour our ship she does ly their
   And I must go to sea my love where the wind it blowes fair
   But if ever i return again how happy i shall be
   With my true love my owne true love set smiling on my knee

6. Fair you well my lovely virgin since i to the sea must go
   Whear their is many a dark and dismal night, and stormy winds do blow
   But if ever i return again unto my native shore
   I will mar[r]y my lovely virgin and go to sea no more

Richard C. Reynolds Dartmouth

93. The Lass of Mohee
[Little Mohee; My Little Mohee; Pretty Mohee; ... Mowee; etc.]
(Laws #H-8)

Integral to the enduring myth of the Enchanted Islands — an element that predates Homer, confounded Odysseus on more than one occasion, provided Saint Amselm potent philosophical analogies, and transfixed European culture since medieval times, occasioning many a young visionary lad to sign articles for a sea voyage—was the allure of the exotic women that seafarers were inevitably expected to encounter in their travels to the farthest reaches of the watery world. In literary and cinematic interpretations, at least, native Tahitian women figure importantly in the drama of HMS *Bounty* and the flight of the mutineers to desolate Pitcairn; Fayaway is a native Marquesan Island lass eager to pledge eternal troth to the protagonist of Herman Melville's *Typee* (1847);[2] and in Eugene O'Neill's *Moon of the Caribbees* (1917), the resonant pulse of native drums haunts and teases modern-day steamship sailors no less than the Sirens affected Odysseus's crew. The theme is often reiterated in whalemen's scrimshaw, shipboard drawings, poetry, and songs; and whether concerning the "Girls Around Cape Horn" on the coast of South America, the tropical South Seas, or the Frozen North, there is an ever-present tension between the exotic allure of remaining in a romantically-perceived State of Nature, versus returning to a State of Civilization back home. "The Lass of Mohee" is an indigenous Yankee sailor ballad along these lines, narrating a sailor's encounter with a beautiful Native woman in the Hawaiian Islands and his reluctant refusal to remain with her rather than return to his lover left waiting back home. The theme and descent of the ballad are intertwined with the closely-related British ballad "The Indian Lass"; and both have a corollary in "The Lake of Ponchartrain" (Laws #H-9), known in Irish tradition and New England: this ballad concerns a sailor's encounter with a lovely Creole woman in the Louisiana bayou. There, the sailor proposes, but *she* refuses, to wait faithfully for the return of her own sailor lad.[3]

Of the popularity of "The Lass of Mohee" among American whalemen there can be no doubt. The Hawaiian outports of Honolulu, Lahaina, and Hilo they regarded as their particular turf; they were not above battling missionaries and other inhibiting interests for freedom of the Hawaiian Sailortowns. Kanaka women they knew first hand. The later song "Rolling Down to Old Mohee" [#143] expresses in lyrics of undisputed sailor origin, in the whalemen's own words, the keen, exuberant anticipation of liberty ashore on Maui after tedious months whaling in the frozen Arctic, and the Island "maidens" who were the principal attraction. Whalemen sometimes mutinied — that is, refused duty — when not afforded sufficient liberty in Hawaiian ports; and this desire was neither fortuitous nor entirely recreational, for here in Polynesia the ancient myth of the Enchanted Islands had become a reality of sorts, especially if the agreeable climate and congenial Island people be compared to the alternatives: a monastic life on shipboard, brutal labor, numbing boredom, the frigid miseries of hunting bowheads in the Okhosk and Bering Seas, and even the snowy winters and humid summers of New England. Many whalemen jumped ship. Some never did return to the girl back home.[4]

---

[2] Expanded from his experience as a deserter from the whaleship *Acushnet* of Fairhaven in 1842 and his subsequent captivity in the Marquesas Islands, *Typee* was Melville's first novel and only commercial success. The sequel is *Omoo* (1847), .

[3] For a discussion of the relationship between "Lass of Mohee" and "Indian Lass," see the note at the end of this section.

[4] Huntington reports four texts of "Lass of Mohee" in whaling journals. One of these he published (with a fragment of a second) in *Songs the Whalemen Sang* (150f), where his disarmingly casual comments effectively expose the often foggy irrelevancies of scholarly "insight": "Barry, in the *Bulletin of the Folk Song Society of the Northeast*, No. 6, pp. 15-16... says 'As the Kanakas were not Indians we conclude that Maui is adventitious, that the ballad originally dealt with the romance of an Indian and a pioneer.' Perhaps so, but this is not the original song 'The Miami Lass,' if that is indeed the original, any more than 'The Boston Burglar' is 'Botany Bay.' This is 'The Pretty Maid of Mohee' or 'The Little Mohee' and it is whalemen's work. For to a whaleman a Polynesian and an Indian would be pretty much the same thing. There were few ethnologists among them."

In recent decades "Lass of Mohee" has customarily been sung to same melody as "On Top of Old Smokey," which does not bear repetition for more than a couple of stanzas, much less than for the entire duration of a narrative ballad.[5] At a sea music festival at Mystic Seaport not long before his death, Stan Hugill suddenly recalled an air for "Lass of Mohee"— never published among his many songs—which turns out to be a form of one of the airs that Kidson gives for his Yorkshire version of "The Indian Lass."

TUNE A - "The Lass of Mohee," from the singing of Stan Hugill of Aberdovey, Gwynedd, Wales (a native of Holy lake, Cheshire, England; and sometime resident of Liverpool); collected and transcribed by Stuart M. Frank, Mystic, Connecticut, June 1990; subsequently also recorded on tape by John Townley, June 1990.

TUNE B - "The Indian Lass," from Frank Kidson, *Traditional Tunes,*" 1891, "second version," p. 111: "noted down by Mr. Lolley [North Yorkshire]."

A.
"THE LASS OF MOHEA." Lyman Holmes, ship *John Howland* of New Bedford, 1841-43. An orthodox text of 10 stanzas not unlike B.

B.
"THE LASS OF MOHEE." Geo. M. Jones & Albert F. Handy, bark *Waverly* of New Bedford, 1859-63. Stanza 1 is missing a line, the remainder is a complete text.

1. As I was a roving and rambling
   For pleasure one day
   [*In loves recreation and love cast away*]
   as I sat a musing myself on the grass
   O who should draw nigh me
   But a sweet Indian lass

2. She sat down beside me and squesed my hand
   Saying I think you are a stranger
       not one of this land
   But if you'll follow after
       you are welcome to come
   For I live by my self in a snug little home

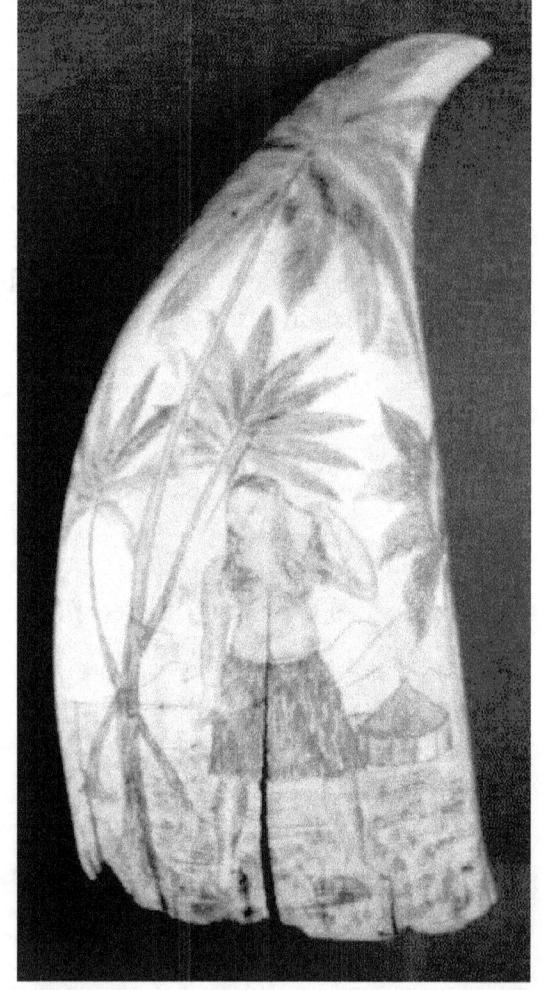

The Lass of Mohee. Sperm whale tooth scrimshaw, engraved and signed by whaleman George O. Hilliot, circa the 1830s-40s. Kendall Collection, New Bedford Whaling Museum.

---

[5] E.g., compare Colcord 199 (Frank 1985 #123, tune A) and Creighton 1933 #51 (Frank 1985 #123, tune B).

3. The sun was fast setting all on the salt sea
   As I wandered along with my pretty Mohee
   We rambled together and together we roved
   Till we came to her home in a coaconut grove

4. As I entered her cottage she lisped in my ear
   I think you are a sailor for so you appear
   But if you ll leave of[f] roving and stay along with me
   I ll teach you the language of the isle of Mohee

5. O no pretty fair maid that never can be
   For Ive a sweetheart in my own country
   And I never will forsake her poor though she be
   For her heart is as pure as my little Mohee

6. Early next morning at the dawning of the day
   It grieved her heart sorely these words I did say
   Farewell my dear jewell farewell my dear
   Our ship has set sail and for home we must steer

7. The last time I saw her twas on the strand
   As my boat shoved of[f] shore she waved her hand
   Saying when you return to the girl that you love
   Remember the lass of the coaconut grove

8. And now I am landed on my own native shore
   Where friends and relations flocked around me once more
   Theres none that came nigh me no not one that I see
   Whose beauty can compare with my pretty Mohee

B.

"THE LASS OF MOHEE." Charles D. Atherton, bark *Oak* of Nantucket, 1869 [MS deposited in the Kendall Whaling Museum from a private collection, courtesy of Mr. & Mrs. Robert D. Webb, Marion, Mass., 1984]. In most respects remarkably like A; verses doubled and misnumbered in the MS, here rectified and regularized into four-line stanzas. Even so, stanzas 6 through 9 appear to be out of order. The line *"as I winder alone"* in stanza 7 (a stanza that does not appear in A) seems to contradict the entire sense of the ballad, that is, that he has forsaken the Lass of Mohee in favor of a woman back home), unless the interpretation be (as could well also be applied to A), that upon reflection back home, he regrets his decision.

1. As I was out walking for pleasure one day
   In loves recreation and love cast away
   As I sat down amusing myself on the grass
   O who should come along but a young Indian lass

2. She sat down beside me and squeezed my hand
   Saying I think you are a stranger not one of this land
   But if you will follow you are welcome to come
   And live along with me in a snug little home

3. The sun was just setting along the salt seas
   As I wandered along with my pretty Mohee
   Together rambled Together we roved
   Until we came to a hut in a cocoanut grove

4. This fond expression she mad[e] unto me
   Saying if you will consent for to live along with me
   No more shall you go a roving all along the salt sea
   But I will learn you to speak the language of the Isle of Mohee

5. Oh no my pretty Mohee that never can be
   For I have an own sweetheart in my own country
   But I will neve[r] forsake her all for her poverty[6]
   For her heart be as true as the lass of Mohee

6. The last time I saw her she sat on the strand
   As the boat passed by her she waved her hand
   Saying when you get over to the girl that you love
   Pray think on the lass in the cocoanut grove

7. This pretty young Indian is pleasant and kind
   She acted her part well in heavens designs
   For I was a stranger and she took me to her home
   And I'll think the Mohee lass as I wander alone

8. The last time I met her was at the break of the day
   And I grieved her heart when these words I did say
   I am going for to leave you so farewell my dear
   For the ship she is now ready and for home we now steer

9. O now I am safe landed on my own native shore
   Where friends and relations flock around me once more
   But as I gaze around me the[re] is none I can see
   That I can compare with the lass of Mohee

Note: Anthologists are fond of quoting George Lyman Kittredge's observation that "Lass of Mohee" is "a chastened American remaking" of "The Indian Lass" (JAF 35:408, 1922), which latter song "had little circulation in the United States" (Mackenzie 155). While there is no doubt that "Lass of Mohee" is intimately related to "Indian Lass," the supposition that "Indian Lass" is actually the ancestor is premised upon insufficient evidence and circular reasoning. The direction of influence remains equivocal. In fact, "Indian Lass" could as easily be "a licentious remake of 'Lass of Mohee.'" Certainly by classifying it among "Native American Balladry" Laws appears satisfied of a sufficiently American origin to constitute its separate standing as a distinct ballad; yet just as certainly, the themes, tunes, and elements of text are held in common. The case for primacy is simply not solved. On the other hand, the byzantine argument that "Lass of Mohee" did not originally refer to a *Kanaka* (Polynesian) woman at all but rather is a corruption of *Maumi* or *Miami* in reference to a squaw of the Miami tribe in the American Midwest, is patent nonsense. By the time this argument was reiterated by Flanders (1931, 146), whose uncharacteristically misguided remarks on this occasion were likely influenced by Phillips Barry, it had already been convincingly debunked by Eckstom & Smith (1927, 233) and by Scarborough (1925, 345). However, not only do the coconut groves and grass shacks in virtually all manifestations of "Lass of Mohee" (including the earliest documented texts) suggest a South Seas locale (versus the Miami Indian homeland in Wisconsin, Michigan, and Ohio), but what even Eckstom & Smith and Scarborough fail to point out is that *Mohee* is a perfectly coherent and irrefutably specific allusion to the Hawaiian Islands. *Mohee* is the antecedent spelling of *Maui,* and was standard usage among sailors, chroniclers, cartographers, and everyone else from the time that Cook first called there in the 1770s—that is, since long before the Old Northwest was settled—until the *Maui* spelling was adopted in the middle 19th century. *Mohee* was one of three Hawaiian Islands (then called the Sandwich Islands) frequented by whalers from 1819 onwards; the others were *Woahoo* or *Wahoo* (Oahu) and *Owayhee* (Hawai'i). Proponents of the Miami Indian theory simply got the transformation the wrong way round: if anything, *Maumi* or *Miami* are the latter-day corruptions in Midwestern tradition. As for the *Indian* reference, Smithyman (1970, 64-70) articulately demonstrates its ambiguous character and applicability to native Hawaiians.

---

[6] See "The Jacket of Blue," #94, stanza 7.

94. The Jacket of Blue

This is an obscure nautical version of "The Bonnet of Blue," itself a fairly obscure Scottish ballad having to do with Highland regiments and clans ("There came a troop of soldiers, as you now shall hear…"); the two are sung to the same air.[7] In whichever form, the ballad is rarely encountered in North America and was evidently unknown to Laws. The nautical rendition here concerns a woman who meets a sailor on the Liverpool docks: he declines her advances and returns to another woman. A broadside printed by Catnach (Holloway & Black #9) has the same title and a similar story, but with the opposite outcome. As Huntington also encountered a text in Benjamin A. Coffin's journal aboard the bark *Catalpa* of New Bedford circa 1856 (where it is entitled "Bonnet of Blue" and which Huntington calls "garbled and full of mistakes"), whaleman Edward J. Kirwin's text of 1872 is not strictly an anomaly: the ballad must have been known in the whale fishery and probably also ashore in New England in the 19th century, but (if it were ever much sung) it had evidently fallen out of tradition by the time ballad collectors took to the field.

TUNE A - "The Bonnet of Blue," from Robert Ford, *Vagabond Songs and Ballads of Scotland,* 1904, p. 212.

TUNE B - "The Bonny Scotch Lad," from Frank Kidson, *Traditional Tunes,* 1891, p. 118.

"THE JACKET OF BLUE." Edward J. Kirwin, cooper, bark *William Gifford* of New Bedford, 1872: "Repeat last two lines of each verse." Similar to Huntington 1964,, 276f, which also has the "ship's crew of sailors" premise, but the Kirwin text is more complete and less garbled.

>   1.   A ship's crew of sailors as you now shall hear
>   A voyage from London to Liverpool did steer
>   There is one lad among that I wish I had never knew
>   He is a jolly sailor lad wears the jacket of blue

---

[7] "The 'blue bonnet'…[is] a distinguishing badge of the Highlanders, and more particularly of those attached to the family of the Royal Stewarts…," says Robert Ford (1904, 214), who gives the complete text of a Highland version set in Yorkshire (pp. 212f), of which the second stanza is:

> There came a troop of soldiers, as you now shall hear,
> From Scotland to Kingston, aboard for to steer:
> There is one man amongst them I wish I ne'er knew
> He's a bonnie Scotch lad and his bonnet o' blue.

2. As I was a walking down by a ship's side
   I listened with pleasure and heard what was said
   His name I'll not mention but his heart it was true
   He was a jolly sailor lad wears the jacket of blue

3. Bright early next morning I arose from my bed
   And called on Sarah my own waiting maid
   Come dress me as sine as your two hands can do
   For I long to see lad that wears the jacket of blue

4. My love he passed by me with a rope in his hand
   I strove to speak to him but my would not stand
   I strove to speak to him but away then he flew
   And my heart it went along with the jacket of blue

5. Said I honored sailor I will buy your discharge
   I will free you from the navy and set you at large
   If you will but love me to you I'll prove true
   And I never will put a stain on your jacket of blue

6. Oh no noble lady I can buy my discharge
   I can free myself from the navy and then be at large
   If I could but love you to you I would prove true
   But you never can have the lad that wears the jacket of blue

7. For I have a girl in my own Country
   Do you think I would slight her in her poverty[8]
   To the girl that I love I'll prove constant and true
   For she never has put a stain on my jacket of blue

8. Now I will go to London where the Artists do dwell
   I'll have my love's likeness drawn out in full
   And in my bed chamber keep it close to my view
   For I long to have the sailor lad wear the jacket of blue

December 28th 1872 Wm. Gifford "bark"
in Lat. 23° 11′ South, Lon. 31° 45′ West
Steering to the north'ard bound home

---

[8] See "The Lass of Mohee," #93, text B, stanza 5.

95. Ellen the Fair
(Laws #O-5)

A cottage-dwelling maiden wins favor and marriage from a landed nobleman, who shows her off at court. Several broadsides and songster texts of this were published (without music), but the ballad was evidently not very widespread in tradition and the tune is virtually extinct. However, despite its rarity elsewhere, it must have been fairly popular on Marthas Vineyard: Captain Rodolphus W. Dexter, the only whaleman known to have transcribed the ballad (the text given here), was from Tisbury, on that island; Huntington found an anonymous transcription in the historical archives at Edgartown; and the tune that Huntington collected from a fellow-Vineyarder and in-law is almost the only one to survive. Its obscurity is easily understood. Neither the music nor the poetry is distinguished by any particular artistic merit. The tune is simplistic and colorless, the lyrics are trite, the syntax formulaic, the rhyme-scheme strained, and the plot virtually non-existent, lacking dramatic tension. Huntington himself reports, "The melody used for this song is the one that Bill Tilton sang it to. I liked the melody but at the time didn't think much of the song and never learned it, or even took down the words…" (MS, 323). Apart from the strong connection to Vineyard tradition, the most appealing and charming feature of the ballad is Captain Dexter's personalized transcription, which he rounds out with an original stanza of his own, dedicated to his wife, Irena, who was thousands of miles away at the time, back on the Vineyard.

TUNE: "Ellen the Fair," from the singing of Bill Tilton, Marthas Vineyard, Mass., collected and reported by Gale Huntington in his unpublished MS, *The Gam,* pp. 321-323, where it accompanies an anonymous text gleaned from the archives of the Dukes County Historical Society, Edgartown.

"ELLEN THE FAIR." Rodolphus W. Dexter, master, ships *Chili* and *Israel* of New Bedford, 1843-46. Captain Dexter's transcription (which contains truly bizarre spelling errors, considering the presentable character of most of the text) is followed by an original stanza of his own, inscribed to his wife.

1. Fair Ellen one morn from hir cottage had strayed
   to the next market town tripped the bautiful maid
   she looked like a goddess so charming and fair
   come buy my sweet posies cried ellen the fair

2. I've cowslips and Jessamines and hair bells so blue
   wild roses and eglantines glistening with dew
   and the lilly the queen of the valley so rare
   come buy my sweet posies cried ellen the fair

3. enraptured gazed on this bautiful maid
   for a thousand sweet smiles on her countenance played
   and while I stood gazing my heart I declere
   a captive was taken by ellen the fair

4. oh! could I but gain this nymph for my wife
   how gladly wold I change my condition in life
   I'd forsake the gay folks of the town and repair
   to dwell in a cottage with ellen the fair

5. but what need I care for the lordly or great
   my parents are dead I've a noble estate
   and no body on earth nor a princess shall share
   my hand and my fortune with ellen the fair

6. In a little time after this nobleman's son
   did marry the maid his affections had won
   when presented at court how the monarch did stare
   and the ladies all envied sweet ellen the fair

Rodolphus W Dexter

*Oh Could I but see my sweet lady so fair I'd
care not for ellen nor lillys so rare but at home
I would stop & always be there to dwell with my sweet
ones in that cottage fair*

this verse is to my wife

*Irena Dexter
oh you charmer*

96. The Sailor and the Shepherdess
[The Shepherdess]
(Laws #O-8)

This broadside-influenced ballad is descended in part from "The Knight and the Shepherd's Daughter" (Child #110). Versions have been collected from tradition in Britain and Maritime Canada, but the song is rare in the United States, where Nantucketer George Snow Cleveland's shipboard manuscript is evidently the only specimen reported. Able Seaman John F. Martin of Philadelphia also mentions this or a similar ballad ("There was a Sheppards daughter Kept sheep on yonder hill") having been performed at sea aboard the whaleship *Lucy Ann* of Wilmington, Delaware, in 1842, but, unfortunately, he gives no text. Ordinarily, the ballad narrates the chance encounter and eventual union of a man and a woman. The whaleman's text, which he evidently regarded as complete, differs significantly from the mainstream in that here the couple do not marry and the narrative remains unresolved: it ends with the woman's objections to sailors' long absences and consequent unsuitability as husbands; and, unlike some versions of the ballad, here the sailor does not forsake his career to remain with her. The few extant tunes appear all to be derivative and corrupt. The greater conservatism in Canadian oral tradition which perpetuated this ballad long after it had evidently dropped out of tradition 'Stateside appears in this instance to have been more conscientious regarding text than tune. One of the tunes collected by Cecil Sharp for "The Knight and the Shepherd's Daughter" is given below for comparison with the only North American tune specimen yet to come to light.

TUNE A - "The Knight and the Shepherd's Daughter," from Cecil J. Sharp, *100 English Folksongs,* 1916, #3, pp. 7f; notes p. xviii. A chorus (not present in "Sailor and the Shepherdess") is "Line, twine, the willow and the dee).

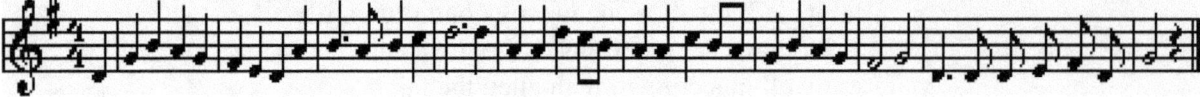

TUNE B - "The Shepherdess," from Helen Creighton, *Folksongs from Southern New Brunswick,* 1971, #37, pp.81f; "Sung by Mrs. Clem O'Connor, Moncton, N.B."; cites alternate titles "The Sailor's Courtship," "The Sailor and the Shepherdess," and "The Lady Shepherd."

"THE SHEPHERDESS." George S. Cleveland, second mate and first mate, ship *Charles* of New Bedford, 1837-40. Creighton (1971, 82) remarks of her version, "Marriage follows meeting so swiftly that this could be another song of the returned lover who is not recognized at first"; but Cleveland's text provides additional evidence that the meeting is indeed fortuitous.

1. It was of a shepherdess a feeding of her flock
   by a rock that was near the seaside
   when A Jolly young sailor by chance came that way
   and fain would have made her his bride

2. The weather being Clear she lie down to sleep
   which caused him to sigh and to say
   he kissed her sweet lips while she lie fast asleep
   saying you have stole my poor heart away

3. She opened her eyes and to her great surprise
   she saw this young sailor standing by
   young sailor she said home Came you here by me
   and by that she began for to sigh

4. I Came from on board of yonder ship you see
   I was cast all alone on the [   ]
   in hope my dearest dear even Comfort to find here
   or else I am forever undone

5. young sailor said she how Could you fancy me
   when you know I can give no Consent
   for when you are on the seas I can never be at ease
   which will cause me to sigh and lament

97. The Jolly Sailor
[The Jolly Sailor, or The Lady of Greenwich]

The whaleman's manuscript is an untitled ballad text that suggests, but is not actually very much like, "The Jolly Sailor and the Beautiful Queen" (Laws #O-13)—a sailors' fantasy-come-true, of marrying a wealthy, beautiful woman and retiring to a life of ease. While the story line develops according to Laws's taxonomic description of "Jolly Sailor and Beautiful Queen," the meter, cadence, phrasing, and syntax of the manuscript differs markedly from the versions cited by Laws (Creighton & Senior 180; Creighton 1933, 76; Doerflinger 298). On the other hand, the manuscript is essentially the same song as a broadside entitled "The Jolly Sailor; or, The Lady of Greenwich" (Ashton 1891, 168), with which it has a plot, a few key phrases, and several stanzas (differently ordered) in common, But the latter ballad is not mentioned by Laws, probably because it has not previously been collected in North America.

[UNTITLED.] John G. Marble, Rhode Island, circa 1846-47: inscribed in the journal of Stephen O. Hopkins, ship *Rosalie* of Warren, 1843; and bark *Perseverance* of Providence, 1849. In stanza 7, Ashton has "*weald* of Kent."

1. A lady lived in London town
   A sailor from the Ocean came
   A lad he was both neat and trim
   The lady fell in love with him

2. Twas unto him she then did say
   Why do you cross the raging sea
   Kind sir I hear that you have no wife
   Why do you lead a single life

3. Tis I poor Sailor he replied
   Who scarcely for myself can provide
   And if I had a wife an family
   I could not al their wants supply

4. Twas unto him she then did say
   O stay at home and leave the sea
   For there is many a lady of high degree
   That fain would wed a man like me

5. O no says he there is one thing more
   I am ofttimes where the billows roar
   And if anything should happen at sea
   There is none on shore to mourn for me

6. O stay at home again says she
   O stay at home and marry me
   Five hundred thousand pounds she cried
   Will make you leave the ocean wide

7. So married they were the very next day
   The sailor and the lady gay
   So hand in hand together they went
   Triumphant to the Isle of Kent

98. The Sailor's Return
[Jack the Sailor]

This broadside-type ballad, not noted by Laws, was evidently transcribed from singing or oral recitation, and seems to be a variant of "Jack the Sailor."

"JACK THE SAILOR" from Kidson, *Garland*, p. 32; and Duncan, *Minstrelsy of England*, p. 136 ("A traditional song which appears in another dress as 'The Tarry Sailor.' (*Christie's Traditional Ballad Airs*, vol. 1, p. 244.)"

"THE SAILOR'S RETURN." Samuel Taylor, ship *Samuel Robertson*, schooner *Oxford*, and bark *Arab* of Fairhaven, fur-sealing at Heard's Island, Antarctica, 1852-60. The final stanza is not complete, and the faulty meter and rhyme-scheme require considerable adjustment for singing.

1. As I walked out one May morning, down by the sea side was a walking
   O there I espied a fair maid unto her father talking

2. She says my true love has come on shoar he is the only lad that I adore
   I pray such fancy does give o'er and ill'd wed with my tarry sailor

3. Five hundred pounds I have left by your aunt, five hundred more Ill'd leave you
   But if you marry without my consent not a farthing will I give you

4. Besides you are a day to young and sailors they have falce flattering tongue[s]
   So quit my premesis and begone if you wed with your tarry Sailor

5. O dear father dont say no nor try to seperate us
   For if you do my hearte youl'd breake greate grief youl'd create us

6. Besides my love is so sincere I love my love forever dear
   I love my love forever dear and ill'd wed with my tarry Sailor

7. Then up steps jack as nimble as a bee Saying whare is my lovely nancy
   She is the onley girl that I adoar the only girl I fancy

8. Saying nancy nancy will you marry me will you marry me say yes or no
   Will you marry me say yes or no will you wed with your tarry Sailor

9. Believe me jack I cant marry you at all with your pockets emty
   O no my dear I have gold in store I have got gold and silver plenty

10. Them down on the table then jack told five hundred gunies all in bright gold
    And into her apron he swept them so bould saying take them from jack your Sailor

11. Her old father a standing by seeing jack behave so clever
    It is a pitty that you two loves should part dam me jack but you Shall have her

12. And since you have parted with all your Store I will do it to you and five times more
    I will double to you and ten times more because you are a clever Sailor

13. Then come brave boys let's drink about and spend this night in pleasure
    Then come brave boys let's drink about for i've got safely Married

14. And now my Ship is riged wright with j[e]wel blocks and sails so white
    Dam me but ill'd board her this night and prove myself

99. The Green Mossy Banks of the Lea
[The American Stranger]
(Laws #O-15)

Despite its English setting and an American protagonist from Philadelphia, the provenance and publishing history of "The Green Mossy Banks of the Lea" are largely Irish. Like the early British broadsides cited by Mackenzie and Cazden, the whalemen's transcriptions lack the usual incongruous flaw (present in most versions gleaned from tradition on both sides of the Atlantic) of locating the River Lea in Ireland, rather than England. (The actual River Lea joins the Thames about four miles east of the City of London, in the Docklands district near the Isle of Dogs—in reality hardly a pastoral setting with "green, mossy banks," but rather a brutally urban Sailortown precinct, where the East Indies, West Indies, and whaling fleets were typically docked and their sailors and cargoes onloaded and offloaded.) Thus, the whalemen's transcriptions as the earliest specimens of the ballad yet recovered, tend to corroborate Mackenzie's claim that the "original" text was corrupted as it became localized in Ireland. However, as *lea* is also a generic noun meaning *meadow* or *grassland* (especially in poetic usage), there may not have been any perceived incongruity in retaining the name of an English river in an Irish setting, and this may also explain the handful of other Irish songs with Irish settings that imply the existence of a River Lea or Lee in Ireland, such as "The Bells of Shandon" by Francis Mahoney (Molloy, 90). Cazden provides a parallel Irish pedigree and has much to say about the provenance of text and tune (Cazden 1982, 130ff). Several tune variants are extant, each quite different in the details, some are in major, others in minor and modal keys, but all are apparently related and perhaps derive from a common ancestor.

TUNE - "The Green Mossy Banks of the Lea," from W. Roy Mackenzie, *Ballads and Songs from Nova Scotia,* 1928, #47, p. 397.

A.

"THE AMERICAN STRANGER." Robert N. Hughson, bark *Java* of New Bedford, 1857-60. In stanza 1, the fourth line is omitted from the transcription (compare B, stanza 1) and is supplied.

1. When first in this country I landed
   Curiosity caused me to roam
   To England I quickly sailed over
   [*And I left Philadelphia my home*]
   I have traveled through all parts of Europe
   Where scenes of great beauty did shine
   T'ill at length I espied a fair damsel
   And I wished in my heart she was mine.

2. One morning as I carelessly did ramble
   Where the pure winds from Heaven do blow
   Down by a clear crystal fountain
   Where the pure sparkling waters they flow.
   T'was there I espied this fair damsel,
   She appeared like a goddess to me
   A plucking of wild those red roses
   On the green mossy banks of the lee.

3. I stepped up and I bid her good morning
    Her cheeks they did blush like the rose
    Said I these green meadows are charming
    Your guardian I'll be if you choose
    Kind sir I do ne'er want a guardian
    Young man you are a stranger to me
    For yonders my Father a coming
    On the green mossy banks of the lee.

4. I waited t'ill up came her father
    And I plucked up my spirits once more
    Said I is this your lovely young daughter
    This beautiful girl I adore
    Ten thousand a year is my fortune
    And a lady your daughter may be
    She can ride in her chariot and horses
    On the green mossy banks of the lee.

5. They invited me home their cottage
    Where in wedlock we soon were to join
    T'was there I erected a castle
    In beauty and splendor doth shine
    But now the American Stranger
    Great pleasure and pastimes doth see
    With adorable gentle Matilda
    On the green mossy banks of the lee.

6. Now come all you pretty fair maids pay attention
    No matter how poor you may be
    For the poor girls are just as handsome
    As those with their large property
    For flattering let no man deceive you
    Who knows but your fortune may be
    Like adorable gentle Matilda, on
    On the green mossy banks of the lee.

B.

"ON THE GREEN MOSSEY BANKS OF THE LEA." Frederick H. Smith, boatsteerer, bark *Roscius* of New Bedford, 1860. A transcription of five stanzas only, lacking the cautionary stanza 6 (see A); in other respects much like A. Stanza 1 here is more typical than the corresponding stanza in A; and *Lea* (rather than *Lee*) is correct throughout. Sample stanzas illustrate principal departures from A; others include: *"guidance"* (rather than *guardian*) in both instances in stanza 3 (i.e., "She says I dont wish any *guidance"*); in stanza 4, "Ten thousand a year is my *portion"* (rather than *fortune*), and *"She shall ride in a Coach with six horses"* (rather than "She *can* ride in her *chariot* and horses"); and in stanza 5, "they *welcomed* [rather than *invited*] me home to their cottage."

1. When first I arrived in this country
    Curiosity caused me to roam
    When I quickly sailed over to England
    And left sweet Philadelphia my home.
    I quickly sailed over to England
    Where the forms of great beauty do shine,
    It was there that I espied a fair maiden
    And I wished in my heart she was mine

2. It was down by a clear crystal river
    Where the pure winds soft breezes do blow
    It was down by a clear crystal river
    Where the sweet water lilies do grow.
    It was there I espied a fair maiden
    Some goddess she appeared to me
    As she stood on the bank [of the] river
    On the green mossey [banks] of the Lea.

Frederick Howland Smith
Dartmouth Massachusetts
on board the barque
in the year of our Lord 1860

100. The Bold Fisherman
[The Sailor Boy]
(Laws #O-24)

What the whaleman calls "The Sailor Boy" is actually an adaptive text of "The Bold Fisherman," with the protagonist's disguise changed from a fisherman to a sailor. The other elements described by Laws—a nautical disguise concealing gold chains, the discovery, apology, pardon, and betrothal—remain intact. The various tunes vary but little. Sharp's has an eccentric meter but is otherwise quite similar to the Down East version given by Flanders & Olney. The air from Hertfordshire (Tune A) is a more interesting variant perhaps older than the others.

TUNE A - "As I Walked Out," from Broadwood & Maitland, *English County Songs,* 1893, p.110: collected from Mr. Thomas Gray of Weston, near Hitchin, Hertfordshire, "who describes it as 'ancients of years old.'"

TUNE B - "The Bold Fisherman," from memory. Compare Flanders & Olney, 218.

"THE SAILOR BOY." George W. Piper, ship *Europa* of Edgartown, 1868-70.

1. As I walked out one May morning down by the river side
   It was there I espied a sailor boy come a roving down the tide

2. Good morning said the sailor boy Good morning sir said she
   I am a looking for some sailor boy For to row o'er the sea

3. He pulled his boat unto the shore and tied it to a stake
   Then he stepped up to this lady fair, a hold of her to take

4. Then he pulled off his morning gown, and laid it on the ground
   When she espied three chains of gold all from his neck hung down

5. Then she fell on her bended knees, Crying O Lord pity me
   For calling you a sailor boy, all on the briny sea

6. Rise up, rise up my fair pretty maid, rise up rise up said he
   You have not said a single word that has the least offended me

7. I will take you to my father's house and married us we will be
   Then you will enjoy your sailor boy, to row you o'er the sea

101. **The Jolly Roving Tar**
[The British Man of War]
(Laws #O-27)

This is a localized Boston version of an English broadside ballad of the 1840s, "The British Man of War." The whalemen's text, transcribed at sea around 1860, is a particularly early specimen recovered from American tradition. Like most other manifestations it relies on catch phrases borrowed from a host of other ballads and incorporates specific search-and-rescue elements of "The Sailor Boy" [#69].

TUNE: "Jolly Roving Tar," from Helen Creighton, *Folksongs from Southern New Brunswick,* 1971, #12, p. 37.

"THE JOLLY ROVING TAR." George M. Jones and Albert F. Handy, bark *Waverly* of New Bedford, 1859-63.

1. It was through the streets of Boston so carelessly I did stray
   There I espyed a sailor lad and a fair young lady gay
   She appeared to me like Venus or some superior star
   As she walked the beach lamenting her jolly roving tar

2. O have you seen my Willie all dressed in sailors clothes
   His cheeks were red as roses his eyes were black as coals
   Her [sic] hair hung down in ringlets and He has gone from me afar
   But my heart lys in the bosom of jolly roving tar

3. O William dearest William why did you sail away
   You knew i'd soon be twenty one and so a lady gay
   I'd command one of my father's ships and brave the storm of chiney war
   I would cross the briney ocean like some jolly roving tar

4. And now she goes to her fathers warfh where his ships are safely moored
   We have provisions plenty and lots of grog on board
   We will sway up our main topsail and sail from here afar
   We will cross the briney ocean like some jolly roving tar

5. And now she takes a small boat and pushes from the land
   And the sailor saw her wave her lilly white hand
   Saying adieu fair maids of Boston I sail from here afar
   To cross the briney ocean like some jolly roving tar

6. Many is the pleasant evening my love and I have had
   She a fair young lady gay and I a sailor lad
   While the harps did sweetly play and so did the guitar
   As we walked hand in hand together like two jolly roving tars

102. The Bold Privateer
(Laws #O-32)

Usually referred to in printed anthologies as an "English folk-song," this is actually a farewell ballad that entered tradition from broadsides. The whaleman's corrupt text fragment is related to (and has a few phrases in common with) the "Farewell, Nancy" ballads [#25 and #26].

TUNE: "The Bold Privateer," from Frank Kidson, *Traditional Tunes*, 1891, p. 101: "The air if from Mr. Lolley, picked up in the East Riding of Yorkshire. In this air there is no indication of the kinds of repeats that form whaleman Donohue's refrain.

A.

[UNTITLED.] James Donahue, ship *Atlantic* of Nantucket, 1850-53. A fragment of two stanzas and "chorus," with the lines undifferentiated in the manuscript, here consolidated into lines and stanzas.*

1. Oh my dearest Molly you and I must part
   I am going oer the Sea love to you I give my heart
   the ship lay A waiting so fare you well my dear,

   Chorus: For I am just going on board of the bold Privateer
       On the bold privateer on the bold privateer.

2. Oh my dearest Johnny great dangers has been crossed
   and many A sweet life by the Seas has been lost.
   You had better stay at home with they …

B.

"THE BOLD PRIVATEER." For comparison, the complete broadside text as given by Frank Kidson, *Traditional Tunes*, 1891, p. 101: "…The words are found on ballad sheets which are sold in Hull and other seaport towns. The story, of course, dates from at least our last French or American war."

1. "O, fare you well, my Polly dear, since you and I must part,
   In crossing of the seas, my love, I'll pledge to you my heart;
   For our ship she now lies waiting, so fare you well my dear,
   For I just now am going aboard of a bold privateer."

2. "You know, my dearest Polly, your friends they do me slight;
   Besides, you have two brothers would take away my life;
   From them I then must wander, myself to get me clear,
   So I am just now going aboard of a bold privateer.

3. She said, "My dearest Jemmy, I hope you will forbear,
   And do not leave your Polly in grief and in despair;
   You'd better stay at home with the girl you love so dear,
   Than venture on the seas your life in a bold privateer."

4. "And when the wars are over, if God does spare our lives,
   We will return safe back again to our sweethearts and our wives,
   And then I will get married to my charming Polly, dear,
   And forever bid adieu to the bold privateer."

103. William Riley

Captain Samuel Bunker's text entitled "William Riley," which he wrote into his journal on an 1824-27 whaling voyage from Nantucket, is one of the earliest transcriptions of a broadside-type ballad recovered from the whaling manuscripts. But it does not correspond to either of the two pieces with similar names classified by Laws among "Ballads of Family Opposition to Lovers," respectively entitled "William Riley" (Laws #M-10) and "William Riley's Courtship" (#M-9). There is no angry father, snobby mother, or overprotective brother here; the meters differ; so, too, the stories. The Nantucketer's "William Riley" is demonstrably neither of these. Rather, it is a reconstituted or foreshortened form of the ballad that Laws calls "John Riley II" or "Young Riley" (Laws #N-37), with which Captain Bunker's text shares key phrases and characteristic elements—notably the lady's refusal to entertain the narrator's suit, the suitor's question about what makes her differ from other women (referring to her unwillingness to marry), and his offer that they "sail to Pennsylvania." However, unlike "Young Riley," here there are no "Lovers' Disguises and Tricks," and the narrator does not produce a token or otherwise reveal himself in the end to be the long-lost Riley. Rather, this "William Riley" is of the type Laws calls "Ballads of Unfaithful Lovers," relating in comparatively straightforward fashion a woman's regret and resentment that William Riley has loved her and left her, and concluding with several stanzas of cautionary lament reminiscent of "The Cuckoo," "O Waly Waly," "Come All Ye Fair and Tender Ladies," "On Top of Old Smokey," and some versions of "The Banks of the Sweet Primroses." As no other manifestation of this "William Riley" has been encountered and no separate tune has been located for it, the best conjecture about what melody the Nantucket whaling master may have intended is the one and only air for "Young Riley" recovered in New England.

TUNE A - MacEdward Leach, *Folk Ballads & Songs of the Lower Labrador Coast*. National Museum of Canada Bulletin Nº 201, Anthropological Series Nº 68. Ottawa, 1965.

TUNE B - "John Reilly," from Helen Hartnett Flanders and George Brown, *Vermont Folk-Songs and Ballads,* 1931, p. 135: collected from the singing of Mr. Josiah Kennison, Townshend, Vermont, 1930.

"WILLIAM RILEY." Captain Samuel Bunker, ship *Alexander* of Nantucket, 1824-27.

1. As I walk'd forth one fine summer's morning
   All for to view the sweet scenes of light
   There I beheld a most charming damsel
   She appeared to me like an angel bright

2. I stept up to her and kindly ask'd her
   If she would be a poor sailor's wife
   Oh no kind sir I had rather tarrey
   I choose to lead a sweet single life

3. I said fair creature what makes you differ
   From all the rest of your female kind
   For you are charming both young and handsome
   Therefore to marrage pray be inclined

4. Oh now kind sir if I must tell you
   I'd ought to bin marrid five months ago
   And to one william riley who lived in this country
   I'm a fraid he's prov'd my sad overthrow

5. O Riley's a man both neat and handsome
   He courted me both by night and by day
   And when he'd gaine'd my whole affections
   He quit this countrey and sail'd away

6. Youth and folley makes young maids marrey
   For when they are married they must obey
   What can't be cure'd must be endur'd
   From all false young men I'm bound away

7. I said fair creature come let us travil
   Unto some foreign distant shore
   And we'll sail over to pennsylvania
   Bid adieu to Riley forever more

8. If we should sail to pennsylvania
   Or to some other distant shore
   Then my poor heart would still be aching
   To think on Riley whom I adore

9. Oh love is wittey and love is prettey
   And love is comely when it is new
   But it grows older and wanes colder
   And fades away like the morning dew

10. The fairest apple it will grow rotten
    The hottest love will soon grow cold
    And young men's vows they're soon forgotten
    Take care pretty maidens dont be control'd

11. O Riley he has gone and left me
    I ne'er expect to see him more
    O Riley there's a place of torment
    To punish you laid up in store

104. Jemmy on the Sea
[The Fair Maid's Lamentations]

This untitled and hitherto unrecorded ballad of lovers reunited is a distinctive, perhaps unique variation on the usual "Lovers' Token" theme, with a "surprise" ending that amounts to a radical departure from the format and formulae of the conventional broadside ballads. The story begins conventionally enough, in the first-person: by the banks of a river the narrator hears a woman singing; he eavesdrops, then asks her why she laments; she explains that her "true lover Jemmy" is away at sea and she fears he will not return. At this point, the formula would lead us to expect that either her lover is dead and the narrator bears some token or deathbed message given to him by Jemmy to be passed along to her; or, more commonly, that the narrator has some token to prove that he *is* Jemmy, perhaps removing a disguise as he discloses his identity; typically, the couple are then married. Here, the narrator does reassure the woman that she has "no cause to weep" for her lover's safety, but in this case it is because her Jemmy is still "ploughing the deep" and will soon return. In support of this claim he offers no evidence and presents no token; and — contrary to the usual ballad convention requiring that, at least, he and Jemmy had been shipmates or comrades, and that he has recently seen Jemmy alive and perhaps bears some message for the lady — it does not appear that the narrator has ever actually met Jemmy in the flesh. Nor does the lady indicate that she believes, disbelieves, or is in any way comforted by the narrator's reassurances. A ship now suddenly appears in view (it is evidently a larger river than one might expect in a purely pastoral setting), flying her true love's "colours" — implying a flag or pennant of some kind — thus signifying to her that Jemmy is safe on board. The "surprise," in terms of its defiance of ballad convention and dramatic exposition, is that neither of the formulaic outcomes turns out to be the case here: the narrator does not turn out to be Jemmy; nor, once this is established, does Jemmy turn out to be dead. From an historical point of view, another surprise is that Jemmy has his own "colours," a distinction usually reserved for monarchs, heads of state, fleet admirals, commodores, and peers of the realm; and in this connection, it may be worth observing that his personal flag (or private signal, if that is what it be), flown from the ship as it approaches the shore, functions in the same way as the more familiar kinds of lovers' tokens in ballads: it symbolizes his faithfulness, signifies the fulfillment of his promise to return, and establishes his identity, providing unequivocal confirmation that it is he and no other. Whaleman George Snow Cleveland, who transcribed the only known text, gives no indication of the air.

[UNTITLED.] George S. Cleveland, second mate, ship *Charles* of New Bedford, 1837-39.

1. twas a bright summers morning as I roved along
   by the banks of a river I heard a fine song
   it was sung by a damsel and her voice was so clear
   saying how happy I should be if my Jemmy was here

2. then I drew a little nearer to a shade that was near
   where this fair maids lamentations I plainly could hear
   oh I asked her what ailed her what caused her for to mourn
   its the loss of my Jemmy who will never return

3. it is morning and evening I am troubled in mind
   since my true lover Jemmy he has left me behind
   in the absence of my Jemmy oh I feel the smart
   every sithe I sithe for him it will soon break my heart

4. oh it's green grow the rushes and the tops of them small
   my true lover Jemmy he is handsome and tall
   in the absence of my Jemmy oh I feel the smart
   every sithe [sigh] I sithe for him it will soon break my heart

5. it is now six months since my Jemmy set sail
   kind heaven did protect him with a sweet and pleasant gale
   oh he hoisted his topsails to the westward did steer
   my true lover Jemmy is drownd I fear

6. says I handsome lady there's no cause for to weep
   for your true lover Jemmy he is ploughing the deep
   he's culvering the ocean from some foreign shore
   you will soon embrace the young man whom you do adore

7. then says I my pretty fair maid there's a ship hove in view
   with colours a flying this damsel she knew
   with colours a flying both blue white and red
   it's my true lovers signal this damsel she said

Scene of a full rigged ship under plain sail, flying signal flags and pennants, passing a rocky headland; engraved on a sperm whale tooth, by whaleman Eli Bangs (1836-1923, originally from Bridgeton, N.J., and Wilmington, Del., ship's cooper in the bark *Helen Mar* of New Bedford during 1856-61. New Bedford Whaling Museum.

105. The Sailor and the Tailor
(Laws #P-4)

The daughter of an affluent tradesman promises to marry a sailor, but during his protracted absence at sea she is betrothed to a tailor, in the belief that the sailor is dead or has forsaken her. But when the sailor shows up at the church on her wedding day, she declares him her true love and leaves the tailor at the altar. Perhaps the most interesting aspect of the text is its conventional stereotyping of occupations. From the point of view of sailors and tailors, the woman's father, a "ship carpenter" (here intended in the capitalist-entrepreneurial sense of *shipbuilder*), would be perceived as quite wealthy, able to provide a handsome dowry. In sailor parlance, tailors and soldiers are the quintessential landlubbers [see "Reuben Ranzo," #47], and it is a tailor whose marital intentions are thwarted by the superior appeal of a sailor. The ballad turns out the way a sailor might prefer, with the sailor getting the woman and the money in the end. However, though the narrative begins in the third person, oddly the final stanza appears to be in the voice of the tailor, who, using a textile-related epithet signifying Jack Tar, warns landlubbers to beware the sailors' wiles, for "Tarpaulin Jack" will steal their women away — a reversal of the sailor's usual worry about what may be going on with the womenfolk back home while he is at sea. The tune, especially the rendition given by Cecil Sharp (which he calls "The Watchet Sailor") is a variant of the same air as the one used for the contemporaneous broadside ballad "Kelly the Pirate (II)."[9]

TUNE: "The Watchet Sailor" (a form of the same ballad), from C.J. Sharp, *100 English Folk Songs*, 1916, #73, p. 164.

[UNTITLED.] Samuel Green, Jr., mate 1835-36 and master 1839-40, ship *Flora*; and master 1844, ship *Neptune*, both of New London, 1844. The meter and rhyme scheme are faulty throughout; stanza 11 is rebuilt from errors in the MS.

1. In London fair sitty its known verry well
   A wealthy ship carpenter daughter did dwell
   She being so beautiful charming and fair
   There was none in the city with her could compare

2. Both lords dukes and nobles and rich squairs of fame
   both noble and simple a courting her came
   For to gain this maids favour they try or their best skill
   But not one could obtain her love and good will

3. Till at length a young sailor a courting her came
   To gain this maids favour he bore a great name
   For to gain this maids favour he tryed his best skill
   Till at length he obtained her love and good will

4. He says my dear juel i sorry it is so
   A long voyage to the indies i must go
   And when I return unto you my dear
   Its we will get married and live in great splender dont fear

---

[9] Laws #K-32; e.g., see Stuart M. Frank, *The Book of Pirate Songs*, #61.

5. Now two years being over and gone
   A handsome young tailor a courting her came
   For to gain this maids favour he tryed his best skill
   Till at length he obtained her love and good will

6. As jack was walking one night through the streets
   One of his old shipmates heed chanced to meet
   You are welcome home ship mate you are welcome home
   In time and good season methinks you have come

7. Its dont you remember you courted a maid
   Now she has agreed with a tailor to wed
   And to morrow church meting its married they be
   And I am invited the [wedding] go see

8. Jack went to his captain got licence that night
   and went to the church long before it was light
   And when he had been waiting in there for a while
   He saw them a coming which caused him to smile

9. Now Jack being dresst in his tarpolin clothes
   Its in to the church after them he goes
   Tuck his true love by the hand which the sailor did crave
   What means you what means you you tarplin brave

10. It was your long absence I thought you was dead
    That made me agree with this tailor to wead
    But to end all dispute this damsel replied
    The Sailor is my true love and I will be his bride

11. Come all you young lands men Where ever you be
    I pray you will take [warning] by me
    Make shure of your true love any time when you may
    Or the tarpolin Jack will steel them away

The End

106. The Pride of Kildare
[Pretty Susan, The Pride of Kildare]
(Laws #P-6)

This ballad takes the form of the first-person narrative of a rejected suitor who regretfully resolves therefore to return to his former seafaring life. Set in Ireland, it is almost certainly Irish in origin and must have been quite popular in the middle of the 19th century: O Lochlainn and Laws report several broadsides, and four American whalemen's texts are known, dating from the late 1840s to circa 1870. It has more often been encountered in tradition in Ireland and the Maritime Provinces of Canada than in the United States.

TUNE - "Pretty Susan, The Pride of Kildare": learned from a fiddler at Truro, Nova Scotia, 1967. Similar to O Lochlainn 1965, #83 (Frank 1985, #119, Tune B); and McCullough, 36. Compare also Manny & Wilson 1968, #88, which has an oddly irregular tempo much adapted to the distinctive singing style of the informant, Angelo Dornin, and which is quite different in transcription, if not in fact, from Dornan's rendition in Creighton 1971, #48.

A.

"PRIDE OF KILDARE." James Donohue, ship *Atlantic* of Nantucket, 1850-53. A disheveled text, undifferentiated into lines and stanzas, but roughly equivalent to a foreshortened rendition of B.

B.

"THE PRIDE OF KILDARE." George W. Piper, ship *Europa* of Edgartown, 1868-70. Except for the first stanza, the transcription indicates that the last two lines of each stanza are to be repeated.

1. When first from sea I landed
   I had a roving mind
   Undaunted I rambled
   My true love for to find
   When I met with pretty Susan
   With her cheeks like the rose
   And her bosom it was fairer
   Than the lily that grows
   And her bosom it was fairer
   Than the lily that grows

2. Her keen eyes they did sparkle
   Like the bright stars at night
   The robes she was a wearing
   Were all costly and bright
   Her bare neck it was shaded
   With her dark raven hair
   And they called her pretty Susan
   She is the pride of Kildare
   And they calls her pretty Susan
   She is the pride of Kildare

3. Long time I courted Susan
   Until I wasted my store
   When her love turned to hatred
   Because I was poor
   Says she I love another
   Whose fortune I will share
   So begone from pretty Susan
   She is the pride of Kildare
   So begone from pretty Susan
   She is the pride of Kildare

4. It was early the next morning
   My heart led me astray
   When I met with pretty Susan
   And her lord so gay
   As I passed by them
   With my heart so full of woe
   I sighed for pretty Susan
   She is the pride of Kildare
   I sighed for pretty Susan
   She is the pride of Kildare

5. Once more to the ocean
   I am resolved for to go
   Unto the East Indies
   With my heart full of woe
   Where there is many a fair maid
   That wears diamonds so rare
   But there is none like pretty Susan
   She is the pride of Kildare
   But there is none like pretty Susan
   She is the pride of Kildare

6. Sometimes I am jovial
   Sometimes I am sad
   When I think that pretty Susan
   Is wedded to another lad
   But since I am at a distance
   No more I'll despair
   So my blessings be with Susan
   She is the pride of Kildare
   So my blessings be with Susan
   She is the pride of Kildare

107. The Rakish Young Fellow
[The Poor Man's Son]

Untitled in the manuscript, this ballad may be a form of "The Poor Man's Son" and is in any case thematically related to "The Nightingale" ("One Morning in May") (Laws #P-14), a British broadside piece widely distributed in North America. Regarding the latter, "Rakish Young Fellow" has an entirely different meter: it cannot be sung to any of the tunes for "The Nightingale" and it fails to exhibit the defining features of that ballad. Characteristically, "Nightingale" has no chorus (though in some manifestations the last line of each stanza is repeated as a refrain), the narration is in the third person (i.e., the narrator and the male protagonist are not one and the same), and the protagonist is a soldier (a "gay cavalier," "brave volunteer," or "bold grenadier"); he seduces the lady with music played on a fiddle and, in the end, refuses her marital overtures and abandons her, sometimes with child: in most manifestations he is already married with children of his own. A text collected in Massachusetts by Flanders & Olney reverses the roles slightly: *he* proposes to *her,* but *she* is already married with children. Accordingly, Laws lists "The Nightingale" as a "Ballad of Unfaithful Lovers." By contrast, this whaleman's text has a chorus, it is narrated in the first person, it does not identify the occupation of the protagonist or his musical instrument (thereby strengthening the double meaning and sexual implications of the tunemaking), and it is resolved much like "The Jolly Sailor" [# 97], with the man marrying the woman and delighting in his unexpected good fortune at making a union above his station. In combination with the incompatibility of meter, these significant departures suffice to identify "The Rakish Young Fellow" as a separate entity which, had it been known to Laws, would have been classified among "Ballads of Faithful Lovers."

The formalistic features and syntax here are also significant. The opening stanza is a formula broadside ballad pastorale; and in the chorus, the association of rosy-red cheeks and sloe-black eyes is ancient, almost to the point of timeworn cliché. For example, in the Arthurian legend of Sir Gawain, a hag who magically transforms herself into a beautiful maiden is described:

> Sweet blushes stain'd her rud-red[10] cheek,
> Her eyes were black as sloe;
> The ripening cherry swelled her lip,
> And all her neck was snow.[11]

And from at least one version of the Czech fairy tale "Grandfather's Eyes," we have:

"… The goats scattered this way and that and Yanechek [the shepherd] sat down on a stone in the shade. He was hardly seated when he looked up and there before him, dressed all in white, stood the most beautiful maiden in the world. *Her skin was red as roses and white as milk, her eyes were black as sloe berries,* and her hair, dark as the raven's wing, fell about her shoulders in long waving tresses. She smiled and offered Yanechek a big red apple."[12]

Unfortunately, though the whaleman-scribe, Frederick Howland Smith, was reputedly an able musician and is known to have been interested in tunes [see Chapter 17], he does not indicate the air to which the ballad is intended to be sung.

---

[10] *Rud*: to redden or make red (as in *ruddy*).
[11] *Percy's Reliques,* iii. 1, 2.
[12] Parker Fillmore, "Czecholovak Fairy Tales" <www.mainlesson.com/display.php?author=fillmore&book=czech&story=eyes> © 2000-2004 Lisa Ripperton. Italics added.

A.

[UNTITLED.] Frederick H. Smith, boatsteerer, bark *Roscius* of New Bedford, 1858-61.

1. As I walked out one May morning
   My fortune for to seek
   Who should I spy but a fair pretty Maid
   And her hands were soft as silk

Chorus: Her cheeks were of a rosey rosey red
   And her eyes were as black as the sloe
   For she is the beauty of this whole world
   For she is blest wherever she goes

2. I says my pretty fair Maid where are you going
   What makes you ramble so soon
   Its I am going to yonder green grove
   For to hear the sweet Nightingale's tune

3. Then I says my pretty fair Maid may I walk along with you
   And I hope their will be no harm done
   Oh yes kind sir you may walk along with me
   Although you are nothing but a poor mans son

4. Oh we walked till we came to the side of the grove
   Where I played her a Virgins tune
   Oh when shall we get married oh kind sir she said
   And I hope it will be very very soon

5. Its little did I think on that very morn
   As I cam out of my door
   That ever I should we[d] with a gay Lady
   That would roll me my riches in store

6. For the drum shall beat and the fife shall play
   And we will bid old England dify [defy]
   For we will rant and we'll roar and we'll bloody call for more
   What a rakish young fellow am I

B.

[UNTITLED.] Fragment of the first stanza and chorus only, from the same source as A; identical to the corresponding portions of A except with "*blessed*" (rather than *blest*) in the chorus.

108. Mary of the Wild Moor
(Laws #P-21)

This is not a proper broadside ballad at all but, rather, a sentimental composition bearing the unmistakable stamp of 19th-century parlor-song bathos in the tradition of Thomas Haynes Bayly's "The Mistletoe Bough." However, because "Mary of the Wild Moor" has occasionally been encountered in tradition it has often been considered "very old" and folkloric in origin. Kidson, who got his version from a singer in Yorkshire, remarks in 1891, "Both air and song appear to be not much earlier than the beginning of the present century." The *Song Index* identifies it only as "old English words and music," but the Oliver Ditson and Century Company catalogues credit it to Joseph W. Turner (b. 1818), the attributed author of "Silver Moon" ("Roll On, Silver Moon"). Helen Kendrick Johnson gives a slightly different story, claiming it to be "a combination of old English words and music. They are both very old; but had never been linked together until Joseph W. Turner united them, added a few lines, and adapted them with a piano accompaniment.... In this form they appeared about 1845." The Ditson anthology *Good Old Songs* may be closer to the mark in stating merely, "By J.W. Turner." Johnson also paraphrases Turner's comments "in a note attached to the music, that the song recites the fate of a beautiful girl, wooed by a young man whose suit was disapproved by her parents. The lovers were secretly married, and when, a year later, the young wife was deserted, she made her way to her old home, only to die upon the threshold." It is this subtext, undisclosed in the ballad itself, that may explain why Laws classifies it among "Ballads of Unfaithful Lovers." The whalemen's texts are evidently copied from printed sources; the tune is also standard, though there are variants in tradition and in revival.

TUNE: "Mary of the Wild Moor," per Helen Kendrick Johnson, *Our Familiar Songs*, 1881, 303f. Compare *Good Old Songs*, 1895, II:82f, which has a chorus neither present in Johnson nor indicated in the whalemen's texts.

A.

"MARY O'ER THE WILD MOOR." George W. Piper, ship *Europa* of Edgartown, 1868-70.

1. One night when the winds they blew cold / Blew bitter across the wild moor
   Young Mary she came with her child / Wandering home to her own father's door
   Crying father O pray let me in / Take pity on me I implore
   Or the child at my bosom will die / From the winds that blow across the wild moor

2. Oh why did I leave this fair cot / Where once I was happy and free
   Doomed to roam without friends or a home / O father take pity on me
   But that father was deaf to her cries / Not a voice nor a sound reached the door
   But the watch dog did howl and the winds / Blew bitter across the wild moor

3. O how must that father have felt / When he came to the door in the morn
   There he saw Mary dead with her child / Folded close in its cold mother's arms
   Then in frenzy he tore his grey hairs / As he gazed on his child at the door
   For Mary had perished and died / From the winds that blew across the wild moor

4. The father in grief pined away / The child to the grave was soon borne
   No one has lived there till this day / The cottage to ruin has gone
   But the villagers point to the spot / Where a willow droops over the door
   Saying there Mary perished and died / From the winds that blew across the wild moor

B.

"MARY OF THE WILD MOOR." William H. Keith, schooners *William Martin* of Boston, *Edith May* of Wellfleet, *Cora Nash* of Boston, etc., circa 1865-71. A similar copy text, sans chorus.

109. Caroline of Edinburgh Town
(Laws #P-27)

Woodcut illustration from *The Forget-Me-Not Songster*, New York, circa 1827.

This widely disseminated ballad concerns a woman who, despite her family's opposition to the union, elopes with her Highland suitor to London; he eventually abandons her and goes to sea, and she takes her own life. The lyrics were often printed in broadsides and songsters, and remained remarkably stable in tradition. Tunes vary. Huntington's (which is not identified and may not be traditional with this text) is unlike most others; Creighton's is quite ornate. Linscott's, collected in Massachusetts, is reminiscent of such come-all-ye ballads as "The Stately Southerner" and some forms of "Girls Around Cape Horn."

TUNE: "Caroline of Edinboro Town," from Eloise Hubbard Linscott, *Folk Songs of Old New England*, 1939, p. 183. Compare "The Stately Southerner" (Colcord 126; Shay 1948, 153) and some versions of "Girls Around Cape Horn" (Colcord 178; compare Vaughan Williams 90) Transposed from the key of E^b.

A.

"CAROLINE OF EDINGBURGE TOWN." James S. Colton, bark *Tenedos* of New London, 1840-43.

1. Come all young maidens attend unto my rhyme
   Its of a young damsel who was scarcely in her prime
   She beat the blushing roses & admired by all around
   Was lovely young caroline of Edingburge town

2. Young Henry was a highland man a courting to her came
   And when her parents came to know they did not like the same
   Young henry was offended & unto her did say
   Arise my dearest caroline & with me come away

3. We will both go to london love & there get wed with speede
   An[d] then my lovely caroline shall have happiness indeede
   Now enticed by young henry she put on her other gown
   And away went young caroline of edingburg town

4. Over hills & lofty mountains together they did roam
   In time arrived in london far from her happy home
   She said my dearest henry pray never on me frown
   Or youll breake the heart of caroline of edingburg town

5. They had not been in london more than half a year
   When harde harted henry prooved too severe
   Said henry I ll go to sea your friends did on me frown
   So beg your way without delay to edinburg town

6. Oh the fleete is fitting out & to Spithead dropping down
   And I will join the Gallant fleete & fight for king & crown
   The gallant tars feel the scares [scars] or in the water drown
   Yet I never will return again to edingburg town

7. Then many a Day she passed away in sorrow & Dispair
   Her cheeks though once like roses were grown like lillies fair
   She cried where is my henry and often did she swoon
   Crying sad is the day I ran away from edinburg town

8. Ore prest with grief without relief this damsel she did go
   Into the woods to eat such fruit as on the bushes grow
   Some strangers did pity her & some did on her frown
   And some did say what made you stray from edingburg town

9. Beneath a lofty spreading oake this maid sat down to cry
   A watching of the gallant ships as they were passing by
   She gave three shrieks for henry & plunged her body down
   And away floated caroline of edinburg town

10. A note liquewise [likewise] her bonnet she left upon the shore
    And in the note a lock of hair with the words I am no more
    And fast asleep I m in the deepe the fish are watching round
    Once comely young caroline of edingburhg town

11. Come all you tender parents ne'er try to part true love
    You re sure to see in some degree the ruin it will prove
    Likewise young men & maidens ne'er on your lover frown
    Think on the fate of caroline of edinburg town

B.

[UNTITLED.] Cornelius H. Beden, ship *Massachusetts* of New Bedford, 1851-53; and ship *South America* of New Bedford, 1855. Fragments, probably transcribed from memory or recitation, nevertheless closely resembling A.

C.

"CAROLINE OF EDINBORO TOWN." George W. Piper, ship *Europa* of Edgartown, 1868-70. A complete text of 11 stanzas; "Edinboro" throughout; otherwise word-for-word remarkably like A.

D.

"CAROLINE OF EDINBURROW TOWN." Fragment of one stanza, undated, appended by the same anonymous scribe to the same sheet on which "Bounding Billows" [#184] is transcribed; as far as it goes, similar to the others and to the *Forget Me Not* version. While the title has "*Edinburrow*," in the text the place-name is "*Edinburgh*."

110. Oxford City
[The Jealous Young Man]
(Laws #P-30)

A ballad of jealousy owing to upward social immobility, remedied by two doses of poison — and thus forging an eternal union where no earthly union was feasible. The whaleman's text is a conventional rendition, possibly copied from one of the several printed broadsides.

TUNE: "In Oxford City," from Helen Hartness Flanders & George Brown, *Vermont Folk-Songs and Ballads*, 1932, p. 92: "Recorded by Mr. Brown, September 12, 1930 (music)…in Bennington…from the singing of Mrs. Ralph Harrington as she remembered it from her father, Mr. Sharon Harrington." The principal air recovered in New England.

"THE JEALOUS YOUNG MAN." Benjamin A. Freeman, Bark *Sea Queen* of Westport, Massachusetts, 1851-55.

1. In Oxford city there lived a fair one
   As fair a one as you shall see
   She was courted by a servant boy
   Who oft times told her he loved her dear

2. This lovely fair one soon shortly after
   Had an invitation to a ball to go
   This jealous young man soon followed after
   All for to prove her sad overthrow

3. He saw her dancing with another
   While jealousy run in his mind
   And to destroy his own true lover
   Was this jealous young mans design

4. He mixed up a dose of poison
   And put it in a glass of wine
   And gave it to his own true lover
   Who drank it off most cheerfully

5. In a short time this lovely fair one
   Cries take me home my dear says she
   For the glass of wine you lately gave me
   Swells my poor heart to a sad degree

6. As they were walking home together
   This jealous young man was heard to say
   O I put poison in your liquor
   All for to take your sweet life away

7. O I drank of the same myself love
   So I am poisoned as well as thee
   So in each others arms they died
   Young man beware of jealousy

Benjamin A Freeman
Bark Sea Queen

111. Jack Robinson

This English comic ballad comprising a poem originally written by Thomas Hudson is sung to "The College Hornpipe," a traditional fiddle-tune always popularly associated with sailors. Part of the supposed humor hinges on the 18th-century slang expression "before you can say Jack Robinson" (meaning *very quickly* or *quick as a flash*)—with regard to which, failing to account for its origin otherwise, Eric Partridge skeptically resorts to quoting Francis Grose's claim in his contemporaneous *Dictionary of the Vulgar Tongue* (1785), that it is "from a very volatile gentleman… who would call on his neighbors and be gone before his name could be announced." The song lampoons ballads about lovers' tokens and lovers' reunions, and ballads about encounters between recently-arrived sailors and tavern landladies; there may also be a prurient subtext, for, according to Partridge, *Jack Robinson* was also a low-slang expression for the male member. A Portsmouth setting places the song in the Royal Navy, but it seems to have been a favorite among sailors of all kinds. The whaleman's version is quite similar to the broadside reprinted by Ashton and the lyrics given by Davidson in his *Universal Melodist.*

TUNE: "Jack Robinson" (actually a variant of "The College Hornpipe"): from *Davidson's Universal Melodist,* 1848, Vol. II, p. 252. A chorus of nonsense syllables ("Tol lol de rol… ") commences at the double bar (not in the MS).

"JACK ROBINSON." George W. Piper, ship *Europa* of Edgartown, 1868-70. Stanza 2 is evidently corrupt.[13]

1. The perils and dangers of the voyage are past
   And the ship has arrived at Portsmouth at last
   The sails all furled and the anchor cast
   The happiest of the crew Jack Robinson
   For his Poll he has trinkets and gold galore
   Besides of prize money quite a store
   And along with the crew he went ashore
   The happiest of the crew Jack Robinson

---

[13] Davidson gives the following for stanza 2: in addition to supplying the correct sequence and the missing portion of the third line, it also reverses the sense of who gave whom the slip among Jack and his messmates:

> He met with a man and he said, 'I say
> May hap you may know one Polly Gray;
> She lives somewhere hereabout.' The man said, 'Nay
> I do not indeed,' to Jack Robinson.
> Says Jack to him, 'I have left my ship,
> And all my messmates giv'n the slip—
> Mayhap you'll partake of a good can of flip,
> For you're a civil fellow,' says Jack Robinson.

2. He met a man and said, I say
   Mayhap you know one Polly Gray
   And the man he said nay
   He then says she lives somewhere here about
   Says Jack to him I have left my ship
   And all my messmates have given me the slip
   Mayhap you will partake of a good can of flip
   For you are a very civil fellow says Jack Robinson

3. In a public house they both sat down
   And talked of admirals of high renown
   And drinked as much as came to half a crown
   This here strange man and Jack Robinson
   The Jack called out, the reckoning to pay
   The landlady came in fine array
   "My eyes and limbs" Why here is Polly Gray
   Who would have though of meeting her here says Jack Robinson

4. The landlady staggered against the wall
   At first she did not know him at all
   Shiver me says Jack Why here is a pretty squall
   Damme! don't you know me I'm Jack Robinson
   Dont you remember this handkerchief you gave to me
   It was three years ago, before I went to sea
   Every day I looked at it, and thought of thee
   Upon my sould I have, says Jack Robinson

5. Says the lady says she I have changed my state
   Why, you don't mean says Jack, that you have got a mate!
   You know you promised me, says she I could not wait
   For no tidings could I gain of you Jack Robinson
   And somebody one day came to me and said
   That somebody else had somewhere read
   In some newspaper as how you was dead
   I have not been dead at all says Jack Robinson

6. Then he turned his quid, finished his glass
   Hitched up his trousers alas! alas!
   That ever I should live to be made such an ass
   To be bilked by a woman says Jack Robinson
   But to fret and stew about it much is all in vain
   I will get a ship and go to Holland, France and Spain
   No matter where, to Portsmouth I will never come back again
   And he was off, before you could say, Jack Robinson

CHAPTER TWELVE
Terra Incognita
Comic and Convivial Songs of Life On Shore[1]

That navigation and commerce enrich and aggrandize a nation none can deny; but what do most mariners profit themselves or their wives and children by all their voyages? The American sailor, I think, may generally claim pre-eminence over mariners of other nations; but even the seaman of the United States is generally treated as if he were a slave, and abused in a worse manner than any favourite brute. All the other classes of useful people seem to prosper more than sailors. Farmers, mechanics and tradesmen, by thousands have smiling families, domesticated in houses which they may call their own; but where will you find a sailor who has the fee simple of any house, except at the bottom of the ocean?

When sailors have been shut up within the prison walls of a ship for months, and sometimes for years, can any wonder that they crave society, and are a little extravagant, so soon as they touch their mother earth? They wish to see and converse with some other beings than the crew of their on vessel. They must have some place of resort; and where decent sailor boarding-houses cannot be found, they are compelled to abide in such as they can find. In foreign ports, especially, a tar is avoided and gazed upon as an ass or a lion; and because people expect no good of him, and show him no civility, he is often reckless in his conduct.

—Ben Ezra Stiles Ely, *There She Blows* (1849).

Hamlet, Prince of Denmark. Ink drawing by R.G.N. Swift from his literate journal aboard the New Bedford ship *Contest*, 1866-70. The title is inscribed above the picture. Note that the king looks suspiciously like the Bard himself; perhaps the prince may be taken as Swift's self-portrait? The captions read: "King: 'I am thy father's spirit Domed for a certain time to walk the night.' Prince: 'O horrible! most horrible!'" Other, illegible notations on the page are in classical Greek. See "The Cove Wot Spouts" [#114]; also #230 and #230. Kendall Collection, New Bedford Whaling Museum.]

---

[1] *Terra Incognita* (Latin for "unknown land") is the classic term used by Renaissance cartographers and voyage chroniclers to refer to unexplored or mysterious regions of the earth—which to common seamen might figuratively include any of the world's seaports, where sailors tended to be ill at ease, vulnerable to slick victimizers, fish out of water at the mercy of land-sharks.

112. All Around the Room
[Ellen Taylor]

This obscure English music-hall song interspersed with spoken passages is of a type that was in vogue in the middle 19th century. It appeared on broadsides but has been encountered in only one other example recovered from tradition, lacking the spoken portions and without a tune, collected in Wiltshire (England) by Alfred Williams, who says that it was not widely known even there, where he "met with it only once" (*Folk-Songs of the Upper Thames*, 1923). It is a comic parody of "All Around My Hat," the lament of a London street vendor who vows to wear a sprig of green willow in his hat "for a year and a day"—a traditional symbol and period of mourning—in remembrance of a woman who was transported to Australia for seven years of penal servitude. Sheet music published in 1838 attributes the words—in dialect—to one John Hansell, Esq[r].; the music of unascribed origin was "arranged by" John Valentine; however, the supposition is probably correct that those lyrics are actually "a perversion of an actual folk song."[2]

> *Chorus:* All round my hat I vears a green willow,
> All round my hat for a twelvemonth and a day,
> If any one should ax it, the reason vy I vears it,
> Tell them that my true love is far, far away.

'Twas going of my rounds in the streets I did meet her,
Oh. I thought she v as an hangel just come down from the sky,

(Spoken) *She'd a nice wegitible countenance, Turnip nose,*
Redish cheeks, and Caroty hair,

And I never heard a woice more louder and more sweeter,
Ven she cried, buy my Primroses, my Primroses come buy,

(Spoken) *Here's your fine Colliflowers!*

For seven long years my love and I are parted
For seven long years, my love is bound to stay…
(Spoken) *Here's your nice heads of Sallary! …*

And vhen she does come back, oh, ve"ll never more be parted,
But ve'll marry, and be happy, oh, for ever and a day

(Spoken) *Here's your fine spring Radishes!*

Writing in 1888 Ashton describes "All Around My Hat" as "one of the most popular of street songs" of the 1830s but "utterly unknown to the present generation." However, it remained in tradition in Ireland, where it was variously adapted as a *woman's* pledge to a fiancé transported to Australia, to a sailor gone to sea for seven years, and as a lament of betrayal. It was revived in the 1970s by the British folk-pop group Steelye Span. A latter-day parody by Irish Republican patriot songwriter Peadar Kearney transforms it into a woman mourning for a lover killed in the Easter Uprising of 1916. Another, entitled "'Round Her Neck She Wears a Yellow Ribbon (For Her Lover Who Is Far, Far Away)," bearing a 1917 New York copyright, is attributed to George A. Norton (Maddy & Meissner, 37), and has been suggested as the source of a yellow ribbon as a symbol of awaiting a soldier's return. The "Yellow Ribbon" spinoff was transformed into a Williams College song by changing *yellow* to *purple* (the school's color). The cheerful air of that version seems well suited to "All Around the Room," which ironically preserves the original street vendor/grocer motif that is mostly lost in the others, but transforms the wares from vegetables to meat. In most respects "All Around the Room" hearkens back to the sheet music lyrics of 1838 more than to any of the folksong variants.

---

[2] www.csufresno.edu/folklore/BalladIndex.html.

TUNE A: "All Around My Hat" ["All Round My Hat"]: "A New Comic Song … as Sung by Jack Reeve, with the most Unbounded Applause. Written by John Hansell Esqr., the Melody Arranged by John Valentine." Sheet music published by George Endicott, New York, circa 1837-39. Compare Lynn, 1961, 42.

TUNE B: "All Around My Hat": Irish traditional song; from the singing of Mary Malloy, learned from an English recording. Compare P.W. Joyce, Kennedy #145, and Creighton 1961, pp. 80f.

TUNE C: "Around Her Hair She Wore a Purple Ribbon": from the singing of Mark Herman, Columbia University, 1967; and Stuart Frank and Tom Berry, Wesleyan University, 1967; learned at Wesleyan as a Williams College song. Compare George A. Norton's "'Round Her Neck She Wears a Yellow Ribbon… " (Maddy & Meissner, 37).

"ALL AROUND THE ROOM." Frederick H. Smith, boatsteerer, bark *Roscius* of New Bedford, 1858-61.

1. All around the room I waltzed with Ellen Taylor
   All around the room until the break of day
   And ever since that time I've done nothing but her beware
   And now she has gone to Margate the summer months to stay

(Spoken) *She was such a divine creature that I fell in love with her the first time I saw her. I looked languishing at her and she did the same. then she gave a sigh, such a heaving one you might have heard it all around the room.*

2. It was at a ball in Islington I first chanced to meet her
   She looked so very fine I could not keep my eyes away
   In all my life before I never saw so sweet a creature
   She danced with me three times and fainted quite away

3. My Ellen is rather tall and my Ellen is rather slender
   Her hair is rather sandy and at singing she is au fait
   But now she has gone to leave me I think it quite a pity
   I am sure I shant be happy all the time she is away

(Spoken) *She was a regular hangell* [angel] *a real natural sort of a woman she wore a bustle that was not very exactural it was rather tergish* [Turkish] *on a modern calculation suppose it would have reached all around the room*

4. For seven long years I apprenticed in the city
   But four of them are gone I have only three to stay
   But if she should refuse me oh crikey what a pity
   I'll go and ask her pa and I am sure he will not say nay

no I dont think the old gentleman will refuse me and than I will marry Ellen and go into business. we will keep a catsmeat shop no a chandlery Ellen will look so nice behind the counter serving the customers to a half pint of treacle a red herring or a pound of butter then we will have a one horse shay and sundays we will take the children out to drive yes we will drive them all around the room

113. Charming Jane Louisa

This rare comic ballad concerns a man's unsuccessful attempt to court a wiley female tailor, who allows him to treat her to meals and entertainments, then abandons him when his money runs out. Very specifically localized to New York City, it flaunts local color, with the rhyming couplets contrived to accommodate some of New York's most popular places of amusement. In part, it is an urban lampoon of the prevalent sailor-and-his-bride ballad pastorale, of which there are numerous examples in nautical lore and in this anthology. It also epitomizes a certain species of mid 19th-century ballad farce with urban-nautical appeal, notably "New York Girls" ("Can't You Dance the Polka") and "Peter Street" ("The Shirt and the Apron"), English sailor-songs set respectively in New York and Liverpool: a mercenary woman in the Big City strings a sailor along, teasing, goading, playing upon his weaknesses, until either he spends all his money on her or she gets him drunk and robs him outright.

Eugene O'Neill's one-act play *The Long Voyage Home* (1917) takes up a similar theme in earnest: liquor and feminine wiles in the Big City derail the Progress of the Innocent and foil his plans to return Home to Mother and a pastoral Farm; the sailor Olsen is a tragic figure unable to resist the ruinous temptations that will shipwreck his life permanently. By contrast, the ballads are played for laughs with self-deprecating, first-person humor: the sailor-in-the-apron tells his own story, playing the fool, and becomes an object of jovial derision among his shipmates ("Sure you could've got a better dress than that for fifty pounds!") while a self-evident moral proclaims: "Any sailor man-of-the-world should've known better in the first place!" In the end, the sailor, more hapless than tragic and wearing a sheepish grin, resolves to know better or do better next time.

Part of the fun in "Charming Jane Louisa" is that "charming" has a double meaning, functioning as both adjective and verb. Only one other example of this ballad has been located, an undated broadside entitled "Charming Jane Louisa" that begins, "It was in the merry month of June when woods and fields were flowery," printed by Wrigley at New York (Wolf #285). No melody has been identified but many ballad airs would fit the lyrics, especially if stretched and molded eccentrically to enhance the comic overtones of the text.

"CHARMING JANE LOUISA." George W. Piper, ship *Europe* of Edgartown, 1868-70.

1. It was in the pleasant month of May when the hills and fields were flowery
   It was on a Sunday in the afternoon as I was going down the Bowery[3]
   And there I met a lovely lass slightly known to me sir
   She was a tailoress by trade and her name was Jane Louisa[4]

   Chorus Right tit fal lal fi lal fal li je bu right tit fal lal fal lie jo
   Right tit fal lal fal lie je bu right tit fal lal li ju

2. I made by bow she took my arm and listened to my flattery
   And together we did walk until we reached the battery[5]

---

[3] The Bowery is a street in lower Manhattan, at one time very fashionable, later New York's most notorious skid row. The name appears in place of "Broadway" in some versions of "New York Girls" ("Can't You Dance the Polka").

[4] It should be noted that in working-class Boston and other sections of eastern and southeastern New England, "Jane Louisa" is commonly pronounced "Jane Looeezer," as if to rhyme with "me sir," "please her," and "sneezer."

[5] The Battery is a district and a park at the southern tip of Manhattan, so called because it is the site of the old Dutch harbor garrison of Nieuw Amsterdam in the seventeenth century: "It was at one time a fashionable quarter, and is now [1889] frequented by the poor of the lower part of the city" (B.E. Smith 1889, 129).

And then she made me understand my manners did much please her
It was then I thought I won the heart of charming Jane Louisa

3. She says kind sir please a wish for all to leave this dry land
Suppose we go and take a walk away down to Staten Island[6]
You may be sure I quickly went determined for to please her
Nor cared I one cent how much I spent[7] on charming Jane Louisa

4. And when we reached the other side[8] and gazed amongst the million
And then together our steps did glide toward the famed pavillion
A chucking[9] in ice cream and cakes O wasn't she a sneezer[10]
Three dollars very soon I spent on charming Jane Louisa

5. And still for more she seemed to lack although my heart was willing
I had tickets for my passage back but in my pockets not a shilling[11]
Says I us had better take a walk the wind here blows a breezer
And quickly I came back to New York with charming Jane Louisa

6. She says kind sir I vow I ought to ask your pardon
But really I should like to go into the Castle Garden[12]
She said so with a winning smile I answered to appease her
My pocket book is left at home my charming Jane Louisa

7. She then began to cry and says you do not treat me right sir
Here comes a gentleman I know and to you I will bid goon night sir
And then she left me by myself beneath a shady tree sir
And that was the way I lost fair false hearted Jane Louisa

8. Since then I never had a girl nor will I unless sir
There is some gentle lady here my loneliness will bless sir
I will treat her as husband ought and do my best to please her
And never more will waste a thought on charming Jane Louisa

---

[6] Staten Island lies across New York Harbor from Battery Park, from which it is accessible by ferry. Since 1898 it has been the Borough of Richmond, an integral component of New York City.

[7] Understandably, there are many variants to the destination, the product purchased, the amount spent, and the nationality of the coinage—for example, "To Tiffany's I took her, I did not mind expense; / I bought her two gold earrings, boys, they cost me fifty cents " or "…fifteen pence."

[8] They have crossed the harbor on the Staten Island Ferry, which remained famous for generations for its five-cent fare.

[9] *Chuck:* "food of any kind"; hence, *chuck,* "to eat" and also "to spend extravagantly"; however, *chuck in,* "to challenge… compete," evidently from a boxing expression (Partridge 1961, 152f).

[10] *Sneezer* (among other meanings): "Something exceptionally good or bad, big or strong or violent, in some specified respect… (19th century slang, 1820); a blow (dialect, became slang circa 1840); a gale (1955, mainly nautical…)" (Partridge 1961, 792).

[11] *Shilling:* the denomination of coinage suggests that the narrator (and hence the song) may be British—and, if an indigent Briton in New York, then likely a sailor.

[12] Castle Garden is a circular fortress on the Battery in New York (see note 3), constructed in 1805 and originally named Fort Clinton, after a renowned governor of New York State. Converted to civic use in 1822, "it was for some years used as an operahouse (Jenny Lind first sang there), and civic receptions were held there. From 1855 to 1891 it was used as a place of reception for immigrants… " (B.E. Smith 1889, 223). As Jane Louisa was hardly likely to have wanted her escort to take her to "a place of reception for immigrants," the Castle Garden allusion suggests that the text predates conversion of the facility in 1855.

114. The Cove Wot Spouts

This Shakespearean romp on the theme The Urban Tough and the Beaux Artes typifies the streetwise Bowery Bhoys music-hall style fashionable in New York in the 1840s and '50s [see "I Am One of the Boys," #115]. In life as in fiction, Bowery Bhoys idolized the eminent American tragedian Edwin Forrest (1806-1872), mentioned here playing the title role in *Richard III* at the Bowery Theatre in Manhattan. The sailor's lyrics are evidently derived from broadsides entitled "The Cove Vot Spouts" (Wolf #402), "The Cove Wot Sings" (reported by Steve Gardham from *The Westminster Review* in 1839), and "I'm One of the Chaps Wot Sings" (Catnach of London and Keys of Devoport) (see also Holloway & Black, p. 16). The tunes named for them are "He was the boy could do it" and "Got 'em," which is also associated with the text "The Devil and Little Mike."

"THE COVE THAT SINGS" from Patrick Shuldham-Shaw, Emily B. Lyle, and Peter A. Hall, eds., *The Greig-Duncan Folk Song Collection*, 8 Vols., Aberdeen: Aberdeen UP, 1987), vol. 3, #563.

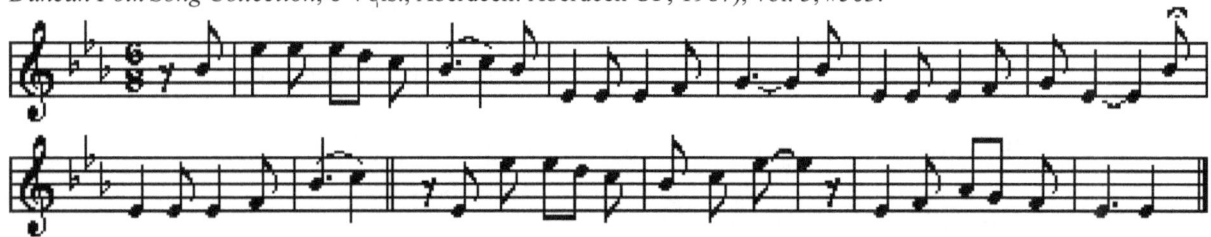

"THE COVE WOT SPOUTS." George W. Piper, ship *Europa* of Edgartown, 1868-70. Slightly realigned from the diarist's slightly irregular division into lines. A long chorus of nonsense syllables is also indicated: "Right tit e fal lal de do / Right tit e fal lal de day / Right tit e fal lal de do / Right tit e fal lal de day."

1. I am going for to sing a song a song what happened the other night
   It will not detain you long And in the end you will say I am right
   My name is no matter what I dont live here about
   But I am welcome everywhere for I'm the Cove wot spouts

2. Last Winter at the Bowery Theatre I saw Edwin Forrest Richard play
   O down down to Hell he cried poor King Henry soon gave way
   I got so careless drunk I began to holler and shout
   A horse A horse My kingdom for a horse Like Richard I did spout

3. A policeman came in and he grabbed me by the collar
   Saying you look here young Man this is no place for to bellow [*holler*]
   He hit me on the head which caused me to shout
   Lay on Macduff and dam[n]ed be him who first cries hold enough
   Like Macbeth I did spout

4. O with that there rushes in about a dozen or more
   It took them all at once for to lay me on the floor
   Say[s] one we got you now you will pay for this no doubt
   O lay me in the grave with Juliet Like Romeo I did spout

5. O they took me off to jail and they put me into bed
   But there I could not sleep for dreams ran through my head
   I got up in the night and seized my comrade by the snout
   Crying Give me my pound of flesh Like Shylock I did spout

6. He commenced for to holler and yell and to kick up the very devil
   O the keeper was at the door and he thought us very uncivil
   He tried to come in but I made the blood [flow] from his nose
   Crying Blood Blood Iago blood run out Like Othello I did spout

7. O the policemen they came in and they took me off to court
   Saying as they went along we will put an end unto your sport
   The judge says who are you that dares kick up such a rout
   I am My Murdered father's ghost Like Hamlet I did spout

8. My father's ghost he cried Why that man is surely mad
   To be insulted on the bench this is really too bad
   For six Months lock him up it is unsafe for to let him out
   And this was a sad recompense for learning how to spout

115. I Am One of the Boys
[One of the Boys; One of the B'hoys]

This slang fest of rowdy shenanigans among firemen in New York's infamous Bowery district is a radical variant of "One of the Boys." A milder, related text of nine stanzas, sans chorus, is printed in *Elton's Songs and Melodies for the Multitudes* (New York and Boston, circa 1848-50).[13] While the lyrics have a distinctly urban flavor,[14] the self-inflating, tougher-than-nails braggadocio and hyperbole of the big-city volunteer firefighters characterizes them as the urban counterparts of contemporaneous American backwoods "heroes"—frontiersmen, Indian fighters, river pirates, even Davy Crockett himself.[15] The song has its roots in a pair of plays by Benjamin A. Baker (1818-1890), staged simultaneously in neighboring New York theatres in 1848. *A Glance at New York: a local drama in two acts,* the first to open, "created a new theatrical genre by its realistic portrayal of Mose, the volunteer fireman and type of the Bowery boy" (Hart, 48), and his female counterpart, Big Lize, "always ready to take up anyone's fight" (Monaghan, 149). They created such a sensation that Baker's sequel, *New York As It Is,* opened while the original was still running: "the leading man, Frank Chanfrau, acted in both plays, dashing from one theatre to the other during the performance" (Ibid, 147). Both leading characters and their gang of "Bowery Bhoys" were soon taken up in a series of prose sequels by popular writer Ned Buntline (pseudonym of Edward Zane Carroll Judson, 1823-1886), catapulting them into the national limelight. Meanwhile, Chanfrau made a career out of playing Mose in numerous sequels and revivals.

---

[13] One or the other is evidently an adaptation, perhaps to avoid a seeming infringement. G.S. Jackson (57) reprints Elton's lyrics and, based on an inconclusive allusion in the text, attributes them to singer T.G. Booth. Compare the first stanza:

"My name is Jack Romaine, and a bull dog I'm in grain
And a might gallus chap, well I am!
I can knock down a watchman or kick up a row,
Or get up a fight, yes I can Jam!
Oh I loves Eliza and I kills for Keyser,
And I runs to fires when I hears the noise,
If you ever see a fuss, you may bet I raised the muss,
Because I am one of the boys."

[14] See Frank 1995, 16ff.

[15] See my article "'I'm One of the B'hoys': A Song about New York Firefighters in the Age of Sail." *Seaport* (South Street Seaport Museum), 37:2-3, special World Trade Center 9/11 issue, Spring/Summer 2002, pp 34-41; and my monograph, *Oooh, You New York Girls! The Urban Pastorale in Ballads and Songs about Sailors Ashore in the Big City* (Kendall Monograph Series N° 9, co-published with the Australian Association for Maritime History; Sharon, Mass., and Perth, Western Australia, 1996).

Audiences never seemed to tire of the actor Chanfrau, in the leading part of Mose, a fireman in a red shirt, boots, and fashionable "soap locks." Moreover, Mose was advertised as a real person, Mose Humphrey, a typesetter on the *Sun* by profession and a foreman socially.... Newsboys packed the gallery cheering the hero, shouting "flashy terms." Half the urchins knew the real Mose and had seen him roistering through the Bowery. Mose became the Paul Bunyan of Manhattan—a fabulous fellow who was said to have jumped across the Hudson, to have blown vessels back down the East River, and to have carried a streetcar with the horses dangling. Chanfrau was Bowery-born himself. As a lad, working behind the scenes of New York theatres, he had made the stagehands laugh with his burlesques of Hamblin, Booth, and Forrest... Now as Mose in 1848 he became famous overnight. (Ibid, 148f)

Unfortunately, while the sense of the action is relatively clear, nowadays some of the slang is impenetrable. *Keyser* is evidently the name of the fire brigade, and *Gotham* one of the engines, after Washington Irving's celebrated nickname for the metropolis. The moniker was coined in his *Salmagundi Papers* (1807) which, analogously to Baker's plays, "was merely a good-natured satire upon the supposed conceit of the author's fellow-townsmen" (Stimpson 1946, 372). One wonders whether any of this was intelligible to the whaleman-scribe, George Wilbur Piper, a country boy from New Hampshire.

"I AM ONE OF THE BOYS." George W. Piper, ship *Europa* of Edgartown, 1868-70. Realigned from 8-line stanzas. The slang is key to bith the ryhes and meaning. The gospel accrding to Eris Partridge is that *spooney* or *spoony* is "A simpleton, a fool" and *luke* is "anothing" (Partridge, pp. 706 and 1131); hence, *spooney lukes* are "foolish non-entities." *Lam* is "To beat, thrash" (p. 663); *spanky*: "Smart; showily smart" (p. 1119), i.e., natty, fashionable; *rig:* is "clothing," derived from nautical usage; *gallus* ("a frequent pronunciation and occasional spelling of *gallows*") is "Enormous; 'fine'" (p. 443). *Tight:*still has the same meaning in modern usage: "close-knit" or "intimate," in the sense of boon companions. And *rhino* is "money"; hence, "the rhino is rough" signifies "the pay is inferior" or "the wages are low."

1

I am one of the boys and up to the joys
Of a New York City life
When Syksez and I gets on a Spree
We are always on hand for a strife
When the boys cry we all aspire
For to be the first on the brakes
We go in for law whenever we can
And carry away the stakes

Chorus: Then hurry hurry up Keyserboys
The Gotham how she flies
For Mose my boys is one of the Boys
And some of the G'Hals is Lize

2

At the fire last night we had a high old fight
When they brought their machine
O the boys stood by on hand for a hie
It was the prettiest sight I've seen
The boys got into a muss somewhere
With a parcel of spooney lukes
They put in their licks like a pile of bricks
And lammed them out of their boots

3

At the Vauxhall Show I thought I would go
So up steps Lize and me
She cut such a swell she was such a belle
I'll be damned if she wasn't sw'ee [?]
I espied a fellow in a spank up rig
And he eyed her rather close
Says I old Guy you had better mind your eye
If you dont want a muss with Mose

4

Then it is hurry along and listen to the song
The Keyser boys are some
Dont you get in a muss if you dont want a fuss
Or a lash with with the Marshal's tongue
The boys are all right all gallus and tight
And down on nothing but Sin
O the rhino is rough and rather tough
But the heart is all right within

116. Sailors Ashore

This jovial sailortown ballad of probable American origin is set in an unspecified port-of-call in the South Seas. It begins conventionally with formula vernal-pastoral imagery drawn from the love ballads but degenerates to describe the rough-and-tumble antics of seamen on liberty ashore, culminating with their awakening to find themselves locked up in the local hoosegow. The song is known only in these two whalemen's texts, transcribed by lads from New Hampshire a decade apart. They are virtually identical except for minor variations, suggesting oral transmission (e.g., "white cora sound" versus "white coral sand"). The original source and melody are unknown but the lyrics are compatible with many ballad airs, especially such traditional Irish jigs as "Rory O'Moore" [#166] and "Old Leather Breeches" [#180].

A.

"SAILORS ASHORE." George Edgar Mills, third mate, bark *Aurora* of Westport, Mass., 1858. Much like B.

B.

"SAILORS SONG." George W. Piper, ship *Europa* of Edgartown, 1868-70. Like A, evidently complete in 2 stanzas.

1. The sweet scented flowers from natures gay bowers
   Were shading their fragrance out on the first breeze[16]
   The village bells ringing the fair maids were singing[17]
   The own native songs amongst the Cocoa nut trees
   When I with some others as dear as my brothers
   All dressed in our long togs[18] we kept in good store
   There was Joe Tom and Jerry and we all being merry
   And bound to have some fun like sailors ashore

2. I being a bruiser and a regular cruiser
   We began as we ended in drinking all around
   With good jokes and loud cheering the Kikoes[19] not fearing
   We started to cruise up the white cora sound[20]
   And some being weary and wishing to tarry
   For the rest in the shade they all felt inclined
   And the next morning found us with iron gates around us
   We had in our rest in the stocks been confined

---

[16] That is, "the smell of the land" as experienced on shipboard approaching the shore: A has "blooming their fragrances."

[17] Text A has the somewhat less tropical-sounding "The tower bells was ringing / The fair maids were singing."

[18] *Long togs:* "Landsmen's clothes; nautical slang" (Partridge 894, citing Marryat and Dana).

[19] *Kiko:* a non-pejorative reference to *aboriginals* or *native people,* most especially Kanakas (Polynesians) and other South Sea islanders, in British and American usage: "Rhyming on *sye* (Cockney for 'say') *so*. It is a Cockney alternative spelling of *cocoa*" (Partridge 1158; thus, see Partridge 167 regarding the confusion between *cocoa-nut* and *coco-nut* and the usage of *cocoanut* or *coco-nut people*.

[20] Text A has "white coral sound," of which the rendition in B is an obvious corruption.

117. He Is Only Gone Home With a Friend

This tragicomic piece about a sailor ashore gradually breaking the news of a shipmate's death at sea is a prime example of a song passed along from one sailor to another on shipboard, in this case from a young seaman to the first mate. The transcription is distinguished by quaint spelling in whaleman Henry George's large, rounded, juvenile hand, for which he politely apologizes at the end. The pious lyrics are of a sort suggesting faithful descent from a printed source (not found), and the structure of the chorus suggests that it is an actual song, intended to be sung, and not merely a poem intended for recitation. However, the esoteric orthography and misguided syntax of this text indicate that it was transcribed from singing or recitation, rather than from print. There is no indication of the tune.

"HE ONLY GONE WITH A FRIEND." Henry George, seaman, inserted in the journal of Austin C. Bennett, first mate, bark *Sunbeam* of New Bedford, 1886-90.

1. A poor sexton woman were longing to see,
   Her husband a sailor return;
   As she sat by the window & anciously wait,
   For some news from a sailor to learn,
   When just around the corner a blue Jacket came;
   Poor woman i saw her turn pale
   As she open the door with a sorrowful sigh
   To listen to the Marrieners tale

Chorus: He is only gone home with a friend
   He is only gone home with a friend
   He told me to tell you he would see you again
   For he is only gone home with a friend

2. I don't understand you she moddesly cried
   For my Jack always come straight to me
   A[s] soon as the ship in the dockyard do lay
   I never knew him for to stay
   Then surely you will tell me what led him astray
   Which made him forget his poor wife
   Then keep your mind easy the sailor replied
   He is free from all care & all strife

3. O man she cried have pitty for me
   O dont fain to utter the truth
   If anything wrong has happen to Jack
   He is the joy & the pride of my youth
   Then trembling a sailor you seldom does see
   The sailor then told her the end
   Your Jacks gone to heaven he is not gone alone
   He is gone with an angellic Friend

Escuse the Wrighting
From Henry George to Mr Bennett

118. Jayne's Hair Tonic
[Dr. Jayne's Hair Tonic]

What is it that a man does not want, and struggles against having as long as possible; But which, when he once gets it, He would not part with it for all the world?   A Bald Head.

— Journal of Charles Atherton, bark *Oak* of Nantucket, 1869.

This comic song text in the snake-oil-and-Yankee-drummer vein, involving a purported cure for baldness, was copied down by cabin boy Jim Stanton, age around 14, from something he calls "The New Yorkers" (possibly Horace Greely's *The New-Yorker*). It has not been found anywhere else, and the tune is unknown.

DR JAYNES HAIR TONIC."   James E. Stanton, ship's boy, ship *Emily Morgan* of New Bedford, 1838: "From the new yorkers."

1. Come all that's bald and all that's gray,
   Come listen to my ditty,
   I Wish to tell you, Without delay
   What brought me to your Citty.

2. It is to clothe your naked heads
   With nature's proper covering;
   Renew the Soil that's Almost dead,
   Nor under Wigs be hovering.

3. My name and fame are outspread Wide,
   Beyond the distant Ocean;
   Both France and England, Spain beside,
   Have all got in the notion.

4. A Bald Head heare Would never be found
   Throughout this might nation,
   if We Would only till the ground
   With this grand preparation.

5. Yourre offered now, both free and pure
   Although youre Case be Chronic,
   A pleasant, shure, And perfect Cure,
   In Dr. Jaynes Hair Tonic.

The End

Note: According to Carl Sandburg, "Earlier than 1880 patent medicine men and their wagons were traveling. Kickapoo Indian Sagwa as a spring tonic and Kickapoo Snake Oil for rheumatism and neuralgia were bespoken and proclaimed by dancing and shouting Indians. The Wizard Oil remedies had their merits sung by slick-tongued comedians with banjos. Flaring gasoline lamps lighted their faces as the throngs surged about listening to the promises made to the sick, lame, sore" (Sandburg, 1927, 52). The Food and Drug Act of 1907, which created the Food and Drug Administration, was the first major government measure to regulate narcotic and alcoholic over-the-counter preparations, and to control the specious and often dangerous claims made by manufacturers, distributors, and drummers.

ROSE OIL (TO MAKE THE HAIR GROW).—Rose petals, beat to a pulp, three or four ounces; olive oil, three quarters of a pint; macerate in the sun or a warm place, in a covered vessel for a week, and press out the oil. Repeat the process with fresh roses till the oil smells sufficiently strong, and then filter.

OIL OF ROSES—Olive oil, two pints; otto of roses one drachm; oil of rosemary, one drachm. Mix. It may be colored red by steeping a little alkanet root in the oil (with heat), before scent-ing it. This oil will make the hair look beautifully glossy, and will help to make it curl.

FAMILY OIL (FOR THE HAIR).—Oil of sweet almonds, one gill; spermaceti, quarter of an ounce. Melt them together over the fire, first breaking the spermaceti into very small pieces. When cold, stir in a few drops of oil of bergamot, rub-bed up with half a grain of civet.

LACQUER FOR BRASS—Take of rectified spirits of wine, two quarts, and three pounds of seed lac, picked particularly clean, and clear of all black and brown specks and pieces, as upon that de-pends the entire beauty of the lacquer; add them together, keep them warm, and shake them often.

OIL FOR THICKENING THE HAIR.—Sweet oil, three ounces, oil of lavender, one drachm. Ap-ply morning and evening to those parts where the hair is wanting, in consequence of a deficiency of moisture in the skin.

QUEEN'S OIL (TO MAKE THE HAIR GROW).—Oil of ben, one pint; civent, three grains; Italian oil of jasmin, three fluid ounces; otto of roses, three minims. If otto of roses is not to be had, ten or twelve minims of common oil of roses may be substituted.

Above: Text of an unidentified newspaper clipping pasted into the whaling journal of William H. Davis, bark Midas *of New Bedford, 1861-65.*

119. Come Landlord Fill the Flowing Bowl

This popular English convivial song seems to have remained in continuous circulation since the 18th century, assisted by its inclusion in many college-song and glee-club anthologies. In the folksong revival of the 1950s and '60s it was also recorded as "Three Jolly Coachmen," after the first line of a lighthearted version popularized by the Kingston Trio.

TUNE - "Come Landlord Fill Your Flowing Bowl," from the *Gentle Annie Melodist Nº 2* (New York, 1859), p. 88.

"COME LANDLORD FILL THE FLOWING BOWL." George W. Piper, ship *Europa* of Edgartown, 1868-70. The MS indicates that the third line of each stanza (and the third line of the chorus) is to be repeated twice; however, the tune requires also that the first couplet of each stanza (as well as of the chorus) be repeated once. It is presumed that the chorus (transcribed at the end in the MS) is to be sung after each stanza.

1. Come landlord fill the flowing bowl
   Untill it does run over
   For this night we will merry merry be
   And to morrow we'll get sober

2. O he that drinks strong drinks
   And drinks without measure
   Lives as he ought to live
   And dies a hearty fellow

3. O brandy it cures the gout
   The cholic and the tisic
   So it is to all men
   The very best of physic

4. O he that courts a pretty girl
   And courts her for his pleasure
   He is a fool if he marries her
   Without store of treasure

5. O he that kisses a pretty girl
   And she runs and tells her mother
   She is a fool for telling her
   For she will never get another

6. O come now let us dance and sing
   And drive away all sorrow
   For perhaps we may not
   Meet again to morrow

Chorus: Come landlord fill the flowing bowl
Untill it does run over
For this night we will merry merry be
And to morrow drunk as ever

120. Lannigan's Ball

This famous Irish comic ballad is often regarded as a folk song, but sheet music already in print by the 1870s attributes it to "Mr. Gavan, the celebrated Galway poet"[21]—according to Steve Gardham, circa 1863: "'Lannigan's Ball', like 'Rocky Road to Dublin' was written by D.K. Gavin of Galway and popularised all over Britain by Harry Clifton," a celebrated music-hall performer; "I would guess that Clifton put the music to it but he often used earlier tunes."[22] American sheet music published in 1868 blithely credits the words to Tony Pastor and the music to Neil Bryant, "as sung by" the famous minstrel Dan Bryant, but these fellows could have done little more than make a few changes. As Gardham notes, "Pastor... nicked many of Harry Clifton's songs." The air is a traditional double jig now commonly known as "Lannigan's Ball" (after the ballad text), but O'Neill identifies it as a form of two older tunes published in Aird's *Selection of Scotch, English, Irish and Foreign Airs* of 1782—a jig called "Dribbles of Brandy," and a hop-jig form of the same, known as "Drops of Brandy" (O'Neill 1910, 139). The whaleman's transcription is testimony to the age of the song and to the remarkable stability of the text: line-by-line, with only a few discrepancies, it follows virtually the same path as the first six (of seven) stanzas reported by O Lochlainn from a version learned by his mother at Kilkee (Ireland) circa 1880.

TUNE - "Lannigan's Ball" (*FEIS-RINCE UI LANNAGAIN*): O'Neill #858.

"LANAGEN'S BALL." George W. Piper, ship *Europa* of Edgartown, 1868-70. (For textual comparison and a few significant departures from O Lochlainn, see "Notes" below.)

1. By the town of Ashthoir lived one Johnny Lanagen,
   Battered away till he hadn't a pound;
   His father, he died and made him a man again,
   Left him [a] farm with an achre of ground.
   He gave a large party to all of his relations
   Who didn't forget him, when sent to the walls,
   And if you will listen t'will make your eyes glissen
   To hear of the ruction at Lanagen's Ball.

2. Myself to be shure got free invertations,
   For all the nice girls and boys that I'd ask;
   In less than a minet his friends and relations;
   Was dancing as merrily as beese [bees] round a cask,
   Miss O Harry the nate little millener,
   Tipped me the wink to give her the call,
   Next we arrived at Timothy Gillergins,
   Just in time for Lanagen's Ball

---

[21] O Lochlainn 1939, p. 223.
[22] 1 May 2009, http://www.mudcat.org/thread.cfm?threadid=8388&messages=24

3. There were lashings of whiskey and whines for the ladies,
   Praties and cake, bacon and tea,
   There were Nolans and Dolans and the Oh Gradiers,
   Were kissing the girls and dancing away
   Songs were as plenty as water shure,
   The harp that once rang in Old Tarras Hall,
   Sweet Nelly Gray and the Rat catchers daughter
   Were dancing in couples at Lanagen's Ball

4. Oh when we got there they were dancing a Polka,
   All around the room in a nate whirlagig;
   Katie and I put a stop to all shuch nonscence,
   And left them the step to an eight irish gig.
   Och Avourneen but wasn't she [proud] of me,
   We danced till we thought the old ceiling would fall
   Shure I spent a whole week at Darlings Academy
   Learning the skekt [steps] for Lanagen's Ball

5. Oh the boys they are gay and the girls they get frisky
   All dancing together in couples and groups;
   Till a accident happened young Bryant Shaugnessy,
   He stuck his right foot through Miss Hagaty's hoops.
   Och this creater [creature] she roared and called Milea Murphy
   She cried for a friend till she gathered them all
   Ned Harding he swore that he wouldn't go fa[r]ther
   Till he had satisfaction at Lanagen's Ball

6. Amidst of them Miss Cavenaugh fainted
   Her cheek[s] all the while were as red as a rose
   Her friends declared her cheeks they were painted,
   But she'd lakened [liked] a small drop to[o] much I suppose.
   Big Ned Courtny so heavy and able
   When he saw his dear collean strecthed down by the wall,
   He pulld the left leg out from under the table
   And broak all the China at Lanagen's Ball.[23]

---

[23] For comparison with O Lochlainn's indigenous Irish text: In stanza 1, he has *ten* acres of ground, a *grand* party, "when *come* to the wall," and *"At the rows and ructions* of Lanigan's Ball"; in stanza 2, he has *merry* (rather than *merrily*), Miss *Judy O'Daly*, and *"And soon I arrived with Peggy McGilligan."* Interestingly, in stanza 3 the whaleman substitutes *whiskey* (American spelling) for *punch,* has the very Irish *praties* where O Lochlainn gives *potatoes,* and *nate* (Irish pronunciation for "neat"; the word recurs in stanza 4, where O Lochlainn has "nice"; also in stanza 3, the list of Irish surnames is the same (though *O'Grady* is misspelled in the whaleman's text); O Lochlainn has *courting* (instead of *kissing*); "The songs they went round as plenty of water, / From the harp that once sounded in Tara's old hall"; and "All singing together at Lanigan's Ball." In stanza 4, O Lochlainn's first line is "They were doing all kinds of nonsensical polkas"; the adjective *nate* is absent in the second line; and he has "But *Julia* and I *soon banished* their nonsense / And *tipped them a twist of a real Irish jig.* / Och *mavrone, how* the girls they got mad on me / And danced till you'd think the ceilings would fall"; and *"three* weeks at *Brooks* Academy." In stanza 5, the boys are *merry* and the girls *hearty;* "*Terence Macarthy...* put his right leg through *Miss Finerty's* hoops"; rather than *fainting,* the "creature" *roared,* and *cried* (rather than *called*) "Meelia murther"—i.e., the equivalent of crying bloody murder—then cried for *her brothers;* and it was *Carmody* who swore vengeance. In stanza 6, Miss *Kerrigan* fainted, and *"some of the lads decreed* she was painted," but "She *took* a small drop too much I suppose, / Her sweetheart *Ned Morgan* so *powerful* and able... *tore* the left leg from under the table / And *smashed all the chaneys* at Lanigan's Ball" (*chaney* is an unsavory epithet for *Chinese*). O Lochlainn's seventh stanza (absent in the whaleman's transcription) is:

Boys, oh boys, 'tis then there was ructions, / Myself got a lick from big Phelim McHugh,
But soon I replied to his kind introduction, / And kicked up a terrible hullabaloo.
Ould Casey the piper was near being strangled, / They squeezed up his pipes, bellows, chanters and all,
The girls in their ribbons they all got entangled, / And that put an end to Lanigan's Ball.

121. The Wild Rover

A mainstay of the pub-singing circuit and a Saint Patrick's Day favorite on both sides of the Atlantic, "The Wild Rover" is popularly regarded as one of the great Irish folksongs. In fact, it is not strictly Irish but, with roots in British broadsides and singing tradition going back to the 17th century it was tinkered with by the Scots-Irish songsmith [George] Alexander Lee (1802-1852). The first American sheet music was published in 1839.

TUNE - "The Wild Rover," generic, after the singing of the Clancy Brothers, Cliff Haslam, Dick Holdstock, etc. Most variants are much alike except Creighton's, which seems to have been corrupted by "Rye Whiskey."

"THE WILD ROVER." George W. Piper, ship *Europa* of Edgartown, 1868-70. The chorus is slightly different than that popularized on the pub circuit, which generally begins, "Then it's no, nay, never / No, never no more...."

1. I have been a wild rover these dozen long years
   I spent all my money on ale wine and beer
   But now I will lay up my money in store
   And I never will play the wild rover no more

   Chorus: Wild rover wild rover and a rover no more
   And I never will play the wild rover no more

2. I went to an ale house where I used to resort
   I began for to tell them my money was short
   I asked them for to trust me but their answer was nay
   Such customers as you we can find every day

3. Then I pulled out a handfull of silver straightway
   And I showed it to them just to see what they would say
   They said what they had told me was only in jest
   And that I was welcome to liquor of the best

4. Nay Nay then said I that never can be
   I will see you all hanged ere I spend one penny
   But now I will lay up my money in store
   And I never will play the wild rover no more

5. But now I am resolved on my future life
   For to settle myself and to marry a wife
   And we will keep out those ravenous wolves from the door
   And I never will play the wild rover no more

CHAPTER THIRTEEN
Lubbers and Swabs
Miscellaneous Songs and Curiosities of Sea and Shore[1]

> … As in a Chinese puzzle, many pieces are hard to place, so there are some unfortunate fellows who can never slip into their proper angles, and thus the whole puzzle becomes a puzzle indeed.
>
> — Herman Melville, *White-Jacket* (1850)

Scrimshaw shot flask made out of a sperm whale tooth, engraved with African-American vignettes copied after book illustrations of the 1830s. Anonymous, American, circa 1840.

Kendall Collection, New Bedford Whaling Museum

---

[1] "Lubbers and Swabs" is quoted from the first line of Dibdin's song "Poor Jack" [#214], alluding to the sailors' occupational pride and disdain for landlubbers' ignorance of nautical ways: "Go patter to lubbers and swabs do you see, about danger and fear and the like." The corollary is the sailors' awkwardness and discomfort ashore, and his ignorance of shoreside manners.

122. The Cobbler or Shoemaker
[The Cobbler; The Cobbler's Jig]

Versions of this folksong have been variously collected from tradition on both sides of the Atlantic but it has not been encountered in any other sailor manifestation than the transcription by whaleman Edward W. Collins, whose text must surely be the earliest known. Miraculously, it may be the long-lost lyrics of an early 17th-century song, "The Cobbler's Jig," which Chappell was unable to locate in 1855. The English words and music were certainly extant prior to 1622, when the melody was published in the Netherlands as an English air, lacking the English title and lyrics, but with the original title and lyrics translated into Dutch. The tune alone was anthologized in the seventh edition of Playford's *Dancing Master* in 1686.[2] Almost two centuries after Playford printed the melody in England, Chappell evidently wanted to reunite the words and music of "The Cobbler's Jig" in his *Ballad Literature and Popular Music of the Olden Time* (published 1855), but reports that he was unable to do so because he did not know and could not find the English lyrics. He was thus obliged to publish the tune with another text, which he selected based on the well-reasoned but erroneous presumption that it "may prove to be the [missing] ballad."[3] Captain Collins gives no hints about the tune. However, the title and subject of his text, the "derry, down" chorus, and the distinctively antique flavor of the ensemble suggest a late 16th- or early 17th-century provenance and indicate that the lyrics were certainly intended for some form of the air of "The Cobbler's Jig." Allowing for minor adjustments to compensate more than two centuries of evolution in tradition between the time the song was translated into Dutch and the time Collins wrote down the words, the lyrics and melody are a surprisingly workable fit. The courtship aspect of the second stanza—peculiar as it is—and especially the *double-entendre* interpretation to which the chorus lends itself, suggest that this little glee could as well have been classified among the amorous songs as among landlubberly occupational ballads.

TUNE: "The Cobbler's Jig," from John Hullah, *The Song Book* (Philadelphia and London, 1866), #26, p. 30, where it accompanies a text entitled "Cold's the wind and wet's the rain": a setting for one voice, after Chappell (1855 I: 278), in which the same text and tune are given in a setting to accommodate four-part harmonies.

---

[2] Concerning the bibliography of the many Playford editions, see: Schnapper I:252; also the facsimile reprint of the first edition (1651), edited by Margaret Dean-Smith (1957), which according to Simpson (1966, xxvi) "includes a descriptive bibliography of all editions, with census of copies known."

[3] Chappell (1855, I:277) cites the titles and dates of two Dutch anthologies in which the tune was published, *Bellerophon* (1622) and *Nederlandtsche Gedenk-Clanck* (1626): "In the index to the latter, among the 'Engelsche Stemmen,' it is entitled 'Cobbeler, of: Het Engelsch Lapperken.' All the English airs in these Dutch books have Dutch words adapted to them; but as I do not know the English words which belong to this, I have adapted an appropriate song from *The Shoemaker's Holiday*, 1600." Thus, in the absence of the original text, the "Cobbler's Jig" air is nowadays better known by the name of the text that Chappell grafted onto it, "Cold's the wind and wet's the rain"; and that is accordingly what is given by those who followed in Chappell's wake, such as Hullah's *Song Book* (1866), where the air is identified as "The Cobbler's Jig" and the source listed as Playford and Chappell.

"THE COBLER OR SHOE MAKER." Papers of Edward W. Collins, master mariner of Fairhaven, Massachusetts, circa 1829-45. In the chorus, "all" should probably be written *awl,* with reference to the cobblers' indispensable tool and possibly with secondary reference to the male member. The significance of the inscription at the end, written large in a fancy version of Collins's hand, is not clear; perhaps it is a toast or a salute.

1. I am A cobler brave
   I've just took up my freedom
   I'le place my Afection now
   All on some fare young damsel

Chorus: Besides my all and my derry derry down
   Besides my all and my d[e]ar o
   With my ring ting ting ting
   A toodle doodle ding dong
   O she was but my dear O

2. Five pounds i'le give you Kate
   If thou wilt but marry
   O no no John she cries
   I think I drother tarry
   Besides my all and my derry derry down &c

3. I have jurney man and boys
   And while they set A mending
   Tis i'le to the ale house go
   And their i'le set A spending
   Besides my all and my derry derry down &c

4. God warns I have lost my wax
   And whare shal I find it next
   I'le turn my self About
   And care it lays behind me
   Besides my all and my derry derry down &c

Edward W. Collins, Fairhaven
Isaac Tinkham, Rochester
this is the glass

123. Dick Turpin's Bonny Black Bess
(Laws #L-9)

Richard Turpin was an English highwayman, notorious in his own time, elevated to legend even before his execution by hanging in 1739 at age 28. Characteristically of glamorous ballad outlaws, in Turpin's case romance has obscured the pedestrian circumstances of his actual back ground and certain unsavory aspects of his history. It is scarcely remembered in the ballads, for example, that Turpin was a failed butcher's apprentice; and that, in addition to being the masked perpetrator of "daring highway robberies" that "struck terror all over the kingdom," as Logan puts it, Turpin was also a cattle rustler and common burglar—by 1735 the leader of an organized ring of housebreakers and petty thieves, more akin to Fagin than to Robin Hood.

This yarn about the outlaw's famous ride on his famous horse, Black Bess, is said to have been based on an actual incident reported by Turpin's biographer, William Maginn (1793-1842), but it is apocryphal—at least in connection with Turpin. As Logan relates, it was fraudulently attributed to Turpin from an episode in the career of an earlier highwayman:

> The description of Dick Turpin's ride from London to York within twelve hours, at a time when it took four days to perform the distance by coach, is most graphic... [but] the circumstance did not actually occur in the case of Dick Turpin, whom by this act the romancist has rendered so interesting. The ride to York is, however, founded on a real incident which took place in 1676. The hero was one Nevison or Nicks, who plundered a traveller at four o'clock in the morning on the slope at Gadshill, and was in the bowling-green at York among the gay company there at a quarter before eight in the evening. The Lord Mayor happening to be there, Nicks sauntered up to him and enquired the hour, and when tried for the Gadshill robbery, and the prosecutor had sworn to the man, the place, and the hour, Nicks brought forward the Lord Mayor of York to prove an alibi. (Logan, 115)

Kennedy deflates the Turpin myth even further:

> No facts seem to support [Turpin's] ride to York, and the same alibi is said to have been used by two other highwaymen. Nor is it known for certain that he had a horse named Black Bess.... It was when he had retired from highway robbery and was living in Welton, near Beverly, Yorkshire, that Turpin was finally arrested for shooting his landlord's cockerel after imbibing too much drink, and it was for this insignificant incident that he was caught and hanged at York on 7th April 1739. (Kennedy, 736)

Several Turpin ballads have survived in tradition in Britain and America, but while examples of the three catalogued by Laws have been collected in Maritime Canada, Michigan, Wisconsin, the American South, and the West, they have been rare in New England, where whalemen Jones and Handy's text of "Dick Turpin's Bonny Black Bess" and John S. Coquin's transcription of "Dick Turpin and the Lawyer" [#124], are the only specimens recorded. Several airs survive from tradition; Gardner & Chickering's is selected here because of the affinity between the texts.

TUNE from Emelyn Elizabeth Gardner & Geraldine Jencks Chickering, *Ballads and Songs of Southern Michigan*, 1939, #130, p. 320, whereof text versions A and B closely resemble the whalemen's transcription.

"DICK TURPIN'S BONNY BLACK BESS." George M. Jones and Albert F. Handy, bark *Waverly* of New Bedford, 1859-63. Employs the standard Robin Hood theme of Gardner's versions A and B, to which most of the Jones & Handy stanzas are similar. The chorus is apparently intended to be sung to the same melody, repeated. Realigned into four-line stanzas to compensate irregular transcription in the MS.

1. When fortune's blind goddess / Forsook my abode
   And friends proved ungrateful / I took [to] the road
   To plunder the wealthy / And relieve my distress
   I took there to aid me / My bonny black bess

Chorus: My bonny my bonny my bonny black bess
   My bonny my bonny my bonny black bess
   When I take a bawber[4] what can I do less
   Than drink to the health of my bonny black bess

2. How silent you stood / When the carriage I stoped
   And the gold and the silver / Their intimates they droped
   No poor man I plunder / Or ere cause distress
   In memory of you / My bonny black bess

3. When justic did me so hyly pursue
   From london to yorkshire / How like lightning you flew
   No toll gate could stop the[e] / The river did brest
   And reached it in twelve hours / My bonny black bess

4. The bloodhounds are approaching / But the[y] never shall see
   The beast that I loved / And as faithful as you be
   Thou must die poor beast / Though it does me oppress
   There there I have shot the[e] / My bonny black bess

5. In after ages when I am dead and gone
   And my tale shall be handed / From father and son
   There is not one but what will confess
   That I shot you in mercy / My bonny black bess

6. It shall never be said that ingratitude did dwell
   In the heart of Dick Turpin / For the one that he loved so well
   I will die like a brave man / And soon be at rest
   So farewell to you my bonny / My bonny black bess

---

[4] *Bawbee:* literally, "baby" (Scots dialect): a copper halfpenny (and, by extension, any copper coin), per the infant portrait of Mary, Queen of Scots featured on a 16th-century halfpenny minted in Scotland. The significance was not necessarily lost on traditional singers, as Creighton illustrates by quoting a New Brunswick informant: "A bawbee is a halfpenny, and the term goes back to the days of Mary, Queen of Scots. They brought out a coin when she was a baby and the baby's head was on it; you know the Scottish drawl and the language, and by and by 'baby' came to be 'bawbee'" (quoted by Creighton 1971, 60). See also OED.

124. Dick Turpin and the Lawyer
[Dick Turpin; O Rare Turpin, Hero; Turpin's Valour]
(Laws #L-10)

Here the wily outlaw exploits his widely-publicized reputation to trick a victim into revealing where he hides his money. The sailor's text is a much simplified variant of the ballad known to Chappell as "O Rare Turpin, Hero" and to Logan as "Turpin's Valour." According to Chappell, "It was evidently written in 1739, just before Turpin was executed"; and Chappell's and Logan's final stanzas (of 18) tells us that, "Now Turpin is condemn'd to die, / To hang upon yon gallows high." But the sailor's rendition omits entirely any notion of Turpin being condemned, creating instead an impression of the outlaw as a successful trickster. Most texts have a chorus, which changes from "O rare Turpin, hero" in the earlier stanzas, to "O *poor* Turpin" in the later stanzas.

TUNE from William Chappell, *Popular Music of the Olden Time,* 661. Also Duncan 1905, II:36; Moffat & Kidson 1900, 160; Palmer 1979b, #19.

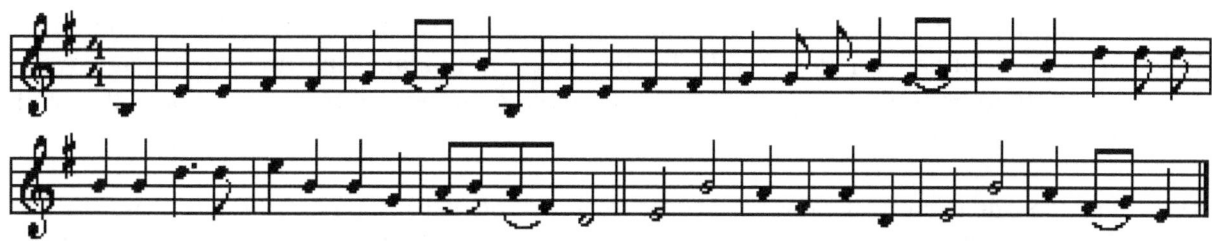

"DICK TURPIN." John S. Coquin, bark *Pacific* of New Bedford, 1867-68; merchant voyages, 1860's-'70s. For the lyrics to be sung to the standard tune requires that the chorus be restored: *O rare Turpin, hero / O rare Turpin O.*

1. As Dick Turpin was riding o'er yon moor,
   He met a lawyer just before;
   And unto him he thus did say
   Have you seen Dick Turpin along this way

2. Oh! no I've not seen Turpin for many a day
   Nor do I wish to all on this way
   For if I should I've got no doubt
   But he would turn my pockets inside out

3. Then says Turpin I'll bet you
   I've got my money all in my shoe
   Then says the lawyer, he feeling very fine
   I've sewed mine up in my coat-cape behind

4. They rode till they came to the foot of the hill,
   When he bade the lawyer to stand still;
   Your coat-cape behind it must come off
   For my bonny black bess wants a new saddle-cloth

5. Now its the very first town that you come to
   Tell them that it was Dick Turpin that robbed you
   And if you should come this way again,
   Why I'd rob you over just the same.

End

125. Johnny Sands
(Laws #Q-3)

Frequently mistaken for a folk song, this is actually an American music-hall piece written by a singer named John Sinclair, who was probably British-born and arrived 'Stateside around 1830. Sheet music issued by Oliver Ditson of Boston in 1842, performance by the Hutchinson Family and their imitators, and publication in Hutchinson Family songsters, broadsides, and eventually *Howe's 100 Comic Songs* (Boston, 1869), launched it into tradition, where the lyrics have been more stable than the tune.[5] On the other hand, the idea of a husband outwitting his virago wife, and even the trick by which Johnny Sands accomplishes it here—homicide by drowning averted by stepping aside at the crucial moment—are not unique. Some manifestations of the theme are certainly folkloric, and there are undeniable textual and plot affinities with "The Old Woman of Slapsadam" ("The Wily Auld Carle"; "The Wife of Kelso") (Laws #Q-2), which Belden traces to Scotland: consciously or unconsciously, Sinclair may have built upon traditional precursors. The song, in original condition, with words and music as issued in 1842, was anthologized in the *Franklin Square Song Collection* (1884), *Good Old Songs We Used to Sing* (1887), and *Heart Songs Dear to the American People* (1909), thus being assimilated into the mainstream American parlor, only to be forgotten again, then "rediscovered" in revival two generations later, with a radically different melody.[6]

TUNE: "Johnny Sands. Comic Ballad composed by John Sinclair." Sheet music, Boston: Oliver Ditson, 1842. The music is through-composed for all four stanzas (and the transcription is so numbered here), and calls for the burden (the repeated lines) of each stanza to be sung three times (not the two times indicated in the whaleman's MS).

---

[5] The song has frequently been recovered from tradition (in Missouri, Arkansas, Florida, Utah, etc.), tenaciously clinging to its title and an orthodox semblance of the original lyrics but often without a tune (e.g., Belden 237); where tunes have been found, most are simplified versions of the A part (first half) of the original (e.g. Randolph #754A); a few are more radical variants (e.g., Randolph #754B). None of the tunes found in tradition are through-composed like the original.

[6] The modal Anglo-Irish melody popularized in the British Isles in the 1970s by Martin Carthy, thence in the Pacific Northwest by Morrigan, is evidently esoteric, but the text is orthodox.

"JOHNNY SANDS." William H. Keith, schooners *William Martin* and *Cora Nash* of Boston, and *Edith May* of Wellfleet, circa 1865-71. A standard broadside copy text.

1.

A man whose name was Johnny Sands,
    Had married Betty Hague,
And though she brought him gold and lands
    She proved a terrible plague;
For O, she was a scolding wife,
    Full of caprice and whim;
He said that he was tired of life
    And she was tired of him.
    And she was tired of him.

2.

Says he, "Then I will drown myself:
    The river runs below:"
Says [s]he, "Pray do you silly elf;
    I wished it long ago:"
Says he, "Upon the brink I'll stand:
    Do you run down the hill,
And push me in with all your might:"
    Says she, "My love, I will."
    Says she, "My love, I will."

3.

"For fear that I should courage lack,
    And try to save my life,
Pray tie my hands behind my back:"
    "I will,["] replied the wife:
She tied them fast, as you may think,
    And when securely done,
"Now stand," says she, ["]upon the brink,
    And I'll prepare to run.
    And I'll prepare to run."

4.

All down the hill his loving bride
    Now ran, with all her force,
To push him in; he stepped aside
    And she fell in, of course;
Now splashing, dashing like a fish,
    "O save me, Johnny Sands!"
"I can't, my dear, though much I wish,
    For you have tied my hands,
    For you have tied my hands."

126. The Farmer's Boy
(Laws #Q-30)

This English agrarian ballad was fairly widely distributed in Britain and America. The folklorists who guessed that it "came [to America] from England as early as 1870"[7] have certainly erred on the side of conservatism regarding its tenure in the New World: its publication in *The Amateur's Song Book* (Boston, 1843) clearly establishes its much earlier introduction and partly explains its wide distribution. Of the four texts recovered from whaling manuscripts, the two reported by Huntington are virtually identical with the lyrics printed in *The Amateur's Song Book*, while the two presented here show significant variations suggesting a different source.

TUNE: "The Farmer's Boy," from *The Amateur's Song Book,* Boston, 1843, pp. 74f.

A.

"THE FARMER'S BOY." Braley family copybook, n.d., inscribed (probably after the fact) in the journal of Jason L. Braley, third and second mate, ship *Stephania* of New Bedford; first mate, bark *Louisa* of New Bedford, 1847-53. Slightly readjusted into lines within stanzas, otherwise uncorrected.

1. The sun had gone down behind yon hill
  And o'er yon dreary moor
When weary and lame a boy there came
  Up to a Farmer's door—
Saying can you tell me if any there be
  Can give to me employ
For to plough for to mow for to reap for to sow
  For to be a farmer's boy

---

[7] Flanders 1932, 118f, quoting Pound, *American Ballads and Songs,* 59.

2. My father is dead my mother is left
    With her five children small
   And what is worse for mother s[t]ill
    I'm the eldest of them all
   Though small I am I fear no work
    If you will give me employ
     For to plough &c

3. If you cannot me employ
    one favor yet I ask
   That is to shelter me this one night
    From the cold winter blast
   At the break of day I will trudge away
    Elsewhere to seek employ
     For to plough &c

4. The farmer says we will try the lad
    No further let him seek
   O yes dear father his daughter cried
    While the tears rolled down her cheek
   For him that can labour it is hard to want
    Or elsewhere to seek employ
     For to plough &c

5. At length of years this boy grew up
    The good old Farmer died
   He left the boy the farm he had
    And his daughter for his bride
   The boy that was, is a farmer now
    And he oft times thinks with joy
   On the happy day he came that way
    For to be a Farmer's boy

B.

"THE FARMER'S BOY." George W. Piper, ship *Europa* of Edgartown, 1868-70. Very similar to A, with the order of stanzas 2 and 3 reversed, and (unlike A) transcribed with the full chorus written out each time. An inscription at the end is a quotation from the last line of the song "The Soldier and the Sailor" (see Doerflinger, 278):

Here is to the honest farmer
Who follows the plough
He earns his living
By the sweat of his brow

<u>*Toast*</u> *He has a wife for a sailor*
and he has a home for a friend

127. Doran's Ass

This Irish comic ballad is sung to a tune also known as "Finnigan's Wake" (O'Neill #265), "The Spanish Lady," and "Red Haired Mary," after the several ballad texts associated with it. As O Lochlainn points out, the air is a variant of "Viva la," a tune presumed to be French in origin, to which the Irish poet Thomas Davis wrote "Clare's Dragoons."[8] The various texts are widely known in Ireland, but "Doran's Ass" is not reported by Laws nor has it generally been recovered from tradition in North America.

TUNE: composite of several generic settings in various keys, otherwise virtually identical: "Red Haired Mary" (sung by Robert Kotta, Sharon, Mass., 1994); "The Spanish Lady" (Loesberg I:33); "Doran's Ass" (Ward, 7); "Finnigan's Wake" (*TORRAM UL FINNGUINE*) (O'Neill #265).

"DORAN'S ASS." William H. Keith, schooners *William Martin* of Boston, *Edith May* of Wellfleet, *Cora Nash* of Boston, etc., circa 1865-71. A well-ordered copy text, possibly from a broadside. Though the punctuation seems to be pretty much intact, customarily (as here) Keith seldom distinguishes between a period and a comma, or between colons and semicolons.

1. One Paddy Doyle lived in Killarney,
   He courted a girl named Biddy Tool;
   His tongue was tipped with a bit of blarney,
   The same to Paddy was a golden rule.
   Both day and dawn she was his colleen;
   When to himself he'd often say,
   What need I cae, when she's my drolleen,
   A coming to meet me on this way?

   Chorus: Whack fol de darrall ido,
              Whack fol de darrall lal la.

2. One heavenly night in last November
   Paddy was out to meet his love;
   What nights it was I don't remember,
   But the moon shown brightly from above.
   That day the boy had got some liquor,
   Which made his spirits light and gay;
   Arrah! what's the use of walking quicker,
   When I know she'll meet me on the way?
       Whack fol &c. &c.

---

[8] "Vive la" is a compound melody (AABB); the Irish cognate is simplex (essentially AA); in fact, the Irish form differs from the AA half of the French version mostly in the cadences: while "Vive la" is in a standard major key (Ionian mode), the Irish variant utilizes a modified pentatonic scale, resolving the cadences on the dominant rather than the tonic note.

3. He tuned his pipes and fell a humming,
   As gently onward he did jog;
   But fatigue and whiskey overcame him,
   So Paddy lay down upon the sod.
   he was not long without a comrade,
   One that could kick up the hay;
   For a big jackass soon smelt out Paddy,
   and lay down beside him on the way.
       Whack fol &c. &c.

4. As Pat lay there in gentle slumbers,
   Thinking of his Biddy dear;
   He dreamt of pleasures without numbers,
   A coming on the ensuing year.
   He spread his arms out on the grass
   His spirits felt both light and gay,
   But instead of Biddy he gripped the ass,
   Roaring out I have her anyway.
       Whack fol &c. &c.

5. He hugged and smugged his hairy missie,
   And flung his hat to worldly care;
   Says Paddy she's mine and may heaven bless her,
   But oh, be [by] my soul! she's like a bear.
   He put his hand on the Donkey's nose,
   With that the Ass began to bray;
   Pat jumped up and roared out:
   Who sarved me in such a way?
       Whack fol &c. &c.

6. Pat ran home as fast as he could,
   At railway speed, or as fast, I'm sure;
   He never stopped a leg or foot
   Untill he came to Biddy's door.
   By that time , twas getting morning;
   Down on his knees he fell to pray,
   Crying: Let me in my Biddy darling
   I'm killed, I'm murdered on the way.
       Whack fol &c. &c.

7. He told her his story mighty civil,
   while she prepared a whiskey glass;
   How he hugged and smugged the hairy divil,
   Go long says she. twas Doran's Ass!
   I know it was, my biddy darling.
   They both got married the very next day.
   But her never got back his old straw hat,
   That the jackass ate up on the way.
       Whack fol &c. &c.

128. Limerick Races

This comic ballad about a day at the races and an evening at the theatre in Limerick (Ireland) is a professionally-written piece, probably produced for the music-hall stage in the 1850s or early '60s. According to Healy (whose tuneless Irish text the sailor's transcription closely resembles), "The theatre to which [the 'Irish lad' in the ballad] wended his way… would probably have been the Theatre Royal, near the Quays which was built in 1841 and burned down in 1882, or maybe at 'The Gaff' (later Courtenay's Theatre) a pretty tough joint where the players had to be good—or else" (Healy 1965, 64). In fact, this song was popularized in England by Sam Collins, "the ex-chimney sweep, who made his first success at the Pantheon in Oxford Street" and later ran a series of music halls of his own (Pulling, 174f). Sailor William Keith's transcription, made circa 1865-71, appears to have been copied from a printed source. The text appears with 19 other sets of song lyrics in *The Popular Songster,* an undated chapbook printed by William R. Walker at Newcastle-on-Tyne (another in the same anthology is "Nelly Gray" [#174], which was first published in 1856); and it was reprinted in 1878 in one of the Beadle Company's many songsters, also without the music. This appears to have been the song's fate throughout its history, the lyrics and melody never appearing together. Joan McDermott of the Irish Traditional Music Archive in Dublin reports, "There are quite a few books containing 'The Limerick Races' but with words only." Healy says that it was sung to "a variant of the traditional air 'Beig Rinnce Againn,'" which does not appear in print anywhere as such; however, Joan McDermott convincingly surmises that the proper reference is a song properly entitled "Beidh Rí l Againn" [tune A], whereof "Beig rinnce againn" is a key line in the Gaelic text. She also located a fiddle tune, sans lyrics and in a different meter, specifically entitled "Limerick Races" [tune B]. Probably by association with a related subject matter, "Limerick Races" was evidently also sung to "The Galway Races," of which Tune C is a close variant in yet another meter. Each of the three tunes requires some adaptation to fit the sailor's lyrics and to accommodate the chorus.

TUNE A - "Beidh Rí l Againn": provided by Joan McDermott, Irish Traditional Music Archive, Dublin: "It appears in *Claiscedal* 1-36 and was collected by Colm Ó Lochlainn."

TUNE B - "Limerick Races": provided by Joan McDermott, Irish Traditional Music Archive, Dublin, from Brendán Breatnach, *Ceol rince Na Hé ireann* (no further citation), in which it is included among the "Irish Airs."

TUNE C - "Limerick Races": generic, learned at coeli sessions hosted by Brendan Boyle and Joel Cowen in Seattle and Bellingham, Washington, 1981. Compare "The Galway Races" in McCullough, 10.

"LIMERICK RACES." William H. Keith, schooners *William Martin, Cora Nash,* and *Edith May,* circa 1865-71.

1. I'm a simple Irish lad, I've resolved to see some fun, sirs,
   So to satisfy my mind, to Limerick town I come, sirs;
   Oh, murther! what a precious place, and what a charming city,
   Where the boys are all so free, and the girls are all so pretty!

   Chorus: Musha ring a ding a da / Ri too ral laddy, oh!
   Musha ring a ding a da / Ri too ral laddy, oh!

2. It was on the first of May when I began my rambles,
   When everything was there, both jaunting cars and gambols;
   I looked along the road, what was lined with smiling faces,
   All driving off, ding-dong to go and see the races.
      Musha ring a ding a da &c &c

3. So then I was resolved to go and see the races, sirs,
   And on a coach and four I neatly took my place, sirs,
   When a chap bawls out, "behind!" and the coachman dealt a blow, sirs;
   Faith, he hit me just as fair as if his eyes were in his poll, sirs.

4. So then I had to walk, and make no great delay, sirs,
   Until I reached the course, where everything was gay, sirs.
   It is there I espied a wooden horse, and in the upper story,
   The band struck up a tune, called "Garry Owen and Glory."

5. There were fiddlers playing jigs, there were lads and lasses dancing,
   And chaps upon their nags round the course sure they were prancing;
   Some were drinking whiskey punch, while others bawled out gaily,
   "Hurrah then for the shamrock green, and the splinter of shillalagh."

6. There were betters to and fro to see who would win the race, sirs,
   And one of the sporting chaps of course came up to me, sirs.
   Says he, "I'll bet you fifty pounds and I'll put it down this minute."
   "Ah then ten to one says I the foremost horse will win it."

7. When the players came to town and a funny set was they, sirs,
   I paid my two thirteens to go and see the play, sirs.
   They acted kings and cobblers, queens and everything so gaily,
   But I found myself at home when they struck up "Paddy Cardy"!

129. The Pearl of the Sea

This anonymous national song has the lyrical and self-consciously literary flavor of the Irish adagio ballads of the middle 19th century, was probably intended to be sung to a traditional air, and was almost certainly transcribed from a printed source. No other reference to it has been located.

"THE PEARL OF THE SEA." George M. Jones and Albert F. Handy, bark *Waverly* of New Bedford, 1859-63.

1. Dear is the white rolling surges commotion
   And welcome there hoarse sounding murmers to me
   As they lash the tall cliffs from over the ocean
   The green cliffs of Erin the pearl of the sea
   Blow on then ye breezes our strained canvas swelling
   Our silver streaked keel like an arrow impelling
   To the fair isle of beauty the home of sweet Ellen
   The mansion of honour the pearl of the sea

2. Her flower spangled valleys her sunset browed mountains
   Her clear silver streamlets that wind through the lea
   The chant of her groves and the health of her fountains
   All these might endear other countries to me
   But the heart that can prize modest merits endeavor
   The free hand of beauty expanded for ever
   And friendship's warm smile that no distance can sever
   Mark the fair isle of beauty the pearl of the sea

3. Thou bright star of even while I watch thy descending
   Thy dimond eyed cresset [crescent] nigh sinking to rest
   I mourn not thy loss since our course we are bending
   To the fair isle of beauty the pearl of the west
   Blow on then ye breezes our strained canvas swelling
   Our silver streaked keel like an arrow impelling
   To the fair isle of beauty the home of sweet Ellen
   The mansion of honors the pearl of the sea

130. Et Tu Bruce

This is a parody of the lullaby "Rock-a-Bye, Baby" ("Hushaby, Baby") lampooning Rhode Island politics and politicians of the era 1841-46. The piece fits right into what was perceived at the time as an unhealthy degeneration of political discourse into slogan-esque verse. As Vera Brodsky Lawrence puts it,

> Under the heading "Making Proselytes by Music," the Albany *Argus* (June 25, 1840) ineffectually grumbled: "A new light has dawned upon the political world. The power of reasoning and argument is to give place to the irresistible influence of poetry and song." The Washington *Globe*, gleefully quoted in the Whig *Madisonian,* (June 25, 1840), protested more passionately, giving a furious annotated catalog of the hated Whiggish electioneering apparatus: "Signs and badges... to *excite the passions* and STULTIFY THE JUDGEMENTS of the people; songs, *inspired by the* FURIES AND WRITTEN *with* FIREBRANDS, and *rabidly clamoured* through the streets; the waving of *itinerant pageants* and banners bearing STUPID MOTTOES... And lastly, to compete with these *ignoble saturnalia*, INTEMPERANCE *itself,* evoked as an auxiliary FIEND in a FIENDISH CAUSE, in the form of a BARREL!! *on which are written the words* HARD CIDER!!! (Lawrence, 285)

To illustrate, Lawrence quotes one such song that is obviously intended to be sung to the air of "Rock-a-Bye, Baby" ("Hush-a-By, Baby"):

> Harping on the same solitary string [of alcoholic excesses], the Albany *Argus* (July 17, 1840) published a sardonic "lullaby" preceded by a note in dubious taste, captioned "sentimental": "A whig paper says Tippecanoe cradles are becoming fashionable among whig ladies (married or single the editor sayeth not). We recommend the following nursery ditty as an accompaniment:
>
>> Hushaby baby,
>> Daddy's a whig;
>> Before he comes home,
>> Hard cider he'll swig;
>> Should he get tipsey,
>> Together we'll fall,
>> Down will come daddy,
>> Tip, cradle and all"

Not long after the second Harrison-Van Buren election, John G. Marble of Warren, R.I., inscribed a similar but much longer and more elaborate political song into his copybook. "Et Tu Bruce," with its Shakespearean title suggesting both tyranny and treachery,[9] primarily concerns congressional and gubernatorial elections in the Ocean State in the 1840s, featuring an array of topical allusions now all but unintelligible (as they would have been at the time to anyone not from Rhode Island). No other version of it has been found.

"ROCK-A-BYE BABY." The familiar melody of the ubiquitous American nursery rhyme, from Albert E. Wier, ed., *The Book of a Thousand Songs*, [1918] 1922, p. 399. (An alternative melody for "Hush a By Baby ... [as] sung by Christie's Minstrels" was not published until 1852, by Firth, Pond & Co. of New York.)

"ET TU BRUCE." John G. Marble, copybook, 1846-47, in the Stephen O. Hopkins's journal of whaling voyages in the ships *Rosalie* of Warren (1843) and *Perseverance* of Providence (1849). Transcription signed "December 12th 1846 / John G. Marble."

---

[9] The allusion is to Caesar's words in *Julius Caesar,* Act III, Scene 1; "Bruce" Americanizes *Brutus* to the generic (=*fellow*).

- 1 -

Hushaby Benjamin
Let the wind blow
Lem shall be governor
Whether or no
We will keep in somehow
If you will be sober
And behave like a man
In the month of October

- 2 -

Hushaby Benjamin
Keep yourself cool
Old James is a Blockhead
And William is a fool
Young Jemmy of Johnston
And Lemuel and you
Are a match for the Antis
and Jackson men too

- 3 -

Hushaby Benjamin
Asher is old
Keep up your spirits
Be valiant and bold
Stick to your party
But mind what you do
Or they that choose Senators
May not choose you

- 4 -

Hushaby Benjamin
Keep yourself still
You know what you can do
Very well if you will
But hearken to Solomon
Make him your guide
And your bark will stay on
With a fair wind and tide

-5 -

Hushaby Benjamin
Trust to your clan
You know you can muster
Full many a man
And among them the Mason
The Lawyer and the Clerck
Who can put a smooth face on
And lie like a Turk

- 6 -

Hushaby Benjamin
Dont make a fuss
Keep yourself quiet
Or things will grow worse
Learn to be prudent
And leave of[f] your fanning
Or down goes your Apple Cart
Spite of your cunning

- 7 -

Then Hushaby Benjamin / But if the bough breaks
On the tree top / Together we'll fall
You shall be put up / And down will come Lemuel
And Asher shall drop / Black Ben and all

Note: Professor Stanley Lemons of Rhode Island College, a specialist in Rhode Island history, generously decoded the allusions in the text and kindly provided the following: "The Benjamin mentioned in the opening line of each stanza is probably Benjamin B. Thurston of Hopkinton who was Lieutenant Governor, 1837-38, then ran (and lost) for lieutenant governor in 1843 on the Democratic ticket. He was elected to the U.S. House of Representatives for 1847-49.... Old James (stanza 2, line 3) is James Fenner, who was on the political scene almost forever in the first half of the 19th century. He was Governor 1807-11, then again 1824-31. He was defeated in 1831 by Lemuel H. Arnold (Democrat). Then in the crisis atmosphere of the Dorr War,[10] he was trotted out again and was Governor again 1843-45, on the Law and Order Party ticket. He lost the 1845 election to Charles Jackson, who ran on the Liberation ticket. In the next election in 1846, Fenner was too old and ill and Bryan Damon, the Lieutenant Governor since 1843, ran for the Whigs (formerly Law and Order Party) and won. William of line 4 is probably William Sprague, formerly the Governor and recently resigned as U.S. Senator. He was Senator from February 1842 to January 1844. He had resigned shortly after the murder of his brother Amasa in December 1843. Young Jemmy of Johnston (line 5) is certainly James F. Simmons of Johnston, Whig, U.S. Senator 1841-1847. Lemuel (line 6) is certainly Lemuel H. Arnold of South Kingstown. In the Liberation campaign of 1845 which resulted in the upset election of the Liberation ticket (Charles Jackson for Governor), both Lemuel Arnold and James F. Simmons espoused the cause of Liberation (Thomas Dorr). Arnold was elected to Congress that year, defeating Elisha Potter, the Whig candidate. I might note that Lemuel Arnold, Democrat, was elected Governor as a in 1831, but lost in the 'fiasco of 1832' when he was opposed by Old James Fenner, Republican, and William Sprague, Anti-Mason. No one was elected, and Rhode Island went without a Governor until 1833 when John Brown Francis was elected. Francis, in turn, lost to Sprague in 1838. Amazing! The Anti's mentioned in line 7 probably are the Anti-Masons, but that is only a guess. Anti-Masonism had considerably faded in Rhode Island by 1841. In fact William Sprague began as an Anti-Mason in the 1830s, but switched by 1841, and was elected by the Democrats to be U.S. Senator in 1842. But the poem's author might still see some Anti-Masonism around in the Whig ranks. The Jackson in the last line is Charles Jackson, a Whig who thought the vindictive treatment of Dorr was excessive, and who then ran on the Liberation ticket in 1845. He was a one term Governor who ran as a Democrat in 1846 and lost to Byron Dimon (Whig). I read the poem to be an anti-Democratic, anti-Benjamin Thurston poem. Or to put it another way, it is pro-Whig. It suggests that Thurston is a drunk...and that he has the support of Masons, Lawyers (horrors!) and Clerks, and so forth." (20 March 1984)

---

[10] Thomas Wilson Dorr (1805-1854) was an agitator for widening suffrage in Rhode Island, forcing a new constitution (1840) which eventually resulted in the election of two separate governments (1842); convicted of treason (1844); pardoned (1845).

131. There's Changes in the Mill

A native Vermonter and adoptive New Hampshireman, Third Mate George Edgar Mills grew up surrounded by the forests with which northern New England is so generously endowed, and spent the better part of his life between voyages amidst timber camps, lumber mills, and furniture factories. He likely had some youthful experience in the woodworking industry, maybe even served part of an official apprenticeship. In 1860, shortly after writing down the words of "There's Changes in the Mill" in his whaling journal, Mills retired from whaling, married the young woman to whom many of his shipboard poems were addressed, and settled in Nashua, New Hampshire, where he took a job as a mill hand. It seems fitting therefore, and perhaps a bit ironic, that of all whalemen it should be George Edgar Mills who transcribed the only known text of a hitherto undiscovered ballad about labor unrest and administrative foibles in the lumber business. Mills was a prolific poet and songwriter, and it is conceivable that he wrote the ballad himself; on the other hand, it is just the sort of thing that might have appealed to his Granite State neighbors, the singing Hutchinson Family. Unfortunately, the authorship is not ascribed and the tune remains a mystery.

"THERES CHANGES IN THE MILL." George Edgar Mills, third mate, ship *James Loper* of Nantucket, 1860.

1. Theres need of all the patience
    That to us all was given
 To keep us serenely in our place
    Nor from the mill be driven
 For all must know the petty ways
    Thats exercised at will
 By all the power of overseers
    Theres changes in the mill

2. Changes, ah yes, there surely is
    From one side to the other
 For surely where those beams now lay
    Are to us quite a bother
 So when you've nothing else to do
    And sitting on the window cill
 We'll have that file moved over there
    Theres changes in the mill

3. Now when tis done, we all can see
    Tis like an old Maids way
 So when we've nothing else to do
    We'll move the beams for play
 So changes there'll be from day to day
    Untill old time stands still
 It is the order of the day
    For changes in the mill

132. Go Down Moses
[Let My People Go]

This classic so-called "Negro Spiritual" is one of the noblest efforts of the African-American singing tradition. With a haunting melody—actually, two haunting melodies—and an abolitionist text preaching the analogy between the Egyptian servitude of the Israelites in the Old Testament and slaves in the American South, it is one of the best known of the freedom songs an spirituals that emerged from the plantations and were actually sung by slaves. The first published report of it was in September 1861, with the Civil War already some months progressed, when it was obtained from slave sources at Fortress Monroe, Virginia. The lyrics were printed in the New York *Tribune* in December of the same year, which "appears to have been the first publication of the text of a Negro spiritual," though some intermediate editing may have been involved (Epstein, 243f). The song became widely known and the lyrics canonized when it was featured in the repertoires of African-American choirs in the Reconstruction era. The very different versions of eh tune in the Marsh and Taylor anthologies of 1880 and 1882 (see below) are likely the earliest appearances of the music in print. Neither of these makes or implies any claim for the song as antebellum folklore; in fact, Taylor attributes the words to "F. Minter" and adds the hymnologists' designation for the metre, "L.M.," implying liturgical objectives. "Go Down Moses" remains one of the finest songs to percolate out of the American land, with authentic African-American roots and a hoary provenance of African-American performance, imparting hope and inspiration to millions of Black Americans in the era of their first emergence from captivity.

TUNE A - "GO DOWN MOSES." From J.B.T. Marsh, *The Story of the Jubilee Singers; With Their Songs*, Boston [1880] 1882, #19, p. 142. The standard tune.

TUNE B - "GO DOWN MOSES." From Marshall W. Taylor, *Revival Hymns and Plantation Melodies*, Cincinnati, [1882] 1888, #86, pp. 148f. Odd variant.

"LET MY PEOPLE GO." Elizabeth Marble, Fall River, Massachusetts: miscellaneous family papers on shipboard and ashore, circa 1845-94. In the characteristic African call-and-response manner (which served as the model for Negro Spirituals and for sailors' chanteys), the lead lines can be sung as a solo and the burden and refrain sung in chorus.[11] Unfortunately, the actual date of Elizabeth Marble's transcription is not known, nor whether it was made at sea or ashore, nor which of the tunes she may have known.

1. When Isreal [sic] was in Egypts land
    Let my people go
   Oppressed so hard they could not stand
    Let my people go

Chorus: Go down, Moses, way down in Egypts land
    Tel Ole Pharaoh, let my people go

2. Thus saith the Lord, bold Moses said
    Let my people go
   If not [I]'ll smite your firstborn dead
    Let my people go

3. No more shall they in bondage toil
    Let my people go
   Let them come out with Egypts spoil
    Let my people go

4. When Israel out of Egypt came
    Let my people go
   And left the proud oppressive land
    Let my people go

---

[11] In the 20th century and perhaps since the 19th, "Go Down Moses" has served African-American menhaden fishermen in North Carolina as a chantey for hauling nets aboard—typically employing the standard solo-and-response form of Tune B, with part-singing on the choruses and intermittently on the burden.

133. The Parson's Narrative

The Very astonishing and surprising, also Astounding; but nevertheless, true; Account of the adventures of the Crew of the Schooner Holy Terror in the land of the Wugger boo foo. Written by the Chaplain

A unique comic ballad narrating in the third person an imaginary voyage to an enchanted — or pixilated — South Sea island. The title notwithstanding, the song has nothing to do with any clergymen other than its frivolous attribution of authorship to "the Chaplain" (in one text) and "Reverend Ah-Chung" (in the other text). What meaning or interpretation may be ascribed to the conceit that the author was a man of the cloth — but what cloth? — can only be conjectural. The sensibilities of this voyage-of-imagination and the made-up, mumbo-jumbo names of people and places, are akin to two precursors, a music-hall song entitled "Tongo Islands" by the British theatrical entrepreneur William Thomas Moncrief (1794-1857)[12] and especially the classic by New York financier Charles Edward Carryl (1842-1920), "The Walloping Window Blind" ("A Capital Ship"),[13] which is sung to the air of "Ten Thousand Miles Away." However, the meter of "The Parson's Narrative" is compatible with neither of these, indicating that the lyricist must have had a different tune in mind.

The interest of this piece is threefold. First, it is highly accomplished and original, at least as clever and substantive as the two aforementioned professional pieces and possessing the same trumped-up exotic tropical appeal. In standpoint of syntax and meter, it is every bit the equal of "Walloping Window Blind" and much superior to "Tongo Islands." Second, it is localized to Acushnet (the birthplace and residence of the scribe, adjacent to New Bedford), and has enough vernacular nautical jargon, accurately employed, that it could only have been written by a sea-wise poet — perhaps Rupert Swift himself, in whose whaling journal of the late 1860s the song was found; but possibly his brother, painter and avocational poet Clement Nye Swift (authorship of the fantasy poem "The Sailor Boy's Dream" [#230] and the superb epic poem "Wood and Black-Skin" [#231] is also equivocal between the two brothers). The sons of a prosperous whaling captain, they were the products of an uncommonly good prep-school education. Rupert read Shakespeare avidly, made journal entries in classical Latin and Greek, and had a singularly whimsical turn of mind and remarkable control of both the language and subject matter. Likewise Clement, whose unpublished poems are complex and literate.

Third and most extraordinary are the two methods of transcription in Rupert's journal: once in the conventional manner, in a cursive hand not necessarily Swift's; and a second time as a broadside that is letterpress-printed right on the ledger page itself. The entire bound volume was evidently placed in the press, as it appears not to have been disbound for the procedure; and as it

---

[12] In *The New Song Book* (Hartford, 1847) "Tongo Islands" is identified "As sung by Mrs. Phillmore at the Warren Theatre." "I sailed rom Port one summer's day, / And to the South seas made my way; / All in the Tongo islands. /The king he made a chief of me, /They called him Ro-ra-ki-ro-kee. /We got as thick as thick could be, /And every night drank strong byshee. /Says he, "will you be my son-in-law, /Marry the princess Was-ki-taw?" /Says I, "Your majesty hold your jaw, /I will accept the princess' paw. / [Chorus:] Swango, Tongo, hoki poki, / hingri, chingri, soki moki, Swango, Tongo, hooki pooki, / All in the Tongo islands." The lyrics can also be found in *Beadle's Songs of the Olden Time* (New York, 1863).

[13] Poor Carryl is almost nowhere credited for what is certainly his best-known work, which is virtually unknown in connection with his name. Written and first published in the Australian Gold Rush era of the 1850s (with oblique allusions to Australia and kangaroos, and using the air of an Australian Gold Rush song), "The Walloping Window Blind" has been widely anthologized and, a masterpiece of its bizarre little genre, has become a classic of "nonsense songs"; however, even such luminaries as Norman Cazden and Oscar Brand have taken all the credit, sans mention of Carryl. An entire illustrated volume for children entitled *The Walloping Window Blind* (Princeton, 1968), subtitled "An Old Nautical Tale," credits both the illustrator and *The Golden Book of Favorite Songs,* indicating that the lyrics were "used by permission of the publishers," but nowhere mentions Carryl. This is brutally unfair, as the piece really is a delight: "A capital ship for an ocean trip was the Walloping Window-Blind; / No wind that blew dismayed her crew or troubled the captain's mind; / The man at the wheel was made to feel contempt for the wildest blow, / Though it often appeared, when the storm had cleared, / That he's been in his bunk below." For citations, see: SIC, PSI, PSIS, and Helen Grant Cushing, *Children's Song Index* (New York: H.H. Wilson & Co., 1936).

would hardly have been worthwhile to hand-compose an entire broadside's-worth of type for the one single impression, it seems likely that "The Parson's Narrative" was also issued as a separate sheet or was also printed in the journals of others. However, as yet no other specimen has come to light and the melody is unknown.

A.

"THE PARSON'S NARRATIVE." R.G.N. Swift, ship *Contest* of New Bedford, 1866-70. Manuscript transcription of five stanzas of 10 lines + one stanza of 8 lines + refrain of 5 lines, surmounted by a subtitle or preamble: "The Very astonishing and surprising, also Astounding; but nevertheless, true; Account of the adventures of the Crew of the Schooner Holy Terror in the land of the Wugger boo foo. Written by the Chaplain." Varies from B only in the one textual instance noted in B, and differences in the preamble and attribution (as noted in B).

B.

"THE PARSON'S NARRATIVE." From the same source as A, B is an actual letterpress impression of an almost identical text, printed directly on the page of R.G.N. Swift's journal volume, lacking the preamble, but with an additional whimsical attribution to "Ah-Chung." The stanzas are not numbered in the MS, and stanza 6 is short, thus may have been intended as a final chorus.

1. They sailed away in a schooner, you know:
    In a schooner they left the bay;[14]
And her name it was the HOLY TER-ROR,
And a prettier craft you never saw
    Upon a summer day.
And when they left Acushnet town
The people all said— "You are bound to drown!"
But they answered them— "Our craft is small,
But we don't care for that—we do'nt care at all;
    We are bound for to go far away.

Chorus: To a land far away in the tropical sea.
    To the land of the WUGGER-BOO-FOO.
Their faces are brown, and their finger nails, black;
And they're tattooed with green in the small of the back:
    And their noses and eyes are blue.[15]

2. They sailed away in a schooner, you see!
    And the schooner did sail very fast;
For the white foam was dancing along the lee rail,
As they hauled aft the sheet of each bellying sail;
    And straining were spar, stay, and mast.
And the old codgers cried as they saw them go by—
"You'll wish yourself back! If you do'nt, say I lie!
For the weather looks bad, and the voyage is'nt short:
And in a typhoon you are bound to get caught
    And go to the bottom at last"[16]

---

[14] Text A has "In a schooner they sailed away." Apart from the prologue (present in A, absent in B) and minor points of punctuation, this is the only textual difference between A and B. B is rather an improvement over A as it eliminates redundancy in the rhyme-scheme, and, as such, suggests itself as the later version.

[15] Compare these humorous, color-conscious descriptions of the fanciful South Sea islanders with Poe's gothic, color-conscious descriptions of his fanciful southlanders in *The Narrative of Arthur Gordon Pym of Nantucket* (1838), a pseudo-whaling narrative partly set in New Bedford which the well-read R.G.N. Swift must surely have known.

[16] In its lighthearted characterization of wharfside doomsayers as "codgers," the ballad plays upon the gloomily "portentous" prophesies-of-doom that are delivered at the outset of voyages by wizened sages, prefigured seriously in Coleridge's *Rime of the Ancient Mariner.* There are also analogies in Homer's *Odyssey* and Melville's *Moby-Dick.*

3. The wind it did blow form the West-Nor-West,
    With a long and flowing sea
And they kept her a-going and crowded on sail
Till the Cat head went under as well as the Rail
    In the white water under he lea.
And they set their sea watch for the rest of the night:
And they said top each other— "I guess it's all right;
For, altho' the voyage is going to be long,
That do'nt make it risky, nor rash, nor wrong:
    And a tough hardy set are we."

4. And for many days they sailed away:
    And whenever the sun did set,
They whistled and shouted a merry tune
To the lively sound of a tin spittoon
    And an ebony clarionet.
"O Hurrah for the land of the WUGGER-BOO FOO!
And the fair Senoritas all waiting for you!
We'll walk with them neath the cocoanut shade
In the land where the olives and figs are all made;
Mongst the orange and lemon and bread fruit trees;
And we'll turn on our toes till we sprain both our knees,
    And we play on the sounding Swinett."

5. And they sailed to the tropical sea, so they did!
    To a land where the water is green.
And they brought home some mud with a savoury smell
And a ton of fine gold in a peanut shell;
    A beautiful sight to be seen!
And they brought home some snakes and some white jackdaws,
And a yellow baboon with red and pink paws;
And a giant sea serpent two feet thick;
And five thousand bottles of 'kill me quick,'
    Which they stole from the Cannibal Queen.

6. And everyone said— "How tall they have grown
Since they went to the isles of the Torrible Zone[17]
    And the country where noses are blue!"
And when they went ashore they had a big feast,
Of Teejees boiled out in soap suds and yeast,[18]
And the old codgers said— "If we live till next May,
We too will get ready and sail right away
    For the land of the WUGGER-BOO FOO."

---

[17] Most texts of "The Walloping Window Blind" (if complete and un-tampered with) mention the "Torrible Zone" or "Torribly Zone," probably homonymously to suggest *horrible* or *horribly*.

[18] "The cook was Dutch and behaved as such, / For the meals that he served the crew / Were a hundred tons of hot-cross buns / Served up with sugar and glue" —"The Walloping Window Blind."

CHAPTER FOURTEEN
There She Blows
Classic Whaling Songs

In taking a general view of the whaling life, we find it replete with incidents of daring adventure, hardship, and deprivation. The vessels first employed in deep-sea whaling were so contracted that no degree of comfort could be afforded to their crews, who, by sheer, ambitious hardihood, maintained existence on board during their short voyages. As the pursuit became extended, requiring larger vessels, the barks and brigs of the fishers were much improved, while the absence from their native shores was more prolonged. At this period a system for fitting out vessels for long voyages was inaugurated as well as the establishment of effective discipline on board, for which well-regulated whale-ships have always been noted; and the whale fishery steadily advanced under judicious management of those able and systematic business gentlemen, whose names have long since become familiar in the remotest parts of the world, as the ships named in their honor. The broad expanse of the Atlantic soon became too limited a field for the vast enterprise, and in consequence of this, the fourth epoch in the fishery was inaugurated, when still larger vessels were sent out to search the nearly unknown waters of the Pacific and Indian Oceans. These vessels doubled Cape Horn and the Cape of Good Hope, in their wanderings, which were so protracted, under the most favorable auspices, that the "green hands," many of whom had never sniffed the ocean's breezes until afloat on board of a whaler, returned to their New England or Western homes, transferred into seamen and whalemen.

— Captain Charles Melville Scammon, *Marine Mammals of the North-western Coast of North America* (1874).

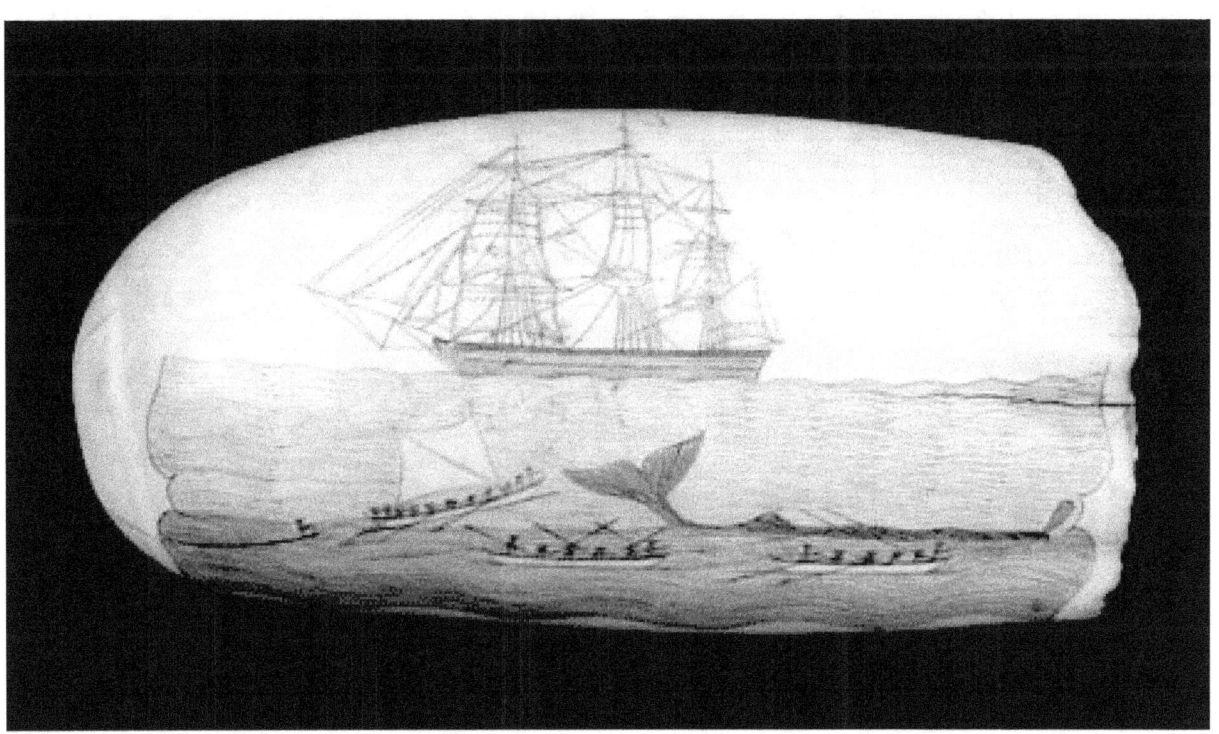

Sperm Whaling: Towing Back. Anonymous whalemen's engraved scrimshaw on a sperm whale tooth, circa 1840-50.
Kendall Collection, New Bedford Whaling Museum

134.
The Greenland Whale Fishery
(Laws #K-21)

This ballad about Arctic whaling off Greenland is the probably oldest extant whaling song in English. Britain first undertook the prosecution of a regular seasonal Arctic whale hunt in the 1610s but was soon eclipsed by Holland, and by the end of the century the British fishery was in decline. From the dates specified in the degraded texts of the ballad published as broadsides and collected from tradition, one might suppose that it emanates from one of the periods of revival of British Arctic whaling in the late 18th and early 19th centuries: for example, the two American whalemen's texts reported by Huntington give the dates 1784 and 1824, two of the three in the Kendall Collection give 1824 and 1841, Greig's has 1801, and according to Vaughan Williams, "Pitts, Such, and Catnach each issued broadside versions, giving 1824 as the date of the incident described. Sharp published a version in which the date is 1861—thirty years too late for Greenland whaling… while Baring-Gould and Whall have unlocated versions giving the date as 1794." However, Vaughan Williams also cites a blackletter broadside of "Greenland Whale Fishery" published prior to 1725, which gives a more accurate notion of the ballad's true antiquity and longevity. Most versions collected from tradition lack the two-stanza preamble ordinarily present in broadsides (present in text A, but absent in C), thereby removing the debt-ridden plight of the narrator and his companions as the rationale for their shipping out; in those instances it is usually the opening stanza that provides the date and destination (such as in B, the first stanza of which corresponds to the third stanza of A); some texts (like C) abandon the date entirely. Likewise, the captain's greater grief over the loss of his men than over the loss of the whale (A) is occasionally reversed (C), however the two whalemen's manuscripts recovered by Huntington eliminate the controversy altogether by omitting any comparison.

TUNE: "The Greenland Whale Fishery," composite; compare Colcord, p. 151. Whall's (71) is an eccentric variant; Karpeles (#42) and Vaughan Williams (50) are significant departures from the conventional mainstream. Of Huntington's variants, the one on p. 9 is conservative; the one on p. 11 (source not identified) is apparently related to the tunes given by Vaughan Williams and recorded by Lloyd. See "Rolling Down to Old Mohee"[#143].

A.

"GREENLAND WHALE FISHERY." Broadside, "Printed by by T. BIRT, wholesale and retail, Great St. Andrew-Street, Seven Dials, London," circa 1831-48: one specimen extracted from an unidentified journal in the Kendall Collection, another found in Joseph Robinson Tallman's journal of ships *Coral* and *Swift* of New Bedford, 1846-52. Not listed in Laws (II: 150), who catalogues broadsides of 12 stanzas by Ashton, Such, Catnach, and Pitts. To fit any of the tunes (and in conformity with the manner in which the song appears customarily to have been sung), the final line of each stanza is repeated (without repeating the coda "brave boys"). Errors in nautical terminology and misstatements of catch phrases are corrected [in *italics* in brackets] in accordance with the manner in which the terms and phrases occur in some other texts. Compare C, a much more nautically-correct text.

    1.   We can no longer stay on shore,
           Since we are so deep in debt,
           So a voyage to Greenland we will go
           Some money for to get—brave boys.

2. Now when we lay at Liverpool,
   Our good-like ship [*goodly ship*] to man,
   'Twas there our names were all wrote down,
   And we're bound for Greenland—brave boys.

3. In eighteen hundred and twenty-four,
   On March the twenty-third,
   We hoisted our colours up to our mast-head,
   And for Greenland bore away—brave boys.

4. But when we came to Greenland,
   Our good-like [*goodly ship*] ship to moor,
   O then we wish's ourselves back again,
   With our friends upon the shore—brave boys.

5. The boatswain went to the mast-head
   With his spy glass in his hand,
   Here's a whale [*a whale-fish*], a whale, a whale, he cried,
   And she blows on every spring [*at every span*]—brave boys.

6. The Captain on the quarter deck,
   (A very good man was he,)
   Overhaul, overhaul, let your boat tackle full [*let your davit-tackle fall*]
   And launch your boats to sea—brave boys.

7. The boats being launch'd and the hands got in,
   The whale fishes appeared in view,
   Resolved was the whole boat's crew,
   To steer where the whale fish blew—brave boys.

8. The whale being struck and the line paid on [*paid out*],
   She gave a flash [*flurry*] with her tale,
   She capsiz'd the boat and [*we*] lost five men,
   Nor did we catch the whale—brave boys.

9. Bad news unto our captain brought,
   That we had lost the 'prentice boys;
   He hearing of the dreadful news,
   His colours down did haul—brave boys.

10. The loosing of this whale, brave boys,
    Did grieve his heart full sore,
    But loosing of his five brave men,
    Did grieve him ten times more—brave boys.

11. Come weigh your anchor my brave boys,
    For the winter star I see,
    It is time we should leave this cold country,
    And for England bear away—brave boys.

12. For Greenland is a barren place,
    Neither light nor day to be seen,
    Nought but ice & snow where the whale-fish blow,
    And the day-light seldom seen—brave boys.

B.

[UNTITLED.] Copybook: Stephen O. Hopkins, ship *Rosalie* of Warren (1843) and bark *Perseverance* of Providence (1849); John G. and Lydia Marble (1846-47); Lemuel C. Richmond, Jr., bark *Perseverance* (1849) and California Gold Rush (1851). Text fragment of 9 lines, beginning, "Twas in eighteen hundred forty one / The fourteenth day of May"; the second stanza is given below; the third has one line only: "Our Captains name was William Moore."

2. And when we came to the cold country
    And our ship lay moored there
    I wished myself in a pretty girls arms
    And a roving round the shore

C.

"GREENLAND WHALES." Robert Nathaniel Hughson, bark *Java* of New Bedford, 1857-60.

1. I can no longer stop on shore
    Since I am so deep in debt.
    So a voyage to Greenland I must go
    Some money for to get Brave Boys

2. Now Greenland it is a very cold coast
    There is nothing but frost and snow
    But it is the place likewise my boys
    Where the whale fish blows Brave Boys

3. Our Chief Mate was at the main mast Head
    With a spy glass in his hand
    Heres a whale, a whale, a whale fish he cries
    And she blows at every span Brave Boys

4. Our Captain was on the quarter deck
    And a very good man was he
    Overhaul overhaul your davit tackle falls
    And launch your boats to sea Brave Boys

5. Now the boats being lowered and all were man[n]ed
    Resolved was each boats crew
    For to steer to sail to paddle and to row
    To the place where the whale fish blows Brave boys

6. Now the whale being struck and the line paid out
    O he gave a splash with his tail
    He capsized the boat and we lost five men
    Nor did we get that whale Brave Boys

7. Now when the news to our Captain came
    He called up all his crew
    For the losing of these five brave men
    He down his colors drew Brave Boys

8. Now the loosing of these five brave men
    Did grieve his heart full sore
    But the loosing of that fine Rite whale
    It grieved him a d - - d sight more Brave Boys

135. Arctic Whaling Song

New Bedford historian Daniel Ricketson was mistaken when he called this "probably the oldest extant" whaling song. "The Greenland Whale Fishery" [#134] is likely somewhat older, and there are a few whaling ballads with lyrics in Dutch that are substantially older. However, "the oldest extant" whaling song in the English language is almost certainly a broadside ballad of 1632 in the Samuel Pepys Collection (Cambridge University) with the unwieldy title, "A wonder beyond mans expectation,/ In the preseruation of eight men in Greenland from one season to another,/ the like neuer knowne or heard of before, which eight men are come all safely from/ thence in this last Fleet, 1631. whose names are these, William Fakely Gunner, Edward Peliham Gun-/ ners Mate, Iohn Wise Robert Goodfellow Seamen, Thomas Ayers Whalecutter, Henry Rett Cooper,/ Iohn Dawes, Richard Kellet Land men" (Rollins II:3015) (registered 2 January, 1632, IV, 268, Fran. Coles & partners, the broadside printed for H. Gosson).

In any case, the Arctic whaling song noted by Daniel Ricketson, of which Captain Charles H. Robbins transcribed the version replicated here, is almost certainly the oldest surviving whaling song of American origin. The lyrics were written by Dr. John Osborne (1713-1753), a physician and poet born at Sandwich, Massachusetts, on Cape Cod. He graduated Harvard in the class of 1735, studied for the Congregational ministry but was not ordained and took up medicine instead, opening a practice at Middletown, Connecticut, in 1739. The text is sufficiently authoritative to suggest that he may have gone on an Arctic whaling voyage himself; if not, he was quite well informed, and whalemen on both sides of the Atlantic seem to have adopted the song as their own. In his volume of naval songs, William McCarty remarks that "Osborn[e]'s famous Whaling Song was for more than half a century on the tongue of every Cape Cod sailor, and it is still [in 1842] frequently heard in the Pacific." The tune, preserved with a derivative, adaptive text in Scottish tradition, is likely also of eighteenth-century vintage, though Ord attributes it to a James B. Allen of Glasgow. A typescript discovered among the papers of Captain Charles H. Robbins, who commanded whaling voyages to Hudson Bay in the middle decades of the 19th century, may have been copied from the text printed in Ricketson's *History of New Bedford* (1858) or, perhaps from McCarty's *Songs, Odes, and Other Poems on National Subjects* (1842), where it is likewise entitled "A Whaling Song." There is also a 19th-century variant referring to an American whaling voyage via the Azores to the South Seas.

TUNE A - "The Whalers' Song," from John Ord, *The Bothy Songs & Ballads,* 1930, p. 317: "Music by Mr. Jas. B. Allan, A.L.C.M., Glasgow." Compare Lloyd 1967, n.p.

TUNE B - Closely related to tune A, this is the traditional form in 20th-century revival, likely influenced by A.L. Lloyd, *Leviathan!* (Topic #12T154), 1967.

"A WHALING SONG." Papers of Captain Charles H. Robbins, 1837-97. Typescript, unascribed. Compare Ord, 317. There is also a variant to the same tune referring to a voyage via the Azores to the South Seas.

1. When spring returns with western gales
   And gentle breezes sweep
   The ruffling seas, we spread our sails
   To plough the wat'ry deep.

2. For killing northern whales prepared,
   Our nimble boats on board,
   With craft and rum, (our chief regard)
   And good provision stored.

3. We view the monsters of the deep,
   Great whales in numerous swarms;
   And creatures there, that play and leap
   Of strange, unusual forms.

4. Cape Cod, our dearest, native land,
   We leave astern, and lose
   Its sinking cliffs and lessening sands,
   While Zephyr gently blows.

5. Bold, hardy men, with blooming age,
   Our sandy shores produce;
   With monstrous fish they dare engage,
   And dangerous callings choose.

6. Now towards the early dawning east
   We speed our course away,
   With eager minds and joyful hearts,
   To meet the rising day.

7. Then as we turn our wondering eyes,
   We view one constant show;
   Above, around, the circling skies,
   The rolling seas below.

8. When eastward, clear of Newfoundland,
   We stem the frozen pole,
   We see the icy islands stand
   The northern billows roll.

9. As to the north we make our way,
   Surprising scenes we find;
   We lengthen out the tedious day,
   And leave the night behind.

10. Now see the northern regions, where
    Eternal winter reigns;
    One day and night fills up the year,
    And endless cold maintains.

11. When in our station we are placed,
    And whales around us play,
    We launch our boats into the main,
    And swiftly chase our prey.

12. In haste we ply our nimble oars,
    For an assault designed;
    The sea beneath us foams and roars,
    And leaves a wake behind.

13. A mighty whale we rush upon,
    And in our irons throw;
    She sinks her monstrous body down
    Among the waves below.

14. And when she rises out again,
    We soon renew the fight;
    Thrust our sharp lances in amain,
    And all her rage excite.

15. Enraged she makes a mighty bound;
    Thick foams the whitened sea;
    The waves in circles rise around,
    And widening roll away.

16. She thrashes with her tail around,
    And blows her redd'ning breath;
    She breaks the air, a deaf'ning sound,
    While ocean groans beneath.

17. From numerous wounds with crimson flood,
    She stains the frothy seas,
    And gasps and blows her latest blood,
    While quivering life decays.

18. With joyful hearts we see her die,
    And on the surface lay;
    While all with eager haste apply,
    To save our deathful prey.

136. The Coast of Peru
(Laws #D-26)

As early as 1800, American whalers were plowing the sparkling waters along the coast of Peru, and their keels cut the equatorial line, north and south, in the Pacific. A favorite cruising-ground was from the Spanish Main, westward, around the Galapagos Islands. There a rich harvest rewarded them, where they labored in a genial climate, with an almost uninterrupted succession of fine breezes and pleasant weather... These periodical breezes, compared with the heavy gales of the Atlantic and the tedious winter about Cape Horn, served only to enliven [the whalemen] into renewed activity under the heated rays of the tropical sun, when in pursuit of the vast herds of Cachalots which were met with, bounding over or through the crested waves.

— Captain Charles Melville Scammon, *Marine Mammals of the North-western Coast of North America* (1874).

Most whaling songs, whatever their additional comic or heroic pretensions, are laments about ill-treatment, the usurious conditions under which the fishery was prosecuted, and the hardships to which whalemen were subjected. This American ballad of early nineteenth-century vintage is the outstanding exception and could have served as an advertisement for the owners. Thoroughly sailor-made and thus distinguished by expert seamanship and authentic whaling episodes, it sings the virtues of the hunt and the prospect of riches to be gleaned. It was widely distributed among American sailors but has not been encountered in tradition in the British Isles or Canada. Each of the whalemen's texts is classic, with B localized to the ship *Europa* of Edgartown.

TUNE A - From Joanna Colcord, *Songs of American Sailormen,* [1924] 1938, p. 194; see also Harlow, 222; and Huntington 1964, 2. The only air definitely and distinctively associated with the text in tradition at sea.

TUNE B - From the singing of Stuart Gillespie, *Sea Chanteys and Forecastle Songs at Mystic Seaport* (Folkways #FTS 37300, New York, 1978); compare A.L. Lloyd, *Leviathan!* Possibly not indigenous to "The Coast of Peru."

TUNE C - From the singing of Bob Webb & Jill King, Vancouver, B.C., 1980; Mystic, Conn., 1980; Sharon, Mass., 1981. Generic come-all-ye air, possibly not indigenous to "The Coast of Peru."

A.

"WHALING SONG." James Donahue, ship *Atlantic* of Nantucket, 1850-53. A corrupt text, lacking a line in stanza 7 and with several metrical anomalies. Reconstituted from undifferentiated lines and equivocal stanzas in the MS.

1. Come all you fellows that has doubled Cape horn[1]
   Come all you young fellows that is bound out for sperm
   for our Captain has told us and I hope it will prove true
   that there is plenty of sperm whales on the coast of Peru

2. We have weatherd cape horn and [are] now on peru
   we are all of one mind our endeavors to do
   our rigging is well fitted our mast-heads well manned[2]
   our boats are all ready when the signal is all plan[n]ed[3]

3. Early one morning just as the sun rose
   A man from the mast-head cries out their she blows
   Where away cries the Captain as he springs aloft[4]
   Two points of[f] the lee-bows and scarce three miles off

4. Get your lines in your boats See you lo[o]se lines all clear
   and up your helm and after them steer
   Sway up your boats boy[s] stand by your boats crew
   lower away my lively lads

5. Spring hard to your oars make your boats Fly
   what ever you do keep Clear of her Eye[5]
   Our chief he has fastened[6] and the whale She went down[7]
   our captain pulled up and Stood by to bend on[8]

---

[1] *Doubling Cape Horn* simply means going around the Cape, in this case west to east, from the Atlantic to the Pacific, a quintessentially stormy and hazardous passage that made it the virtual archetype of hard duty among square-rig sailors.

[2] Once on the whaling grounds, lookouts are posted in the mastheads high aloft to keep a sharp eye for whales.

[3] The whaleboats (normally numbering between three and five) are ready and fully equipped with oars, paddles, rudder, tiller, removable mast and sail, harpoons, lances, line-tubs containing carefully coiled rope, bomb-guns, bomb-lances, knives, a hatchet, casks of water, and a few provisions) to be lowered when whales are sighted—which occurs in stanza 4; and signals are arranged so that the boat crews can communicate with one another and with the mother-ship during the chase.

[4] The captain verifies the sighting, typically using a telescope.

[5] The whalemen's idea here is to approach at an oblique angle from the stern-quarter of the whale, to avoid the whale's seeing the boat and thus attempting to swamp or squash it with powerful tail-flukes. The mystique of the whale's eye has ever been a fascination to whalers and naturalists (see *Moby-Dick,* chapters 55 and 74).

[6] That is, *fastened-on* to the whale, i.e., harpooned it and thus made a line (a rope) *fast* (attached) to the whale.

[7] The whale *went down*: the whale dove into the sea (*sounded*) in an endeavor to escape the hunters.

[8] The captain and each of the mates commands his own boat; and each boat has a complement of six men, consisting of a *boat-header* (the officer in command), a *boatsteerer* (the harpooner), and four oarsmen. The harpooner rows the bow oar and initially stands in the prow of the boat to harpoon the whale, the officer is in the stern to steer. The harpoon, with barbs or toggles, is used to fasten on to the whale; and once the whale is fast to the mate's boat, the captain comes up in his boat, attaches his line to the whale-lines, and orders the other boats to do the same, thereby adding to the drag that the whale must pull through the water. This is to tire out the whale sooner. At this point in the hunt, with the whale secured to the boat and tiring from the chase, the harpooner and officer exchange places: it is the officer, now in the prow, who *lances* the whale, that is, strikes the killing blow.

6. The whale arose to the Windward and like a log she lay
   I can say no other but she showed us fair play
   In less than five minutes we caused her blood to spout
   and in less than ten minutes we caused her to turn fin out[9]

7. We towed her along side with many a shout
   that day cut her in next day tryed her out
   and stowed her down below[10]
   ... [*Line absent*]

8. Now when our ship is full boys to new bedford we shall steer
   where their is plenty of good liquor and plenty of good cheer
   we will spend our money freely with the lasses on shore
   and when its all gone we will go a spouting for more

   James Donahue

B.

"WHALING SONG." George W. Piper, ship *Europa* of Edgartown, 1868-70. A complete and representative (if not especially early) text, slightly localized to Edgartown, Martha's Vineyard. For annotations of some technical terms, see text A.

1. Come all you bold seamen that's bound round Cape Horn
   Come all you bold seamen who are bound after Sperm
   For our Captain has told us and I hope it will prove true
   There are plenty of Sperm Whales on the Co[a]st of Peru

2. Now we are around the Horn boys on the Coast of Peru
   Each man knows his station, has chose his boat's crew[11]
   Our rigging is rattled our mastheads are all manned
   Our boats are all ready and the signals are at hand

3. The first whales we saw boys being late in the day
   Our old man came on deck and these words he did say
   Go down to your bunks boys there quietly be
   For to morrow we will see them right under our lee

4. It was early the next morning just as the sun arose
   When the man from our masthead sings out there she blows
   Where away cries our Captain and springing aloft
   Three points on our lee bows and scar[c]e two miles off

---

[9] Wielded by the boat's officer, the sharp-pointed and long-handled *lance* is thrust into the whale's lungs and, if possible, churned, until the whale spouts blood and turns *fin-out* (or *fin-up*), dead.

[10] The carcass is towed alongside the mother-ship for processing. *Cutting in* is flensing or butchering the blubber; *trying-out* is rendering or boiling-down the blubber into oil, which on American whalers took place in a *tryworks* (oven apparatus) on deck. The oil is then cooled and placed in wooden barrels, which are lowered into the hold belowdecks (*stowed down*) for storage until it can be returned to market in Massachusetts or abroad.

[11] The master and mates customarily choose their respective boat's crews at the commencement of the voyage, much as school children choose-up sports teams on the playground. The common seamen seldom have any voice in the process.

5. We hauled back our main yard[12] the whales they drew near
   Then standby your boats boys see your box lines all clear[13]
   Swing your boat tackles stand by your boats crews
   Now lower away roundly lower away brave boys do

6. And now to your oars boys and make your boats fly
   Whatever you do boys keep clear of his eye
   Our chief mate is fast boys the whale has gone down
   Our Captain he pulls up for all to bend on

7. We gave him six lances, six lances or more[14]
   And the blood from his spout hole in torrents did pour
   We caused him to vomit thick blood for to spout
   And in less than two minutes we rolled him fin out

8. We towed him along side with many a shout
   We commenced cutting in likewise trying out
   And now he is tried out boys and safely stowed down
   He is more in our pockets than one thousand pounds[15]

9. And now come my brave boys we have had a long chase
   We will all go on board and we will splice the main brace[16]
   Here is success to the Europa wherever she may be
   She is as good an old ship as sails over the sea

10. Here is success to our chief mate and to his boat's crew
    And to all whalemen who are now on Peru
    And if you want money I advise you to go
    On the Coast of Peru where the Sperm Whales do blow

11. We have got our ship full boys and now she is bound home
    And the glass of good brandy will merrily go around
    [Here] is success to our sweethearts who live upon shore
    We will spend our money with them and go spouting for more

---

[12] This refers to the means of "putting on the brakes"—that is, to back-wind the sail and arrest the forward progress of the ship and bring it to as much of a standstill as possible at sea.

[13] If the line should become fouled the whale could be lost, the boat could be lost, or men could be lost. Being fouled in a line and dragged overboard, or being crushed in a boat that is upset or crushed by a whale, or being drowned after a whale has upset a boat, were the most prevalent hazards and greatest causes of death-by-injury among whaling crews. Even very experienced men could lose their lives this way, as happened to the great scrimshaw artist Edward Burdett, first mate of the Nantucket whaleship *Montano*, in 1833.

[14] That is, struck him six times with lances.

[15] British unit currency (pounds sterling) is explicable here by reason of rhyme scheme, in addition to it being the international standard of exchange on the Peru coast (as elsewhere). It may also be a remnant of the Nantucket and Boston custom (in colonial days when John Hancock and Josiah Quincy were exporters of whale oil to England) of figuring the value of a catch by its worth as an export commodity on the London exchange. Well into the Federal era, whale oil was one of few cash commodities produced in America; as such, by virtue of fluidity, it had an effective commercial influence far exceeding its empirical dollar value.

[16] *Splice the main brace* is nautical lingo for the ingestion of alcoholic beverages. Unlike the British naval and merchant services, which featured a daily grog ration—typically watered rum—on American whaleships spirituous liquors were offered up (if at all) only as a reward or on special occasions. This was usually rum or brandy; however, *genevra* or Holland gin ("genever" or "geneca" gin) also seems to have been common [see songs #230 and #159].

137. Diego's Bold Shores

Like "The Coast of Peru" [#136], this ballad from the classic era of Yankee whaling is cast in the heroic mode. The setting is the Diego Ramirez Islands, barren rocks off Cape Horn, beyond what James Fenimore Cooper calls in *The Sea Lions* the "Ultima Thule" of the Americas—and, by implication, the very frontier of human experience and endeavor. Here, on the threshold of Antarctica, is no mere hunt, no mere story of oil-gathering from large animals. Perhaps more than any other authentic whaling song, it ennobles the whalers' occupation from the excitement of the chase itself to the sweet anticipation of homecoming. The literate text, which survives in sperm-whaling and right-whaling adaptations, is interrogative—"Have you ever..." done such and such?—and while it is hardly a metaphysical treatise, it speaks fluently of the whalemen's heroic self-image, flowing Coleridge-like through visions of victory, death, and destiny at sea, perhaps as much in pursuit of ideas as in pursuit of whales. As in *Moby-Dick*, the implication here is that the whale-hunter's participation in primordial battle may yield a teleological vision available nowhere else.

TUNE: "Diego's Bold Shores," from Joanna C. Colcord, *Songs of American Sailormen*, [1924] 1938, p. 196: "The air was furnished by Joe McGinnis." Transposed from the key of B♭.

A.

"ORIGINAL WHALEMAN'S SONG... BY ONE OF THEM." Jason L. Braley, third mate and second mate, ship *Stephania*, 1847-50; first mate, bark *Louisa*, 1851-53; master, ship *William Badger*, 1853-57, of New Bedford. A right-whaling version probably copied from a contemporaneous periodical.

1. Has a love of adventure and a promise of gold
   Or an ardent desire to roam
   Ever tempted you far over the watery world
   Away from your kindred and home
   With a storm beaten captain freehearted and bold
   And [a] score of brave fellows or two
   Inured to the hardships of hunger and cold
   A fearless and Jolly good crew

2. Have you ever stood watch where Diego's bold shore
   Looms up from the Antarctic wave
   Where the snowy plumed Albatross merrily soared
   O'er many a poor mariner's grave
   Have you heard masthead men sing out "there she blows"
   Seen the boats gaily leave the ship's side
   Or the giant fish writhe 'neath the harpooner's blow
   While the blue sky with crimson was dyed

3. Have you seen the foam fly when the mighty right whale
   Thus boldly attacked from his lair
   With a terrible blow of his ponderous tail
   Sent the boat spinning up in the air
   Or where the fair isles of the evergreen glades
   Are teeming with dainties so rare
   Have you ever made love neath the cocoa's shade
   To the sweet sunny maids that dwell there

4. And have you e'er joined in the boisterous cheer
   Ringing far through heaven's blue dome
   When rich in the spoils you had purchased so dear
   You hoisted your topsails for home
   Or when the dark hills of Columbia rose
   From out the blue waves of the main
   Have you e'er realized the unspeakable joys
   Of meeting with loved ones again

5. Let those who delight in the comforts of home
   And the joys of a warm fireside
   Who deem it a peril the ocean to roam
   In the cots of their fathers abide
   But not a day nearer we reckon our death
   Though we daily sport over our graves
   Nor sweeter they'll slumber the green sod beneath
   Than we in the boisterous wave

B.

"THE WHALEMANS SONG / BY ONE OF THEM." William F. Keyser, bark *Midas* of New Bedford, 1861-65. Dated at the end: "Barque Midas / Jan 20th 1862." Essentially the same A, with minor differences: stanza 1, line 5, "storm *beating* captain"; stanza 2, line 3, *"soars"* (rather than *soared*); line 4, "masthead *man*" (rather than *men*); line 8, *"skies"* (rather than *sky*); stanza 3, line 2, "attacked *in* his lair" (rather than "attacked *from* his lair"); line 7, "cocoa's *green* shade" (rather than "cocoa's shade"); stanza 4, line 2, "through *the* heaven's blue *domes*"; line 5, *"arose"* (rather than *"rose"*); stanza 5, line 6, *"grave"* (rather than *graves*).

C.

"WHALING SONG." George W. Piper, ship *Europa* of Edgartown, 1868-70. Per stanza 3, a sperm-whaling variant similar to A and B; a lesser, less complete text with textual differences; reverses the order of quatrains in stanza 2.

3. Have you ever seen the mighty Sperm Whale
   Thus boldly attacked in his lair
   With one sweep of his mighty and ponderous tail
   Send the boat springing into the air
   Where the fairy green isles of the evergreen glades
   Are teeming with dainties so rare
   Have you ever enjoyed neath the Cocoa nut shades
   All the beauties of nature so fair

D.

[UNTITLED.] Fragment of stanza 2 only, in an anonymous journal of three voyages in the bark *Mermaid* of New Bedford, 1883-90.

138. There She Blows
[The Wounded Whale]

> During a "gam," sleep is out of the question. News from other ships of the fleet is rehearsed, books are exchanged, yarns are swapped, experiences related, and the hours slip rapidly by.
>
> At such times the ship that has a fiddler or a good singer on board is very popular with the crews of vessels not so fortunate, and man y pleasant hours are passed in visiting each other at sea, when, for the time being, all care and hardships are forgotten in boisterous merrymaking. Tales, well told, are eagerly listened to, and truth and fiction are retailed for the benefit of the visiting crews.
>
> Among others there was a song that was popular above any which I heard, possibly because the last four lines of each verse were repeated as a chorus, in which the entire crew usually joined, making at all times a burst of doubtful melody that was exhilarating, to say the least. Who the composer may have been, or how much the original might have gained in passing from mouth to mouth, I will not venture to guess, but will give the words as I heard them sung to the tune of "Hail to the Chief:"
>
> — J.F. Beane, bark *Java* of New Bedford, circa 1864,
> from his narrative *From Forecastle to Cabin* (1905)

"There She Blows," as it was known to Colcord, is a lyrical American sperm-whaling song, technically flawless and one of the most literary and dramatic of all authentic sailor songs. It is also perhaps the most fully descriptive of the actual chase and capture in the boats. Accordingly, it was popular among whalemen, who often recorded it in their journals, but it apparently was not much in vogue with sailors in other trades—unlike "The Greenland Whale Fishery" [#134] and "The Coast of Peru" [#136], which were perennial favorites among mariners of all kinds. "There She Blows" is known to have been sung to the tune of "Hail to the Chief," a poem by Sir Walter Scott, but to which one of the several standard airs has not been definitively ascertained. One [Tune A] is actually a form of the Scottish traditional air "The Hills of Glenorchy" ("The Boat Song"). Another [Tune B], composed by James Sanderson (1769-1841) and published in New York in conjunction with Scott's text perhaps as early as 1812, is the setting familiar today as the standard salute to the President of the United States, in which capacity the piece may have made its debut as long ago as the inauguration of Martin Van Buren in 1837 (Lawrence, 188). A third [Tune C], attributed to Henry Rowley Bishop (1786-1855), is the melody given by Colcord.

TUNE A - "Hail to the Chief" (actually the traditional Scottish air "The Hills of Glenochry," also known as "The Boat Song"), from *The Lyric Gems of Scotland,* Glasgow (circa 1875), I:52; likewise per S.T. Gleadhill, *Kyle's Scottish Lyric Gems,* Glasgow (circa 1880), pp. 238f. Transposed from the key of B$^\flat$ Major.

TUNE B - "Hail to the Chief," composed by James Sanderson; from a facsimile of the original sheet music (New York: Wm. Dubois, [1812] 1817); also quoted in Lawrence, 188f.

TUNE C - "Hail to the Chief," attributed to Henry Rowley Bishop, from Helen Kendrick Johnson, *Our Familiar Songs,* [1881] 1889, pp. 499f. This is the air given by Colcord, sans the repeats in the final 12 measures.

A.

"A SPERM WHALING SONG." George Edgar Mills, fourth mate, ship *Java* of New Bedford, 1854-55; third mate, ship *Leonidas* of New Bedford, 1855-56; second mate bark *Mary Frances* of Warren, 1856. First line "Bright as the sun from its ocean bead springs"; a less complete text than B, C, or D; like C, transcribed as 8 stanzas of 4 lines each, with textual variations, most significantly the absence of two stanzas (corresponding to stanza 4 of B and D).

> 5. ! Row Hearties pull, if you love your ambition,
>   Spring to your thwarts let the reeking sweat flow
>   Now if you've got blood let it have demonstration
>   Bend to your oars and give way all you know

B.

"WHALING SONG." George W. Piper, ship *Europa* of Edgartown, 1868-70. More complete than A, with the stanzas doubled, in conformity with the tune. The usual opening line is "Lo as the sun… " (as in C; compare D).

> 1. Low as the sun from its ocean bed rises
>   Broad o'er the waters its glistening beams throws
>   Hark from our masthead the joyful sound ringing
>   Hard on our lee beam a whale there she blows
>   Call up the sleepers then larboard and starboard men
>   Main yard aback man your boats lower away
>   Hard on our lee beam see the white water gleam
>   Wreathing, her foam in a garland of spray

> 2. Now the Leviathan in vastness is Lying
>   Making the sea a luxurious bed
>   While reeling over her the sea birds are flying
>   A watching the billows that break over ahead
>   Broad, high, and close to there she goes flukes in air
>   So stately and slowly she sank in the main
>   Peak all your oars awhile rest from your weary toil
>   Waiting and watching her rising again

3. Row hearties row for the pride of your nation
   Spring to your thwarts let the reeking sweat flow
   Now if you have blood let it have circulation
   Ben[d] to your oars and give way all you know
   See each boat advance as gaily as to a dance
   A gliding like shadows across the blue sea
   Stand up and give him some send both your irons home
   Stern all trim the boat see the line all free[17]

4. Wounded and sore fins and flukes in commotion
   Black skin and oars contending with the spray
   So loud and so shrill rings the horn of the ocean
   Fettered and fast she brings to in dismay
   Haul line every man gather in all you can
   Lances and spades from your thwarts clear away
   Peak all your oars again let each boat fast remain
   Safely and surely whilst we hold her in play

5. Surrounded with foes yet with strength undiminished
   So wildly she lashes the sea in her ire
   A lance in her life and the struggle is finished
   So slowly she sinks with her chimney on fire[18]
   Loud rings the joyful sound from each stout seaman's heart
   Matching the sea in its turbulent roar
   Look from the spout hole see the red signals fly
   So slowly she dies and the struggle is o'er

C.

"WHALEMENS SONG." John S. Coquin, bark *Pacific* of New Bedford, 1867-68; and merchant voyages out of Boston, circa 1860's-'70s. First line "Low [sic] as the sun from its ocean bed springing"; similar to B, and like B transcribed as 5 stanzas of 8 lines each, but with a few interesting differences, such as: in stanza 2, "*See* the leviathan in *his* vastness lying / Making the *deep* his *voluptuous* bed"; line 4, "Combing the billows that break o'er *his* head"; final line "Slowly he dies & the conflict is o'er."

D.

[UNTITLED.] Emma McInness, bark *Josephine* of San Francisco, 1891-92. Transcribed as 10 stanzas of 4 lines each; otherwise quite similar to B. The last line is: "So slowly she dies and the conquest is o'er."

1. Lo as the sun from its ocean bed springing
   Bright o'er the waters its glittering beams glows
   When from our masthead the joyful cry ringing
   "A whale off the lee beam, a whale there she blows"

---

[17] *Stern all!* is the command to row backwards (astern), quickly to get the boat clear of the whale's dangerous tail flukes. The harpoon, now plunged deep in the whale's back and holding fast, is attached to thousands of feet of sturdy line (rope) which must be free of all kinks, tools, and legs, so that it can uncoil—reel out—as the whale swims or dives. This line is *paid out* —let out gradually—and, when the opportunity arises, hauled in; but for the most part, as the whale swims it tows the boat along after it; and the crew stands ready to sever the line with a hatchet if there be any danger of the boat being dragged underwater.

[18] *Chimney on fire:* i.e., the spout-hole is pouting blood, a sign that the whale is fatally wounded.

139.
Blow Ye Winds
[It's Advertised in Boston; 'Tis Advertised in Boston]

> Wanted immediately, 100 enterprising young men, Americans, to go on whaling voyages in first-rate ships. Carpenters, coopers, and blacksmiths are all wanted. The present is a very desirable opportunity for those who wish to take a voyage to sea to learn navigation or nautical improvement. All clothing and other necessary articles furnished on credit. Apply to S. & J.N. Luckey, 106 South Street, upstairs.
>
> Wanted thirty young men for two ships at New Bedford, twenty-five men for two ships at Fairhaven, twelve men for a ship at New London, two men for a ship at Sag Harbor. By applying immediately at Thomas Lewis' clothing store, No. 15 James Slip, they can have their choice of ships and places. All clothing furnished on credit.
>
> — New York *Sun,* 14 July 1839[19]

    This New Bedford ballad, perhaps the best known and certainly the most often extemporized American whaling song, recounts the miseries of the fishery that plagued whalemen—unsavory recruiting tactics, usurious outfitting and in-fitting practices, dreadful food, miserable shipboard conditions, and various hazards, duplicities, and injustices. Topical though it be, the words and music are descended from an earlier English sea song called "Blow Ye Winds in the Morning," which according to Captain Whall "is based on a ballad in Percy's *Reliques* [1765], 'The Baffled Knight'" (Child #112). However, Whall's notion that "'Blow, Ye Winds, in the Morning'… was a song of the midshipmen's berth rather than the forecastle" does not apply here: the American whaling ballad "Blow, Ye Winds" was clearly an anthem of foremast hands, sometimes actually used as a chantey. The tune is essentially the same as the air used for "The Baffled Knight," which, in turn, is actually a form of "The Derby Ram" (e.g., see Waite I:37). Harlow is the single notable exception: he gives "Derby Ram" as the melody for "The Merman" and for a Yankee capstan chantey he calls "Blow Ye Winds," which has an entirely different text; meanwhile, his rendition of the windlass chantey that he calls "It's Advertised in Boston" (which has a version of the standard New Bedford lyrics) is set to an innocuous but distinctive variant.[20]

    In his memoirs of a fifty-year career at sea, including an apprenticeship in the Royal Navy, many Cape Horn passages in latter-day clipper ships and China traders, and one whaling voyage in the schooner *Franklin* of New Bedford (1889-91), Canadian mariner E. C. Sears attributes to the master and first officer of the *Franklin* a compelling vindication of the good seamanship of American whaleman, thus contradicting the Dana's disparaging remarks in *Two Years Before the Mast.* On his way aboard the *Franklin* before embarking on his whaling cruise Sears quotes or paraphrases the mate, a Mr. Linscombe of Mattapoisett, Massachusetts, as saying, "I have served my early boyhood in deep water ships and when I left them to enter the [whale] fishery I could not handle an oar or row, seen a kedge anchor run out. Believe me you will see more sea manship in those months [whaling] than you could expect to see in ten years in any other class of ships." This opinion is reinforced in Sears's description of the captain's abilities and insistence upon high standards aboard the *Franklin*: "Believe me, the sails when bent to the yards were as carefully furled as were ever furled in any warship, bunts were square and every bunt gasket in its proper place before leaving the ship." However, unlike Sears, who was a seasoned veteran of the naval and merchant services, when they first came on board most first-time whalemen were hopelessly unacquainted with seafaring and sailor ways. Many were refugees from New

---

[19] Quoted from Spears 1908, p. 246.

[20] Harlow is mistaken that Admiral Luce "gives the same air" (a form of "Derby Ram") for "The Merman": Luce's air for "The Merman" is actually a form of an earlier tune, "The Budgeon It Is a Delicate Trade," the same air that Hugill gives for "Rolling Down to Old Mohee" [#143].

England farms or the big manufacturing towns; others were former tradesmen's apprentices, farmhands, and disgruntled shop clerks hoping to see the world. A few, like Sears, were out-of-work seamen looking for a paying berth. And many of all types were, like Sears, recruited in the big cities and brought to the whaling ports by independent agents who were paid a fee per each man enlisted. So close was the ballad to Sears's own experiences (though "Blow Ye Winds" must already have been at least 40 or 50 years old when Sears was first recruited by a Manhattan "crimp"), that he wrote it into his memoirs, the only song he "collected" and transcribed among hundreds of pages of memoirs and lore.[21]

TUNE A -"Blow, Ye Winds," composite: compare Colcord, 191; Harlow, 130; Hugill, 219; Shay 1948, 126; Whall, 21.

TUNE B - "It's Advertised in Boston," from Frederick Pease Harlow, *Chanteying Aboard American Ships,* 1962, pp. 211ff: "Windlass chantey."

A.

"CHEER UP MY LIVELY LADS WE'LL ALL GO HOME TOGETHER." George W. Piper, ship *Europa* of Edgartown, 1868-70. The unusual title (unequivocal in the MS) derives from the unconventional chorus, which seems more akin to "The Bold Harpooner" [#140] than to any standard rendition of "Blow Ye Winds." A lengthy and well-wrought text with many whaling allusions. Regularized from several different schemes of transcription in the MS.

1. They advertized in Boston New York and Buffalo
   Five hundred bold Americans awhaling for to go

   Chorus: Cheer up my lively lads in spite of wind and weather
   Cheer up my lively lads we'll [all] go home together

2. They'll take you to New Bedford, that famous whaling port
   They'll take you to a S— of a B—, and he will fit you out

3. O we'll s[h]ow you the Clipper Ship built so strong and stout
   They'll say you'll have $500 before you're six months out

4. And now the ship is out to sea and the wind begins to blow
   Some are sick as the very old nick[22] and the rest are all below[23]

---

[21] E.C. Sears, manuscript memoirs, 3 vols., vol. 2, n.p., n.d.

[22] *Old Nick:* a euphemism for the Devil; thus, "sick as the devil."

[23] That is, *belowdecks,* in the forecastle, presumably recuperating from drunken debauches ashore.

5. When first you leave New Bedford, They will treat you very kind;
But when they get you round Cape Horn It['s] then they chang their mind

6. The Capt[ai]n he will flog you, The Mate will curse and swear;
Saying lay aloft you lousy slops Take hay seed out of your hair

7. They send you to the masthead, But that's against your wil
Saying if you raise a whale my boy I'll give you [a] ten dollar bill

8. You will crawl behind the try works, A trying to get a nap
The Mate will come along and, Give you a smarting rap

9. Then comes the running rigging, It must be learned you know,[24]
And if you dont learn [it] in a week You lose your watch below.[25]

10. Then comes the darn old compass It will grieve your hart full sore
The[re] are two and thirty points to learn[26] And you'll find forty more[27]

11. Then comes the cursed grub my boys, And that is little enough,
There's stinking meet all the week And on sunday a little duff.[28]

12. Now we are on the coast of Peru, Where the whales begin to blow,
Its lower away the boats my boys, And after them we'll go

13. And now the boats are lowered my boys, And we are on the level,
And if you dont look out for flukes[29] They will knock you to the devil

14. And now we have the whale fin up, And brought him alongside,
It's then we put the fluke chains on And rob him of his pride.[30]

15. The boatsteerer is overboard[31] The tackles overhauled,
The captain in the [rigging chair?] And loudly does he bawl

---

[24] See "The Sailor's Alphabet" [#44].

[25] Like other sailors, whalemen worked alternating watches, on American ships customarily a four-hour rotation on and off duty (however, when actually on the whaling grounds the schedule was revised to accommodate the hunt during daylight hours). The sense here is that if a sailor does not "learn the ropes" right away, he will be required to spend his off hours at work until he does.

[26] That is, the 32 compass directions (which can also be subdivided again into 64): to recite them all in order is called *boxing the compass,* a standard nautical skill required as a prerequisite for advancement. The grade Able Bodied Seaman is not automatically attained. Among mainstream American writers who served in square-rig—including Dana, Melville, and Cooper—only O'Neill held A.B. papers, earned in his youth and a lifelong source of pride (though Cooper had served as a midshipman in the U.S. Navy and probably also could have qualified). See "The Schooner *Varnum Hill,*" stanza 5 and footnotes.

[27] The arithmetic here (variously represented as 40 or 44) has ever been a mystery in manifestations of the song in which this line appears. "No modern whaleman has been able to say what is meant by the reference to forty-four points [in her version] of the whaler's compass" (Colcord 190f). The line is likely merely a corruption of 64. In any case, the significance of the line is not lost: whatever task be accomplished, the officers will always find something else—or, as it is put in "The Whaleman's Lament" [#154], "…The best that you can get from them / Is plenty more work to do" (Huntington 1964, 7).

[28] *Duff:* a "pudding" of crushed sea biscuit and flour, sometimes blended with raisins and molasses, usually regarded by seamen as a treat, common in all maritime services, typically served up on Sundays.

[29] That is, beware of the tail of the whale.

[30] See "Boston" [#33], footnotes.

[31] That is, on the *cutting stage,* a wooden platform rigged on the starboard side of a whaleship to accommodate *cutting-in* the *blanket-pieces* of blubber while the whale is tied alongside; or, alternatively, on the back of the whale itself.

16. Now we have the whale tried out, And are stowing him away;
    There's fifty casks a coming to you Of the two hundred lay.[32]

17. Now liberty we do go, To Tombez[33] or some such port,
    Where if [you] try to run away, You'll shurely will get caught.[34]

18. When for Talkwaner[35] we do go When you're in the Captain's power
    The American Consul he can buy For half a barrel of flour.[36]

19. And now our ship is full my boys, And we don't give a damn
    To bend on all our lofty sails And steer for Yankeeland.[37]

20. And now we're in New Bedford, And lay along the side of the dock,
    And if I ever go whaling again I hope I will be shot.

B.

"BLOW YE WINDS." MS memoirs of E.C. Sears, schooner *Franklin* of New Bedford, 1889-91. Five-stanza fragment of a standard text with the standard chorus. Lines and stanzas regularized.

1. Tis advertised in Boston New York and Buffaloa,
   Five hundred brave Americans, A whaling for to go, singing

Chorus: Blow ye winds in the morning, Blow ye winds high O!
   Clear away your running gear, And blow ye winds high O

2. They send you to New Bedford, that famous whaling port
   They'll take you to some land sharks to board and fit you out

3. They send you to a boarding house there for a time to dwell
   The thieves are thicker [there] than the other side of hell.

4. They tell you of the clipper ships a going in and out,
   And say youll take five hundred sperm before youre six months out

5. Its now we are out to sea, my boys the wind comes on to blow;
   One half the watch is sick on deck, the other half below

---

[32] This is more arithmetical gibberish representing owners' promises unkept. A *two-hundredth lay* is a fractional share amounting to 1/200th of the crew's portion of the catch—*before* sundry deductions for expenses. See Hohman 1928, 217-288.

[33] Tumbez: one of the whalers' principal ports-of-call on the coast of Peru. See "The Coast of Peru" [#136].

[34] There were strict prohibitions governing *jumping ship* in any port-of-call; in foreign ports the American Consul (or in some cases by prior agreement, the British Consul) had jurisdiction over American ships and crews to arbitrate disputes and enforce the law. See biographical notes on Daniel Kimball Ritchie in Appendix 6; also Hohman 1952, Parts II-III).

[35] *Talcahuano:* on the Chile coast, like Tumbez, was a major South American watering and provisioning port much frequented by New England whalers.

[36] As Hugill points out with reference to Colcord's version of the same song, "The last line has been camouflaged. It was a common line in shanties, forebitters, and whaling songs: Where the Old Man bought a whore-house out for a half a barrel o' flour" (Hugill 223). See "The Coast of Peru" [#136].

[37] By the 1850s, on square-rigged ships, barks, and some brigs. when actually on the whaling grounds, the uppermost square sails (usually royals) were sent down and *masthead hoops* (crow's-nest rings) were mounted in their place. At the end of whaling, the masthead hoops were sent down and the royal yards reinstalled ("bent on") for the homeward passage. This and the dismantling of the brick *tryworks,* also customary on American vessels, were symbolic signs that whaling was done and the ship was homeward bound.

140. The Bold Harpooner
[The *Diamond* Ship; The Bonnie Ship the *Diamond;* Captain Bunker; Nantucket Song]

> So be cheery, my lads, let your hearts never fail,
> While the bold harpooner is striking the whale!
>
> — "Nantucket Song"
> in *Moby-Dick*.

This ballad is of Scottish origin and, like "The King of the Southern Sea" [#229], it also has an American literary context. However, unlike "King of the Southern Sea," various forms of "The Bold Harpooner" appear actually to have been sung by whalemen in the 19th century (as well as aboard floating-factory ships in the 20th). Among several extant variants of the lyrics, the name Captain Bunker appears only in the tortured text quoted by J. Ross Browne in *Etchings of a Whaling Cruise* (1846). The Bunkers were a venerable Nantucket family that over several generations produced numerous whaling masters, a few of whom in the late 18th and early 19th centuries were expatriate commanders of South Seas whaling voyages out of various British, French, and Canadian ports. Thus, on both sides of the Atlantic, "Captain Bunker" became a generic name associated with the eminent whaling heritage of Nantucket, and it is frequently encountered in whalemen's songs and poems (e.g., Colcord's version of "The Coast of Peru"). It was likely from these Nantucket associations that Melville identified the fragment he excerpted from Browne, and, omitting the Bunker name, spliced into *Moby-Dick* with the vague designation "Nantucket Song." Whaleman George Wilbur Piper's rendition [A] unaccountably mentions the *Mary Jane* of Sunderland (England), and the names and places mentioned in it do not coincide with the historical record. Sunderland was not much of a whaling port and, while the records are not entirely conclusive, it is unlikely that any whaleship *Mary Jane* ever sailed from there. Even so, Piper's lyrics are more complete and less corrupt than Browne's or Melville's. A fragmentary text from an anonymous journal of the *Mermaid* [B] is localized to that particular New Bedford bark, corroborating the suspicion that there may have been other localized adaptations in Britain and America which, whether or not they were ever committed to paper, do not survive. The most intact form of the ballad is "The Diamond Ship" ("The Bonnie Ship the *Diamond*"), which Greig obtained from Ord: the lyrics refer to the Arctic whaling fleet of Aberdeen (Scotland) but it has a similar chorus:

> So be cheery, my lads, let your hearts never fail,
> While the bonnie ship the *Diamond* is a-fishing for the whale!

In the 1960s A.L. Lloyd popularized an adaptation from Peterhead (Scotland), also known as "The *Diamond*," which he ostensibly collected in the 1930s from the singing of a British factory-ship whaleman. His tune is evidently a form of the same air that Greig names as a variant of "The Hook and the Plaid."

TUNE - "The Diamond" (according to Greig, a variant of the Scots air "The Hook and the Plaid"): from the singing of Stuart Gillespie, Louis Killen, Robert Kotta, Alan MacLoed, Jeff Warner, etc., after A.L. Lloyd et al., *Leviathan!* (Topic #12T154, 1967), thence tracing to Greig and Ord.

A.
"WHALING SONG." George W. Piper, ship *Europa* of Edgartown, 1868-70. Lines regularized into stanzas.

1. The Mary Jane of Sunderland[38] is under our lee
   She is trying for to weather us but that can never be

   Chorus: So be cheerful my lads let your hearts never fail
   While the bold harpooneersman Is a striking of the whale

2. The Captain walks the quarter deck crying Steady as she goes
   When the man from the mast head sings out there she blows

3. Our Captain takes his spy glass and springing up aloft
   Crying where away O where away and how far is she off

4. The answer from aloft my boys which caused us all to smile
   Three points on our lee[ward] bow and distance scarce a mile

5. Then lower away your boats my boys and after them we will go
   For I know that they are sperm whale because they spout so low

6. O we pulled up alongside and we hove two irons in
   Then the whale he struck us with his flukes and killed one of our men

7. O the loss of that big whale my boys it grieved the captain sore
   But the loosing of that one brave man it grieved him ten times more

8. Now our ship is full my boys So pass around the can of gin
   For we and the Mary Jane Are homeward bound again

B.
[UNTITLED.] Fragment of the chorus only, in an anonymous journal of three voyages in the bark *Mermaid* of New Bedford, 1883-90.

Then come search her up My lively lads
Let your hearts never fail,
While the saucy little Mermaid,
is a Cruising after Whales

---

[38] Sunderland, an industrial seaport in County Durham, had a comparatively minor role in the revival of British whaling during the 1780s and '90s, but whaling there had declined to inactivity before the close of the Napoleonic Wars and there is no evidence that the port reentered the fishery at a later date. "The *Diamond*" concerns Scotland's Davis Strait whale fishery and names several well known Scottish whaling vessels.

141. The Wonderful Whale
[Jack and the Whale; Wonders, Or The Whale]

This tall tale is indebted to two ancient legends that have had enduring religious and cultural significance: St. Brendan the Voyager, a 6th-century Irish abbot who held mass on the back of an enormous sea monster in the mistaken belief that it was an island; and Jonah, of Biblical fame, who was swallowed by a "great fish" and emerged unscathed. The comic ballad also presumes a knowledge of the once-popular song "The Great Sea Snake," of which "The Wonderful Whale" declares itself the sequel; oddly, "The Great Sea Snake" actually seems to presume a knowledge of itself:

> Perhaps you have, all of you, heard a yarn,
> Of a famous large Sea Snake,
> That was once seen off the Isle of Pitcairn,
> And caught by Admiral Blake:
> Now list not to what land lubbers tell,
> But give an air to me,
> And I'll tell you what to me befel,
> 'Cause I'm just come from Sea.[39]

The promise of adventure goes unfulfilled. The yarn has no plot, really, but simply hyberbolizes the extraordinary size of the sea-serpent: it takes six months to sail from head to tail; mistaking him for their "promised lands," a thousand pilgrims "with oxen, pigs and sheep" build houses and a church on his back while the monster sleeps; but "The Snake left them in the lurch, / By diving down below." It ends with a warning to landsmen to give ear, take pity, and have more respect for the wonders of the deep. "The Wonderful Whale" is not a precise adaptation but transforms the scenario into a whale hunt, with the beast represented as a kind of comical foil to Moby Dick, The Greatest Whale You Could Ever Imagine. Jack is swallowed by the whale, lives comfortably inside, and winds up selling the carcass for oil. Whaleman George W. Piper's shipboard text is in many respects similar to one printed a generation earlier in *The American Sailor's Songster* (circa 1840), but with many changes, possibly the result of oral transmission. That version is in turn based upon broadsides printed in England, with the lyrics attributed to J.C. Davidson to be sung to "The Great Sea Snake." The ancestor of these is a broadside titled "Wonders; Or, The Whale," printed circa 1809 by J. Jennings of London, subtitled "A comic song, by Joannot, at the Royal Circus/Written by Mr Lawler/Tune—The Pyeman's Trip to Bagshot Health Camp." A third farce along similar lines is "How to Catch a Whale" [#142]. "The Wonderful Crocodile" is yet another. All four manifestations of these zoological lyrics—a sea serpent, two whales, and a crocodile—are sung to a melody that is identified by its association with an 18th-century text having to do with an analogous culinary gargantuanism, "The Great Meat Pie" [see #142], which seems to be simply another name for the "Pyeman" air named in the broadside.

TUNE - "The Crocodile," from Broadwood & Maitland, *English County Songs,* 1893, pp. 184f (nonsense-syllable chorus omitted). Compare: "Great Meat Pie" [#142].

---

[39] Ashton 1888, 147: a text of six stanzas. Robert Blake (?1598-1657) was a naval hero in the wars against Holland and Spain. Pitcairn was not discovered until 1767 and was so remote from the regular sea-lanes (and from anyplace that Admiral Blake had ever been!) that after the *Bounty* mutineers settled there in 1790, their presence was unknown for almost two decades.

"JACK AND THE WHALE." George W. Piper, ship *Europa* of Edgartown, 1868-70. Sequel to "The Great Sea Snake." The repetitions are consistently through-transcribed as a refrain for each stanza, per the first stanza, but are not here repeated from the MS.

1. About the great sea snake you have heard in a rare astounding tale
   So now I will tell you what occurred with a monster South Sea whale

Chorus: With a monster South Sea whale / With a monster South Sea whale
   So now I will tell you what occurred with a monster South Sea whale

2. It was in the Autumn of the year that we left the river's mouth
   And with a spread of sail did steer towards the Sunny South

3. We steered our course then by degrees and we weathered many a gale
   When all at once our Captain sees a thumping great big whale

4. It crawled along like any snail in a scorching sun at noon
   But we very soon put into its tail a jolly sharp harpoon

5. Right mad with pain it quickly turned and flew at harpoon Jack
   But he it's malice cooly spurned by striking at its back

6. The whale enraged then flew at Jack while he for aid did bawl
   With a gaping mouth and in a crack it swallowed him boat and all

   Bully for Jack. That must have been
   the whale that swallowed Jonah.

7. And now in the whale's inside poor Jack was safely stowed
   And when he came to himself he cried I am in it now I am blowed

8. But I will not sink in sight of rocks, and in that he was right
   So out he lugged his tobacco box and lighted up his pipe

9. The smoke it was so very dark, and it grew uncommon thick
   The whale unused to such a lark it soon grew uncommon sick

10. This brought a thought into his head to force Jack from below
    But Jack having passed his teeth clear once, he held fast and cried no go

11. The whale he then did roll over he rolled over on his side
    And though it was must against his will he soon gave it up and died

12. And when Jack the land did reach he jumped ashore with a smile
    He drew the whale upon the beach And the carcass sold for oil

13. Our crew received this with a smile they tell it with a grin
    And I only say if it is all a lie, You are fairly taken in

142. How to Catch a Whale

The whaleman's transcription includes a preamble, "A popular Comic Song / now singing with great applause / by Messrs H. Fox / W. Warde &c &c / Tune — Great Meat Pie," indicating that "How To Catch a Whale" was copied from a published text. While this preamble may be a hoax (as no record of any such sheet music or songster text has been located), the song is in any case a parody of "The Great Meat Pie," a British folksong that nowadays (if it be remembered at all) is usually relegated to the nursery.

> The great meat pie was a tidy size,
> And it took a week to make it,
> A day to carry it to the shop,
> And just a week to bake it.
> And if you'd seen it, I'll be bound,
> Your wonder you'd scarce govern.
> They were forced to break the front wall down
> To get it in the oven.[40]

According to Kidson, the song was "suggested by similar exaggerative ditties, and probably by the monster meat pies made on certain occasions in Denby Dale in Yorkshire. The first Denby Dale pie was baked in 1788 to commemorate the recovery of George III; the second in 1815 on the victory at Waterloo; another on the repeal of the corn laws in 1846… "; and others in 1877 and 1896 (Kidson & Martin, 47). Unlike the original comic verse in R.G.N. Swift's journal, such as "The Parson's Narrative" [#133] and "The Sailor Boy's Dream" [#230], there is nothing about "How to Catch a Whale" of which a generic landlubber lyricist would not have been capable, or which might require a whaleman's esoteric nautical insights to find humorous: it has little of the professional lingo or technical proficiency by which "real" deepwater songs and whalemen's ballads are distinguished. On the other hand, young Swift was evidently a clever lyricist and enjoyed the kinds of puns and hoaxes exemplified here: he could have written it himself.

TUNE: "The Great Meat Pie," from Frank Kidson and Martin Shaw, *Songs of Britain*, n.d., 46: "The song and tune printed about 1830." Transposed from B^b. It is substantially the same as the version of "Great Meat Pie" given for "The Wonderful Whale" [#141]; compare Leisy #43; Kennedy #292.

---

[40] Quoted from Leisy 1974, 130f.

"HOW TO CATCH A WHALE." R.G.N. Swift, ship *Contest* of New Bedford, 1866-70.

1. O I'm come for to go for to sing a song
    Tis neither Dutch nor Turkey,
   I know I'm either right or wrong,
    For I had it from a Yankee.
   'Tis all about a wonderful whale—
    Tis the truth I'm going to patter,
   A Sailor swam from the head to the tail,
    And was ten years reaching the latter,
        Fol lol &c.

2. When at her tail Poor Jack arrived,
    The smallest part about it,
   We crawleth up upon her, then she dived
    Two thousand miles—d'ye doubt it?
   For full three years disappeared,
    With Jack in the ocean treasured,
   One day with Jack on land she steer'd,
    And she, miles one million measured.
        Fol lol &c.

3. On land Poor Jack secured his prize,
    He stuck a knife in her belly,
   Which made her whaleship[41] roll her eyes,
    And look like a lump of jelly,
   But when Jack let the daylight in
    Between her ribs so bulky,
   She wagged her tail and gave a grin,
    Then looked to Jack quite sulky.
        Fol lol &c.

4. She turned a flip flop onto her back
    And kicked the bucket—a wonder
   She gave a groan which frightened Jack
    Twas ten times louder than thunder.
   Jack cut her open as soon as she died,
    And found as he was bewailing,
   Five hundred ships in her inside,
    And of oceans people sailing.
        Fol lol &c.

5. The ships from her sailed one by one,
    All in a terrific motion,
   And the water from her whaleship ran
    In partnership with the ocean
   Jack took her body inside out
    And onto her skin went jumping,
   Then up and down he floated about
    And set all the ships a bumping.
        Fol lol &c.

6. The people from the island all
    To Jack in their ships were advancing
   For Jack invited them to a ball
    And deck's the whale out for their dancing
   Some thousand slipt about so rash
    Which previously did rock her
   But the ship went to pieces and with a crash
    The whole went to Davy's Locker.[42]
        Fol lol &c.

---

[41] *Whaleship*: a pun turning on two implied senses of the word: as a form of address (as of the nobility, e.g., "your worship," "her ladyship," "his lordship"), here addressing and comically personifying the whale; and as a vessel used for hunting whales.

[42] *Davy Jones* signifies the spirit of the sea, a personification common among British, American, Dutch, and other seamen since the eighteenth century; also *Davy, Old Davy, David Jones,* etc. *Davy's Locker* (more commonly nowadays *Davy Jones's Locker*) is the sea, "especially as an ocean grave." Partridge gives the derivation as "*Jonah>Jonas>Jones,* the *Davy* being added by Welsh sailors." The term is nautical usage but, as it is supposed to have originated in print with Smollett's *Peregrine Pickle* (1750), it is presumed to have been in very wide circulation in ordinary language ashore.

143. Rolling Down to Old Mohee

In George Wilbur Piper's shipboard copybook of 1868-70, this ballad of the Western Arctic bowhead whalemen is entitled "Song of Songs: Rolling Down to Old Mohee," and, indeed, it is arguably the greatest whaling song of all. Thoroughly American in origin, it seems to have arisen in the 1850s and briefly recounts in rugged detail the hardships and exigencies of whale hunting among the floes, and expresses the gleeful anticipation with which the whalemen contemplate their end-of-season layover at Lahaina, on Maui ("Mohee"), in the lush, tropical Sandwich Islands (Hawaii). The three whalemen's texts reported here are intrinsically just about the best — and the first two probably the earliest — encountered anywhere to date. Jones & Handy's rendition of seven stanzas [text A] is especially powerful and eminently complete, and all three specifically refer to the Kamchatka Sea (adjacent to Siberia) and St. Lawrence Island (in the Bering Sea, now part of Alaska), both important Arctic whaling grounds.

When Colcord published her text in 1924 and again in 1938 she was unable to locate a tune, but several have since been connected with the song. Harlow obtained his from Captain R.W. Guy "of the bark *Guy C. Goss,* who had seen service in early days on whalers"; but this (later reprinted in a garbled adaptation by Huntington) is little more than a generic hodgepodge of bits-and-pieces spliced together from other songs, including "Greenland Whale Fishery," "Tenting on the Old Camp Ground," and "The Marine Corps Hymn." It could not be indigenous to the 19th-century original, sung by whalemen on shipboard. In 1967, A.L. Lloyd, a folksong collector, BBC Radio personality, and sometime collaborator of Ralph Vaughan Williams, recorded a version of "Mohee" with a melody he does not identify and which many in his audience have since assumed to be indigenous. In actuality, both the tune and the harmonization (which has the semblance of old shape-note or "Sacred Harp" *a capella* harmony) are merely adaptations of Vaughan Williams's 1906 arrangement of something he identifies only as a "Traditional English Melody": it appears twice in Broadwood & Maitland, as the air for a text of "Lazarus" ("Dives and Lazarus") collected in Middlesex in the 1890s, and for a text of the ballad "The Thresher and the Squire" from Oxfordshire; it is known to liturgical music as "Kingsfold" and in Irish tradition as "My Love Nell" and "The Star of the County Down" [see also "Columbia's Ships," #53]. *The Oxford Book of Carols* associates it with texts of "Job" and "Dives and Lazarus," while *The English Hymnal* (#101), current in the Episcopalian Church in the USA and the Anglican Church worldwide, combines the Vaughan Williams arrangement with a Rogation Days text. Hugill's tune, which he himself made popular in revival, is by far the strongest and the only one with any plausible claim to being the "original" sung by 19th-century whalemen on shipboard. It has not generally been recognized by the thousands who sing it that Hugill's melody is a fairly orthodox rendering of a hoary English ballad air, "The Budgeon It Is a Delicate Trade," which traces back at least to 1725. Since 1762 it has perhaps been better known as "The Jolly Miller," after a text by Isaac Bickerstaffe (c1735-c1812), which was set to this tune in the play *Love in a Village* (1762), where the music was composed and arranged by Thomas Arne (1710-1778).[43] Hugill's rendition sports a full-scale chorus. Only one of the whalemen's texts has such a chorus [B], one explicitly specifies that the last two lines of each stanza are to be repeated as a refrain [A], while the third gives no indication of a chorus or refrain.

---

[43] Notwithstanding such sharp distinctions of provenance, there remains a close melodic affinity between Lloyd's and Hugill's tunes. Mary Malloy, who transcribed Lloyd's recorded rendition, suggests that they are variants of the same tune, and offers the hypothesis that their close resemblance (masked by the Sacred Harp vocal arrangement) may be responsible for a subtle subversion of memory on one part or the other, in consequence of which one traditional air may have been substituted for the other. Nevertheless, be there any doubt, whereas Lloyd's association with Vaughan Williams raises doubts about the provenance of his melody, Hugill's recollection of the tune is so classic a rendition of "The Budgeon it is a delicate Trade" that it cries out as authentically indigenous to the piece.

TUNE A - "The Budgeon it is a delicate Trade," from John Hullah, *The Song Book,* 1866, p. 55, where it is given for the text "There Was a Jolly Miller"; after Chappell II:668, who remarks: "The air… is from *The Triumph of Wit* [and also] in a collection of songs 'in the canting dialect' (1725) [etc.]…. The tune of *The jolly Miller* was one of those harmonized by Beethoven for George Thomson, in 1824" (II:666-668). Also reprinted in Duncan I:134f.

TUNE B - "Rolling Down to Old Maui," from the singing of Stan Hugill (see also Hugill, *Songs of the Sea,* 1977, p. 120): a straightforward adaptation of "The Budgeon it is a delicate Trade (The Jolly Miller)" [tune A], converting from 6/8 to 4/4 time. Note that the subtonic (here a G#) is sometimes flattened (to G natural) in 4th and 12th measures, as would be the case with a classic modal air. The chorus, not indicated in tune A, is merely a repeat of the second part of the melody, as shown.

A.

"ROLING [sic] DOWN TO OLD MOHEE." George M. Jones and Albert F. Handy, bark *Waverly* of New Bedford, 1859-63. A robust, complete text, more literate in content than in transcription. Slightly regularized into stanzas from inconsistencies in the MS. No chorus or refrain is indicated.

1. Onse more with a favring northern breese
   We are bounding o're the main
   And soon the hills of the tropic isles
   will be in view agane
   Five slugish months have past and gone
   Sinse first from your shores sailed wee
   But now we are bound from the Arctic ground
   Roling down to old Mohee

2. In vapors neath the chilly sky
   Aurora colerd the wave
   and slumbers beneath the moon beams smile
   In the dark St Lorance Bay
   For many a w[e]ary day we toiled
   In the wild Kamtschatka Sea
   But as we've toiled we've laughed and sung
   Of the girls of Old Mohee

3. Welcom the seas where the fragrant breeze
   Filled with oders rare

       Whare the suny glades and pretty maids
       are gentle kind &fair
       Tis there bright eyes look forthe each way
       in hopes some day to see
       Our snow white sails before the gale
       roling down to Old mohee

4.   We heave the lead[44] where old dimes head[45]
       Looms up in Old Oahu
       Our decks and riging are clear of Ice
       Our sails are free from snow
       The hoary heads of the sea gurt Isles
       that deck the artic sea
       are many and many a legue astern
       Since we steered for Old Mohee

5.   An ample shair of toil and cair
       we whalemen undergo
       But our labor's ore what cair we more
       How oft the wind may blow
       Tis homeward bound that thriling sound
       Although it nare may be
       When we think of that we'l laugh and chat
       With the girls of old mohee

6.   Once more we're bound with a favering breeze
       On tord our distant home
       Our mainmast sprung we're almost wrecked
       still she proudly rides the foam
       Our studding sail booms are carried away
       What care we for that sound
       a living gale is after [us]
       Hurah we're homeward bound

B.

"ROOLING [sic] DOWN TO OLD MOWHEE." William A. Abbe, bark *Atkins Adams* of Fairhaven, 1859. An abbreviated text of only four stanzas, no chorus is indicated but stipulating that the last two lines of each stanza are to be repeated as a refrain, and with interesting variations and a few phrases not encountered elsewhere.

1.   Once more we are waved by the norther gales & bounding oer the main
       And now the hills of the Tropic Isles we soon shall see again
       Five sluggish moons have waxed & waned since from the shore sailed we
       But now we are bound from the Arctic ground—rooling down to old Mowhee

---

[44]   *Heave the lead:* to *take soundings,* i.e., manually to determine the depth of water with a lead weight rigged to a long rope. Samuel Clemens's nom de plume, Mark Twain, derives from the analogous process aboard Mississippi River boats.

[45]   *Diamond Head* is a rock promontory by which Honolulu Harbor is distinguished. Jones & Handy have it right; Piper (who, it seems, actually shipped at Honolulu for his cruise in the *Europa*) confuses the allusion, interpreting it figuratively as if to refer to a geographical feature in the Arctic.

2. Through many a blow of frost & snow & bitter squalls of hail
   Our spars were bent & canvass rent as we braved the northern gale
   The horrid Isles of ice cut ties that deck the Arctic Sea
   Wer many – many leagues astern as we sailed for old Mowhee

3. Through many a gale of snow & hail—our good ship bore away
   And in the midst of the moon beams kiss—she sleeps in St. Lawrence Bay
   Many a day we have whiled away in the wild Kamskatka Sea
   But we'l think of that as we laugh and chat with the girls of Old Mowhee

4. An ample share of toil & car we whalemen undergo
   But when its labor oer what care we how bitter the blast may blow
   We are homeward bound—that joyful sound—and yet it may not be
   When we'l think of that as we laugh & chat With the girls of old Mowhee

Repeat last two lines of every verse —
Wm A Abbe—
Barke Atkins Adams
Dec 25th 1859
Bound for St Felix & Masafuera

C.

"SONG OF SONGS. ROLLING DOWN TO OLD MOHEE." George W. Piper, ship *Europa* of Edgartown, 1868-70. A complete text, more literate than most but somewhat corrupt in the geographical details. Unlike A, it includes a chorus, per Hugill.

1. Once more we are waved by the Northern gale,
   We are bounding o're the main;
   The verdant hues of the tropic gale,
   We soon shall see again.
   Five sluggish months have waxed and waned,
   Since from the shore sailed we;
   But now we are bound from the Arctic sea,
   Rolling down to Old Mohee

Chorus: Rolling down to Old Mohee my boys,
   Rolling down to Old Mohee
   But now we are bound from the Arctic ground
   Rolling down to Old Mohee.

2. Through many a blow of frost and snow,
   And bitter squalls of hail;
   When spars are bent and canvas rent
   We braved the Northern gale.
   The hoary piles of seagirt isle[s],
   That decked the Arctic sea;
   Are many and many a league astern,
   As we sail from [sic] the Old Mohee

3. The Northern winds they do blow strong,
   Old [   ] rolls away
   Or sleeps in the midst where the moon beams kiss,
   On the wide St. Lawrence bay.
   We have toiled our way for many a day
   On the wide Kamshatka sea
   But we think of that and we laugh and chat
   With the girls of Old Mohee.

4. We heave our lead where the diamonds head
   Looms up through the waste of snow,
   Our masts and rigging were covered with ice,
   Our decks were white below.
   The hurricanes on our weather beam
   The breakers on our lee;
   It seemed that the blast as it whistled past,
   Brought tidings of Old Mohee.

5. And now we have reached our destined port,
   No more we'll plough the sea;
   Our cruise is done our anchor's gorn,
   Our head swings in the breeze.
   Our yards are square our decks are clear,
   Now to the shore haste we
   And we'll laugh and sing till the nut groves ring
   On the Isle of Old Mohee

6. Our ample share of toil and care
   We whalemen undergoe;
   But when its o'er we care no more,
   How keen the blast does blow,
   We['re] homeward bound that joyful sound
   But yet that may not be;
   But we'll think of that as we laugh and chat,
   [With the girls of Old Mohee]

7. Now its heartfelt joy without alloy,
   That fills each manly breast;
   And dearer yet far dearer yet,
   Bound home on the far wide sea west.
   We'll tread once more on our native shore,
   The land of the brave and free,
   And we'll think when at home how we used to roam
   On the Isle of Old Mohee

144. No Ke Ano Ahiahi
[Hawaiian Song]

> In this night's watch Jack of Hawaii, our Kanaka bard, chanted to us the song of the Haleakala…
> The more I see of the Kanakas of the Sandwich Islands, the more I am drawn to them…
> —William M. Davis, *Nimrod of the Sea* (1874).

This classic Native Hawaiian ballad is virtually the only specimen of the *hula ku'i* tradition to survive the assimilation and hybridization of Hawaiian culture in the 1870s — a unique jewel, the presence of which in a contemporaneous whaling journal is little less than miraculous. It is the first-person narrative of a Kanaka (Native Hawaiian Islander) who makes a whaling cruise to Alaska in an American ship. Its very existence is remarkable on several counts, not the least of which being that Yankee whaleman George W. Piper was able to record an intelligible text in the Hawaiian language. The song itself is a transitional artifact, a rare textual remnant of an age-old narrative singing-and-dancing tradition that became extinct within a decade of the whaleman's transcription (after the introduction of the ukulele to the Hawaiian Islands in 1874). According to Amy Stillman, the text "retains elements of the original Hawaiian oral narrative conventions" and "stands near the beginning of an acculturated genre of music accompanying the *hula ku'i* which we know was established by the mid 1880s. Although early *hula ku'i* songs were chanted to sparse melodies and little accompaniment, further acculturative processes included addition of [ukulele and] guitar, and melodies conforming more closely to Western temperament and harmonization. Thus, much later nineteenth-century repertory is extant today in both 'traditional' and 'modern' versions. This particular song is unique in being one of the very few *datable* pieces,"[46] and is especially significant for having ascertainably antedated the hybridization of Hawaiian music. The ballad specifically mentions the "island of America" (*maleka 'ailana*) and the "cold of Alaska" (*hau la no alika*), unequivocally indicating a bowhead-whaling cruise to the Western Arctic of the sort for which Hawaiian natives were regularly recruited in substantial numbers at Honolulu, Lahaina, and Hilo. George Piper may have obtained this song from such a Kanaka whaleman, perhaps one of the more than two dozen who signed aboard the *Europa* for seasonal cruises during her sojourn of almost six years in the Pacific (1866-72); or perhaps from someone he met ashore in the Islands — for Piper himself, like the Hawaiians, came aboard in the Pacific when the voyage was already in progress, signing on for seasonal cruises over a period of a year or two, then signing off before the *Europa* returned to Edgartown.[2]

TUNE A - "No ke ano ahiahi," from Amy K. Stillman, Harvard University, Cambridge, Massachusetts, August 1984: learned from tradition in childhood in Hawaii, transcribed after additional research from recordings.

No ke a - no a - hi a - hi ke a — lo — ha la i ka ha - li -'a — li - a -'a - na mai

TUNE B - "No Ke Ano Ahi Ahi," from *Ritual Song: A Hymnal and Service Book for Roman Catholics* (Chicago, [1996] 1998), where it is used as the tune for "Canció n del Cuerpo de Cristo" / "Song of the Body of Christ."

---

[46] Amy K. Stillman, letter to Stuart M. Frank, 23 August 1984. Ms. Stillman, who was also the source of the traditional air, is a native Hawaiian who was working in 1984 as a consultant to the Peabody Museum (now the Peabody Essex Museum) of Salem, Mass., while pursuing doctoral studies in Hawaiian language and literature at Harvard University.

A.

"HAWAIIAN OR SANDWICH ISLANDERS SONG." George W. Piper, ship *Europa* of Edgartown, 1868-70. A fair transcription of Piper's mildly corrupt Hawaiian text copied directly from the manuscript, which consists of 24 lines undifferentiated into stanzas (though divided between stanzas 8 and 9). Initial transcription by Amy K. Stillman. Compare renderings into standard Hawaiian (B1 and B2) and translations into English (C1 and C2).

1　No keano ahihi kealoha la
2　nokohali alia anamai
3　ewikioi epualokeoiai ka hoa iu kane
4　O kou laholo keia ke lu mai ne napea
5　kiai ui neiikahe leu na uiakaeu e ka hae moko
6　Ao le wau epa huana ika pohi
7　holo ika nia kani
8　Ahia hoopau laina kepeii nei ikalu hihau

9　hau ealo e nele kaeu
10　Oiai ka moana lipo li po
11　ewaiho o e a huali ho i mai
12　ekauepa po no na ia
13　eia kana kani mahope
14　Anui kahu wilahepeuiwini
15　kauiliki kaihu ehoi ai
16　ikeia o male ailana
17　Ma he hau la noali ka
18　eka we we ihu o ka moku
19　A o leauepu nia kiu
20　ike kaeua maiakehoa
21　ho mai kaihu wali wali
22　ehoni kiu ili a kui ai
23　ha ina kaino o lohe
24　A o pilikoahu aikeanu

B.

Renderings of the text into standard Hawaiian: by Amy Stillman, Harvard University, 1984 [left];[47] and by Elizabeth Tatar and Patience W. Bacon, Bishop Museum, Honolulu, 1984 (right).[48]

1	No ke ano ahiahi ke aloha ka	No ke ano ahiahi ke aloha la
2	No ka hali'ali'a 'ana mai	No ka hali'ali'a 'ana mai
3	E wiki 'oe [h]e pua loke 'oia i ke hoa 'iu kane	E wiki 'oe [h]e pua loke 'oia i ke hoa 'iu kane
4	'O ko'u la holo keia [la] ke lu mai ne[i] na pe'a	'O ko'u la holo keia [la] le lu mai ne[i] na pe'a
5	Kia'i u'i nei i ka heleu 'iu a ka 'eu a ka hae moki	Ke 'iu nei i ka haleuma ua kau e ka hae mahope
6	'A'ole wau e pa huana i ka pohi	'A'ole wau e pahu ana i ka poki
7	Holo i ka ni'a [nia?] kani	Holo i ka makani
8	Ahia [Ahea?] ho'opau laina ke pi'i nei i ka lu lihau	Ahia [Ahea?] ho'opau laina ke pili nei i ka lihihau

---

[47] "An educated attempt at intelligible Hawaiian... The story is basically a sailor's reminiscence in the manner of a travelogue, describing things such as billowing sails (line 4: *ke lu mai nei na pe'a*), quitting the lines and climbing in the billows (line 8: *ho'opau laina ke pi'i nei*), the wheel spinning as the boat [sic] encounters a storm (line 14: *A niu ka huwila*), and seeing mainland America (line 16: *Maleka 'Ailana*, a Hawaiianization of 'American Island')" (Amy K. Stillman, 23 Aug. 1984).

[48] "We came to the conclusion that the American was given several songs, not just the one we all recognized [as 'No ke ano ahiahi'] which is now a name song for Lunalilo, one of the [Hawaiian] kings... I recognized some phrases from another sailor's song, 'Kuu aloha la, kuu aloha.' Words such as 'Poki' or boat were used in these chants... The American was not consistent in how he spelled the Hawaiian words and I suspect he missed a few words in dictation" (Elizabeth Tatar, letter, Dec. 1984). Ms. Tatar, an ethnomusicologist at the Bishop Museum, indicated that lines 1, 2, 4, 5, 9, 10, 15, 16, 23, and 24 are still sung today.

9	Hau e alo e nele ka'eu	Huli au a hele kaua
10	'Oia ai ka moana lipolipo	Eia ka moana lipolipo
11	E waiho 'oe a huali ho' i mai	E waiho ioe [a huali?] ho'i mai
12	E ka uepa pono na i'a	E kau ka'ea pono la
13	Eia kana kani ma hope	Eia ka makani ma hope
14	A niu ka huwila ke peu 'iwi nei	A nui ka huwila [ke peu?] uwini
15	Kau 'ilik[a]i ka ihu e ho'i ai	Kau aku kaua a ho'i ai [la] e ho'i ai
16	'Ike 'ia 'o Male[ka] 'Ailana	'Iks au Male[ka] 'Ailana
17	Me he hau le no 'Alika	Me ke hau la no 'Alika
18	E ka wewe ihu o ka moku	E kawewe ihu o ka moku
19	'A'ole au e puni a kiu	'A'ole au e puni aku
20	'Ike ka ua mai a ke hoa	'Ike kaua mi ai ke hoa
21	Ho mai ke ihu waliwali	Ho mai ka ihu walwali
22	E honi kiu ili a kui ai	E honi kuwili a kaua
23	Ha'ina ka inoa a lohe	Ha'ina ka inoa a lohe
24	A'o Pilikoahu ai ke anu	A'o Pilikoahu ai ke anu

C.

Partial translation by Elizabeth Tatar and Patience W. Bacon, Bishop Museum, 1984: "It certainly was difficult to decipher... Some of these lines just don't make sense in Hawaiian; lines 3 and 20 stumped us totally." The significant portions that are translated are highly specific text about the Kanaka bard's firsthand experience in bowhead whaling. Text D is perhaps typical of the lesser, generic texts in more recent circulation.

1 For the evening there is love
2 For fondly recollecting
3 [*unintelligible*]
4 This is the day I am sailing away, the sails are unfurled
5 The anchor is lifted [*weighed*] the flag flutters at the stern
6 I will not push the boat
7 Running before the wind
8 When the line [is pulled?] close to the edge of the ice
9 Turn around and let us go
10 There/Here to the deep blue ocean
11 You outside [   ] return
12 ? sea-spray rises well
13 Here the wind behind
14 Big wheel [   ] wind
15 We two go back and return
16 I saw the island of America
17 The cold of Alaska
18 The bow hums in the sea
19 I did not go around thee
20 [*unintelligible*]
21 Turn to me soft nose
22 Let us kiss and embrace
23 This is the name heard
24 Of [Pilikoahu] in the cold

D.

"NO KE ANO AHIAHI." "Modern" translation of a later, analogous text dating from during or after the reign of Lunililo (1873-74); from *The Musicians,* the liner notes enclosed with the 1971 LP recording *Sons of Hawaii*: "An imaginary [sic] trip to the 'island' of America [Alaska]. Lyrics provided by Elizabeth Tatar, ethnomusicologist, Bishop Museum, Honolulu, and graduate student at Harvard University, 1984.*

The evening hours I dearly love
When fond memories come back to me.

This is the day I am sailing away
The sails are being unfurled.

The anchor is lifted now
The flag flutters at the stern.

Turn about and let's set forth
Out to the deep blue sea.

Let us return home now
After seeing the land of America

This is my praise to the Chief
Lunalilo is his name

* The record-album annotator is clearly mistaken that this is an "imaginary" voyage, and his comment is telling evidence of the great extent to which the heritage of Kanaka seamen on American deepwater vessels has faded from Polynesian cultural memory. Such voyages were very common among Native Hawaiians, many of whom actually processed hides on the California coast, went whaling for full seasons in the Alaskan or Siberian Arctic, as well as in the South Pacific, and traveled to distant ports as foremast hands. No fewer than 27 Kanakas are recorded in the crew of Piper's own ship, the *Europa* of Edgartown, making seasonal passages out of Honolulu to the Northern and Southern whaling grounds during 1868-74.

Note on the Text of "No Ke Ano Ahiahi":

It is not clear whether the apparent corruptions and problems of Hawaiian syntax in the whaleman's text are entirely due to the scribe's own errors in transcription. The source of his text was unlikely a seasoned lexicographer or grammarian, and the text probably arrived in his hands corrupt; also, especially given the inability of the translators to account for some of the words and phrases, the text may employ conventions of terminology pertaining to ships and whaling that are now obsolete in Hawaiian—that is, technical terms and allusions that were subsequently "lost" to the Hawaiian language and hence lost to modern philologists. Some of the wording is quite specific and clearly characterizes a whaling voyage. Lines 6 and 7 indicate that the narrator will not be rowing or paddling the "boat" (as he would a Kanaka canoe) because it will be "running" (sailing) by the wind. In Line 12, translated as "sea-spray rises well," one wonders whether this might actually refer to *spray* (as opposed to *sea-spray*) rising well, and is thus perhaps an allusion to the whale's spout, rather than to ocean foam. In Line 14, what is translated as "Big wheel [   ] wind" Amy Stillman interprets to mean that the ship's wheel *spins around* in a storm. Lines 16 and 17 are among the most significant, as *Maleka* refers to "America" and *Alika* to "Alaska," specifically corroborating the origins and destination of the voyage. According to Elizabeth Tatar, the phrase "Let us kiss and embrace" (Line 22) is "From Kalakaua's song, 'Aloha no wau ikou maka, Kou ihu waliwali ka'u i honi' (I love your eyes, your soft nose I kiss)." Line 24 may also be quite revealing, as *Pilikoahu* is evidently the Hawaiian form of some place-name, almost certainly in or adjacent to Alaska and probably the Pribilof Islands, an important whale- and seal-hunting ground in the Bering Sea.

Note on the Significance of "No Ke Ano Ahiahi":

A variety of non-whaling texts of "No ke ano ahiahi" are still in tradition and popular circulation in the Hawaiian Islands, where the *hula ku'i* dance is performed and the song has been collected and recorded: tune B and text D (above) are examples. The introduction of the ukulele to Hawaii in 1874 (shortly after whaleman George Wilbur Piper visited there in the *Europa*) precipitated a revolution in Hawaiian music, creating its own Island genre and virtually obliterating, or at least thoroughly hybridizing much of the pre-existing musical tradition. Supposing the *hula ku'i* tradition to predate the advent of the ukulele, scholars have had no verifiably earlier specimen of a text to place in evidence. The whaleman's manuscript, transcribed in corrupt and somewhat enigmatic, but nevertheless recognizable, authentic Hawaiian, not only demonstrates an earlier provenance of the song than has been documented hitherto, but also illustrates the influence of the Yankee whalers on the Native Hawaiian genre. Despite the difficulties of Piper's text, it is abundantly clear that it is a special case and a unique relic. Allusions to the Alaska coast and Arctic ice vividly and unequivocally indicate its Yankee bowhead-whaling context, for which allusions there can be no other reasonable explanation, and no other version has come to light in which these elements are fully present. In fact, later examples (of which text D is perhaps typical) are bland and unspecific, as though filtered down through many hands until they were several generations removed from the actual event. Such later manifestations, the evolved descendants of the original "No ke ano ahiahi," emerged only after the revolution in Hawaiian music and were "preserved" in an atmosphere where the American whaling presence was no longer influential and Yankee square-riggers had become only a distant memory.

References: Stuart M. Frank, "'No Ke Ano Ahiahi': A 'Lost' Hawaiian Narrative Ballad," *Mains'l Haul: A Journal of Pacific Maritime History* (Maritime Museum of San Diego), 38:3, Summer 2002, pp 22-27. Also: Frank 1985 #165; Frank 2001 #144; Gabby Pahinui and the Sons of Hawaii, liner notes for the LP recordings *Folk Music of Hawaii* (Honolulu: Panini, n.d., #24209) and *Gabby Band Vol. II* (Honolulu: Panini, n.d., #PS 1008); *The Musicians* (liner-notes for the LP recording *Sons of Hawaii*, Honolulu: Island Heritage Panini, 1971, #KN 1001). Other citations refer to private communications from Amy Ku'uleialoha Stillman, at the time a graduate student at Harvard University and an Associate of the Peabody Museum of Salem, Mass., lately Associate Professor of Music and American Culture at the University of Michigan; and Elizabeth Tatar and Patience W. Bacon, Bishop Museum, Honolulu, all in 1984.

CHAPTER FIFTEEN
The Whaleman's Lament
Original Whaling Songs

> I wonder whether these jolly lads bethink them
> of what they are dancing over.
>
> — Old Manx Sailor,
> *Moby Dick,* Ch. 40.

Some whalemen were prodigious writers of original lyrics. As a junior mate aboard a series of Yankee whalers, George Edgar Mills composed a variety of comic songs, love poetry, romantic ballads, short fiction, discursive essays, and even one-act dramas, styling himself in his journals not only "Officer in the United States Merchant Navy" but also Poet, Playwright, and Novelist; he also experimented with different forms of his name and signature — George Edgar Mills, G.E. Mills, G. Edgar Mills — evidently to increase the literary effect. The brothers Rupert G.N. Swift, a whaleman and sea captain, and Clement Nye Swift, an artist-illustrator of some reputation, were the well educated sons of a New Bedford whaling master and scrimshaw maker: singly and collaboratively they authored verse of genuine quality and occasional brilliance. "The Parson's Narrative" [#133] and "The Sailor Boy's Dream" [#230] are imaginative, clever, sophisticated, and complex, the latter particularly so, exhibiting a highly developed control of the narrative voice in a distinctively nautical comic-gothic vein. "Wood and Black-Skin" [#231] is arguably the finest narrative poem about whaling ever written in English, and could only have been composed by an insightful poet and seasoned whaleman. However, unlike George Edgar Mills, "Rupe" Swift seems never to have turned his considerable talents to producing a chronicle-in-verse of his own shipboard experiences, or a even a singable song about the whale hunt. Many lesser saltwater bards did try their hands at such ballads and songs, with varying degrees of success, imparting a personal dimension and whaler's-eye-view of the fishery, and occasionally revealing a glimpse of deep-seated hopes and cherished dreams.

For these sailor-made songs about whaling only a few of the tunes are known. In rare cases the diarist indicates the air to which his ballad is to be sung; in some instances the intended tune, though unstated, is apparent, such as "All the Whales Are Wild and Ugly" [#158], an obvious parody of Stephen Foster's "Old Folks at Home." In others, the tune may be ascertained from textual analogues, such as the pronounced affinities between "One Year in Blubber Hunter" [#145] and "The Limejuice Ship." Still, a handful of tunes remain mysteries.

145. One Year in a Blubber Hunter

[November 1856:] On the night of the 7th while standing watches the fore topsail was torn completely to pieces in a squall, and the following day it was replaced by the main topsail and a new one in its stead. Such is the merry whalemen's life.

> Swiftly through the foaming sea
> Shoots our vessel gallantly
> And yet approaching as she flies
> The Western sun and radiant skies

— Benjamin Franklin Gallup,
bark *South America*, 1856.

"One Year in a Blubber Hunter" was written in 1856 by Benjamin Franklin Gallup of Poquonnock Bridge, Connecticut, a foremast hand in the New Bedford bark *South America*. Like the ballad "The Schooner *Varnum Hill*" [#147] by fellow-whaleman B.F. Rogers, it chronicles some of the men and events of the diarist's own voyage and, unfortunately, was never finished. Another narrative stanza in the same meter, written a few months later, seems to have been intended to augment the original ballad, and has been integrated into the main text as stanza 2. An identical meter and unmistakable similarity of the choruses indicate that "Blubber Hunter" is a cousin of the latter-day British sailor song that Hugill calls "The Limejuice Ship" or "According to the Act"—that is, Gallup's ballad appears to be based on the same unidentified seamen's-discharge song that was later transformed into "Limejuice Ship," which, according to Hugill, was a chantey occasioned by the British Merchant Shipping Act of 1894. Significantly, both of the choruses appear to have been suggested or influenced by "The Old Ship of Zion," an authentic African-American slave spiritual employing a nautical metaphor for salvation. Thus, "Old Ship of Zion" is probably a common ancestor of both "Blubber Hunter" and "Limejuice Ship," which must both descend through an earlier seamen's-discharge song, now apparently extinct.

TUNE - "The Limejuice Ship," learned from Stan Hugill, North Stonington, Connecticut, June 1975; per *Shanties from the Seven Seas,* 1961, p. 58, where text and tune are a composite of versions learned from Hugill's own father, Henry James Hugill, a Royal Navy sailor and Coast Guardsman; and from a shipmate named Arthur Spencer.

"ONE YEAR IN A BLUBBER HUNTER." Benjamin Franklin Gallup, Jr., bark *South America* of New Bedford, 1855-59. As the text is not complete, the last two lines of the final stanza are added from a separate poem written by B.F. Gallup aboard the *South America* around the same time. Stanza 2 is added from a later entry in Gallup's journal.

1. Come all ye young and jolly lads, come listen to my song
   T'is of a blubber hunter which in Bedford does belong,
   T'was in the year of 55 that she from Bedford went,
   And when we had been out a year, we hadn't made a cent.

Chorus: Then come along, come along, then come along I say,
   Come along, my jolly lads, we'll go another way
   And when we've been a season North, with this true and steady barge
   We'll then go into some good port, and get a true discharge.

2. It was one summer morning when my mind was not at ease
   That I picked up my traps[1] and started to sail upon the seas.
   The voyage was long and tedious, as around the world we went
   And when at Bedford we arrived, we did not have a cent[2]

3. We had on board a mixed up crew, as ever went to sea,
   The nations they did number 10, besides the Pourtigee [Portuguese][3]
   Some were white, and some were black, and some to sea were sent
   And some had been to great expense, to our Federal Government[4]

4. Some of the boys did feel all right, and some were very sick
   And some did get an extra rap, and some an extra kick
   And some now I'll tell the honest truth, as I had it told to me
   If you wish to see the elephant,[5] you'd better go to sea

5. The residence of Capt[ain] Glass was the first that we did make
   We came so near of being wrecked it made the Capt[ain] shake
   The boats were lowerd the boys did pull as well as Jaccob Snider
   And when the danger was all past, they had a tot of Cider

6. From thence our bark did speedy go, to the new discovered land
   When Smith he stood upon the beach, and swore he took command
   …

---

[1] *Traps* in the sense of *belongings* or *gear* (Partridge, 907).

[2] As Hohman explains (1928, passim)—and for reasons touched upon in "Address to Young Sailors" [#151], "The Lay System" [#152], and "Landsmen One and All" [#153]—the *lay system,* by which whalemen, rather than receiving regular wages, were theoretically paid a fractional share in the proceeds of the voyage, was rigged against them from the start, and few ever made any money on their first or second voyages (see Frederick Howland Smith's autobiography, headnotes to Chapter 17).

[3] Portuguese-speaking crewmen, black and white, were signed on in large numbers by outward-bound Yankee whalers at land falls in the Azores and Cape Verde Islands. Many of the recruited men returned with their ships to New England and settled there permanently, often bringing their families over later; and more than a few followed the whale fishery from New England to California in the latter decades of the 19th century. See Donald Warrin, *So Ends This Day: The Portuguese in American Whaling, 1765-1927* (New Bedford, 2010).

[4] *great expense, to our Federal Government:* The Yankee whaling fleet was not exactly brimming over with felons and prison escapees—their numbers were probably few—but a whaleship could be a good place to lay low for a couple of years, including for escaped slaves and refugees from European military conscription. Because of the clandestine character of such origins, it is virtually impossible to construct a statistical profile of exactly how many or what proportion of such men served in the fishery.

[5] *See the elephant*: American slang for "see the world," i.e., gain worldly experience (from circa 1840).

146. The *Aurora's* Whaling Song

Though it begins like a ballad, this is actually a kind of love song. It is inscribed by the whaleman-author, third mate George Edgar Mills, to his ladyfriend back home, Mary Frances Hopkins of Milford, New Hampshire. He pined for her the whole time he was at sea, wrote a lot of poetry dedicated to her, and wrote her name several times conjoined with his in his journal. It is perhaps gratifying to know that the couple were later married. The tune is not explicitly indicated, but textual evidence indicates resoundingly that the lyrics are based on "The Coast of Peru" [#136] and they certainly fit the "Coast of Peru" melody.

TUNE: See "The Coast of Peru" [#136].

"THE AURORA'S WHALING SONG." George Edgar Mills, third mate, bark *Aurora* of Westport, Mass., 1858.

1. We came round Cape Horn boys
   To capture sperm whales
   And in catching of which
   There's many tough tales
   But now we are ready
   The voyage to commence
   And when we get all full
   So gaily we'll dance

2. There's many a danger
   that to us will come
   As in search of sperm whales
   The ocean we roam
   But where we may wander
   What e're our luck be
   I'll be to the[e] ever
   What thou art to me

   George E. Mills
   To M. F. H.

Anonymous whaleman's scrimshaw engraving on a sperm whale tooth, circa 1840-60. Kendall Collection, New Bedford Whaling Museum

147. The Schooner *Varnum Hill*

> ... The crew came aboard, surely a motely gang. With the exception of some five or six men most of them had never been to sea before. One particular outstanding personage was a professor of history from some Western state colledge. It may be added here before the voyage was over [he] proved to be an apt pupil. And a great man at an oar. There was also a vaudeville artist who by his constant wit and good nature helped to while away many a dog watch below. They were far above the average class of men picked up to man the general run of whale ships.
>
> — E.C. Sears, manuscript memoirs, schooner *Franklin* of New Bedford, 1889-91.

The Canadian-born whaleman E.C. Sears mentioned his forecastle menagerie only in passing (in the passage quoted above), but Chicagoan Benjamin F. Rogers made it a point to immortalize his shipmates individually in outward-bound verse. Stanza-by-stanza he benignly caricatures each of the members of the crew (stanza 17 is a self-portrait); and while he fails to identify an actual vaudevillian or college professor, he nevertheless manages to make them interesting, ending on a note of homeward-looking optimism and the expectation of future nostalgia. It is a pity that he never completed the ballad, which appears to have been conceived as a chronicle of the voyage itself that evidently never materialized. The lyrics seem to have been inspired by the English broadside ballad "William and Nancy" (which manifests itself as "Lisbon" and "Banks of the Nile," Laws #N-8 and N-9), whereof one version begins:

> 'Twas on a Whitsun Wednesday, the fourteenth day of May,
> We untied our anchor, and so we sailed away,
> Where the sun do shine most glorious, to Lisbon we are bound,
> Where the hills and fields are daintied with pretty maidens round.[6]

and another:

> 'Twas in one summer season, / The twentieth of May,
> That we hoisted up our English colors, / And we did make for sea....[7]

This may provide a clue to the tune, but the many variant airs for "Lisbon" seem too dreary for the *Varnum Hill* ballad; and, with some adjustments, many other melodies in circulation at the time fit equally well—"Oh! Susanna" [#177], "Vilikins and His Dinah" [#81], "Blow Ye Winds" [#139], "The Wearing of the Green" ("The Bonny Blue Flag"), and a host of others.

[UNTITLED.] Song by Benjamin Franklin Rogers, in the journal of Solomon P. Nickerson, schooner *Varnum H. Hill* of Provincetown, Massachusetts, 1863-65.

1. It was the 14th of April
   i remember well the day
   as our gallang little schooner
   lay at anchor in the bay
   our hearts were light and buoyant
   as we striped ourselves for toil
   it is heave up the anchor boys
   and of[f] we go for oil

2. There is manuel and two Johns
   Making three in all
   They are the Valiant Portuegues
   From the island of Fayal
   There wants must be attended to
   By Gleason or else Bill
   For they are the gay Boatsteerers
   of the schooner Varnum Hill

---

[6] Vaughan Williams, 58.

[7] Mackenzie, 35.

3. In speaking of the Portugues
   I thought i'de said enough
   I will mention the young steward
   For he gives us pork and duff[8]
   And soft tack[9] he gives us to[o]
   As much as ere we please
   Oh spare a place in Heaven
   For the blackeyed Portugues

4. There are twelve of us before the mast
   Three have been to sea before
   There is Ebe and Sam and Seaman Jack
   From the Yankee man of war
   And Tom and Jim and Gleason
   Charley George Steve Frank and Bill
   For we are the gallus Bummers[10]
   Of the schooner Varnum Hill

5. First before the mast comes Jack
   From some Southern state[11]
   Before we sailed from Provincetown
   He said he would be mate
   But to talk about such things
   It seames all very nice
   He shipped as able seaman
   And can neither reef nor splice[12]

6. Next comes Sam a Boston chap
   Who is some among the girls
   His hair is black as midnight
   And hangs in graceful curls
   Once before he's been a whaleing
   And cruised round center bay[13]
   He made 12 & 30 cents
   And got the 150 lay

7. Ebe hails from New Hampshire
   And been to the Black Sea
   He also went to China
   Where we get our Hongkong tea[14]
   But when we go to Faialard
   And anchor safe and sound
   we will go ashore together
   And take a drink around

8. The largest man before the mast
   George Kelley he by name
   He fought in Buells army[15]
   And came back home quite lame
   But now he things that Whaleing
   Is more successful than the sword
   And he will fight no longer
   In the army of the Lord

9. There is Bill he is quite a genius
   And from the west he came
   He did not like the country
   And he is much to blame
   He thought he'd be a sailor
   And plough the raging main
   But if he once gets home again
   He will never come again

10. Tome is a mischeavous chap
    He came from Ballyrooe[16]
    He sailed in a packet ship
    From Cork to Liverpool
    He came to America
    Sweet Freedom to enjoy
    He is the spring of shelaiegh
    And the broth of a boy

---

[8] *Duff*: a bread pudding customarily served on shipboard on Sundays. See "Blow Ye Winds" [#139], footnote xx.

[9] *Soft tack*: bread, as opposed to *hardtack* (sea biscuit).

[10] *Gallus*: "frequent pronunciation and occasional spelling of *gallows,* adverb," meaning "very, extremely, from circa 1820... Byron, 'Then your Blowing will wax gallus haughty' (Partridge, 313)." *Bummers*: bums, ne'er-do-wells, loafers.

[11] *Southern state*: The Civil War was going on at the time, and a Yankee whaleship could not have been a very hospitable environment for a Confederate sympathizer; on the other hand, the whale fishery was a common refuge for dissidents and draft evaders on both sides of the conflict.

[12] *Reefing sail* and *splicing line* (rope) were two of the skills required for an Able Bodied Seaman's rating; another was *boxing the compass*. See "Blow Ye Winds" [#139], fn.

[13] *Center Bay:* not identified; presumably a whalers' local place-name.

[14] The China trade, in which American merchants had been active and prosperous since shortly after the Revolution, and in which the Americans had made significant advances during the Clipper Ship era of the 1850s, was increasingly dominated by Britain in the 1860s when the United States was preoccupied with the Civil War. Hong Kong was one of the four so-called Treaty Ports—Chinese ports-of-entry that were open to limited foreign trade before the Opium War. The others were Canton, Shanghai, and Macao.

[15] Don Carlos Buell (1818-1898) was a Union brigadier and major general early in the Civil War, later relieved of command after his failure to monopolize upon a rout of Confederate forces at Perryville (October 1862); resigned from the Army 1864.

[16] *Ballyrooe*: As a prefix in Irish Gaelic place-names, *Bally* (*Bala* in Welsh Gaelic) signifies *town* or *village*. *Ballyrooe* could refer to any of several hamlets of similar name in the west of Ireland.

11. Next in rhyme comes Jimmy
    He is one of the boys
    He plays with Stephens Windmill
    And various other toys
    He worked in a glass house
    But did not learn to Blow
    He came from that happy land
    Called Canida & Oh[17]

12. How are you gay young Gleason
    All the way from York
    Oh what a mug he has boys
    For stowing beef and pork
    And when it is his watch on deck
    Against the windlass he will sit
    And as often as he falls asleep
    As often he gets wet

13. How are you next little Frank
    Some sixteen years of age[18]
    He is the smallest boy aboard
    His surname it is Page
    He draws water for the steward
    For he has to clean no craft[19]
    He gets the cakes and puddings
    The steward brings from aft

14. There is Steve the Nova Scotian
    He can eat his weight in sails
    He blows about Victoria
    Likewise the Prince of Wales
    He grumbles continually
    From morning untill he is asleep
    He is the shape of a dolphin
    And has scales upon his feet

15. The last in line comes Charley
    But though he is not least
    He has three hairs upon his head
    And comes from way down east[20]
    He thought he'd be a soldier
    And go down to Bull Run[21]
    And when he returned again
    Twas with two fingers and a thumb

16. I must not forget the Cook
    If he is so very slow
    He gives us soft tack every day
    And that is mostly dough
    He has a lively little gait
    About as fast i think
    As a Mississippi Crockodile
    Going down to drink

17. Now comes your humble servant
    B Frank Rogers you all know
    His fighting weight is 7 stone 10
    And he came from Chicargo[22]
    And when the Voyage is over
    to the westward he will steer
    And never go so far again
    From Whisky and Lager beer

18. And when we all return again
    To drift on the sea of Life
    Or each has settled down
    And taken to himself a wife
    And when the final day arrives
    We will blow to Heavens high will
    Memory will bring back the hours
    Spent on the schooner Varnum Hill

---

[17] This is an allusion to an important broadside ballad known as "Canaday-I-O" (Laws #C-17), which was much in circulation among lumberjacks in New England, the Maritime Provinces, and eventually the Upper Midwest and the Pacific Northwest. It depicts Canada as anything but a "happy land": akin to the Seamen's Lament and Sailor's Complaint species of shipboard song, it complains about rotten food, hard conditions, inclement weather, and ill treatment in the logging camps.

[18] Sixteen is not atypically young for a lad on a whaleship or even in the Navy. Many were younger, some only twelve or thirteen years old when they shipped out.

[19] *Craft:* short for iron *whalecraft:* harpoons, lances, bone spades, flensing knives, etc., for hunting, butchering, and processing whales.

[20] *Down East* can have various contexts within or without New England and the Maritime Provinces of Canada. In this context it refers specifically to Maine.

[21] *Bull Run,* a small river in eastern Virginia, gives its name to two Civil War battles, both Confederate victories, in July 1861 (under General P.G.T. Beauregard) and August 1862 (under Robert E. Lee). The battles are also known as First and Second Manassas. Symbolic of the Union loss (and perhaps of the as-yet-undetermined outcome of the war itself) is that Charley, the veteran described here. lost at least a couple of fingers in the battle.

[22] It is ironic that the whaleman-scribe misspells the name of his own hometown, as though it were pronounced with a New England accent.

148. Stanzas from the *Mermaid*

These verse vignettes were inscribed in an anonymous journal of three whaling voyages in the bark *Mermaid* of New Bedford during 1883-90. They are widely distributed throughout the manuscript and it is presumed that some are intended to be sung to the air of "Blow Ye Winds" [#139] and others to "Auld Lang Syne." Some are fictitiously or pseudonymously signed.

When we've but little money
and that is all gone
We will jump on board a whaling bark
bound around Cape Horn

When we have but little money
and that we have is gone
We will jump on board a whaling bark
bound around Cape Horn

Oh now we are homeward bound, my boys
And we have done our sailing
We will drink success to every lass
And d———m & bugered whaling

E.P.Q.

We will sing the song of Auld Lang Syne
When we get on shore
We will spend our money with the girls
But a whaling go no more

Our anchor's dropt the sails are furled
On Bedford wharf we stand
With much delight we view the past
No more spouting band.

Next came the sound to Port we are bound
With a stock of education
Where liberty Men both Now and then
Bring trouble and vexation

Old Commodore

We had a fiddler on board
N. Durfee was his name
He used to keep us well supplied
With Musick on the brain

Next he got [a] Cornet
to match with that above
And any one would think,
the ship was in a fog

B. Morrison

149. On a Passage to the Crozet Islands

This is one of several amateurish whaling ballads written by boatsteerer Richard C. Reynolds of Nantucket aboard the New Bedford ship *Janus* in the early 1840s. It is not clear what tune or tunes he may have had in mind for any of them, but they are unmistakably the products of a seasoned whaleman, in this case one who grew up in the wholly whaling-oriented atmosphere of Nantucket. As the title implies, the lyrics here chronicle the outward passage from New Bedford to the Crozet Islands whaling grounds in the southern Indian Ocean, including a disappointing sojourn in the frigid waters of High Latitudes South—the actual route taken by the *Janus*. There are a pronounced chronological and thematic redundancy and a decided paucity of literary art in Reynolds's ballads—in addition to atrocious spelling and poor syntax—but these are partly compensated by the young whaleman's sincerity and authoritative authenticity. "Cape Horn" [#150], extolling the virtues of his ship and providing a kind of sequel to the Crozet piece, is even more reserved in its criticism of the whale fishery than "On a Passage to the Crozets"; however, his other compositions — "Address to Young Sailors" [#151], "The Lay System" [#152], and "Landsmen One and All" [#153] — constitute a veteran whaleman's embittered cautions to young would-be mariners, landlubbers, and women ashore.

"ON A PASSAGE TO THE CROZETTS ISLANDS." Richard C. Reynolds, boatsteerer, ship *Janus* of New Bedford, 1842-44.

1. In the month of october on the 22 day
   Weigh our anchor to leave buzards Bay[23]
   With thoughts in my head how long it may be
   Before my native land again I shall see

2. We then spread our canvas with a head wind
   To leave all our friends and [ ] truelove behind
   Dismal it looked as we sailed in the wind
   And leaving behind my own native land

3. Torents of rain quickly did come
   Which made every man wish himself at home
   But repenting the day it was to[o] late then
   For far over the ocean our ship she does swim

4. The pleasures of a new ship to[o] I will relate
   You begin in the morning no rest untill night
   It will so keep you goin for months 2 or 3
   So now you may know what pleasure their be

5. We stopped to St gago[24] their to recruite
   With hogs and oranges and other kinds of fruit
   Likewise a native we took from of[f] their
   To go in the ship our company to have

---

[23] *Buzzards Bay* is an inlet of the Atlantic Ocean in southeastern Massachusetts, adjacent to Vineyard Sound and forming the estuary of the Acushnet River, on which the whaling ports of New Bedford and Fairhaven are situated.

[24] *St. Jago* (São Tiago): one of the Cape Verde Islands, at the time a Portuguese colony. The port of Praia was a frequent calling place for outward-bound Yankee whalers, and recruiting provisions and signing-on of locals to fill vacancies in the crew was a common practice here and was perhaps even more common on the Cape Verde island of Brava.

6. We then squared our yards on our passage procede
   And with a strong breese go with great speede
   No ships that we meet with can hold us any play
   We run by them all and go on our own way

7. On the western ground the first wright whale we see
   We came into contact with him only in the day
   Soon killed the monster and brought him alongside
   He a hundred barrels made us and some gallons besides

8. Instead of stopping their some more for to get
   We squaired in our yards and bore for the Crozettes
   So onward we proceded in our litle barge
   Saying now we will go whear the whales they [are] large

9. But when we cam their that desolate hole
   Their was plenty of rain and the weather was Cold
   No whales to be seen only once in a while one
   Which would go to windward[25] like a ball from a gun

10. It is but a short time that we can stay hear
    For seeing no whales our captain is in fear
    Our ship she is costly so new and so gay
    No oil a getting and the time roling away

11. Now we must start for a more desolate place
    Wheare their is hail and snow and islands of ice
    Besides the wind in gales it does blow
    For ten or twelve days you must heave your ship to

12. Our captain aloft and this he will say
    Every man be readdy the boats clear away
    The thoughts of getting wet if you fasten to a whale
    Dose make us all shiver but nothing can prevail

13. Our boats they are down readdy for the chase
    After a long pull probearly get fast
    Then he will run to the windward eyes out
    Every man in the nation trying to trim boat

14. I am now about ending my rime
    And this as true as the stars they do shine
    You that donte believe it try it and see
    And if you donte find it so call and see me

Richard C. Reynolds

---

[25] If a whale swims off into the wind, pursuit becomes difficult or impossible.

150. Cape Horn

This original little ballad by boatsteerer Richard C. Reynolds bespeaks the pride he took in his ship, the *Janus*—notwithstanding that, as most of his other ballads relate, he was fed up with whaling and retired from the fishery as soon as he returned to New Bedford in the *Janus*.

"CAPE HORN." Richard C. Reynolds, boatsteerer, ship *Janus* of New Bedford, 1842-44. Regularized from inconsistent division into lines and stanzas in the MS.

1. O now we have doubled cape horn my boys
   And the cold weather has now all past
   The wind is on our quarter boys
   We known not how long it will last

2. And we have got as fine a ship
   as crosses ore the seas
   And all that she requires
   it is a pleasant breese

3. For she is long legged
   and quick uppon the heal
   For she will run ten [k]nots and hour
   with a good man at the wheel

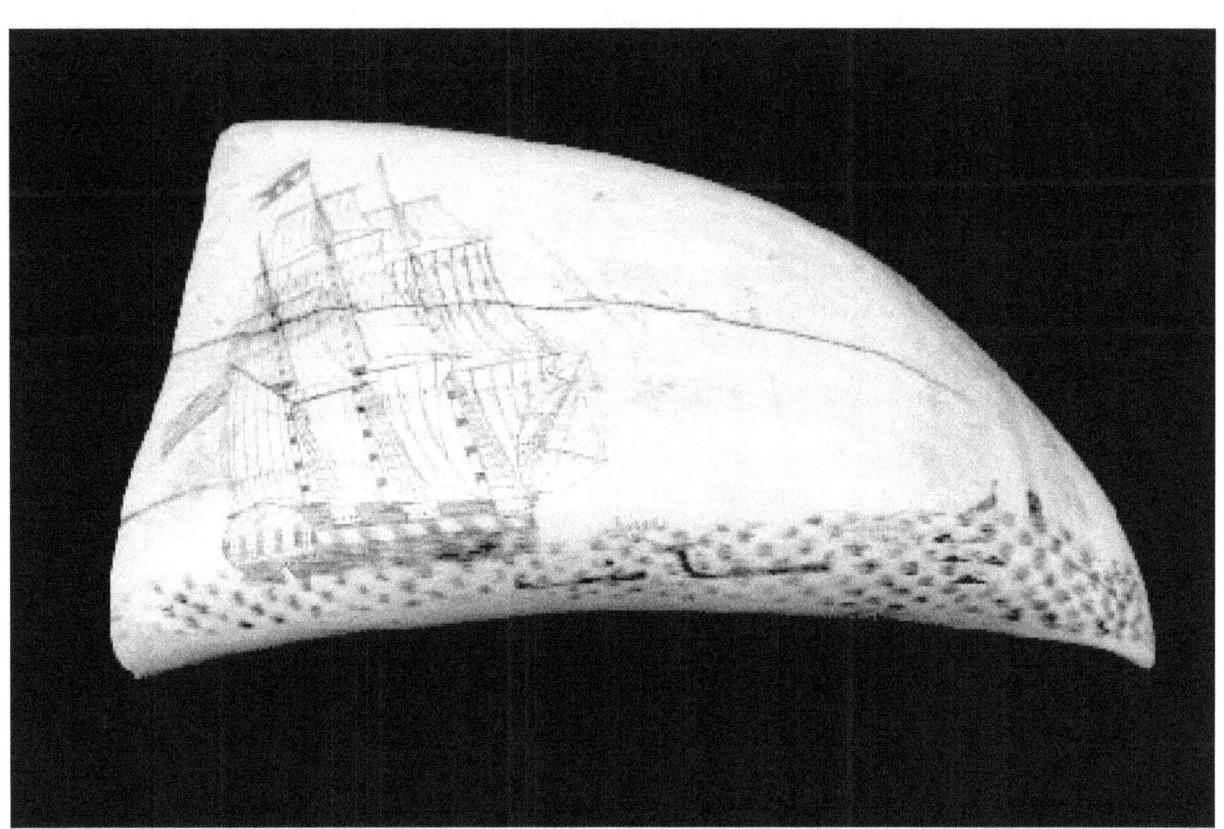

Whaleship underway, Anonymously engraved scrimshaw on a sperm whale tooth, depicting a ship the whaling grounds with boats lowered. The ship portrait is actually based upon an image of a warship on an engraved official document. American, mid 19th century. Kendall Collection, New Bedford Whaling Museum.

151. Address to Young Sailors

Richard C. Reynolds will not be winning any posthumous literary awards for the come-all-ye stanzas he composed as a seasoned boatsteerer aboard the New Bedford ship *Janus* in the 1840s; nor are most of his lyrics sufficiently complete to be considered actual full-scale ballads, though they were undoubtedly intended as ballads and are in many respects ballad-like. However, his crudely-wrought fragments resonate with the age-old tradition of Seamen's Complaints about the exploitation of mariners, warning would-be sailors against the dangers and deprivations of life at sea and against the usurious practices of landsharks ashore. What the author lacks in polish he makes up in credibility, and though the poetry is not beautiful the sentiments are legitimate.

"ADRES TO YOUNG SAILORS." Richard C. Reynolds, boatsteerer, ship *Janus* of New Bedford, 1842-44. Basically compatible with "The Croppy Boy" (the air for "Lady Franklin's Lament" [#67]), which was extremely well known at the time and is suitably elastic to accommodate the irregular meter here.

1. Come now brother sailors a warning take
   I would have you quit rambling and the seas forsake
   If you donte you will be ondone
   And curse the day you first began

2. I have followed it for several years
   Its often filled my eyes with tears
   I have often said when I returned again
   That [I] would quite forsake the main

3. But hear i am now caught again
   And for tow years or mire i must remain
   A catching whales it is my toil
   For New Bedford onyrs [owners] to have the oil

4. In doing this it is no fun
   For in a hundred barrels i have nary one
   I do not think that this is right
   For we must shurely work day and night

5. To think of this it does me greive
   By cheating sailors they do live
   They are not satisfied with their one
   But take it all and leave me none

6. The janus is the ship that I am now in
   As fine a little ship as dose on the ocean swim
   Our mate will call jack crosstrese
   He is always a yelling when it blows a heavy breese

7. As I am now to end my yarn
   The weather grows cold insted of warm
   I hope you will look before you leap
   And see what dangers poor sailors escap

152. The Lay System

This short ballad by boatsteerer Richard Reynolds, untitled in the manuscript, together with another untitled set of lyrics ["Landsmen One and All," #153], constitute at the same time a kind of parallel and a series of sequels to his "Address to Young Sailors" [#151]. All of them are spoken in the voice of a veteran whaleman, and all of them caution how sailors are shortchanged and victimized by the agents and owners. "The Lay System," localized to New Bedford and to his ship, the *Janus,* emphasizes the financial coercion by which otherwise happy seamen are ensnared. It is particularly notable for its specific mention of the *dead horse,* the sailors' burden of debt from having received at the outset of the voyage an advance against future pay [see "Old Horse," #48]; and the so-called *lay system* by which whalemen, in lieu of wages, theoretically receive a predetermined fractional share of the profits of the voyage, in this case a 1/200th "lay." An extremely rare, possibly unique feature is that it enumerates (in stanza 4) some of the hidden fees and expenses that are customarily charged by the owners against the sailors' puny share in the profits, by which, Reynolds contends, the owners and agents provide themselves still another opportunity to cheat sailors out of their rightful earnings.

[UNTITLED.] Richard C. Reynolds, boatsteerer, ship *Janus* of New Bedford, 1842-44. To the degree that it is regular, the meter is compatible with the air for "The Sailor's Alphabet" [#44]; and with "Derry Down" and other airs used for "The Dreadnought" [#36].

1. Come all my jolly Sailors wough ever you be
   I will sing you a song uppon the high sea
   On board of the janus wheare singing is free
   The sailors are happy on land or at Sea

2. All you that are to New Bedford a stranger
   Look out very sharp or you will fall into danger
   Fine yarns they will tell and lead you astray
   And then ship you of[f] your debts for to pay

3. A small sum when you start you have to pay
   But a dead horse[26] is a drug on the 200 hundredth lay[27]
   It will so encrease while you are gorn
   When you return their will be ten to one

4. Tis wharfage gauges pilotage and all
   And when you do settle things they will have it all
   They will then say this is the first voyage
   Go again my lad and keep up good courage

---

[26] *Dead Horse* is sailor lingo for the indebtedness incurred by accepting an advance against future wages, to pay for outfitting expenses and lodgings ashore until sailing day. One month's wages was customary in the merchant service, but in the American whale fishery, where each seaman was paid a share in the net proceeds of the voyage, amounts varied; moreover, were the hapless neophyte recruited by a *crimp* (a recruiting agent or boardinghouse master who received a fee for each man signed to a particular ship), the fee paid to the crimp was customarily levied against the sailor before the final settling-up was concluded at voyage's end. See "Old Horse," #48.

[27] *Lay* refers to the fractional share of the profits of a voyage to be paid to each member of a ship's company. The *lay system* descends from medieval Viking-era practices and has its direct ancestry in the Colonial epoch, in which New England and Long Island shore whaling was essentially a communal enterprise with each participant sharing equally in the proceeds. American whalemen, instead of receiving set wages (as did mariners in the merchant and naval services), signed articles in advance of the voyage to be paid a predetermined fraction of the net proceeds of the voyage, but only after certain expenses of outfitting, port visits, and the various other charges Reynolds enumerates—and after the owners' half of the proceeds—had been deducted.

153. Landsmen One and All

In this fragmented text, untitled in the manuscript, boatsteerer Richard Reynolds somewhat awkwardly anticipates a better ballad called "The Whaleman's Lament" [#154], which was transcribed by someone else on another ship at least a dozen years later. This earlier piece exhibits most of the distinguishing features of the later one, including the narrator's presumption of his hypothetical listener's reluctance to appreciate the veracity of his account ("you may think it's a lie but I'll ensure you it's true"); the warning to stay ashore rather than "venture your life on the sea"; and a final stanza qualified by the cautionary "if ever I return again." However, Reynolds's lament has a different meter and cannot be merely another form of the same ballad. In another entry in the same journal, the whaleman extends his warning to the folks on shore, cautioning landsmen who may be contemplating a voyage and women who might be tempted to fancy a sailor (text B). Such warnings to women that stereotype sailors as "a wild and roving set" are typical of the broadside genre, but the words are usually mouthed by a woman scorned or a woman betrayed. Here, they are the confidences of a seasoned boatsteerer, as weary of his shipmates as he is of the whaling life. In the absence of any title, one is adopted from the opening stanza of this second set of lyrics.

[UNTITLED.] Richard C. Reynolds, boatsteerer, ship *Janus* of New Bedford, 1842-44.

A.

1. O come all my young Seamen whough ever you be
   May this be a warning to you tis to me
   Never to venture your life on the sea
   But stay on the land where liberty is free

2. For heare in bondage for years two or three
   And nothing but troubles and trials to see
   The hard squalls and raine that you must beat through
   You may think it a lie but I ll enshure you its true

3. If ever I return back to the land that is free
   I am in hopes that it will be a warning to me
   When I think of the dangers that I have escaped
   But now I am safe landed in the united States

B.

1. Lan[d]smen one and all wough ever you be
   Do not venture your life uppon the high sea
   This is a warning to all that is young
   And to save your life you should better be hung

2. For Sailors they are a wild & roveing set
   They often do promis but soon do forget
   So girls I advise you never to wed
   With a jolly young sailor they are not the lad

154. The Whaleman's Lament

Seamen's Complaint ballads trace back at least to the Tudor navy, and numerous examples survive from the naval and merchant services of the three ensuing centuries. Reformist zeal and an increasingly Dickenisan appreciation of the plight of the labor force in the 19th century notwithstanding, the Industrial Revolution did little to alleviate and evidently much to compound tendencies to depersonalize ship's crews and treat them with cruelty.

In 1825, and again in 1835, laws were passed which sought to protect seamen from their own officers. Under certain circumstances fines and imprisonment were provided for assault, beating, wounding, the infliction of "any cruel and unusual punishment," and forcing ashore or leaving a seaman in a foreign country. In 1850 the culmination of a long period of agitation was marked by writing into the statutes a single sentence: "Flogging on board vessels of commerce is hereby abolished."[28]

A quarrel between two of the men resulted in Antonio, a Portuguese, drawing a knife on his shipmate .... The second mate reported the row to the supreme authority, and the fiery Antonio was summoned to the quarter-deck to answer. His offense was serious; it was shown that he meant mischief, and we could not seriously demur when we saw him lashed to the weather main-rigging, and his yellow back exposed to the rope's-end. But however much we condemned Antonio's act, when we saw and heard the rope's-end cut the writhing flesh, and heard the man's moaning supplication to "Santa Marie" and "Jesu Christo," we forgot it. Very serious thoughts occupied my mind as I looked on the cruel scene; and for the first time in the voyage the life became horrible and hateful to me. [circa 1835][29]

Jack's wrists were lashed to a ratlin on the starboard side, and Bully's to a ratlin on the larboard. The captain then provided himself with a piece of tarred ratlin, and, standing up to Bully, bared the man's back.
"Remember, now, this is for fighting."
"Oh, for God's sake, don't flog me, captain!" said Bully, sensible of the degradation of the punishment about to be inflicted on him.
"Not a word!" said the captain, whose blood was boiling with passion. Take that! and that! and that! Do you feel it? Will you fight again?" Poor Bully groaned and writhed with agony. Each stripe of the ratlin raised a blood-red mark on his back.
"I'll show you how to fight!" roared the captain, swinging the ratlin over his shoulder, and raising the stripes with every blow. "I'll make an example of you! Take a warning, all of you. You see what you get for fighting. If that ain't enough, I'll lay it on heavier next time. I'll skin your back worse than that! Cut him down now! See if he'll behave himself!"
Jack's turn came next. At the first stroke he yelled with all his might.
"Oh Lord, captain! Oh, for God's sake! Oh, don't flog me! I'll never fight again!"
"I'll take care you won't. If you do, I'll lay you up for a month. Your back's been itching for a flogging. Now take it! Take that! take that! Yes, you feel it, don't you? Cut him down, Mr. D—."
[circa 1842][30]

There were probably many happy ships — see, for example, the circumstances surrounding "A Voyage on New Holland" [#161] aboard the bark *Kathleen* [Chapter 16] — but mistreatment of sailors was common, no less aboard whalers than elsewhere at sea. In fact, accountability of officers in the whale fishery appears actually to have been even less than in the navy or merchant service, and avenues of redress for seamen even fewer. Ship owners and consular authorities are not renowned for having taken the sailors' part in complaints lodged against their officers, and few cases of brutality aboard whaleships were ever prosecuted in a court of law.

---

[28] Elmo P. Hohman, *The American Whaleman*, 1928, p. 75.

[29] William M. Davis, ship *Chelsea* of New London, 1834-38, as recounted in *Nimrod of the Sea*, New York, 1874, 198f.

[30] J. Ross Browne, ship *Bruce* of Fairhaven, 1842-43, as narrated in *Etchings of a Whaling Cruise*, New York, 1846, 222f.

"The Whaleman's Lament" is a firsthand indictment of whaling, emphasizing brutality on board and culminating in an articulate formulation of the age-old sailors' resolve to go seafaring no more. The journal of Nantucketer Benjamin A. Coffin is the only place it has been found. When Huntington published this same text he garbled the lyrics, neglected to identify the journal keeper (who may have been the original author), and failed to identify the tune, which may not be indigenous to the song. However, the text and tune as printed were taken up by A.L. Lloyd and a host of others, and have become inseparable in revival; thus, in the absence of any better candidate for a melody, Huntington's choice is the one given here.

TUNE generally after Huntington 1964, 15ff, where the tune is not identified; per the singing of Ellen Cohn, New Haven, Conn.; Mary Malloy & Stuart Frank, Sharon and Foxborough, Mass. (various performances preserved in the Mystic Seaport Museum and Kendall Collection audio archives); also Lloyd 1967, etc.

THE WHALEMANS LAMENT. Benjamin A. Coffin, bark *Catalpa* of New Bedford, 1856-57; and ship *James Loper* of Nantucket, 1857-60 [Nicholson Collection, Providence (R.I.) Public Library]. Verbatim from the original MS, correcting numerous errors and various unaccountable changes made by Huntington, who evidently tried to smooth out the text for singing, but in so doing unwisely corrupted the 19th-century syntax and true nautical flavor of the original lyrics. (For example, in stanza 4, line 3, where Huntington has *"So do it now or damn your eyes / I will flog you till you're blue"*: the manuscript is actually quite clear here, and the whaleman's syntax is better and certainly more authentic than Huntington's: *"O do it now or dam[n] your eyes I will flog you till you do."* On the other hand, in the manuscript, line 3 of stanza 5 is flawed: Huntington's serviceable rendition is "I will stay at home [contented] and I will roam no more.")

1. It was on the Briny ocean in a whailship I did go
   oft times I thought of distant friends oft times I thought of home
   Remembering of my youthful days it grieves my heart full sore
   and fain would I Return again to my own Native Shore

2. Though Dreary discontented then I then resolved to Rome [roam]
   to try my fortune on the sea to ease me of my woe
   I shipped onboard of a Whale ship to sail without delay
   to the pacific ocean their for a while to stay

3. Through dreary storms and tempest and t[h]rough some heavy gales
   around cape horn we ste[e]red our way to look out for spirm whales
   the[y] will rob you the[y] will use you worse than [any] slaves
   before you go a whaling boys you best within your graves

4. They will flog you for the least offence and that is frequent to[o]
   and the best that you get from them is plenty of work to do
   O do it now or dam your eyes I will flog you till you do
   my Boys I would [not] say it all But it is all to[o] true

5. but if ever I Return again a solemn vow I will take
   that I will never go a Whailing my liberty [to] stake
   I will stay at home [contented] And [I will] Rome no more
   For pleasures are but fiew my Boys [far] from our native shore

155. I and Betty Martin
[My Eye and Betty Martin; Hey, Betty Martin]

This comic-ironic whaling song recounts (as a first-person narrative) the proverbial injustices suffered at the hands of New Bedford chandlers and outfitters, this ballad is a clever reworking of a comic Yorkshire-dialect song, "My Eye and Betty Martin":

> In Yorkshire I wur born and bred,
> And knows a thing or two, sir,
> Nay, what be more, my father said,
> My wit would bring me through, sir;
> At single stick or kiss the maids,
> I wur the boy vor sartin,
> Zays I, push on, to be afraid's
> My eye and Betty Martin.

The whaleman's parody is as interesting for its language as for its whaling lore. Indigenous to the fishery and highly localized to New Bedford, it combines the technical syntax of whalers' occupational songs with the subterfuge of the music-hall genre (especially evident in the refrain), monopolizing upon indirectness and even duplicity of phrasing. The narrator signs articles to go on a whaling voyage, goes "down to Old Seabery's shop" to obtain "a tall fit out," and only later, at sea, discovers that he has been cheated and rags substituted for the new clothing he thought he had purchased. He laments that "the biggest part" of his wages will now have to go for clothing, and vows vengeance: "I will go and smash old rascal Seabery / When I get back from whaling."

The song's interest is both substantive and literary. Secondhand deceptions of land sharks in sailortowns the world over are legion, but this ballad constitutes a rare firsthand recitation by a Yankee whaleman. Cast in the role of villain is Otis Seabury, a highly visible Union Street retail merchant and partner in O. & E.W. Seabury, who were shareholders in whaling vessels (not to be confused with his more famous kinsman and co-owner of some of the same vessels, Captain Humphrey W. Seabury, who, after his retirement in 1861, was a major figure in New Bedford business and banking circles). Equally compelling for its literary value is that, even more than the original "My Eye and Betty Martin," the refrain of the whaleman's text turns on a series of puns and slang expressions that reinforce the theme of deception and duplicity, the understanding of which requires winking participation in the joke (and it must be understood that obsolete slang terms that require etymological exegesis today were common parlance that anyone would likely have understood in the whaleman-scribe's era). *My eye and Betty Martin* was a common 19th-century slang expression meaning *Nonsense!* (the shortened form *My eye!* is the more prevalent 20th-century remnant).[31] In the whaleman's hands, this becomes a pun, *I and Betty Martin;* and to this he adds *Oke Walker!,* another slang expression of the era with much the same meaning: "*Walker!* originally and properly *Hock(e)y Walker!* 'Signifying that the story is not true, or that the thing will not occur,' *Lexicon Balatronicom,* 1811" (Partridge, 1305). In the whaleman's song, *Oke Walker* may additionally be contrived as a secondary pun, as if to say "Okay, Walker," with *Walker* literally signifying a *walker* (*landlubber*) as opposed to a *sailor.* Through these various subversions of "My Eye and Betty Martin," the whaleman's song incorporates the expletives into the meaning of the narrative, and increases the dramatic effect of the double entendre. In this song the phrase "my eye and Betty Martin" is no longer the superfluous non sequitur it is in

---

[31] Partridge gives the definition as "Nonsense!": *all my eye* is "perhaps the earliest form (Goldsmith has it in 1768)"; *that's my eye, Betty Martin* was "already familiar in 1765"; and the *my eye* part (suggesting the form and its derivatives in use today) is possibly derived from the French *mon oeil!* But he disparages as "too ingenuous" the derivation of the expression as a corruption of *Oh, mihi, beate Martine,* claiming "the *Betty Martin* part... remains a mystery. It is, however, interesting to note that Moore the poet has, in 1819, *all my eye, Betty,* and Poole, in *Hamlet Travesties,* 1811, has *all that's my eye and Tommy... .*"

the Yorkshire prototype, or in such minstrelsy parodies current in the 1860s as "Milly Martin,"[32] where ugly racial stereotypes run rampant and the original meaning of the catch-phrase "my eye and Betty Martin" seems to have been lost, replaced by "Like lubly Milly Martin."

TUNE - "Hey, Betty Martin, Tip Toe Fine," per Edward Arthur Dolph, *"Sound Off!,"* 1942, p. 437: "The fifers and drummers frequently played this tune during the War of 1812"; the text is "In Yorkshire I was born and bred...."

"WHALING SONG." George W. Piper, ship *Europa* of Edgartown, 1868-70. Lines regularized to compensate inconsistent transcription in the MS. Requires some adaptation to fit the tune.

1. In New Bedford I got on a lark, I shipped myself on board of a bark
   For to plough the waters dark and go on a voyage a whaling

   Chorus: Oke Walker
   Done me up for sartin[33]
   Does your mither[34] know you are out
   Sure I and Betty Martin

2. I went down to Old Seabery's shop and there I got a tall fit out
   I never knew what I had got, untill I went a whaling

3. One day I overhauled my store I found two shirts worn out and tore
   And Scotch cap and a few things more with me to go a whaling

4. My heart strings broke I gave a start, The blood it curdles in my heart
   For to think my bill is the biggest part[35] When I get home from whaling

5. But now I am far out to sea I am obliged to let this gum game
   But I will go and smash old rascal Seabury When I get back from whaling

---

[32] "Milly Martin" (words by G.S. Lee, music by G. Swaine Buckley, sung by Buckley's Seranaders, circa 1863).

[33] *Sartin:* Scots, Northumbrian, and Yorkshire dialect for *certain.*

[34] *Mither:* Scots, Northumbrian, and Yorkshire dialect for *mother.*

[35] That is, the biggest part of the debt incurred by a whaleman against an advance made by the owners prior to sailing. See "Old Horse" [#48] and "The Lay System" [#152].

156. Indian Ocean Whaling Song

This original ballad recounts the deprivations, inconveniences, and shortages—many of them having to do with food—to which the Yankee whaleman was subjected, replete with vernacular sailor jargon and specific references to the geography of the so-called New Holland whaling grounds, including Amsterdam Island, Desolation Island (the nearest land mass to Antarctica), and Rottenest Island, all in the Indian Ocean; Roti Bay ("Rotter Bay"), near Timor, in the East Indies; and Fremantle, Western Australia, the principal whalemen's port-of-call in the region [see "A Voyage on New Holland," #161]. The song may or may not be indigenous to the voyage on which it was transcribed, but is localized to the ship *Europa* and her home port of Edgartown, Marthas Vineyard. Like the "Bowhead Whaling Song" [#157] and "Blow Ye Winds" [#139], of which the same whaleman-scribe also made comprehensive transcriptions, the narration here is more than incidentally concerned with whalemen's woes suffered at the hands of his employers. The distinctive chorus seems to be derivative and may have been inspired by "My Eye and Betty Martin," or by the whaleman's variant "I and Betty Martin" [#155, from the same manuscript source], which analogy is likely the best clue to the air (not found).

"WHALING SONG." George W. Piper, ship *Europa* of Edgartown, 1868-70. Stanzas regularized.

1. Come lads and listen to me,
   I will sing you a song for company
   About a devilish high old spree
   I had upon a voyage a whaling
   I shipped in a place called Edgartown
   Somewhere in the Vineyard Sound
   And I assure you it cost me many a pound
   before to home I got around

Chorus: Scraping, scrubbing all the day,
   Always to work, and never to play
   And if you say a word the devil is to pay,
   When you go a voyage a whaling

2. They gave me a box within some clothes,
   A pair of shoes and two or three hoes
   And two or three pipes for to warm my nose
   And sent me off a whaling
   I signed the articles to work,
   up to my middle in grease and dirt
   And something else that ain't so neat
   for to live three years on stinking beef

3. To Desolation's weary hole,
   where the water is wet and the weather is cold
   For to get some oil to put in our hold
   We went on a voyage a whaling
   We found that we had got there betimes,
   but found that we were short of line
   So then we all made up our minds
   for to give it up and go it blind

4. We beat about through storms and calms,
and arrived at a place called Amsterdam
For to go a fishing was our plan
Which was one of our cruises a whaling
The Captain, the old hoggish elf,
kept all the best fish for himself
And fed us the rest both salt and fresh
till the very bones stuck out of our flesh

5. We found that our grub was getting short
They said we ate more than we ought[36]
So we squared away to make a port
Which spoiled our cruise a whaling
We went to a place called Rotter Bay
Where after sounding we made our way
So we came to anchor and there did lay
and we lived on nothing for many a day

6. At length we arrived in Fremantle Town,
where in a minute you will spend a pound
And tick it boys around the town,
and then we are off a whaling
There is plenty of games and plenty of cards,
and rum that will kill you [at] five hundred yards
And every thing else you get on a loose,
for to make you all right for a sperm whale cruise

7. Near Turtle Isle where the Humpbacks blow,
and ginger rolls are all the go
We took four dozen to stand a show
and then we were off a whaling
We had turtle fried, and turtle boiled,
turtle baked, and turtle spoiled
O Lord God it would set you wild,
for to cruise three months around Turtle Isle

8. A little more oil and all will end,
then homeward bound with money to spend
And then our troubles will be at an end,
when we get home from whaling
There is short-legged Jim with his fists so close
And long-shanked Bill with his crooked nose
They will all have cause to remember well,
their humble servant for a spell[37]

---

[36] There were very specific, though seldom strictly enforced regulations in maritime law pertaining to per diem allotments of beef, pork, flour, potatoes, bread, water, and other rations for merchant sailors. See Richard Henry Dana, Jr., *The Seamen's Friend* (Boston, 1841), passim.

[37] The *Europa* voyage actually lasted almost six years, during which the turnover of crew was considerable; in fact, the captain was the only man to remain from start to finish. Thus, it is pointless to sift through all the various Jims and Bills represented in the incomplete crew lists that survive, in the speculative hope of identifying the particular men Piper sought to memorialize here —if, indeed, he had anybody in particular in mind.

157. Bowhead Whaling Song
[The Captain's Wife]

The ship *Europa*'s whaling voyage to the Western Arctic under Captain Thomas Mellen that commenced in August 1866 was not completed until just short of six years later, in August 1872. While this was by no means a record—in terms of years at sea or barrels of oil and pounds of bone returned to New England—it was a much longer and somewhat more lucrative voyage than average, and certainly more eventful.[38] The final months, from October 1871 onward, were consumed by the frustrating and debilitating chore of rescue operations in the icy Beaufort Sea, well above the Arctic Circle and far beyond the Bering Strait on the north coast of Alaska; and thence in transporting the rescued crews to safe harbors in the Temperate Zone. As one of few ships in that remote region still able to do so, the *Europa* was recruited, grudgingly, to help off-load men, cargoes, and equipment—and more than a few women and children, the wives and families of bowhead whaling captains—from the thirty-three American whaling vessels trapped in the floes in an unusually early autumnal freeze.[39] Beyond being a harrowing ordeal for the victims, and one that resulted in financial reversals among owners, officers, crewmen, and insurers by way of loss of vessels, oil, bone, and equipment (miraculously, not a single life was lost among the 1200 persons stranded in the ice), it was also an unwelcome intrusion upon the regular, money-making activities of the reluctant rescue ships. Their whaling season was unexpectedly curtailed, their provisions and stores were consumed at a stupendously accelerated pace by hundreds of uninvited passengers, and their agents and owners were to be embroiled in litigation for twenty years (the suit for damages was not settled until 1891). Even in cases where the principals were eventually to recover some portion of their losses, the delay tied up their capital for a while and inhibited or disabled some from mounting subsequent voyages.[40] Few of the common whalemen would ever recover a particle of their lost revenue. Nor was the lesson of Arctic cold well enough learned by whaling masters: the 1871 disaster proved to be only the first and largest of a series of periodic mishaps in the decades following, in most of which the serious fiscal consequences were tragically overshadowed by human suffering and death.

Seaman George Piper could hardly have foreseen any of this when, aboard the *Europa* a year or two previous, he assembled his voluminous copybook of songs; nor when he transcribed this partly humorous, partly serious, wholeheartedly critical "Whaling Song" in 1870. His ship had already completed several seasons on the Arctic grounds that voyage, in the Kamchatka and Okhotsk Seas on the Siberian side of the North Pacific as well as off the Alaska coast. There had been layovers among the *wahinees* in the Hawaiian Islands, commemorated in his transcription of "Rolling Down to Old Mohee" [#143]; they had been sperm-whaling on the coast of Peru and in the South Pacific, and had taken aboard four years of water, four years of salted-meat rations, four years of fresh fruit, kindling wood, ink, dungarees, and tobacco, from outports in the remote and well-traveled regions alike. In his song transcriptions, at least, including several he obtained from shipmates along the way, he marked the progress of the voyage by characterizing the progress of all such voyages, documenting the love, hatred, retribution, charity, faith, and remorse as he found them in the sailor-world of songs, immersed in sailor-lore, enmeshed in sailor ways. If

---

[38] The total cargo returned was 1556 barrels of sperm oil, 3100 barrels of whale oil, and 39,293 pounds of bone (baleen), of which only a small percentage was actually carried home in the *Europa;* the rest was sent back in other vessels (Starbuck, 612f). Based on Starbuck's tabulation of average oil and bone prices for 1872 (p. 661), and on the basis of 31 $^{1}/_{2}$ gallons of oil per barrel (the standard varied upward), the *Europa*'s cargo would have been worth in the aggregate $185,000.

[39] Of 33 vessels nipped in the ice, only one was subsequently freed and restored to service. Comprehensive accounts of the 1871 Arctic disaster include Starbuck, 109; Hohman 1928, 293ff; Bockstoce 1977; Bockstoce 1986; Gilkerson & Bockstoce 1982.

[40] The *Europa* carried 244 rescuees, the largest number of passengers among the six vessels that participated in the rescue. Her owners filed for reparations in the amount of $71,000. "On February 21, 1891, long after many actors in the drama had passed away, Congress awarded damages to the owners on the basis of $138.89 for each passenger carried from the scene of the disaster to Honolulu." The *Europa*'s share was $33,889.16 (Hohman 1928, 294).

he had thoughts about any of it or drew any conclusions, they elude us, as he wrote down nothing but the songs and poems themselves, with scarcely a remark.

This ballad, which like several others the whaleman-scribe calls merely "Whaling Song," is of unknown origin. Its meter and content closely resemble "The Whaleman's Lament" [#154], but this one is lighter-hearted and more specific. Individual phrases seem to have been influenced by Piper's own transcription of "Blow Ye Winds" [#139]. It is particularly distinguished by its vituperative portrait of the captain's wife, who is characterized in seven of the seventeen stanzas as a fool and a virago—in sharp contrast to the portrait of Lizzie Marble in "A Voyage on New Holland" [#161]. That the syntax resorts to formula and cliché is apparent; but that it is authentic whalemen's work is also abundantly evident. Beneath its crude superfice lurks the kernel of a naive truthfulness that, despite stylistic unsophistication—and perhaps partly because of it—expresses at once the humor, the irony, and the desolate inhumanity of the whalemen's lot.

"WHALING SONG." George W. Piper, ship *Europa* of Edgartown, 1868-70. For singing to an appropriate ballad air, the stanzas would likely need to be doubled.

1. Come all you bold Americans wherever you may be
   O never go a whaling up in the Ockotsk Sea

2. We sailed from Oldtown Harbor[41] on the 21st of May[42]
   With twelve bold Yankees forward,[43] who were merry, blithe and gay

3. We sailed into Flores for men we were distressed[44]
   And there we shipped some Portuguese for to hug and hold the mast[45]

4. Then away for the Okhotsk Sea away we did go
   For to cruise upon two meals a day and see the bow heads blow

5. The bowhead whale he was struck by the Yankee who steered the mate[46]
   He raised his flukes and stove the boat which was to be our fate

6. And now about our Captain I hope you hope you will not think it hard
   Fourteen miles to windward he hauled back his main yard[47]

7. And when we hoisted up our waifs[48] to signal our sad tale
   Says he O let the buggers drown Since they did not get the whale

---

[41] *Old Town:* popular local name for Edgartown, Martha's Vineyard, Massachusetts, the *Europa*'s port of registry.

[42] The sailing date specified in the text ("the 21st of May") bears no relation to the actual sailing date of the *Europa* (29 August 1866); but as Piper himself was not yet in the crew when the *Europa* sailed from Edgartown, the significance of this "error" is equivocal.

[43] That is, twelve Americans among the common seamen—foremast hands—who live in the forecastle, in the prow of the ship.

[44] *Flores* is the westernmost of the Azores Islands, a frequent port-of-call for outward-bound American whalers as it lay conveniently on a prevailing-winds path to Cape Horn and the Cape of Good Hope. Labor shortages in New Bedford and the other New England and New York whaling ports often obliged vessels to fill out their crews along the way, which was typically done in the Azores and the Cape Verde Islands.

[45] *hug and hold the mast:* This is disparaging of the Azorean whale-hunters; but see "The Schooner *Varnum Hill*" [#147].

[46] *the Yankee who steered the mate:* That is, the harpooner (*boatsteerer*) assigned to the mate's boat.

[47] That is, brought the ship to a virtual standstill. The significance here is that the ship is to windward of the boats, and instead of the captain sailing out to pick up the men (and they being unable to sail the boats against the wind), they must now row fourteen miles back to the ship. This is characterized as an inconvenience, and as somewhat unkind and unnecessary.

[48] *Waif:* a signal device carried in whaleboats, usually made of wood or of canvas and wood in the shape of a lollipop or in the form of a flag.

8. Our Captain has got his wife on board, and by her he is ruled
   And of all the women that I ever did see She is the biggest fool

9. And when we cam on board of the Ship as in a chair she sat
   The very first words she said to us O did you get all wet?

10. A sperm whale broke our third mate's leg which made him take his bed
    And if it will not detain you I'll tell you what she said

11. And when we told her our sad tale She swore by the Son of Mars
    That instead of being an officer she wished that it was one of the tars

12. Our captain spoke the bark Eugene[49] the old woman used her tongue
    Saying ask him through your trumpet has he got any onions

13. Our captain's wife is almost starved which causes her to droop
    The reason is the captain gives the boat steerers all the soup

14. Our captain to get grub for her has tried by every means
    He has even told the steward not to give the boat steerers beans

15. Come all you bold Americans and listen to what I say
    Before you go to the Okhotsk Sea you had better throw yourself away[50]

16. For Bow-Heads are like spirits though once they were like snails
    I really believe the devil has got into the bowhead whales[51]

17. But now we are in New Bedford and lay alongside of the dock
    And if I ever go a whaling again I hope that I may be shot[52]

---

[49] The mention of the *Europa* having spoken the *Eugene* may be corrupt or apocryphal, but it suggests a much earlier possible date of the events narrated in the ballad than the *Europa* voyage or Piper's transcription. The only American whaler named *Eugene,* a bark of Stonington, Connecticut, was "sold to New Bedford and broken up [in] 1858" (Starbuck, 513), so it could not have been around in Piper's time. On the other hand, the New Bedford bark *Eugenia* (whose three-syllable name does not fit the meter of the lyrics as well as the two-syllable name *Eugene*) made two voyages to the North Pacific and Western Arctic whaling grounds in the period 1865-71, where she may have encountered the *Europa* more than once. Starbuck also reports a New Bedford bark *Eugenia* on the Atlantic grounds during a voyage of June 1864 to April 1869; but as she did not venture beyond the Capes it is extremely unlikely the vessel referred to in the song. The name *Eugene* thus appears to be a substitution for *Eugenia,* or apocryphal or, in any case, not actually related to the events narrated in the ballad.

[50] Before you would go whaling boys, you'd best be in your graves" ("The Whaleman's Lament," #154, stanza 3).

[51] See "All the Whales Are Wild and Ugly" [#158].

[52] And if I ever go whaling again I hope I will be shot" ("Blow Ye Winds" [#139-A], stanza 20); "Do not venture your life upon the high sea… to save your life you should better be hung" ("Landsmen One ands All" [#153], stanza 2).

158. All the Whales Are Wild and Ugly
[Song… to Captain S.D. Oliver]

This delightful parody of Stephen Foster's "Old Folks at Home" [#182] was written somewhere in the Pacific in 1855 by the prolific George Edgar Mills, third mate of the New Bedford whaleship *Leonidas*. It takes the form of a plea addressed to the captain, Samuel D. Oliver, that, instead of continuing to waste time contending with ornery and cantankerous gray whales, he should please take the ship north into the Arctic Ocean, where they can hunt the more valuable and more docile bowhead whale. The title derives from the first line of the chorus, a reference to the "wild and ugly" grays. "Old Folks at Home" had been published only four years before, in 1851, and was at the time still climbing the heights of its long-lived popularity.

TUNE: "Old Folks at Home" by Stephen Collins Foster, which Mills specifies as the melody (and which is intrinsically obvious from the text). From the original sheet music published at New York by Firth & Pond, 1851 (also repr. in R. Jackson, 101). See #182.

"SONG… TO CAPTAIN S.D. OLIVER." George Edgar Mills, third mate, ship *Leonidas* of New Bedford, 1855.

1. Far, Far to the Arctic Ocean
   Where the Bow Heads Blow,
   There's where my mind am turning ever
   There's where I want to go.
   All this Ocean am sad and dreary
   Every where we stray
   O Captain will you go to that Ocean
   Go where the Bow heads Lay

   Chorus: All these whales are wild and ugly
   All those we see
   O Captain will you go to that Ocean
   Go where the Bow heads Be.

2. All up and down this sea we've wandered
   Since I've been with you
   Then Captain let us go to the Northard
   Then we will see something new
   All the whales that are in this ocean
   All are wild we see
   Then Captain will you go to the Northard
   To where the Bow heads Lay

3. When shall I see the hills and valleys
   Far away on the Nor west shore
   O Captain let us leave this Ocean
   And not cruise here anymore
   All this ocean am sad an dreary
   Every where we stray
   O Captain will you go to that Ocean
   Go where the Bow Heads Lay

159. A Song of the Hatteras Whale

The New Bedford schooner *John R. Manta,* built in 1904, turned out to be the last American sailing vessel to complete a whaling voyage, commanded by Antone J. Mandly in 1925. (A final attempt, under Captain Joseph Edwards in 1927, was foiled by a gale that forced the schooner to turn back before having taken any whales.) On an earlier voyage, registered in Provincetown and commanded by Joseph Luis, the *Manta* sailed for the Atlantic grounds on 22 October 1908 and took 2,130 barrels of sperm-whale oil before returning to Cape Cod a few weeks short of three years later, on 12 September 1911. On the homeward-bound leg of this successful cruise, some member of the ship's company penned these stanzas anonymously on a single sheet of paper in clear italic capitals, with a fancy, ornamental title and illustrated with five charming ink vignettes of whaling scenes. The lyrics are carefully numbered and dated, and while the melody is not specified it appears likely to have been Ord's old Scots tune for "Arctic Whaling Song" [#135].

"A SONG OF THE HATTERAS WHALE." Anonymous, schooner *John R. Manta* of New Bedford, 1911. From a contemporaneous photograph of the manuscript taken by William H. Tripp (1880-1959), who later chronicled and photographed the last American whaling voyage, aboard the *John R. Manta* in 1925 (recounted in his book *There Goes Flukes,* 1938).

I
To an ebbing tide, all sail apeak
And a blustery freshening wind,
The good ship ploughs her way to the deep
Land fading in haze behind.

II
Four moon's rise to a south'ard course
And the lair of the game is sought,
The eye is keen and the arm is strong
For the battle which must be fought

III
A cry of "Blow" from the mainmast head
A splash of boats in the sea,
Then the rhythmic swing of swaying backs
For the prey lies far to the lee.

IV
A sailor's dash to the monster's side
A form at the cutter's prow,
A deadly lunge from cruel harpoon
And the combat awaits us now.

V
A swirl and a plunge to old ocean's depths
A tug on the singing line,
Then thrust on thrust from the langer's hand
While the blood flows warm like wine.

VI
A bellow and rush of the mighty hulk
A crimson spout to'rd the sky,
A cauldron of foam in the water's blue
As the king rolls over to die.

VII
A joyous pull to the distant craft
A draught of burning gin,
A word of praise from the master's lips
For the lay we helped to win.

VIII
Sing ho! for the tang of the salt sea air
Sing ho! for the whistling gale,
Sing ho! for the ones we left at home
Sing ho! for the Hatteras whale.

At sea, Aug 3ᵈ 1911

160. I Was Once a Sailor Lad

Let the wealthy and great live in splendour and state,
I envy them not, I declare it;
For I grow my own hams, my own ewes, my own lambs,
And I shear my own fleece, and I wear it.

I have lands, I have bow'rs, I have fruits I have flow'rs,
And the lark is my morning alarmer;
So you jolly boys, now, here's God speed the plough,
Long life and good health to the farmer.

— Anonymous 19th-century song[53]

This delicately haunting ballad, untitled in the manuscript, is about as splendid a poem as was ever created by a whaleman, and perfectly characterizes the sailor's age-old tension between land and sea—sea-dreaming while on shore, wishing for home while at sea, aspiring someday to retire to a secure pastoral life behind the plough. Playwright Eugene O'Neill observed and must have felt the same dialectical longings during his own youthful tenure at sea. He explored them over and over again in plays written throughout his career, and exploited them for a romantic not much present elsewhere in his works. He is quite explicit about them in the so-called Glencairn Plays, written around the time of the first World War. In *The Long Voyage Home,* these notions of land-wishing and sea-dreaming materialize in Olson's perpetually-frustrated hope to return to his family farm in Norway. In *Bound East for Cardiff* they are represented in Yank's unrealized dream—and dying wish—to retire from the sea to a farm in Argentina. They reverberate through O'Neill's later plays, accounting for the evocative title and complex fraternal rivalries of *Beyond the Horizon,* and lurking within and behind *Desire Under the Elms, Anna Christie, Mourning Becomes Electra,* and in Edmund's nostalgic sea-dreaming of *Long Day's Journey into Night.* The gentler sentiments and subtle maturity of "I Was Once a Sailor Lad" express kindred notions far beyond the years of the young lad who likely wrote it, journal-keeper, James W. Hutchins (or Hutchings) of Fairhaven, Mass., age about 23. Its most compelling feature may be that the poet, far at sea on a whaling voyage to the other side of the world, was able to anticipate a wisdom and contentment that, even then, he aspired to acquire in later years.

Though whaling is nowhere specifically mentioned in Hutchins's lyrics, Huntington rightly classifies the piece among the whaling songs and gives the same text (erroneously transcribed), with a melody he does not identify. *Songs the Whalemen Sang* is a pioneering work, useful in its way, but appearances to the contrary, throughout the book Huntington consistently fails properly to identify the diarists, the dates of the voyages, or the repositories that hold the journal volumes from which he harvested his texts. Superficially, the documentation appears comprehensive and correct, but many of the texts are corrupt and, in fact, many of his citations are badly garbled or downright incorrect. In this instance he also neglects to provide any information about the tune, which (whether Huntington knew it or not) turns out to be a fairly conservative form of "The Collier Boy"; and this, in turn, is actually a degraded variant of the hoary, traditional Scottish air "The Broom of Cowden Knowes."[54]

---

[53] Probably English; transcription from an ironstone pitcher of circa 1800 presumed to have been owned by Washington Irving, in the collection of Sunnyside, Irving's former home at Tarrytown, N.Y.; and an English ironstone cup-and-saucer in the author's collection. There are also several variants on anonymous printed broadsides of similar vintage.

[54] No particular melody is indicated in the whaleman's manuscript. Without explanation, Huntington does not identify his tune, which may or may not be indigenous to the text. Ellen Cohn has refined and improved upon it tune and added repeats at the end of each stanza: the result is even closer to pure Scots forms of "The Broom of Cowden Knowes." In this instance, Huntington's melodic instincts are sound, and Cohn's exquisite: various contemporary forms of "The Broom of Cowden Knowes" are eminently well suited to the meter and mood of the whaleman's lyrics.

TUNE: "The Broom of Cowden Knowes," a traditional Scottish ballad air: composite, after the air to "New England Home" (which is actually a form of "The Broom of Cowden Knowes"), published in *The Singer's Companion,* New York, 1855, p. 177; the singing of Paddy Hernon of Victoria, British Columbia ("The Broom of Cowden Knowes," San Francisco Maritime Museum, 4 Sept. 1979; Frank 1980b; etc.), wherein the melody diverges primarily in the cadences of the second and third lines; and the singing of Ellen Cohn of New Haven, Conn. ("I Was Once a Sailor," revised from Huntington; Kendall Whaling Museum Symposium Archive; and Sea Music Festival Archive, Mystic Seaport Museum), but without the repeats she introduced to the tune and lyrics printed by Huntington.

[UNTITLED.] James W. Hutchins, ship *Florida* of New Bedford, 1843-46 [collection of the New Bedford Free Public Library].

1. Yes I was once a sailor lad
   I plowed the restless sea
   I saw the sky look fair and glad
   And I felt proud and free

2. I breathed the air of many a clime
   Saw beauties fair and gay
   My hopes were fixed on future time
   The present slipped away

3. Experience sad hope's brilliant view
   Like mist dissolved away
   I found small harvest did accrue
   To plowmen of the sea

4. I found my team would range and rove
   'Twas but the fickle wind
   That plowing o'er the rolling sea
   No furrow left behind

5. Days have passed by I'm snug on shore
   Safe from the sea's alarms
   I have a never failing store
   A fifteen acre farm

6. Oh, sweet it is to till the soil
   'Neath our New England sky
   And sweet when I have eased my toil
   To muse on days gone by

CHAPTER SIXTEEN
"Plenty of Music"
Two Voyages of the Bark *Kathleen*

> I think we shall have plenty of music for we have a flute player an accordion player and one that plays the most pieces I ever hurd and he plays some Operah pieces beautifully and I think we have some good singers.
>
> — Elizabeth Marble, outward bound aboard the bark *Kathleen* of New Bedford, 17 September 1857.

The bark *Kathleen* was destined to become one of the most famous vessels in the annals of the whale fishery, when, *Pequod*-like, on Saint Patrick's Day in 1902, she was stove by an angry sperm whale and "went down in less than a half hour" (Hegarty 1959, 35). Frederick Howland Smith, many of whose songs and tunes are included in this anthology and who had been master of the *Kathleen* on the voyage immediately previous, was one of her owners at the time; and the income he might have realized in his retirement from the *Kathleen*'s future successes was obliterated in a flash of flukes and brine, as, no doubt, were the fortunes of the many others connected with her, despite that no lives were lost in the misfortune.

But when she set sail on 25 August 1857, bound for sperm whaling in the Indian Ocean, the *Kathleen* was a young vessel relatively new to the whale fishery. Built at Philadelphia in 1844 for the merchant service, she had been carrying cargoes until purchased by New Bedford owners in 1851 — the year *Moby-Dick* was published — and fitted out for whaling.[1] This would be her third whaling voyage, her first under the auspices of managing owners J. & W.R. Wing, New Bedford's leading whaling merchants at that time. Her captain, John C. Marble of Fall River, was embarking on his fifth command. He took more family with him than was usually the case even in the often nepotistic whale fishery. Also on board were John's brother George, junior by three years and himself a former whaling captain, who signed as first mate; John's wife, Elizabeth, called "Lizzie," and their son, George Frederick, age seven when the voyage commenced, known to the family and crew variously as "Georgie" and "Freddie." It was their first whaling voyage together, and might have been the first of many. John Marble, scarcely 44 years old, was in good health and at the top of his profession. He would die at sea four years later as master of the bark *Awashonks*, with the same family circle folded around him.

Regarding empirical considerations of whaling, the *Kathleen* voyage was unremarkable. She returned to New Bedford about thirty months later with a respectable catch of sperm and whale oil, having visited the "New Holland" whaling grounds off the west coast of Australia, and the region of Java and Sumatra. A few hands left the ship and were replaced along the way; one man died; a boat or two was lost to angry whales during the hunt; there were a few visits ashore in Western Australia and on torrid tropical islands in an ocean wilderness domain traversed almost exclusively by whalemen. Statistically, it was a whaling voyage among whaling voyages.

What is remarkable about the *Kathleen* voyage is the unusually rich and insightful vision of life at sea in a Yankee whaler provided by the journal and letters of the captain's observant wife. Born Elizabeth Church Wrightington at Fall River in 1825, she came from a family long associated with the whaling industry. Her younger sister Sarah was married to John's brother George, the first mate. Her respect for and understanding of the whaling trade grew out of long years of familiarity and an innate curiosity about the world around her, which she first visited in its full extension when she accompanied her husband and brother-in-law to some of its most distant corners.

Music was an integral part of daily life in the *Kathleen*, and Lizzie's account of the voyage is

---

[1] The *Kathleen*'s registry dimensions for 1852 are: 306 $^{12}/_{95}$ tons, length 106.4 feet, breadth 25.6 feet, depth 12.5 feet.

noteworthy for its attention to musical activities on shipboard, any record of which is scarce. She embraced any opportunity to become involved in the entertainments and amateur theatricals the crew undertook. On 19 October 1857, only a couple of months out, she writes, "thare is quite a band on deck. thare is an accordion a gatar a violin and two pare of clackers and a triangle. they play a while and then they sing a while." A musical crew with an easygoing a captain inevitably resulted in musical soirees on special occasions. Christmas night, 1857, was especially memorable:

> we had a very good concert last night and every thing went along as regular as if they were at home in a hall. they had their hand bil pasted up and a program of the pieces. thare was nine of them, all but the cook foremast hands and six pieces of music and it was performed well. the cook was dressed as a woman with hoops on and he acted his part well. before they got through John treted them. they then gave him a very good torte and a song in cornection with it, so all things considered we had quite a time.

As she illustrates a couple of days later, there were many instances of extemporaneous music and a bevy of talented individuals to provide a constant supply of music for the aftercabin:

> we had some music on the serapheam[2] last night. one of our foremast hands can play on moste every instrument. he played the Organ in chirch a year before he left home. his name is Avery. thare are two brothers of them George and James and they both play and sing and they understand it. John asked George into the cabin and he played for us two hours. [28 Dec. 1857]

Before very long, the Captain's wife was recruited to assist in the costuming department:

> I have had an invitation to day to make fancy dresses for the company forward. thare name is the kathleen seranade band… I have spent this weak so far in making fancy dresses for our band. I have made one white skirt with three stripes of calico around the bottom, and one white skirt with five rows of ribon, two of broad blue satin and three of red satin. the wasts were made of blue flaniel and trimed with ribon. [11 and 15 Jan. 1858]

Lizzie's subsequent output for the musicians included "a swallow tailed coat out of calico," "a pare of knee britches," two "pare of man of war pants… bound foreleg and top with black white and read," and other sundries. The Kathleen Serenade Band continued to function throughout the cruise, providing many hours of welcome respite from the long, boring intervals between whales, and the hazards, discomforts, and inclement weather of the Indian Ocean grounds.

In addition to chronicling these quaint but morale-boosting musical rituals, Lizzie performed a meritorious service to posterity by preserving among her papers transcriptions of two original songs written by inmates of this musical ship's company. "A Voyage on New Holland" is a ballad of 71 extant stanzas, one of the most comprehensive and, in places, well crafted original songs to emerge from the fishery, a veritable voyage journal in itself. The other is an equally well-crafted anonymous ballad of 14 stanzas describing the *Kathleen*'s next voyage under Captain Charles C. Mooers. How Lizzie obtained copies of the song about her own voyage is no great mystery: her husband and brother-and-law each transcribed it themselves, perhaps directly from the author's original manuscript. But how she got hold of the ballad about the *next* cruise is a minor mystery; for while Captain Mooers was doubling the Cape of Good Hope in the *Kathleen,* Lizzie was with John aboard the *Awashonks* on a whaling voyage that neither would complete. But New Bedford whaling circles were small and closely circumscribed. No doubt after she returned to Fall River following her husband's untimely death at sea thousands of miles from home, someone, probably William Butts, second mate on both of these *Kathleen* voyages — remembering the joy Lizzie derived from musical gaiety aboard the *Kathleen,* and realizing that those years in the *Kathleen* with John and Freddie and George were the happiest she had ever known—did her the kindness of passing the song along to her, proof that the *Kathleen*'s musical legacy was still intact.

---

[2] The *seraphin* or *seraphina* is a small, portable, foot-pedal organ; its invention is attributed to John Green in 1833 (OED 9:491).

161. A Voyage on New Holland

This original ballad constitutes a veritable journal in verse. In 71 stanzas, it narrates a three-year whaling voyage to the Indian Ocean in the bark *Kathleen* of New Bedford during 1857-60, presenting a good-natured chronicle of people, places and events. External evidence indicates that it was written by either the third mate, John C. Sullivan, or the second mate, William T. Butts. It affords a favorable glimpse into the life and affairs of a fundamentally happy ship with a worthy skipper, in contrast to the stream of Sailor's Complaints and Whalemen's Laments by which shipboard ballad-writing is often characterized. It may be the most complete ballad ever written about an individual whaling voyage. The tune "Vilikins and His Dinah" [#81] is specified in text B. (For a discussion of Captain John C. Marble, the family members he brought along with him from Fall River, and the important role that music played on this voyage, see the chapter headnotes to this chapter and the biographical Appendix.)

TUNE - "Vilikins and His Dinah," after the original sheet music published at Boston by Oliver Ditson, 1855; and at Baltimore by George Willig, Jr., 1860; reprinted in Sigmund Spaeth, *Reed 'em and Weep,* 1926, p. 56. Transposed from the key of Eb.

A.

"A VOYAGE ON NEW HOLLAND." Captain John Marble, master, bark *Kathleen* of New Bedford, 1860. Only a fragment of 15 stanzas survives on three leaves from what was likely originally a complete transcription of 71 or 72 stanzas on 15 leaves; attributed to Captain Marble's hand; preserved among the papers of his wife, Elizabeth. Virtually identical with the first 15 stanzas of B.

B.

"A VOYAGE ON NEW HOLLAND." George D. Marble, first mate, bark *Kathleen* of New Bedford, 1860. A complete or near-complete transcription of 71 stanzas (of a possible 72; stanza # 66 is unaccountably absent) on 9 leaves, evidently in George Marble's hand.

1. Come all you bold whalemen that plow the rough main
   Of[f] the coast of New Holland or off that of Spain
   Give ear to my ditty I'll tell what I've seen
   While cruising the Ocean in the Bold Kathleen

2. Dear friends you have all heard of that City no doubt
   Where sharks in men's clothing[3] go prowling about
   Where they fit out bold seamen and send them away
   With a box of sea clothes and the 200th lay

3. If you cruise down south water street there you may see
   J & W R Wings shop as snug as can be
   There we all signed our names a fine crew to be seen
   For a thirty months voyage in the Bark Kathleen

---

[3] That is, so called *land sharks*—the merchants, boardinghouse keepers, and shoreside *crimps* who preyed upon the naïveté and spendthrift tendencies of sailors in every service. See Richard H. Dillon, *Shanghaiing Days* (New York: Coward-McCann), 1961; Hohman 1928 ; Hugill 1969; Knut Weibust, *Deep Sea Sailors* (Hardlingar: Nordiska Museets), 1969.

4. Near the last part of August on the 25th day
   With colors all flying we got under way
   Bade adieu to New Bedfords sweet maidens so fair
   With their low necked pink dresses and black curly hair

5. Now we're on the Atlantic and the voyage is begun
   If you dont like the business there's no chance to run
   You can mourn for your sweethearts and they may for you
   But the day you left Bedford is the day you will rue

6. Our course is now eastward and mast heads all manned[4]
   Our harpoons are ready and lances at hand
   Our small boats in order each man knows his place
   And all hands seem eager the prize for to chace

7. We touched at the Azores and then bore away
   To the Cape De Verd Islands and stopped there one day
   We next saw the Trusteens[5] and there took a slope[6]
   And with a fine breeze passed the Cape of Good Hope

8. When on the Trusteen ground we lowered for right whales
   And trying to work careful took paddles and sails
   But the whales smelled a rat and they gave us the slip
   So the whales went to windward and us to the ship

9. Now whaling in Wings shop is all very fine
   Or up to Spink Greens Hall[7] when sipping your wine
   With a girl on your knee you can cut in with ease
   But its different business when on the salt seas

10. The first whales we saw we down boats and got three
    And got alongside as sung as could be
    But night coming on and one boat out of sight
    And the weather looked stormy that very same night

11. The Capt[ain] in order to save the boats crew
    He cut from the whale and what more could he do
    The crew in the boat they got tired of the chase
    So they came alongside and we spliced the main brace[8]

---

[4] That is, lookouts were posted aloft to watch for whales. The line is borrowed from "The Coast of Peru" [#136].

[5] Tristan da Cunha is an archipelago in the South Atlantic at 37°3' South, 12°18' West consisting of three principal and two minor islands. A British dependency after 1816, it was sparsely populated and was visited mostly by whalers and navy squadrons.

[6] *Slope:* a diagonal or "turn" in course; alternatively, a navigational sighting, an angle or declension of the sun or a star.

[7] Spink Green's Hall was a local watering place in New Bedford frequented by whalemen.

[8] *Splice the main brace*: Captain Marble was more generous with spirituous liquors than many, which is interpreted here as an admirable kindness, defying the unfavorable stereotype of the bucko whaling master whose first concern is the whale, or his own comfort, and not the welfare of his crew [see "Boston," #33].

12. We arrived off cape Leuwin[9] in season to see
    The Pamelia[10] cutting right under our lee
    The Lapwing[11] a boiling off our weather beam
    A fine place for spirme off cape Leuwin it would seem

13. After cruising a few days and seeing no spout
    For Geograph bay[12] then we tacked the ship about
    We passed by Cape Natches[13] oh that is the rub
    And in two hours time anchored off the tub[14]

14. We'll gam with old Forest of course as we pass
    And he'll sell us poor liquor for six pence a glass
    From Forests to Earnshaws[15] oh yes its all right
    And by that time of course you'll be pretty tight

15. Now adieu to Australia's fair maids for a while
    We're going off the west coast to cruise for sperm oil
    From there to the Rosemary Isles[16] in July
    We to make out 600 this season must try[17]

16. Now we're off to the west coast of New Holland all right
    A cruising for sperm what a beautiful sight
    To see old square head alongside of the ship
    And the Capt[ain] singing out there boys heave and slip

17. For the owners at home a few words I will say
    We'll do all the work and they'll get all the pay
    You will say to yourself tis a curious note
    But dont growl for some day you may chance steer a boat[18]

18. When your fast to the whale running risk of your life
    Your shingling his houses and dressing his wife
    Your sending his daughter off to the high school
    When your up to your middle in grease you great fool

19. We took a few good cuts between March and June
    Of regular old sperm oil oh that is the tune
    We then went to Bally which lies down in nine[19]
    We got some good water but not so good wine

---

[9] Cape Leuwin is in the extreme southwest of Western Australia, on the Indian Ocean.

[10] Bark *Pamelia* of New Bedford, 300 tons, Edward Coggeshall, then nearing the end of her voyage (4 June 1855 - 22 Aug. 1858).

[11] Ship *Lapwing* of New Bedford, 432 tons, Michael Cumisky, came more recently to the grounds (3 June 1856 - 4 Nov. 1859).

[12] *Geographe Bay*: an inlet of the Indian Ocean on the southwest coast of Western Australia, much frequented by whalers.

[13] *Cape Natches* is a corruption of Cape Naturaliste, a promontory at the head of Geographe Bay.

[14] *The Tub* has not been identified. It may be a whalers' local place-name or esoteric usage for a bay or whale habitat; or it may be intended in the sense of the nautical colloquial expression meaning "to make a ship fast to a buoy" (Partridge 1961, 914).

[15] *Forest*'s and *Earnshaw's* evidently refer to inns or taverns at Bunbury.

[16] *Rosemary Island* is in the Indian Ocean on the northwest coast of Western Australia near the entrance to Nickol (Nichol) Bay, at approximately 20°30' South, 177° East.

[17] That is, 600 barrels of oil (not 600 whales or 600 miles):. In American usage at the time 1 barrel = ± 31.5 or 32.5 gallons.

[18] That is, don't complain, for you may stand a chance of promotion to boatsteerer (harpooneer).

[19] *Bally*: the island of Bali in the Dutch East Indies (now Indonesia), lying between 8° and 9° South latitude, i.e., "in nine."

20. To the Rosemary Islands our ship she now sent
    To capture the Humpback it was our intent
    We thought that for two months 440 would pay[20]
    So in July we anchored in deep water bay[21]

21. We lay there at anchor quite nice for a while
    We then dropped our ship down towards spectacle Isle[22]
    The Capt[ain] aloft with a glass in his hand
    Sings out for a cow and a calf close to land

22. A word about Humpbacks now my dear friends
    To you that to try this fine business intend
    To see what a fine sport it is cutting them in
    And we skin the gut fat off as clean as a pin

23. We gut the poor Humpbacks and eat up her calf[23]
    And to see how the deck looks I bet you would laugh
    All covered in gurry, guts, flukes, and big fins
    And to get around the deck you may break your poor shins

24. We took most 700 then we got under way
    And being short of water we went to Mew Bay[24]
    On the Island of Java got water and wood
    Then put her for Anger[25] as fast as we could

25. Of the maidens of Anger I'll tell you some day
    Why dont he tell now I suppose you will say
    But twould injure the feelings of shipmates I fear
    So you'll get all the news from old Mrs Burtonear[26]

26. Now we'll boldly up anchor from Anger my men
    And try our luck off Cape Leuwin again
    Old Lewin received us as it done before
    The seas mountains high and the tempests did roar

27. We cruised off Cape Lewin and took one big whale
    Cut in and tryed out then for Port we made sail
    Tis only ten months since we sailed for Vasse[27] clean[28]
    And we've taken 1200[29] in the Bold Kathleen

---

[20] That is, the cruise might be worth 400 barrels of oil.

[21] *Deep Water Bay:* a generic place name, specific reference not identified; perhaps esoteric to whalers.

[22] *Spectacle Island:* not identified, probably a whalemen's place-name.

[23] *Humpback calf:* Dining on whale meat was not common in American ships, though dolphins were sometimes taken for their meat. Sperm whale meat was generally considered unpalatable to European- and African-Americans (though, taken in small quantities, it is regarded as a delicacy in Japan); however, some of the *mysticetes* (baleen whales, including humpbacks) were, occasionally exploited for fresh meat, evidently as they were in this instance.

[24] *Mew Bay:* on the Sunda Straight, island of Java in the Dutch East Indies (now Indonesia).

[25] Anjer: port in the northwest extremity of the island of Java, across the Sunda Straight from Sumatra.

[26] Not identified.

[27] *Vasse:* there is not "city" of this or any similar name in this region, but it was evidently a place on Geographe Bay, Western Australia, in the vicinity of Bunbury (a frequent whalers' port-of-call) and Busselton.

[28] *Clean:* That is, without any oil.

28. No we'll go see Vasse citys sweet maidens so fine
    You may drink to your true love and I'll drink to mine
    We will drink to the girls that are so far away
    While lying at anchor in Geograph Bay

29. Now our ship is recruited[30] we'll get under way
    And cruise a few weeks of[f] Cape Lewin they say
    We'll leave Mrs Marble and Georgie on shore[31]
    And knock about Leuwin where tempests do roar

30. When Lewin bore N[orth] E[ast] a big whale hove in sight
    But our boats were turned up for it blowed so that night
    And the gale still continues so we lay there hove to
    And looked at old square head what more could we do

31. Next morning we manned out mast heads at daylight
    As the gale it abated in the course of the night
    We soon saw a big whale bound into the land
    And the Capt[ain] rings out lower the boats bear a hand

32. The mate lowered and struck one and turned him fin out
    We took him alongside with many a shout
    He made 70 barells we then bore away
    For that place fame for beauty called Geograph Bay

33. We attended the races this time in the Bay
    Saw fighting and fooling and dancing and play
    Saw old mother Forest selling poor gin
    And Mary her daughter dressed neat as a pin

34. The race being over Ben Bolt[32] won the prize
    But to see all the fair sex it dazzled my eyes
    But it dazzles them more to see Duff day come round[33]
    And its so with the moste of the crew I'll be bound

35. Now we've started again on a cruis Jolly tars
    And got a few miles out and in comes the Mars[34]
    So we shipped some oil by her for home or elsewhere
    Which caused Katys crew for to grumble and swear[35]

---

[29] That is, 1200 barrels of oil.

[30] *Recruited:* That is, "provisioned": took on water, supplies, probably fresh fruit, and possibly livestock.

[31] It was not unusual for a whaling master's family to enjoy a hiatus of a few days or weeks ashore in a friendly foreign port-of-call. Lizzie and young George Frederick, now eight, no doubt lodged with a respectable family in Bunbury or Busselton.

[32] *Ben Bolt:* the fictitious title character in a very popular sentimental song written in 1842 by a Philadelphia doctor, Thomas Dunn English (1819-1902), and set to music by Nelson Kneass (1823 - circa 1869).

[33] *Duff day:* usually Sunday, when this pudding concoction of flour or crushed hardtack, water, and raisins, molasses, or plums, was sometimes served up as a treat.

[34] Bark *Mars* of New Bedford, 270 tons, Gerardus P. Harrison, sailed 10 June 1856. In stanza #68, the *Kathleen* and the *Mars* are racing to New Bedford. As it turned out, they both arrived on the same day, 13 April 1860 (Starbuck, 549).

[35] They *grumble* because the standard practice is to head for home only when the ship is "full"; each barrel of oil sent home by

36. Now adieu for the last time to this City of sand
    Adieu to the maids of this far distant land
    Good by uncle Herring look out for the mail
    Our anchor is catted and we're under sail

37. For the port of Freemantle[36] our course is now laid
    We're going to touch there to seek medical aid
    We stopped there one week then we maid sail again
    To cruise for sperm whales and to plow the rough main

38. Now sad is the story I'm going to relate
    The loss of our shipmate oh sad was his fate
    He was called from our number he the sumons obeyed
    And his body down deep in the ocean is laid

39. No pale slab points out where he sank in the deep
    No loved ones ere stands o'er his grave for to weep
    But the stormy winds whistle their dirge o'er his head
    As he lies far from home in his deep ocean bed

40. But the lord he knows best when to call us away
    May each one be prepared for that much dreaded day
    Farewell to our shipmate we'll ne'er see him more
    Till the dead shall arize from the sea and the shore

41. Now the wheel of dame fortune is rooled round anew
    But did not forget Kathleen and her crew
    She showered down her blessings casks filled up fast
    We've taken 400 since we sailed from port last

42. Of the Ships on N[ew] Holland I'd have you to know
    Some sails very fast and some sail very slow
    There's the Oriole, Swallow, and Eagle likewise[37]
    To beat little Katy the whole of them tries

43. There's the Mars and the Martha are cruising about
    There's the Draco and Dunbar they lately come out
    And last but not least in the list to put down
    The clipper Bark Sunbeam of fame and renown[38]

---

other means leaves room for more oil to be taken on the grounds, thereby lengthening the voyage and delaying the homecoming. However, Starbuck makes no mention of the *Kathleen* shipping oil home on this voyage.

[36] *Fremantle:* on the Swan River, the port for the city of Perth and the principal port of Western Australia.

[37] This was the *Oriole*'s first voyage: a bark of 404 tons, she was built and registered at Fairhaven in 1857, sailed 8 July 1857 under Captain Thomas Mickel, returned 11 Sept. 1861, then was sold to New Bedford (her portrait was expertly painted by New Bedford-Fairhaven artist William Bradford. Ship *Swallow* of New Bedford, 430 tons, Herman N. Stewart, was also newly built at Fairhaven (1856; sailed 9 Oct. 1856, returned 22 Dec. 1860). Bark *Eagle* of New Bedford, 336 tons, John McNally, was much older, built at Amesbury, Mass., in 1816, converted for whaling in 1827, and recently converted from a ship (1856; sailed 22 Oct. 1856, returned 28 Mar. 1861). None of these except the *Oriole* returned a cargo equal to the *Kathleen*'s.

[38] The bark *Sunbeam* of New Bedford, 300 tons, Samuel H. Cromwell, at this time, could hardly have been "renowned" for anything but her good looks—unless Captain Cromwell's bucko methods (as the ballad describes them in the next few stanzas) were already notorious—for the *Sunbeam* was a new vessel making her first voyage. Built at Mattapoisett, Mass., in 1856, she sailed 21 July 1856 and returned 13 April 1860, the same day as the *Kathleen* and the *Mars,* with a substantial cargo of sperm oil

44. She's commanded by Cromwell not Cromwell of old[39]
    But one of more recent date I am told
    With his cutlass in hand he will chop off your head
    So you wake up next morning to find yourself dead

45. He half starves his crew and he locks up the bread
    Goes growling around like a dog with sore head
    But he missed jist one figure devilish old Bipp[40]
    When he trod on the toes of his mate Mr Tripp[41]

46. We cruised until august the season being over
    The Capt[ain] says boys we will cruise here no more
    So we then spoke the Eagle and the capt[ain]s agreed
    They'd go to Mauritius[42] with all haste and speed

47. We arrived at Mauritius all safe and all sound
    Cruised over the City all through and all round
    We recruited our ship and we then put to sea
    And we'll be home in April the Capt[tain] tells me

48. We stood to the westward and at night shortened sail
    In hopes to fall in with a good large sperm whale
    With the Island of Bourbon[43] close under our lee
    And our foretopsail in we were as snug as can be

49. One day we raised whales with the Sunbeam in sight
    Her 3d mate he struck one of course he done right
    But he being a kind hearted and jenerous man
    Says stern, out the was boys as fast as we can

50. Our boats being close to we will mate was the cry
    And they soon made the blood from his spouthole to fly
    So Katy being close to and in search of her pray
    She backed her foretopsail and quietly lay

51. So we've got him alongside the Kathleen now
    He's fast by a fluke chain to our starboard Bow
    Where many just like him have been fast before
    And in hopes before long we'll see one or two more

---

greater in value than the total catch of the *Kathleen* or *Mars* (Starbuck 538f).

[39] *Cromwell of Old:* The whaleman-author is probably referring to Oliver Cromwell (1599-1658), the Puritan revolutionary and Lord Protector of England (1653-58), seminal figure in history; but he may have had in mind the Lord Chamberlain of England under Henry VIII, Thomas Cromwell (1485-1540), created Earl of Essex in 1540 and, soon after, was executed for treason.

[40] *Old Bipp:* This is by way of a curse, "Bipp"—chosen to rhyme with "Mr. Tripp"—being intended to signify the Devil.

[41] The specifics of the incident are nowhere disclosed, but the ballad author evidently considered Mr. Tripp, one of the mates, a man to be reckoned with and a match for Captain Cromwell—and thus something of a hero among the crew.

[42] *Mauritius*: This island in the Indian Ocean—with Reunion Island forming the Mascarene Group east of Madagascar—was a port-of-call where the U.S. Consul was kept busy adjudicating and adjudicating whaling-related disputes and legal transactions.

[43] *The Island of Bourbon*: refers to the French name for Reunion Island (see footnote #42).

52. Next morning at daylight we overboard hook
    And off of this perm whale his jacket we took
    He hove in his head yes his case and his Junk[44]
    While the only dry place in the ship was your bunk

53. We worked here in water chock up to our knees
    Our bark she lie rooling and shipping in seas
    Our chain straps they parted and our hooks they tore out
    While Katy lie rooling and tumbling about

54. Now our try works is going and the fires blazing bright
    And the oil slewing out what a beautiful sight
    Blind jacks at the wheel and the watch's gone below
    Your landsmen would envy such <u>comfort</u> I know

55. So we'll cruise the wide Ocean where stormy winds blow
    Its hard to leave home such a long time we know
    But if duty commands it we'll never say die
    And out motto while cruising is always <u>we'll try</u>[45]

56. Next with the ship Martha[46] we mated[47] one day
    She got a big whale to windward we lay
    She saw Katy coming at double quick rate
    So they run up their ensign at the mizzen to mate

57. Our Capt[ain] says boys now come set ours with speed
    And twas lucky we did so quite lucky indeed
    Our Capt[ain] he smiled for he very well knew
    That ½ of the whale was for Katy and her crew

58. Now we'll ship by the Martha our share of this whale
    And for Madagascar we'll quickly make sail
    We arrived off Fort Dauphin[48] and took a look round
    We saw plenty [of] ships but no whales on the ground

59. Now boys says the Capt[ain] with his good natured smile
    We'll go round the Cape[49] and cruise there for a while
    So we made sail next day for the Capt[ain] thought best
    To set the sea watches and steer off South west

60. We took one more whale then we went into Cape Town
    The day before Christmas our anchor went down
    Oh the Cape is a fine place and the girls like Hop Beer
    But I wont say much more for friend Borden is near[50]

---

[44] Spermaceti from the head-case and "junk" were regarded as of the best quality and commanded premium prices.

[45] This is a pun on *try* (to endeavor or attempt) and *try-out* (to render or boil-down blubber into oil).

[46] Ship *Martha* of Fairhaven, 301 tons, Timothy C. Spaulding, sailed 20 May 1856, returned 1 April 1860.

[47] *Mated*: That is, the *Kathleen* and the *Martha* went whaling together, referred to as whaling "in company.".

[48] *Fort Dauphin*: a fortified seaport on the Indian Ocean coast in the extreme southeast of Madagascar.

[49] That is, the Cape of Good Hope and thence into the Atlantic.

[50] *Mr. Borden* was fourth mate of the *Kathleen*. At Cape Town he was evidently involved in an affair of the heart or got inebriated on "hop beer": the ballad does not specify which, but after embarrassing Borden by bringing up the matter at all, spares him the humiliation of spelling out the details. The ship's company was undoubtedly familiar with the incident; and poor Borden, whatever his indiscretion, must certainly have suffered the indignity of a few guffaws at the hands of his shipmates.

61. Our stay at the Cape was quite brief it is true
    So our course to the westward again we'll pursue
    In long[itu]de three east we wore ship around
    To cruise and look over the Waldwich Bay ground[51]

62. We arrived on the ground and we cruised east and west
    And to raise a sperm whale why each man tried his best
    But our search it was fruitless and never would pay
    So for St Helena[52] we then bore away

63. Now about St Helena a few words I will say
    My friend lost his Boots while ashore there one day
    And instead of his Boots he found gaiters I vow
    A very good swop I suppose you'll say now

64. Next morning quite early the Boots hove in sight
    But he hung to the gaiters and I think he done right
    For they was a nice pair and they fit to a T
    But you wont hear no more about gaiters from me

65. Now all brother seamen whose Boots need repair
    Of those fancy gaiters I'd have you beware
    For you know they cost money as well as I do
    When the money's all gone then the gater's gorn too[53]

66. [stanza omitted]

67. Now the voyage is moste over our ships Homeward Bound
    We'll all Jump for Joy at that thrice welcome sound
    For we're thirty months absent from our dear native shore
    And to get to N[ew] Bedford will take us two more

68. Oh the 18th of February was a fine pleasant day
    When the Mars and the Kathleen they got under way
    With a fair wind a blowing and studding sail set[54]
    We'll beat the old Mars to N[ew] Bedford I bet

69. Now we're rooling along with the wind at south East
    Our good ship is plowing four knots at least
    We're bound for N[ew] Bedford for our cruising is oer
    And we're steering the good course of N[orth] W[est] once more

---

[51] *Waldwich Bay*: corruption of Walvis Bay (from the Dutch *Walvisbaaij*, literally "Whalefish Bay"), a harbor and town on the Atlantic Ocean coast of Southwest Africa. It was an important whaling ground in the 18th century and remained an occasional port-of-call for Yankee whalers in the 19th.

[52] *St Helena*: remote island in the South Atlantic at 15°57' South, 5°42' West, infamous as the place of final exile and original interment of Napoleon (until his remains were moved to the Palace des Invalides in Paris in 1840). It was an extremely important port-of-call and consulate, visited by American whalemen and British garrison troops usually on the homeward passage from the Capes. See "Bonaparte on the Isle of St. Helena," #62.

[53] This is refers to a tendency among sailors to pawn anything of value when in need of cash. Gaiters may have been more saleable than sea boots and a sailor would be more likely to part with them.

[54] *Studding sails* are lightweight, light-weather ails rigged to *studding-sail booms*, athwartships extensions of the conventional square-rig yards, developed in clipper-ship times to increase speed and subsequently in common usage on whalers; sailors often objected to the danger and trouble to which they were subjected in setting and taking in the "stu'nsls" [see "Boston," #33].

70. Now the hardships and dangers of the Voyage are all past
Our ship lies snug in New Bedford at last
Her sails are all furled and her anchor is down
And she rides to her anchor off N[ew] Bedford town

71. Hurrah for our good Bark she's carryed us safe o'er
The dark stormy waters where tempest do roar
Through cold and through heat and through tempests and rain
And landed us safe in N[ew] Bedford again

72. So good by to old Ocean I've done with you now
No more o'er your dark stormy billows I'll plow
Our friends here at home they all greet us with Joy
Welcome home Welcome home to the Bold Sailor Boy

162.
Song Composed aboard the Bark Kathleen

Preserved among Elizabeth Marble's papers, this anonymous ballad-like song was written on the homeward-bound leg of a whaling voyage to the New Holland grounds in the New Bedford bark *Kathleen* under Charles C. Mooers (AKA Moore and Mover) during 1861-64. It begins with the narrator going to New Bedford from New York in response to one of J. & W.R. Wing's recruiting advertisements, the sort of thing that the principal whaling agents had been placing in newspapers and posting in shop windows in the major cities since the 1830s [see "Blow Ye Winds" or "It's Advertised in Boston," #139]. How Lizzie Marble obtained the lyrics is not documented. She had accompanied her husband, Captain John Marble, on the previous voyage of the *Kathleen* (1857-60), where she had written an articulate journal and letters, and one of the mates had written a long, explicitly affectionate narrative ballad entitled "A Voyage on New Holland" [#161] that presents a generous portrait of Captain Marble's kindness and good nature. Lizzie was widowed aboard the *Awashonks* soon afterwards, in 1861.

At the time, the *Kathleen* was still at sea under Captain Mooers. When John Marble died suddenly, Lizze left the *Awashonks* in mid passage and returned to Fall River with her young son and brother-in-law (George Marble, who had been first mate). This second *Kathleen* ballad, was produced at sea in 1864 long after she had gone home, and must have been passed along to her as a tribute after the *Kathleen*'s return, probably by William T. Butts, who was second mate on both outings. An appreciative veteran of service under John Marble, and undoubtedly fond of Lizze, a favorite among the *Kathleen* crew whose kindness and maternal interaction with the lads helped make it an ideally companionable voyage, he may have written the lyrics himself, based on the earlier ballad; he may even have written both ballads (it was either he or third mate John Sullivan who wrote the first one). In fact, Butts may well have been doubly appreciative because, as comparison of the ballads makes clear, unlike John Marble, Captain Mooers was hardly a genial commander. Whether it was Butts or Sullivan who wrote the first *Kathleen* ballad, it is clear that the first one influenced the second. Yet they are quite different, providing interesting contrasts not only between the two captains but also in the respective dramatic emphases of the texts. The first is construed as a sequential narrative, the second is more a series of enthusiastic portraits of the captain, officers, and ratings. While no tune is specified in the manuscript, the second ballad is presumed to have been intended for the same melody as the first, the air of "Vilikins and His Dinah" [see #81], which fits it admirably.

A.

"SONG COMPOSED ABOARD THE BARK KATHLEEN." Marble Family Papers, Fall River, circa 1860s. A fragment of five stanzas (#1-5) in Elizabeth C. Marble's hand identical to the corresponding stanzas in B. The MS was badly water damaged and separated from the sequel pages long before it came into the Kendall Collection in 1981. B appears to be a verbatim transcription in another hand, made while the prototype was still intact.

B.

"SONG COMPOSED ABOARD THE BARK KATHLEEN." Marble Family Papers, Fall River, circa 1860s. An apparently complete text of 14 stanzas (the first 5 of which are identical with A), transcribed in an unidentified hand not that of John, George, or Elizabeth Marble, unaccountably writtenon the stationery of the New Haven [Conn.] Lawn Club. Parenthetical annotations ( ) are original to the MS. Eleven officers and crewmen are named in the portion of the lyrics that survives, but nineteen men listed on the outward manifest are not named at all (see fn. 75).

1. As I was a walking on South St. so wide,[55]
   On the corner of Dors, this note I espied,
   There's twenty young seamen now wanted to sail
   In the Kathleen of Bedford in search of sperm whales

2. I went to New Bedford, all's true that I sing,
   I went to New Bedford & shipped with J (& R) Wing
   On[e] outfit he gave me, and a dollar or two
   Then wished me good luck, and on board had me go.

3. Next morning we sailed & O Lord & O Dear
   Our stomachs were heaving, we felt very queer,
   But better we got, and quite well, and quite smart (sound)
   We arrived in safety, on the Western Ground[56]

4. We sailed for Flores,[57] before a fine breeze,
   We sailed for Flores, to get Portugees,
   Two green hands we got, who the sea had ne'er seen
   Likewise two young fellows, who sailors had been

5. We sailed for Fyall,[58] as you may have heard
   We sailed for Fyall, likewise Cape de Verd[59]
   The we doubled the East Cape[60] with the wind strong and free
   And sailed for Australia, the port of Bunbury[61]

---

[55] *South Street* was New York's principal waterfront street at the time. South Street Seaport and the remnants of the old Fulton Street Fish Market are located there today as reminders of the city's extremely vigorous maritime heritage.

[56] The so-called Western Whaling Grounds in the Atlantic Ocean, which (from a British point of view) was known to mariners in the Age of Sail as the Western Ocean.

[57] *Flores:* westernmost of the Azores Islands; its port is Santa Cruz.

[58] *Faial* [*Fayal*]: one of the Azores Islands, on which the port of Horta was the most frequent calling port for Yankee whalers.

[59] *Cape de Verd:* the Cape Verde (or Cabo Verde) Islands, off the coast of West Africa, a Portuguese dependency at the time, peopled by Creoles (Criollios) of mixed African and European ancestry, a frequent outward-bound stopover for the Yankee whaling fleet and a perpetual source of able personnel. The principal whalers' ports-of-call were the islands of Brava and Fogo.

[60] *East Cape:* the Cape of Good Hope, as opposed to the "West Cape," Cape Horn.

[61] *Bunbury:* seaport in Western Australia on the Indian Ocean coast ±200 kilometers (120 miles) south of Perth and Fremantle.

6. Cha[rle]s C. Moores is our Captain,[62] a man of great name
   From the outcast of nations, Nantucket he came,
   He's hasty in temper, and it rules supreme,
   But since I've been whaling worse captains I've seen

7. [Mr.] Craw[63] is our first mate, from Fall River he hails
   None better than he out of Bedford now sails
   He's liked by the officers, obeyed with a will,
   we would ask for none better, his office to fill

8. Mr. Butts[64] is our second, who is known far and wide
   For as bully a whaleman, as e'er stemed the tide
   As an officer just, as kind as he can
   He's liked by the officers, and wo[o]ed by the men.

9. Mr. Anderson[65] is our third mate and better than he
   Ne'er trod on the green earth, nor sailed the salt sea
   He's [a] man and a Christian a sailor also
   And well knows his duty aloft and alow

10. Mr. Harpes[66] is our fourth mate a cooper by trade
    And if its a keg or a cask you'd have made
    A box to be scrimshawed a desk or a swift
    Just ask Mr. Harpes and he'll give you a lift

11. Boatsteerers we have, in number but three
    None better there are, for none better can be
    There's Jim, and there's Charles, there's Peter also[67]
    Just give them a chance, and you'll see what they'll do

12. The Carpenter[68] swears if I his name do write
    He'll kick, and he'll tear, and he'll somebody fight
    But it's useless for him to be taking such paines
    He's famous for his boxes, likewise for his canes[69]

---

[62] In all, Charles C. Mooers commanded seven whaling voyages, of which the Kathleen was his sixth: barks *Maria* of New Bedford (1849-52 and 1852-56), *Iowa* of Fairhaven (1852, 1856, and 1856-59), *Kathleen* of New Bedford (1860-64), and *Sea Queen* of Westport (1866-69).

[63] Henry T. Craw, first mate, age 27 when the *Kathleen* sailed, had been third mate and boatsteerer on the bark *Mattapoisett* (1853-54) and second mate on the bark *D. Franklin* (1855-56), both out of Westport and both under Captain Leander Smith.

[64] William T. Butts, second mate, age 26 when the *Kathleen* sailed, was from Dartmouth, Mass., and was one of four men who made both of the *Kathleen* voyages. In fact, he made three: he was a boatsteerer on the 1855-57 voyage of the Kathleen under Captain William Allen, and second mate under John Marble during 1857-60 and under Charles Moores on this voyage.

[65] James Anderson, 25, from Utica, New York.

[66] Reuben C. Harps, Jr., was born on Nantucket in 1835 and trained there as a cooper (Frank 1991, 64). (See below.)

[67] Jim was James McQuade, 21, from Middleborough, Mass.; Charles F. Smith, 17, was from Dartmouth, Mass.; and Pedro João Delgado, a native of the Azores. Delgado and McQuade had also been on the previous *Kathleen* voyage, Delgado as a boatsteerer, McQuade as an ordinary seaman. Benjamin A. Allen of New Bedford was also a boatsteerer on the previous voyage and, from his position on the NBPS crew list of the 1860-64 voyage, he appears to have been a boatsteerer on it, too. The outward manifest lists his age as 14, but he was probably 24 when the ship sailed.

[68] It is not possible to identify the carpenter from the incomplete data on the surviving crew list.

13. There's Steward[70] and Johnson[71] both great on a song[72]
    There's Charlie[73] the Blacksmith to make up the throng
    There's Kelly[74] the cook for shortness called Mick
    From Boston he comes and you can swear he's a brick

14. And now we've been cruising on the Australia shore
    For the last thirty months but will be no more
    And we challenge you all both old ships and new
    To equal the Kathleen in officers and crew[75]

Bark *Kathleen,* sperm whaling, by E.N. Russell, painted in 1902, the year the *Kathleen* was stove and sunk by a sperm whale.

---

[69] References to scrimshaw—pictorial engravings, carvings, boxes, swifts (yarn-winders), sewing implements, tools, etc., made from sperm whale ivory, walrus ivory, or baleen, often mixed with other "found" materials—are surprisingly scarce in whalemen's journals. *Canes* refers to walking sticks carved or turned on shipboard out of sperm whale jawbone and fitted with fancy handles. *Boxes* constructed of various combinations of wood with sperm whale or walrus ivory, skeletal bone, baleen, abalone, mother-of-pearl, tortoise shell, and wood, were among the standard forms. It was not unusual for a skilled ship's carpenter or cooper to assist his shipmates with some of the finer points, or even to produce scrimshaw for others in trade. The carpenter and cooper of the *Kathleen* seem to have been such celebrated craftsmen. Captains sometimes commissioned scrimshaw from able subalterns, though John Marble did his own scrimshaw on the earlier *Kathleen* voyage; so, too, third mate John Sullivan (see Frank 1991, pp 89 and 128).

[70] It is not possible definitively to identify the steward from the incomplete data on the surviving crew list.

[71] George C. Johnson, 26, of New York City.

[72] The *Kathleen* had been quite a musical ship on the previous voyage, with amateur theatricals, frequent skylarking, and private recitals in the aftercabin—matters about which Lizzie Marble, the captain's wife, comments frequently in her letters and journals. Unfortunately, there is no equivalent record of musical doings on this second voyage, and the lyrics here are the only specific evidence of music on board.

[73] It is not clear whether this is Charles McEaton, 22, from Saugus, Mass., or Charles Hess, 22, from Philadelphia, both of whom are named on the crew list but in unspecified capacities.

[74] Michael Kelley, 22, originally from Manchester, N.H., but evidently a Boston resident at the time.

[75] Eleven officers and crewmen are named in the portion of the lyrics that survives, but nineteen men listed on the outward manifest are not named at all: Benjamin A. Allen of New Bedford, already mentioned, whose residence is listed as New Bedford and his age as 14, but who was a boatsteerer on the previous *Kathleen* voyage and was probably one of the boatsteerers on this one, too; one or the other of the two Charlies (Hess or McEaton); five of the six Portuguese in the crew: Frank Gomes, Manuel Frates, Joseph Roderick, and Andrew Martina; Christiana Ferrara, a foreign seaman of unknown nationality; a German named Jacob Hershler, age 23, who had been cook on the previous *Kathleen* voyage; and thirteen other Yankees: George A. Archer, listed as 14 years old, from Nantucket; John Collins, 21, of Providence; William Emerson, 22, Boston; Matthew Kennedy, 20, Roxbury, Mass.; Felix Roth, 22, Aurelius, N.Y.; Lyman St. Clair, 21, Topsham, Maine; Nelson Stone, 21, from New Hampshire; Thomas J. Taylor, 22, Fairfield, Maine; Harrison G. Thompson, 20, Weymouth, Mass.; and Ellery H. Butts, 13, the son of the second mate.

CHAPTER SEVENTEEN
"Musick on the Brain"
Frederick Howland Smith's Tune List

> We had a fiddler on board N. Durfee was his name
> He used to keep us well supplied with musick on the brain
> Next he got a Cornet to match with that above
> Anyone would think that the ship was in a fog
>
> — B. Morrison, from an anonymous journal of
> the New Bedford bark *Mermaid,* 1883-90[1]

Captain Frederick Howland Smith was one of the most interesting and versatile fellows ever to carve out a niche for himself aboard a Yankee whaler; however, his terse autobiography hardly does justice to his experiences:

> Sailed in the Lydia Oct 9" 1854 Capt John W Leonard gone 4 years—Cabin Boy—1300 bbls [barrels of oil]. In 1858 sailed as Boatsteerer in Bark Roscius, Capt Fred Howland, on Sept 1. Arrived Home in August 1861. 1800 bbls. Enlisted in 18" Mass Volunteers Aug 6" 1862. Discharged in August 1864. Shipped as 3d Mate and sailed April 16 1865 in Ship Herald Capt John Hunewell [sic] gone 19 months 575 bbls. Sailed again in the Herald as Second Mate Capt Seth Nickerson on a Two years voyage. I cleared on this Voyage 1966$, about the first money made Whaling. In August the 31st I sailed in the Barque Hecla as Master; on the morning of Dec 29" 1870 struck on Bird Island and ship & cargo were a total loss. Came home by way of Suez & England. Expecting to be hung; But the same Owners gave me the Barque Petrel and July 20th 1871 I started for another Voyage. May first 1874 arrived home—1800 Bbls. July 5" 1875 sailed in Barque Ohio was gone 38 months and arrived with 2000 Bbls., Oct 17" 1878—May 24" 1882 sailed in John P West, arrived home May 22d 1886, 2000 bbls. sperm. June 19" 1900 sailed in the Barque Kathleen arrived home Sept 28" 1901 Dismasted, 920 bbs sperm[2]

Beyond this rough outline, Smith's career was a colorful one in which music and the arts played a significant role. An able scrimshanderer (maker of scrimshaw) and skilled marlinspike seaman (maker of fancy ropework), he was also a collector of songs and tunes and a shipboard musician in his own right. Raised in Dartmouth, Mass., just outside New Bedford, he first went to sea as a cabin boy at age 14, conscientiously learned the art and craft of whaling, applied himself to the study of navigation, and rose through the ranks. At 22 he enlisted in the Union Army, saw action during two or three years' service, and after the war resumed whaling and continued his progress in the fishery. Shipwrecked on his first command, he returned home via the new Suez Canal—as he put it, "expecting to be hung"—but thanks to enlightened owners he was exonerated from blame, given another command, and emerged as a respected and beloved whaling captain for over thirty years. His wife, Sallie, accompanied him on a couple of whaling voyages and appears to have been as accomplished as he, collaborating with him on scrimshaw, macramé, journal-writing, even celestial navigation. Fred was evidently a violinist, and certainly a fiddler; uncorroborated lore suggests that Sallie played the piano and the guitar. After Captain Smith finally retired, he was widowed and remarried; then part of his assets were wiped out in the wreck of the *Kathleen*—of which he was one of the owners at the time and which he had actually commanded on the voyage immediately previous—when in 1902, *Pequod*-like, she was struck by a sperm whale and sank "in less than half an hour."

---

[1] See "Blow Ye Winds" [#139].

[2] Transcribed in its entirety from the untitled original of Smith's one-page autobiography, in Smith's own handwriting, in the Kendall Collection, New Bedford Whaling Museum.

Most of Fred Smith's known song and tune collecting was been done during his first four voyages, when he was a cabin boy, seaman, boatsteerer, and deck officer in three whaleships and before he ascended to the responsibilities and distractions of marriage and command. He kept journals of all four voyages in a single volume, which also became his reference library of song texts and tunes (he transcribed many; q.v. in Appendix 6). It also became his notebook and study guide in matters of seamanship and celestial navigation. In one instance, as a second mate, he carefully recorded, in the manner of a legal document, a complaint evidently lodged against him by the captain about some aspect of his work—apparently for future reference should the issue ever be brought up before the owners or consul.[3] An intriguing and endearing feature of this volume is its preoccupation with The Education of Frederick Howland Smith, Mariner, and his own earnest conscientiousness, tempered by a wry wit and an irrepressible love of drawing, sketching, and music. This provides an instructive contrast to the sober and more self-confidently professional tone of his mature journals, written in the full flower of command, but which nevertheless, though they contain few drawings and no songs, retain the easy style, keenness of perception, and tendency toward humor and irony apparent in his more youthful manuscripts.[4]

It would undoubtedly delight folklorists and performers today had Fred Smith or some other whaleman seen fit to transcribe shipboard fiddle and dance tunes, note-for-note, just as he knew them—preferably with grace notes and ornamentation, the way they were played in the forecastle and aftercabin at sea. But, so far, no such transcriptions have emerged, and Smith's mere list, inscribed on a single page of his journal, is about the best and most extensive documentation of such tunes on American whaleships. Fortunately, the tune list is sufficiently detailed, and the musical literature sufficiently explicit, to enable a comprehensive and virtually complete reconstruction, presented in this chapter in the order in which the diarist listed them.[5]

It is difficult to know precisely what original purpose Smith intended his list to serve; but it seems to be just the kind of inventory that many musicians regularly maintain, just to remind them of what tunes—and the names of the tunes—they already know and might be called upon to play. This bit of organization in the often chaotic world of tune-playing and tune-remembering imparts a kind of structure to any programme of tune-learning. In Smith's case, judging from the context of his shipboard journals—tools he employed conscientiously and scrupulously in his steady rise from cabin boy to Master Mariner—his compendium of tunes appears to be yet another List of Things Learned a-Whaling between 1854 and 1869, probably written down while serving as third mate of the ship *Herald* just after the Civil War. He carried this early journal of four voyages with him on subsequent cruises over many years as captain, and so perpetually had the songs and tune list with him at sea, including the voyages with his musician-wife on board.

---

[3] The ship agent-owners were, of course, responsible in part for determining or approving the advancement of a young whaleman's career and his eventual promotion to captain. The American Consul in any foreign port was the local authority responsible for adjudication of any dispute between captain and crew; this was effective only in varying degrees (see the biographical note on Daniel Kimball Ritchie in Appendix 6).

[4] Smith's early journals are in the Kendall Collection at the New Bedford Whaling Museum. Fred and Sallie Smith's parallel journals of the barks *Ohio* and *John P. West,* and Sallie's scrapbook (begun circa 1877), are preserved at the G.W. Blunt White Library at Mystic Seaport Museum.

[5] Of the 21 titles inscribed on Smith's list, 20 are anthologized here; unfortunately, one title has been omitted as illegible.

361

163. Fisher's Hornpipe
(O'Neill #1575, #1576)

Our blacksmith—we called him "Smut"—was one of the "darndest fiddlers," as Shanks expressed it, that I ever knew. He was born a-fiddling, he said, and it came so natural to him that he couldn't help it,—he had to fiddle. He used to tell us that he had done nothing but kill cats for a month, before beginning the voyage, so that he would be sure to have strings enough for his fiddle. The old Toms made the best of strings, but he preferred the little kittens for the upper notes.

— "Whaling on the Crozets" by 'An Old Salt' (1876).

Setting A: "FISHER'S HORNPIPE (*CRANNCIUIL FISUIR*) - 1st SETTING." O'Neill #1575.

Setting B: "FISHER'S HORNPIPE (*CRANNCIUIL FISUIR*) - 2nd SETTING." O'Neill #1576.

Setting C: "FISHERS' OR SAILORS' HORNPIPE." Lucien O. Carpenter, *J.W. Pepper's Universal Dancing Master*, 1889, p. 92: "First couple down the outside, back; down the centre, back; cast off; swing 6 hands quite round; right and left." (*1000 Fiddle Tunes,* 95: tune and dance figure similar to New England form reported by Linscott, 76ff).

164. The White Cockade
(O'Neill #1803)

A hornpipe and march traditional in the British Isles and North America, published in David Herd's *Ancient and Modern Scottish Songs, Heroic Ballads, etc.* in 1776, "The White Cockade" is sung in Ireland with a traditional Gaelic text and is used for a variety of dances, including the Virginia Reel and a contra dance known as "The White Cockade." There are two theories about the significance of the title. One is that it is derives from a decorative embellishment on military headgear, "a knot of ribbons or a rosette worn as a badge… The Stuart badge was a white rose, and the resulting white cockade figured in Jacobite songs after the downfall of the dynasty… Originally, the wearing of a cockade, as soon as it had become a badge, was restricted to soldiers, as 'to mount a cockade' was 'to become a soldier'" (*Enc. Brit.*). This explanation is strengthened by the Northern English folk ballad "The White Cockade," which concerns army recruitment and specifically mentions the white cockade as a military insignia; and by the historic military associations of the hornpipe and its frequent use as an army and navy march. An alternative theory is: "'The White Cockade' (*Cnotahd Ban*) means literally a bouquet, and has nothing to do with the military cockade, as some authorities state, but is a bouquet or plume of white ribbons with which the young women of Munster adorn the hair and headdress on wedding and other festive occasions. The custom prevailed early in the seventeenth century" (Fitz-Gerald, 358).

Setting A. "THE WHITE COCKADE." From Eloise Hubbard Linscott, *Folk Songs of Old New England*, 1939, p. 120; associated with a contra dance of the same name. Similar to Linscott, p. 117, the given for the Virginia Reel.

Setting B. "THE WHITE COCKADE (*AN CNOTAN BAN*)." O'Neill #1803.

165. Zip Coon
[Old Zip Coon; Turkey In the Straw]

Every night in pleasant weather, Smut would bring up his fiddle, and "make it talk." Then things would be lively. The waist of the ship was the ball-room, and every one who could dance a jig, horn pipe, or breakdown, performed; while Smut sat on the carpenter's bench, and fiddled and cracked his jokes. I used to think that sometimes he would fiddle too much. But no ill effects ever came from his music, and I am quite sure now that a fiddle is a good thing to have at sea.

— "Whaling on the Crozets" by 'An Old Salt' (1876).

One of the most popular American tunes of all time, this unascribed minstrel song was first published in 1834 and blazed through the blackface era. Early editions of sheet music allege that it was popularized by George Washington Dixon (1808-1861), the "celebrated buffo singer" who was performing by 1827 and introduced "Coal Black Rose" in 1829; but rival minstrel Bob Farrell also claimed it. According to S. Foster Damon, Farrell "is usually credited with the authorship" even though Dixon, "who also featured it, insisted that it was his." A New York edition published by Thomas Birch, dated 1834 (thus certainly one of the first) advertises itself as "sung by all the celebrated comic singers." The original text is riddled with the kinds of racial stereotypes characteristic of the genre. An variant form of the tune is known as "Turkey in the Straw" after a text written for it in 1861 by minstrel Dan Bryant (né Daniel W. O'Brien, 1833-1875).

"ZIP COON." From *Minstrel Songs, Old and New,* Boston, 1882, pp. 120f, where it appears with a full text.

166. Rory O'More
(O'Neill #856)

The song "Rory O'More," written by Irish novelist, painter, lyricist, and tunesmith Samuel Lover (1797-1868), was first published in 1826. It became extremely popular, was adapted as a jig (likely the form in which Fred Smith knew it), and circulated in many forms and variants on both sides of the Atlantic, becoming the source of many imitations and "sequels"—such as the "Rory O'Moore Quickstep… as performed by the Boston Brigade Band, arranged for the pianoforte by B.A. Burdett" (Boston: C.H. Keith, circa 1837-46). Lover later expanded his character into a novel, entitled *Rory O'More, a National Romance* (1837). The novel, in turn, was made into a play, with Tyrone Power (1797-1841) in the title role (*Webster,* 924), which ran for 108 nights on the London stage (B.E. Smith 1897, 625).

Setting A. "RORY O'MOORE (*RUAIDRI UA MOROA*)." O'Neill #856.

Setting B. "RORY O'MORE—JIG." From *1000 Fiddle Tunes,* p. 62. A representative American setting.

167. Oh, Dear, What Can the Matter Be?
[What Can the Matter Be?; Johnny's So Long at the Fair]

According to Chappell, "This song must have come into favour not later than 1792. *The Bristol Lyre or Muses' Repository,* Jan. 5th, 1793, calls it the favourite duet. It is thought not to be much older than the first date." It was still in tradition in the late 20th century, when it was often relegated to the nursery.

"O DEAR WHAT CAN THE MATTER BE." From undated sheet music (New York: E[dward] Riley, 29 Chatham St., circa 1819-31). A standard form of the tune. Compare Chappell 1855, II:732; and *Accordion Music* (London, circa 1860), p. 89, where in the third measure, the dominant has been substituted for the subdominant.

168. Harvest Home Waltz

What Fred Smith intended by "Harvest Home Waltz" has not been definitively ascertained. It is probably "Harvest Home," an English song which, though it is not customarily printed in 3/4 ("waltz") time, it is usually in 6/8 time—for practical purposes virtually undistinguishable from a waltz, especially if it be learned from performance rather than from printed music.

"HARVEST HOME." From John Hullah, *The Song Book,* London, 1866, p. 31; after Chappell.

Note: "Harvest Home" is also the name of an Irish hornpipe that is easily rearranged into waltz time; it could be to such an adaptation that Smith refers: a similar metrical transformation, "Home as a Waltz" (Boston: C.H. Keith, circa 1843-46) is a waltz-time adaptation of "Home Sweet Home" [#181]. Alternatively, Smith may have had in mind an extremely obscure tune entitled "The Joys of Harvest Home. Adapted to the Much Admired Hungarian Waltz. Written by S. Richards. Arr[anged] by T. Munro," which was still available at the time in sheet music published at Boston by C. & E.W. Jackson, circa 1822 (Dichter #952).

169. Soldier's Joy
(O'Neill #1642)

This ubiquitous hornpipe was in circulation throughout the British Isles and North America. It appears in most of the principal anthologies of Irish traditional tunes and in various British and American collections. A circle-dance of the same name is particularly associated with the tune: according to Linscott, "'Soldier's Joy' is one of the earliest dances recorded in England, but no date of origin has been established" (Linscott, 110).

Setting A: "THE SOLDIER'S JOY (*LUT GAIR AN SAIGEADOR*)." O'Neill #1642.

Setting B: "SOLDIER'S JOY." From Eloise Hubbard Linscott, *Folk Songs of Old New England,* 1939, p.110: given as a circle-dance of the same name (compare another setting on p.341).

170. Pop! Goes the Weasel

This is an English tune that takes its name from the text, a venerable occupational song in which *weasel* (in the title and the chorus) refers both to the wily animal and to a component of the hatter's and shoemaker's apparatus named for the animal. Linscott identifies it as a popular singing game of unknown origin dating "as far back as the seventeenth century." It was quite popular during the minstrel era of the middle 1800s, when several editions of sheet music were issued and it was often performed on stage, but it is now usually regarded as a children's song and is so classified in the *Song Index*. The melody makes a nice jig but is most often published as a reel. A set-dance format traditional in New England may be the way whaleman Fred Smith knew it in the 1850s. At around the same time, fellow-whaleman George Edgar Mills transcribed in his journal the text of a comic parody entitled "Matrimony," addressing a rather more adult perspective on gamesmanship. Mills was a prolific poet and the parody may be his own original composition, though it does reflect a rather higher order of literary sophistication than even Mills was ordinarily capable. In any case, the lyrics have not been located anywhere else.

"POP GOES THE WEASEL." Composite: compare Lucien O. Carpenter, *J.W. Pepper's Universal Dancing Master*, 1889, p. 97; Linscott, *Folk Songs of Old New England*, p. 107 (contra dance of the same name) and, p. 117 (a quite similar setting given for the Virginia Reel, but with fewer embellishments).

"MATRIMONY." George Edgar Mills, third mate, bark *Aurora* of Westport, Massachusetts, 1858.

1. Matrimony is a must
   For every mans digestion
   When the shell is fairly cracked
   Pop, goes the question

2. Pretty girls will sign and blush
   Simper all they can sir
   Till from out their pouting lips
   Pop, goes the answer

3. Cupid fans the hold flame
   Rankest kind of arson
   When it gains a certain height
   Pop, goes the parson

4. Quite throughout the honeymoon
   Made of rosy colors
   Into sundry good [sic] till
   Pop, goes the dollars

5. When a year has shown its tail
   Round the corner maybe
   Out upon the happy world
   Pop, goes a baby

6. Mother gives it catnip tea
   Father gives it Brandy
   And adown its gastric tube
   Pop, goes the candy

7. All the sweets the earth can yield
   Wont suffice to calm it
   Daddy screws his lips and then
   Pop, goes a Damn it.

March 28th [18]58

171. Yankee Doodle

… Hautboy forthwith got out his dented old fiddle and, sitting down on a tall rickety stool, played away right merrily at "Yankee Doodle" and other off-handed, dashing, and disdainfully carefree airs. But as common as were the tunes, I was transfixed by something miraculously superior in their style.

— Herman Melville, "The Fiddler."

The persistent story that "'Yankee Doodle' was introduced… by one mischievous Dr. Richard Shuckburgh of the British army" in 1755 (Nason) may be apocryphal; so, too, the contention that it was later adopted by the King's troops to ridicule the rebellious colonists, thus giving rise to the ostensibly pejorative epithet "Yankee." But with lyrics playfully reverent of Washington and the Continental Army, the song was proudly, and with more than a bit of irony, adopted as the anthem of the American Revolution and the epithet embraced as a badge of honor. The unvaryingly stable tune has been immensely popular and has hosted an enormous assortment of textual adaptations. It has been very much anthologized, reprinted, and parodied, mostly along patriotic lines, extolling American naval prowess in the War of 1812, commemorating milestones of national history (like the latter-day Boston Tea Party text below), or lampooning political opponents. It was as popular at sea as on shore. John Jones alludes to it in his meandering journal of the *Eliza Adams* in 1852, it appears on Fred Smith's tune list a few years later, and John Martin mentions it as a kind of oddball chantey aboard the whaler *Lucy Ann* of Wilmington in 1842. A clipping pasted into John Marble's journal of the *Pilgrim* of Somerset that same year attributes the music to "one Dr. Shachburg, an English surgeon" in 1775, and gives lyrics purporting to be original, taken "from Farmer & Moore's Historical Collections, published in 1820." Marble also reports a yarn about "Yankee Doodle" being ill used by the captain as a whaleboat chantey on some previous voyage:

Saturday Sept 10th [1842] Blowing a gale of wind from the N & W. laying to… In the evening Jim a color'd fellow was amazing us by telling us how the old man acted on board ship when the boats were about to fasten. he says he sings to the tune of yankee doodle such words as these: O pull my good fellows, you dont pull a bit. O you molly horns pull. there he stands up give it to him solid, he's fast, he's fast, he's fast. there he lances him there he spouts thick blood; cocka doodle doo— with a throwing of his arms about & kicking up his heels. I expect he sang a different song when he saw us come alongside with no whale. Lat 34.48.S Long: 123.°58' E.

Tune and later text from the *Excelsior Song Book* by B.F. Baker (Boston, 1860), page 101 (facsimile).

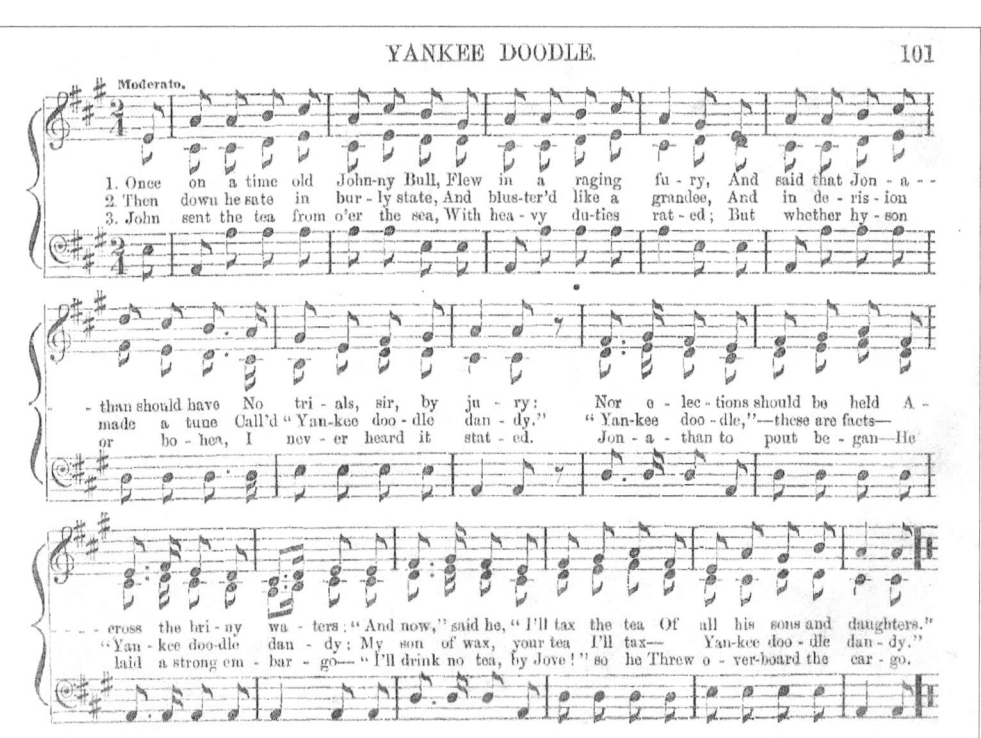

"YANKEE DOODLE." Facsimile or a clipping from an unidentified periodical, reprinting a text "from the Albany Argus," pasted into the journal of John C. Marble, first mate, bark *Pilgrim* of Somerset, Massachusetts, 1842-43.

In the summer of 1775 the British army, under command of Abercrombie, lay camped on the east bank of the Hudson river, a little south of the city of Albany, awaiting reinforcements of militia from the Eastern States, previous to marching upon Ticonderoga. During the month of June these raw levies poured into camp, company after company, each man differently armed, equipped and accoutred from his neighbor, and the whole presenting such a spectacle as was never equaled, unless by the celebrated regiment of merry Jack Falstaff. — Their *outre* appearance furnished great amusement to the British officers. One Dr. Shachburg, and English surgeon, composed the tune of Yankee Doodle, and arranged it to words, which were gravely dedicated to the new recruits. The joke took, and the tune has come down to this day. The original words, which we take from Farmer & Moore's Historical Collections, published in 1820, we have not, however, met with before in many years:—

General George Washington with an attendant and his stallion. Anonymous whalemen's scrimshaw on a sperm whale tooth, circa the 1840s-50s. Kendall Collection, New Bedford Whaling Museum

Father and I went down to camp.
  Along with Captain Goodwin,
And there we saw the men and boys
  As thick as hasty pudding.

And there was Captain Washington
  Upon a slapping stallion,
A-giving greets to all his men—
  I guess there was a million.

And then the feathers on his hat,
  They looked so tarnal finey,
I wanted teskily to get
  To give to my Jemima.

And there they had a swampin' gun,
  As big as a log of maple,
On a deuced little cart
  A load for father's cattle.

And every one then fired it off
  It took a ton of powder
It made a noise like father's gun,
  Only a nation louder.

I went as near to it myself
  As Jacob's underpinnin',
And father went as near again—
  I thought the deuce was in him.

And there I see a little keg,
  Its heads were made of leather;
They knock'd upon't with little sticks,
  To call the folks together.

And there they'd fife away like fun,
  And play on cornstalk fiddles,
And some had ribbons red as blood
  All bound around their middles.

The troopers, too, would gallop up,
  And fire right in our faces;
Its scar'd me almost half to death
  To see them run such races.

Uncle Sam came there to change
  Some pancakes and some onions,
For 'lasses cakes to carry home
  To give his wife and young ones.

But I can't tell you half I see,
  They kept up such a smother;
So I took my hat off—made a bow,
  And scampered home to mother.

172. Russian Waltz

Fred Smith lists "Russian Waltz" among his tunes. A set of lyrics in *The Universal Songster* (3 vols., London, 1825), entitled "My Love Is Returned" and attributed to William Ball, specifies "Russian Waltz" as the air, but no trace of the melody has been found.

173. The Poor Old Slave

An American minstrel song with abolitionist sentiments, with words and music by G.W.H. Griffith, published in 1851. The fraudulent racial stereotyping that typifies many of the merrier so-called "plantation" songs of the blackface-minstrel era tends to be less prevalent—or at least more subtle—in such tear-jerkers as this. It must have been fairly popular on shipboard, for not only does it appear on Fred Smith's tune list but full texts are transcribed in five other journals surveyed.

"THE POOR OLD SLAVE." From *Minstrel Songs Old and New*, 1882, p. 190.

A.
"THE POOR OLD SLAVE." George Edgar Mills, third mate, bark *Aurora* of Westport, 1857. Dated "June 15th 1857 / Galipagos [sic] Islands," text A begins "It is just one year ago today" and comprises elements of the other whalemen's texts, with variations suggesting an oral source; transcribed as 3 stanzas of 8 lines each (like B), but the final 2 lines of the chorus are: "Now side by side they take their sleep / Way down in Tennessee."

B.
"THE POOR OLD SLAVE." Robert Nathaniel Hughson, bark *Java* of New Bedford, 1857-60. Standard text much like the others, beginning "Twas just one year ago to day that I remember well," and (like A) transcribed as 3 8-line stanzas, but with the standard chorus (as in C); stanza 3 has "But since that time *how* things have changed."

C.
"THE POOR OLD SLAVE." George M. Jones and Albert F. Handy, bark *Waverly* of New Bedford, 1859-63. This is a slightly eccentric text, resembling text E with minor variations (note stanza 3). The chorus (absent in A) is usually transcribed as four lines, but is given as two in the MS. "Toiled" in stanza 1 tends to impart a more sympathetic and compassionate view of the slave than the corresponding "lived" in D and E.

1. Twas just one year ago to day that I remember well
   I sat down by Nelly side a story she did tell
   Twas about a poor unhappy slave that had toiled for many a year
   But now he's dead and in his grave no master does he fear

Chorus: The poor old slave has gone to rest we know that he is free
Disturb him not but let him rest way down in Tennessee

2. She took my arm we walked along to an open field
Twas there she paused to breathe and then to his grave did steal
And kneeling down upon that little mound she softly whispered there
Come to me father she said and gently dropped a tear

3. Many a change has taken place since Nelly was my bride
For now she's dead and in her grave with her father by her side
I planted there upon their graves a weeping willow tree
And bathed its roots with many a tear that it might shelter me

D.

"POOR OLD SLAVE." Horace Wood, bark *Andrews* of New Bedford, 1866-67. A standard text of three stanzas, similar to E, with the standard chorus transcribed as four lines, exhibiting only minor variations.

E.

"THE POOR OLD SLAVE." George W. Piper, ship *Europa* of Edgartown, 1868-70. Apart from Piper's tendency to deconstruct contractions ("now *he is* dead," rather then "now *he's* dead") and formalize syntax ("*Away* down in Tennessee," rather than "*Way* down... "), few variations from C. However, such differences of emphasis as those in the last line of stanza 2 and throughout stanza 3, are worthy of comparison.

1. It is just one year ago today, that I remember well
I sat down by Nelly's side, a story she did tell
Twas about a poor unhappy slave, that lived for many a year
But now he is dead and in his grave, no master does he fear

Chorus: That poor old slave has gone to rest
We know that he is free
Disturb him not, but let him rest
Away down in Tennessee

2. She took my hand we walked along, into an open field
Twas then she paused to breathe awhile, and to his grave did steal
She sat down on that little mound, and softly whispered there
Come to me father, it is your child, and gently dropt a tear

3. But since that time all things have changed, poor Nelly that was my bride
Now lies beneath the cold green sod, close by her father's side
I planted near that little spot, a weeping willow tree
And I bathed its roots with many a tear, that it might shelter me.

174. Nelly Gray
[Nellie Gray; Darling Nelly Gray]

This minstrel song with abolitionist overtones, published in 1856 and widely disseminated in print and on stage for at least a decade thereafter, is the most famous composition of Benjamin Russell Hanby (1833-1867), "the Stephen Foster of Ohio." The author claimed that it was based on actual events in his own family's history. It is also a prime example of how even a professionally composed, commercially viable piece can enter tradition and tenaciously remain there, spawning numerous progeny—including at least one authentic sea chantey, at least one original sailors' parody, and, indirectly, an entire family of authentic cowboy songs.

The historical basis for "Nelly Gray" is said to be "a runaway slave named Joseph Selby who died at the home of Hanby's father while on his way to Canada to earn money to buy the freedom of his lover named, yes, Nelly Gray" (R. Jackson, 267). "A fairly elaborate story about the background of the song and the real-life prototypes of the characters," together with an account of "Hanby's brief career and family background," was read into the *Congressional Record* (89th Congress, First Session, 1965): "a long address by Judge Earl R. Hoover entitled 'Benjamin R. Hanby—"The Stephen Foster of Ohio"'" (Ibid, 267).

In the eleven decades intervening between its publication and its apotheosis in the House of Representatives, the song had developed a national appeal and exerted great influence, much of it unacknowledged. In the Northeast, "'Darling Nellie Gray' and 'The Girl I Left Behind Me' are two square dances which originated in New York State... [and] became established throughout southern New England" (Tolman & Page, 78). Out West, when the great cowboy poet-songwriter Jack Thorp wrote the lyrics to his classic "Little Joe the Wrangler" in 1898, he claimed W.S. Hays's "Little Old [Log] Cabin in the Lane" (1871) as the inspiration for the tune. What Thorp evidently did not realize, and what cowboy-song historians (e.g., Fife, 214; Lomax & Lomax, 91-93; Tinsley, 84-86) have not realized ever since, is that "Little Old Log Cabin in the Lane" is derived from "Nelly Gray"—so much so that Mr. Hays is indeed fortunate not to have been prosecuted for plagiarism. (Perhaps is was the Confederate sympathies of the Old West at the time that obliterated the Hanby legacy.) Thorp's "Little Joe the Wrangler," definitely an improvement on both originals, in turn provided the tune for "The Cowboy's Dance Song," "Roy Bean," and, as late as the 1940s, "Reuben James"—all of which can trace their ancestry through Thorp, to Hays, and ultimately to "Nelly Gray." Meanwhile, soon after it was published in 1856 it was making the rounds at sea. Sailors in uncommonly large numbers transcribed the words into their journals, a hit-parade level of popularity on shipboard in the 1850s and '60s. Also, almost certainly within the first couple of years after the first publication of "Nelly Gray," the derivative "Maggie May" (Hugill, 307) arose as a chantey, likely debuting on British merchant ships; and on a voyage out of New Bedford during 1857-59, whaleman Charles B. Swain wrote a parody of his own (text E).

"DARLING NELLY GRAY." From the original sheet music, Boston: Oliver Ditson & Co., 1856.

A.
"NELLY GRAY." Substantial fragment transcribed between voyages by Helen M. Tinkham in the journal of Daniel L. Tinkham, bark *Samuel & Thomas* (1852) and brig *March* (1855-56) of Mattapoisett, 1855. (5/4 +chorus/4)

B.
"NELLY GRAY." Freeman A. Smith, schooner *Varnum H. Hill* of Provincetown, 1857-58. Standard copy text (5/4 + two choruses/6).

C.
"NELLY GRAY." George Edgar Mills, third mate, bark *Aurora* of New Bedford. "Copied from Barque John A. Parker, Nov. 22, 1858. off Galapagos Islands." Standard copy text (5/4 + two choruses/6).

D.
"NELLY GRAY." George W. Piper, ship *Europa* of Edgartown, 1868-70. Line 3 of stanza 4 is obviously corrupt; C has "Hark's: there's somebody knocking at the door"; in stanza 4, C has "And I never shall see her any more."

1. There's a low green valley on the old Kentucky shore
   Where I have wiled many happy hours away
   A setting and a singing by the little cabin door
   Where lives my darling Nelly Gray

   Chorus: O my poor Nelly gray
   They have taken you away
   And I will never see my darling any more
   I am setting on the river
   And I'm weeping all the day
   For you have gone from the old Kentucky shore

2. When the moon had climbed the mountain and the stars are shining too
   I will take my darling Nelly Gray
   I will paddle down the river in my little light canoe
   And so sweetly the banjo I will play

3. One night as I went to see her she had gone the neighbors say
   The white man had bound her with a chain
   They have taken her to Georgia, for the wear her life away
   As she toils midst the cotton and the cane

4. My canoe is on the river and my banjo is unstrung
   I am tired of living any more
   My song shall be ended, and my banjo unstrung
   While I stay on the old Kentucky shore

5. My eyes are getting blinded, and I cannot see my way
   I am tired of living any more
   I hear the angels calling and I see my Nelly Gray
   Farewell to the old Kentucky shore

Chorus: O my poor Nelly gray
It is up in Heaven so they say
And they will never take you from me any more
I am coming, coming, coming
And the angels clear the way
Farewell to the old Kentucky shore

E.
"NELLIE GRAY / WORDS BY C.B. SWAIN." Charles B. Swain, bark *Cachalot* of New Bedford, 1857-59.

1. Neath the shady forest trees by the silent river side.
   Stood the cabin of my darling Nelly Gray;
   There in our light canoe, on its gently rippling tide
   Together us have floated all the day.

   Chorus: But my poor Nelly Gray! / They have taken her away;
   I ne'er shall see my darling Nelly more,
   Now I'm sitting by the river, and weeping all the day,
   Farewell! to my old Kentucky shore.

2. Where the wild roses blossom, and the violets twine,
   And the lily reigns queen among them all;
   There on a mossy bank together we'd recline,
   And we envy'd not the master in his hall.

3. On that old cottage doorsill, my Nelly sat and spun;
   Singing joyous and happy as a bird;
   Now all is lone and silent since my darling Nelly's gone,
   And that song now there never more is heard.

4. Now weary sad and lonely, I would lay me down and die,
   For my heart it is breaking here alone;
   Theres no one heeds or listens to my wild entreating cry,
   Oh! take me where my darling Nellys gone.

5. Oh dig me a grave in yonder shady grove
   That stands near my Nellys cabin door
   There my rest shall be so peaceful whilst the wild flowers wave alon[ ]
   Near the river by the old Kentucky shore

175. Nelly Bly

With words and music by Stephen Collins Foster (1826-1864), copyrighted in 1849, "Nelly Bly" was introduced by Christy's Minstrels in 1850. Like everyone else, whalemen in the 1850s and '60s were evidently quite fond of Foster's songs, several of which appear in their journals.[6]

"NELLY BLY." From the original sheet music, New York: Firth & Pond, 1849 (also repr. in R. Jackson 1974, 77ff).

"NELLY BLY." George W. Piper, ship *Europa* of Edgartown, 1868-70.

1. Nelly Bly Nelly Bly bring the broom along
   Sweep the kitchen clean my dear, we will have a little song
   Poke the wood my lady love, and make the fire burn
   And while I get my banjo down just give the mush a turn

   Chorus: Hi Nelly Ho Nelly / Listen love to me
   I will sing for you, play for you / A dulcum melody

2. Nelly Bly shuts her eye when she goes to sleep
   And when she wakens up again, her eye balls begin to peep
   The way she walks she lifts her foot and then she puts it down
   And when it lights, there is music up there, in that part of the town

3. Nelly Bly has a voice like the turtle dove
   I hears it in the meadow I hears it in the grove
   Nelly Bly has a heart warm as a cup of tea
   And bigger dan the sweet potatoe away down in Tennessee

4. Nelly Bly Nelly Bly never never sigh
   Never bring the tear drop to the corner of your eye
   For the pie is made of pumpkins and the mush is made of corn
   And there is corn and pumpkins plenty love love a lying in the barn

---

[6] In addition to "Nelly Bly," "Oh! Susanna" [#177], and "Old Folks at Home" [#182], which appear on the tune list, one or more transcriptions of each of the following Foster compositions were encountered in journals: "Dolcy Jones" (1849); "Ellen Bayne" (1854); "Farewell, My Lilly Dear" (1851); "Gentle Annie" (1856); "Hard Times Come Again No More" (1854); "Jeanie with the Light Brown Hair" (1854); "Maggie By My Side" (1861); "My Old Kentucky Home" (1853); "Nelly Bly" (1849); "Oh! Lemuel" (1850); "Oh! Willie We Have Missed You" (1854); "Old Dog Tray" (1853); "Ring, Ring the Banjo" (1851); and "Under the Willow She's Sleeping" (1860).

176. Augusta's Favorite
[*Ah! Vous Derai-je, Maman;* Twinkle, Twinkle, Little Star]

In English-speaking countries the 18th-century French traditional air "Ah! Vous Derai-je, Maman" is formally known as "Augusta's Favorite." Both Mozart and Dohanyi wrote sets of variations on it for the classical repertoire; but nowadays it is most often identified with a modest poem by Jane Taylor (1783-1824) first published in 1805. Originally titled "The Star," it is has been far better known by its first line, "Twinkle, twinkle, little star." The fundamental simplicity of the tune, perhaps, made it a fixture in the nursery, universally coupled with Taylor's innocuous lyrics.

"AUGUSTA'S FAVORITE." From Paul de Ville, *The Concertina and How to Play It* [1915], p.20; variants omitted.

177. Oh! Susanna
[Susanna]

This Stephen Foster classic, published in 1848, was soon transformed by sailors of the Gold Rush era into a Cape Horn chantey localized to Salem, Mass., beginning "I come from Salem City with a washbowl on my knee" (Shay 1948, 114). Colcord (with Hugill in her wake) presents a fragment of another midcentury American chantey adaptation of "Oh! Susanna," reportedly used for holystoning the deck and localized to the famous clipper ship *Sovereign of the Seas*. Hugill advances the esoteric theory that "Oh! Susanna" is essentially derivative, and with "Camptown Races" (also by Stephen Foster), may descend from what Hugill calls a "Negro" chantey, "The Sailor Fireman"; however, there is no evidence for this, and the extraction is almost certainly in the opposite direction. Meanwhile, text, tune, and variants of "Oh! Susanna" have had a remarkable international circulation. There are close cognates in what Shay calls "hog-German" (*"Ich komm dem Salem City mit dem washbowl auf dem knee..."*) and in Swedish—notably "Susannavisan" ("The Susanna Song"), of which Sternvall makes the spurious claim that "both text and melody can be traced back to the 1750s"! (*Sång under Segel,* quoted by Hugill). Oddly, perhaps, none of the whalemen, not even the exhaustively acquisitive George W. Piper or George Edgar Mills, saw fit to transcribe the words into their journals.

"OH! SUSSANA." From the original sheet music, New York: C. Holt, Jr., 1848 (also reprinted in R. Jackson 1974, 89ff).

178. Fanny Elssler Leaving New Orleans
[Fanny Elssler; Grog Time o' Day]

The florescence of sailors' chanteys in the 19th century is closely tied to the influence of black stevedores in the Southern cotton ports, with whom deepwater sailors increasingly came into contact in the expansionary post-Napoleonic era. Deckside worksongs grew out of age-old call-and-response traditions imported from Africa, enhanced by the related phenomenon of the so-called Negro Spirituals. These were nurtured as cultural touchstones through the anguish of slavery and transmuted through generations of singing at hard labor in the cotton fields and cane-brakes. Mixed and blended with the songs of the sailors themselves—Irish tunes, English music-hall pieces, American stage-minstrelsy, and the miscellaneous singing traditions of a remarkably polyglot class of sea-laborers—the result was a piquant soup of worksongs, respecting which the only rule was that they provide utilitarian, workable rhythms and some slight diversion from the labor at hand. Many authentic chanteys survive; probably at least as many have been lost since steam propulsion supplanted the sailing ships on which chanteys had once thrived. But comparatively few unadulterated cargo-loading songs remain. "Fanny Elssler Leaving New Orleans" appears to be one of these, evidently originating with African-American longshoremen in New Orleans and occasioned by the much-acclaimed American tour of the Viennese superstar dancer Fanny Elssler (1810-1884) during 1840-42.[7] The lyrics are miraculously preserved through ephemeral publication in *The Negro Singer's Own Book* (circa 1845). That the song may also have been making rounds on the music-hall circuit is suggested by an allusion on an earlier page of the same songster (196), in a section entitled "Conundrums," intended as a collection of vaudeville-like dialect quips for "Negro" musicians. It is attributed to the so-called "Black Apollo," whose real name was Charles White, "and all the Colored Savoyards at the Principal theatres in the United States":

> Why is Fanny Elssler like the Bunker Hill Monument?
> Because they are both out ob town.

The search for other manifestations of "Fanny Elssler Leaving New Orleans" or any cognate worksongs revealed that whatever survived into the field-collecting era did so in the West Indies, where the old cotton-steeving and cargo-loading chanteys persisted long after becoming extinct in the Southern states. Sailors' and longshoremen's worksongs arrived with American, African-American, British, and Irish mariners well before the 1830s, at which time the anonymous author of *Service Afloat*—who identifies himself only as "A Naval Officer"—remarked on local singing practices at work (as quoted by Abrahams, 11; italics added):

> Rowing in boats or other kind of labour, when a simultaneous effort is required, they have generally a song formed of extempore verses, the improvisatore being the stroke oar, the driver, or one superintendent among the rest for the talent. He in a minor key gives out *a line or two in allusion to any passing event,* all the rest taking up the burthen of the song, as a chorus, in a tenor, and this produces a very pleasing effect.

---

[7] Fanny (1810-1884) and her sister Therese (1808-1878) were daughters of Johann Elssler of Vienna, described as the factotum of composer Joseph Haydn. Their successful careers as ballerinas led both to wealth and fame. Therese, after several morganatic liaisons, married Prince Adalbert of Prussia and eventually had the title Baroness von Barnim conferred by Friedrich Wilhelm IV. Fanny "amassed a fortune and retired from the stage in 1851" (*Webster*). This was nine years after the conclusion of her charismatic North American tour, where her popularity prefigured the subsequent greater success of the Swedish Nightingale, *chanteuse* Jenny Lind, about whom songs were written and tunes named. If Fanny Elssler was similarly honored, the accolades were less luminous and few of the pieces can have survived: her portrait and some small notices appeared on the lithographic cover-art of a few generic compositions not named for her—such as "La Cachucha," which in sheet music published at New York in 1845 was billed as a "Celebrated Castanet Dance by Fanny Elssler" and "As danced by Fanny Elssler" (Dichter & Larrabee #1005f). Apart from these, the obscure heaving-and-hauling song is the only remnant of an American musical tribute to Fanny Elssler.

These chanteys were anything but stable and canonical. Rather, they were adopted, adapted, and reconfigured in the various islands, and the words altered and extemporized with "a line or two in allusion to any passing event." The "grog time of day" refrain in the example that the author of *Service Afloat* gives to typify Antigua is clearly related to the chorus of "Fanny Elssler":

> Massa lock de door, and take away the key,
> Hurra, my jolly boys, grog time a day.
> CHORUS— Grog time a day, my boys, grog time a day
> Hurra, my jolly boys, grog time a day, &c.

Hugill also quotes a snippet of *Service Afloat,* reiterated by Abrahams, in which the same song is specifically presented in a cargo-loading context:

The harbor work was performed by a gang of Negroes. These men will work the whole day at the capstan under a scorching sun with almost no intermission. They beguiled the time by one of them singing one line of an English song, or a prose sentence at the end of which all the rest join in a short chorus…

> Grog time of day, boys
> Grog time of day
> *Ch:* Huro, my jolly boys,
> Grog time of day[8]

Unfortunately, the author of *Service Afloat* did not see fit to provide tunes for these boat-rowing and cargo-loading chanteys; but another British commentator, touring the West Indies at around the same time, graciously prints the words and melody of "Fine Time o' Day,"[9] a boat-song that is certainly a parallel version of the "Fanny Elssler" cargo-loading chantey. It is the only extant tune than can be attributed to "Fanny Elssler Leaving New Orleans," perhaps the very tune that Fred Smith played on board the *Herald* thirty-five years later.

> Hur-ra my jol-ly boys,
> *Fine time o' day.*
> We pull for San Thamas, boys.
> *Fine time o' day.*

"FINE TIME O' DAY," from Trelawney Wentworth, *The West India Sketch Book* (London, 1834), II:240; quoted by Abrahams 1974, p. 18.

Hur-rah, my jol-ly boys, *Fine time o' day.* We pull for San Tha-mas, boys. *Fine time o' day*

"FANNY ELSSLER LEAVING N. ORLEANS." Text from *The Negro Singer's Own Book* (Phila: & New York: Turner & Fisher, n.d.), p.337. Through-composed, no differentiation into stanzas (of which there are actually three).

> Fanny, is you gwyne up de riber,
>   Grog time o' day;
> When all deese here got Elslur feber,
>   Oh, hoist avay.
> De Lord knows what we'll do widout you,
>   Grog time o' day;

> De toe an' heel won't dance widout you,
>   Oh, hoist avay.
> Dey say you dances like a fedder,
>   Grog time o' day;
> Wid tree tousand dollars al togedder,
>   Oh, hoist avay.

---

[8] Hugill 8; Abrahams 16.
[9] In fact, given the stultified England of William IV, *"Fine Time o' Day"* may be a euphemism for *"Grog Time o' Day."*

179. Off She Goes
(O'Neill #914)

> "Are you ready there forward?"
> "All ready, Sir."
> "Heave away. What kind of a drawling tune is that you Fifer? Strike up *Off She Goes* or *Drops of Brandy.* Aye, that is the tune. Keep step there, all of ye, stamp and go. Light round the messenger there, aft, hand forward the nippers, you boys.
>
> — Robert Hay, *Landsman Hay,* with reference to the sailing of HMS *Culloden* for the East Indies in 1804[10]

A traditional jig, probably Irish in origin, "Off She Goes" is widely distributed throughout the British Isles, North America, and the Antipodes. It has been a military march since the 18th century and, as the quote from HMS *Culloden* illustrates, it was occasionally used to coordinate work-rhythms on shipboard — especially in the Navy, where chanteying was not generally permitted.

Setting A. "OFF SHE GOES! (*TA SI AG AMTEACD!*)." O'Neill #914.

Setting B. "OFF SHE GOES—JIG." From *1000 Fiddle Tunes*, p. 58.

---

[10] Quoted by Hugill, 7.

180. **The Old Leather Breeches**
[Leather Breeches; Nell Flaherty's Drake]
(O'Neill #167, #763)

[24 November 1854] After supper in the wa[i]st fiddling
and dancing to amuse the captain and his Wife.

— William Gifford, Third Mate,
ship *Benjamin Cummings*
Lat 34:13 Long 52:33

Called "Leather Breaches" in Frederick Howland Smith's shipboard tune list, this traditional Irish air is also known in modern times by the names of the several texts that became attached to various forms of it, notably the metaphorical Irish Republican ballad associated with the patriot Robert Emmet, "Nell Flaherty's Drake."[11]

Setting A. "THE OLD LEATHER BREECHES (*AN SEAN BRISTE LEATAIR*)." O'Neill #167. Compare O Lochlainn 1939 #67A, entitled "The Old Leather Breeches (Nell Flaherty's Drake)," annotated: "To the same tune [as 'Nell Flaherty's Drake'] or one very like it... ."; also Ward 1947, #30 ("The Old Leather Breeches"), which differs significantly from Ward #47 ("Nell Flaherty's Drake").

Setting B. "NELL FLAHERTY'S DRAKE (*BARDAL EIBLIN NI FLAITBEARTAIG*)." O'Neill #763. Compare O Lochlainn 1939 #67A; Clancy 1964, 47; and Ward 1947 #47 ("Nell Flaherty's Drake"), which differs significantly from Ward #30 ("The Old Leather Breeches")

Setting C. "NELL FLAHERTY'S DRAKE." Learned from Tommy Makem at Newport, R.I., 1965.

---

[11] "The main character of this anonymous nineteenth-century ballad ['Nell Flaherty's Drake'] is said to be a secret code name for Robert Emmet, an exceptionally charming youth who led a small uprising in Dublin in 1803, for which he was publicly hanged" (Clancy 1964, 47).

181. Home, Sweet Home

With the classic lyrics by the American actor and dramatist John Howard Payne (1792-1852) set to music by Englishman Henry Rowley Bishop (1786-1855), "Home, Sweet Home" debuted in the operatic melodrama *Clari, or the Maid of Milan* in 1823. It took hold with an enthusiastic public and rode a groundswell of popularity through the next several decades and well into the next century, becoming the best-known popular song of its era and the most widely anthologized. The tune also had independent status and was often published separately in musical tutors, sheet music, and dance-music books. John Jones alludes to it in his journal of the New Bedford ship *Eliza Adams* in 1852, as have many other sailors before and after. Captain Samuel Bunker and seaman George Wilbur Piper actually transcribed the lyrics into their journals; but in this case one of the reasons that the words do not appear more often in the journals may be that the song was so frequently committed to memory and was so widely available in print that one hardly needed to make a manual copy.

TUNE - "Home, Sweet Home," from *Maynard's New German Concertina Tutor and Budget of Popular Songs and Ballads,* London, n.d. (circa 1860), p. 25.

A.

"HOME SWEET HOME." Samuel Bunker, master, ship *Alexander* of Nantucket, 1824-27. An early transcription of four stanzas + chorus, produced when the song was new; phonetically corrupt but otherwise orthodox.

B.

"SWEET HOME." George W. Piper, ship *Europa* of Edgartown, 1868-70. A text of two stanzas transcribed around the time that Frederick Howland Smith compiled his tune list.

1. Mid pleasures and palaces
   Though we may roam
   Be it ever so humble
   There is no place like home
   A charm from the skies
   Seems to hallow us there
   Which search through the world
   Is not met with elsewhere

2. An exile from home
   Pleasure dazzles in vain
   O give me my lovely
   Thatched cottage again
   For birds are gaily singing
   They come at my call
   O give me these with peace of mind
   That's dearer than all

Chorus: Home Home Sweet Sweet Home
Be it ever so humble
There is no place like home

182. Old Folks at Home
[Swanee River]

This was one of Stephen Foster's best known and most influential hits, published in 1851. As late as 1870 it was fraudulently attributed to Edwin P. Christy (1815-1862), who had purchased the rights and whose minstrel troupe popularized it on stage (Dichter #184; Ewen, 293f). It was ubiquitous on shore and seems to have been suitably popular at sea. Two of the whalemen's renditions (A and B) are variants of the standard lyrics, and the third (C), an original parody, is a whaling song. There must have been other whalemen's parodies that did not survive.

"OLD FOLKS AT HOME." From the original sheet music, New York: Firth & Pond, 1851 (also repr. R. Jackson, 101).

A.

"THE OLD FOLKS AT HOME." George W. Piper, ship *Europa* of Edgartown, 1868-70.

1. Away down upon the Swaney River
   Far far away
   There is where my heart is turning ever
   There is where the old folks stay
   All up and down the whole creation
   Sadly I roam
   Still longing for the old plantation
   And for the old folks at home

   Chorus:
   All the world is sad and dreary
   Everywhere I roam
   O darkies how my heart grows weary
   Far from the old folks at home

2. All up and down the hills I wandered
   When I was young
   Many is the happy days I squandered
   Many is the song I've sung
   When I was playing with my brother
   Happy was I
   O take me to my kind old mother
   There let me live and die

3. One little cot among the bushes
   One that I love
   Still fondly to my memory rushes
   No matter where I rove
   When shall I see the bees a humming
   All around the comb
   When shall I hear the banjo tumming
   Down in the good old home

B.

"THE OLD FOLKS AT HOME." Harvey R.C. Phillips, ship *Gladiator* of New Bedford, 1853. Partial adaptation after Stephen Foster, beginning "Away down by the deep flowing river."

C.

"SONG... TO CAPTAIN S.D. OLIVER." George Edgar Mills, third mate, ship *Leonidas* of New Bedford, 1855. An original parody relating to the gray whale fishery and Arctic bowhead fishery, first line "All the whales are wild and ugly" [q.v. among the whaling songs, #158].

CHAPTER EIGHTEEN
Hurrah for the Sea
Parlor Songs of Ships and Seafaring

In the terms "folk song," "folk music," and "traditional music," *folk* and *traditional* refer to the spontaneous musical activities that are said to arise "unselfconsciously" among ordinary "folks," and within such specialized occupational groups as cowboys, lumberjacks, weavers, soldiers, and sailors. Melville establishes a nautical context for the point in *White-Jacket* (1850), where—in conformity with standard naval usage—he refers to common seamen as "the People"; that is, the crew, as opposed to the officers. That which is of "the folk" is neither of the Academy nor of Commerce: the anonymous lyricists and musicians who produced and performed the old songs that we now call "traditional" are presumed not to have had formal literary or musical training (though some inevitably did); more to the point, their music—or, at least, its performance by "the folk"—was not typically commercially or academically motivated. Rather, the folk genre is a pursuit of "amateurs," music emanating from and continuous with the circumstances of ordinary daily life and labor. Often greatly changed through years or generations of being passed along, handed down, reconstituted, personalized, localized, "improved," and modernized, some of the songs made up by ordinary folks survived by virtue of a seemingly mystical but quintessentially democratic process of selection by collective consensus. The survivors are the songs that "the People" liked and persisted in singing, songs that were "popular" in Francis J. Child's sense of the phrase "Popular Ballads" (though not necessarily in the same sense as the actual ballads in Child's collection)—music created and preserved not so much *for* the people as *by* the people, ostensibly out of sheer aesthetic enjoyment and practical necessity. "Folk songs" and "traditional music" are components of a shared linguistic, ethnic, cultural, or occupational heritage, and, often, the songs that popular opinion regards as the "best" can transcend parochial boundaries and become the cherished property of all.

On the other hand, "parlor songs" and "minstrel songs" refer to music created *for* somebody *by* somebody else, in this case 19th-century music intended to amuse the masses in music halls or entertain them at home in their own middle-class parlors. Rather than springing spontaneously from the collective ebullience of the common people (as some theoreticians might characterize the folk process), parlor songs were "written" and "composed" by occupational songwriters — forerunners of Tin-Pan Alley penny-liners, Madison Avenue and Fleet Street ad-men, and the highly-charged music-industry tunesmiths of 20th-century show biz. Or they were written by *aspiring* occupational songwriters, or by *imitators* of occupational songwriters, some of whom were ordinary non-professionals—motivated by fashion or pretense, striving to adopt the *style* of occupational songwriters. The ostensibly *individualistic* or *collaborative* (rather than *collective* and *generational*) processes of composition and transmission of parlor songs and minstrel songs, and the alleged "purity" of folk music — that is, the supposed absence of any of the mercenary or predatory objectives that may be ascribed to commercial songwriting — separate parlor songs and stage songs at least one remove from the spontaneous common heritage of "the People."

Of course, many a song that began its career in the hands of a music-hall hack came eventually to be adopted by "the folk," entered "tradition," and was handed down through "oral transmission" by means analogous to the Homeric epics, Norse sagas, and bardic poems of old; but in this case usually without any recollection of, homage paid to, or inhibiting influence exerted by whomever may originally have created the songs. In this way, a few parlor songs and minstrel compositions have effectively "become" folksongs. However, for the most part the longevity of parlor songs, like the contrived popular music of any age or generation, is a function of transient fashion. Unlike so many folk songs and traditional ballads (including a few adoptive specimens that originated in the parlor-song repertoire), comparatively few parlor songs — even ones that were commercially viable in their own time, survived to be handed down for the enjoyment of future generations. The overwhelming majority have been relegated to a richly-deserved obscurity. To recapture them today would require excavation from old songbooks or original sheet music. The effort is seldom worth the trouble, for many 19th-century parlor and minstrel songs are caught up in the politics, fashion, maudlin sentimentality, gaudy patriotism, and jingoistic bigotries of the Victorian epoch and can appear rather silly to us today.

On this point, Nicholas Tawa provides provocative and compelling insights. Characterizing John Ordway's saccharine Civil War-era song "Let Me Kiss Him for His Mother" [Appendix 7, #351] as "an exercise in bathos," Tawa astutely discusses what makes us sophisticated modern folks shudder with disdain, then goes on to vindicate the genre by measuring it on its own terms, terms by which the sailor-diarists certainly appreciated it. One has only to run a cursory tabulation of the song texts catalogued in Appendix 7 to verify that seamen painstakingly collected, transcribed, performed, and, according to their own testimony, enjoyed, literally hundreds of shallow parlor songs and minstrel showtunes, in hugely greater numbers than they bothered with ancient ballads, authentic deepwater songs, or even their own sea chanteys:

> ... To twentieth-century tastes... excessive emotionality shrinks to nothing the aesthetic distance between author and subject, his studied simplicity exploits one strong though stereotyped experience to the exclusion of depth, variety, subtlety—a criticism which is levied on most parlor-song texts.
>
> On the other hand, these lyrics were not meant for reading but for singing strophically, thus encouraging an overall unity of expression to accommodate the repetition of the melody. At the same time, the music, unassuming as much of it is, remains in the brighter major, rather than the minor, mode. In this fashion the composer relieves the sentimentality of the text and contributes an extra dimension to the whole that is difficult to define. When one lives day after day with these parlor compositions and hears them as songs (that is, at all times as a unity of words and music), a good number of them seem to shed their excessive sentimentality and emerge as fundamental and moving statements on the human condition. Furthermore, the real beauty of several of their melodies, though incapable of being readily analyzable, has merits comparable to that of the better art and folk songs. (Tawa, 152)

This constitutes almost the only credible explanation for why any two-fisted professional sailor might have put up with, might even have relished mawkish Victorian misrepresentations of the shipboard life and work he knew so well. It is one thing for landlubbers to romanticize and sentimentalize Jolly Jack Tar, to be seduced by the cloying superficiality of trivial, patronizing songs that tend to minimize the hardships and heroism of seafaring and depreciate the dignity of the mariners' experience; but it is quite another thing for an actual deepwater sailor to be taken in by the same ruse. As Melville writes in *Moby Dick* about one of what he calls "Monstrous Pictures of Whales," "Before showing that picture to any Nantucketer, you had best provide for your summary retreat from Nantucket"; that is, while a landlubber might be hoodwinked, any real whaleman would easily see through the fraud.

There is an additional contributing cause of the sailors' affection for the dripping sentiments of parlor confections on nautical themes. Unlike Melville aboard the *Acushnet* of Fairhaven, or Ishmael aboard the *Pequod,* most Yankee whaling lads were barely out of puberty. The typical foremast hand was between 17 and 23 years old; some were much younger, not many much older. And while a majority of native-born American whalemen had a grade-school education or better (a few were college trained; some were functionally illiterate), whalemen were not characteristically highly educated, worldly, sophisticated, or well traveled outside the fishery. The boys who scribbled song texts in their journals may have been aspiring lyricists and singers, but at a more fundamental and visceral level they were trying to survive seasickness, homesickness, and heart-sickness; they were training to be officers, or planning their escape, and learning how to be adults. Melville's autobiographical remark in *Moby Dick* that the ocean was his Yale College and his Harvard is a more poignant factual generalization about deepwater mariners than may be commonly supposed. The young sailor at sea was incalculably far removed from home and hearth, perpetually deprived of the security of mother and family, parted from boyhood friends, absent from the regular ministrations of the church and inculcation in normative moral, social, and intellectual values that family, school, or a viable community might impart. He had no choice about the hours or company he kept, the food he consumed, the job he performed, or the direction of his life: imprisoned for weeks and months at a time aboard some ship on the trackless deep, he was forbidden by law from unilaterally quitting his job; he endured miserable fare, slept in a filthy hovel, daily performed hazardous, backbreaking labor in all kinds of foul weather, and, often, was subjected to the cruelest personal humiliations and occupational indignities. Entirely lacking female companionship, he was eliminated from even the remote possibility of forming conventional romantic attachments at the very time of life when inclinations in that direction are at their keenest and when the relevant protocols and social skills are normally acquired and developed. All this went on day after day, week after week, month after month. At sea, even more than on shore, a young man was susceptible to what Tawa describes as the alluring subtext of the parlor-song genre:

> In the restless, constantly changing nineteenth-century social environment, where mobility and competition allowed little room for the development of warmth and intimacy between individuals, the relationship of suitor to beloved, husband to wife, and children to parents became of great consequence. The importance of love and the other "pure" emotions in cementing personal relationships, therefore, was stressed.
>
> It is clear that these Americans lived constantly with life's harsh truths. It is just as clear that when they turned to song for entertainment, they preferred that these truths be softened with sentimentality. To relieve the actualities of the American experience in song that held nothing back would have seemed incomprehensible to them. Instead, they wished for some relief from the stark reality of their existence. For sentimental songs to take on a recreative and therapeutic function, realistic details were suppressed, situations generalized and the violent emotions muted…
>
> Given the dramatic temper of the time and the felt need to articulate what was a "peoples music," the creators of the American parlor song behaved like representatives of the people and did give shape to a musical genre with meaning for their own age. For this, at least, they should receive credit, and their compositions respect. (Tawa, 153f)

In any large shipboard anthology, like William Histed's copybook aboard the ship *Cortes* of New Bedford, circa 1847 (whereof the songs form an important component of Gale Huntington's *Songs the Whalemen Sang*), or the even larger compendium made by George Wilbur Piper in the ship *Europa* of Edgartown during 1868-70 (wherefrom many of the songs have been excavated and anthologized here), the representation of parlor songs and minstrel songs is likely to be commensurately numerous. Their presence in such significant numbers in these compilations, notwithstanding also in dozens of other small and medium-sized collections made by whalemen, should suffice to demonstrate that gender stereotyping does not adequately explain the popularity of the songs among young men as well as women. This being said, it is nevertheless worth pointing out that a significant minority of the transcriptions of parlor songs, minstrel songs, and sentimental poetry recovered from the whale fishery were actually done by women on shipboard, a class that on Yankee whaleships was limited to the wives of whaling masters only. Accordingly, in the "Parlor Songs" chapter as well as other sections, it will be found that many of the songs were recovered from the papers of Elizabeth Marble of Fall River, Massachusetts, wife and shipboard companion of New Bedford whaling captain John Marble in the 1850s.

With some allowances made for thematic continuity—such as among songs about pirates and piracy—the songs in this chapter are arranged in the approximate chronological sequence of their original publication.

183. The Heart that Can Feel for Another
[Jack Steadfast]

The lyrics of this obscure British composition and an unascribed variant are printed in *The Universal Songster* (London, circa 1825) and, it would appear, nowhere else. The words are attributed to W. Upton, who also wrote "The Village Born Beauty" [#442] and whose poetry is primarily associated with melodies by William Thomas Parke, most notably "The Garden Gate" and "Old England the Mariner's Glory"; but there is no clear clue about the tune in this instance.

"SAILOR'S SONG." George W. Piper, ship *Europa* of Edgartown, 1868-70. Compared with the *Universal Songster* lyrics, the only significant simplification or Americanization is the substitution of "between the water and the sky" for "'twixt water and sky" (stanza 2); and "We will pass around the grog" for "Toss the can, boys, about" (stanza 3). The last couplet in the manuscript is evidently corrupted: the *Universal Songster* text reads, "And, what's more, they love, what I hope you all wish, / 'Tis the heart that can feel for another."

1. Jack Steadfast and I were both messmates at sea
   And had sailed half this wide world together
   And many hard battles encountered had we
   Strange climates and all sorts of weather
   For sailors you know are inured to hard gales
   Determined to stand by each other
   For the boast of a tar where so ever he goes
   Is the heart that can feel for another

2. When often suspended between the water and the sky
   And death yawned on all sides around us
   Jack Staeadfast and I scorned for to murmer or sigh
   For dangers could never confound us
   Smooth seas and rough billows to us were the same
   Convinced that we must brave the one and the other
   And the toast that we gave through life's checkered game
   Was for the heart that can feel for another

3. Thus smiling at dangers on sea or on shore
   We will box the compass right cheerily
   We will pass around the grog and a word or two more
   We will drink to the girls that we love dearly
   For sailors you know though green kinds of fish
   Love the girls [just] as dear as their mother
   And the toast that we give is toast that we all wish
   Is for the heart that can feel for another

184. Bounding Billows, Cease Your Motion

These lyrics are attributed to English stage actress Mrs. Mary Darby Robinson (1758-1800), but the composer is not identified. The text here is from an anonymous manuscript of mid 19th-century vintage, written in a feminine hand on stationers' foolscap. From its context in the Kendall Collection, it is presumed to have had some connection to the whale fishery, now lost.

TUNE from H.K. Johnson, *Our Familiar Songs,* [1881], 345; sheet music, John Aitkin, Philadelphia, circa 1808.

"BOUNDING BILLOWS." Anonymous MS, n.d. H.K. Johnson's stanzas correspond to 1, 2, 4, 8, 9, 5, and 15 here.

1. Bounding billows cease thy motion
   Bare me not so swiftly ore
   Cease thy roaring foming Ocean
   I will tempt thy rage no more

2. Ah! within my bosom beating
   Varying passions wildly reign
   Love with proud resentment meeting
   Throbs by turns with joy and pain

3. Joy that far from foes ive wandered
   Whare there taunts can reach no more
   Pain that womans heart grows fonder
   When the dreams of bliss are ore

4. Proud has been my fattel passions
   Proud my injured heart shall be
   while each thought and inclination
   Still shall prove me worthy thee

5. Not one sigh shall tell my story
   Not one tear my cheek shall stain
   Silent grief shall be my glory
   Grief that stoops not to complain

6. Let thy bosom prone to ranging
   Still from ranging seek a cure
   Mine disdains the thought of changing
   Proudly destined to endure

7. Joy by fickle fancy banished
   Spurned by hope indignant flies
   But when love and hope are banished
   Restless memory never dies

8. Yet believe no servile passion
   Seeks to charm thy vagrant mind
   Well i know thine inclination
   Wavering as the passing wind

9. For i go where fate may lead me
   Far acrost the troubled deep
   Where no friendly ear can hear me
   Where no eye for me shall weep

10. But ere far from all ive treasured
    Dearest girl i bid adieu
    Ere my days of pain are measured
    Take the song that is still thy due

11. I have loved thee dearly loved thee
    Through an age of worldly woe
    How ungrateful i have proved thee
    Let my mournful exile show

12. Ten long years of anxious sorrow
    Hour by hour ive counted o're
    Looking forward till to morrow
    Every day i've loved thee more

13. Power nor splendor could charm me
    I no joy in wealth could see
    Nor could threats or fears alarm me
    Save the fear of losing thee

14. When the frowns of fortune pressed thee
    I have wept to see thee weep
    When relentless cares distressed thee
    I have lulled those cares to sleep

15. When with thee what ill could harm me
    Thou coulds every pang assuage
    But when absent nought could charm me
    Every moment seems an age

16. Fare the well ungrateful lover
    Welcome calia's hostile shore
    Now yon breezes waft me over
    Now we part to meet no more

185. Lashed to the Helm

This song by Englishman James Hook (1746-1827) is rare in North America. Sabine Baring-Gould remarks,

> James Hook is said to have set over two thousand songs to music; among these a large number were imitation Scottish songs. They were composed for Vauxhall [i.e., the theatre]. Hook produced a "Monthly Banquet of Apollo," in 1795-96, and a number of ballad operas. Amongst all this profusion it is not easy to find a single pure melody that is a real creation of genius. The song we now give is an echo of the robust sea-songs of his age, but nothing more than an echo." (Baring-Gould 1895, II:xi)

TUNE from S. Baring-Gould, *English Minstrelsie*, 1895, II:81. Transposed from Bb Major.

"LASHED TO THE HELM." Robert N. Hughson, bark *Java* of New Bedford, 1857-60. The third chorus is inconsistently transcribed in the manuscript and is here reconstituted according to Hughson's scheme for the first chorus. To be sung, the text requires repeats as shown in italics (but not transcribed in the manuscript).

1. In Storm when clouds obscure the sky
   And thunders roll and lightnings fly
   In midst of all them dire alarms
   I think my [Sally] on thy charms
      The troubled main
      The wind and rain
      My ardent passion prove
      Lashed to the helm
      Should seas o'erwhelm
      I'd think on thee my love
      [*I'd think on thee my love*]
      [*I'd think on thee my love*]
      [*Lashed to the helm*]
      [*Should seas o'erwhelm*]
      [*[I'd think on thee my love*]

2. When rocks appear on every side
   And art in vain the Ship to guide
   In various shapes when death appears
   The thoughts of thee my bosom cheers
   [*Chorus repeats per stanza 1*]

3. But should the gracious heavens prove kind
   Dispel the gloom and still the wind
   And waft me to thy arms once more
   Safe to my long lost native Shore
      No more the rain
      I'd tempt again.
      But tender joys improve
      O then with thee
      I should happy be.
      And think on nought but love

186. Saturday Night At Sea
[The Sailor Boy]

This anonymous parlor song is known only in two rather different transcriptions in whaling journals (a text with the same title cited by Huntington from the *Mammoth Songster,* published at Boston in 1866, is likely a different song altogether, with a kindred refrain). Whaleman James W. Hutchins's transcription aboard the New Bedford ship *Florida* in 1843 (Huntington 1964, 65) is more elaborate than George Edgar Mills's text aboard the bark *Aurora* of Westport in 1857: the former requires repeats by way of slightly varying refrains appended to each stanza which the latter does not include. By contrast, a stanza Huntington quotes from the *Mammoth Songster* is "written-through"—that is, it fills out the music with lyrics, rather than repeats.[1] The melody or melodies are unknown. But with its theme and key phrases indebted to Charles Dibdin, it is small wonder that the tune Huntington assigns to the Hutchins text in *Songs the Whalemen Sang* is Dibdin's "Saturday Night at Sea" ("'Twas Saturday night, the twinkling stars...") [#215]. However, Huntington's miscalculation may be inadvertent, as he obtained the melody not from any anthology of Dibdin's songs, but from *The American Musical Miscellany* (1798), where the music to Dibdin's "Saturday Night at Sea" is unascribed.

"THE SAILOR BOY." George Edgar Mills, third mate, bark *Aurora* of Westport, 1857. To fit the tune, the lyrics require adaptation, doubling of verses, or the kind of repeats given in Hugill's text (see footnote 1, below).

1. The sailor loves a gallant ship
   And shipmates bold and free
   And ever welcomes with delight
   Saturday night at sea

2. One hour each day we'll
       snatch from care
   As through the world
       we roam
   To think of dear
       ones far away
   And all the joys
       of home

3. We'll think of those bright beings who
   Bedeck with joy our lives
   And raise to Heaven a prayer to bless
   Our sweethearts and our wives[2]

Saturday Night At Sea. Wood engraving drawn by George Cruikshank as an illustration for the book *Songs, Naval and National, of the late Charles Dibdin,* by Thomas Dibdin (London, 1841).

---

[1] The first stanza of Huntington's text:

    A sailor loves a gallant ship
    And messmates bold and free
    And ever welcomes with delight
    Saturday night at sea
    Saturday night at sea my boys
    Saturday night at sea
    Let every gallant sailor sing
    Saturday night at sea

The stanza Huntington reprints from *Mammoth Songster*:

    Come messmates fill the cheerful bowl
    Tonight let no one fail
    No matter how the billows roll
    Or roars the ocean gale
    There's toil and danger in our lives
    But let us jovial be
    And drink to sweethearts and to wives
    On Saturday night at sea

[2] See "Saturday Night at Sea" (1788) (also known as "Sweethearts and Wives") by Charles Dibdin [#215, in Appendix 1].

187. The Minute Gun at Sea

Minute gun refers to the procedure of firing ship's cannon at one-minute intervals in foggy or stormy weather as a means of ship location and warning, the equivalent of a modern foghorn. Minute guns were also fired as salutes at military and naval funerals. The music was composed by Matthew Peter King and varies little among published versions, but there are two distinct manifestations of the lyrics, originally written by Englishman R.S. Sharpe (1776-1822). The prevalent form—beginning, "Let him who sighs in sadness / Rejoice to know a friend is near"— is usually printed as a song intended to be sung. With minor differences from text to text, it emphasizes the Coast Guard's readiness and heroism as monitors of shipping. The other form is differently ordered, contains additional material, and in printed versions is usually noncommittal whether it be intended as a song or poem (for example, William Cullen Bryant's anthology makes no mention that singing is an option). On the face of it, it might seem that this "poetic" form is the original, and the other a later adaptation to fit M.P. King's music. However, the "poetic" form is actually more ballad-like, with the opening line, "'Twas in the storm on Albion's coast," establishing a context for the narrative: it is easily adapted to King's tune, and the systematic textual repetitions indicated in the whaleman's text (which are not indicated in Bryant's rendition) suggest that it was intended to be sung, almost certainly to King's standard musical setting.

TEXT AND TUNE of the prevalent form of the song, from Rear-Admiral S.B. Luce, *Naval Songs,* 1889, pp. 208f. Virtually identical to the original American sheet music (New York: William Dubois, n.d.)[3] and essentially the same as Johnson 122f. Set as a vocal duet for "Voice 1" and "Voice 2" (italics).

---

[3] The dates of original composition and first American publication, and the dates of composer M.P. King's birth and death, are unknown. According to Dichter & Shapiro, publisher William Dubois was doing business as such at various New York City addresses during 1813-21, 1839-50, and 1853-54; between times he was associated in various partnerships.

"THE MINUTE GUN AT SEA." George W. Piper, ship *Europa* of Edgartown, 1868-70.

T'was in the storm on Albion's coast
The night watch guards his weary weary post
From thoughts of danger free
When we mark some vessels well known form
And hears among the howling storm
The minute gun at sea, the minute gun at sea
    And hear amidst the howling storm
        The minute gun at sea

Quick on the shore the hardy few
The life boat manned with a gallant crew
To face the dangerous waves
Through the wild surf they [cleave] their way
Lost in the foam there is no dismay

In they go the crew to save,
        for they go the crew to save
    Lost in the foam there is no dismay
    For they go the crew to save

What joy what rapture fills each breast
The hapless crew on the ship distressed
When landed safe on shore to tell
Of all the dangers that had befell
Then was heard no more
        by the watch on shore
The minute gun at sea, the minute gun at sea
Then was heard no more
        by the watch on shore
    The minute gun at sea

188. Steady She Goes

This text typifies the process by which English patriotic songs were Americanized for the Yankee market. The original lyrics by Thomas Morton (1764-1838), as printed in the *Universal Songster* (London, circa 1825), begin "The British tar no peril knows," and they later mention an English vessel coming into view. To render the lyrics suitable for Yankee sailors and American audiences—for whom such cheaply-printed and widely-circulated vehicles as the *Forecastle Songster* and *American Sailor's Songster* were intended—American editors simply redirected the offending patriotic sentiments by substituting "Yankee" or "Columbia" wherever "British" or "England" occur. The whaleman's text below is undoubtedly a copy from one of these derivative American sources. Unfortunately, no tune has been located on either side of the Atlantic.

"STEADY SHE GOES." George W. Piper, ship *Europa* of Edgartown, 1868-70.

1. The Yankee tar no danger knows,
    but fearless braves the angry deep
  The ship is his cradle of repose,
    and sweetly rocks him to deep sleep
  He though the raging surges swell,
    in his hammock swings
  When the stern man sings
    Steady she goes! All's well.

2. While on the maintop yard he springs
    Columbia's vessel heaves in view
  He asks, but she no letter brings,
    from bonny Kate he loved so true
  Then sighs he for his native dell,
    yet to hope he clings true
  While the steersman sings,
    Steady she goes! All's well.

3. The storm is past the battle o'er
    Nature and man repose in peace
  The homeward bound on Columbia's shore
    The hope of joys that never will cease
  His Kate's sweet voice those joys foretell,
    And his big heart springs
  As the steersman sings
    Steady she goes—all's well.

The Yankee Tar. Colored lithograph co-published by J. Baillie & Co., New York; and J. Sowle, New Bedford, circa the 1840s. New Bedford Whaling Museum

189. The True Yankee Sailor
[The True British Sailor; Harry Bluff]

Like "Steady She Goes" [#188], this is a slightly Americanized form of an English patriotic song. The original words are by Isaac Pocock, circa 1820, loosely emulating the style of Dibdin; the adaptation is by some anonymous American songster editor; and the music is unattributed.

"THE TRUE YANKEE SAILOR." Unattributed, from Rear-Admiral S.B. Luce, *Naval Songs,* 1889, 120f.

"HARRY BLUFF." George W. Piper, ship *Europa* of Edgartown, 1868-70. Here regularized into lines and stanzas, per Luce. The first line is usually rendered, "When a boy, Harry Bluff… " (Forecastle 150; Luce 120).

1. Harry Bluff when a boy left his friends and his home
   And his dear native land over the ocean to roam
   Like a sapling he sprung he was fair to the view
   And was true Yankee oak boys when older he grew
   Though his body was weak and his hands they were soft
   When the signal was heard He was first up aloft
   And the old sailors all cried He will one day lead the van
   Even though rated a boy He had the soul of a man
   And the heart of a true Yankee sailor

2. When to manhood promoted and burning for fame
   Still in peace or in war Harry Bluff was the same
   To his love was so true and in battle so brave
   That the rose and the myrtle entwine over his grave
   For his country he died when the victory crowned
   And the flag shot away fell in tatters around
   The foe thought that he had struck but he sung out avast
   And the colors of Columbia he nailed to the mast
   Then he died like a true Yankee sailor

190. The White Squall

Not to be confused with a more famous poem of the same name by William Makepeace Thackeray, the lyrics of this parlor piece are variously attributed to a Captain Johns of the Royal Marines; to George A. Barker (1812-1876), who undoubtedly composed the music; and to Barry Cornwall, pseudonym of Bryan Waller Procter (1787-1874), who is unequivocally credited as the author on sheet music issued by Oliver Ditson (Boston, n.d., circa 1844-57).

TUNE ascribed to George A. Baker, from Rear-Admiral S.B. Luce, *Naval Songs,* 1889, 108-112; per sheet music of circa 1844-57.

"THE WHITE SQUALL." George W. Piper, ship *Europa* of Edgartown, 1868-70. To fit the tune, several repeats are required in each stanza, which are only partly indicated in the MS. Additional repeats required for singing the complicated, through-composed third stanza are indicated in italics in brackets.

1.
The sea was bright and the bark rode well
And the breeze bore the tole of the vesper bell
It was a gallant bark with a crew as brave
A eer was launched on the heaving wave
A eer was launched on the heaving wave
For she shone in the light of declining day
And each sail was set and each heart was gay
For she shone in the light of declining day
And each sail was set and each heart was gay
And each heart was gay

2.
Then she neared the land where in beauty smiled
The sunny shores of the Grecian Isles
All thought of home and friends so dear
That soon should greet each wanderers ear
That soon should greet each wanderers ear
Then in fancy joined the social throng
The festive dance and the joyous song
Then in fancy joined the social throng
The festive dance and the joyous song
And the joyous song

3.
Now a white cloud rides through the azure sky
What means that wild despairing cry
Farewell thou visions scenes of home
[*Farewell thou visions scenes of home*]
That cry is for help when no help can come
That cry is for help when no help can come
[*Farewell thou visions scenes of home*]
[*Farewell thou visions scenes of home*]
For the white squall rides on the surging wave
And the bark is engulfed in an ocean grave
For the white squall rides on the surging wave
And the bark is engulfed in an ocean grave
[*For the white squall rides on the surging wave*]
[*And the bark is engulfed in an ocean grave*]
[*For the white squall rides on the surging wave*]
[*And the bark is engulfed in an ocean grave*]
[*In an ocean grave, in an ocean grave*]

191. The Sailor's Consolation
[Barney Buntline]

This is a clever parody of a close-knit family of "Sailors' Come-All-Ye" folk ballads which extol the virtues of the hard, heroic life at sea and lampoon the pastoral pleasures of the farm. The deepwater prototype, known in various manifestations as "The Sailor's Complaint," "The Sailor's Come-All-Ye," and "Jolly Sailors Bold" [#33], descends from a broadside of circa 1635 entitled "Neptune's Raging Fury" (Ashton 1891, 223) and another entitled "To All You Ladies Now On Land," published in 1686 (Baring-Gould 1895, VIII:92). The evolved "Complaint" seems to have been immensely popular at sea. Colcord, Harlow, and Hugill collected specimens from the merchant service, Masefield and Palmer from the navy, Mackenzie from sources ashore in Nova Scotia. Its life in tradition may have been extended by publication of variant texts in *The American Singer's Own Book* (Philadelphia, 1841) and *The American Vocalist* (New York, 1856), but some of the shipboard appearances are demonstrably earlier. Huntington's fine text, which he calls "Hearts of Gold," he found in William Silver's journal of the Salem ship *Bengal* (1832). Thomas Bennett, a mate in the ships *Condor* of New Bedford (1839-40) and *William Baker* of Warren (1840-41), dubbed his text "Nantucket Whaling Song" [#33A]; and George W. Piper on the ship *Europa* of Edgartown (1868-70) entitled his merely "Sailors Song" [#33B] (qq.v.).

"The Sailor's Consolation," which arrived on the scene before the songster texts were printed and had an independent life of its own, genially provides a comical counterpoint to "The Sailor's Complaint." Unaccountably, William Cullen Bryant attributes it to Thomas Hood, though he does note that it is "sometimes erroneously attributed to Charles Dibdin" (Bryant II:590), this possibly in confusion with analogous themes in Dibdin's "The Best Bower Anchor" (q.v., Luce, 170) or, more likely, in confusion with an unrelated Dibdin song entitled "The Sailor's Consolation; or, Grieving's Folly," better known as "Spanking Jack," after the first line (Hogarth I:131; T. Dibdin 1841, 64; T. Dibdin 1860, 64). Moffat credits the lyrics to George Colman (Moffat 1901, 89). But the actual author was probably William Pitt of the Royal Navy (not to be confused with the famous father-and-son Parliamentarians of the same name), who was master attendant at the naval dockyard at Jamaica in the West Indies and was later stationed at Malta, where he died in 1840 (H.K. Johnson, 114). The tune is merely a degraded adaptation of John Davy's classic "Bay of Biscay O" [#3], which was featured in the ballad opera *Spanish Dollars* in 1805. There is also an obscure setting by John Farmer (Farmer 1896 #86; Griggs 1900, 148). "Sailor's Consolation" seems never to have been as much in vogue with sailors as "Sailor's Complaint," but it circulated ashore and was widely anthologized. It must have had a certain currency at sea in the middle 19th century — or such is the implication of its inclusion in two whalemen's journals (below and Huntington 1964, 68), in *Naval Songs* and the Luce anthology, and by Hugill's discussion of it as the original on which the capstan chantey "The Drummer and the Cook" is based (1969, 460).

TUNE from *Naval Songs*, New York, 1883, 124; see Luce 1889, 190; Farmer #86. A version or loose adaptation of "The Bay of Biscay O," originally composed by John Davy.

"THE SAILOR'S CONSOLATION." From a clipping pasted into the whaling journal of Jeremiah C. Norton, first mate, ship *Swift* of New Bedford, 1849-52. The printed source is unidentified but is the same source as #192-A.

1. One night came on a hurricane,
   The sea was mountains rolling,
   When Barney Buntline turned his quid,
   And said to Billy Bowling:
   "A strong nor'wester's blowing, Bill;
   Hark! Don't ye hear it roar now?
   Lord help 'em, how I pities all
   Unhappy folks on shore now!

2. "Foolhardy chaps who live in town,
   What danger they are all in,
   And now are quaking in their beds,
   For fear the roof should fall in;
   Poor creatures, how they envies us,
   And wishes, I've a notion,
   For our good luck, in such a storm,
   To be upon the ocean.

3. But as for them, who're out all day,
   On business from their houses,
   And late at night are coming home,
   To cheer the babes and spouses;
   While you and I, Bill, on the deck,
   Are comfortably lying,
   My eyes! What tiles and chimney-pots
   About their heads are flying!

4. "And very often we have heard
   How men are killed and undone,
   By overturns of carriages,
   By thieves, and fires in London.
   We know what risks all landsmen run,
   From noblemen to tailors;
   Then, Bill, let us thank Providence
   That you and I are sailors!"

192. A Wet Sheet and a Flowing Sea
[The Mariner's Song; The Sailor's Song]

… I might fill pages in recording the pleasant memories of my Greenwich [Rhode Island] home and its pleasant incidents. My favorite amusement and recreation was fishing and yachting on the Bay [Narragansett Bay]. I became quite a skillful and venturesome sailor, taking more pleasure in strong winds and rough seas than in a calm. I had read Dana's *Two Years Before the Mast* and learned to sing "A Life on the Ocean Wave," "A Wet Sheet an a Flowing Sea," "Britannia Rules the Waves," etc. These things and a restless, excitement-loving disposition will in part account for my longing for the life of a sailor which finally led me to leave my home to date the dangers of the deep.…

On Monday, January 18th, 1847, we had a fine breeze, and sailed with "a wet sheet and a flowing sea," for my own dear native land.

—Ben Ezra Stiles Ely, *There She Blows* (1849).

Written by Scottish poet Allan Cunningham (1784-1842) to the traditional French military air "Le Petit Tambour," the song was first published in Cunningham's *Songs of Scotland* (1825). It became very popular and was widely disseminated in sheet music and various anthologies in the British Isles and America. It was often performed in music halls and other venues at home and abroad; it was wholesomely well suited for singing in the family fold; and with the text severally reprinted in periodicals and songsters of the kind that circulated among China traders and the whaling fleet in the Pacific, the song could hardly have escaped the attention of Ben Ezra Stiles Ely and a host of other mariners. Huntington reports two texts, from the New Bedford ships *Citizen* (1844) and *Cortes* (1847); Ely alludes to it twice in his narrative of a whaling voyage in the ship *Emigrant* of Bristol, R.I. (1844-47); and it is represented here by two virtually identical texts, one from a clipping in Jeremiah Norton's log of the New Bedford ship *Swift* (1849-52) and the other as transcribed in George W. Piper's copybook aboard the Edgartown ship *Europa* (1868-70). The jaunting melody, known by the name of Cunningham's text, was occasionally adopted for parodies and other lyrics, among them a pirate song "The Low Black Schooner," printed anonymously in *The Pirate's Songster* of circa 1845 (Frank 1998 #45).

TUNE from *Naval Songs,* New York, 1883, p. 7; and Luce, *Naval Songs,* 1889, p. 202 (in both of which the song is attributed to Allan Cunningham, who wrote the lyrics but not the music). Identified by Helen Kendrick Johnson and in *Miller's British Songster* as the French military air "Le Petit Tambour."

A.

"A WET SHEET AND A FLOWING SEA." From a clipping pasted into the whaling journal of Jeremiah C. Norton, first mate, ship *Swift* of New Bedford, 1849-52. The printed source is unidentified but is the same as #191.

1. A wet sheet and a flowing sea—
   A wind that follows fast,
   And fills the white and rustling sail,
   And bends the gallant mast—
   And bends the gallant mast, my boys,
   While, like the eagle free,
   Away the good ship flies, and leaves
   Old England on the lee.

2. Oh, for a soft and gentle wind!
   I heard a fair one cry;
   But give to me the snorting breeze,
   And white waves heaving high—
   And white eaves heaving high, my boys,
   The good ship tight and free!
   The world of waters is our home,
   And merry men are we.

3. There's tempest in yon horned moon,
   And lightning in yon cloud;
   And hear the music, mariners!
   The wind is piping loud—
   The wind is piping loud, my boys,
   The lightning flashing free;
   While the hollow oak our palace is,
   Our heritage the sea.

B.

"A WET SHEET AND A FLOWING SEA." George W. Piper, ship *Europa* of Edgartown, 1868-70. Quite similar to A, except B is personalized ("our" ship) and omits Cunnigham's last two lines (stanza 3), for which it substitutes a repetition of the last two lines of stanza 2.

193. The Sea

[The Sea, the Sea, the Open Sea]

The lyrics were written by "Barry Cornwall," literary pseudonym of the distinguished British attorney and public administrator Bryan Waller Procter (1787-1874), a sometime schoolmate of Lord Byron and Sir Robert Peel. They were set to music sometime after 1830 by the Austrian composer Sigismund von Neukomm (1778-1858), a pupil of Haydn and intimate of Tallyrand and Brazilian Emperor Dom Pedro I. Such illustrious pedigrees of author and composer virtually assured immediate acceptance of "The Sea" in polite society. Throughout the 19th century it was regarded as an "art song" worthy of genteel audiences and respectable households, and frequently appeared in secular anthologies in England and America. It has not been encountered in oral tradition, yet it was probably more popular among sailorfolk than its unseamanlike syntax might suggest. The poetry was printed in 1841 in *The Sailor's Magazine,* a widely circulated missionary monthly; Huntington found a text in William Histed's copybook of the whaleship *Cortes,* circa 1847; Admiral Luce included it in his collection of navy songs; and Hugill reports that his father, a British coast guardsman around the turn of the 20th century, used to sing and play it on the button accordion (private communication). It was certainly known on shipboard (as it was ashore) in its incarnation as a song, probably also as a poem. A chronic shortage of reading material in the Pacific left whalemen always on the prowl, typically passing from hand to hand and from ship to ship whatever books and periodicals they could get—including back issues of all sorts of newspapers and magazines. *The Sailor's Magazine* was one of the most ubiquitous, undoubtedly circulating at sea over a period of many years. Indeed, it could well have been Lizzie Marble's source for her transcription in her husband's journal in the 1850s.

TUNE from Rear-Admiral S.B. Luce, *Naval Songs,* 1889, p. 212.

"THE SEA." Elizabeth Marble, inscribed after the fact (in connection with her subsequent voyages, circa 1850-61) in the journal of John C. Marble, ship *America* of Hudson, N.Y., 1839-40.

1. The Sea the sea the open sea
   The blue and fresh the ever free the ever ever free
   With out a mark without a bound,
   It runneth the earths wide regions around.
   It plays with the clouds it mocks the skies
   Or like a cradled creature lies
   Or like a cradled creature lies
   I'm on the sea I'm on the sea I am where I would ever be
   With the blue above and the blue below
   And silence where-so-ever I go
   If a storm should come and a wake the deep what matter
   I shall ride and sleep what matter what matter I shall ride and sleep

2. I love, O how I love to ride
   On the fierce, foaming, bursting tide the foaming bursting tide
   When every mad wave drowns the moon,
   Or whistles aloft his tempest tune
   And tells how goeth the world below,
   And why the souwest blast doth blow,
   And why the souwest [blast doth blow]
   I never was on the dul[l] tame shore,
   But I loved the great sea more and more
   And backward flew to her billowy breast,
   Like a bird that seeketh its mothers nest;
   And a mother she was and is to me
   For I was born was born on the open sea
   For I was born on the open sea

3. The waves wore white and red the moon,
   In the noisy hour when I was born the hour when I was born
   And the whale it whistled the porpoise rolled,
   And the dolphin bared their backs of gold
   And never was heard such an outcry before
   As welcomed to life the ocean child,
   As welcomed to [life the ocean child]
   I have lived since then In calm and strife
   Ful[l] fifty summers a rovers life
   With wealth to spend and power to range
   But never have sought or sighed for change
   And death whenever he comes to me
   Shall come shall come on the wide unbounding sea
   Shall come shall come on the wide unbounding sea

194. The Sailor Boy's Last Dream

The lyrics by English poet William Dimond (1800-1837) were widely anthologized on both sides of the Atlantic. There were two American musical settings. The first, by Thomas Van Dyke Wiesenthal (1790-1830) [Tune A] has a Navy provenance circa 1819. The other, by Isaac Baker Woodbury (1819-1858) [Tune B], was the one popularized in America by the Hutchinson Family in the 1840s. In addition to the two whaleship texts given below, "The Sailor Boy's Last Dream" is mentioned by whaleman William Gillaspia, who evidently intended to write the words into his copy book aboard the ship *Atlantic* of Nantucket (1846-49) but never got around to it.

TUNE A - "The Sailor Boy's Last Dream... Composed and Arranged... and Dedicated to Robt. M. Rose Esq. of the U.S. Navy by T.V. Wiesenthal, " from the original sheet music (Boston: G. Graupner & Co., n.d., circa 1819).

TUNE B - "The Sailor Boy's Last Dream... Words by Dimond, composed and inscribed to the Hutchinson Family by I.B. Woodbury," from the original sheet music (Boston: C. Bradlee & Co., 1846): Prints 11 stanzas.

A.

"THE SAILOR BOY'S LAST DREAM." Elizabeth Marble, inscribed after the fact (circa 1850-61) in the journal of John C. Marble, ship *America* of Hudson, N.Y., 1839-40. A copy text corresponding to the stanzas in the sheet music, consisting of stanzas 1, 3, 4, 5, 6, 7, 8, 9, 10, and 13 of B (q.v.), and one stanza not found in B, viz:

> 7. He springs from his hammock and flies to the deck;
> Amazement confronts him with images dire—
> Wild winds and mad waves drive the vessel a wreck—
> The masts fly in splinters, the shrouds are on fire!

B.

"THE SAILOR BOY'S DREAM." George W. Piper, ship *Europa* of Edgartown, 1868-70. Much like A except as noted in A. Compare Bryant II:567f; and Bruce, 293.

> 1. In slumber of midnight the sailor boy lay
> His hammock swung loose at the sport of the wind
> But watchworn and weary his cares flew away
> And visions of happiness danced o'er his mind

2. He dreamt of his home and his dear native bowers
   And the pleasure that circled around life's merry morn
   While memory stood sideways half covered with flowers
   And restored every rose but deserted the thorn

3. Then fancy her magical pinions spread wide
   And bade the young damsel in extacy rise
   Now far far behind him the green waters glide
   And the cot of his forefathers gladdens his eyes

4. The jessamine chambers in flowers o'er the thatch
   And the swallow sings sweet from her nest in the wall
   All trembling with transport he raises the latch
   And the voices of loved ones reply to his call

5. A father bends over him with looks of delight
   His cheek is impearled with a mother's warm tear
   And the lips of the boy in a love kiss unite
   With the lips of the maid whom his bosom holds dear

6. The heart of the sleeper beat high in his breast
   Joy quickens his pulse all his hardships seem o'er
   And a murmer of happiness steals through his rest
   O God thou hast blest me I ask for no more

7. Ah whence is that flame which now bursts on his eye
   Ah what is that sound which nor larums his ear
   T'is the lightning's red glare painting hell on the sky
   T'is the crashing of thunders the groan of the sphere

8. Like mountains the billows tremendously swell
   In vain the lost boy call[s] on Mary to save
   Unseen hands of spirits seem ringing his knell
   And the death angel flaps her broad [wings] o'er the wave

9. A sailor boy woe to thy dream of delight
   In darkness dissolves the gay frost work of bliss
   Where now is the picture that fancy touched bright
   The parents fond pressure and love's honey'd kiss

10. O sailor boy sailor boy never again
    Shall home love or kindred thy wishes repay
    Unblessed and unhonored down deep in the main
    Full many a score fathom thy frame shall decay

11. No tombstone shall plead to remembrance for thee
    To redeem form or frame from the merciless surge
    But the white foam of waves shall thy widow's sheet be
    And the winds in the midnight of winter thy dirge

12. On beds of green sea weed thy limbs shall be laid
    Around thy white bones the red coral shall grow
    Of thy fair yellow locks threads of amber be made
    And every part suit to thy mansion below

13. Days months years and ages shall circle away
    And still the vast water above the[e] shall roll
    Earth loses thy pattern for ever and aye
    O sailor boy sailor boy peace to thy soul

195. Over the Mountain Wave

According to *The Young Minstrel* (Boston, 1848), "Over the Mountain Wave," with lyrics by George Lunt and music by Edward L. White, was "sung at the Second Centennial Anniversary of the settlement of the ancient town of Newbury [Massachusetts], May 26, 1835" (Johnson & White, 72). This is the form in which the song was later anthologized by McCaskey and by Levermore in the 19th century. However, Elizabeth Marble transcribed lyrics (probably a copy text) that has the same title, first stanza, and chorus, but lacks Lunt's second and third stanzas, substituting instead a different second verse.

TUNE from J.P. McCaskey, ed., *Franklin Square Song Collection Nº 2*, 1884, p. 165. Identical to Levermore #78.

"OVER THE MOUNTAIN WAVE." Elizabeth Marble, miscellaneous family papers on shipboard and ashore in Fall River, circa 1845-61. The first stanza is virtually identical to American printed texts but there are minor differences in the chorus; but lacking Lunt's stanzas 2 and 3, substituting instead an entirely different second stanza.

1. Over the mountain wave
   See where they come;
   Storm cloud and wintry wind
   Welcome them home;
   Yet where the sounding gale
   Howls to the sea
   There their song peals along
   Deep tones and free;

2. England hath sunny dales
   Dearly they bloom;—
   Scotia hath heather-hills
   Sweet their perfume:
   Yet throu the wilderness
   Cheerful we stray,
   Native land—native land
   Home far away

   Chorus: Pilgrims and wanderers,
   Hither we come
   Here the free dare to be,
   This is our home

196. Poor Bessy
[The Parting]

The music of this English parlor song was composed by George Alexander Hodson to lyrics by Isaac Pocock entitled "The Parting." American sheet music was issued circa 1836 by James L. Hewitt & Co. of New York, with a lithograph by N. Currier on the cover (Dichter #1857); and the poetry was printed in *The Sailor's Magazine,* a New York missionary monthly that circulated widely among sailors in the Pacific. But the piece never seems to have achieved much popularity 'Stateside and was seldom anthologized. Its inclusion in Admiral Luce's *Naval Songs* and two whaling-journal transcriptions by the Marble family of Fall River are the only real indications that "Poor Bessy" was ever sung at sea or had much of a life in tradition. It is interesting to note in connection with this sad song, concerning a sailor who returns from a voyage to find that his beloved wife and son had died while he was at sea, that when Captain John Marble shipped out as master of the whaler *Gold Hunter* of Fall River in 1846, his wife Lizzie was pregnant; but their infant son, born while the father was at sea, died before the Captain came home in 1848. So Marble retired temporarily from whaling and for the next few years worked in the coastwise trade as master of the local schooner *Chesapeake,* which made shorter cruises, enabling him to spend much more time at home. It was only in the wake of the successful birth and good health of another son that Marble resumed whaling in 1853; and once they felt the son was old enough to accompany them, Elizabeth and their boy, George Frederick, went along on John's next voyage, as master of the bark *Kathleen* of New Bedford, 1857-60, with his brother George serving as first mate. They were an uncommonly happy family and the *Kathleen* an uncommonly happy ship [see Chapter 16, "'Plenty of Musick': Two Voyages on the Bark *Kathleen*"; and "A Voyage on New Holland," #161]. However, misfortune would follow. On their next outing, with John serving as captain of the New Bedford bark *Awashonks* and all four of them on board, he fell ill a few months out and died at sea in October 1861, leaving the widow, the orphan, and the brother to find their own way home from the Pacific in mourning.

TUNE A - from sheet music published by Oliver Ditson of Boston circa 1835.

TUNE B - from Rear-Admiral S.B. Luce, *Naval Songs,* 1889, 107. Through-composed for the first and second stanzas. Transposed from Bb and slightly corrected.

A.

"POOR BESSY." Marble Family copy book: inscribed (probably after the fact) in the whaling journal of George D. Marble, brig *Le Baron* of Rochester, Mass., 1837-39. Essentially the same text as B (q.v.).

1. Poor Bessy was a sailors bride
   And he was of[f] to sea
   Their only child was by her side
   And none as sad as she
   Forget me not, Forget me not
   When youre away from me
   And what ever poor Bessys lot
   Still, still, remember me.

2. Scarce twelve months, was past and gone
   Ere it was told to me
   That William with a gladsome heart
   Returned home from Sea,
   He clambered up the craggy path
   And sought his cottage door
   But the lovely wife and pretty child
   He never saw them more.

3. Forget me not—Forget me not
   The words rang in his ear
   He asked the neighbors one by one
   Their answer was their tears.
   They pointed to the old Church yard
   And their his lovely bride
   And the pretty child he loved so well
   Lay resting by her side

B.

"POOR BESSY." Marble Family copy book: inscribed (probably by Elizabeth Marble) in the journal of John Marble, ship *America* of Hudson, 1839-40. Essentially the same as A; minor differences in spelling and punctuation.

197. The Fisher's Wife
[She Wanders By the Ocean; The Fisherman]

This obscure piece concerns a widow who waits by the sea in the futile hope that her husband will return from a voyage that has "sunk his bark beneath the wave." With words and music by the American basso Joseph Philip Knight (1812-1887), composer of "Rocked in the Cradle of the Deep," it was originally published as "The Fisher's Wife" (New York, 1837); but probably because it became popularly known by its first line some subsequent editions take the title from the first line, "She wanders by the ocean," Interestingly, the sailor's title transfers emphasis from the fisher's *wife* (per the title on the original sheet music) to "The Fisherman," which is the whaleman's title in his journal, suggesting that the sailor-diarist may have identified with the poor dead fisherman in much the way Arctic whalemen identified with John Franklin's ill-fated crew [see #67].

Tune "SHE WANDERS BY THE OCEAN," written and composed by J.P. Knight, from the sheet music (New York: Firth Pond & Co., 1 Franklin Sq., n.d., circa 1848-53).

"THE FISHERMAN." George M. Jones, bark *Waverly* of New Bedford, 1859-63. Verses regularized and clarified from the MS.

1. She wanders by the ocean
   From mornings dawn till dark night
   And she watches from her casement door
   But no bark is there in sight
   From yonder ocean
   She has vanished long ago
   And the sound of distant billows
   Come silently and slow

2. Every morning before the sun shines bright
   Upon the dashing sea
   It was the fisherman['s] delight
   Upon the waves to be
   But a sudden tempest riseing
   Sunk his bark beneath the wave
   And his dirge is now the wild winds
   That murmer o'er his grave

3. Every dark and dreary night
   A beacon light had burned
   And though the years have rolled over
   She's expecting his return
   She knows not on his wave rent form
   The sun no more will shine
   And she feels as if her body was
   Some find, delusive dream

4. Day by day she gazes
   on the distant breaking sea
   And at night she listens
   to the oceans murme[re]d breeze
   She questions them as they pass by
   Do they still in safety keep
   The fisherman that long ago
   Was buried in the deep

198. A Life on the Ocean Wave

The lyrics by American poet Epes Sargent (1813-1880) are said to be based on S.J. Arnold's poem "The Death of Nelson"; they were published in a musical setting by the celebrated English composer and baritone Henry Russell (1812-1900) in 1838. Popularized by the immensely influential Hutchinson Family, the song was a best-seller at sea and ashore. It enjoyed a long life on shipboard, and seems to have been especially popular among such young *literati* of genteel background as Ben Ezra Stiles Ely of Greenwich, Rhode Island, who had been expelled from the Lawrenceville School and dropped out of Delaware College before going to sea in the 1840s; and Daniel Kimball Ritchie of Needham and Canton, Massachusetts, a slightly older product of a respectable classical education, who was whaling around the same time. Disparities between the glowing, romantic picture of the seafaring life promoted in Sargent's lyrics and Russell's lilting melody—by Ely's own testimony, the song played a part in inspiring him to go to sea in the first place [see #192]—versus the hard-bitten realities these young lads encountered in the actual fact, seems not to have tarnished their admiration for the song even after their opinion of seafaring had —at least in the case of the disgruntled, mildly paranoiac Ritchie—degenerated into disgust. Huntington has two whalemen's texts, and two more are noted below, in the aggregate spanning a period of just under forty years. Hugill reports having heard it sung in square-rig and steam in the 20th century, it has been a perpetual fixture in the glee-club repertoire, and it is one of few 19th-century parlor-songs-of-the-sea that are still sung today, notably including a vigorous revival of popularity quayside among the many so-called "sea-chantey choirs" that emerged in northern Europe in the 1980s. In the 19th century the lyrics were occasionally parodied using the same melody, such as in "The Life of the Bold Buccaneer," an anonymous pirate song printed in *The Buccaneer Songster* (New York and Philadelphia, circa 1845) and *The American Sailor's Songster* (Philadelphia, New York, and Boston, circa 1848), and reprinted in Rinder's British *Naval Songs* anthology (circa 1895) and *The Book of Pirate Songs* (Frank 1998, #44). The manner of the whaleman's transcription in his journal (for example, the notations "Repeat: A life &c———" and "Sung by Miss Juliet Rose") indicate that he copied it directly from the sheet music.

TUNE by Henry Russell, from an early American sheet music edition, New York: Hewitt & Jaques, 1838 (Dichter & Shapiro, 56). See also *Naval Songs,* 1883, 20; Luce, 68f.

A.

"LIFE ON THE OCEAN WAVE." Daniel K. Ritchie, second mate, ship *Massachusetts* of New Bedford, 1847.

1. A life on the ocean wave,
   A home on the rolling deep
   Where the scattered waters rave,
   And the winds their revels keep.
   Like an eagle caged in pine,
   On this dull unchanging shore;
   But give me the flashing brine
   With the spray and tempests roar.
   Repeat: A life &c———

2. Once more on the deck I stand,
   In my own swift gliding Bark;
   Set sail, farewell to land,
   And the wind that follows aft,
   We shoot through the sparkling foam.
   Like an ocean bird set free
   Like an ocean bird our home,
   Will find far out to sea.
   A Life &c

3. The land is no longer in view
   And the clouds have begun to frown
   But with a stout vessel & crew
   We'll stay, let the storm come down:
   And the song of our heart shall be
   While winds and waters rave,
   A life on the heaving sea
   And a home on the bounding wave
   A Life &c.

Sung by Miss Juliet Rose
Written on board ship Massachusetts, Capt. Wm. Cash, on Japan cruising for Sperm Whales, 2100 bbls sperm oil on board and looking for more, by Daniel K Ritchie who is 43 mos from home the 5th of July 1847.

B.

"OCEAN WAVE." Anonymous miscellaneous papers, bark *Mars* of New Bedford, George W. Allen, master, 1869-73. The scribe may have been one E. Nash of Westerly, Rhode Island. Virtually identical to A.

199. The Sailor Boy's Carol

Written circa 1841 by Thomas Power to an air called "The Alpine Horn," "The Sailor Boy's Carol" was one of the "Celebrated Melodies of the Rainer Family." This was a singing troupe also known as the Tyrolese Family Rainer that specialized in so-called "Alpine" music, a faddish confection of the era that about as closely approximated the genuine Swiss article as blackface banjo doggerel resembled authentic plantation songs; which is to say, not very much at all. Parker & Ditson of Boston issued the original, unornamented sheet music for "'The Sailor Boy's Carol' Adapted to the 'Alpine Horn'" in 1841. When successor Oliver Ditson reissued it couple of years later, there were no changes made to the music itself (*inside* the sheet), but it had a new cover featuring a prominent Thayer & Company lithograph of the Rainer Family in elaborate Alpine costume, with Mr. Power's original song-title reduced to a mere footnote under Rainer Family billing and the title "The Alpine Horn (sailor boy's carol)." In the wake of the famous Hutchinson Family, the Rainer Family was only modestly successfull their star was not very long-lived and most of their songs are unknown today. This one was anthologized in Johnson & White's *Young Minstrel* (1848) but appears otherwise to survive only in antique sheet music. Part of its failure to make the hit parade may be credited to the fact that the song is rather stagey, with a long, repetitious refrain of *la la la la las*, and is accordingly difficult to sing effectively without the sort of part-harmonies and flashy string band or brass ensemble accompaniments in which 19th-century minstrel troupes specialized.

"THE SAILOR BOY'S CAROL Adapted to the Alpine Horn": from the sheet music, Boston: Oliver Ditson, 1843, a reissue of the Parker & Ditson first edition of 1841 but with a new, illustrated cover crediting the Rainer Family.

"THE SAILOR BOY'S CAROL." Elizabeth Marble, inscribed after the fact (in connection with subsequent whaling voyages, circa 1850-61) in the journal of John C. Marble, ship *America* of Hudson, 1839-40.

1. Theres joy upon the sparklin Sea
    Sparklin Sea
    For blithe and gay the sailor tells
    Of merry hours when pleasure dwells
    Who so happy Who so free
    Hurra Hurra Hurra

    Repeat:
    List to his note list to the song
    Marked with the gayest measure
    Thoughts of his home thoughts of his fair
    Bring the truest pleasure   la la la

2. Though tempest swell the boundless main
    Boundless Main
    His song is heard amid the gale
    That swells the vessels graceful sail
    Dear the feeling sweet the strain
    Hurra Hurra Hurra

3. Come then to the sparklin sea
    Sparklin Sea
    Where pleasure dwells without a care
    Where skyes are bright and winds are fair
    For the joyous and the free
    List to his note list to his song

200. The Soldier's Tear

Apart from having been popular at sea in its own right this Anglo-Scottish sentimental song is included here primarily because it was the model for "The Sailor's Tear" [#201]. The original lyrics by the prolific Irish songwriter Thomas Haynes Bayly (1797-1839) are here somewhat toned down from the manipulative bathos of Bayly's three-handkerchief favorite, "The Mistletoe Bough" [Appendix 7, #370]: "The Soldier's Tear" is more an apologia for the sensitive modern male hero. There are two mainstream musical settings. Michael R. Turner calls the one by the Scots-Irish singer-impresario George Alexander Lee (1802-1852) [Tune A] "unpretentious," having "distinctive charm, with (in the original orchestral version) its bugles in the introduction and horns, everlasting symbols of the pastoral, under 'And the soldier leant upon his sword'" (Turner, 76). Another setting was composed by Sidney Waller [Tune B] for a coupling of the "The Soldier's Tear" with the parody by F.W.H. Bayley entitled "The Sailor's Tear" [#201].

TUNE A - The original music composed by George Alexander Lee; slightly adapted from Helen Kendrick Johnson, *Our Familiar Songs,* [1881] 1889, p. 504f (see also Wier 1918, 427).

TUNE B - "The Sailor's Tear and The Soldier's Tear," composed by Sidney Waller; from the original sheet music (New York: James L. Hewitt, Nº 31 Broadway, n.d., circa 1830-35) [Peabody Essex Museum of Salem, Mass.]

A.

"THE SOLDIER'S TEAR." Theodore D. Bartley, ship *California* of New Bedford, 1851-54. A standard text, somewhat modified from the published version.(e.g., the first line, of which B exemplifies the usual). Unfortunately, the payoff in stanza 3 is corrupted; the phrasing in B is clearer.

1. He stood upon the hill / To take a last fond look
   Of the valey & the village church / And the cottage by the Brook
   He listened to the sounds / So familiar to his ear
   And the soldier leaned upon his sword / And wiped away a tear

2. Beside that cottage door / A girl on bended knee
   Held aloft a snowy scarf / And it fluttered in the Breeze
   She breathed a silent prayer for him / A prayer he could not hear
   But he paused to bless her as he stood / And wiped away a tear

3. He turned to leave the spot / Oh! do not deem him weak
   For dauntless was that soldier's heart / Though a tear was on his cheek
   Go watch the foremost in the ranks / Of Battles wild career
   Believe the hand most dauntless there / Has wiped away a tear

B.

"THE SOLDIER'S TEAR." George W. Piper, ship *Europa* of Edgartown, 1868-70. Much like A, except the first line ("Upon the hill he stood to take a last fond look," which is more standard; sometimes "Upon the hill he *turned*"); and the final stanza, viz:

3. He turned and left the spot O do not deem him weak
   For dauntless was that soldier's hear[t], though tears were on his cheeks
   Go watch the foremost ranks in danger's dark career
   Be sure the hand most daring there, Has wiped away a tear.

201. The Sailor's Tear

"The Sailor's Tear" is a nautical adaptation of "The Soldier's Tear" [#200], devised to ride to fame and glory on the coattails of the prototype. The sheet music attributes the derivative lyrics to F.W.H. Bayley, Esq.—not to be confused with (but intended to be confused with) the famous Thomas Haynes Bayly, who wrote "Soldier's Tear." A New York edition of circa 1830-35 (which may not be the first issue) has both "Soldier's Tear" and "Sailor's Tear" printed together with a musical setting by Sidney Waller. The cover, which sports a generic Sailor's Farewell lithograph by Pendleton's of Boston, proclaims only, "The Sailor's Tear, written & composed for & sung by Madame Vestris.[4] Poetry by F.W.N. Bayley, Esq. Music by Sidney Waller" (see below). Inside, neither song is ascribed and the words are conjoined vertically as if they were stanzas of the same text, the clear implication being that "Bayley" is *the* "Bayly" and that "The Sailor's Tear" is an authorized adaptation and expansion of the original text. On the other hand, the adaptation is in some respects more interesting than the original, notably the last two lines, where what in the original is a predictably sentimental ploy becomes in the nautical rendition a stronger dose of patriotic resolve. The American whaleman's version (below) takes this transformation a step further, turning the British patriotism of the "original" into a bit of "Yankee thunder."[5]

TUNE by Sidney Waller — see "The Soldier's Tear" [#200 – Tune A and especially B].

"THE SAILOR'S TEAR." George W. Piper, ship *Europa* of Edgartown, 1868-70.

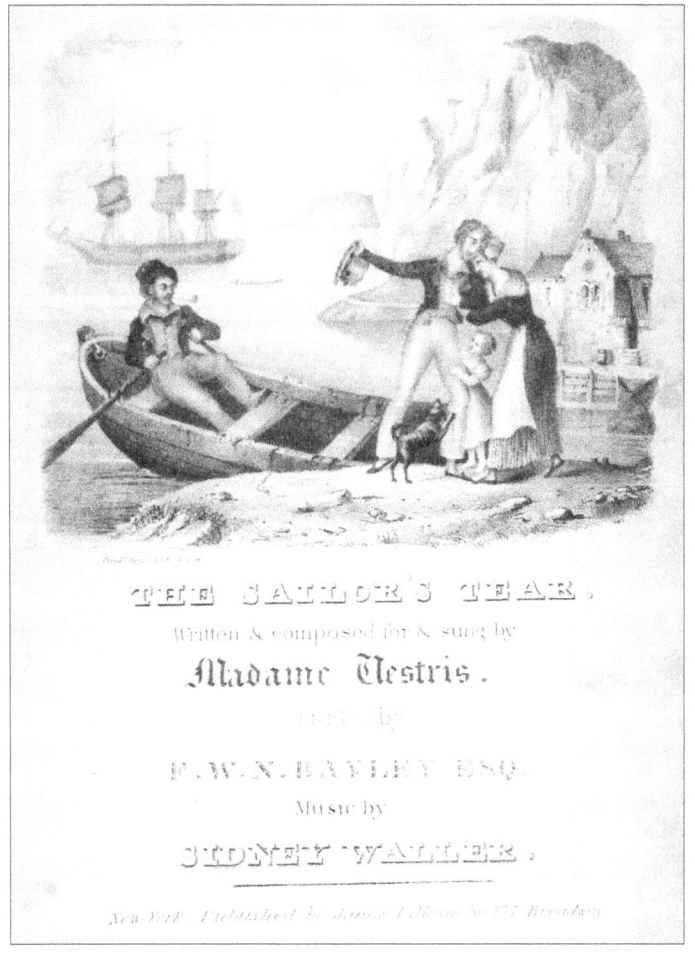

1. He jumped into the boat
    as it lay upon the strand
  But O his heart was far away
    with his friends upon the land
  The thought of those he loved the
    best, a wife and infant dear
  A feeling filled the sailor's breast
    The Sailor's eye a tear.

2. They stood upon a far off cliff
    and waved a kerchief white
  And gazed upon his gallant bark
    until she was out of sight.
  The sailor turned to look at them
    and shook, but not with fear
  He raised his hand up to his eye,
    And wiped away a tear

3. Ere long over the ocean's blue expanse, his gallant bark had sped
  The gallant sailor from her prow,
    descried a sail ahead
  And then he bared his mighty arm
    for Columbia's foes were near
  And then he bared his arm but not
    To wipe away a tear

---

[4] *Madame Vestris:* stage name of Lucia Elizabeth Matthews (1797-1856), wife of actor/playwright Charles James Matthews.

[5] *Yankee Thunder* is the title of at least one early American Navy song and appears as a phrase in several others (see Luce 28f and *passim*), thus became both epithet and cliché, alluding to cannonfire but signifying also American bravado, ferocity in defense of freedom, and grandness of scale—grand not so much geographical as symbolic, with much the same impact as "by thunder!"

202.
Hurrah for the Sea
[A Bold Brave Crew; A Home on the Mountain Wave; A Song of the Sea; The Sea Witch]

The lyrics by H.W. Rockwell are suspiciously reminiscent of "A Wet Sheet and a Flowing Sea" [#192] by Allan Cunningham (1825) and "A Life on the Ocean Wave" [#198] by Epes Sargent (1838). Rockwell's lines lines appeared anonymously in the February 1841 issue of *The Knickerbocker* magazine, they were reprinted anonymously five months later in *The Sailor's Magazine* (published by the American Seamen's Friend Society), and were anthologized under various titles in songsters intended for seamen. Music was added in 1842 by Thomas Bricher [Tune A], perpetrator of "The Homebound Whaleman" [Appendix 4]. A second setting, by W.J. Wetmore, M.D., appeared in 1853 [Tune B]. Captain Harlow says that it was "sung in New Bedford by my father and brothers before I was born, or before any of us went to sea. I have never seen the music, but give it as my brother Willy sang it" (Harlow 1962, 216); and its inclusion (with a much-simplified melody) in his fine anthology indicates that at least a few sailors evidently liked it well enough to sing it. However, whalemen Georeg M. Stockbridge (in the 1840s) and George W. Piper (in the 1860s) are the only ones known to have committed the lyrics to paper at sea.[6]

TUNE A - "A BOLD BRAVE CREW AND THE OCEAN BLUE." Music by Thomas Bricher, from the original sheet music (Boston: Oliver Ditson, 1842).

TUNE B - "THE SEA WITCH. A SONG OF THE SEA … Composed and cordially dedicated to Geo. W. Frazer, Esq. (Captain of the 'Sea Witch') by W.J. Wetmore, M.D."; from the sheet music (Philadelphia: J.E. Gould, 1853).

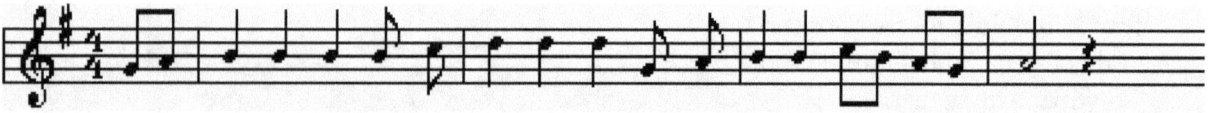

---

[6] Another song of the same name ("Hurrah for the Sea") has lyrics by Captain Willes Johnson, beginning "your poets may sing of the pleasures of home," and two musical settings: one by Philip Klitz (Philadelphia: J.C. Smith, circa 1844-48), advertised as "From the Songs of the Mid Watch"; and another from the repertoire of New Hampshire's singing Baker Family, published as "Hurra for the Sea Boys" and ascribed only "composed and arranged by John C. Baker" (Boston: Oliver Ditson, 1845).

A.

"A SONG OF THE SEA." George M. Stockbridge, green hand, ship *Gratitude* of New Bedford, 1841-45. Neither the whaleman nor the printed songsters—nor Harlow—indicates the many repetitions present in Text B, at least some of which are required to fit either of the two melodies. Harlow's lyrics are served up as 8-line stanzas, with the second stanza indicated as a chorus.

B.

"SAILOR SONG." George Wilbur Piper, ship *Europa* of Edgartown, 1868-70. This text clearly indicates the many repetitions required to fit the lyrics to the melodies. The sheet music gives a different sequence of repeats (see C).

1. A bold brave crew on an ocean blue
   And a ship that loves the blast
   And a good wind piping merrily
   In the tall and gallant mast
   Ha! Ha! my boys, these are the joys
   That suit the noble and the brave
   Who love a life in the tempest strife
   And a home on the mountain wave
   Who love a life in the tempest strife
   And a home on the mountain wave
   And a home on the mountain wave
   And a home on the mountain wave

2. When the driving rain of the hurricane
   Puts the lights of the lighthouse out
   And the growing thunder around is going
   On the whirlwind's battle rout
   Ha! Ha! do you think that the valiant shrink
   No, no, we are bold and brave
   We love to fight in the wild midnight
   With the storm on the mountain wave
   We love to fight in the wild midnight
   With the storm on the mountain wave
   With the storm on the mountain wave
   With the storm on the mountain wave

3. Breezes that die when the greenwoods sigh
   To the landsmen sweet may be
   But give to the brave, the broad backed wave
   In the tempests' midnight glee
   The howling blast, and the rocking mast
   And the dashing angry wave
   The thunder's jar o'er the seas afar
   Are joys that suit the brave
   The thunder's jar o'er the seas afar
   Are joys that suit the brave
   Are joys that suit the brave
   Are joys that suit the brave

4. There is lightning in your horned moon
   There is tempest in your cloud
   And hard to leeward mariners
   The wind is piping loud
   Ha! Ha! to night boys, we must fight
   The winds they roar and wave
   No storm can scare the mariner
   As he rides on his mountain wave
   No storm can scare the mariner
   As he rides on his mountain wave
   As he rides on his mountain wave
   As he rides on his mountain wave

C.

Example of the sequence of repeats as shown in the sheet music (Boston: Oliver Ditson, 1842).

With a good wind piping merrily,
In the tall and gallant mast.
Ha! ha! my boys, these are the joys,
Of the noble and the brave,
Who love a life In the tempest's strife,
And a home on the mountain wave;
Who love a life In the tempest's strife
And a home on the mountain wave.
Ha! ha! my boys, these are the joys,
Of the noble and the brave,
Who love a life, In the tempest's strife,
And a home on the mountain wave,
Who love a life in the tempest's strife,
And a home on the mountain wave.

203. Away, Away o'er the Boundless Deep
[The Buccaneer's Bride]

The fragment from the bark *Oak* of Nantucket (1869) is related to two, more complete texts reported by Huntington in journals of the New Bedford ship *Hillman* (1854) and bark *Pacific* (1870). All three are evidently derived from "Away! Away We Bound o'er the Deep," written and composed by Joseph Rodman Drake (1795-1820) and published circa 1834 in a setting by Thomas Van Dyke Wiesenthal (1790-1830), a naval surgeon and prolific composer. Variations among the manuscript texts suggest oral transmission, and the abortive *Oak* version (short as it is) is the most interesting because it has the surprising phrase, "Man your brake... with a song of your island home" — an allusion to chanteying while manning the brake windlass, absent in the other two whalemen's texts. To fit any of the sets of lyrics to Drake's melody requires adjustments of text or tune, including more extensive repeats than are suggested either in the printed broadside or any of manuscript texts.

"AWAY! AWAY WE BOUND O'ER THE DEEP" by Joseph Rodman Drake, arranged by T.V. Wiesenthal, from the sheet music (Baltimore: George Willig, n.d., circa 1834). Compare *Davidson's Universal Melodist* (1848), II: 327.

A.

"SONG." Charles D. Atherton, bark *Oak* of Nantucket, 1869. Fragment only. Reconstituted into stanzas for clarity.

1. Away away oer the boundless deep / we ll merrily merrily roam
   Come man your brake while the mermaid sleeps / with a song of your island home
   repeat with a song of &c

2. On the decks I stand / [end]

B.

One of two whalemen's texts collected by Huntington (MS 198). He credits the source as the ship *Hillman,* 1854, in the collection of the New Bedford Whaling Museum (MS, 611); however, no such journal exists there; it is actually from a journal of the ship *Hillman* of New Bedford, 1854-57, in the collection of the Peabody Essex Museum of Salem, Mass.:

1. Away away o'er the boundless deep
   On merrily they roam
   Wake lady disturb the mermaid's sleep
   With the songs of thy Highland home

2. On the deck they stand that gallant band
   To bear my love o'er the sea
   To the spicy isles where the bright sun shines
   And a home in the woods for me

3. Look up look up my bonny bride
   Say where does the find heart roam
   Does it sigh for Glenlock with its silvery sky
   Or the halls of thy Highland home

4. Sleep on sleep on that virgin sleep
   That dreams of thy Highland halls
   Thy brothers shall watch for the bucaneer
   Till no dew by the twilight falls

This sheet music cover for John M. White's setting of Eliza Cook's famous poem "I'm Afloat, I'm Afloat" [#204], published by Henry Prentiss of Boston in 1841, features a lithograph by the renowned Boston firm of B.W. Thayer depicting a pirate ship in a heavy sea, flying the black Jolly Roger flag. However, White's composition never displaced the earlier musical setting by Henry Russell, which remained the popular standard throughout the 19th and 20th centuries.

204. I'm Afloat, I'm Afloat
[The Rover of the Sea]

Huntington collected text A from the Kendall Whaling Museum years ago and printed a poor transcription of it in *Songs the Whalemen Sang,* failing to identify the lyrics and giving no tune. Of course what he and the diarists call "The Rover of the Sea" is the famous poem by the British poet Eliza Cook (1818-1889), which is better known by its first line, "I'm Afloat, I'm Afloat." It became even more famous in a musical setting by Henry Russell (1812-1900), published before 1840. A second musical setting by John M. White (Boston: Henry Prentiss, 1841) never achieved the huge popularity of Russell's composition, despite that it was printed with an attractive three-color lithographic cover by the Boston firm of B.W. Thayer (illustrated on the previous page). The text, of course, romanticizes the seafaring life of pirates "on the account," and ignores the fundamental evil and cruelty of their predatory, often murderous livelihood.

TUNE by Henry Russell from the sheet music (Boston: George P. Reed, 1847). Compare Kieth, Prowse & Co., *Accordion Music,* London, circa 1860, pp. 202f.

A

"THE ROVER OF THE SEA." Charles C. Evans, in the journal of Daniel A. Chapel, cooper, ship *Benjamin Tucker* of New Bedford, 1851. This verbatim transcription supersedes Huntington's corrupt text (1964, 80f), in which he unaccountably gives the date 1849: the MS is clearly dated "May 14th 1851," at which time the ship would have been on the last homeward-bound leg approaching New Bedford, where she arrived June 1st.

1. I'm a float I'm a float on the fierce rolling tide
   The ocean is my home and the barque is my pride
   Up up with my flag let it wave o're the sea
   I'm a float I'm a float and the Rover is free

2. I fear not the monarch I heed not the law
Ive a compass to steer by Ive a dagger to draw
And never as a coward or a slave will I kneel
While my guns carry shot or my belt bears a steel

3. Quick Quick trim the sails let the sheets kiss the winds
And I'll warrant we ll soon leave the seagull behind
Up up with my flag let it wave o're the sea
I'm a float I'm a float and the Rover is free

4. The night gathers o're us the thunder is heard
What matters our vessel skims on like a bird
What cares she for the storm-ridden main
She had braved it before and she'll brave it again

5. The light gleaming flashes around us may fall
They may strike they may cleave but they cannot appall
With lightnings above us and darkness below
Through the wide wast[e] of waters right onward we go

6. Hurrah my brave boys may ye drink may ye sleep
The storm fiend is hushed we;'re alone on the deep
Our flag of defiance still waves o'er the sea
Hurrah boys hurrah boys the Rover is free

May 14th 1851   well what of it   Chas C Evans

B.

"ROVER SONG." Thomas D. Bartley, ship *California* of New Bedford, 1852. Virtually identical to A, except that B is more literate, with better spelling and punctuation. Transcription dated:

At Sea   Feb 9th 1852

C.

"I'M AFLOAT." Martha Ann Tray, Monmouth, Maine, 1846: inscribed after the fact in the whaling journal of George A. Gould, ship *Columbia* of Nantucket, 1841-46; dated:

Tuesday Feb 30th / [18]46
Martha Ann Tray, Monmouth

205. The Pirate of the Isles

   This song, about the defeat of a self-confident and unaccountably gleeful pirate by a British man-of-war, was certainly in tradition among deepwater sailors in the mid 19th century. On the basis of a remarkable interview conducted "in the field" by Henry Mayhew and published in *London Street Folk* (1851), the first of four volumes in his massive *London Labour and the London Poor* (1851-64), the song can be confidently attributed to the London street author and broadside pamphleteer whom Mayhew identifies only by the initials J.H., who wrote it for the London stage in the 1830s:

> "Above fourteen years ago I tried to make a shilling or two by selling my verse. I'd written plenty before, but made nothing by them. Indeed I never tried. The first song I ever sold was to a concert-room manager. The next I sold had great success. It was called 'The Demon of the Sea,' and was to the tune of 'The Brave Old Oak.' Do I remember how it began? Yes, sir, I remember every word of it. It began: 'Unfurl the sails, / We've easy gales; / And helmsman steer aright. / Hoist the grim death's head / The Pirate's head / For a vessel heaves in sight!' That song was written for a concert-room, but it was soon in the streets, and ran a whole winter. I only got 1 s[hilling] for it. Then I wrote 'The Pirate of the Isles,' and other ballads of that sort. The concert rooms pay no better than the printers for the streets." (Mayhew, I:302f)

Captain Harlow's lyrics, "sung by Wm. R.B. Dawson, an old-time chanteyman," are virtually the same as those given by Admiral Luce, including the variant final chorus; the two tunes are also related and harmonically compatible. William Histed's copybook text aboard the ship *Cortes* of New Bedford, circa 1847 (Huntington 1964, 72), varies from these two in subsidiary features only, stanza for stanza following the same general scheme and preserving some of the same stilted syntax (with such "artistic" lines as "Proud Gallia's sons and Spanish dons"). Huntington claims to have obtained his melody from Harlow's book but he transposes the key and makes capricious changes, resulting in some peculiar variations and stigmatizing it as a deliberate corruption. The two whalemen's texts the Kendall Collection resemble the other known texts, with few significant variations: only enough to suggest active transmission as a song.

TUNE A - from *Naval Songs,* 1883, p. 71, where it is presented without comment; likewise Luce 1889, p. 66.

TUNE B - "The Pirate of the Isles," from Frederick P. Harlow, *Chanteying Aboard American Ships,* 1962, pp. 172f: "Sung by Wm. R.B. Dawson, an old-time chanteyman."

A.

"PIRATE OF THE ISLE." George E. Sanborn, in the journal of shipmates George M. Jones and Albert F. Handy, bark *Waverly* of New Bedford, 1859-63. Subscribed "Written by [in the sense of *written down by*] G E Sanborn."

1. [leaf missing]

2. I love to sail in a pleasant gale / Oer the deep and boundless sea
    With our prize in view we'll heave her to / And take her under our lea
    Then we'll give three cheers and homeward steer / Whilst fortune on us smile
    For there's none dare cross the famous Ross / Until me his cross he strikes

Chorus: For my men's well tried my barque my bride &c.

3. Ye noble sons of spanish dons / Of proud and noble mein
    Who left your homes to capture me / But ne'er returned again
    Old England to[o] doth me persue / While at his threats I smile
    For her ships I take and her men Ive slain / And burnt and sank them in the main

4. And as he spoke there hove in sight / A ship of might a british seventy four
    She hailed the corsair stoped her course / While into him a broadside did pour
    The pirate soon returned the boon / Whilst proudly he did smile
    Till a fatal ball witch caused his fall / When loud for quarters his men did call

Chorus: In the briny deep there lies to sleep / In the briny deep there lies to sleep
     Once the pirate of the Isle / Once the pirate of the Isle
     Once the pirate Once the pirate / Once the pirate of the Isle

B.

"THE PIRATE OF THE ISLES." George W. Piper, ship *Europa* of Edgartown, 1868-70.

1. I command a band a sturdy band / Of pirates bold and free
    No laws I own my ship is my throne / My kingdom is on the sea
    My flag flies red at my royal mast head / And at my foes I smile
    No quarters show where so ever I go / For soon the prize we will take in tow

Chorus: For my men I have tried, my bark is my pride
     For my men I have tried, my bark is my pride
     I'm the pirate of the isles, I am the pirate of the isles
     I am the pirate   I am the pirate
     I am the pirate of the isles

2. I love to sail in a pleasant gale / On the wide and raging sea
With a prize in view we will heave her to / And haul her under our lee
Then we will give three cheers and for home we will steer / While fortune on us smiles
For there is not dare cross that famed Le Ross
Unto his flag they will strike of course

3. Proud galleon sons and Spanish Dons / With pride and fury burn
They have crossed the seas for to fight with me / But never more again returned
Then England too doth me pursue / But at her threats I smile
Her men I have slain her ships I have ta'e / I have burned and sank them in the main

4. At length there is in sight a ship of might / An English man of war
She hails Le Ross and stops his course / And a broadside unto her she poured
The pirate the returned the fire / And proudly he did smile
But a fatal ball soon caused him to fall / And loud for quarters his men did call

Chorus for the last stanza
In the briny deep he is laid to sleep / In the briny deep he is laid to sleep
Once the pirate of the isles / Once the pirate of the isles
Once the pirate   Once the pirate   Once the pirate of the isles

206. The Robbers of the Glen

This rare song of uncertain origin is styled as the first-person testimony of the chief of a band of highwaymen, merrily extolling the virtues of his Robin Hood-like career in the forest, but with an ultimate sense of tragic futility. It is included here primarily because of its close affinities with "The Pirate of the Isles" [#205], with which "The Robbers of the Glen" is paired in each of the few instances in which it has been found in sailors' manuscripts. Like "Pirate of the Isles," "Robbers of the Glen" was certainly in circulation among American whalemen in the mid 19th century, but is rather too stable and formal to suggest a truly folkloric genesis; perhaps both were written by the same London street author, who is known only by the initials J.H. [see #205]. However, unlike "Pirate of the Isles," which was evidently fairly widely known at sea and on shore and is mentioned in Mayhew's *London Street Folk* (1851), "Robbers of the Glen" is not recorded elsewhere than an extremely rare broadside (Hewins Coll. #537A; Carnell, 21) and two texts in whaling journals in the Kendall Collection at the New Bedford Whaling Museum — the same two journals in which its seafaring *doppelganger,* "The Pirate of the Isles," also appears. The air is unknown.

A.

"THE ROBBERS OF THE GLEN." George M. Jones, bark *Waverly* of New Bedford, 1859-63. Neither as literate nor as clear as B; A reverses the order of stanzas 4 and 5; some of the lines garbled in A can be resolved by referring to B. A indicates that the last two lines in each stanza are to be repeated (in B, no repeats are indicated in the MS).

1. Stand stranger stand your jewills give me
Your gold we must obtain
Tis useless with your fate to strive
Resistance is in vain
Look at that band of mountaineers
Both bold and active men
At cares they laugh no danger fear
We are the robbers of the glen

2. When first we steal at dark midnight
Like owls we shun the day
When the tell tale morn obscures the day
Then we secure our prey
No violence save self defence
Whilst I command my men
No blood is shed on no pretence
By the robbers of the glen

3. When all the festive board we meet
   I with my men all game
   They my welcome loudly greet
   My heart still slings to fame
   The ruby wines that seem in flame
   We all looked forward then
   But I cursed the hour that I became
   A robber of the glen

4. Through fate my prospects darkened and
   My friend was once my pride
   He like a traitor proved [to] me false
   And then seduced my bride
   I sought him but he would have fled
   We fought and he was slain
   And since that hour this life Ive led
   A robber of the glen

5. Through cards and dice my wealth Ive lost
   I once had wealth and fame
   But now alass they are no more
   And friendship but a name
   Yon stately castle there below
   In Its wide and broad domains
   They once were mine what am I now
   A robber of the glen

6. Come fill your [ ] with the livening glass
   Bid all dull cares be gone
   No more we'll think on scenes that have past
   Let the worlds dull cares alone
   Come sing the song and toast the glee
   And shout my merry men
   With a loud hurrah and three times three
   For the robbers of the glen

B.

"THE ROBBERS OF THE GLEN." George W. Piper, ship *Europa* of Edgartown, 1868-70. A more cogent and more precise text than A. The sequence of stanzas 4 and 5 in B is reversed in A. Unlike A, no repeats are indicated in B.

1. Stand stranger stand your jewels give
   Your gold I must obtain
   T'is useless now with fate to strive
   Resistance is in vain
   Look at that band of mountaineers
   Both tried and active men
   At care they laugh nor danger fears
   The robbers of the glen

2. When forth we steal at dark midnight
   Like owls that shun the day
   When the tell tale moon doth shed her light
   Then we will secure our prey
   No blood is shed on no pretence
   Whilst I command my men
   No violence shown save self defence
   By the robbers of the glen

3. When at the festive board we meet
   I with my men look gay
   They at my welcome loudly greet
   But my heart still longs for prey
   The ruby wine the scene inflames
   We all look merry then
   But I curse the hour that I became
   A robber of the glen

4. Through cards and dice my wealth Ive lost
   I once had wealth and fame
   But now alas they are no more
   And friendship is but a name
   Yon stately castle there below
   With all its wide domain
   It once was mine what am I now
   A robber of the glen

5. But my prospects darkened o'er
   My friend was once my pride
   He like the traitor played me false
   And then seduced my bride
   I sought him then he would have fled
   We fought and he was slain
   And since that time this life I have led
   A robber of the glen

6. Come fill your sould with livening glass
   Avaunt all cares begone
   No more we will think of things that's past
   Of worldly cares be done
   Come give the song and toast the glee
   And shout my merry men
   With a loud huzza and three times three
   For the robbers of the glen

207. Pirates' Chorus

This theatrical aria by the Irish-born composer Michael William Balfe (1808-1870), from his light opera *The Enchantress* (1845), commits the usual sin of the comic stage and its fictional pirates, portraying them as affectionate, romantic, perhaps even jovial, rather than endeavoring to capture the brutal misanthropy by which actual piracy on the high seas was characterized.

TUNE from *Heart Songs Dear to the American People,* 1909, p. 237 (also Frank 1998, #33, p. 82). Requires at least two pirates to sing it properly; three if the um-pah bass be added per Balfe's original score.

"PIRATE'S CHORUS." William H. Keith, whaling schooners *William Martin* of Boston and *Edith May* of Wellfleet, 1865-69; and merchant schooner *Cora Nash* of Boston, circa 1869-71. Repeats required by the tune but not included in the MS are indicated in italics brackets.

Ever be happy and light as though art
Pride of the pirate's heart!
   Long be thy reign
   O'er land and main:
By the glaive, by the chart,

Queen of the pirate's heart.
Ever happy and light as thou art,
Pride of the pirate's heart
[*Pride of the pirate's heart*]
[*Pride, pride of the pirate's heart*]

208. The Life of a Tar

This obscure American parlor song, in print by 1847, is known only from songster texts. Neither author nor composer has been identified, and the air has not been discovered.

"THE LIFE OF A TAR." George W. Piper, ship *Europa* of Edgartown, 1868-70.

1.
The life of a tar is the life I love
The sea beneath us, the Heavens above
Our reign undisputed from the sky to the sea
Whose life can compare to the mariner free,
When winds whistle loud, still in safety we ride
Through waves which never overwhelm us
   as we merrily stride
No life half so happy, no life half so free
While we skim undismayed over the rolling sea

2.
The hope of our maidens, the pride of our isle
The heart is a stranger to falsehood and guile!
His ship is his home, his nation the world,
His boast is his flag never wrongly unfurled
His heart his true honor, how happy is he
While we skim undismayed over the rolling sea
No life half so happy, no life half so free
While we skim undismayed over the rolling sea

209. Our Way Across The Sea

This is an obscure parlor song of American origin circa the 1830s, authorship unknown. Two transcriptions were found in whaling journals.

TUNE: unascribed "adapted to a favourite French air... La Serenade Nº 3," in sheet music published by Geo. Willig, Philadelphia, n.d. [circa the 1830s]; reprinted as "arranged from a Swiss air," in C.E. Leslie, *Cyclone of Song,* 1888, 160ff; and H. Griggs, *Beacon Song Collection Nº 2,* 1900, 160f.

A.
"OUR WAY ACROSS THE SEA." Asaph S. Wicks, bark *John Dawson* of New Bedford, 1853-58.

1. Home fare thee well the ocean storm is o'er
   The weary pennant woos the seaward wind
   Fast speeds the bark and now the lessning shores
   Sinks the wave with those we leave behind
   Fare fare the[e] well / Land of the free
   No toung can tell / The love I bear to the[e]

2. We wreath no bowl to drink a gay good bye
   For tears would fall unbidden in the wine
   And while reflected was the mournful eye
   The sparkling surface e'en would cease to shine
   Then fare fare well / Once more once more
   The ocean's swell / Now hides my native shore

3. See where yon star its diamond light displayed
   Now seen now hid behind the welling sail
   Hope rides in gladness on its streaming ray
   And bids us on and bribe[s] the favoring gale
   Then hope we bend / In joy to thee
   And careless wend / Our way across the sea

B.
"OUR WAY ACROSS THE SEA." Marble Family copy book, inscribed (after the fact) in the journal of John C. Marble, ship *America* of Hudson, 1839-41. Virtually identical to A.

210. Jamie's On the Stormy Sea
[My Jamie's On the Stormy Sea; My Lover's On the Stormy Sea]

Helen Kendrick Johnson concurs with the sheet music in attributing the melody to American songwriter Bernard Covert, though, perhaps because of its characteristically Scots-Irish flavor, it is sometimes credited to George Alexander Lee. But Johnson errs in claiming, "There is no clue whatsoever to the authorship of these words." Though the lyrics are unattributed on the sheet music, both Charles Bruce, editor of *Poems, Songs and Ballads of the Sea* (Edinburgh, 1874), and William Cullen Bryant, the celebrated American poet and anthologist, are unequivocal in ascribing them to David Macbeth Moir (1798-1851), a Scottish physician who used the pseudonym "Delta." The text is a kind of imitation of the broadside ballad genre, in this case the ballads of the Sailor's Return: the woman is encountered pining for her lover in a pastoral setting; he is a sailor "on the stormy sea"; she sings, as the woman often does in the ballads; the narrator reveals himself to be the long departed Jamie; only there is little real drama in the sadness or the reunion here compared with authentic ballads on similar themes. Nevertheless, the song has often been reported in tradition, and on shipboard by Huntington, who gives a text from the ship *Euphrasia* of Salem, circa 1849. In addition to the two whalemen's texts given below, the song is mentioned by William H. Keith on whaling and merchant voyages in the 1860s and '70s.

"JAMIE'S ON THE STORMY SEA." From the original sheet music (Boston: Oliver Ditson, 1847), undoubtedly the source for H. K. Johnson and *Heart Songs Dear to the American People*. Transposed from Eb.

A.

UNTITLED. Edward McCleave, master, ship *Roscoe* of New Bedford, 1847-51. A substantial fragment, consisting of two 7-line stanzas. One line of each stanza may be missing; or a repeat may have been intended, not indicated in McCleave's manuscript. However, comparison with B is helpful in clarifying anomalies in that more complete but corrupted text.

1. Ere the twilight bat was flitting
   In the sunset at her knitting
   Sang the lovely maiden, sitting
   Underneath her thersehold [*threshold*] tree
   And ere daylight died before us
   Fitful rose her tender chorus
   Jamie, on the stormy sea

2. Warmly shone the sunset glowing
   Sweetly breathed the young flowers blowing
   Earth with beauty overflowing
   Seemed the home of love to be
   As those angel tones ascending

Ever had the same low ending—
Jamie, on the stormy sea

B.

"MY LOVERS ON THE STORMY SEA." George M. Jones, bark *Waverly* of New Bedford, 1859-63. Differs markedly from Moir's original in that it reconstitutes the original 8-line stanzas into 4-line verses; simplifies, with a more frequent refrain; shortens, eliminating portions of the original; substitutes new text of its own; and confuses syntax.

1. Ere the twilight bat was flitting
   In the sunset sat her knitting
   Sang a lovely Maiden singing
   My lovers on the stormy sea

2. And as daylight died before us
   And the vesper star shone oer us
   Shrillful rose they louder chorus
   My lovers on the stormy sea

3. Warmly shone the sunset glowing
   Sweetly grew the wild flowers glrowing [sic]
   Gayly sat the maiden singing
   My lovers on the stormy sea

4. Nearer as I drew and nearer
   Softer grew the voyce and clearer
   Oh it was heaven itself to hear her
   My lovers on the stormy sea

5. How could I but list and linger
   To the song and near the singer
   Sweetly wooing heaven to bring her
   Lover from the stormy sea

6. Blow ye winds and blandy hover
   Oer the bark that bears my lover
   Gently blow and bear him over
   To his own dear home and me

7. For when the night wind bends the willow
   Sleep forsakes my lonely pillow
   Gently thinking of the lonely billow
   My lovers on the stormy sea

8. And while yet her lips did name me
   Forth I sprang my heart oercame me
   Weep no more I am here to claim thee
   Home returned to love and thee

211. Willie's On the Dark Blue Sea

An obscure American parlor song by H.S. Thompson (circa 1825-circa 1865), published in 1849, encountered in tradition only in several Yankee whalemen's transcriptions.

TUNE from two editions of the original sheet music (Boston: Oliver Ditson, 1849 and 1853).

A.

"WILLIE ON THE DARK BLUE SEA." Asaph S. Wicks, bark *John Dawson* of New Bedford, 1853-58. What Wicks transcribes here as a chorus appears in Huntington's *Euphrasia* version as stanza 2.

1. [My] Willie's on the dark blue sea
   He's gone far o'er the main
   And many a weary day will pass
   Ere he'll come back again

2. I love my Willie best of all
   He e'er was true to me
   But lonesome dreary are the hours
   Since first he went to sea

3. There's danger on the water now
   I hear the blond billy cry
   And moaning voices seem to speak
   From out of the cloudy sky

4. I see the vivid lightning's flash
   And hark the thunder roar
   Oh Father save my Willie from
   The storm king['s] might[y] power

5. And as she spoke the lightning ceased
   Hush'd was the thunder's roar
   And Willie clasp her in his arms
   To roam the sea no more

6. Now blow gentle winds o'er the dark blue sea
   No more we'll stay thy hand
   Since Willie safe at home with me
   In his own dear native land

Chorus: Then blow gentle winds o'er the dark blue sea
   Bid the storm king stay his hand
   And bring my Willie back to me
   To his own dear native land

B.

"THE DEEP BLUE SEA." George Edgar Mills, third mate, bark *Aurora* of Westport, 1856-59. Similar to C, lacking stanzas 4 and 6 of A.

C.

"MY WILLIE IS ON THE DEEP BLUE SEA." George W. Piper, ship *Europa* of Edgartown, 1868-70. Similar to B, lacking stanzas 4 and 6 of A.

212. **Good News from Home**

The morning of the 5th of Oct [1857] we safely anchored in Honoruru [sic] harbor. Ever thing then seemed like home except the swarm of native boys that gathered upon the wharf and aroun[d] the ship. After giving necessary orders the Capt. took a boat and went on shore and returned again in a short time with the letters for the ship. No pen can describe the anxiety that was felt within me to once more hear from home. After receiving my letters I became so much excited that I heeded not the date of the letter but broke open the first within my reach... Many news I received and I think that which most rejoiced me, as pertaining to home affairs, was in may father purchasing the old homestead. Many hours of happiness have I spent within its walls in my younger days, when the youthful heart seemed blithe and gay... O! for another visit to those scenes again, to those scenes of happiness & enjoyment. O! for another visit among friends, brothers & sisters, that our voices may mingle again together, within that parental cot. How many times during the reading of my letters did I repeat,

>Home, sweet home, there is no place like home.

>— Benjamin Franklin Gallup, Jr., bark
>*South America* of New Bedford, 1857

The cover of the original sheet music for "Good News from Home" (published in 1854) is inscribed, "Poetry and Music Composed and most affectionately dedicated to his MOTHER by P.S. GILMORE, Leader of the Boston Brigade Band," surmounted by a Stephen Foster-like portrait of the composer with ships in the background. Inside, the publisher proudly proclaims, that "G.P. Reed & Co. have just published 'Sad News from Home.' Composed as a companion to this song." There is more salesmanship than seamanship in pieces of this ilk, and no matter what the merits of the music, the lyrics reveal that the Irish-born songwriter Patrick Scarsfield Gilmore (1829-1892) was no sailor and no Stephen Foster. Yet even stilted palaver may surround a kernel of insight. Weak as this little ditty may appear today, it seems perfectly in accord with young Franklin Gallup's equally stylized sentiments as a young Connecticut sailor in Hawaii when Gilmore's song was still new, and, if the number of per capita transcriptions be any measure, the song was quite popular in the whale fishery.

TUNE from the original sheet music (Boston: G.P. Reed & Co., n.d., circa 1854-56), ascribed and quoted as above; simplified from the through-composed setting.

A.

"GOOD NEWS FROM HOME." George Edgar Mills, third mate, ship *Aurora* of Westport, dated "August 23rd. 1857. Galapagos Islands. Albarmarle." Virtually identical to the text in the sheet music and with B. Minor spelling and grammatical variations suggest possible transcription from singing or oral recitation.

B.

"GOOD NEWS FROM HOME." George W. Piper, ship *Europa* of Edgartown, 1868-70. Virtually identical to the text in the sheet music and to A.

1. Good news from home good news for me
   Has come across the deep blue sea
   From friends that I have left in tears
   From friends that I've not seen for years
   And since we parted long ago
   My life has been a scene of woe
   But now the joyful hour has come
   For I have heard good news from home

   Chorus: Good news from home good news for me
   Has come across the deep blue sea
   From friends that I have left in tears
   From friends that I've not seen for years

2. No father's near to guide me now
   No mother's tear to soothe my brow
   No sister's voice falls on my ear
   No brother's smile to give me cheer
   For though I have wandered far away
   My heart is filled with joy today
   For friends across the ocean's foam
   Have sent to me good news from home

3. When I shall see the cottage door
   Where I've spent years of joy before
   My heart then knew no grief nor care
   For I was always happy there
   But should I never see them more
   Nor stand upon my native shore
   Where'er on Earth I am doomed to roam
   My heart will be with those at home

C.

"GOOD NEWS FROM HOME." William H. Keith, whaling schooners *William Martin* of Boston and *Edith May* of Wellfleet, 1865-69; and merchant schooner *Cora Nash* of Boston, circa 1869-71.

D.

"GOOD NEWS FROM HOME." Undated in the journal/copybook of Richard C. Reynolds, boatsteerer, ship *Janus* of New Bedford, 1842-44, but, given the publication date of the song, evidently inscribed after the fact.

APPENDIX 1
Dibdin's Songs

There can be little doubt that among landsmen and seamen alike, songs by the English tunesmith Charles Dibdin (1745-1814) were some of the most popular of their day. During a career that extended from the Colonial wars almost to the end of the Napoleonic era, Dibdin produced a staggering number of compositions, mostly for the comic and semi-operatic stage: about seventy operatic productions between 1762 and 1822, thirty-five musical entertainments, and more than a thousand songs, writing the words not only for his own music but also for many other composers (*Minstrelsy of England,* 192). Some of these achieved wide circulation in the music halls and among soldiers and sailors, and Dibdin is remembered today for having contributed importantly to the morale and hence the success of Nelson's navy. As Melville observes, in later life Dibdin was awarded a government pension for his service to the crown. His musical and theatrical compositions encompassed such a variety of topics as few lyricists would dare attempt, ranging from life in the British infantry to American slaves playing the "banjar." A few of his "patriotic verses, full of sea chivalry and romance" were adopted as anthems in the army and navy—if not officially by the Admiralty in a tacit conspiracy to promote conscription and morale, as Melville implies in *Whie-Jacket* and *Billy Budd*, then certainly among common sailors themselves, from whom there is reliable firsthand evidence that Dibdin's songs were sung enthusiastically and often. They were extensively anthologized during his own time and in the next two generations, in anthologies entirely devoted to Dibdin, in general anthologies like the *Universal Songster* and *Forecastle Songster,* and in a collected works edited by George Hogarth and by Dibdin's sons, Thomas and Charles, Jr., who successfully carried forward the family songwriting tradition and also advised Hogarth.[1] In fact, so thoroughly was the elder Dibdin's name associated with songs of the sea, that nautical ditties of any analogous type were often erroneously attributed to him in print and the actual poets slighted thereby. The titan cast his shadow across British patriotic song in the Age of Nelson and earned the attention, at least, if not the wholehearted approval, even of the likes of Melville. Though Melville differed with Dibdin politically and philosophically he could neither ignore him nor help but admire some of his songs.

Perhaps not surprisingly, Dibdin's compositions are rare in the copybooks of Yankee seamen. In his extensive gleanings from whaling manuscripts in several archives, Huntington turned up not even a single stanza by Dibdin. This is probably due to the reasons Melville suggests—that Dibdin's lyrics are not true to the hard lot and bitter resentments of the ordinary Jack Tar, that they are patronizing and tend to stereotype the common sailor, and that by reason of their royalist chauvinism, many are unsuitable to be sung by patriotic Americans. They were also obsolescent by the time whalemen began copying down songs in their journals. Dibdin's greatest and only truly enduring song is "Tom Bowling" [#2], which appears on both Melville's and Dana's lists of so-called "classical songs of the sea." Interestingly, all seven texts of the six other Dibdin songs come from only two journal sources: Daniel Kimball Ritchie, the troubled young product of a classical education, serving as second mate in the New Bedford ships *Israel* and *Herald* (1843-47); and the inexhaustible New Hampshire scribe George Wilbur Piper, an eclectic, voluminous, and proficient copyist aboard the whaler *Europa* of Edgartown (1868-70). The songs, which are almost never sung nowadays, are presented in chronological order of their composition.

---

[1] It should be noted that while Hogarth's editions were prepared in good faith and are not controversial, they are not identical with the songs as Dibdin originally composed and produced them. However, until such time as a scholarly revision supersedes Hogarth, his renditions will likely remain definitive. For the purposes of the present anthology, inasmuch as Hogarth's arrangements were evidently vetted by Dibdin's sons, are contemporaneous with the whalemen's manuscripts, and probably constitute a fair representation of the way the songs were known and sung in the middle decades of the 19th century, the Hogarth anthology is probably the best authority on the state of Dibdin's art at the time.

213. The Signal to Engage

Words and music by Charles Dibdin, from *The Impostor; or, All's Not Gold that Glitters* (1776). One of Dibdin's earlier and lesser-known songs, it has seldom been published since. In some ways the poem is one of his best. Compared to many of his later works, the lyrics are straight forward and unimpeded by cumbersome, caricatured jargon, thus the poetry is nicely suited to the stirring simplicity of the subject, a navy boatswain's beefy instructions and encouragement to the crew just as the enemy is about to be engaged in battle. On the other hand, the melody is through-composed (that is, rather than repeating, it differs from stanza to stanza) in a difficult key, and rather complicated, perhaps accounting in part for its failure to attract a permanent following.

TUNE from George Hogarth, *The Songs of Charles Dibdin,* I:73-80.   Through composed.

"THE SIGNAL TO ENGAGE." George Wilbur Piper, ship *Europa* of Edgartown, 1868-70. A copy text that varies from the published original in that it is not transcribed into verses, does not indicate that "The signal to engage &c." is a refrain repeated after each fourth line (per the tune), and is slightly Americanized in stanza 3. Reconstituted into stanzas, but otherwise uncorrected from the MS. Variations from Hogarth's text are indicated in italics in brackets.

1. The signal to engage shall be,
   a whistle and a halloa;
   be one and all but firm like me
   And conquest will soon follow:

2. You Gunnel, keep the helm in hand,
   thus, then boys steady steady
   Till right ahead you see the land
   then soon [*soon as*] we are ready

3. Keep boys, a good lookout,
   do you hear [*d'ye hear*],
   It is for bold Columbia's honor
   [*'Tis for old England's honor*]
   Just as you've brought your lower tier,
   Broadside to bear upon her

4. All hands, then, lads [*boys*], the ship to clear,
   load all your guns and mortars
   Silent as death, the attack prepare,
   and now all to your quarters.

214.
Poor Jack

Words and music by Charles Dibdin, from *The Whim of the Moment* (1788). One of few Dibdin sea songs that enjoyed a degree of popularity and staying-power among seamen. It was evidently still in circulation after a hundred years, when Admiral Luce anthologized it. Betweentimes it appeared often in songsters and was evidently a staple of the British and American naval repertoire. *Davy* refers to Davy Jones' Locker below the sea, a nautical slang term for the afterlife

TUNE from George Hogarth, *The Songs of Charles Dibdin,* I:189-192.

"POOR JACK." George W. Piper, ship *Europa* of Edgartown, 1868-70. In the MS some lines are doubled and Dibdin's characteristic jargon conjugations ("d'ye see," "'twas," etc.) are redivided into whole words ("do you see," "it was," etc.). Reconstituted into verses per Hogarth. Variations from printed texts indicated in italics in brackets.

1. Go patter to lubbers and swabs do you see,
   about danger and fear and the like
   A tight water boat and good sea room give me,
   and it aint [*and t'ent*] to a little I'll strike
   Though the tempest top gallant masts smack smooth should smile
   And shiver each splinter of wood
   Clear the wreck, stow the yards, house [*and bowse*] everything tight,
   and under reefed foresail we will scud
   Avast nor dont think me a milksop so soft,
   To be taken by trifles aback,
   For they say there is a Providence sits up aloft
   To keep watch for the life of Poor Jack

2. Why I heard the good chaplain palaver one day
   about souls, heaven, mercy and such
   And, my timbers! what lingo he would coil and belay,
   Why it was just all to one as high dutch
   But he said how a sparrow cant founder do you see
   without orders that come down below
   And many fine things that proved clearly to me
   that Providence takes us in tow
   For says he, do you mind, let storms ever so oft,
   take the topsails and sailors aback
   There is a sweet little cherub that sits up aloft,
   to keep watch for the life of Poor Jack

3. I said to our Poll, for you see, she would cry,
   when last we weighed anchor to sea
   What argufies snivelling and piping your eye,
   What a dam—d fool you must be
   Cant you see the world is wide, and there is room for us all,
   both for seamen and lubbers ashore
   And if to old Davy I should go, friend Poll [*old Davy I go, dear Poll*]
   Why you never will hear of me more
   Why then all is hazard, come dont be so soft,
   perhaps I may laughing come back
   For do you see there is a cherub sits smiling aloft,
   to keep watch for the life of Poor Jack

4. Do you mind a sailor should be every inch,
   all as one as a piece of the ship
   And with her brave the world, without offering [to] flinch
   from the moment the anchor is atrip
   As for me, in all weathers, times, sides, and ends
   Nought is a trouble from duty that springs
   For my hearts is my Polls, and my rhino is my friends'
   And as for my life, why its the kings
   Even when the time comes never believe me soft,
   as for grief to be taken aback
   That [*For*] the same little cherub that sits up aloft,
   Will look out a good berth for Poor Jack

215. Saturday Night at Sea

The sailor who transcribed this song seems to have confused the title with Dibdin's "Wives and Sweethearts," from *The Whim of the Moment* (1788), but it is actually a nearly verbatim text of the song properly known as "Saturday Night at Sea," from Dibdin's *The Oddities* (1789). The theme is familiar of course, and often encountered in sea songs. The ship as metaphor for a woman is usually fraught with transparent double entendre, as in "The Fire Ship" and some forms of "Blow the Man Down" (qq.v. in Colcord, 38; Shay 1948, 40 and 205; Doerflinger, 18; Hugill, 203f). But the apparent double meaning in Dibdin's composition here is likely unintentional and more the result of modern than contemporaneous slang usage of "tight." However, the last lines of the final stanza may not be entirely innocent. This song should not be confused with other songs of the same name —notably #186; and another that may have been adrift in the 20th-century American Navy, a drinking song by one H.P. Smith (Trident 23).

Saturday Night at Sea. Anonymous mezzotint issued by Laurie & Whittle, London, 1796. New Bedford Whaling Museum

TUNE A - from George Hogarth, *The Songs of Charles Dibdin,* I:226ff.

TUNE B - from *The American Musical Miscellany,* Northampton, Massachusetts, 1798, pp. 120f.

"SWEETHEARTS AND WIVES" [sic]. Daniel K. Ritchie, second mate, ships *Israel* and *Herald* of New Bedford, 1843-47. Copy text of "Saturday Night at Sea," unaccountably mis-titled in evident confusion with a Dibdin song published the preceding year. The one significant variation from Hogarth is indicated in italics in brackets; one word is missing in the MS and is likewise supplied from Hogarth, in italics in brackets. The song is also mentioned but no text is given by John Jones, steward, ship *Eliza Adams* of New Bedford, 1852.

1. 'Twas Saturday night, the twinkling stars
   Shone on the rippling sea;
   No duty called the jovial tars,
   The helm was lash'd a-lee:
   The ample can adorn'd the board,—
   Prepares to see it out,
   Each gave the girl [*lass*] that he ador'd
   And pushed the grog about

2. Cried honest Tom, my Peg I'll toast
   A frigate neat and trim,
   All jolly Portsmouth's [*fav'rite*] boast;
   I'd venture life and limb—
   Sail seven long years, and ne'er see land
   With dauntless heart and stout,
   So tight a vessel to command:
   Then push the grog about

3. I'll give, cried little Jack, my Poll,
   Sailing in comely state;
   Top-gan't sails set, she is so tall,
   She looks like a first rate:
   Ah! would she take her Jack in tow,
   A voyage for life throughout,
   No better a berth I'd wish to know:
   Then push the grog about.

4. I'll give, cried I, my charming Nan,
   Trim handsome, neat, and tight;
   What joy so fine a ship to man,
   She is my heart's delight:
   So well she bears the storms of life,
   I'd sail the world throughout,
   Brave every toil for such a wife:
   Then push the grog about.

5. Thus to describe Poll, Peg, or Nan,
   Each his best manner tried;
   Till, summon'd by the empty can,
   They to their hammocks hied;
   Yet still did they their vigils keep,
   Though the huge can was out,
   For, in soft visions, gentle sleep
   Still push'd the grog about.

216. Who Cares?

Words and music by Charles Dibdin, from *The Will o' the Wisp* (1795).

TUNE from George Hogarth, *The Songs of Charles Dibdin*, II:70f.

"WHO CARES." George W. Piper, ship *Europa* of Edgartown, 1868-70. In the MS some lines are doubled, conjunctions are remade into whole words and punctuation is largely omitted; otherwise much like the texts in the *Universal Songster* and Hogarth. Reconstituted into stanzas per Hogarth, whereof differences are noted in italics in brackets.

1. If lubberly landsmen to gratitude strangers,
   still curse their unfortunate stars
   Why what would they say, did they try but the dangers,
   encountered by true hearted tars
   If life's vessel they put before the wind or they tack her,
   Or whether bound here or [bound] there
   Give them sea room, good fellowship, grog and tobacco [*tobacker*]
   Why then darn me [*well, then, damme!*] if jack cries [*cares*] where

2. Then your stupid old quidnuncs,[2] to hear them all clatter,
   the devil can [*can't*] tell you what for
   Though they dont know a gun from a marlinspike chatter,
   about and concerning of war
   While for king, wife, and friend he is through everything rubbing
   With duty still proud to comply
   So he gives but the foe of America[3] a drubbing
   Why then darn me [*damme!*] if jack cares why

3. And then what good fortune has crowned his endeavors,
   and he comes home with shiners[4] galore
   Well, what if so be he should lavish with favors,
   on every poor object along shore
   Since money is the needle that points to good nature,
   friend, enemy false or true
   So it goes to relieve a distressed fellow creature,
   Well then darn me [*damme!*] if jack cares who

4. Dont you see how some different thing every one is twigging[5]
   to take the command of a rib[6]
   Some are all for the breast work, and some for the rigging,
   and some for the cut of her jib
   Though poor, some will take her in tow to defend her,
   and, again some are all for the rich
   As for I, so she is young her heart honest and tender
   Why then darn me [*damme!*] if jack cares which

5. Why now if they go for to talk about living,
   my eyes, why a little will serve
   Let each small part of his pittance be giving,
   and who in this nation can starve
   Content is all the thing, rough or calm be the weather
   the wind on the beam or the bow
   So honestly he can splice both ends together
   Why then darn me [*damme!*] if jack cares how

---

[2] *Quidnuncs:* from the Latin, literally, "what-now"; "One who is constantly asking: 'What now?' 'What's the news?'; hence, an inquisitive person; a gossip; a newsmonger" (OED).

[3] In the MS Piper has crossed out "old England" and substituted "America."

[4] *Shiners:* coins, money.

[5] *Twigging:* seeking for or trying to figure out (see *twig* in OED).

[6] *Rib:* London slang term for a woman, in the Biblical sense of Eve having been created from Adam's rib. Then ensues a double-entendre metaphor of ship-as-woman.

6. And then for a bring up do you see about dying,
   on which such a racket they keep
   What argufies if in a church yard you are lying,
   Or find out your grave is the deep
   Of one thing we are certain whatever our calling,
   death will bring us all up And what then?
   So his conscience's tackle will bear overhauling
   Why then darn me [*damme!*] if hack cares when

217. Nature and Nancy

Words and music by Charles Dibdin, from *Tom Wilkins* (1799).

TUNE from George Hogarth, *The Songs of Charles Dibdin*, II:235ff.

"NATURE AND NANCY." Daniel K. Ritchie, second mate, ships *Israel* and *Herald* of New Bedford, 1843-47. A proficient copy text. However, there is no indication that when sung the tune requires repeating the last few lines in each stanza: the repeats (from Hogarth) are indicated in a chorus appended to the first stanza; the same procedure should be followed for each ensuing stanza. Other textual differences with Hogarth are noted in italics in brackets..

1. Let swabs with their vows, their palaver, and lies
     Sly flattery's silk sails [*still*] be trimming
   Swear their Polls all be angels dropped down from the skeys,
     I your angels dont like,—I loves women,
   And I loves a warm heart and a sweet honest mind,
     Good as truth, and as lively as fancy;
   As constant as honor, as tenderness kind;
     In short I loves Nature and Nancy

[Chorus: *Good as truth, and as lively as fancy,* (2x)
   As constant as honour, as tenderness kind; (2x)
   In short, I loves Nature and Nancy; (2x)
   Nature and Nancy; As constant as honour, as tenderness kind;
   In short, I loves Nature and Nancy.]

2. I read a song about Wenus, I thinks
   All rigged out with her Cupids and graces;
   And how roses & lillies, carnations and pinks,
   Was made paint to daub over their faces.
   That they loves it may take all such art for their pains,
   For mine 'tis another guess fancy;
   Give me the rich health, flesh and blood, and blue veins
   That pays [*paints*] the sweet face of my Nancy

3. Why, I went to the play, where they talk'd well at least
   As to act all their parts they were trying;
   They were playing at soldiers and playing at feast
   And some they were playing at dying
   Let them hang, drown, or starve, or take poison d'ye see
   All just for their gig and their fancy;
   What to them was but jest is right earnest to me
   For I live and I [*I'd*] die for my Nancy.

4. Let the girls then, like so many Algerine Turks,
   Dash away, a fine gay-painted galley,
   With their jacks and their pennants and ginger bread work
   All for show, and just nothing for value
   False colours throw out, decked by labour and art,
   To take of pert coxcombs the fancy;
   They are all for the person, I'm all for the heart,—
   In short I'm for Nature and Nancy

   —*Dibdin*

218. The Lass that Loves a Sailor
[*Formally known as* "The Standing Toast"]

Words and music by Charles Dibdin, from *The Round Robin* (1811).

TUNE from George Hogarth, *The Songs of Charles Dibdin*, I:171f. See also Hullah #75; and Luce, 211, presumed to reflect the state of the song as sung in the U.S. Navy in Luce's time.

A.

"THE LASS THAT LOVES A SAILOR." George W. Piper, ship Europa of Edgartown, 1868-70. The patriotic features are "Americanized" similarly to Luce; Johnson's third stanza, absent in Luce, is present here.

1. The moon on the ocean was dimmed by a ripple
   Afffording a checkered light
   The gay jolly tars passed the word for a tipple
   And the toast, for it was Saturday night
   Some sweetheart or wife / He loved as his life
   Each drank, and he wished he could hail her
       But the standing toast / That pleased the most
       Was the wind that blows / The ship that goes
       And the lass that loves a sailor

2. Some drank to his country,[7] and some her brave ships[8]
   And some the Constitution
   Some may the French and all such rips
   Yield to American[9] resolution
       That fate might bless / Some Poll or Bess
       And that they soon might hail her
       But the standing toast / That pleased the most
       Was the wind that blows / The ship that goes
       And the lass that loves a sailor

3. Some drank to the Navy,[10] and some our land
   This glorious land of freedom
   Some that our tars would never want
   Heroes bold to lead them
   That she who in distress may find
   Such friends that ne'er will fail her
       But the standing toast / That pleased the most
       Was the wind that blows / The ship that goes
       And the lass that loves a sailor

B.

[Fragment.] George W. Piper, ship *Europa* of Edgartown, 1868-70. Folkloric variant of Dibdin's refrain.

    The wind that blows the ship that goes
    And the lad that fears no danger
    The ship lying to in a pleasant gale
    And the girl that loves a sailor

---

[7] In her British version, Helen Kendrick Johnson has "some drank 'the *Queen*'" (which would be "the *King*," in Dibdin's era); the American Admiral Luce substitutes "some drank 'the *Flag*.'"

[8] Johnson has "some '*our* brave ships'"; but Luce has "and some our land / Our glorious land of freedom."

[9] Johnson has "*English* resolution'; the phrase is lacking in Luce.

[10] Johnson has "the *Prince*" (Dibdin's original was published in the first year of the Regency).

APPENDIX 2

How Cheery Are the Mariners:
Miscellaneous Parlor-like Songs of Ships and the Sea

"Hardened deepwater tars," "shellbacks," and "swabs," as common seamen were often called by fellow mariners, were not above imitating parlor songs, folk songs, and sentimental poetry, occasionally waxing rhapsodic about the joys and hardships of the seafaring life. They were not really so hardened. Most Yankee whalemen, and probably a majority of merchant and navy seamen, were no older than their early twenties, with many of them still in their teens and most of them having spent the formative years of early adulthood on the rolling deck and lurching spars of a square-rigger. While other lads were in high school and college, or working on the family farm, clerking in shops, or serving trade apprenticeships ashore, the sailor was far out at sea dreaming of home. Young, uprooted, removed from normal life ashore, as a class, rather than being jaded or cynical, sailors tended to be callow, moonstruck, and impressionable, thus perhaps especially susceptible to the allure of poetry and song. For those with musical predilections and literary aspirations, this led, naturally enough, to imitation. Surprisingly many of these sailor-wrought imitations achieve a fairly respectable literary standard, while others are just sentimental exercises by mere boys. One, at least, "Norfolk Girls" [#11] by U.S. Navy Midshipman William Spicer, with its lyrical original melody and engaging poetry, actually had some currency in the naval repertoire (though the song seems to have had little to do with the composer's eventual rise to Commodore): it is certainly one of the best, less a parlor song than a navy song about women left behind. Seamen were often capable of appreciating or writing viable poetry when they abandoned highbrow pretension and concentrated instead on authentic seafaring experiences and their own genuine hopes and aspirations. But even the least of their parlor songs on sea-themes seem no worse to our latter-day ears than most of what the professional parlor songsmiths and stage minstrels were turning out. Whatever their relative merits as songwriters, it is worth noting that some of these young seafaring fellows were able, even quite heroic practitioners of their life-threatening trade, as the following poem attests. It is the mature work of a Boston physician, written aboard the Boston ship *Olive Branch* while a passenger from California to Panama in Gold Rush days. It is dedicated to Nicholas Kirby, Jr., first mate of the *Olive Branch,* who on that same cruise authored one of the songs in this section ["O Think of the Sailor," #223] and transcribed the doctor's poem into his journal, with the annotation "Panama March 27th 1851":

From a Friend

Youthful sailor, ere we part,
I for my home, you for the sea,
Accept these cherished, kind regards
Of passengers and friends to thee.
When on this gallant vessel's deck,
You I beheld, a stripling youth,
And heard you in that manly way
Give orders, though, to me, uncouth:
I thought it very strange to see
The office held by [a] boy like thee.

'Twas next upon the open sea,
When stormy winds and thunder roared;
Thy voice, as calm and firm I heard
As when thou stood upon the shore,
Contenting with the angry waves
Our ship and life both for to save.
I watched thee then; and since that hour
Felt no distrust, though youth thou art;
But all can say with heart sincere:
Thou bravely, nobly done thy part

Dr. Wm Cutler

219. **The Sailor**

This is so polished a homeward-bound song that it is difficult to imagine a seaman having written it; and a real sailor was likely to be more declarative than the speculative sentiments expressed in the subjunctive in stanza 3. But it is the sort of thing that whalemen often copied down among the songs and poems in their journals. James S. Colton, in the New London bark *Tenedos* during 1840-43, evidently got hold of it somewhere before it was reprinted in *The Sailors' Magazine* two or three years later (17:2, Oct 1844, 56). Verse could be obtained from the endless stream of schoolboy songbooks produced to foster wholesome values, and from any of the innumerable morally-uplifting periodicals that circulated among sailors in the Pacific in the mid 19th century. This one has about it the patronizing ring of the seamen's Christian benevolent organizations that were springing up at the time, whose purpose was to save mariners from themselves and coerce them into thrift, temperance, chastity, and compliance.

1. Behold the stately merchant ship / Come dancing ore the tide
   Her streamers floating gracefully / Her wide [*white*] sailes spreading wide

2. How proudly from her bow she heaves / The white topped curling waves
   As onward to her destined port / Her homeward path she weaves

3. What joy must thrill her hardy crew / When first the hills arise
   And in the azure distance spread / Their country meets their eyes

4. And on the bounding deck there stands / The sailor brave & free
   And in his heart he gently says / Im coming love to thee

5. For fancy with her giddy train / Of visions wild & sweet
   Reveals to him some cherished one / His homeward steps to greet

6. Who would not love the sailor bold / Who leaves his native land
   And braves the oceans stormy path / And [   ] a foreign strand

7. He fears no dangers that might well / The boldest heart abash
   The tempests might the fitful gale / The lightnings fiery flash

8. Welcome the sailor to his home / Ye daughters of the land
   And greete him with the dance & song / And take the proffered hand

9. For, neath his weather beaten heart / There beats a heart as true
   As ever cherished memorys tread / Or loves sweet influence knew

10. Then welcome him into your hearts / Ye smiling virtuous fair
    Protect him by your filial love / From sins alluring snare

220. How Cheery Are the Mariners

Stephen O. Hopkins, ship *Rosalie* of Warren, 1843. *The New Naval Song Book,* selected by J.E. Carpenter (1865, p. 121) attributes the lyrics to the American poet Park Benjamin, Sr. (1809–1864) with music by William Richardson Dempster (1809-1871). Despite the predictably formulaic exposition, it has a small dose of accurate nautical lingo.

1. How cheery are the mariners / Those lovers of the sea
   Their hearts are like the yeasty wave / As bounding and as free
   They whistle when the storm-line wheels / In circles round the mast
   And sing when deep in foam the ship / Ploughs onward to the blast

2. What care the mariners for gales / There's music in their roar
   When wide the berth along the lee / And leagues of room before
   Let billows toss to mountain heights / Or sink to chasms low
   The ship so stout will ride it out / Nor reel beneath the blow

3. With streamers down, the canvas furled / The gallant hull will float
   Securely, as on island [*inland?*] lake / A silken-tassled boat
   And sound asleep some mariners / And some with watchful eyes
   Will fearless be of dangers dark / That roll along the skies

4. God keep these cheery mariners / And temper all the gales
   That sweep against the rocky coast / To their storm-shattered sails
   And men on shore will bless the ship / That could so guided be
   Safe in the hollow of his hand / The wave the mighty sea

221. On New Year's Day

Original verse by Richard C. Reynolds, boatsteerer, ship *Janus* of New Bedford, 1843; signed "By R.C. Reynolds 1843," recounting in a ballad format the hardships, privations, and character of the sailors' life. Bits of the orthography are even more original than the sentiments expressed, in stanza 2 quaintly capturing the phonetics of a New England drawl. Air not identified.

1. This is the Begining of the year / Which every Sailor ought to fear
   That when he is to sea so Far / That he has Got a leding Star

2. Wheare ever he is at Land or sea / I wold have hime take warning to day
   How the Last year has Past and Gorn [gone] / And how another is rowling on

3. When he is far upon the seas / Although it blows a pleasant Breese
   He knowes not what a storm he'll have ; That will lay him Beneath the dark Blue wave

4. When you are toasting to and Fro / Think on whough guides you safe through
   He can guide from all harm / And when you are cold can make you warm

5. Sailors they are wild you know / And many hardships do go thorough
   And when they do get on shore / Some are resolved to go no more

6. And when they have shipped again / They are so happy until she haules in the stream
   Soon on board no they must go / To plough the ocean through and through

7. For several days when they are first out / The thoughts of leaving dose not them suit
   But when to some port draw near / Every heart begins to cheere

222. [The Sailor Is a Wanderer Free]

Joseph W. Tuck, brig *E. Nickerson* of Provincetown, 1850. Origin and air unknown; not found elsewhere. Neither Stan Hugill nor William Doerflinger could identify the text or the air, but both agreed it seems more like a song than a poem. Possibly only a fragment; possibly an original composition, but scant evidence of the mariner's technical expertise suggests that it is more likely something copied from a contemporaneous periodical or schoolboy song book, not identified. Frank 1985 #20.

1. The sailor is a wanderer free / and like the breezes fly
   Far o'er the wide & tractless sea / Where waves roll mountains high

2. A Lion's heart that knows no pain / A soul that knows no care
   He gayly sings, & toils for gain / That others too may share

223. O Think of the Sailor

Original lyrics written " off Guatemala March 12th 1852" by Nicholas Kirby, Jr., first mate, ship *Olive Branch* of Boston, on a Gold Rush voyage to California, 1850-52. Kirby was the subject of Dr. William Cutler's poem "From a Friend" (quoted above).

1. O think of the sailor, his hardships and dangers
   And of the privations he has to know
   Far away from his friends and home [he remembers]
   On the dark ocean where high winds do blow

2. Come for a while, let imagination
   Go with me down on the bright rolling wave
   See that noble ship so majestic'ly rolling
   High on the air the bright pennants [play]

3. Now in their berths so snugly they're sleeping
   Dreaming of home and [of] friends that's so dear
   Hark for a cry from the deck it comes sweeping
   All hands on deck for a squall it is near

4. Now from their hammocks so quickly they['re] spring[ing]
   Hurry on deck to prepare for the [blow]
   Then to the yards [they] quickly go [climbing]
   'Mid thunder and lightning 'mid sleet, hail, and snow

5. All is now darkness the rain is down pouring
   The bright lightnings flash and the thunders do roar
   Then it's clew down your topsails, haul out your reef tackles
   Lively, my lads, we are on a lee shore

6. Then up on the yard every man to his station
   The earrings and dog's ears being both of them manned
   Haul out to the leeward reef away to the windward
   Then knot your points lively [and] to deck you descend

224. [We're Bounding o'er the Dark Blue Sea]

Benjamin Franklin Gallup, Jr., bark *South America* of New Bedford; signed "F.M. Gallup / Barque South America / Dec. 31st 1856." A formula parlor-type song with whaling allusions in stanzas 1 and 4, it may be the diarist's own original composition. Frank 1985 #169.

1. We're bounding o'er the dark blue sea
   Who are so happy or so free?
   We're a jovial band, to each other true,
   And the king of the Ocean we pursue.

2. We love to plough the raging main
   And trace old Neptune's dark domain!
   What though the raging tempests rise,
   And foaming billows reach the skies!

3. Our bark is strong and will bide the gale,
   Not a heart is fain not a cheek is pale,
   But with joyous song our sails we'll trim,
   As long as her gallant hull shall swim.

4. The ocean's our home on its bosom we'll sail
   In search of our prey the huge sporting whale
   With joy from aloft we love to descry
   His breath as a banner sent up to the sky

Notes: The transcription is in B.F. Gallup's hand and is unaccountably signed pseudonymously: there was no other Gallup in the crew at the time; the diarist was customarily known as (and often signed his name) "Franklin Gallup," as distinguished from his father and namesake; thus "F.M. Gallup" must refer either to the diarist himself (possibly experimenting with an alternative form of his name) or to some member of his family, with whom any connection to the song is unknown.

225. [The Sailor On the Ocean Wide]

Frederick Howland Smith, boatsteerer, bark *Roscius* of New Bedford, 1861. Likely an original composition by the diarist, age about 20 at the time; air unknown.

1. The sailor on the ocean wide / Thinks little of his life;
   He laughs to see the wind and tide / Engaged in endless strife.

2. He laughs in scorn to hear the roar / Of breakers all around;
   And steers his Ship from off the shore / Whence comes the dismal sound

3. Away he flies before the gale / And singing as he goes;
   His men he tells to trim the sail / And snug the hatches close.

4. Brave man is he who thus can dare / The wrath of Neptune grim;
   But naught thinks he of freight [fright] or care / If his stout Ship is trim

5. 'Tis calm at last—the sky serene / Looks down upon the ships
   It seems as though no storm had been / Disturbing its fair trips.

6. All things are close—the ropes are taut / And jolly sings the crew
   Their songs of war, as if they sought / To bring the storm anew

226. The Mariner's Song

George W. Piper, ship *Europa* of Edgartown, 1868-70. A homeward-bound pastorale, origin and air unknown, not located elsewhere. It is unlikely a whaleman's original; in any case, Piper is not known to have composed original lyrics and seems scrupulously to have credited the ones he obtained from shipmates. "The white cliffed isles" could refer to the proverbial white cliffs of Dover or to Marthas Vineyard, where the *Europa*'s home-port is located.

1. Gaily we go o'er the salt blue sea / And the waves break white before us
   The crowded canvas bends to the breeze / And home points the pennant o'er us
   Speedily, speedily, bound we on / As if with the wind contending
   Now high the heaving surge upon / Now its yawning gulf descending

2. Our ship spreads wide her snowy wing / Like another bird of ocean
   As she shapes her way like a living thing / Of graceful make and motion
   Then speed thee speed, my home bound bark / Till thy native harbor nearing
   Soon the white cliffed isles shall the mariner mark / O'er the azure deep appearing

3. Yet no charms for me hath the fairest vale / Like the wilderness of waters
   When the vessel stoops to the freshening gale / And the spray around her scatters
   Then may the hammock my death bed be / And my grave beneath the billow
   There as well will I anchor under the lee / Of the wave as of the willow

227. A Seaman's Life

George W. Piper, ship *Europa* of Edgartown, 1868-70. There were several London broadsides with the lyrics but the melody is unknown. Not to be confused with "A sailor's life's the life I trow" ("The Sailor's Life") in Wilson, 78.

1. A seaman's life is the life I love
   The life I will live and die
   The sea below and the sky above
   And the billows run mountains high
   I love to hear the waters dash
   The wild waves roaring round
   The thunders roar the lightning's flash
   The sea birds welcome around

   Chorus:
   Then hurrah for the deep the briney deep
   The bright the glorious sea
   In the calm or the storm or any other form
   A Seaman's life for me

2. Some make their boast of a distant land
   Of the peaceful joys of home
   But I envy not their chosen lot
   Give me the sparkling foam
   Through the golden air our bark will steer
   On the rippling moonlight wave
   We laugh at the joys a toast my boys
   To the seaman's welcome grave

3. I love to hear the water's dash
   To hear the boatswain call
   All hands reef topsails be quick my lads
   The storm is coming on
   Aloft we flew with a gallant crew
   While the sun was sparkling bright
   I am a merry laughing sailor lad
   And the sea is my delight

4. When first I left my father's land
   What cares had life for me
   I love the strife of the seaman's life
   With the noble and the free
   O my heart was light and the sea was bright
   When I joined that gallant crew
   Our anchor is weighed our sails are unfurled
   To our friends we will bid adieu

5. Sometimes all in the midnight watch
   When on the boundless sea
   I think of her in a foreign land
   She was a good mother to me
   I love her still and always will
   When years have past and gone
   I may return to my native land
   But the sea shall be my home

228. Farewell to the Arctic

Robert N. Hughson, bark *Java* of New Bedford, 1857-60. In more capable sailors' hands the same themes that drive this insipid piece became the gutsy whalemen's homeward-bound ballad "Rolling Down to Old Mohee" [#143].

1. We are bound for the land of the glorious and brave
   That land the fair Jem of the sea
   Where the Stars and the Stripes, in triumph still wave
   Oer the home of the happy and free
   T'is there w[h]ere dwells those that we love
   Although now far from them we may be
   And a wide span of water between us doth roll,
   Yet our hearts are still ever with the[e] / Then let each heart with joy encore
   Let each note die away in the wind / An bid adieu to the Arctic Shores
   As we leave it far behind

2. As each day passes by to that land we draw near
   Where the eagle of freedom doth soar
   And we shout as each mountain of snow disappears,
   Farewell thou Arctic Shores
   Farewell and forever thou Ice bound North,
   To thy barren lands adieu
   As our Bark through the waters goes merrily forth
   We give three Cheers to you. / Then let each heart with joy encore
   Till each note dies away in the wind / Let us bid adieu to the Arctic Shores
   As we leave it far behind

3. Blow on thy cold wind blow on
   Our stay with the[e] is passed
   No more thy shores we will gaze upon
   Nor feel the bitter blast
   Our sails fill gently in the wind
   And each young heart bounds with glee
   As thy shores we leave far behind
   For that land of liberty / Then let each heart with joy encore
   Till each note dies away in the wind / Let us bid adieu to the Arctic Shores
   As we leave it far behind

4. Now the sun grows warmer with each mornings dawn
   And brightens all around
   Our little Bark glides swiftly on
   As though it knew it was homeward bound
   Our Ship is full all hands rejoice
   And each seamans bosom swells
   As they gather around and with one voice
   Shout to the Arctic Shores Farewell / Then let each heart with joy encore
   Let it echo far oer the sea / As we give three cheers for freedoms Shores
   And the land of Liberty

APPENDIX 3
The King of the Boundless Sea
Selected Whaling Poems

> "Oh the rare old Whale, mid storm and gale
> In his ocean home will be
> A giant in might, where might is right,
> And King of the boundless sea."
>
> — *Whale Song*
> from "Extracts," in *Moby Dick.*

Some whalemen's shipboard journals are peppered with copy-texts of songs and poems extracted from various periodicals and the occasional anthologies and gift-books that circulated around the fleet. Some of the magazines, like *The Seaman's Friend,* were specifically produced by seamen's benevolent organizations for the moral improvement of American sailors abroad. The evangelistic motives of the publishers generally eliminated from editorial consideration any but the most conventionally and unequivocally uplifting verse—preferring the pedestrian formulae of Mrs. Hemans and Isaac Baker Woodbury over the bold iconoclasm and disquieting vigor of Walt Whitman or Edgar Allan Poe. What little whaling-related material there was tended to be the product of well-meaning landlubbers, some of them professional poets but virtually all of them strictly amateur in standpoint of seamanship. Their poetry was calculated more to encourage Christian virtue than to characterize the empirical realities of the whaling business. "The King of Southern Sea" [#229], which evidently originated in Scotland, is a cut above most. Though it has little of the blood-and-guts drama of an actual whale hunt, it does capture a sense of the majestic gargantuanism that also inspired Melville's reverence, hence his use of the poem in "Extracts." Once it was reprinted in the American press and circulated around the Pacific in the 1840s, it caught on with whalemen, who sometimes pasted clippings of it or copied the lyrics into their journals. The whalemen's own poetic efforts only seldom achieved so high a literary standard. Even if they possessed talent and the inclination to write, the young lads in the fishery were, by and large, insufficiently experienced and insufficiently tutored to produce literary art of intrinsic quality or enduring value (though, given the context in which they were produced, some of their original poems are remarkably worthwhile; see Miller 1979). Brothers Rupert and Clement Swift, attributed authors of the comic ballad "The Parson's Narrative" [#133] (it is not certain which one actually wrote it), are notable exceptions. The sons of a distinguished New Bedford whaling master, the Swift boys were beneficiaries of a fine education at the Friends Academy; thus, before "Rupe" went whaling he had an opportunity, rare among whalemen, to pursue systematically the study of English syntax and to acquire a working knowledge of Greek, Latin, and Shakespeare. But this no more adequately accounts for the brilliance of his (or his brother's) poetry than it can explain Clement's precise draftsmanship and sensitive pictorial renderings. Greatly enhanced by the kind of wide reading and formal training that might also have turned the likes of George Edgar Mills, Daniel Kimball Ritchie, and Benjamin Franklin Gallup into competent writers, rather than the awkward neophytes they remained, the Swifts's exquisite literary genius transcends the received conventions and simplistic formulas of Victorian versifying, and elevated their efforts above the merely imitative. The gothic-comic poem "The Sailor Boy's Last Dream" [#230] is an achievement that bears comparison with Poe's *Narrative of Arthur Gordon Pym of Nantucket;* and the lyric-epic character and vivid imagery of "Wood and Black-Skin" [#231], which could only have been written by an expert whaleman—or the son of an expert whaleman—is hardly less than a poetic sidebar for *Moby Dick:* they are among the best poems ever produced by a sailor in English and perhaps the best ever produced by anyone about whaling.

229. **The King of the Southern Sea**
[The Rare Old Whale; Whale Song]

This poem of unknown authorship was reprinted from the *Glasgow Chronicle* in the May 1840 and December 1843 issues of *The Sailor's Magazine,* a monthly published in New York by the American Seamen's Friend Society which had a wide circulation among Pacific Ocean mariners. It is excerpted in "Extracts" in *Moby-Dick,* where it is identified as a "Whale Song"; however, it was never a *song* in the musical sense of lyrics intended to be sung: it has not been encountered in tradition and is not anthologized with musical notation; there is no evidence that it was ever issued as sheet music, that a setting was ever composed for it, or that it was ever sung at all, on shipboard or elsewhere, except as a lark by whaleman-biologist Robert Cushman Murphy circa 1913. It is included here because Melville's implication has understandably misled readers into presuming it to be a traditional whaling song, and scholars have searched in vain for the tune. The existence of whalemen's transcriptions attests to a certain popularity it must have enjoyed in the fishery when the poem was new, and vindicates Melville—more poet than musician—that he did not somehow betray shipboard culture by representing as genuine an academic parlor piece that was almost entirely unknown to his seafaring brethren.

A.

Joseph H. Eayrs, boatsteerer, bark *Gratitude* of New Bedford, 1841-45. A complete verbatim copy text entitled "The South Sea Whale," per *Sailor's Magazine,* December 1843, "From the Glasgow Chronicle," transcribed at sea when the poem was newly published. In stanza 3, replaces "shall" with "will"; extra exclamation points (!!!) are added before and after the refrain; otherwise identical with the *Sailor's Magazine* text and text B.

B.

Randall Himes, second mate, bark *Emma* of New Bedford, 1847. Untitled; verbatim copy text inscribed "From the Glasgow Chronicle," almost certainly transcribed from the *Sailors' Magazine* of 1843 (reprinted in Frank 1985 #162 and Frank 1985c).

1. Oh! the whale is free, of the boundless sea;
   He lives for a thousand years;
   He sinks to rest on the billow's breast,
   Nor the roughest tempest fears.
   The howling blast, as it hurries past,
   Is music to lull him to sleep;
   And he scatters the spray in his boisterous play,
   As he dashes—the king of the deep.
   Oh! the rare old whale, mid storm and gale,
   In his ocean home will be
   A giant in might, where might is right,
   And king of the boundless sea.

2. A wondrous tale could the rare old whale
   Of the might deep disclose,
   Of the skeleton forms of bygone storms,
   And of treasures that no one knows.
   He has seen the crew, when the tempest blew,
   Drop down the slippery deck,
   Shaking the tide from the glassy side
   And sporting with the ocean and wreck.
   Then the rare old whale, &c.

3. Then, the whale shall be still dearer to me,
   When the midnight lamp burns dim;
   For the student's book, and his favourite nook,
   Are illuminated by the aid of him;
   For none of his tribe could be e'er imbibe
   So useful, so bless'd a thing.
   Then we'll on land go hand in hand,
   To hail him the Ocean King!
   Oh! the rare old whale, &c.

230. The Sailor Boy's Dream

These 18 stanzas of uneven length in the journal of R.G.N. Swift aboard the ship *Contest* of New Bedford, 1866-70, constitute an epic gothic tall tale rich in nautical lore and color: a first-person narrative that achieves an uncommonly high literary standard. Its vernacular accuracy and specificity suggest that it must have been written or heavily revised by an experienced whaleman, and its localization to the *Contest* suggests the author was likely the whaleman-diarist himself (whose other original compositions demonstrate that he was an accomplished writer of poetry and prose). It has not been found elsewhere in any form. Note that in stanza 4 *lay* is a pun on *lay on* (thrust the harpoon); *Rupe* (stanza 10) is the diarist's name, a nickname for Rupert; the *Flying Dutchman* (stanza 10) is a legendary ship and sea captain condemned to eternal, pointless wandering over the sea; *tin* (stanza 10) is a common slang term for *money,* from coinage; *Skidam* is poor spelling but adequate pronunciation for the Dutch manufacturing and shipbuilding town of Schiedam on the Rijn, adjacent to Rotterdam, noted for production of so-called *genever* or *geneva* gin (which adjective is a corruption of the Spanish noun *genevra* or *ginebra,* meaning *gin*); *scudding* (stanza 13) is the fishermen's activity of shaking fish out of nets, and may here refer to a vessel being analogously shaken by wind and waves (it is also general parlance for skimming, sliding, or running along, as before a gale of wind); and *skeleton crew* (stanza 17) is another clever pun: sailors commonly refer to a "skeleton crew" as a minimum-maintenance measure, a term now in common parlance in the construction industry and law enforcement. The inscription at the end, in quotes in Swift's hand, is unascribed.

1. One day while sleeping, the other side of land,
   Where the broad Pacific laves the strand,
   Where the sun, by day, shines warm and bright,
   And the Southern Cross looks down at night
   Where the Magellan clouds gleam white in the sky
   And stars, at noon, at times you may descry,
   Far up in the zenith, withe the naked eye.

2. While calmly sleeping, as I said just now,
   On board the "Contest," in my bunk at the bow:
   Surrounded by shipmates, strong and true,
   As ever formed a whaleman's crew
   As ever sprung to the trough and oar
   Or listened to the sound of the norther's roar.
   I dreamed a dream, whose horror quite
   Gave me the blues, for a day and a night;

3. Methought, we had fastened to a big old bull,
   Who had given us a long and exhausting pull
   O'r the boiling sea, under a broiling sun.
   To[o] tired to cheer now our work not near done,
   We sat on the thwarts, sullen and sore,
   While the whale made his run, ten miles and more;

4. When suddenly the mate sang out, with an oath,
   Haul in the line quiet, he stops, by my troth!
   I'll give him the lance, and "as sure as you'r born"
   Will lay him as straight as a crocked ram's horn!
   Lay me on! and I'll insure your lay
   Is better by a hundred barrels today!

5. Forgetting fatigue, we work[ed] with a will,
   Our thoughts all bent, the whale to kill.
   Silent we paddle the boat to his side—
   One moment the mate stands up, in his pride,
   The next c[h]aos night in my wandering mind,
   Flashing lance, foul line, descending flukes with boat behind,
   The stern orders half drowned in the water's roar,
   Stern all! pay out! and I know no more.

6. At last I awake, or dream so, you know,
   At the bottom of the sea, some miles below,
   On walking about, Yankee like, to discover
   How things were going on, or something or other:
   I spied a big ship, wedged in between rocks,
   Resting as quite [quiet] as if on her stocks.

7. For shipmates, you know, she was far down below
   The rushing of currents, or gales that blow.

8. The boat and my shipmates had passed from my dreams
   And naught seemed present but the water's dull gleam.
   Alone in the waste of waters I stood,
   Alone with that dark mass of iron and wood,
   Her model is ancient, her look forlorn,
   Made me feel "streaked," as sure as you'r born.

9. One moment prompted to climb her dark side,
   Creeping fear, the next my purpose denied,
   Fear of the unknown, intangible things,
   Magicians, ghosts, or uncharted wings,
   All the ghost stories ever heard by me,
   Reached into my mind in those moments, you see.

10. But plucking up courage, in a little while,
    I said to myself, with a passing smile,
    "Rupe," my boy, you may "stinks ile,"
    If the "Flying Dutchman" this sure to have gin,
    If a "Spanish Gallion" there's lots of tin:
    If the ghost speaks Dutch I'll call for Skidam

      And if they talk Spanish, my pockets I'll cram
      With the bright gold of the "Inca," the noble chief,
      So cruelly despoiled by Pizar[r]o, the thief.

11.   If afloat, we would "gam" her, like another ship,
      And, darn it! I'll keep a stiff upper lip!
      And show them a Yankey ain't afraid to pry
      Into any darned mystery under the sky.

12.   My mind made up, I boarded the wreck,
      Touching my hat as I sprung up on deck.
      Not a soul to salute, you may well guess that
      But respect for the dead brought my hand to my hat.

13.   Shipshape she looked, made snug for a gale,
      With hatches battened down with tarpaulin and nails—
      The helm lashed amidships, as if scudding before,
      The waves had sent her to an untimely shore.

14.   Going down in the forecastle, I was taken aback
      By a sight that made my heartstrings crack;
      I rubbed my eyes and scratched my head,
      And, shiver my timbers, to myself I said,
      Am I asleep or am I dead?

15.   Stretched on each bench, prone there lay
      a ghostly skeleton, stark and gray.

16.   Some men when scared swift ran away,
      Others, by whistling their fears betray,
      My feet now rooted on the vessel's deck,
      My heart did n't seem to beat a speck.
      I thought, by Gosh, if I did not holler,
      My life wasnt worth a [*Yankee?*] dollar

17.   So touching one of the skeleton crew
      I said, how long have you slept there, you?
      I spoke as if speaking to living men.
      He replied, since eighteen hundred and ten.
      I started, for to tell you the truth, flat and plain,
      I did not expect an answer to gain.
      But quickly recovering, I thought he's so civil
      I'll pump the old fellow in spite of the Devil.
      For if anyone will answer it is my own true
      That a Yankey will question 'til all is blue
      And I guess our folks will be tickled to death,
      To learn how these fellows came to slip their breath.

18.   So, turning again to the skeleton loon,
      I said, old chap, wont you turn out soon?
      No bloody [   ], the grim voice replied,
      The watch aint called yet, and he turned on his side.
      Just then a rap, on the deck overhead,

Resounding like doom to "the quick and the dead,"
And a voice called out with an awful roar
Never heard, I ween, by fellows on shore,
Turn out there! wise out, Sarbotine Ahoy!
Come and get your grub! you lazy boy.

"And when thy soul is buried in a sleep, in midnight solitude, and little dreaming of such a spectre—what if I should creep, within thy presence in such dismal seeming? Thine eyes will stare themselves awake, and weep, and thou wilt cross thyself with treble screaming. And pray with mingled penitence and dread that I were less alive—or not so dead."

231. Wood and Black-Skin

Whaleman Rupert Swift and artist Clement Nye Swift were the sons of New Bedford whaling master and scrimshaw artist Rodolphus Nye Swift. Which of the two brothers composed the lyrics of this extraordinary poem is not known for certain. It survives as an insert in Rupert's journal of the New Bedford ship *Contest,* 1866-70; but the transcription is in Clement's hand. Rupert's handwriting was so bad (as shown elsewhere in the journal) and Clement's so good (he was a gifted artist) that even had Rupert written the lyrics he might have had his kid brother write them down. Alternatively, Clement may have written the poem and presented it to Rupert to take on the voyage; or it could have been the product of a collaboration between the two. Drawn on epic proportions, it is experientially authentic and technically accurate in every compelling detail. It is arguably the most lyrical and powerful of all poems to describe the technology and sensibilities of the whale hunt, and in its vivid articulation of a profound veneration of the whale, it is akin to the most lyrical passages of *Moby Dick*. Perhaps even more so than *Moby Dick,* it could only be the work of a professional whaler or someone intimately familiar with the nuances of the hunt.

1. The whale was off at a furious pace
    And the whale was fast to the boat
    My collar was open wide at the throat
    And I felt the wind on my face
    As we followed the order to "FACE ABOUT"
    And haul and surge on the line
    In the furnace heat of the fierce sunshine
    And we all turned to with a shout

2. "HEAD AND EYES OUT" The great whale ran
    A black spot far in the lead
    Dead to windward with furious speed
    And we were drenched to a man
    For a smothering curtaining cloud of wet
    Hung at the bow and convex walls
    Like two inverted waterfalls
    O'er topped each rail like a parapet

3. The smooth walls of glistening green
    As from an emerald chiseled and cut
    The sleek sides hissed as we passed between
    And the boat slid on in the gleaming rut

> In the wide foam-road of the whale's wake laid
> On the tumbling wave-hill's wide expanse
> That vast blue prairie devoid of shade
> Then the Mate wet forward to take the lance

4. And the Mate yelled— WOOD AND BLACK SKIN!
   When he stood in the whaleboat's bow
   "NOW PULL ME UP TO THAT WHALE!" he said
   As he dashed the sweat from his brow
   "Just lay me on, and give me a SETT
   And I'll make it worth your while
   For the whale that's runnin ahead of us there
   Has a hundred barrels of ile"

5. "WOOD AND BLACK SKIN!" The mad crew yelled
   As wildly they tugged and hauled
   "WE'LL BEACH THE BOAT ON THE WHALE'S BARE BACK!"
   And we staggered and strained and bawled
   And as we took in the wet line's "slack"
   when it reached the TUB-OARSMAN
   He threw it out in the boat's churned track
   While the white foam-eddies ran

6. Shoulder to shoulder we pulled with a will
   We lost, we gained, we lost
   As the blistering line slipped through our clutch
   When the flying boat was tossed
   But inch by inch we got it back
   Three fathom for one that slipped
   Though once we fell and rolled in a heap
   When Josiah Wormwell tripped

7. But not a man lost hold of the line
   And though our gain was slow
   We brought her up to the churning flukes
   As near as was safe to go
   The Mate he turned to the port gunwale
   And steadied him on his feet
   And lifted the whale-line out of the "chocks"
   And into the "BOWING CLEAT"

8. The boat now ranged abreast of the whale
   And soo we had her there
   Not six feet off from his rolling bulk
   And his spout was a cloud in the air
   To starboard and port the crank boat heeled
   And the Mate six times essayed
   To sink his lance in the monsters side
   But the boat's wild roll delayed

9. But at last she ran on an even keel
   For one short instant's space

Then the Mate stood high and thrust deep down
With an iron look on his face
And as he recovered his twisted lance
He straightened it on the rail
Then steadied himself on his feet again
And thrust it deep in the whale

10. Then he suddenly cried—THERE'S TAR! THERE'S TAR!
    As the whale's spout reddened and threw
    Barrels of thick black blood to the sky
    Which rained in a hideous dew
    And the great whale LOB-TAILED and smote the sea
    With the sound of a cannon shot
    While the crimson foam rose up like a wall
    And the black spout rained down hot

11. STERN ALL! STERN ALL! we backed away
    To wait till the whale was dead
    While each man sat to his knees in blood
    And he saw his comrades red
    BAIL OUT! BAIL OUT! we bailed with a will
    And through the blood-stained air
    The sea birds circled and swooped and shrieked
    And fought for the blood clots there

12. When the boat was bailed and washed "SMOKE, OH!"
    The soothing pipe was passed
    Each man sank and lay where he dropped
    For the fight was finished at last
    Each sailor felt that his strength was done
    Most grateful it was to feel
    The fearful tension relaxed at last
    And the boat on an even keel

13. Three hours it had been, thre[e] minutes it seemed
    As we lay and smoked at ease
    Though bruised and battered, we to the skin
    And soaked in blood to the knees
    And while we waited the coming ship
    We watched as the great whale turned
    His dying head to the crimson disk
    Where the tropic sunset burned

14. WOOD AND BLACKSKIN! pull up and lance him
    Cling like a bull dog that sinks his teeth
    Bumped on the whale till the planks are shattered
    Now skimming the red foam now buried beneath
    Smothered in steam of his wild spout rising
    Drenched by the black blood his death-spout sends
    Grapple him! cling to him! cedar to BLACK SKIN
    And never let go till his great life ends.

APPENDIX 4
The Homebound Whaleman

"The Homebound Whaleman" is precisely the sort of confection that a real whaleman would scrupulously endeavor to avoid: its inaccuracies and the liberties it takes with the profession are too close to home, its shallow cheerfulness too ludicrous to be taken seriously by anyone even marginally familiar with the whale fishery. The sheet music was published in 1844 with three different covers: one plain, with no illustration; one with an inoffensive scene of a generic ship under sail, though precariously close to a rocky shore; and one with what purports to be a full-scale whaling scene. And like the lyrics, the whaling scene, an anonymous and superficially attractive lithograph, is a transparent fraud. The ship, which is incorrectly rigged for whaling, is under full sail (rather than hove-to) while the men are lowered for whales, and is sailing off as if to abandon them. There are nine men in a whaleboat that should contain six. The boat itself is not the right kind, the oars are too short and not of the distinctive whaling type. The boat-steerer or harpooner is standing precariously high in the prow, without resting his knee in the crotch for stability. The boatheader (the officer in the stern) is using a *rudder and tiller* to steer, as if the boat were under sail, rather than the long *sweep oar* used when the oars are employed. He is also sitting too high in the gunwales and is likely to be dumped overboard at the first pitch in the excitement immediately to ensue. Another man appears to be crouching idly in the bow—unless he is grasping the tow-line on a "Nantucket sleighride" (the draftsmanship is too ambiguous for certainty on this point), in which case the oars should be inboard and the crew working like fury or hanging on for dear life. The crew are dressed neat as pins in what appear to be naval uniforms, which a real whaleman would scorn as ridiculous getup for boat work and inappropriate for a whaleman in any case.

The whale itself is an amorphous, ill-begotten lump that seems not to disturb the surface of the sea in any of the manifold characteristic ways in which the surface of the sea is ordinarily disrupted by a spouting, fifty-ton leviathan defending its life. The spouts are the very quintessence of the "jets d'eau, hot springs and cold, Saratoga and Baden-Baden, come bubbling up from his brain" that Melville ridicules in his chapter "Of the Monstrous Pictures of Whales" (*Moby Dick,* Ch. 55). And the flukes are hardly convincing. Any whaler sufficiently proud of his profession to sing about it—and to be *cheerful* about it—would likely have agreed with Melville that "it is time to set the world right in this matter, by proving such pictures of the whale all wrong." Not surprisingly, "The Homebound Whaleman" has yet to be found written down or even mentioned in any of the whalers' journals or copybooks; nor has it been reported in tradition elsewhere.

The music was composed and the lyrics probably written by Thomas Bricher, "author of 'A bold brave crew' [#202], etc.,'" and the sheet music was issued in Boston by Kieth's Musical Publishing House in 1844, "as sung with most enthusiastic applause by Leonard Marshall." It appeared briefly in the three editions and then descended into a richly deserved obscurity, where the song has remained ever after (even if the sheet music itself be rare and collectible today: the edition with the generic ship is common; the one with the whaling scene is extremely scarce). The song is included here by way of contrast with the authentic whaling songs—and the handful of respectable parlor-songs—preferred by the men and women who actually lived and worked aboard whaleships and knew what they were about.

232. The Homebound Whaleman

Words, melody, and punctuation as found in the sheet music, "Composed and respectfully dedicated to Sumner Hudson, Esq. by T. Bricher" (Boston: Kieth's Musical Publishing House, 1844." The same firm published another edition of the sheet music the same year, with a different lithograph on the cover; also an edition with no cover illustration.

1. Blow on, blow on wild gale,
   My heart is bounding, too.
   O fill the spreading sail,
   While we dash through the waters blue
   I have play's with the ocean king,
   I have chas'd him from his lair,
   And with many a shout did ring,
   The sky, the wave, the air;
   I have play'd with the ocean king,
   I have chas'd him from his lair,
   And with many a shout did ring,
   The sky, the wave, the air

2. Our ship is homeward bound
   My heart exulting braves,
   Yes it braves the tempest sound,
   Nor fears the mountain wave
   Then blow, blow on wild gale;
   In hope we'll firmly stand
   O fill our spreading sail
   'Till we touch our native land
   Then blow, blow on wild gale.
   In hope we'll firmly stand,
   O fill our spreading sail
   Till we touch our native land

Chorus: Cheerily O my boys we go, O cheerily O we go
Cheerily O my boys we go, O cheerily O we go

APPENDIX 5
"Music and Deviltry"
John Martin's Musical Programme

Monday July 4th ... In the afternoon music with dancing, cheering and all sorts of nonsense... in the evening singing music & deviltry.

Wednesday Feby 16th. We are now in sight of land part of the coast of Brazil. we shall be obliged to come to shortly as we are out of wood. This evening being pleasant & calm—we are now in sight of Cape Freo [Frio] or cape cold. but the sun is hot enough to roast potatoes. We finished this day with a grand concert given by the whole crew. the audience were sea gulls. the following is the program of the concert. Lat. 23.26 S[outh] Long. 41.42 W[est]

—John Martin's, ship *Lucy Ann* of Wilmington, 1842

The practice of producing concert bills on shipboard, detailing musical and theatrical performances by the crew, was not uncommon and was certainly influenced by the concert programs that sailors encountered in theatres and music halls ashore. Aboard whalers and merchant vessels, which lacked the facilities for letterpress printing, any invitations or programs were handwritten for informal distribution. However, the clipper ships of the 1850s and later passenger steamers commonly carried presses to produce weekly newspapers. Amidst the usual shipboard gossip and myriad other trivial items, these typically listed the programs of upcoming entertainments organized and performed by the passengers, whose primary duties were to avoid seasickness and amuse themselves on the several weeks' passage across the Atlantic or the four or five months' journey around Cape Horn to San Francisco. A kindred practice in the navy, where things would necessarily have been more formal, is suggested by Melville in *White-Jacket* (1850): there the theatrical soiree is perhaps included more for its artistic and symbolic value than as testimony about life in the navy; but it is nevertheless quite a formidable document, ostensibly founded in Melville's firsthand experience.

In his splendid illustrated journal of a whaling voyage in the ship *Lucy Ann* of Wilmington, Delaware in the 1840s (quoted above), John F. Martin describes shipboard musical activities in charming detail [see Introduction]. He also provides particulars of a performance held aboard ship on 16 February 1842, in which many of the crew participated as singers, musicians, and comics. Analogous concert bills were produced by later mariners, especially whalers wintering-over with the fleet in the Arctic, where such entertainments were necessary to maintain morale during the long, dark, icebound winter months.[1]

John Martin's is the earliest example yet to come to light. His account is merely a list, cryptic in places, requiring substantial reconstruction to discern its full measure. Even so, a few mysteries remain; and as a Delaware ship with a crew drawn largely from the Southern and Middle Atlantic states—with fewer New Englanders, New Yorkers, Africans, African-Americans, and European foreigners in her crew than would typically have been the case in a New Bedford blubber-hunter —the *Lucy Ann* is not entirely representative of the repertoire one might expect to find in the mainstream. Nevertheless, Martin's concert bill is the most specific description yet discovered of a shipboard musical soiree in this era, and seems to capture something of the essentially frivolous spirit of comical songs and amateur theatricals that must have been enacted countless times on countless vessels on countless occasions. And like the drunken skylarking on deck among the sailors in Eugene O'Neill's one-act play *Moon of the Caribbees*—which is set on a steamship at the time of the first World War—the frolic threatens to come to an abrupt end by order of an impatient mate, who in neither case takes part in the fun. However, unlike the O'Neill play, the

---

[1] This was certainly the case at Herschel Island, adjacent to Alaska, in the 1890s (see John R. Bockstoce, *Whales Ice and Men*, 1986; and Gilkerson & Bockstoce, *American Whaling in the Western Arctic*, 1983); and in Hudson Bay in the 1860s (see the theatrical and musical programs from Charles Durgin's journal in Frank, *More Scrimshaw Artists*, 1998, Appendix VII).

Lucy Ann performance never turns bitter or violent. If the whalemen's journals be any reliable guide, few ever did.

John Martin's concert bill aboard the *Lucy Ann* is transcribed below, with notes on the songs on the next page in the order in which they appear on the programme.

Programme.

Part 1st

Song.	One eyed Riley	
	with chorus by the whole crew by Chubb	[*performer*↓]
"	There was a Sheppards daughter	
	Kept sheep on yonder hill	Lightning
Song	I hit her right in her stinking machine	by Hominy head
Solo.	on Kent Bugle by	— myself

Part 2nd

Song.	Cant you wont you stay a little longer	by —Turpin
"	Turkish Lady " "	Black Leg
	Duette with Drum & Fife	Chub & [ ]

Part 3rd

Song.	My Dogs eyes makes mince pies —Steward	
"	Morgan Ratler	—Spunyarn
"	The Mermaid in three parts by	—Hardy
"	Trayum with chorus by crew	

Part 4th

Song.	Kelly the Pirate.	King David
"	Tally ho	Spunyarn.
"	Lord Lovell that went to strange	
	countries for to see	Hardy.
Solo.	on Flute by	Young Nowal

Part 5th

Song.	Fanny Blair	Turpin
"	French Lady	Mizen
"	All the girls in our town	Steward

Part 6th

Song.	So early in the morning the	by Mocha
	sailor loves the bottle O	a color'd Gentleman
"	Milkmaid	Hominy Head
"	Two little sisters walking up the street	Jersey

Grand Chorus
by the whole crew on Bugle, Drum, Fife, Flute, Violins, Triangle & wound up by the Mate telling us if we did not quit making such a damned noise he would heave a bucket of Stinking water over us. Ends the same.

Notes on the Songs in John Martin's Musical Programme

One-Eyed Reilly [*Reilly's Daughter*]. Irish folk song known in expurgated and unexpurgated "military" versions, the latter (with "one-eyed Riley" a reference to the male member) scarce or nonexistent in print, the former rather stable in most Irish and American versions. Healy II #39; Clancy Brothers 1964, 37; Loesberg 1981, 3:72; etc.

The Shepherdess. Likely some form of "The Sailor and the Shepherdess" [#96]; alternatively, possibly "The Knight and the Shepherd's Daughter" (Child #110) or a bawdy parody. Laws #O-8; SI; PSI; PSIS; Creighton 1961, 17; Creighton 1971 #37; Greenleaf #15; Mackenzie #53; Sharp 1916 #3. See also Child #110; Huntington 1964, 185.

I Hit Her Right On Her Stinking Machine. Unknown. Occasionally cited (but never identified) in connection with Martin's journal, probably because of the intriguing title: Ellen R. Cohn, "Shipboard Music: a Report from American Whaling Journals," *Essays in Arts and Sciences,* 10:2 (March 1982), 189; Creighton, *Dogwatch & Liberty Days* (Salem, 1982), 52. The song is probably original to "Hominy Head," from his name apparently a Southerner.

Can't You, Won't You Stay a Little Longer. Obscure British music-hall piece properly entitled "Stay a Little Longer," for which the tune has not been located nor authorship attributed, probably much changed in performer Turpin's hands. *Universal Songster* I:333. See "All Around the Room" [#112] for a similarly-constructed piece.

Turkish Lady. Extremely common popular variant of "Young Biechan" (Child #53), widely published in broadsides and songsters, as was "Young Bateman" ("Lord Bakeman"), another derivative of "Young Beichan." SI; SI2; SIC; PI; PSI; PSI-1; PSI-2; Rosenberg #141G; Am. Sailor 131; Bell 1856, 144; Bell 1857, 68; Bronson I:409-465 (numerous airs, citing many versions of text); Howard Mayer Brown, *Theatrical Chansons of the Fifteenth and Early Sixteenth Centuries* (Harvard, 1963); Cox #8; Creighton 1933 #13; Creighton 1961, 7; Arthur Kyle Davis, *More Traditional Ballads of Virginia* (University of North Carolina Press, 1960); Eddy #10; Flanders 1932 #204; Flanders 1953 #54; Forget Me Not (2 versions), 169, 171; Gardner #49; Greenleaf #7; Huntington 1964, 141; Karpeles 1970 #7, #33; Kidson 1926; Mackenzie #15, #17; Moore & Moore; Randolph, I:80; Sharp 1916 #6; Sharp 1932 #13; Sharp & Karpeles; etc. See also Child #17, #53, and #226, and corresponding tunes in Bronson I-III.

My Dog's Eyes Makes Mince Pies. Unknown. Whaleship stewards did the baking, and pie making was his most time-consuming occupation (see quotes from John Martin's journal in the Introduction; also "Six Months Outward Bound: John Jones, steward, Ship *Eliza Adams* of New Bedford, 1852," in Frank 1991b, 14-30; and Robert Cushman Murphy, *Logbook for Grace,* 1947, pp. 69, 130). If the steward of the brig *Daisy* could bake cakes with penguin eggs (Murphy, 205), the *Lucy Ann*'s steward could joke about making mince pies out of dog's eyes as a self-deprecating commentary about culinary arts on whaleships—an odd occupational song he probably cooked up himself.

Morgan Rattler. "Rattler" was "the inevitable nickname of men surnamed Morgan," signifying "anything first-rate" (Partridge 1961, 689)—for reasons unknown to the lexicographers, but almost certainly after the title of the popular song and tune. The lyrics were written by Thomas Hudson, author of "Jack Robinson" [#111]. The air is not specified in the *Universal Songster* I:430, but see the jig "Morgan Rattler" in *1000 Fiddle Tunes* (p. 53).

The Mermaid. Attributed by Chappell to poet Charles Sloman, but very widely circulated and known in tradition, localized to England, Scotland, New Bedford, and other places. SI; SIC #9467 A-E; PSI; PSIS; Child #289; Rosenberg #896 A&B; Ashton 1891; Belden 101; Bronson III; Cox #33; Creighton 1961, 26; Davis & Tozer #48, #49; Forget Me Not 79; Hugill 1961, 560; Luce 118; Mackenzie #116; Vaughan Williams 70 (unusual modal tune).

Kelly the Pirate. Martin's journal entry of 30 March 1842 describes an encore performance of "Kelly the Pirate" by Chub and the steward, "which they sang together holding on to each others hands & when they came to the part we'll clap a few Yankee pills into her tail [a double entendre, the literal meaning of which is to fire cannonballs into the stern quarters of the pirate ship] they throw their hats & Jackets on deck with furious looking countenances which never fails to produce a roar among the crew." Two principal variants (Laws #K-31 and K-32) are known and were widely disseminated in broadside and songster texts. Both forms appear with music and a songster illustration in Frank, *The Book of Pirate Songs,* 1998, #21 and #22. PSI; Rosenberg #739; Creighton 1961, 151; *Forecastle* 1847, 213; *Forecastle* 1850, 241; *Forget Me Not,* 75; 60; Greenleaf #43; Healy 1967 #24, #45; Mackenzie #81.

Tally Ho. Almost certainly "Tally Ho" by E.M. Steel (Duncan, v2), which was paraphrased by steward John Jones aboard the *Eliza Adams* of New Bedford in 1852: "I am off with poor tally i ho you know / O, tally hy ho you served me so" (Frank 1991b, 18). The song may be related to the chantey "Cheer'ly, Man," known to Dana and Melville (see Frank 1985a, "'Cheer'ly Man': Chanteying in *Omoo* and *Moby-Dick*"; Colcord 77; Hugill 1961, 317; Shay 1948, 32), and is alluded to among the sea-songs in the song "The Ballad Seller" (*Universal Songster* I:9; Frank 1998, 48). Dibdin also wrote a song entitled "Tally Ho!" concerning the fox hunt ("At the sound of the horn... "), which is not the sort of subject matter that would ordinarily be expected to turn up on a Yankee whaler but which might have found its way aboard the *Lucy Ann* with one of the many southerners in her crew.

Lord Lovell. Venerable British ballad (Child #75) known in a stable popular version issued in American sheet music circa 1835 ("Lord Lovell and Nancy Bell," arranged by John Smith, published by George Willig, Baltimore [Dichter #858]), and thereafter much parodied and the tune often adopted for other lyrics. SI; SIC; PSI; PSIS; Dichter #858; Child #75; Rosenberg #834 A-F; Am. Songster 145; Cox #12; Eddy #13; Flanders 1932, 215; Flanders 1953, 200; Franklin Songster 55; Gardner #6; Linscott 233; New Song Book 203; Sharp 1916 #26; Sharp 1932 #21. See also the Brown University song "Old Sukey," in H.R. Waite, *Carmina Collegiensa*(Boston, 1876), 94; and the Whig campaign song (1840) "King Matty and Blair," from *A Miniature of Martin Van Buren,* in Lawrence, 278.

Fanny Blair. English and (perhaps originally) Irish folk song of indeterminate ancestry only rarely encountered in tradition, perhaps because of its controversial and unseemly theme, which concerns a man accused of rape. Compare the version in *The Forget Me Not Songster* (102) with Sharp 1916 #46. Also SI.

All the Girls In Our Town. Of several possibilities here, the most likely is "Nancy Dawson," which begins, "Of all the girls in our town, / The black, the fair, the red, the brown, / That prance and dance it up and down, / There's none like Nancy Dawson." Miss Nancy Dawson (circa 1730-1767) was a popular dancer who first received notice for her extemporaneous performance in a 1759 revival of John Gay's *Beggar's Opera* at Covent Garden, London. The text, attributed to Scotsman George Alexander Stevens (d. 1784), was set to a dance tune known as "Miss Dawson's Hornpipe" or merely "Nancy Dawson," published in London with the text circa 1760. Chappell (II:718) gives text, air, and historical particulars; Simpson (503) also mentions the inevitable parodies. Some he does not mention are the sea chanteys that preserve her name, offshoots of "Cheer'ly, Man," known to both Dana and Melville (see Frank, "'Cheer'ly Man': Chanteying in *Omoo* and *Moby-Dick*"; Colcord 77; Hugill 1961, 317; Shay 1948, 32). Another candidate for the identity of the song is "Sally in Our Alley," in which the first lines, "Off all the girls that are so smart, / There's none like pretty Sally," written by Englishman Henry Carey (1685-1743), have occasionally been corrupted to "Of all the girls in our town…," and were, in any case, the inspiration for "Nancy Dawson." Carey wrote his song to a tune of his own composition (circa 1719), but by 1760 it had become obsolete, eclipsed by "the much older ballad tune of *The Country Lass,*" also known as "Cold and Raw," which had been in tradition since circa 1620: Chappell (II:645) and Duncan (I:46) each give texts and both airs; Chappell also gives what he calls an "older version" of "The Country Lass"; Simpson (134) has two versions, and on the evolution of the tune cites R.G. Noyes, "The Contemporary Reception of 'Sally in Our Alley'" (*Harvard Studies and Notes on Philology and Literature,* 18 [1935], 165-175). Yet a third possibility is "The Bailiff's Daughter of Islington" (Child #105), known in many versions and variants, such as "All the girls in Exeter town / O they did sport and play" (Bronson I:536, #27). All of these songs are susceptible to bawdy parody. There is also "Toutes les dames de la ville / Soni alentour qui dasant…" (J. Murray Gibbon, *Canadian Folk Songs,* London: J.M. Dent, [1929] 1947, p. 43) — a most unlikely candidate for the *Lucy Ann*'s steward, who also gave his cohorts "My Dog's Eyes Makes Mince Pies."

French Lady [The Landlady of France; Brandy O]. Original lyrics by George Coleman the Younger (1762-1836) to the traditional marching-tune "Brandy O" became widely known and much parodied, the tune used at the capstan (see quotation from *Landsman Hay* in connection with the jig "Off She Goes" [#179] and in Hugill 1961, 7), and adopted for other lyrics, notably the hugely popular American patriotic song, "The *Constitution* and the *Guerriere*" [#52], and its English counter-song, "The *Shannon* and the *Chesapeake.*" Arthur Schrader gives "Pretty Maid of Derby O" as an alternate title, after a related text of that name. Universal Songster II:225; Am. Songster 110; tune: see #52.

The Sailor Loves His Bottle O. An important but not very widely distributed chantey, called by C. Fox Smith "a real old stager" and already an old song when it became popular with London sailors in the 1850s (Smith 1927, 42). Colcord's version is presumed to be the closest to what American sailors might have sung aboard the *Lucy Ann.* SI; SIC; Colcord 74; Davis & Tozer #29; Hugill 56 (3 versions); Smith 1927, 43.

The Milkmaid. One of the most widely dispersed of all mildly bawdy folk songs, it is usually known as "Dabbling in the Dew" or "Rolling in the Dew," which Kennedy (420, 436) indicates was also known as "The Milkmaid's Song," and for which he gives a detailed provenance. SIC; PSI; Laws #O-10; Rosenberg #905; Am. Singer's Own Book 110; Cox #125; Creighton 1933 #46; Eddy #52; Greenleaf #77; Kennedy #189; Sharp 1916 #44; Warner #52.

The Two Sisters [more often *The Two Little Sisters*]: an old ballad (Child #10) much changed in tradition and often parodied in bawdy and "clean" adaptations. SI; SIC; PSI; Child #10; Bronson I and III; Gardner #2; Sharon 1932 #5.

Dingi I Otten Dotten. Extremely rare "Negro" minstrel song, a version or variant of "Who Dare?," with the chorus "Dingee I otten dotten, ballio otten dotten, / Dingee I otten dotten, WHO DARE?" Possibly a precursor of scat singing in jazz. Found only in *The Negro Singer's Own Book* (circa 1840), 338f; not found in songsters of similar vintage.

Also cited by John Martin on 26 January 1843:

Oh, If I Had Her [Were You Ever in Dumbarton?]. Scottish song, susceptible to bawdy parody, sometimes used on shipboard ship as a chantey, as cited by Melville in *Omoo* (1848). See Doerflinger 306; Frank 1985, p. 136; Hugill 9; Frank 1985a, "'Cheer'ly Man': Chanteying in *Omoo* and *Moby-Dick.*"

APPENDIX 6
Biographical Notes on the Diarists and Journal-Keepers

Sources: Ancetry.com; City Directories of Boston, New Bedford-Fairhaven, Providence, and San Francisco; Ferguson 1984; Frank 1985; 1991a, 1998, Frank MS 2010; Index of Seamen's Protection Papers and Index of Whalemen's Shipping Papers, New Bedford Free Public Library; Haskins 1890; Hegarty 1959; Hegarty 1964; Kendall Whaling Museum Archive; *Kendall Whaling Museum Newsletter*; Lund 1997; Martin 1982; Miller 1979; New London Crew Lists, Seamen's Protection Certificate Register, and Salem, Mass. Crew Lists Index posted online by Mystic Seaport; New Bedford Port Society Crew Lists, New Bedford Whaling Museum; Sherman et al., 1986; Ship Registers of Barnstable, Dighton-Fall River, and New Bedford, Mass., and of Providence and Newport, R.I.; Spinazze 1976; Starbuck 1878; Vital Records of Barnstable, Brewster, Chilmark, Dartmouth, Dennis, Edgartown, Fairhaven, Falmouth, Nantucket, New Bedford, Orleans, Plymouth, Rochester, Tisbury, West Tisbury, Westport, and Yarmouth, Mass.; U.S. Census Records; WPA *Whaling Masters*; manuscript genealogical records in the Sturgis Library, Barnstable, Mass., and the New Bedford Free Public Library. [For complete citations, see Bibliography.]

Abbe, William Alanson (Tolland, Conn., and Boston.) Born in Tolland in 1835; green hand and seaman, bark *Atkins Adams* of Fairhaven, 1858-63. The son and brother of physicians, at the time he embarked on his one whaling voyage he was living in Boston with his family and was listed as a law student, but instead of taking up the law, in later life he was an oil merchant in New Bedford. He evidently retired to Tolland, where he died in 1892. [Song #93]

Atherton, Charles D. (Sandwich, Cape Cod, Mass.) Born circa 1849; seaman, bark *Oak* of Nantucket, 1867-69. The son of Charles Atherton, a dry goods merchant associated with Hammett & Atherton of New Bedford, young Charles may or may not have been aboard the *Oak* for the entire voyage. His extant journal covers only the final, homeward-bound passage from Barbados to Nantucket in 1869. Even so, it has a couple of good song texts. The *Oak* was the last whaler registered in Nantucket and was sold on her next voyage to a consortium of New York owners. Atherton sailed in the bark *Cornelia* of New Bedford for a Pacific Ocean whaling voyage in October 1871, but the vessel was condemned and sold en route at Paita on the Peru coast in March 1873, and Atherton must have found other means to return home to Cape Cod. [Songs: #67, 93, 203.]

Bartley, Theodore D. (Norwalk, Huron County, Ohio.) Born at Granby in Oswego County, N.Y., in 1830, he later moved with his family to Norwalk, Ohio, and served as a seaman in the ship *California* of New Bedford, 1851-54. His journal of the 43-month voyage to the North Pacific is rendered in a strong and well-tutored, though occasionally careless hand, and contains an interesting array of his drawings and sketches. After he returned from whaling in 1854 he stayed a few days at the Boston Mariners' Home, then shipped in the merchant brig *Matanzas*, bound from Boston to Charleston, South Carolina, with a cargo of ice. He remained several months with that vessel, married a woman from Dresden, N.Y., and from the 1860s to the '80s was in the merchant trade as captain of a sailing barge on Lake Champlain in upstate New York and Vermont, usually bringing his family on board with him. (Selections from his journals were published by the Lake Champlain Maritime Museum.) He died at Dresden Center in 1914. [Songs: #23, 39, 74, 89, 200, 204, 360, 370, 371, 382.]

Beden, Cornelius H. (Dartmouth, Mass.) Born circa 1825. His first voyage was as a green hand for a 1/170th lay in the bark *Canton* of New Bedford, 1841-42. The source of his songs is his later journal aboard the New Bedford ships *Massachusetts* (1851-53) and *South America* (1855). [Songs: #109, 238, 298, 368, 405, 442.]

Bennett, Austin C. (Fall River, Mass.) Born in 1853, he had a long whaling career, including an unrecorded outing as a green hand (circa 1874-76), followed by an unusually long string of five voyages in the bark *Sunbeam* of New Bedford, as seaman (1876-78 and 1878-82), boatsteerer (1882-86), fourth mate (1886-89), and second mate (1890-93). His one song comes from the journal of his last voyage. [Song #117.]

Bennett, Thomas (Kent County, Delaware.) Born circa 1814; seaman, ship *Condor* of New Bedford, 1839-40; second mate, ship *William Baker* of Warren, 1840-41. It is not clear from the whaling records where this particular Thomas Bennett served previously or in which of several New Bedford whalers he may have served subsequently. But having embarked as an able seaman in the ship *Condor* under Captain Harding in 1839, and perhaps having been promoted along the way, his work was evidently good enough for Captain Bowen to take him aboard the *William Baker* as second mate only eight months later, in March 1840. This Thomas Bennett is not the one listed in the New Bedford City Directory (1845 et seq.) as a clerk and, later, as superintendent of the Wamsutta Mills textile manufacturing plant, but he is probably the one identified as "Thomas Bennett 2d," who served in the whaleship *Gratitude*, 1845-48. [Songs: #32, 62, 84.]

Braley, Jason L. (Rochester, Mass.) Born 1824; third mate, ship *Stephania* of New Bedford, 1847-49; second mate, 1849-50; first mate, bark *Louisa* of New Bedford, 1850-53; master, ship *William Badger* of New Bedford, 1853. The younger brother of Captain Samuel T. Braley (q.v.), Jason also grew up on the family farm, shipped out at 17, and progressed up the ranks even more rapidly than Samuel had done. His first voyage was as a green hand for a short Atlantic whaling cruise, probably in the brig *Agate*, and after this few months' experience he shipped as boatsteerer (harpooner) in the bark *Newton* (1843-46). This voyage is noted for the crew's mutiny, refusing duty at Oahu; as a petty officer, Braley remained with the ship when the crew was discharged and another crew shipped. However, the *Newton*'s woes did not end there. In December 1844, the captain fell ill and died at San Diego, and the voyage was disrupted until another commander could be installed. Braley was third mate in the *Stephania*, and was promoted to second mate during the voyage. It was on this cruise that he began the journal from which his songs were recovered, a journal that he continued as mate of the *Louisa* and captain of the *William Badger*. During this later period he seems to have had a close collaborative relationship with his wife, Eleanor ("Nellie"), who may have contributed some of the songs Jason took with him to sea. [Songs: #91, 126, 137, 237, 243, 259, 260, 333, 348, 394, 431.]

Braley, Samuel Tripp (Rochester, Mass.) Born 1817; died at Mahe, Seychelles Islands, Indian Ocean, 1870; master, ship *Arab* of Fairhaven, 1849-52. Captain Braley was a complex and somewhat enigmatic character, and despite that he was a distinguished whaling master, successful farmer, respected citizen, and town selectman, his career at sea was not an entirely happy or lucrative one. A farmer's son and elder brother of whaling captain Jason L. Braley (q.v.), Sam shipped out for the first time at age 16 and continued in the whale fishery until the day he died, interrupting his whaling activities intermittently to engage in farming at Rochester-in his younger years on the family homestead and later on a farm that his wife, Mary Ann King, had inherited. He was shipwrecked on his second voyage, rose to a captaincy at 28, and commanded six whaling voyages. His first four commands were none too successful financially; on the fifth he lost his ship in a wreck off Zanzibar; and on his sixth he died in the Seychelles, about as far away from home and hearth as a Yankee whaleship could have carried him, but where he had an extracurricular wife and children, and where, through repeated visits, he had made a second home. It is unfortunate that, as he was an accomplished accordionist and singer, he did not record or transcribe more of the songs and tunes that he used to occupy the countless hours at sea on the whaling grounds. A son, Henry King Braley (1850-1929), was an attorney, Mayor of Fall River, and justice of the Massachusetts Superior Court and the state Supreme Court. Another son, Jason T. Braley, Jr. (1858-1940), educated at MIT, was a mechanical engineer at Rutland, Vermont- where the son of L.C. Richmond, Jr. (q.v.) was serving as mayor. (Additional source: Pamela A. Miller, unpublished typescript, KNB archive.) [Songs: #11, 343.]

Bryant, Thomas R., Jr. (New Bedford.) Born 1828; seaman, ship *Elizabeth* of New Bedford, 1847-51. The son of a New Bedford shoemaker and retail merchant, he embarked on his first whaling voyage in the ship *Hercules* in 1843 at the tender age of 15. At the time, his Seamen's Protection Paper described him as only 4 feet 10 inches (147.3 cm) tall. After two voyages in that vessel, by which time he was 19, well experienced, and presumably taller, he shipped aboard the *Elizabeth* as an able seaman in 1847, the voyage covered in the journal from which his songs were recovered. He served as fourth mate on her next cruise (1851-55), later as third mate in the bark *Stafford* (1860-64), and in some unrecorded capacity in the bark *Osprey* (1865-67), after which he likely turned to farming in the New Bedford area. [Songs: #69, 371, 424.]

Bunker, Samuel (Nantucket.) Born circa 1786-96 into one of Nantucket's hoary families of seafarers and whaling masters, he was mate of the Nantucket ship *Alexander* (1821-24) and commanded two Pacific Ocean voyages in the same vessel (1824-26; 1827-31). The journal in which he wrote down the lyrics of three songs is from the second of these. He also skippered a voyage in the Fairhaven bark *Arab* (1831-34). [Songs: #69, 103, 181.]

Cahoon, Stephen, Jr. (Orleans, Cape Cod, Mass.) Born in 1772, he made only a few whaling cruises to the Atlantic grounds, notably as a seaman in the ship *Polly* of Gloucester during 1794-95. His sporadic journal of that voyage is the source of two song texts anthologized here and several others he transcribed at sea and later ashore. He married Phebe Kendrick (1775-1848) of Harwich in 1799, fathered ten children (of whom nine survived to adulthood), and died in 1842. His lyrics — where possible, re-joined with the original music — were published with biographical notes in Frank, *Songs of the Polly, 1795: A Garland of Songs, Ballads, and Ditties from Stephen Cahoon's Journal aboard the Whaleship Polly of Gloucester, Massachusetts* (Kendall Monograph N° 15, 2001). [Songs: #24, 85.]

Chadwick, Matthew Anderson (New Bedford and Tisbury, Mass.) Born in 1832, he was a green hand in the New Bedford bark *Ohio* (1850-54) and is believed to have written the lyrics of "Bark Ohio Outward Bound" (#28-A). After another voyage of which the details are not recorded, he was fourth mate and boatsteerer in the New Bedford bark *Roscius* (1858-61), and on that voyage passed the Ohio song along to a young shipmate and fellow boatsteerer, Frederick H. Smith (q.v.), who transcribed the original and also an adaptive text, localizing it to the *Roscius* (#28-B). Chadwick continued in the whale fishery but never made it to captain, serving as fourth mate in the New Bedford bark *Virginia* (1862; captured and burned by the Confederate commerce-raider *Alabama*); second mate in the New Bedford bark *Osceola 3rd* (1866-68); and first mate in the brig *Mercy Taylor* of Tisbury (1868-70), bark *Sarah* of New Bedford (1871-73), and brig *Rosa Baker* of Boston (1874-75). [Song #28.]

Chappell [Chapel], Daniel A. (New Bedford.) He made several voyages as cooper in the ship *Benjamin Tucker* of New Bedford, on the last of which (1849-51) he kept the journal in which he transcribed a song and several stanzas of verse obtained from shipmate Charles A. Evans (q.v.). After another whaling cruise, in the ship *Rambler*, 1852-53, he worked as a shoreside cooper in New Bedford. [Song #204.]

Chase, Elijah Pitts (Nantucket.) Born in 1822, he transcribed his song as a seaman during 1845-49 in the Nantucket ship *Navigator*. A later family member summarized his biography: "Elijah Pitts Chase, ship[p]ed on boa[r]d of the Navigator Sept. 1841 at 19 years of age. Born on the island of Nantucket Oct 1st 1822. Spent 8 years on board the Navigator. 1st voyage from Sept. 1841 to May 1845. At home 8 weeks. 2nd voyage from July 3rd 1845 to June 4th 1849. 1st voyage Elihu Fisher, Capt. 2nd voyage George Palmer, Capt." (annotation on the reverse of a fine watercolor portrait of the Navigator in Chase's journal, painted by shipmate George Clark of Nantucket). [Song #41.]

Cleveland, George Snow (Nantucket.) Born in 1815, he grew up in the whale fishery and made voyages as third mate (1833-37) and second mate (1837-39) of the New Bedford ship *Charles*; his songs were transcribed on the latter voyage. After another whaling cruise, at age 25 he married Harriet B. Huntington of Nantucket in 1841. [Songs: #43, 96, 104, 306, 324.]

Coffin, Benjamin A. (Nantucket). Born in 1835, he served in the New Bedford bark *Catalpa*, 1856-57 (the journal of this voyage, in which he transcribed "The Whaleman's Lament," #154, is in the Nicholson Collection, Providence Public Library); also the Nantucket ship *James Loper*, 1857-60; and bark *Sunbeam* of New Bedford, 1860-64. He later married Lydia M. Ray (born 1843) of Nantucket. [Song #154.]

Collins, Edward Willson (Dartmouth and Fairhaven, Mass.). Born at Dartmouth in 1809, he followed his older brother Silas into the whale fishery. In 1829 he transcribed unique texts of "The Bold Trinity" and "The Lowlands of Holland" into his brother's journal of the brig *By Chance* of Dartmouth (1826-27), served two voyages in the New Bedford ship *Condor* (1832-33 and 1833-34), married Esther D. Tinkham of Rochester, Mass. (1834), and was first mate of the New Bedford ship *Endeavor* (1835-37) and master of the ships *Phocion* of New Bedford (1839-40), *Stephania* of New Bedford (1841-44), and *Midas* of Fairhaven (1844-45). He died at sea at age 35 aboard the *Midas* in February 1845, 230 days out of New Bedford, bound for the Indian Ocean and Northwest Coast whaling grounds. He had married Esther Tinkham, and in 1855 their son Hananiah followed his father's footsteps and went whaling. It is not known at what point Captain Collins transcribed his text of "The Cobbler," which is to date the only known text of this ballad in English to survive since the 1620s. [Songs: #6, 19, 122.]

Colton, James S. (Munson, Hampshire County, Mass.) Born circa 1808, he was a New London resident and made both of his known whaling voyages (and probably others) from that port: in the ship *John and Edward*, 1831-33, and bark *Tenedos* as second mate, 1840-42. It was on the latter voyage that he recorded the lyrics to five songs. He later returned to Western Massachusetts, where he was living in the 1840s. [Songs: #65, 109, 219, 241, 379.]

Coquin, John S. (New Bedford.) Born in 1848, he was a seaman in the bark *Pacific* of New Bedford (1867-68) and on a series of merchant voyages out of Boston (1860s-'70s). In addition to his interest in songs he was a scrimshaw artist whose several extant journals reveal much about scrimshaw practice on shipboard (Frank 1991a, 38; Barbeau, 5f; Gilkerson, frontis); he also copied down a large number of poems and aphorisms. In his *Pacific* journal he transcribed 25 songs — mostly pedestrian parlor pieces but also a few good deepwater songs and broadside ballads. He also made whaling voyages in the New Bedford barks *Napoleon* (1864-67), *Globe* (1869-72 and 1872-76), and *Europa* (1876-79), interspersing them with occasional merchant voyages that he also recorded in his *Pacific* journal. [Songs: #36, 49, 79, 88, 124, 138, 205, 257, 281, 294, 343, 359, 366, 373, 377, 382, 399, 401, 415, 428, 453, 460.]

Davis, William H. Seaman, bark *Midas* of New Bedford, 1861-65. There were two whalemen of this name active at about the same time in New Bedford. The other William H. Davis must have had a terrible time of it, with two vessels (the bark *Eben Dodge* and ship *Oneida*) burned out from under him by the Confederacy, while the William H. Davis who wrote the words of parlor songs into his journal was aboard the *Midas* [songs: #271, 291, 319, 350, 392, 426]. It is not known which of the two namesakes was previously Ordinary Seaman in the ship *Marengo* (1855-59) or carpenter in the ship *India* (1858-61). In fact, there were so many sailors named William Davis whaling out of New Bedford at one time or another that it is impossible, among the not-very-specific records, to distinguish which is which—as if to vindicate the prophetic truth of the traditional Irish tune TA DHA UILLIAM DÀ IBHÌ S ANNSAN À ITSE ("There are Two William Davis's In this Place"), from P.W. Joyce, *Old Irish Music and Songs* (London, 1909), #307:

Dexter, Rodolphus W. (Tisbury, Martha's Vineyard, Mass.) The namesake of a prominent New Bedford whaling captain, he was a successful whaling master in his own right. He grew up on Marthas Vineyard, made his mark as a whaleman, and married Irena Clifford in 1838. His songs come from voyages as master of the New Bedford ships *Chili* (1843-45) and *Israel* (sailed 1846-47), in the latter of which he was shipwrecked at the Cape of Good Hope in 1847. His journal is filled with excellent vignette drawings of vessels encountered along the way. [Songs: #21, 95.]

Donahue, James (Liverpool, Onandagua County, N.Y.) Born circa 1826, he was from a town just outside Syracuse. As inscriptions in his journal indicate, he was proud of his Irish heritage and this influenced his selection of songs to transcribe. On a voyage in the ship *Atlantic* of Nantucket (1850-53), which was evidently his second whaling cruise, he collaborated with Nantucketer William Gillaspia (q.v.) on a journal that includes their jointly transcribed songs. [Songs: #16, 34, 102, 106, 136, 283, 292, 318, 335, 371.]

Eayrs, Joseph H. (Boston). Born circa 1814, he sailed in the ship *Mercury* of New Bedford (1837-40) at age 23, rather older than average for a first voyage. In 1841 he signed articles as boatsteerer in the bark *Gratitude* but was promoted to third mate even before the voyage commenced. His brothers Augustus and Henry also made whaling voyages at that time. The *Gratitude* voyage (1841-45) appears to have been Joseph's last. Around 1855 he married a woman named Mary who was 19 years younger. They lived in her native New York State until circa 1861, and their first two daughters were born there. Unaccountably for a Yankee family, during the Civil War and until 1870 they were living in Texas, where they had three more daughters. They then moved to Chicago, where Joseph worked as a cabinetmaker and died of Bright's disease in 1880 at age 66. [Song #229.]

Evans, Charles Albert (Sanbornton, Belknap County, New Hampshire.) Born circa 1829, he contributed a song [#204] and several stanzas of verse to the journal of Daniel A. Chapell (q.v.) on the New Bedford ship *Benjamin Tucker* (1849-51). He was later a boatsteerer in the New Bedford ship *Caravan* (1856-60).

Fisher, Holmes C. (Edgartown, Marthas Vineyard.) He contributed a song to the copybook of George W. Piper (q.v.), ship *Europa* of Edgartown, 1868-70. Born circa 1845, he was the son of whaling captain Lorenzo Fisher of Edgartown, and the younger brother of whaleman Lozenzo Fisher, Jr. In later life he was a house painter. [Song #7.]

Fisher, Nathan C. (Sandwich, Cape Cod, Mass.) His voyage as first mate of the bark *Ocean* of Sandwich (1856-57) could not have been very satisfying. He had evidently been aboard for one or two voyages before, as a boatsteerer and deck officer; but the unsuccessful cruise of 1856-57, of which Fisher's journal is the outstanding record, might well have soured a man on whaling altogether. Having sailed from Sandwich on 26 June 1856, there is no record of the *Ocean* taking any whales during the ensuing eleven months. According to Fisher's account, they lowered often enough but either the harpoons drew out or the whales were gallied or the line parted or some other mishap occurred to prevent the men from taking any oil, except for a few porpoises. In May 1857, eleven months out, they called at St. Helena, where the crew refused duty "on account of the vessel being rotten." The hull was surveyed, and a compromise between captain and crew was mediated by the American Consul whereby the men agreed to return with the vessel to an American port where she could be properly surveyed and repaired. Starbuck reports that she returned "clean" — that is, without any cargo of oil on board — on 20 July 1857; and in his notes for her next voyage, he remarks that the *Ocean* had "returned once, the crew having mutinied," an obvious allusion to (if an extreme characterization of) the incident at St. Helena. She sailed again on 29 September under another captain but with many of the same men aboard, including Fisher as first mate; but neither this cruise (1857-59) nor her subsequent one (1859-61) was distinguished by anything more than very modest success. Fisher, who is to be admired for sticking with it for so long under such circumstances, never went whaling again. [Songs: #40, 91.]

Freeman, Benjamin Allen (Sandwich, Mass.) Born in 1836, at age 15 he shipped as a green hand in the bark *Sea Queen* of Westport (1851-55), where he transcribed his songs. He made a second whaling voyage as a boatsteerer in the New Bedford bark *Mermaid* (1855-60). [Songs: #65, 110.]

Fullmoon, Sylvanus C. (Long Island, N.Y.) A Native American career whaleman, aboard the ship *Nimrod* of New Bedford, 1842-45, Fullmoon transcribed texts of "The Indian's Lament" ("The Indian Hunter's Prayer"; "The Indian Hunter"; "White Man, Let Me Go") and "The Jewish Maid," both of which are sympathetic to the plight of downtrodden minorities. His next voyage was in the New Bedford ship *Canada* (1846-49). [Songs: #333, 340.]

Gallup, Benjamin Franklin, Jr. (Poquonnock Bridge, Groton, Conn.) Born in 1836, he was a green hand in the bark *South America* of New Bedford, 1855-59. His father was a builder and "pioneer in the menhaden industry" (Kimball 1984, 50), and archives in the New Bedford Free Public Library indicate that he shipped as "green hand and carpenter" in the *South America*; but Gallup's own journal does not bear this out. The actual ship's carpenter, whom Gallup mentions frequently as such, was a shipboard friend and shoreside companion on liberty days. Gallup lists himself among the foremast hands but for some reason lives aft, "in the cabin," though he is not the cook, the steward, or "boy," each of whom he mentions in context and names in his crew list. The captain called upon him periodically to perform special duties, such as preparing for a gam. Whatever his function or the odd interpretation he may have placed upon it in the journal, the remuneration could not have been great. Despite that the captain left the ship because of illness before the voyage was completed, the *South America*'s combined cargo of oil and bone amounted to a particularly lucrative catch; but as Gallup had signed for a 1/225th lay, a mere pittance, his share of the proceeds could hardly have been princely. The most unusual and compelling feature of the voyage is Gallup's journal, which betrays the diarist's fair education, rigorous religious upbringing, and engaging fluency in the language, exemplified in several prose passages and original poetic compositions. It also shows him experimenting with various forms of his name, alternately referring to himself as Franklin, B.F., and F.M. Gallup. He died in 1883. (Additional sources: B.F. Gallup Papers, G.W. Blunt White Library, Mystic Seaport Museum; Gallup & Peck, *Gallup Genealogy,* # 1612; Sunnee Gallup Spencer, private communications.) [Songs: #70, 145, 224, 413, 438.]

Gibson, Henry ["Harry"]. (Tremont: probably Tremont, Maine, but possibly Tremont, Pennsylvania.) Born circa 1846, his name appears on the flyleaf of the whaling journal of William Keith and Charles W. Kinney, 1865-71 (qq.v.), and he may have contributed one or more of the many songs there (though none are signed by or credited to him). During 1868-72 Gibson was evidently aboard the whaling bark *Atlantic* of New Bedford.

Gifford, George H. (Westport, Mass.) Born at Westport in 1808, he married Rebecca Davis of that town in 1826, and was first mate of the Westport brig *Elizabeth* (1837-38) when he transcribed his one song. In the 1840s he was a Justice of the Peace and Town Assessor, and in the 1860s presided as a judge of the criminal courts. [Song #458.]

Gillaspia [Gillespie], William (Nantucket.) Born in 1827, at the time he transcribed his songs he was serving as seaman (1846-49) and boatsteerer (1850-53) in the ship *Atlantic* of Nantucket. A shipmate, James Donahue (q.v.), contributed songs and collaborated on the journal during the second of these voyages. [Songs: #9, 25, 79, 258, 327.]

Gilman, Benjamin J. (Fairfield, Maine.) Born circa 1822, he served in the ship *Virginia* of New Bedford (1840-43) before making the voyage in the New Bedford ship *Mary* (1844-47) on which he transcribed one song. [Song #48.]

Gorham, Joseph R. (Nantucket.) Born 1817; carpenter, ship *Columbia* of Nantucket, 1841-45. He contributed verse to the journal of shipmate George A. Gould (q.v.), where his name is recorded as "J. Goram"; he also collaborated with Gould on a number of drawings (illustrated in Martin 1983). After his return from the *Columbia* voyage he married Eliza F. Brown of Portland, Maine. Some of his original poems are anthologized in Miller 1979.

Gould, George A. (Gardiner, Maine.) Seaman, ship *Columbia* of Nantucket, 1841-45. Gould, who later served as second mate in several Down East merchant vessels on the Liverpool run, kept a journal of his whaling cruise in the *Columbia*, to which his shipmate Joseph Gorham (q.v.) and an acquaintance or relative of Gould's in Maine, Martha Ann Tray (q.v.), contributed poems and songs. [Songs: #42, 204; 253.]

Green[e], Samuel, Jr. Born in 1815 in Waterford, Conn., he was one of the most distinguished and long-tenured whaling masters from the neighboring town of New London. He went to sea at age 13, was first mate and, at the uncommonly early age of 21, relief master of the ship *Flora* of New London, 1835-36; then master of the New London ships *Neptune* (3 voyages, 1839-44), *Morrison* (1844-48), *Catherine* (1848-50), and *George and Mary* (1850-53), and the New Bedford ships *Nassau* (1863-65; captured and burned by the Confederate States commerce-raider *Shenandoah*) and *Trident* (as relief captain in the Arctic, 1868-70). He married Mary A. Crandall in 1839. During his long retirement he was a well-known figure around New London, where he died in 1898. Biographical sketches in Frank 1991a, 62; Colby, 68ff; Webb, 107-111. [Songs: #87, 105.]

Halstead, Israel T. (Newburgh, N.Y.) Born in 1819; fourth mate, ship *Mt. Vernon* of New Bedford, 1843-46. His early whaling voyages have not been identified. Martin (1983, 146) speculates that "he may have spent his early years aboard whalers out of his home town of Newburgh, N.Y."; however, as his Protection Paper was issued at New Bedford in 1838, it is just as likely that he commenced his whaling career out of New Bedford at that time. His first documented whaling voyage was as boatsteerer in the New Bedford bark *Newton* (1841-43); this was followed the by two voyages in the *Mt. Vernon*. His song "The Ship Is Ready" is connected to the first of these. When, on the second *Mt. Vernon* voyage, First Mate John L. Spooner was killed by a whale, Halstead was likely promoted in the general reorganization that followed. His activities during 1846-54 have not been discovered and he may have been engaged in other activities ashore, but he was issued a new Protection Paper in 1854 and served as first mate of the New Bedford bark *Ionia* (1854-57), his last recorded voyage. A charming sketch in his journal, signed and dated 7 June 1856 by his sister Henrietta (who also gave him the one song in his journal), suggests a certain domestic tranquility on the banks of the Hudson between voyages which may at last have wooed him permanently away from the fishery. He was later a farmer at Salisbury Mills, in the town of New Windsor, N.Y. [Song #30.]

Handy, Albert F. (Binghamton, N.Y.) Born at Colesville, N.Y., circa 1838; seaman, bark *Waverly* of New Bedford, 1859-63. He collaborated with George M. Jones and George E. Sanborn (qq.v.) in collecting songs and keeping an intermittent journal on his maiden voyage in the *Waverly*. Of the three, Handy was the only one to go whaling again. He obtained a berth as Ordinary Seaman in the bark *Stella* of New Bedford, but the unfortunate vessel was "lost off Foggy Island, Gulf of California, August 11, 1867,"suffering two men lost. Though Handy was evidently not one of the hands killed, the harrowing incident may have dissuaded him from a seafaring career. There is no further record of him in the whale fishery. [Songs: see George M. JONES.]

Himes, Randall (New Bedford.) Born circa 1820; second mate, bark *Emma* of New Bedford, 1847-48. His one song was transcribed in the middle of a rather long and successful whaling career that eventually brought him to the quarterdeck and part-ownership in a New Bedford whaler. His Protection Paper was issued at New Bedford in 1836, and at 5 feet 7 ¾ inches (172 cm) tall, with red hair and blue eyes, he was rather taller than many full-grown men of the era and must have cut quite a commanding figure as a lad of 16. The name of his first vessel is not recorded (1836-39), but he is known to have been in the New Bedford ships *Frances Henrietta* (1839-43) and *Falcon* (1843-46) before becoming second mate of the *Emma* (his journal records only a portion of the voyage of 1847-51). He was afterwards first mate of the bark *Laetitia* (1852-54), and as master of the same vessel on her next voyage (1854-57), in addition to his lay as captain he received a 1/32nd share of the profits — an ownership interest that carried over to the next voyage, under Captain Joseph Stowell (1857-60); but his own voyage as skipper of the *Laetitia* is Himes's last recorded outing in the whale fishery. [Song #229.]

Hopkins, Stephen O. (Athens, Pennsylvania.) Born circa 1821; green hand and seaman, ships *China* of New Bedford and *Rosalie* of Warren, 1843-44; seaman, bark Perseverance of Providence (and Newport), 1849. He served the first part of his apprenticeship in the *China* (these early pages are missing from his journal) and presumably transferred to the *Rosalie* a few weeks later (his journal provides only a fragmentary account aboard the *Rosalie* during part of 1843). Whatever he may have been as a whaleman, he was not a conscientious journal-keeper: the narrative trails off long before revealing whether he remained with the *Rosalie* for the duration, returning to Warren in April 1845 (the *China* arrived home the following October). The winter of 1846-47 finds the journal at least, if not Hopkins himself, in the temporary custody of John G. Marble and Lydia Marble (qq.v.), Rhode Islanders who transcribed a number of songs into it, many of them signed and dated: the impression is one of Hopkins spending the Yuletide season with relatives or friends in Warren, far from his home in Pennsylvania. By June 1849, the volume was certainly in his possession again when he sailed from Providence in the *Perseverance* on a Cape Horn voyage to San Francisco. His journal describes episodes of lowering unsuccessfully for pilot whales ("blackfish") and porpoises in the Atlantic — seemingly an odd pastime for a vessel presumably bound in a hurry for the gold fields, but evidently intended to raise capital for a grubstake in California. His journal ends abruptly in July 1849, with the *Perseverance* still on the coast of Africa. After a hiatus of 17 months, the narrative is resumed by L.C. Richmond, Jr. (q.v.), carpenter in the *Perseverance*, now on the California coast, and there is no further mention of Hopkins in the journal. "S O Hopkins" is duly listed among those who embarked in the *Perseverance*, as is one "Gt Richmond" [sic] (Haskins, 472); but there is no clear indication whether Hopkins actually landed in San Francisco. Did he desert ship in some African or South American port-of-call? Did he fall from aloft one dark night, to find a watery grave? Or did he again simply tire of journal-keeping, and pass off the ledger volume to a shipmate? And if he ever did reach California, how did he fare in the gold fields? [Songs: #53, 134, 220.]

Howland, George Washington (Dartmouth, Mass.) Born circa 1856; seaman, bark *Pioneer* of New Bedford, 1875-77. Miller (p. 77) calls Howland "one of the last creative writers on board whaleships," and so he may have been, as the industry was changing and with it the fashion in journal-keeping and verse composition. The Victorian morality and home-sweet-home sentimentalism that prevailed at mid century — in journals that were often designed as gifts and souvenirs for loved ones at home — in later years were more often infused with irreverence and iconoclasm, manifestations perhaps characteristic of the naturalism, social Darwinism, political disillusionment, and decadence of the Reconstruction and Post-Reconstruction eras. The poems of George W. Howland and sometime collaborator Frederick Russell (q.v.) are a case in point. Yet their bawdy song "Frozen Limb" is virtually unique in whaling lore. Even after many subsequent additions to museum manuscript collections and several full-scale surveys of their contents since Miller's remarks were published in 1979, with only one or two exceptions her observations still hold true, that Howland and Russell co-authored "the only openly pornographic, or even bawdy, work uncovered in the journals. In fact, extremely few pornographic items, copied or original, are in the major public whaling collections ..." (Miller, 77) — or in private collections, for that matter [but see songs #15 and #16 for recent additions to the known literature]. By the time he and Russell wrote their song, Howland was already an experienced whaleman, having gone to sea in the *Emma Jones* of New Bedford at age 16 (1871-74). Nor was the *Pioneer* cruise his last. He made two voyages in the New Bedford ship *Horatio* and another in the *Stafford* during 1877-89. [Song #17.]

Hughson, Robert Nathaniel (Hamilton, Ontario; and Albion, N.Y.) Born circa 1833, he held an American citizenship paper issued at New Bedford in October 1857, the day before he sailed in the bark *Java* (1857-60). The paper gives his age as 24 and his residence as Albion, N.Y., but his own manuscript crew list in his journal gives his home as "Hamilton, Canada West." This equivocation, and the fact that his songs include an unusually high proportion of farewell ballads and Irish emigration songs, together with a few British parlor songs not found in other whalemen's journals, suggest that Hughson may have been an emigrant from Ireland to Canada, subsequently naturalized in the United States. For reasons not explained, at the end of the *Java* voyage Hughson's journal seems to have fallen into the hands of boatsteerer David McFall (McFalls) of New York City. Hughson himself continued whaling right into his forties. His next voyage was in the New Bedford ship *Reindeer* (1860-64), he was probably in the bark *Camilla* during 1867-71, and he is known definitely to have been in the bark *Helen Mar* during 1875-76, as his *Helen Mar* journal is also preserved in the Kendall Collection. His songs are all from his first outing in the *Java*. [Songs: #65, 67, 99, 134, 173, 185, 228, 233, 277, 290, 292, 328, 349, 448, 460.]

Hutchins, James W. (Bath, Maine.) Born circa 1820, he went on his first whaling voyage in 1838 (vessel not identified), was shipwrecked on his next voyage as a seaman in the ship *Cadmus* of Fairhaven (1841-42), and was boatsteerer in the ships *Florida* of New Bedford (1843-46) and *Samuel Robertson* of Fairhaven (1846-49). His original stanzas, "I Was Once a Sailor Lad," do not appear in his own *Florida* journal (New Bedford Free Public Library) but are among the songs and poems he transcribed into someone else's anonymous journal aboard the *Florida* (New Bedford Whaling Museum) when Hutchins himself was already aboard the Samuel Robertson. [Song #160.]

Jenney, Japhthah, Jr. (New Bedford). Born circa 1803; ship *Hercules* of New Bedford, 1827-28. He may have made his maiden voyage in the brig *Planter* (1818), another in the brig *Alliance* (1820-21), and probably one or two others before his time in the *Hercules*, where he transcribed the text of one song. He lived in Fairhaven, was twice married, and eventually served as first mate of the New Bedford ship *Nassau*, 1841-54. [Song #92.]

Jones, George M. (Milford, New Hampshire.) Born circa 1837; seaman, bark *Waverly* of New Bedford, 1859-63. On his four-year whaling cruise in the *Waverly* he and two shipmates — Albert F. Handy and George E. Sanborn (qq.v.) — collaborated casually in collecting songs and keeping a sporadic journal, all three of them at one time or another making entries in a single ledger volume. It was evidently begun as a copybook by Jones, whose first entry, a version of "Lady Franklin's Lament," is inscribed "On board ship / Sept 15th 1859," about five months out. While a few pages were removed from the journal at some point, this and five other songs remain intact from the early part of the voyage. Most appear to have been copied down in 1859, after which the copybook was abandoned for a while. Two years later, in April 1862, Albert Handy began to keep a journal in diary form in this same volume but kept it up only until August, when Jones himself picks up the daily entries, which, in his own words, he continued "during the remainder of the voyage." In the meantime, they resumed the practice of writing down song lyrics, this time using the back pages of the ledger (though one of the songs in the early section is apparently in Handy's writing). Here, too, several leaves are missing. But the complete texts of 24 more songs were transcribed, mostly during 1862 and 1863, some of them signed and dated by George Sanborn, the most senior of the three and the only one who had been whaling before. After the *Waverly* voyage, Jones appears to have gone back to the Granite State to follow other pursuits. Of the three, only Handy was to go whaling again, and then only briefly. [Songs: #10, 14, 33, 39, 67, 89, 93, 101, 123, 129, 143, 173, 197, 205, 206, 210, 248, 252, 276, 284, 289, 293, 308, 319, 359, 389, 404, 416, 434.]

Jones, John (Craftsbury, Vermont.) Born 1822; steward, ship *Eliza Adams* of New Bedford, 1851-52. When he sailed in the *Eliza Adams*, his third whaling cruise, he was only recently back from three years in the New Bedford ship *Marengo* (1848-51); however, his unconventional journal of the *Eliza Adams* is the only relic of his career, and, alas, it is but a fragment, comprising only the first five months of a five-year voyage. That it is not complete is one of the minor tragedies of whaling lore, as it provides a delightfully witty and eccentric commentary on shipboard life, punctuated by song allusions and snippets of lyrics erratically and somewhat compulsively interwoven into the narrative (the annotated journal fragment has been published in its entirety in Frank 1991b, 13-30). Jones was "well read in low literature, worldly, somewhat jaded, whimsical to the point of frivolousness. When the mood strikes, he effervesces over the passing parade, quoting popular song lyrics, paraphrasing Shakespeare, and using and abusing platitudinous aphorisms and sayings" (Ibid, 3). Unfortunately, the journal ends abruptly without explanation with the entry for 22 April 1852, 171 days out of New Bedford, and is resumed exactly three months later in another hand, without any mention of John Jones, whose subsequent fate is unknown. But his voice from steerage provides a small window on the life and times of the Yankee whale fishery and intriguing clues about "what was hot and what was not" aboard blubber-hunters in the early 1850s. [Song #341.]

Keith, William H. (Mattapoisett, Mass.) Born circa 1844, he was the youngest of four whaling brothers, of whom Charles Frederick, second oldest, was a distinguished whaling master and sometime captain of the barks *Triton* and *Charles W. Morgan*. After his maiden whaling voyage in the Mattapoisett bark *John Dawson* (1862-64) William recorded songs in a journal he kept aboard the whaling schooners *William Martin* of Boston and *Edith May* of Wellfleet (circa 1865-69) and on a series of coastwise merchant cruises aboard the Boston schooner *Cora Nash* (circa 1871), among others. According to a rare annotation in his journal, when Keith went to sea in the 1860s he brought along a small inventory of essentials: a "Pocket Clasp Bible," a copy of "Worcester's Comprehensive Dictionary" [sic], evidently as yet unread, "Sargent's Fifth Reader," a blank book "for songs" (which turned out to be his combined journal and copybook), lead pencils, watercolor paints, and an ivory ruler. Some of his songs were actually transcribed by shipmates Henry Gibson and George R. Worth (qq.v.); others may have been written down by Charles M. Kinney, who evidently took the volume with him on a later voyage in the Provincetown schooner *Mary D. Leach*. [Songs #5, 10, 29, 31, 59, 86, 103, 108, 125, 127, 128, 182, 207, 212; also 63 additional song texts listed in Appendix 7, and 22 additional titles mentioned.]

Keyser, William F. (Southwick and Chester, Pennsylvania). Born circa 1830, he first went to sea in 1851 and transcribed one song aboard the whaling bark *Midas* of New Bedford, 1861-65. [Song #137.]

Kinney, Charles M. He may have transcribed some songs in the former journal of William Keith (q.v.) while on a voyage in the schooner *Mary D. Leach* of Provincetown in the 1870s.

Kirby, Nicholas, Jr. (Dartmouth, Mass.) Born circa 1826, he must already have been an experienced seaman when in 1849, at age 23, he obtained a new Protection Paper at New Bedford, for less than a year later he was serving as first mate in the merchant ship *Olive Branch* of Boston (1850-52). It was aboard the *Olive Branch* that Kirby transcribed a few songs; and it was one of the *Olive Branch* passengers, Dr. William Cutler, a Boston physician, who wrote a poem about him [see "To a Friend," headnotes to Appendix 2]. In the 1870s Kirby was still a professional mariner, living in New Bedford. [Songs #37, 223.]

Kirwin, Edward J. (New Bedford) Born circa 1851, he was a seaman or green hand (and ship's cooper?) in the bark *William Gifford* of New Bedford during 1872-73. His father, James Kirwin, was a New Bedford cooper who worked for Lorenzo Pierce in the 1840s and '50s, went to sea as cooper in the whaling bark *Belle* of Fairhaven, then worked for Pierce again until about the time of the Civil War; by 1865 he had become a cooper for New Bedford's Seneca Oil Works, where he was later made foreman cooper. Edward, who undoubtedly came properly armed with an extensive knowledge of cooperage gained from years of apprenticeship under his father, undertook his initiatory whaling voyage at around age 21, but did not persist in the fishery. After the one whaling cruise he made a couple of merchant voyages in the New Bedford bark *Veronica* and was later a glass maker in New Bedford. [Songs: #67, 94, 443.]

McCleave, Edward (Nantucket.) Born in 1813, he made many whaling cruises, collected scrimshaw and souvenirs in the Pacific, and commanded several merchant voyages. His one song was transcribed as master of the whaleship *Roscoe* of New Bedford during 1847-51. He married Martha C. Coleman in 1840. [Song #210.]

McInnis, Emma Lapointe Taber [Mrs. John McInnis]. (Acushnet and Dartmouth, Mass.; and San Francisco.) Born circa 1861, she was a widow of 29 living in Acushnet when she married Captain John McInnis in 1890. The following year, she accompanied him to sea aboard the San Francisco bark *Josephine*, and it is from her journal of that voyage (1891-92) that their only song in this anthology was recovered. Her husband's career typifies the peripatetic fortunes of the whaling industry itself in its declining years. Born around 1845 at Dartmouth, in the heart of whaling country, adjacent to New Bedford, John McInnis was only 13 when he embarked on his maiden voyage. He emerged a professional whaleman who rose through the ranks to command three New Bedford vessels and came to specialize in the North Pacific and Western Arctic bowhead fishery then the most productive and, by reason of ice, the most dangerous. He moved with the fishery out to San Francisco when because of its proximity to Alaska the Golden Gate was becoming the new hub of Yankee whaling. He lost a vessel in a devastating shipwreck among the floes, but lived to be rescued (with his entire crew) and resume whaling. After their marriage in 1890, Emma was his almost constant companion at sea and on shore. He skippered one of those newfangled steam-powered barks on two voyages, and, after retirement from command, finished out his career as boatheader in the same steam-whaler. The catalogue of his senior posts is impressive: mate of the ship *Jireh Perry* of New Bedford (1875-79); master of the

New Bedford barks *Hercules* (1879-82) and *Swallow* (1883-87); two voyages the San Francisco bark *Jacob A. Howland* (1888-89), on the second of which he was wrecked and the crew rescued by the bark *Abram Barker*; master of the barks *Josephine* (1890-91, 1891-92) and *Wanderer* (1893), with Emma aboard; two outings as master of the auxiliary steam bark *William Baylies* (1894-95, 1896) and one as boatheader (whaling supervisor) in the *Baylies* under Captain D.F. Davoll (1897). He was next master of the famous schooner *Effie F. Morrissey* (made famous by Bob Bartlett, later converted to a Brava packet re-named *Ernestina*, and now preserved as a museum ship in New Bedford): McInnes took her to Newfoundland for the winter herring season of 1898-99, and sold the cargo in New York; then went dory fishing in the 1899 season. See Bockstoce 1977 and 1986. [Song #138.]

Marble, Elizabeth Church [née Wrightington] [Mrs. John C. Marble]. (Fall River and San Francisco.) Born 1825; New Bedford barks *Kathleen*, 1857-60; and *Awashonks*, 1860-61. She married whaling captain John Marble (q.v.) in 1845 and bore him a son while her husband was away on a three-year voyage. The infant died in 1848 before Captain Marble's return. When he finally did come back he resigned temporarily from whaling and entered the coastwise and California trade, which enabled him to come home more often and stay longer. Another son, George Frederick ("Freddie"), was born in 1850. Once the child's good health seemed assured, Marble returned to whaling; and in 1857, when he was given command of the *Kathleen* and a substantial share in her profits, he arranged to bring Lizzie and seven-year-old Freddie to sea with him, a privilege extended only to captains, and only with the permission of the owners (whom a captain was required to reimburse for the extra expenses of board and upkeep). John's younger brother, George D. Marble (q.v.), who was married to Lizzie's sister Sarah, went as first mate, an unconventional arrangement between brothers resulting in an unusually close-knit family circle in the aftercabin. Lizzie, aged 32 when the voyage commenced — the only woman on board, good-natured, gregarious, and substantially older than any of the officers or crew — embraced with gusto the roles of helpmate, mother hen, theatrical costumer, soprano, and advisor-to-the-lovelorn that her new circumstances suddenly thrust upon her [see Chapter 17]. Meanwhile, she maintained a frank and expansive correspondence with her mother and sisters back home. Lizzie, John, and George, who had each been writing down songs and poems all along, now gathered them collectively, transcribing them into their journals. Lizzie also wrote down many on the blank, leftover pages of John's and George's journals of voyages past; and it was she who, long after her husband and brother-in-law were gone, cherished and preserved the songs, with the journals, letters, scrimshaw, souvenirs, and other memorabilia of the *Kathleen* and *Awashonks*. These came to Freddie as a family legacy after her death at San Francisco in 1895. Unfortunately, most of the transcriptions are undated, frustrating any hope of connecting them with particular voyages. But thanks to her, the Marble Family archive remains substantially intact, to shed unique light on life and labor in the Yankee whale fishery, and on the unique plight of an endearing, reflective young woman contending with the joys and sorrows of marriage, child rearing, friendships, and death over several years at sea, and, ultimately, revealing the bravery and nobility of a young widow crossing oceans and broad continents to return with her son to the family fold. (Additional sources: biographical sketch of John Marble in Frank 1991a, 89f; the late Mrs. William H. Holmes, West Hartford, Conn, a descendant of John and Elizabeth Marble; Marble Family Papers and a Charles P. Worth sketchbook in the Kendall Collection.) [Songs: #132, 161, 162, 193, 194, 195, 196, 199, 209, 244, 252, 262, 265, 274, 295, 311, 331, 332, 333, 334, 339, 348, 356, 376, 387, 390, 421, 427, 436, 437, 447, 450.]

Marble [Marbel], George D. (Fall River.) Born at Assonet, Mass., 1816; seaman, brig *Le Barron* of Rochester, 1837-38; boatsteerer, bark *Roscoe* of New Bedford, 1839-42; second mate, ship *Caroline* of New Bedford, 1842-46; first mate, bark *Octavia* of New Bedford, 1846-48; master, ship *Helen Augusta* of Newport, 1854-56; first mate, New Bedford barks *Kathleen*, 1857-60; and Awashonks, 1860-61; ashore from 1861; died at Florence, Mass., 1885. The younger brother of Captain John Marble (q.v.), George "Marbel" never switched to the consistent use of the other spelling (as the rest of the family did circa 1845). His first and only command, the *Helen Augusta*, was a troubled voyage, the details of which are not entirely clear even from George's own journal. What is clear is that they sailed in 1854; and in 1856, after persistent unrest among the crew, they finally mutinied and burned the ship at Manganui, New Zealand. The owners, Josiah Munroe & Co., apparently blamed the captain for the incident, and he was thereafter unable to obtain, or unwilling to accept, any other command. (An analogous situation turned out very differently for Captain Frederick Howland Smith: see Chapter 18.) The mishap effectively ruined his career and might have ended the career of a less tenacious man; but George was not too proud to come back from misfortune to serve again in a lesser capacity. Far from leaving the whale fishery in disgrace, Captain George cheerfully signed articles as chief mate of the *Kathleen* under his brother's command, an arrangement to which the *Kathleen*'s owners, J. & W.R. Wing, must certainly have agreed. On this voyage, his double sister-in-law (Elizabeth Marble, wife of John Marble, was also the younger sister of George's wife, Sarah) was also on board, along with John and Lizzie's young son. It was a happy voyage that the family — intact except for Sarah, who as the wife of a mere mate could not accompany the entourage to sea — hoped to repeat on the next cruise. Thus, when John was given the *Awashonks* in 1860, Lizzie and young Freddie joined him in the aftercabin and George shipped as mate. Tragically, John died in the Pacific about thirteen months into the voyage. George left the ship with Lizzie and the boy to see them safely home. According to family tradition, George had been "sent to art school" in his early years, an aspect of his activities of which his elegant handwriting is the only evidence. It is presumed by Marble descendants that after George's return to Fall River in 1861 he utilized this talent and training as part of his livelihood, but neither the family nor any other source has been able to provide particulars. Other family testimony suggests that George was associated with Freddie in the fish business at Florence, Mass., his own son (John W.P. Marble, called William) having died in infancy. See Chapter 17. (Additional sources: the late Mrs. William H. Holmes, West Hartford, Conn, a Marble descendant; Marble Family Papers, Kendall Whaling Museum). [Songs: See Elizabeth C. MARBLE.]

Marble, John (Fall River.) Born at Assonet, Mass., 1813; green hand, ship *Java* of New Bedford, 1832-33; seaman, boatsteerer, and junior mate, ship *William Wirt* of Fairhaven, an unidentified vessel, and ship *America* of Hudson (1833-41); mate, brig *Pilgrim* of Somerset, 1842-43. Master: brig *Leonidas* of New Bedford, 1843-45; ship *Gold Hunter* of Fall River, 1846-49; schooner *Chesapeake* of Fall River (merchant and Gold Rush voyages, 1849-53); bark *A. Houghton* of Fall River, 1853-56; bark *Kathleen* of New Bedford, 1857-60; and bark *Awashonks* of New Bedford, 1860-61; died at sea, 1861. In 1845, following his debut as captain, he was married to Elizabeth ("Lizzie") Church Wrightington of Fall River; and she, with their son George Frederick (born 1850), accompanied him on two voyages, in the *Kathleen* and *Awashonks* (1857-61). John's younger brother, George D. Marble (q.v.), went along as first mate on both of these voyages. The family were uncommonly close: the brothers were married to sisters; their professional relationship as brothers serving together as captain and executive officer on two voyages was virtually unique; the sisters maintained an articulate and extremely affectionate correspondence; and, especially during the five years that John, Lizzie, and George were at sea together, they gathered and transcribed songs and poems collectively. Their cooperation, kindness, and nobility of spirit carried over to respectful, humane, even generous treatment of the officers and crew, distinguishing this voyage in the *Kathleen* as one of the happiest in the annals of whaling, and probably one of the most musical. A wealth of memorabilia survives from the *Kathleen*: journals by the captain, the first mate, and the second mate, William T. Butts; scrimshaw by the captain and the third mate, John C. Sullivan; Lizzie and Sarah Marble's letters; inlaid wooden furniture made and presented by whaling captain Charles P. Worth of Nantucket, upholstered at sea by John Marble with needlepoint made by Lizzie on shipboard; splendid souvenirs collected by the family from exotic islands and landfalls; and a particularly engaging chronicle in the form of a song, "A Voyage on New Holland" [#161], written by either William Butts, second mate, or John Sullivan, third mate. The voyage was also an economic success. Captain Marble, still holding a 1/62nd share in the profits of his former command, the *A. Houghton*, and with his regular master's lay and an additional 1/16th ownership share in the *Kathleen*, had set himself up for what would have been a very comfortable retirement after another voyage or two. But it was not to be. With his wife, son (now age ten), and first-mate brother again on board, he sailed from New Bedford as master of the *Awashonks* in September 1860. Taken sick a few months later, he died on board in October of the following year. (Additional sources: biographical sketch in Frank, 1991, 89f; the late Mrs. William H. Holmes, West Hartford, Conn, a descendant of John and Elizabeth Marble; Marble Family Papers and the Charles P. Worth sketchbook in the Kendall Collection.) [Songs: See Elizabeth C. MARBLE.]

Marble, John G. and Lydia (fl. Warren, Rhode Island, circa 1846-47.) After Pennsylvanian Stephen O. Hopkins (q.v.) returned from a whaling voyage in the ship *Rosalie* of Warren (1842-45), husband and wife John G. and Lydia Marble, who may have been Hopkins's relatives, transcribed several poems and nine song texts into his journal. A few of these they signed and dated. Hopkins took the journal with him in 1849 when he joined a party of former whalemen who outfitted the bark *Perseverance* for a Gold Rush voyage to California; the journal later came into the hands of Lemuel C. Richmond, Jr. (q.v.). The Warren Historical Society reports that John Marble was a local ship-smith and a distant relation of the whaling Marbles of Tiverton, R.I., and Fall River, Mass. (see John C., Elizabeth, and George D. MARBLE). [Songs: #1, 66, 80, 89, 97, 130, 261, 356.]

Martin, John F. (Philadelphia.) Born circa 1820; seaman, ship *Lucy Ann* of Wilmington, Delaware, 1841-44; died in California, circa 1880. A Pennsylvanian who later became a California pioneer, John Martin produced a lavishly illustrated journal of his third whaling voyage, in the *Lucy Ann*. He had been a green hand in the bark *Superior* of Wilmington (1836-39) and a seamen in the ship *Jefferson* of that port (1839-41) on whaling voyages to the Pacific Ocean and sperm whaling in the Atlantic. The *Lucy Ann* was quite a musical ship. Martin himself played the bugle and participated in many after-hours soirees, chronicling many instances illustrating that music and musical shenanigans were important features of shipboard life. In addition to some of his remarks and observations quoted throughout, his evening programme of musical entertainments — "a grand concert given by the whole crew" on shipboard, on 16 February 1842 — is a prime example of the kind of thing that must have taken place at sea fairly often but which was seldom recorded in such detail. After disembarking in Wilmington in 1844, disillusioned with whaling, Martin served for a few years on Philadelphia merchant vessels, then, in 1854, went to California to try his hand at prospecting. While he never made a fortune in gold, he did take over a ferry operation on the Klamath River at a site still known as Martin's Ferry. He was also a sometime rancher, bridge-builder, justice of the peace, and respected local citizen. (Additional sources: Kenneth R. Martin, ed., *In the Way of the Whale: John Martin's Journal...*: unpublished manuscript, Kendall Collection archive; Kenneth R. Martin and James A. Frazier, private communications; biographical sketch of John F. Martin in Frank 1991a.) [Songs: see Appendix 5.]

Merrill, Frederick (New York City.) Born circa 1854; green hand, bark *Janus* of New Bedford, 1875-77; seaman, schooner *Eothen* of New York, on a voyage to transport Frederick Schwatka and his exploration party to Hudson Bay, 1878. [Song #35.]

Mills, George Edgar (Grafton, Vermont; Milford, New Hampshire.) Born circa 1828; fourth mate, ship *Java* of New Bedford, 1854-55; third mate, ship *Leonidas* of New Bedford, 1855-56; second mate, bark *Mary Frances* of Warren, 1856; third mate, bark *Aurora* of Westport, 1856-59; third mate, ship *James Loper* of Nantucket, 1859-60. Though his skills may not have been so highly developed as those of, say, Daniel K. Ritchie or R.G.N. Swift (qq.v.), nor his education so demonstrably thorough, Vermonter George Mills had pronounced literary proclivities and, at least half seriously, thought of himself as a poet, novelist, playwright, and gentleman. Some of his original work is quite sensitive and well wrought, as, for example, his philosophical treatise on death at sea (Miller 112f). In other moods he is whimsically allusive, as in "All the Whales Are Wild and Ugly" [#158]. With some justification, Miller regards him as one of the most interesting and prolific of whalemen-writers. He undertook his first whaling voyage at 21, shipping as a green hand in the New Bedford ship *Triton*, 1849-51. He must have been quite a "good hand on an oar," for he rose steadily through the ranks. His two voluminous journals as a young deck officer, brimming over with original poetry, song lyrics, and prose, and with dozens of songs, poems, aphorisms, and miscellanea copied down or collected from shipmates, are addressed to his wife, Mary Frances (née Hopkins), in Milford. Homesick and mourning their separation during long years at sea, upon his return in the *James Loper* he gave up whaling and settled down permanently in New Hampshire, where he worked as a mill hand at Nashua. He likely knew whalemen George M. Jones (q.v.), a native of Milford; and George W. Piper (q.v.), a younger fellow from Concord. Partially through regional predilections, and perhaps through personal acquaintance, there are numerous significant overlaps in the songs and texts transcribed by these three Georges from New Hampshire. Of the three, Mills seems to have had the most pedestrian taste, gravitating towards parlor songs and minstrel tunes destined to descend into well-deserved obscurity during his own lifetime. But his journals are distinguished for his own original compositions, two or three good whaling songs, and such unique materials as "There's Changes at the Mill" [#131]. [Songs: #18, 38, 68, 116, 131, 138, 146, 158, 170, 173, 174, 186, 211, 212, 263, 265, 277, 285, 286, 301, 362, 368, 386, 391, 400, 407, 417, 448.]

Nickerson, Solomon R. (Provincetown, Mass.) Born circa 1848, he came from an enormous family of Nickersons in Harwich and Provincetown on Cape Cod, where he was trained as a carpenter. In his journal aboard the Provincetown schooner *Varnum H. Hill* in 1863 he transcribed an original ballad by shipmate Benjamin Franklin Rogers (q.v.). [Song #147.]

Norton, Jemeriah C. (Edgartown, Marthas Vineyard) Born circa 1819; first mate, New Bedford ship *Swift*, 1849-52. He may have begun his whaling career from his native island, where whaling was already a century old when New Bedford was founded in the 1760s, but at age 22 he shipped as seaman in the Fairhaven ship *Cadmus* (1841). It was not an auspicious beginning, as the vessel was lost on Cadmus Island (named for the wreck) about nine months out, in August 1842. He appears then to have joined the bark *Mars* of New Bedford on a voyage already in progress (1841-45), married Margaret S. Vincent at Edgartown in October 1845, and undoubtedly served as a mate on at least one other whaleship (circa 1846-49) before shipping as mate in the Swift in 1849. It was on this voyage that he transcribed the songs anthologized here, but on his next that he was admitted to the fraternity of whaling masters that was the object, at one time or another, of virtually every whaling career. He commanded two New Bedford vessels, the ship *Louisiana* (1853-57) and bark *Andrews* (1858-62). Neither voyage was more than marginally successful; but it was probably more by reason of the Civil War than any prior misfortune that Norton retired from whaling and returned to the Vineyard in 1862. [Songs: #191, 192.]

Peacock, James S. (New York City.) Born circa 1836. Boatsteerer, ship *Hiawatha* of New Bedford, 1856-61. He was the source of a text of "The Prince of Morocco" (#88) in the copybook of George W. Piper (q.v.) aboard the ship *Europa* of Edgartown, 1868.

Pettey, Henry Tripp (New Bedford.) He made voyages in New Bedford barks, as a seaman in the *Mary Ann*, 1853-55, boatsteerer in the *Chili* (1856-59), and second mate in the *Atlantic* (1859). The journal in which his songs are recorded is from the first two voyages. [Songs: #9, 247.]

Piper, George Wilbur (Concord, N.H..) Born in 1840 either at Hopkinton, N.H., or Topsham, Vermont; raised at Concord; ship *Europa* of Edgartown, 1868-70. Little is known about this young New Hampshireman whose shipboard collection of songs is by far the largest ever yet encountered among seamen's manuscripts. His Protection Paper, issued at New Bedford scarcely a month before the *Europa* weighed anchor in August 1866, indicates that Piper set off a-whaling on this or some other vessel around that time. The official logbook, kept by successive first mates William Earle and James Green during the first four years of what was to be a six-year voyage (1866-72), presents only incomplete data about the crew, which turned over several times during the *Europa*'s inordinately long sojourn in the Pacific, and Captain Thomas Mellen was evidently the only member of the original ship's company who stayed on for the duration. It appears that Piper joined up as part of a large rotation of officers and crew at Honolulu in 1868, and he may have left the ship in 1870 or '71 (a consular "Settlement of Voyage" dated 19 December 1870 at Honolulu lists a "G.W. Pope" among the 15 crewmen amicably discharged at that time). Meanwhile, in his comparatively short tenure aboard the *Europa* Piper was an eclectic collector of songs. His inventory is not only large (comprising 156 song texts, in addition to dozens of poems and literary excerpts) but also eccentric and quirky in its sources and catholic in its tastes. Folksongs, parlor songs, music-hall comic pieces, minstrel tunes, broadside ballads, deepwater songs, and traditional whaling come-all-ye's, are all represented in surprisingly rich variety, in a literate, legible hand. Song texts vastly outnumber the other verse and prose pieces, and there are ample indications that Piper intended his texts for singing: the transcriptions often conform to musical and vocal phrasing, rather than to strict poetic conventions of rhyme and meter; and frequently, where a song runs to multiple pages the chorus is repeated on each page, as though not to inconvenience the singer and accompanist by requiring that the pages be turned any more than necessary. It was also Piper's custom occasionally to have shipmates inscribe a song or two into his copybook. His "Hawaiian Song" ["No Ke Ano Ahiahi," #144], transcribed in his own hand in the Hawaiian language, is an extraordinarily rare traditional hula narrative, undoubtedly obtained from one of the many Kanakas who shipped in the *Europa* for seasonal whaling cruises out of the Hawaiian Islands. But, alas, Piper wrote nothing in the volume to explain the context and circumstances in which the songs were sung, or the role of music aboard the *Europa* in those years. After 1870 he evaporates from view. (Additional source: logbook of the *Europa*, 1866-70, New Bedford Whaling Museum.) [156 ballads, songs, and variants.]

Phillips, Harvey R.C. (Massachusetts) Born circa 1820, he was a professional whaleman who lived variously at Dartmouth, Westport, Taunton, and New Bedford and made a long string of voyages in New Bedford and Marion schooners during a whaling career that spanned over 40 years. His one song, a text of "Old Folks at Home," was transcribed aboard the New Bedford ship *Gladiator* in 1853, when the song was still new. When he finally retired, Phillips was one of the most unusual of all species of whaleman, still an Able Seaman at age 63. [Song #182.]

Poole, William H. (Dartmouth, Mass.) Born circa 1844, at age 19 he shipped in the New Bedford bark *Morning Star* (1864-65) and served as boatsteerer on the next voyage of the same vessel (1866-67). It was on his outing as a junior officer in the ship *Minnesota* of New York during 1868-72 that he transcribed the songs in this anthology. He afterwards served as mate in the Westport bark *Platina* (1872-75), and rose to command the New Bedford barks *Bartholomew Gosnold* (1881-85) and *John and Winthrop* (1885-88) (his journals of the *Minnesota, Platina, Bartholomew Gosnold,* and *John and Winthrop* are in the Kendall Collection). He then retired from whaling for a while, reemerged as mate of the *Wanderer* (1892) and boatheader (whaling supervisor) of the *Reindeer* (1893), both out of San Francisco, and skippered the *Canton* of New Bedford on an Arctic whaling voyage to Hudson Bay (1895-96). [Songs #89, 236, 271, 314, 330, 357, 384, 397, 419, 425, 439, 440, 451, 455.]

Prescott, G.H. As a seaman in the ship *Ocean* of New Haven (1860-61) and bark *Belle* of Fairhaven (1861-62), he transcribed the lyrics of "Lady Franklin's Lament" (#67).

Reed, Israel (Dartmouth, Mass.) Born circa 1834; seaman, bark *Black Eagle* of New Bedford, 1860-61. His brother Isaac, older by four years, was master of the bark *Thomas Winslow* of Westport during 1857-59. Israel, who never made it to captain, followed Isaac into the whale fishery in 1848, when he was only 14 years of age and only 4 feet 10 inches (147 cm) tall. When he shipped in the *Black Eagle* at age 26, he had grown 8 inches (20 cm) taller and, presumably, proportionally more skillful on an oar. This voyage took him to the Davis Strait whaling ground off Greenland, in former days the traditional hunting ground of the British and Dutch whaling fleets, and into Hudson Bay. Reed's only song transcription was Stephen Foster's "Hard Times Come Again No More," a possible reflection of his attitude about the whale fishery, to which he seems never to have returned. [Song #313.]

Reynolds, Richard C. (Freetown, Mass.) Born in 1822, he embarked on his first voyage at age 17. It was on his second or third outing, as boatsteerer in the ship *Janus* of New Bedford during 1842-44, that he wrote a number of original ballads and ballad fragments. These [#149-153] are notable as warnings to young would-be sailors and land-lubbers not to go whaling — advice that Reynolds himself evidently followed. He also collected a few songs aboard the *Janus*, including one or two very good ballads; and afterwards, both ashore and on merchant voyages into the mid 1850s he continued to collect songs, transcribing the texts in this same volume. Sadly, except for a handful of popular songs published in the 1850s, it is not always possible to distinguish which lyrics were transcribed when. In the case of "My Mary Ann" [#27] this results in an unfortunate quandary regarding the original date of the song, of which Reynolds's text is evidently the earliest ever recovered from tradition. [Songs: #27, 51, 75, 76, 79, 92, 149, 150, 151, 152, 153, 170, 212, 221, 250, 289, 314, 429, 454.]

Richmond, Lemuel C., Jr. (Bristol, R.I.) Carpenter, ship *Perseverance* of Providence (and Newport), 1849; drayman, San Francisco, circa 1851. The son and namesake of a prominent Bristol merchant after whom the whaleship *L.C. Richmond* was named in 1834, young Richmond was evidently apprenticed to a carpenter in his home town; he probably also made some youthful sea voyages. In 1849 he joined a party preparing to take the *Perseverance* on a Cape Horn voyage to the Golden Gate for prospecting. Another member of the group was Stephen Hopkins (q.v.). At some point en route, Hopkins's journal — in which he had transcribed some songs on an earlier whaling cruise in the ship *Rosalie* of Warren, and in which a few songs were written down for him in Rhode Island by John G. and Lydia Marble (qq.v.) — came into Richmond's possession. Richmond and Hopkins both embarked from Providence in the *Perseverance*, but there is no clear evidence that Hopkins actually arrived at San Francisco and his subsequent activities have not been discovered. But what became of Richmond is abundantly clear from his intermittent remarks in the much-traveled secondhand journal. Rather than striking it rich in the gold fields he was unable to raise a grubstake, remained with the ship for a while as it plied coastwise between San Francisco and San Diego, and was finally stranded on the California coast (1851) and forced to accept employment as a day laborer and drayman, pining for his Annie back home: "the Devil is in all the wimmen in frisco having there husbands & going with others. this is a grate cuntry, I hope I shall leave it soon for Bristol & Anny. I feel tired, worn, Draying all day... I am home sick & hartsick, of staying in this Cuntry all alone." How he got back to New England is not recorded: so many men were deserting their ships in San Francisco Bay to head for the hills and go prospecting that outward-bound berths for experienced hands were not difficult to obtain. By 1854 he was an officer on the sloop *Thomas Jefferson*, carrying lumber, produce, and other goods coastwise among Marthas Vineyard, Providence, and Bristol. By 1857 he may also have been doing some farming, as his terse accounts of sales of onions and hay during that year are also preserved in the back pages of the journal volume. Around that time, he moved his family to Vermont, where his son, Rollin Lemuel Richmond, was born at Barnard in 1858, graduated from the Randolph State Normal School, and became influential in banking, insurance, and local politics, serving as a justice of the peace and Mayor of Rutland. (Additional source: *Who's Who in New England,* 1908.) [Songs: see Stephen O. HOPKINS; and John G. and Lydia MARBLE.]

Ritchie, Daniel Kimball (Needham and Canton, Mass.) Born 1817; green hand and boatsteerer on two successive voyages of the ship *Portland* of Newburg, N.Y., circa 1835-39; after at least one additional voyage, second mate, ship *Israel* of New Bedford, 1843-45; ship *Herald* of New Bedford, 1845-47; ship *Massachusetts* of New Bedford, 1847. His whaling journal is one of the most interesting and intriguing anywhere, a narrative of shipboard rivalries, retribution, incarceration, psychological instability, and principled self-sacrifice, with several novelistic twists, including, as the result of a verbal altercation with Captain James Finch of the *Israel*, a sojourn of four weeks as an inmate at "The Fort" Prison in Honolulu in 1845. A young man of obvious education and breeding whose writing and handwriting both attest to his literary accomplishments and training, whose taste in songs tended toward the rarefied and neoclassical, Ritchie must have been quite a character on board ship, with highly developed principles and unwavering, self-righteous dedication, yet evidently much troubled by a kind of persecution complex that everywhere interferes with his career. One is never quite certain what it is that motivates and moves him, despite that his narrative is introspective, frank, well organized, and articulate. His journal trails off, with the Massachusetts on the North Pacific whaling grounds in 1847. Perhaps he returned to New Bedford with the ship in June 1848; perhaps he came back to New England by other means. In any case, the last we know of him is that he was in New Bedford again in 1849; for in March 1849 he applied for and received a new Protection Paper, and on the same day finalized the registration of the 350-ton ship *Mayflower*, in which he and about a dozen others were shareholders for a Gold Rush voyage to San Francisco under shareholder-captain George Randall. With the promise of fabulous riches on the horizon in the West, the adventurers rounded Cape Horn, sold the vessel in San Francisco, and disappeared into the hills. [Songs: #2, 198, 215, 217, 265, 356, 424.]

Robbins, Charles H. (Rochester, Mass., and New Bedford) Born in 1822, his long and distinguished career of 41 years at sea (1837-78) was crowned by his articulate memoir, entitled *The Gam: Being a Group of Whaling Stories*, published in 1899 (with a revised edition issued in 1913). Contrary to the prevailing custom among whalemen, Robbins wrote down the words to chanteys as well as songs, and they seem not to have been written into a journal or copybook — at least, such a copybook is not known to survive — but were found in holograph and typescript among the papers Robbins assembled in his retirement when he was writing *The Gam*. (The texts printed in *The Gam* differ in various particulars from the manuscripts; the songs are given in this anthology verbatim from Captain Robbins's originals). The manuscripts themselves and the contexts in which Robbins presents the songs in *The Gam* suggest that they are the accumulation of an entire career, beginning as a cabin boy in the New Bedford ship *Swift* (1837-41), followed by two astounding leaps in rank to third mate (1841-45) and first mate (1845-49) in the ship *Balaena* of New Bedford, then master of the barks *Hope* of New Bedford (1850-53), *Clara Bell* of Mattapoisett (1855-58), *Thomas Pope* of New Bedford (1859-63), *Kathleen* of New Bedford (1864-65), *Cape Horn Pigeon* of Dartmouth (1866), and *General Scott* of New Bedford (1875-78). Between times, he commanded merchant voyages out of New Bedford in the bark *Elisha Dunbar* (circa 1854-55), brig *William Shepherd* (1867-68), and bark *Sacramento* (1868 - circa 1874). Aboard the *Clara Bell*, which furnished part of the background for *The Gam*, one of his charges was young Robert W. Weir, Jr., alias Robert Wallace, black sheep of the famous Weir family of American artists and an accomplished marine painter, caricaturist, and cartoonist in his own right (see Frank 1990; Frank 1991a). Along the way, Robbins found time to marry Hannah P. Warren and he survived to 1903. An appreciation by Zephaniah W. Pease appears in the posthumous 1913 edition of *The Gam*, 240-242. [Songs: #45, 46, 54, 135.]

Rogers, Benjamin Franklin (Chicago.) Seaman, schooner *Varnum H. Hill* of Provincetown, 1863-65. Some of his original verse composed aboard the *Varnum Hill* has been anthologized by Miller (1979), who is mistaken that this voyage was his first. In fact, his whaling career of three voyages coincides almost precisely with the Civil War era, from the spring of 1860 to just about the time of Lincoln's assassination in April 1865. His first was to the Davis Strait grounds in the ship *Ansel Gibbs* of Fairhaven, 1860-61; he next spent nine months in the ship *Northern Light* of New Bedford to Hudson Bay during 1861-62. Thus, by the time he composed the clever lyrics praised by Miller, Rogers was already a seasoned hand on an oar as well as with a pen. His one song, "The Schooner Varnum Hill," was included for its Portuguese interest in *Afonso, Mar de Baleias...*, 1998. [Song #147.]

Russell, Frederick H. (Dartmouth, Mass.) Born 1847; second mate, bark *Pioneer* of New Bedford, 1875-78. Russell was the songwriting collaborator of his younger cousin and shipmate George Howland (q.v.), with whom he authored the mildly pornographic ballad "Frozen Limb" (#17), portions of which appear in each of their parallel journals of their voyage together in the *Pioneer*. Russell was quite a literary fellow in his own way. In his journal he made a list of 59 novels and nine stories he read during the voyage, with reference to which Miller observes, "While he did read such popular and now classic novels as *The Black Tulip, The Woman in White, Oliver Twist,* and *Our Mutual Friend* most of Russell's list is comprised of sensational literature. At least eight stories are from Beadle's series of dime novels, and many have titles like *Adelaide the Avenger* and *Chenga the Cheyenne*"(Miller 1979, 18f). Russell was raised on a farm and made his first whaling voyage in the bark *Henry Taber* New Bedford (1864-65). He also made two or three other voyages, including in an officer's berth in the Westport bark *Sea Queen* (1870-73). His outing in the *Pioneer* appears to have been his last. He later worked as a machinist in New Bedford. [Song #17.]

Sanborn, George E. (Lowell, Mass.) Born circa 1836; seaman, bark *Waverly* of New Bedford, 1859-63. A year or two older than his shipboard song-collecting collaborators George M. Jones and Albert F. Handy (qq.v.), Sanborn is the only one of the three who had been whaling before, as a green hand in the Westport schooner *Kate Cory*, 1857-58. The *Waverly* voyage was his second and last. When he came ashore, he married a woman named Sarah from Watervleit, N.Y., and became the proprietor of George Sanborn & Co., house painters, in the town of Cohoes, N.Y. Somehow, it was he who retained custody of Jones and Handy's shipboard journal-copybook. In the back pages he later recorded some business transactions; there are also a few doodles by one J. Sanborn, Jr., probably a nephew or grandson, who must have got hold of the old ledger after the songs and business records were no longer considered important by the family. [Songs: see George M. JONES.]

Sears, E. C. (Montreal, Quebec.) Born circa the 1860s; seaman, schooner *Franklin* of New Bedford, 1889-91. An English-speaking Canadian from Montreal who served for a time in the Royal Navy, he first went to sea as a young man in 1883. According to his account, he arrived in New York in 1889 in the crew of a British skysail-yarder with an offer of a berth on the next cruise. But, as he explains, such vessels were rapidly becoming obsolete; and this one, which her owners no longer found useful, was sold, leaving Sears "on the beach" in Gotham. In the classic manner of the New Bedford whale fishery of a generation earlier, he was recruited in Manhattan, had his passage paid to the whaling mecca, and was shipped in the *Franklin*. He absorbed enough on this one relatively brief voyage — with a bit of additional research and the benefit of a long subsequent career in deepwater ships—to begin a book of essays and memoirs that was evidently planned to include much about whaling history and technology, and to concentrate even more heavily on the naval architecture, decorative arts, technology, and shipboard practices of the British naval and merchant services. The unpublished result was three volumes of pictures and essays (preserved in the Kendall Collection), an unfinished magnum opus laboriously compiled over a period of fifty years, from his youthful days at sea in the 1880s and '90s to a comfortable retirement in Montreal in the 1940s. It reveals Sears as one of the most eclectic, technically proficient, and versatile sailor-writer-artists of the many whose analogous work has survived. The sketchbooks overflow with over 400 pencil and ink drawings and watercolors (in various stages of completion) meant to illustrate brief "articles," written in his own hand, pertaining to all manner of things nautical: watercraft, deepwater and riverway commerce, naval and fisheries hardware, shipboard procedures, historic naval engagements and their influence on technology, rigging and bowsprit details through the ages, ancient and modern, European and nonwestern. Among all of these are only two songs, but good ones: the classic whaling song mirroring some of his own experiences in the whale fishery, "Blow Ye Winds" ("Tis Advertised in Boston"); and an original composition, entitled "Navy Song" ("We Ride Head to Wind"). [Songs: # 60, 139.]

Short, Robert, Jr. The manuscript credits him with being the author of "The Carpenter and the Maid," the lyrics of which were copied into an anonymous commonplace book on the ship *Warren* of Warren in 1832. He is presumed to have been in the crew, but no actual record of his presence has been discovered. [Song #15.]

Smith, Frederick Howland (Dartmouth, Mass.) Born 1840; boy and seaman, ship *Lydia* of Fairhaven, 1854-58; boatsteerer, bark *Roscius* of New Bedford, 1858-61; 18th Regiment of Massachusetts Volunteers, Union Army, 1862-64; third mate, bark *Herald* of New Bedford, 1865-66; second mate, bark *Herald* of New Bedford, 1866-69. A Renaissance Man among sailors, he had a colorful career in which music and the arts played a large part. An able whaleman and venerated whaling master for over thirty years, he was a collector of songs and tunes and a musician in his own right, scrimshaw artist, marlinspike seaman (maker of fancy ropework), and diarist whose work is preserved in the Kendall Collection, New Bedford Whaling Museum, Mystic Seaport, and private collections. His wife, Sallie (née Sarah G. Wordell, 1840-1896), who accompanied him on several voyages, seems to have been equally accomplished and collaborated with him on scrimshaw, fancywork, journal-keeping, and even celestial navigation. He first went whaling at age 14 as boy in the *Lydia*, and was promoted to seaman during the voyage. After a turn as boatsteerer in the *Roscius*, he enlisted in the Army and was mustered out in 1864. At the close of the war he signed on as third mate in the *Herald*, and was second mate on her next voyage, when he received a share of a reasonably good catch and a bonus for 70 pounds of ambergris that brought $97.50 per pound. As Smith puts it in his terse auto biography [see headnotes for Chapter 17]. It was on these first four voyages that he collected the songs and tunes anthologized here. Upon his return in the *Herald* in 1869, he was given his first command, bypassing the customary intermediate stint as chief mate; but the way this voyage in the bark *Hecla* of New Bedford turned out, his first command could well have been his last: The *Hecla* went aground and was wrecked on Bird Island in the Indian Ocean, with ship and cargo a total loss. But right afterwards the same owners gave him command of the bark *Petrel* (1871-74), then he and Sallie were in the bark *Ohio* (1874-78), and, following a hiatus of three and a half years, the bark *John P. West* (1882-86), "greasy luck" voyages in which Fred and Sallie maintained parallel journals, carved scrimshaw, did fancy ropework, and (though there is no specific record of it one way or another) probably continued the long-standing interest in music that he displayed in his earlier cruises. He retired from whaling at the hoary age of 46; Sallie died in 1896, and Fred later remarried. In 1900, he came out of retirement to become master and 2/32nds owner of the bark *Kathleen*, the same vessel on which, almost a half-century earlier, John and Lizzie Marble, their son Freddie, John's brother George Marble, and two of the mates (qq.v.) collected some of their songs. On this, his last active whaling voyage, Captain Smith returned in slightly over 15 months with a handsome catch. He retained his owner's share on the *Kathleen*'s next voyage, which turned out to be her last: one of the most infamous disasters in the annals of whaling. For, under the command of Thomas H. Jenkins, a monstrous fate befell her that had only two precedents—the ships *Essex* of Nantucket in 1820 and *Ann Alexander* of New Bedford in 1851 (just after *Moby Dick* was published): on 17 March 1902 the Kathleen was stove by a whale and foundered at sea; she "went down in less than a half hour. Captain and Mrs. Jenkins and the crew took to the boats" (Hegarty 1959, 35). While no lives were lost and some insurance compensation was likely forthcoming for the loss of vessel and cargo, Smith's shares had gone the way of the *Pequod*. The strange accident put an ironic end to a whaling career that, despite occasional setbacks, had been little less than brilliant. He seems to have spent his remaining years in quiet retirement, and died in 1924. See Chapter 17, "'Musick on the Brain': Frederick Howland Smith's Tune List"; and Frank, ed., *"Musick on the Brain": Frederick Howland Smith's Shipboard Tunes, 1854-69*; Kendall Monograph N° 12, Sharon, Mass., 2000. (Additional sources: F.H. Smith, [Autobiography] (see Chapter 18); Barbeau 1952; Frank 1991a; Malley 1983. [Songs: #28, 58, 99, 107, 112, 163-182 (tunes), 219, 235, 249, 277, 304, 345, 359, 412.]

Stanton, James E. (Rochester and Dartmouth, Mass.) Boy, ship *Emily Morgan* of New Bedford, 1837-41. He was born in Rochester, Mass., the son of Captain Giles E. Stanton and the former Hannah Beebe; the family later moved to Dartmouth. His juvenile journal chronicles the first of a dozen or more whaling voyages in a seafaring career that spanned 46 years, after which, in comfortable retirement, he was owner-agent for a series of whalers. A scrimshaw rolling pin by his hand is in the New Bedford Whaling Museum. His Protection Paper, issued in 1837 about a month before the *Emily Morgan* sailed, describes him as only 13 years of age, standing 4 feet 8 $^{3}/_{4}$ inches tall. His one song, "Jayne's Hair Tonic," a comic music-hall piece, was transcribed on this voyage, which he completed at age 17. He afterwards rose through the ranks, and beginning in 1853 commanded a series of voyages in the New Bedford barks *Pauline, Osprey, George, Martha, Cleone,* and *Tropic Bird*, retiring from active service in 1883 but continuing to own and manage whalers until around 1903. Two of his four brothers also became whaling captains. James's callow, Miranda-like journal of his maiden voyage not only provides a child's coda to whalemen's songs, but also offers an interesting contrast to the mature reflections and habituated professionalism of the much more senior officers and master mariners — men not unlike Stanton himself in later life. (Biographical sketches in Frank 1985, pp 1145f; and forthcoming in Frank, *Scrimshaw and Provenance*.) [Song #118.]

Stockbridge, George M. (Hanover, Mass.) Born in 1821, he transcribed one song on his maiden voyage, as a green hand in the New Bedford ship *Gratitude*, 1841-45. His second voyage was as boatsteerer in the New Bedford bark *Russell* (1845-49); he then disappears from the whaling records. [Song #202]

Sullivan, John C. (New York City.) Born circa 1834; third mate, bark *Kathleen* of New Bedford, 1857-60. Little is known of his career outside the *Kathleen* voyage, where he served under Captain John Marble and First Mate George D. Marble (qq.v.). But something is known of his character from Elizabeth Marble (q.v.), the captain's wife, who sailed with them in August 1857. In a letter written home less than one month out, she says, "Mr Sulavan the 3 mate [whom] I think is a very fine man ready and wilin to do his duty but I do not think he enjoys good health but he does not say but what he is well." Whatever Sullivan's physical condition may have been, a scrimshaw sperm whale tooth he engraved later in the voyage, inscribed to one "Miss F. Rioth" (Kendall Collection), indicates that he was lovesick at the time, missing his sweetheart. Lizzie Marble continued to hold him in high regard, he proved himself to be an able and faithful officer, and at the end of the voyage he may have been the author of "A Voyage on New Holland," a song of 71 stanzas that chronicles virtually the entire whaling cruise, to the tune of "Vilikins and His Dinah." The text survives in a complete transcription and a fragment found among Lizzie Marble's papers (Kendall Collection). The lyrics testify to the clever, whimsical, and sensitive nature of whatever man wrote it: though no literary paragon, he could deliver a compliment as well as a barb, knew the business of whaling well and professionally, and had an eye for the anachronistic and incongruous. He also knew how good he had it on the *Kathleen* under Captain Marble. It may be the best piece of its kind ever produced. (Biographical sketch in Frank 1991a.) [Song #161.]

Swain, Charles B. (Nantucket.) Born in 1829 or 1833, he was in the crew of the New Bedford bark *Cachalot* (1857-59) when he wrote two original Sailors' Farewell songs [#12 and #13] and an original parody of "Nelly Gray" [# 174D]. He was afterwards aboard the bark *Islander* of Nantucket, specific dates unknown. (Not to be confused with the Nantucket whaling master of the same name.) [Songs: #12, 13, 174.]

Swift, Clemet Nye (Acushnet, Mass.) Marine and animal painter, born in 1846, died in 1918, the son of whaling captain Rodolphus Nye Swift and younger brother of Rupert G.N. Swift [see below]. Both sons were given a substantial classical education at the Friends Academy in New Bedford. But, unlike Rupert, Clement never went whaling and never became a ship captain. Instead of going to sea he went to Paris to study art, lived for a while in France, exhibited at the Paris Salon and the National Academy in London from 1877 to 1896. Today, many of his pictures are in the permanent collection of the New Bedford Whaling Museum. He was an accomplished poet and short-story writer but remained unpublished in his lifetime, and it is not known whether it was he or Rupert who authored "Wood and Black-Skin" [#231], which is in Clement's hand but survives as an adjunct to Rupert's whaling journal; "The Parson's Narrative" [#133], which survives in two transcriptions in Rupert's journal; and "The Sailor Boy's Dream" [#330], which is also in Rupert's journal. See Rupert G.N. SWIFT, below.

Swift, Rupert G.N. (Acushnet, Mass.) Born circa 1845; seaman, ship *Context* of New Bedford, 1866-70. The son of whaling captain Rodolphus Nye Swift (see Frank 1991a; Frank 1995) and brother of marine artist and animal painter Clement Nye Swift (q.v.), R.G.N. Swift (he calls himself "Rupe" in his journal) was highly educated, articulate, well read in Shakespeare, reasonably fluent in Classical Latin, less so in Greek — altogether as literary as his father was mechanical and his brother artistic. But it is not clear which of the brothers wrote the poem "Wood and Black-Skin" [Appendix 3, #231], perhaps the finest narrative poem ever written about whaling and one that would have required an intimate knowledge of Yankee methods, whaleboat procedures, and sailor jargon. Rupert's two compelling comic songs, "The Parson's Narrative" [#133] and "The Sailor Boy's Dream" [#330], are devilishly clever, sea-wise, and highly amusing. After a brief whaling career in his youth, Rupert continued as a professional deepwater sailor and went on to skipper his own coastwise trading vessels. His songs and poems appear in conjunction with his journal of the *Contest*. [Songs: #133, 142, 230, 231.]

Taylor, Samuel. In August 1856 the ship *Samuel Robertson* sailed from Fairhaven on an elephant-sealing voyage to Antarctica, the first vessel from the New Bedford District to go sealing on Heard's Island. There she was joined by the schooner *Oxford* and bark *Arab* of Fairhaven. Crews were deposited ashore on various islands for the season, then were picked up in rotation in alternate seasons for the three vessels to go whaling in company. Taylor appears to have served on all three; and in his journal of a portion of the voyage (1858-60) he recorded the lyrics of his one ballad. No further details of his biography and career have been definitively ascertained, but he may have been the

Samuel A. Taylor of Pennsylvania, born circa 1828, a green hand in the ship *Nassau* of New Bedford (1850-53) and boatsteerer in the ship *Montezuma* of New Bedford (1854 - circa 1856). [Song #98.]

Tinkham, Daniel L. (Rochester, Mass.) Born 1832, he went whaling at 15-he was only 4 feet 7 inches (1.4 m) tall at the time-making a voyage as a green hand (1848-49) and another as seaman (1850-51) in the brig *America* of Mattapoisett. On his third voyage he was boatsteerer in the Mattapoisett bark *Samuel and Thomas* (1852-54); and it was on that voyage and his next one, as boatsteerer in the Mattapoisett brig *March* (1855-56), that he transcribed his songs. His last recorded voyage was as second mate of the schooner *Palmyra* of Mattapoisett (1858-60). [Songs: #29, 174, 240, 312, 380.]

Tray, Martha Ann. (Monmouth, Maine.) She signed and dated a copy text of Eliza Cook's "I'm Afloat, I'm Afloat" ("The Rover of the Sea") in the journal of George A. Gould (q.v.) in February 1846, about two months after his return from a whaling voyage in the ship *Columbia* of Nantucket, and just before he embarked on a career in the North Atlantic carrying trades. [Song # 204.]

Tuck, Joseph Washington. (Provincetown, Mass.) Born circa 1824; mate of the brig *E. Nickerson* (1850-52); mate (1852-53) and master (1857-58) of the bark *F. Bunchinia*. Provincetown, his home town and the home-port of all his vessels, was a small Cape Cod community, and Tuck's experiences in the local whale fishery were largely a family affair: he served under kinsmen on at least two voyages, owned a share in his vessel while still only a mate, and ascended to command a ship owned and managed by relatives. His wife, Maria C.B. Tuck, was related to other principals in the local whaling industry and to various owners of the vessels in which her husband served. His 1857-58 outing was actually the second of five consecutive voyages as master of the *F. Bunchinia* (1855-61), after which he left the whaling fleet and joined the Union Navy. As a deck officer in the Commodore McDonough up to the middle of 1864, he participated in several major campaigns and saw action on coastal patrol and blockade duty in the South. His two extensively illustrated journals and lavishly ornamented copybooks aboard the *E. Nickerson* and *F. Bunchinia*, in which later entries also recount his war experiences-were produced as souvenirs for presentation to Maria, and it was for her sake as well as his own that he committed a few songs to paper. He died in 1902. [Songs: #222, 235 277, 347.]

West, Benjamin L. As a young seaman in the ship *Leonidas* of Fairhaven during 1843-46, he wrote the lyrics of a song he called "West's Farewell," expressing his intention to join Zachary Taylor's expedition against Mexico. As no further record of him in the whale fishery has been found, it seems that he may actually have gone. [Song #22.]

Whalon, Jonathan (Westport, Mass.) He transcribed two songs on his seventh whaling voyage out of New Bedford (his first as master), aboard the ship *Henry Kneeland* during 1854-56. He was previously a green hand (1841-43) and boatsteerer (1843-44) in the bark *President*, boatsteerer in the ship *Sallie Ann* (1844-47), second mate in the ship *Phoenix* (1847-51), and mate of the *Henry Kneeland* (1851-54). [Songs #23, 78.]

Wicks, Asaph S. (Falmouth, Mass.) Green hand (1853-55), then seaman (1855-59), bark *John Dawson* of New Bedford. Considering this Cape Codder's long and distinguished career, which spanned the remarkable period of 53 years as a whaleman and whaling master, surprisingly little is known about him. Apart from his longevity at sea, an extraordinary feature of his career is that he spent the first 20 years of it in one vessel, rising from green hand to command six voyages in the *John Dawson*. He retired for a while during 1872-78, during part of which he acted as relief master of the *Greyhound*, resumed a more active role as master of the bark *Mars* (1878-81), and made his last voyage as skipper of the bark *Rousseau* (1882-86). The journal in which he transcribed his three songs is from the earliest part of his career. [Songs: #209, 211, 376.]

Wood, Horace (New Bedford.) Born in 1847, the son of merchant James B. Wood (J.B. Wood & Co., Commercial Wharf, New Bedford), he and his brother James, Jr., served in the Union Navy during the Civil War, Horace aboard the *Oneida* and James in the *Matanzas*. Horace then made two Atlantic Ocean whaling voyages, the first as a green hand in the New Bedford bark *Andrews* (1866-67), when he transcribed seven songs in his journal, and the other as a boatsteerer in the New Bedford schooner *John W. Dodge* (1868-69). He later married Ella M. Wood and worked as an engineer in New Bedford. [Songs #7, 38, 67, 173, 316, 354, 365.]

Worth, George (Siasconset Village, Nantucket.) Born circa 1846, as a young seaman in the 1860s he contributed a text of "The Lily of the Lake" ("The Lily of Lake Champlain") to the journal of William Keith (q.v.). [Song #10.]

Wright, Dean C. (Avon, N.Y.) Born circa 1818; boatsteerer, ship *Benjamin Rush* of Warren, 1841-45. This voyage was his third and probably his last, but the "Commonplace Book" he compiled during its course proposed to include "a little bit of everything-poetry, prose, anecdotes, tales, etc." Much of what he did produce remains of considerable interest today: firsthand essays and philosophical reflections on "Whales, Whaling, and Whalemen" and the plight of "A Boatsteerer" (complete annotated text with illustrations and biographical notes in Frank 1991b, pp. 2-12 and 31; drawings also illustrated in Martin 1983). His one song is a remarkable piece, of interest to naval historians, students of James Fenimore Cooper, and devotees of Melville's sources for Billy-Budd: a full-scale contemporaneous ballad of the famous *Somers* mutiny, which actually unfolded while Wright was aboard the *Benjamin Rush* — told from a young mariner's sympathetic point of view (see Frank 1998c). [Song #56.]

APPENDIX 7
Inventory of Additional Song Texts Found in the Manuscripts

Key to Listings (alphabetical by title)

N°. **TITLE** [Alternate and Variant Titles] (Reference numbers from relevant taxonomies)
¶ *First line of text.* Source of the text (unless otherwise indicated, refers to manuscripts in the Kendall Collection)
(A) First version, where more than one text was found: *First line.* Source. (Number of stanzas / number of lines each stanza).
(B) Second version, where more than one text was found: *First line.* Source. (Number of stanzas / number of lines each stanza).
(C) Third version; etc.
Type / classification of song. w: author of the words (birth-death dates, if known); m: composer of the music (birth-death dates, if known). Bibliography: beginning with song indexes; then taxonomic and bibliographic compilations; then anthologies of songs, scholarly works, literary citations; other remarks. For full citations refer to the general bibliography.

Symbols and Abbreviations Used in the Listings

¶	Manuscript citation in the Kendall Collection	m:	music (air; melody) composed by…
(A)	First version (of two or more collected)	misc.	miscellaneous
(B)	Second version (of two or more collected); etc.	MS	manuscript
Am.	American	n.c.	no city indicated
Br.	British	n.d.	no date indicated
btstr.	Boatsteerer (harpooneer)	n.p	no page number(s) indicated
Ch.	Chapter	Ntk.	Nantucket, Massachusetts
Chs.	Chapters	p.	page
cho.	chorus	pp.	pages
Coll.	Collection	ref.	refrain
f.	following page	schr.	schooner
ff.	following pages	w:	words (lyrics) written by…
frag.	fragment	w&m:	words and music by…

Hailing Ports and Home Towns Referred to in the Notes

Boston	Capital and metropolis of Massachusetts, and principal port of New England; a minor whaling port.
Dartmouth	Massachusetts; a whaling port and shipbuilding center adjacent to New Bedford.
Edgartown	On Martha's Vineyard island, Massachusetts; previously known as Holmes' Hole.
Fairhaven	Across the Acushnet River from New Bedford, Mass. Melville sailed from here in the *Acushnet* in 1841.
Fall River	Massachusetts; a textile-manufacturing town, also home to a few whaleships and many whalemen.
Falmouth	Massachusetts; on the southernmost part of the Atlantic Ocean coast of Cape Cod.
Holmes' Hole	Former name of Vineyard Haven, Marthas Vineyard, Massachusetts.
Hudson	New York State; riverport on the Hudson River midway between Poughkeepsie and Albany.
Marion	Whaling and shipbuilding town adjacent to Mattapoisett and Rochester in the Sippican region of Massachusetts.
Mattapoisett	Massachusetts; shipbuilding and whaling town, adjacent to Rochester on the south (Buzzard's Bay) coast.
Nantucket	Nantucket Island, Massachusetts; the quintessential and most-storied American whaling port.
New Bedford	Massachusetts, adjacent to Buzzard's Bay; the preeminent capital of the 19th-century whaling industry.
New Haven	Connecticut; a major cultural center and minor whaling port on Long Island Sound.
New London	Connecticut; a major whaling port at the mouth of the Thames River estuary on Long Island Sound.
New York	Metropolis and principal port of the United States; a significant whaling port up to the 1850s.
Newburg	New York; one of several minor upstate whaling ports on the Hudson River.
Newport	Aquidneck Island, Rhode Island; at one time important in the West Indies, coastwise, and foreign trades.
Providence	Capital and metropolis of Rhode Island, at the head of navigation on Narragansett Bay; a minor whaling port.
Provincetown	Cape Cod, Massachusetts, noted for its latter-day sperm-whale fishery in schooners and local oil industry.
Rochester	Massachusetts; shipbuilding and whaling town, adjacent to Mattapoisett on the south (Buzzard's Bay) coast.
Salem	Massachusetts, on the North Shore of Massachusetts Bay; leading China Trade port, sometime whaling port.
San Francisco	The first metropolis of California and the preeminent whaling center and entrepôt of the West Coast.
Stonington	Important whaling, fur-sealing, and elephant-sealing port in New London County, Connecticut.
Warren	Rhode Island; the state's principal whaling port, on Narragansett Bay.
Wellfleet	Cape Cod, Massachusetts; a small fishing and coastwise-trading port.
Wilmington	Metropolis of Delaware, on the Delaware River below Philadelphia; a minor whaling port in the 1840s.

Manuscripts Referenced in Appendix 7

Anonymous	"Scraps, Odd-thoughts & Tag Ends of a Rope Hauler," ship *Warren* of Warren, 1832
Bartley	Theodore D. Bartley, ship *California* of N.B., 1851-54
Beden	Cornelius H. Beden, ship *Massachusetts* of N.B., 1851-53; ship *South America* of N.B., 1855
Braley	Papers of Eleanor Braley and Jason L. Braley, N.B.
	Braley family copybook and Braley family papers, n.d.
Bryant	Thomas R. Bryant, Jr., ship *Elizabeth* of N.B., 1847-51
Cleveland	George S. Cleveland, second/ first mate, ship *Charles* of N.B., 1837-39
Colton	James S. Colton, bark *Tenedos* of New London, 1840-43
Coquin	John S. Coquin, bark *Pacific* of N.B., 1867-68; merchant voyages out of Boston, 1860's-'70s
Davis	William H. Davis, bark *Midas* of N.B., 1861-65
Donahue	James Donahue, ship *Atlantic* of Ntk., 1850-54
Fullmoon	Sylvanus C. Fullmoon, ship *Nimrod* of N.B., 1842-45
Gallup	Benjamin F. Gallup, bark *South America* of N.B., 1855-59.
Gifford	George H. Gifford, brig *Elizabeth* of Westport, 1837-38
Gillaspia	William Gillaspia, ship *Atlantic* of Ntk., 1850-53
Gorham	Joseph R. Gorham, ship's cooper (transcribed lyrics in the journal of his shipmate George A. Gould, ship *Columbia* of Nantucket, circa 1845)
Handy	Albert F. Handy, bark *Waverly* of N.B., 1859-63 (see also Jones & Handy)
Hopkins	Stephen O. Hopkins, ship *Rosalie* of Warren, 1843
Hughson	Robert Nathaniel Hughson, bark *Java* of N.B., 1857-60
Jones (George)	George M. Jones, bark *Waverly* of N.B., 1859-63 (see also Jones & Handy)
Jones (John)	John Jones, steward, ship *Eliza Adams* of N.B., 1852
Jones & Handy	George M. Jones and Albert F. Handy, bark *Waverly* of N.B., 1859-63
Jones et al.	George M. Jones, Albert F. Handy and George E. Sanborn, , bark *Waverly* of N.B., 1859-63
Keith	William H. Keith, circa 1865-71
Kirby	Nicholas Kirby Jr., First Mate, 1850-52
Kirwin	Edward J. Kirwin, cooper, bark *William Gifford* of N.B., 1872-73
Lepetit	Eugene A. Lepetit, ship *Josephine* of N.B., 1859-62
Marble (I)	Papers of Elizabeth Marble, Fall River: inscribed after the fact in the journals of John Marble and George Marble, various vessels *America* of Hudson, N.Y., 1839-61
	Elizabeth Marble, Fall River: misc. family papers on shipboard and ashore, circa 1845-61
	Elizabeth Marble or George D. Marble, Fall River (inscribed after the fact in the journal of George D. Marble, ship *Le Baron* of Rochester, 1837-39).
	journal of John Marble, ship *America* of Hudson, N.Y., 1839-40
	Marble family copy text
Marble (II)	John G. Marble, Rhode Island, circa 1846-47: inscribed in the journal of Stephen O. Hopkins, ship *Rosalie* of Warren, 1843; bark *Perseverance* of Providence, 1849
Merrill	Frederick Merrill, bark *Janus* of N.B., 1875-76; and schooner *Eothen* of New York, 1878
Mills	George Edgar Mills, third mate, "The Boatman's Song," obtained from William Painter, ship *James Loper* of Ntk., "bound home off Bermuda Island," 1860
	George Edgar Mills, third mate, bark *Aurora* of Westport, 1858
Peters	Joseph Peters, ship *Congaree* of Stonington, Connecticut, 1846-50
Pettey	Henry Tripp Pettey, bark *Mary Ann* of N.B., 1853-55; bark *Chili* of N.B., 1856-59
Piper	George W. Piper, ship *Europa* of Edgartown, 1868-70
Poole	William H. Poole, ship *Minnesota* of New York, 1868-70.
Reed	Israel Reed, bark *Black Eagle* of N.B., 1860-61
Reynolds	Richard C. Reynolds, boatsteerer, ship *Janus* of N.B., 1842-44
Ritchie	Daniel K. Ritchie, second mate, ship *Israel* of N.B., 1843-45
Sanborn	George E. Sanborn—see Jones et. al
Smith	Frederick H. Smith, btstr., bark *Roscius* of N.B., 1858-61
Tinkham	Daniel L. Tinkham, transcribed between voyages in the bark *Samuel and Thomas* (1852) and brig *March* (1855-56) of Mattapoisett, Mass.
Tuck	Captain Joseph W. Tuck, bark *F. Bunchinia* of Provincetown, 1857-58
Wicks	Asaph S. Wicks, bark *John Dawson* of N.B., 1853-58
Wood	Horace Wood, bark *Andrew* of New Bedford, 1866-67

233. ADIEU MY NATIVE LAND, ADIEU
Adieu my native land adieu. Hughson, bark *Java*, 1857-60 (3/8)

There are two parlor songs of this name, one by someone named Chandler (Baring-Gould, *English Minstrelsie*), the other by Joseph Labitzky (McCaskey v3); Huntington 1964, 238f identifies this with the latter. SI; PSI.

234. AMERICA [National Hymn; My Country, 'Tis of Thee] (Frank 1985, #d59)
(A) *My country 'tis of thee, Sweet land of liberty.* Piper, ship *Europa*, 1868-70. (4/5)
(B) *ditto.* Piper, ship *Europa* , 1868-70. (transcribed as 4/2, but generally the same as A)
¶ Title entered (but no text given) by Keith, circa 1865-71.

American patriotic song in emulation of the English national anthem "God Save the King" by Henry Carey (English, 1685-1743). w: Samuel Francis Smith (American, 1808-1895); m.: *God Save the King.* SI; Dichter #1, #2; Dichter & Shapiro 46; very widely anthologized. Luce (1) presents a variant tune, composed by one James J. McCabe, that apparently had some currency in the Navy. Lawrence 262; Sonneck 1909, 73-78.

235. ANNIE LAURIE [Bonnie Annie Laurie] (Frank 1985, #85)
(A) *Maxwelton's Banks are bonnie.* Tuck, bark *F. Bunchinia*, 1857-58. (3/8)
(B) *Maxwell braes are bonny.* Smith, bark *Roscius*, 1858-61. (3/4)
(C) *Maxwelton' braes are bonnie.* Keith, circa 1865-71. (3/8)

Scottish parlor song. w: William Douglas of Fingland, 17th C.; m: Lady John Scott [née Alicia Anne Spottiswoode] (1810-1900), circa 1838. Popularized by Jenny Lind, notably on her American tour of 1850-51, the song has had an extraordinarily extensive publishing history and remains in print and in wide circulation today. SI; PSI; PSIS; SIC #3405; Dichter #1017, #1477; Dichter & Larrabee #1112, #1114; *Beadles' N° 1*; Gleadhill 80; *Good Old Songs* I:81; H.K. Johnson 364; Miller's 7; Wier 1918, 28; etc.

236. ANNIE OF THE VALE
The young stars are glowing. Poole, ship *Minnesota*, 1868-70. (12+ lines)

Parlor song, circa 1861; w: George P. Morris (1802-1864); m: John R. Thomas (1829-1896). Dichter #1554; Dichter & Larrabee #775; *Beadle 8.*

237. THE APPEAL [*version of* The Missionary Hymn, *q.v.*] (Frank 1985, #39)
From many a noble vessel. Papers of Eleanor Braley and Jason L. Braley, N.B. (6/4)

American hymn in 14s & 12s meter. w: Mrs. C.T. Putnam, published in *The Sailor's Magazine*, 18:2 (Oct. 1845), 22. m: either the air for *The Missionary Hymn* by Lowell Mason (1792-1872), circa 1829, as specified in *The Sailor's Magazine* and the Braley MS; or the air entitled *The Millennial Dawn* (*The Morning Light Is Breaking*) by George James Webb (1803-1887), circa 1844, as given in Stowe's *Ocean Melodies* (1852). Butterworth 179.

238. ARABY'S DAUGHTER (Moore)
Farewell farewell to the araby daughter. Beden, ships *Massachusetts* and *South America* 1851-55.

Poem by Thomas Moore (Irish, 1779-1852) in *Lalla Rookh*, for which George Kiallmark composed the tune, which is also used for the hymn "Requiem on the Death of a Mariner" (q.v.). SI; SI2; SIC; Dichter #942, #979; McCaskey v5; H.K. Johnson 307; Wier 1918, 22.

239. AWAY DOWN EAST
There is a land of notions, of apple sauce and greens. Keith, circa 1865-71. (7/4)

Classic minstrel piece, a signature song of the Hutchinson Family of New Hampshire, circa 1846; w: Arthur Morrell; m: E.L. White. Dichter #686; *Beadles' N° 10*. See Brink, *Harps in the Wind*, 1947; Tawa 71-75.

240. AWAY DOWN IN OLD VIRGINIA
Away down in old Virginia. Tinkham, transcribed between voyages, "March the 11, 1855." (3/4 + cho./4)
Unidentified minstrel-type song.

241. THE BACHELORS SONG
Im a jolly old rebel as ever you met / And I live the happiest life. Colton, bark *Tenedos*, 1840-43 (8/4).
Unidentified.

242. THE BALLET GIRL
I once did know a ballet girl. Keith, circa 1865-71. (5/11 + 7)

Minstrel-era song. There is a text version from the repertoire of Dan Lewis—who was evidently an actual black man, rather than a mere blackface performer—in *Dan Lewis' "Oh She Is" Songster* (Chicago & Boston: White, Smith & Co., 1881).

243. THE BAREFOOT OLD LADY (Frank 1985, #d1)
The old lady sat in her rocking chair. Braley family copybook (stanzas undifferentiated).
Unidentified; not found elsewhere; air unknown. Refrain: "Darn, darn, darn."

244. BE KIND TO THE LOVED ONES AT HOME (Frank 1985, #77)
(A) *Be kind to thy father, for when thou wert young.* Papers of Elizabeth Marble. (4/8)
(B) *Be kind to your father, for when thou wert young.* Piper, ship *Europa*, 1868-70. (4/8)
(C) *Be kind to thy father.* Keith, circa 1865-71. (4/8)

American parlor song, circa 1847; w&m usually attributed to Isaac Baker Woodbury (1819-1858), but some editions of the sheet music indicate "Author unknown. Music by I.B. Woodbury." SI; Dichter #52, #53; Dichter & Larrabee #31; Dichter & Shapiro 140; Century 19; Rosenberg #80. Beadle's N° 6; McCaskey v3; *Good Old Songs* I:11; *Heart Songs* 488; Spaeth 1927, 165.

245. **BEAUTIFUL ISLE OF THE SEA**
  Beautiful isle of the sea. Keith, circa 1865-71. (3/3 + 1)
Minstrel song; w: George Cooper (1838-1927); w: J.R. Thomas (1829-1896). SI; SIC; Dichter & Shapiro 140; *Heart Songs* 224.

246. **BEGONE! DULL CARE** [Dull Care] (Frank 1985, #d3)
  Begone dull care I pray thee begone from me. Piper, ship *Europa*, 1868-70. (6 lines)
English song. w: authorship unknown; m: 17th-century air *The Queen's Jig*; first published in *Playford's Musical Companion*, 1687 (Baring-Gould 1895 VI:20; Mackay 58); known as "Begone *Old* Care" until 1793 (Baring-Gould). SI; Amateur 50; Grigg's 63; H.K. Johnson 454; *Singer's Gem* 224; Wier 1918, 32.

247. **BELIEVE ME IF ALL THOSE ENDEARING YOUNG CHARMS** (Moore)
  Believe me if all those endearing young charms. Pettey, barks *Mary Ann* and *Chili*, 1853-59. (4/4)
Irish lyric song. w: Thomas Moore (1779-1852); m: English air "My Lodging It Is On the Cold Ground." Very widely anthologized (e.g., Chappell, Hullah, Molloy, Page, etc.).

248. **BELLE BRANDON** (Frank 1985, #d4)
  Beneath the tree by the margin of a woodland. Jones & Handy, bark *Waverly*, 1859-63. (3/8 + cho.)
American parlor song. w: T. Ellwood Garrett; m: Francis Woolcott; 1854. PSI; Dichter & Shapiro 140; Rosenberg #81; Beadle's N° 1; Fife #48; De Ville #93.

249. **THE BLUE JUNIATA** [Bright Alfarata] (Frank 1985, #d5)
  Wild roved an Indian girl bright Alfaretta. Smith, bark *Roscius*, 1858-61. (14 lines)
American parlor song inspired by a river in Pennsylvania. w&m: Marion Dix Sullivan, 1844. Listed by Laws among "ballad-like pieces" (I:277). SI; SIC #3673; PSI; Dichter & Shapiro 74; Rosenberg #136; Beadle's N° 6; McCaskey v3; *Heart Songs* 154; *Good Old Songs* I:93; H.K. Johnson 279; Wier 1918, 36.

250. **BOBBING AROUND**
  All you fellows just listen to me. Reynolds, ship *Janus*, 1842-44; possibly after the fact, circa the 1850s.
Not identified. Evidently not the song of the same title by W.J. Florence (SIC #1086).

251. **BONNIE DOON** [Ye Banks and Braes] (Burns) (Frank 1985, #d7)
  Ye banks and braes of bonnie doon. Piper, ship *Europa*, 1868-70. (2/8)
Scottish song. w: Robert Burns (1759-1796); m: James Miller. SI; Rosenberg #60; Century 20; Amateur 62; Am. Songster 242; *Beadles' N° 9*; *Good Old Songs* I:162; Grigg's 58; Mackay 275; Miller's 144; McCaskey v1; H.K. Johnson 343; Wier 1918, 43.

252. **BONNIE ELOISE** [Bonny Eloise; The Belle of the Mohawk Vale] (Frank 1985, #86)
(A) *Sweet are the scenes / Where the Mohawk gently glides.* Jones & Handy, bark *Waverly*, 1859-63. (2, irregularly transcribed + cho./4)
(B) *Sweet is the vale where the Mohawk / Gently glides on its Clear winding way to the sea.* Papers of Elizabeth Marble, circa 1845-61. (3/4 + cho./4)
(C) *O sweet is the vale....* Piper, ship *Europa*, 1868-70. (3/4 + cho:/4)
(D) *ditto.* Keith, circa 1865-71. (3/4 + cho./4)
American parlor song, 1858. w: John Rogers Thomas (1829-1896); m: C. W. Elliott. SI; SIC #3735; PSI; PSIS; Dichter & Shapiro 140; Beadle's N° 8; Beadle's Dime Melodist 5; *Heart Songs* 108; Wier 1918, 51.

253. **BOUND HOME** (Frank 1985, #179)
  Our ship no longer braves the seas. Gorham, in the journal of shipmate George A. Gould, ship *Columbia*, circa 1845. (7/4)
Original end-of-voyage poem by whaleman Joseph Gorham of Nantucket, possibly intended to be sung, air unknown. Miller 26. See "We'll Soon Be There" (#42).

254. **THE BOWLD SOLDIER BOY** (Frank 1985, #d6)
  There is not a trade going worth showing or knowing. Piper, ship *Europa*, 1868-72. (3/11+)
w&m: Samuel Lover (1797-1868); 1845. SI; Dichter #1500; McCaskey v7; *Heart Songs* 241; H.K. Johnson 446; Wier 1918, 42.

255. **LE BRAVO** [The Graggart; The Outlaw] (Frank 1985, #72)
  Devant St. March un homme est en priè re. Lepetit, ship *Josephine*, 1859-62. (4/4/10)
Lyrical song concerning an outlaw (possibly a political expatriate) lurking in the shadows of Venice. Text and journal in French. Not found elsewhere; possibly an original composition by whaleman Lepetit; air unknown.

256. **BREAK IT GENTLY TO MY MOTHER**
  See! ere the sun sinks behind those hills. Keith, circa 1865-71. (2/8 + cho./4 + 7 lines intro)
Civil War sentimental song inspired by a death at the Battle of Gettysburg in 1863; w: Mary A. Griffith; m: Frederick Buckley. Dichter & Larrabee #885; *Buckley's* 12.

257. **BRIGHT-EYED LITTLE NELL OF NARRAGANSETT BAY**
  Full well do I remember my boyhoods happy hours. Coquin, 1860's-'70s. (3/8 + cho./4)
Anonymous sentimental song. SI2; Beadle's N° 7; Rosenberg #135; Spaeth 1927, 30.

258. **THE BROKEN CIRCLE**
  We morn for the loved and cherished. Gillaspia, ship *Atlantic*, 1850-53. (2/8)

259. **THE BROKEN HEART** (Moore) (Frank 1985, #d8)
She is far from the land where her young hero sleeps. Braley family copybook. (4/4)
w: Thomas Moore (1779-1852), from *Irish Melodies;* m: Irish air *Open the Door.* SI; SIC #6012 A&B; Miller's.

260. **BROTHERS FAINTING AT THE DOOR** (Frank 1985, #d9)
Yonder comes a weary soldier. Braley family copybook. (3/8 + cho./4)
American parlor song. The MS attributes the song to Belle F. King; the sheet music (1863) ascribes the lyrics to E. Bowers and the music to P.B. Isaacs; Century and Ditson mention Isaacs but neither Bowers nor King. Dichter #281.

261. **THE BURIAL OF SIR JOHN MOORE** (Frank 1985, #43)
(A) *Not a drum was heard...* John G. Marble, 1846-47: journal of Stephen O. Hopkins, 1843-49. (8/4)
(B) *Not a drum was heard...* Piper, ship *Europa*, 1868-70.
Parlor song. w: Rev. Charles Wolfe (1791-1823), Irish-born Anglican priest, 1817. m: (1) Thomas Williams (British, 1761-1844), "The Soldier's Grave: Monody on the Death of Sir John Moore," circa 1827; (2) John Barnett (1802-1890). SI; *Am. Singer* 105; Davidson II:380; Farmer 18; Grigg's 270; H.K. Johnson 560; Miller's 102; O'Reilly 672; *Universal* II: 241. Evidently not found in tradition elsewhere. Not to be confused with the song text by Frome, "The Death of Sir John Moore" (*Universal* III:189).

262. **CALIFORNIA GOLD-DIGGER'S SONG** (Frank 1985, #64)
Bear me far from all the pleasures. Papers of Elizabeth Marble, inscribed after the fact in the journal of John Marble, ship *America* of Hudson, N.Y., 1839-40.
American gold rush song about the hardships and futility of prospecting for gold. Sheet music for something called "California gold digger," ascribed to Barker [? George A. Barker (1812-1876)], was published by Oliver Ditson of Boston by 1852. (Not the same song as "The California Gold Diggers: Song and Chorus," m: adapted and arranged by Nathan Barker, w: Jesse Hutchinson [Jr.], first line: *We've formed our band and we're all well mann'd;* Boston: S. W. Marsh, 1849.)

263. **CANADIAN BOAT SONG** [The Boatman's Song] (Moore)
Faintly as tolls the evening chime. Mills: "The Boatman's Song," obtained from William Painter, ship *James Loper* of Nantucket, "bound home off Bermuda Island," 1860.
Poem by Thomas Moore (Irish, 1779-1852), sung to a French-Canadian *voyageur* air. SI; Rosenberg #113; Amateur 30; Beadle's N° 9; McCaskey v4; H.K. Johnson 204; Mackay 363 (includes Moore's own extensive notes on the tune); *Naval Songs* 80; Wier 1918; etc. There is also a setting by Maurice Arnold (*Laurel Song Book*).

264. **THE CAPTAIN WITH THE WHISKERS** (Frank 1985, #d10)
As they marched through the town withe their banners so gay. Piper, ship *Europa*, 1868-70. (4/8)
English parlor song. w: Thomas Haynes Bayly (1797-1839); m: Sidney Nelson (1800-1862); n.d. PSI; Dichter & Shapiro 120; Rosenberg #169; Randolph #228, II:287; Warner #69.

265. **THE CARRIER DOVE** [The Captive Knight; The Spirit Bird] (Frank 1985, #109)
(A) *Fly away to my native Land sweet dove.* Ritchie, ship *Israel*, 1843-45: "This song given me by Andrew Haskins of Middlebury [Vermont], one of the crew of the ship Israel. He left [the ship] at Ghoa & shipped as a Musician on board of the U.S. Frigate Brandewin [*Brandywine*], Comodr. F.O. Parker." (3/8)
(B) *Fly away to my native Land sweet dove.* Elizabeth Marble or George Marble, inscribed after the fact in the journal of George Marble, ship *Le Baron*, 1837-39. (3/8)
(C) *Fly away to my na---tive Land sweet dove.* Marble family copy text showing evidence of transcription from sheet music with musical notation and syllabic divisions of words, for singing: inscribed after the fact in the journal of John Marble, ship *America*, 1839-40. (3/8)
(D) *Fly away to the promised land, sweet dove.* Marble family copy text entitled "The Spirit Bird," in the same hand as C: inscribed after the fact in the journal of John Marble, ship *America* of Hudson, N.Y., 1839-40. (5/8)
(E) *Fly away to my native land sweet dove.* Mills, bark *Aurora*, 1856-59. (4/8)
(F) *I can bear in a dungeon to waste away my youth.* Mills, bark *Aurora*, 1858: an edited and (judging from Mills's other literary efforts elsewhere) deliberately corrupted, transformed text. (4/8)
Parlor song, circa 1836-39. w: anonymous; m: Daniel Johnson. SI; PSI; Dichter #1382; Dichter & Shapiro 58; Beadle's N° 6; McCaskey v2; *Heart Songs* 486; H.K. Johnson 100; Wier 1918, 81. Not to be confused with "The Captive Knight" by Mrs. Hemans (H.K. Johnson 533). A sequel, "Answer to the Carrier Dove," composed by James G. Meader with words "by a lady," appeared in 1841. Marble family text E is a derivative parody on a sacred theme, authorship unknown.

266. **CARRY ME BACK TO OLD VIRGINNY** (Frank 1985, #d11)
On the floating scow in Old Virginny. Piper, ship *Europa*, 1868-70. (3/8 + cho./4)
Minstrel song. w&m: attributed to Edwin P. Christy (1815-1862), circa 1850. SI; Wier 1918, 75. Not to be confused with a later song of the same title by the African-American songwriter James A. Bland, 1878, adopted as the state song of Virginia in 1840.

267. **A CHILD'S CONFIDENCE** (Frank 1985, #137)
It was when the sea with an awful roar. Piper, ship *Europa*, 1868-70. (1/12 = 3/4)
Anonymous poem text suspiciously like "The Tempest" by James T. Fields (Bryant II:585; *Sailor's Magazine,* 25:11 [Jul 1849], 342), which probably inspired it; air unknown. Not found elsewhere.

268. **THE CHILD'S WISH**
O I long to lie, dear mother. Keith, circa 1865-71. (5/8)
American sentimental song. Beadle's N° 1. See also "The Dying Child's Request (w: Mrs. Mary Scrimzeour Whitaker; m: Scottish air "House of Glams") in *Singer's Companion,* 142.

269. **CHRISTIAN CONSOLATION** (Frank 1985, #d12)
Jesus, I my cross have taken. Piper, ship *Europa*, 1868-70. (4/8)
Standard-type hymn in 8s. & 7s. double meter, with the tune unspecified.

270. **COME HOME, FATHER** (Frank 1985, #d13)
(A) *O father, dear father, come home with me now.* Inscribed long after the fact in the journal of Joseph Peters, ship *Congaree* of Stonington, Connecticut, 1846-50. (fragment of 10 lines)
(B) *Father, dear father, come home with me now.* Keith, circa 1865-71. (3/8 + 1/4 + cho./2)
Temperance song, one of "two poems that the modern public considers the apex of temperance verse" (Ewing 16; the other is "The Face on the Floor"); w&m: Henry Clay Work (1832-1884); featured in the play by William W. Pratt, *Ten Nights in a Barroom*, 1858. SI; SIC #4105; PSI; PSIS; Rosenberg #226 A-D; Dichter #1965; Dichter & Larrabee #1069; Dichter & Shapiro 141; Beadle's Nº 15; *Heart Songs* 230; Wier 1918, 83; Randolph #308, II:396; Spaeth 1926, 57; Turner 264. "A song like 'Come Home, Father' is subject to at least four interpretations: (1) it can be taken as a lesson in temperance; (2) it can be sung satirically to disparage th etemperance movement, as it often is today; (3) it can be sung to ridicule the bathetic ballad, as it might be at a modern Sunday school party; or (4) it can be presented as simply a bathetic song. It was in this last fashion, probably, that it was put into 19th-century songbooks" (Ewing 16).

271. **COTTAGE BY THE SEA** (Frank 1985, #d14)
(A) *Childhoods days now past before me.* Davis, bark *Midas*, 1861-65. (3/8)
(B) *Childhood's days now pass before me.* Keith, circa 1865-71. (3/8)
(C) *ditto.* Poole, ship *Minnesota*, 1868-70. (3/8)
American parlor song. w&m: John Rogers Thomas (1829-1896), 1856. SI; Dichter & Shapiro 142; Beadle's Nº 4; *Good Old Songs* II:152; Kieser 73.

272. **DEAREST MAE** (Frank 1985, #d16)
O come and listen darkies. Piper, ship *Europa*, 1868-70. Title: "Dearest May." (4/8 + cho./3)
American minstrel song. w: Francis Lynch; m: (1) L.V.H. Crosby; (2) James Power, "as sung by the Harmoneons," 1847. SI; Brown Coll. 3&5:#405; Century 22; Dichter & Larrabee #107; Beadle's Nº 6; McCaskey v6; *Good Old Songs* II:60; *Heart Songs* 158; *Minstrel Songs* 143; Morrison & Whitney; Noble; Wier 1918, 109.

273. **DEAR MOTHER, I'VE COME HOME TO DIE**
Kind friends, I bid you adieu. Keith, circa 1865-71. (3/4)
Civil War-era sentimental song, 1863; w: E. Bowers; m: Henry Tucker. PI; Dichter #284; Dichter & Larrabee #770, #891, #970; Note the comic parody "Dear Mother, I've Come Home to Eat" (Charles Magnus song-sheet, Dichter & Larrabee #761).

274. **THE DEAREST SPOT ON EARTH IS HOME** [The Dearest Spot of Earth... ; Home] (Frank 1985, #d17)
¶ *The dearest spot on earth to me is home sweet home.* Marble family copybook. Title: "Home." (2/6 + cho./2)
¶ Title entered (but no text given) by Keith, circa 1865-71.
American parlor song, 1852; w&m: William Thomas Wrighton. Largely derived from "The Dearest, Sweetest Spot Is Home," by J. Sullivan (Universal I:287) and "Home, Sweet Home" (q.v.). The MS is inscribed "By Miss Ida Philips," perhaps in reference to Elizabeth Marble's immediate source. SI; SIC #4117; PSI; Century 22; Ditson 14; Dichter & Larrabee #108, #775, #1070; Beadle's Dime Melodist 36; McCaskey v1; *Heart Songs* 8; Wier 1918, 207.

275. **DEATH AND THE DRUNKARD** (Frank 1985, #d18)
His form was fair, his cheek was health. Piper, ship *Europa*, 1868-70. (57 lines)
Anonymous temperance song, articulately construed on themes of bankruptcy, ruin, remorse, and redemption. "There were dozens of compositions called 'The Dying Drunkard' or 'Death of the Drunkard' depicting the hopelessness of the situation..." (Ewing 178). Not found elsewhere.

276. **DEATH OF A SHIPMATE** (see Frank 1985, #36)
¶ Cited by Jones as having been sung in conjunction with a burial at sea aboard the bark *Waverly* of N.B., 1863.
Anonymous hymn in 8s. meter. "I rejoice for a brother deceased," in a copy of *Seamen's Hymns and Devotional Assistant* (New York: American Seamen's Friend Society, 1859, #446), embossed in gold on the cover, "New Bedford Seamen's Bethel" (3/8).

277. **DO THEY MISS ME AT HOME?** [We Miss Thee at Home] (Frank 1985, #79)
(A) *Do they miss me at home, do they miss me.* Tuck, bark *F. Bunchinia*, 1858. (4/8)
(B) *ditto.* Hughson, bark *Java*, 1857-60. (4/8)
(C) *ditto.* Mills, bark *Aurora*, 1858. (4/8)
(D) *ditto.* Smith, btstr., bark *Roscius*, 1858-61. (4/8)
(E) *ditto.* Piper, ship *Europa*, 1868-70. (4/8)
American parlor song, 1852. w: Caroline Atherton [née Briggs] Mason (1823-1890); m: Sidney Martin Grannis (1827-after 1906). At least one edition of the sheet music indicates that it was in the repertoire of the Amphions (Boston: Oliver Ditson, 1853). SI; SIC #1350; PSI; Dichter #83; Dichter & Larrabee #110; Dichter & Shapiro 142. Beadle's Nº 1; H.K. Johnson 68; McCaskey; *Good Old Songs* I:127; Randolph #858, IV:385; Wier 1918, 110.

278. **DO THEY THINK OF ME AT HOME?** (Frank 1985, #d19)
Do they think of me at home, do they ever think of me. Piper, ship *Europa*, 1868-70. (4/4)
American parlor song. w: J.E. Carpenter; m: C.W. Glover; undoubtedly based on "Do They Miss Me at Home?" (q.v.) by Mrs. Mason and S.M. Grannis (1852). SI; Dichter & Larrabee #768; Rosenberg #306; Golden Robin; McCaskey v2; *Heart Songs* 430; Spaeth 1927, 19; Wier 1918, 207. Note also "Do They Pray for Me at Home?" by W.O. Fiske (Century 22, Ditson 15).

279. **DOLCY JONES** [Dolcie Jones] (Foster)
   Oh! White folks do not wonder when I again appear. Keith, circa 1865-71. (3/4 + cho./4)
Minstrel song by Stephen Collins Foster, 1849. SI; Whittlesey & Sonneck 11; Beadle's N° 7; Wier 1929, 123.

280. **DON'T BE ANGRY, MOTHER**
   Don't be angry, Mother. Keith, circa 1865-71. (3/8)
Obscure sentimental song. Beadle's N° 1. Possibly related to "Don't Be Angry With Me, Darling," w: W.L. Gardner, m: H.P. Danks, 1870 (Dichter #977; Dichter & Shapiro 142).

281. **THE DRUNKARD'S DOOM**
   I saw a man at early dawn. Coquin, 1860's-'70s. (6/4)
American temperance song fairly widely distributed in oral tradition (hence Ewing's observation that the song "has found its way into several folksong collections," p. 177). SI lists only Arnold, *Folksongs of Alabama,* 58; also: Lomax & Lomax 1934, 174; Sandburg 104.

282. **THE DRUNKARD'S DREAM** [The Husband's Dream] (Frank 1985, #d20)
   O Harry tell me how it is. Piper, ship *Europa*, 1868-70. (8/10)
Temperance song on the theme of the Prodigal Son. SI calls it an "old American song," Laws lists it among "imported ballads and songs" (I:179), but Ewing (who may be referring to another song of the same formulaic title) seems to attribute the lyrics to Charles W. Denison (p. 144). SI; Rosenberg #322 A-H; Belden 469; Brown Coll. 3&5:#22; Cox #129; Eddy #101; Greenleaf #73; Randolph #307, II:393; Spaeth 1927, 193.

283. **THE DYING AMERICAN OILY TAR**
   His couch was his shroud. Donahue, ship *Atlantic*, 1850-54 (5/4).
Parlor song or poem. Not found elsewhere. Whaleman James Donahue seems to have added the adjective "oily," a kind of pun in reference to *tar* and the greasy "blubber-hunters" of the American whale fishery.

284. **THE DYING CALIFORNIAN** (Frank 1985, #31)
   (A) *Lay up nearer brother nearer.* Jones, bark *Waverly*, 1859-63. (8/8)
   (B) *Lay up nearer brother nearer.* Piper, ship *Europa*, 1868-70.
   (C) *Lie up nearer, brother, nearer.* Keith, circa 1865-71. (8/4)
American religious-sentimental poem subtitled "The Last Bequest" or "The Brother's Bequest," first published in a Rhode Island temperance magazine in February 1850, and reprinted there "by popular demand" less than a month later. m: A. L. Lee (sheet music Boston: Oliver Ditson, 1855). SIC #7561; PSI; Century 23; Ditson 16; Dichter #87; Jackson III:55; Rosenberg 333 A&B. Beadle's N° 1; Belden 350; Cazden 1982 #86; Cox #49; Creighton 1971, #58; Eddy #126; Fife #15; Greenleaf #117; Lingenfelter & Dwyer 34 (excellent publishing history); *The New England Diadem and Rhode Island Temperance Pledge,* 5:6 (Providence, 9 Feb 1850) and 5:9 (2 Mar 1850). See also A.H. Tolman and M.O. Eddy #126, JAFS, 35 (1922), 364.

285. **THE DYING GIRL**
   Are we almost there, are we almost there. Mills, ship *James Loper*, 1859-60. (7/4). Not found.

286. **THE DYING SAILOR** (Frank 1985, #32)
   (A) *The sailor was dying and none could save him.* Mills, bark *Aurora*, 1858. (4/8)
   (B) *The sailor was dying and none could him save.* Piper, ship *Europa*, 1868-70. (4/4)
Sentimental song, origin uncertain. A is labeled "Original by George E. Mills." From several surviving journals, Mills is known to have written many songs and poems, often emulating maudlin Victorian fashions (see P.A. Miller, passim). However, the existence of a second, similar (though shorter) text in the Piper MS casts doubt upon Mills's implication that he was the one-and-only lyricist. In the absence of evidence that Piper got it directly from Mills (they did live in neighboring New Hampshire towns in the 1860s and it is conceivable that it could have been passed along there), more likely Mills added original verses or revisions to a published text (not located) and, a dozen years later, Piper independently copied that or a similar text into his copybook.

287. **THE DYING SAILOR BOY**
   See yon vessel swiftly sailing. Keith, circa 1865-71. (8/4). Sentimental song, origin unknown, not found elsewhere.

288. **EIGHTEEN HUNDRED FORTY-NINE** [Gold Rush Voyage Song]
   In eighteen hudred forty-nine / We left our native land behind. Lyrics by George H. Ashley, ship *Olive Branch* of Boston, on
      the coast of California, 1850-52, transcribed by Nicholas Kirby Jr., First Mate, in his journal of the voyage. (4/4)
Original lyrics by George H. Ashley on a Gold Rush voyage in the ship *Olive Branch* of Boston, on the coast of California, 1850-52, transcribed by Nicholas Kirby Jr., First Mate. Tune: *The New York Trader* (related to the text).

289. **ELLEN BAYNE** [Ellen Bane] (Foster) (Frank 1985, #d21)
   (A) *Soft by thy slumbers rude cares depart.* Jones & Handy, bark *Waverly*, 1859-63. (3/4 + cho./4)
   (B) *ditto.* Inscribed circa the 1850s by Reynolds, former boatsteerer, ship *Janus*, 1842-44.
w&m: Stephen Collins Foster, 1854. SI; SIC #1112; PSI; Dichter #91; Dichter & Larrabee #145; Whittlesey & Sonneck 13f; Century 23; Beadle's N° 8; Golden Robin; Kieser 200; Wier 1918, 121.

290. **THE EMIGRANT'S FAREWELL**
   Fare well to the[e] Erin fair jewel of the north. Hughson, bark *Java*, 1857-60 (5/4)
Not found. Possibly related to "The Emigrant" ("Farewell to poor old Erin's isle...") (JFSS 18: 53). Not the same song as the well known song "The Emigrant's Farewell" in *Beadle's N° 3*.

291. **ERIN IS MY HOME** (Frank 1985, #d22)
   Oh, I have roamed in many lands. Davis, bark *Midas*, 1861-65. (2/8 + cho.)
w: Thomas Haynes Bayly (1797-1839), ostensibly to an old German air. SI; Beadle's Nº 4; H.K. Johnson 88; Wier 1918, 121.

292. **THE EXILE OF ERIN**
(A) *There came to the beach A poor exile of Erin.* Donahue, ship *Atlantic*, 1850-53 (5/8).
(B) *There came to the beach a poor exile of Erin.* Hughson, bark *Java*, 1857-60 (5/8).
British parlor song written by Thomas Campbell (1777-1844) to the Irish air "Savourneen deelish." SI; SI2; McCaskey v4; H.K. Johnson 91; Mackay 135; Molloy 100.

293. **FADED FLOWERS** (Frank 1985, #d23)
   The flowers that I saw in the wildwood. Jones, bark *Waverly*, 1859-63. (3/8)
American parlor song. w: J.H. Brown; m: settings by (1) James Power (McCaskey v6); (2) William Willing (*Good Old Songs* II:134; Ditson 17). SI; Dichter & Larrabee #773; Rosenberg #373. Not Belden 216: this is the "other" song he mentions. Not to be confused with "'Tis But a Little Faded Flower," 1860 (Dichter & Shapiro 152).

294. **FAREWELL, MY LILLY DEAR** (Foster)
   O, lilly dear it grieves me the talke that I have to tell. Coquin, bark *Pacific*, 1867-68; and merchant voyages out of Boston, circa 1860's-'70s. (4/4 + cho./2)
w&m: Stephen Collins Foster, 1851. SI; SI2; Dichter & Shapiro 93; Whittlesey & Sonneck 15; *Minstrel Songs* 92; Wier 1918, 136.

295. **FAREWELL SONG OF ENOCH ARDEN** (Frank 1985, #d24)
   Cheer up, Annie darling, with helpful emotion. Papers of Elizabeth Marble. (3/4 + refrain/4)
Written and composed by Septimus Winner (1827-1902) in 1865 to monopolize on the transient popularity of Tennyson's poem "Enoch Arden" (1864). Dichter #97; Beadle's Nº 17; Brown Coll. 3&5:#684; Century 24; Ditson 17; Golden Robin.

296. **THE FIELDS OF MONTEREY** (Frank 1985, #d25)
   The sweet church bells are pealing forth a chorus wild and free. Piper, ship *Europa*, 1868-70. (3/4)
Early, influential Mexican War song written by Mrs. Marion Dix Sullivan, 1846. SI; Dichter & Shapiro 81; *Heart Songs* 318.

297. **FIGHT FOR THE UNION** (Frank 1985, #d26)
   So let the rebels fight as they will. Piper, ship *Europa*, 1868-70. (fragment of 4 lines)
Union song of the Civil War, not otherwise identified.

298. **A FINE OLD DIETSCHEN** [sic] **GENTLEMAN** [Fine Old Dutch Gentleman] (Frank 1985, #d27)
   I am going to sing a dichen song. Piper, ship *Europa*, 1868-70. (5/6 + refrain/2 + recitations)
English music hall song, one of the "Fine Old Gentlemen" series by Charles Henry Purday (SI) and/or John Brougham (SIC). Beadle's Nº 3. See "Fine Old English Gentleman" (Baring-Gould 1895 I:16; Singer's Gem, 14; etc.).

298. **FLOW GENTLY, SWEET AFTON** [Afton Water] (Burns)
   Flow gently sweet afton among thy green braes. Beden, ships *Massachusetts* and *South America*, 1851-55. (fragment/4)
One of the most popular and best known Scottish songs, w: Robert Burns (1759-1796), m: (1) traditional air "Afton Water"; (2) setting by Alexander Hume; (3) setting by Jonathan E. Spilman (1812-1896). SI; SI2; SIC; PSI; Dichter #778. Beadle's Nº 83; McCaskey v2; *Good Old Songs* I:139; *Heart Songs* 15; *Home Songs*; Mackay 272; H.K. Johnson 322; Wier 1918, 141; etc., etc.

300. **THE FLYING TRAPEZE** [The Man on the Flying Trapeze]
   Once I was happy but now I'm forlorn. Keith, circa 1865-71. (3/8 + 1/3 + cho./4)
Extremely popular and widely disseminated comic music-hall song, circa 1868, controversially attributed to either Gaston Lyle (Dichter #269) or George Leybourne (Dichter #270). PSI erroneously attributes the song to Walter Michael (born 1900). Dichter & Shapiro 131; Beadle's Nº 21; Spaeth 1926, 73.

301. **THE FORESTER'S SONG**
   O I dearly love on my bonnie steed. Mills, bark *Aurora*, 1856-59. (3/4)
Unidentified minstrel-era song, possibly an original imitation by the diarist.

302. **GAILY THE TROUBADOUR** [The Troubadour] (Frank 1985, #d28)
   Gaily the troubadour touched his guitar. Piper, ship *Europa*, 1868-70. (3/2, actually 3/4)
English romance on the theme of Blondel's rescue of King Richard. w&m: Thomas Haynes Bayly (1797-1839). SI; Beadle's Nº 15; McCaskey v1; *Good Old Songs* I:141; *Heart Songs* 149; H.K. Johnson 521; *Singer's Gem* 126; Wier 1918, 165.

303. **GALLANT WILL**
   Oh! the stormy times we knew in our suits of army blue. Keith, circa 1865-71. (4/4 + cho./4 + cho./4)
Post Civil War-era sentimental song about a lost comrade. Not found.

304. **GENTLE ANNIE** (Foster) (Frank 1985, #d29)
   Thou wilt come no more gentle Annie. Smith, bark *Roscius*, 1858-61. (3/4 + cho./4)
w&m: Stephen Collins Foster, 1856. SI; SIC #1114; PSI; Dichter #103; Dichter & Larrabee #1856; Rosenberg #441; Whittlesey 17; McCaskey v7; *Good Old Songs* II:62; *Heart Songs* 354; R. Jackson 1974, 33; Kieser 32; *Minstrel Songs* 52; Randolph #701, IV:159; Wier 1918, 172.

305. **GENTLE NETTIE MOORE** [Little White Cottage] (Frank 1985, #d30)
In a little white cottage / Where the trees are ever green. George Gregson, in Piper, ship *Europa*, 1868-70. (5/6 + cho./6)
Minstrel song. w: Marshall S. Pike; m: G.S. Pike (arranged by J.S. Pierpont); 1857. SI; Dichter #148; Dichter & Shapiro 147; Beadle's N° 6; *Good Old Songs* I:16; Wier 1918, 167.

306. **THE GIPSY CHANT** (Frank 1985, #d31)
We roam through the forest Glade. Cleveland, 1837-39. (1/4 + cho./4). Not identified.

307. **THE GIRL WITH THE WATERFALL** (Frank 1985, #d32)
As you go out for a walk on a windy day. Piper, ship *Europa*, 1868-70. (5/4 + cho./4)
Copy text from a broadside; the air is specified as *The dark gal dressed in blue;* quite different from the specimen quoted by Laws (#H-26, "The Girl that Wore a Waterfall"; see also 'The Ballad of the Waterfall," Laws 1950, Appendix II, 261, citing M.E. Henry, *Folk-Songs from the Southern Highlands,* New York: J.J. Augustin, 1938, 307). PSI; Fife #64; Randolph #389, III:110.

308. **THE GOLD DIGGER'S LAMENT** [The California Gold Hunter] (Frank 1985, #63)
I'm going far away from my Creditors just now. Jones & Handy, bark *Waverly*, 1859. (2/4)
Fragment of an anonymous ballad about the futility of prospecting for gold; published as a broadside in New York by J. Wrigley, n.d.; to be sung to the air *Jeanette and Jeanot,* composed by Charles William Glover (1806-1863) for a text by Charles Jefferys (1807-1865). SI; Beadle's N° 3; McCaskey v2; H.K. Johnson 338). Lingenfelter & Dwyer present the complete text and publishing history, 91. The same year as Jones & Handy's transcription, William Batchelder Bradbury (1816-1868) issued the parody "The California Gold-Hunter," written by Asahel Abbott with music by Bradbury (*Alpine Glee Singer,* 141).

309. **GOOD-BYE**
Farewell! farewell! is a lonely sound. Keith, circa 1865-71. (4/4)
Sentimental song attributed to J.C. Engelbrecht (Ditson 20).

310. **THE GRAVE** (Frank 1985, #d34)
There is a calm for those who weep. Piper, ship *Europa*, 1868-70. (8/4) Not identified.

311. **THE GRAVE OF WASHINGTON** (Frank 1985, #d35)
(A) *Disturb not his slumbers, let Washington sleep.* Marble family copybook. (2/8)
(B) ditto. Marble family copybook (second copy).
w: Marshall S. Pike; m: L.V.H. Crosby (Century lists Crosby and E.L. White; Ditson lists only Crosby). SI; PSI; Beadle's N° 6; McCaskey v6; Wier 1918, 159.

312. **GUM TREE CANOE** [Tom-Big-Be River]
(A) *On the Tombigbe river so bright I was born.* Transcribed between voyages by Helen M. Tinkham of Mattapoisett, Mass., in the journal of Daniel L. Tinkham, March 1855. (4/4 + cho./4 [2])
(B) *On the Tombiggee river so bright I was born.* Keith, circa 1865-71. (4/4 + cho./2)
American minstrel song, 1847; w&m: S.S. Steele. SI; SI2; SIC; Dichter & Larrabee #1183; Beadle's N° 5; Chamberlain & Harrington; *Minstrel Songs* 208; Wier 1918, 476; Wier 1929, 243. See "*Florida's* Crew," #59.

313. **HARD TIMES COME AGAIN NO MORE** (Foster) (Frank 1985, #84)
Let us pause in life's pleasures. Reed, bark *Black Eagle*, 1860-61. (2 stanzas of 4 + cho.)
w&m: Stephen Collins Foster, circa 1854. SI; SIC #1115; PSI; Dichter #1604; Dichter & Larrabee #199, #1081; Whittlesey & Sonneck 20; Beadle's N° 1; *Heart Songs* 82; R. Jackson 1974, 46; Kieser 8; *Minstrel Songs* 184; Taylor & Howard 23; Wier 1918, 203. Jackson (1974, ii) remarks, "The printed 1854 [on the sheet music] is incorrect." Whittlesey & Sonneck also list "Sorrow Shall Come No More" (words by A.K., arranged by A. Cull, 1863), an adaptation as a sacred song.

314. **THE HAZEL DELL**
(A) *In the hazel dell my Nellys sleeping.* Inscribed circa the 1850s in Reynolds, ship *Janus*, 1842-44.
(B) *In the hazel dell my Nellie's sleeping.* Poole, ship *Minnesota*, 1868-72. (2/8)
Parlor song by "Wurzel" [pseudonym of George Frederick Root], 1853. SI; SI2; Dichter #110; Dichter & Shapiro 144; Rosenberg #666; *Good Old Songs* II:18; *Heart Songs* 212; Wier 1918, 206; Wier 1929, 26.

315. **HE DOETH ALL THINGS WELL**
I remember how I loved her. Keith, circa 1865-71. (6/4)
"The subject of Isaac B. Woodbury's *He Doeth All Things Well* (Boston, 1844) is really the death of a sister" (Tawa 145); the sheet music went to 16 editions (Tawa 101). Beadle's N° 6.

316. **HEENAN AND SAYERS [PRIZE FIGHT OF HEENAN AND SAYERS]**
O ye lovers of the fisty corps, attention to my song. Wood, bark *Andrew*, 1866-67. (10/4)
Anonymous ballad commemorating a celebrated bareknuckles boxing bout between American champion John C. Heenan ("The Benicia Boy") and the English champion, Tom Sayers, held at Farnborough, Hampshire (England) on 17 April 1860. The tune is "Morrissey and the Russian Sailor," reported to be a lumberjack song of folkloric origin (compare texts and tunes in Charles J. Finger, *Frontier Ballads,* Garden City, N.Y.: Doubleday Page, 1927; Peter Kennedy, *Folksongs of Britain and Ireland,* New York: Schirmer, 1975; and Carl Sandburg, *American Songbag,* New York: Harcourt, Brace, 1927. For biographical details, see *Encyclopedia Britannica,* 11th ed., XXII, "Pugilism," Cambridge, 1911; and Richard J. Purcell, "John Carmel Heenan," *Dictionary of American Biography,* VII, New York, 1946.

317. **HER BRIGHT SMILE HAUNTS ME STILL**
'Tis years since last we met. Keith, circa 1865-71. (3/12)
Parlor song. w: Joseph Edwards Carpenter; m: William Thompson Wrighton. SI; SI2; Colcord 93; McCaskey v6; *Good Old Songs* II:157; *Heart Songs* 380; Wier 1918, 192.

318. **HIGHLAND MARY** (Burns)
Ye bonny banks and braes and streams around. Donahue, ship *Atlantic*, 1850-53 (2/6).
The celebrated poem by Robert Burns (1759-1796) is sung to the traditional air "Lady Katherine Ogie" (the prevalent setting) or to music by H.N. Bartlett. SI; SI2; SIC; PSI; McCaskey v6; H.K. Johnson 359; Kidson 1891, 84; Wier 1918, 192. Not to be confused with the folk ballad "Burns and His Highland Mary" ("The Parting of Burns and His Highland Mary") (Laws #O-34), which is is reported to have been written circa the 1850s "by a West of Scotland police constable named Thompson, who subsequently emigrated to Canada" (Laws, quoting Greig 1914); see Creighton & Senior 159, Doerflinger 312, Ord 354.

319. **HOME AGAIN** (Frank 1985, #82)
(A) *Home again home again.* Jones, bark *Waverly*, 1863. (3/8 + cho./4)
(B) ditto. Davis, bark *Midas*, 1861-65. (3/8 + cho./4)
(C) ditto. Piper, ship *Europa*, 1868-70. (3/8 + cho./4)
¶ Title entered (but no text given) by William H. Keith, circa 1865-71.
American parlor song, 1850 (sometimes erroneously given as 1851). w&m: Marshall S. Pike. SI; SIC #2828; PSI; Dichter & Larrabee #220; Dichter & Shapiro 144; Rosenberg #551; Beadle's N° 1; McCaskey v5; *Good Old Songs* I:121; *Heart Songs* 327; Wier 1918, 202.

320. **A HOME BEYOND THE SEA**
I have told you how fair the roses are. Keith, circa 1865-71. (2/8) Not found.

321. **A HOME IN THE VALE** [O Give Me a Cot] (Frank 1985, #d33)
O give me a cot in the valley I love. Handy, bark *Waverly*, 1859-63. (4/4 + cho./4)
English parlor song. w: Charles Jefferys (1807-1865); m: Stephen Glover (1812-1870). Miller's 74.

322. **THE HUNTER'S GLEE**
Some love to ride the ocean tide. Keith, circa 1865-71. (22 lines + repeats) Not found.

323. **[HYMN, untitled]** (Frank 1985, #d36)
Dear Father ere we part now let thy grace descend. Piper, ship *Europa*, 1868-70. (2/4 + repeat)
Anonymous hymn in Long Meter, origin unknown, tune not indicated.

324. **[HYMN, untitled]** (Frank 1985, #40)
With outstretched necks and longing eyes. Cleveland, ship *Charles*, 1837-39. (5/4)
Anonymous hymn in slightly corrupt Common Meter, origin unknown, tune not indicated. Possibly an original composition.

325. **I DREAM OF ALL THINGS FREE** (Frank 1985, #d38)
I dream of all things free / of a gay and gallant bark. Hopkins, ship *Rosalie*, 1843. (1/7 + 1/8)
w: Mrs. Felicia Dorothea [née Brown] Hemans (1793-1835); m: (1) Karl M.F.E. von Weber (1786-1826); (2) Alexander Ball, the tune most often encountered in the rare instances in which the song been printed in America. SI; Dichter #853; McCaskey v2.

326. **I HAVE NO MOTHER NOW**
The midnight stars are gleaming. Keith, circa 1865-71. (2/8)
Sentimental song, circa 1858; w&m: T. Smith. Dichter #131; Dichter & Larrabee #244. Ditson 23 lists a setting by F. Staab.

327. **I KNEW NOT TILL WE PARTED**
I knew not till We parted. Gillaspia, ship *Atlantic*, 1846-49 (9/4). Not found.

328. **I'D OFFER THEE THIS HAND OF MINE**
I would offer thee this hand of mine. Hughson, bark *Java*, 1857-60. (3/8)
Anonymous parlor song. SI; SI2; McCaskey v5; *Good Old Songs* I:40; Wier 1918, 229. Attributed to J. Winter (Ditson 25).

329. **I'LL THROW MYSELF AWAY** (Frank 1985, #d39)
Now ladies your attention. Piper, ship *Europa*, 1868-70. (4/8 + cho.)
Minstrel song attributed to Edwin P. Christy (1815-1862), 1853. Century 29; Ditson 25; *Christy's Plantation Melodies* II:10.

330. **I'M LONELY SINCE MY MOTHER DIED**
I'm lonely since my mother died. Poole, ship *Minnesota* of New York, 1868-72. (3/8)
American parlor song, 1863; w&m: H.S. Thompson. Century 29; Ditson 25; Dichter #124.

331. **THE INDIAN HUNTER** (Frank 1985, #65)
The father above thoght fit to give. Papers of Elizabeth Marble. (2/16)
English parlor song. w: Eliza Cook (1818-1889), circa 1835 (first line: *Oh, why does the white man follow my path*); m: (1) Frederick C. Leader (cited in *Miller's New British Songster*, n.d.; not found in North America); (2) Henry Russell (1812-1900), circa 1836-37 (the composer with whom Cook's poetry is most closely associated and the version popular in America). The MS unaccountably reverses the order of the stanzas, hence the disparity in the first line. SI; Dichter & Shapiro 75; Beadle's N° 3; Beadle's N° 4; McCaskey v7; Miller's 418; Randolph #781, IV:297; see Rosenberg #656-659.

332. THE INDIAN WARRIOR'S GRAVE (Frank 1985, #67)
Green is the grave by the wild dashing river. Marble family copybook. (3/4 + refrain/2)
Minstrel song by Mashall S. Pike. Beadle's N° 4; Century 30; Ditson 26.

333. THE INDIAN'S PRAYER [The Indian's Lament; The Indian Hunter's Prayer; White Man, Let Me Go] (Frank 1985, #66)
(A) *Let me go to my home in the far distant west.* Marble family copybook. (6/4)
(B) *Let me go to my home in the far distant west.* Marble family copybook (second copy). (6/4)
(C) *Let me go to my home that is far distant west.* Sylvanus C. Fullmoon (Native American), ship *Nimrod*, 1842-45.
(D) *Let me go to my home that is far distant west.* Braley family copybook, N.B., n.d. (5/4)
(E) *Let me go to my home.* Keith, circa 1865-71. (4/4 + repeat)
American parlor song that entered oral tradition among whalers and in Maritime Canada. Original w&m: Isaac Baker Woodbury (1819-1858); sheet music Boston, 1846. Seldom attributed; but see Howard, 148. SIC; PSI; Century 22; *Beadle's N° 3;* Brown III, #270; Howard, 148; Fowke & Johnston, 33 ("White Man, Let Me Go": they state erroneously, "It does not seem to have appeared in any published collection, and the Library of Congress has no information about it"); Huntington 1964, 180 (2 texts; erroneous tune, in confusion with #331); Thompson #76, p. 172. See also Dichter & Shapiro 75; Rosenberg #656-659.

334. THE IRISH EMIGRANT'S LAMENT [The Lament of the Irish Emigrant] (Frank 1985, #d41)
(A) *I am sitting on the stile Mary.* Marble family copybook. Probably transcribed from singing or recitation. (8/8)
(B) *I am sitting on the stile Mary.* Marble family copybook (second copy). Probably a copy text. (8/8)
(C) *I'm sitting on the stile, Mary.* Keith, circa 1865-71. (8/8)
Irish parlor song. w: Helen Selina Sheridan [Mrs. Price Blackwood], Lady Dufferin (1807-1867), a granddaughter of R.B. Sheridan; m: (1) William Richardson Dempster (1809-1871), by 1840; (2) George A. Barker (1812-1876). SI; PSIS; Dichter #146; Rosenberg #673; Beadle's N° 5; McCaskey v7; *Good Old Songs* I:46; H.K. Johnson 85; Miller's 383; Turner 116; Wier 1918, 221.

335. IRISH MOLLY O
As I walked out one morning in the month of May. Donahue, ship *Atlantic*, 1850-53.
Irish folksong. SI; PSI; Rosenberg #674; *Beadle's Half-Dime Singer's Library N° 13* (1898). Note first line, "When first unto this country a stranger I came" (Morris, *Folk Songs of Florida*).

336. IRISH SONG (Frank 1985, #d40)
O the sweetest of all was the dear little maid. Piper, ship *Europa*, 1868-70. (2/4 + refrain/8)
Parlor song, not found elsewhere.

337. IS IT ANY BODY'S BUSINESS?
Is it any body's business? Keith, circa 1865-71. (6/4)
Comic song on the theme "mind your own business"; m. (and possibly also w.) by O.R. Donderup (Century 30). *Howe's 100*.

338. JEANIE WITH THE LIGHT BROWN HAIR (Foster)
I dream of Jeanie with the light brown hair. Keith, circa 1865-71.
w&m: Stephen Collins Foster, 1854. SI; SI2; SIC; Dichter & Larrabee #318; Dichter & Shapiro 92; Whittlesey & Sonneck 24f; Beadle's N° 8; R. Jackson 1974, 53; etc.

339. JENNY WITH THE BONNY BLUE E'E (Frank 1985, #d42)
Ive strolled on the banks of the bright rolling tweed. Marble family copybook. (2/9)
Attributed to John C. Andrews, in apparent imitation of English North Country and Scottish Border ballads. Beadle's N° 9; Beadle's Dime Melodist 59.

340. THE JEWISH MAID
No more shall the Children of Judah sing. Fullmoon (Native American), ship *Nimrod*, 1842-45 (2/8).
American parlor song that likely owes much to the popularity of Walter Scott's *Ivanhoe* (1819), to the renown of Rebecca Gratz of Philadelphia, upon whom Scott's Jewish Maiden charteter in *Ivanhoe* is based, and possibly to an obscure opera, *The Maid of Judah,* which may have been produced in Boston circa 1837 (Dichter & Shapiro 79). The song itself has not been found.

341. JONES'S ALE [John's Ale; Joan's Ale; Johnson's Ale; When Joan's Ale Was New; etc.] (Frank 1985, #138)
old darby he sat and played the fiddle. John Jones, ship *Eliza Adams*, 1852 (fragment only).
Anglo-American convivial song — a progressive song of occupations set in a tavern, in which several *bon vivants* enter one-by-one with implements and idiosyncrasies characteristic of their respective trades. Chappell I:187; Doerflinger 167, 358; Emrich II:A; Frank 1985, #138, note 5, pp. 720-722; JFSS; Palmer 1979, #117; Simpson 387; Walser.

342. JOSIE AT THE GATE [Meet Me Josie at the Gate]
Wilt thou meet me tonight, at the old garden gate? Keith, circa 1865-71. (2/8 + cho./4)
Sentimental song, circa 1868; m: George M. Clark. Dichter #158.

343. JUST BEFORE THE BATTLE, MOTHER (Frank 1985, #d43)
(A) *Just before the battle, mother, I'm thinking most of you.* Keith, circa 1865-71. (3/8 + cho./4)
(B) ditto. Coquin, 1860's-'70s. (3/8)
(C) ditto. Inscribed more than a decade after the fact in Braley, ship *Arab*, 1849-52. (3/8)
Civil War-era song expressing Union sentiments, widely parodied in the South. w&m: George F. Root (1820-1896), 1862. Listed among "ballad like pieces" (Laws I:278). SI; SIC #3071; PSI; PSIS; Dichter #304; Dichter & Larrabee #909; Dichter & Shapiro 116; Beadle's N° 12; Cox #74.

344. **KATE KEARNEY** (Frank 1985, #d44)
 O did you ever hear tell of Kate Kearney. Piper, ship Europa, 1868-70. (4/4)
British parlor song. w: Sidney [née Owenson] Morgan, Lady Morgan (1783?-1859); m: said to be a traditional air, *The Beardless Boy* (SI), but elsewhere attributed to [George] Alexander Lee (1802-1852) (Morrison & Whitney, 336). Describes a *femme fatale* to an extreme just short of Nathaniel Hawthorne's "Rapacini's Daughter." SI; Beadle's N° 1; Grigg's 101; H.K. Johnson 418; Kieser 120; O'Reilly 825; Page 44.

345. **KATHLEEN MAVOURNEEN** (Frank 1985, #d45)
(A) *Kathleen Mavourneen the bright day is breaking.* Smith, bark *Roscius*, 1858-61. (4/4)
(B) *Kathleen Mavourneen, the gray dawn is breaking.* Keith, circa 1865-71. (2/8)
Parlor song first published in 1837 or 1839, thereafter ascending to tremendous popularity and giving rise to a host of imitations and parodies, of which "Katty Avourneen" (q.v.) is one. w: Mrs. Louisa Matilda Jane [née McCartney or Montague] Crawford (1790-1858) (sometimes wrongly attributed to Anne Barrie Crawford, 1731-1801); m: Frederick William Nicholls Crouch (1808-1896). SI; SIC #734; PSI; PSIS; Dichter #1367; Beadle's N° 2; McCaskey v2; *Good Old Songs* I:148; *Heart Songs* 376; H.K. Johnson 333; Page 46; *Singer's Gem* 106; Wier 1918, 242. See "'Kathleen Mavourneen' and 'Katty Avourneen,'" in Fitz-Gerald, 132-145. An earlier song "Kathleen Ma Vourneen Cushlah Ma Chree" is sung to "The Humours of the Glen" (*Universal* II:271).

346. **KAT[T]Y AVOURNEEN**
 'Twas a cold winters night and the tempest was snarlin' Keith, circa 1865-71. (3/8)
Comic parody of "Kathleen Mavourneen" (q.v.), variously attributed to J.E. Johnson or Desmond Ryan. SI2; Beadle's N° 11; *Songs of Ireland* 1890. See "'Kathleen Mavourneen' and 'Katty Avourneen'" in Fitz-Gerald, 132-145.

347. **KITTY CLYDE** (Frank 1985, #d46)
 Who has not seen Kitty Clyde who lived at the foot of the hill. Tuck, bark *F. Bunchinia*, 1858. (3/8)
Minstrel song. w&m: L.V.H. Crosby (1853), who also produced a sequel, "Minnie Clyde, Kitty Clyde's Sister," with the sheet music illustrated by Winslow Homer (Boston: Oliver Ditson, 1857; Dichter #704; Beadle's N° 6). Crosby's inspiration was no doubt Charles Dibdin's "Kitty of the Clyde" (*Universal* II:332). The popularity of either Dibdin's or Crosby's composition may have inspired the title of *Kitty Clyde's Reel,* evidently a homegrown American tune (1000 FT 36; not in O'Neill), now virtually extinct. Dichter & Larrabee #347; Dichter & Shapiro 146; Beadle's N° 1; Brown Coll. 2&4:#198.

348. **THE LAKE OF THE DISMAL SWAMP** (Moore) (Frank 1985, #133)
(A) *They made her a grave, too cold and damp.* Marble family copybook. (8/4 + prose preamble)
(B) *They made her grave, too cold and damp.* Braley family papers. (8/4)
Poem by Thomas Moore (Irish, 1779-1852), written in connection with his visit to the Great Dismal Swamp (Virginia) in 1803. It was anthologized as a song but without an air in *The Songster's Companion* (1815), the *Universal Songster* (I:422, c1825), the *American Songster* (c1835), etc. There were evidently two settings, by Bernard Covert (Century, 22) and T. Wood (Ibid, 29), but neither has been found. The Marble MS includes a verbatim transcription of Moore's prose introduction; the Braley MS does not; absent in both MSS is a quotation in French from d'Alembert often published with the poem (in Waller 444 but not Bryant II:782).

349. **LASHED TO THE HELM**
 In Storm when clouds obscure the sky. Hughson, bark *Java*, 1857-60 (3/4 + cho./4)
Parlor song by James Hook (1746-1827). SI; Baring-Gould, *English Minstrelsie*; Mofat & Kidson, *English Songs of the Georgian Period*. *Beadle's Pocket Songster N° 5* (1867) has a selection eneitled "Lashed to the Mast."

350. **THE LAST ROSE OF SUMMER** (Moore) (Frank 1985, #d49)
 'Tis the last rose of summer. Davis, bark *Midas*, 1861-65. (2/8)
w: Thomas Moore (Irish, 1779-1852), from *Irish Melodies* (1813; however, Dichter #1237 lists American sheet-music published c1811); m: traditional Irish air *Groves of Blarney*. Turner (214) gives a provenance, tracing it to street balladry in 1660 and its appearance on stage. SI; SIC #5291; PSI; PSIS; Century 78; Dichter & Larrabee #771; Amateur 52; Beadle's N° 5; McCaskey v1; *Good Old Songs* I:168; *Heart Songs* 146; H.K. Johnson 219; Kieser 60; Miller's 51; Page 111; *Singer's Gem* 128; Wier 1918, 258.

351. **LET ME KISS HIM FOR HIS MOTHER**
 Let me kiss him for his mother. Keith, circa 1865-71. (3/8 + cho./4)
An "exercise in bathos" (Tawa 152) by John Ordway; sheet music issued by the author, Boston, 1859. Dichter & Larrabee #772; Dichter & Shapiro 146; Beadle's N° 4; unattributed in PI. Comic parody "Let Me Spank Him for His Mother" (Beadle's N° 21).

352. **LINES** [*Where are the soldiers...*] (Frank 1985, #d50)
 Ah! Where are the soldiers that fought here of yore? Piper, ship *Europa*, 1868-70. (7/4)
Not identified. The pastoral setting suggests American origin, but the use of "sod" and "turf" (but not "soil") suggests Ireland.

353. **A LITTLE MORE CIDER** (Frank 1985, #d51)
 O I love the white folks and the black. Piper, ship *Europa*, 1868-70. (4/8 + cho./4)
Minstrel song, w&m: Austin Hart, 1852. SI; Dichter & Shapiro 147; Century 33; Ditson 31; Beadle's N° 6; *Heart Songs* 372; Wier 1918, 274.

354. **LIZETTE [THE YOUNG RECRUIT]**
 See those banners gaily streaming. Wood, bark *Andrews*, 1866-67. (3/6)
The original words by George Linley (with additional stanzas by Arthur Nash), to the music of Friedrich Wilhelm Kücken (1810-1882), are much changed and only barely recognizable in the sailor's MS. SI; Chamberlain & Harrington 244; Wier 1918, 311.

355. **THE LONE STARRY HOURS** (Frank 1985, #d52)
(A) *O the lone starry hours give me love.* Piper, ship, 1868-70. (2/12)
(B) *ditto.* William H. Keith, circa 1865-71. (2/8)
Minstrel song. w: Marshall S. Pike; m: James Power (sometimes wrongly attributed to J.P. Ordway, who was actually the Boston publisher in 1849). SI; Dichter & Larrabee #381; Dichter & Shapiro 147; Rosenberg #822; Beadle's N° 8; Century 33; Ditson 31; McCaskey v8; *Good Old Songs* I:64.

356. **LONG, LONG AGO** [The Long Ago] (Frank 1985, #73)
(A) *Oh where are the friends that to me were so dear.* Ritchie, ship *Israel*, 1843-45. (frag.1/4)
(B) *ditto.* Fragment, Ritchie, ship *Massachusetts*, 1847. (fragment 1/2)
(C) *Where are the friends that I once loved so dear.* John G. Marble, circa 1846-47, in the journal of Stephen O. Hopkins, ship *Rosalie*, 1843, and bark *Perseverance*, 1849. (3/8)
(D) *Tell me the tales that to me were so dear.* Marble Family Papers.
English parlor song, 1830s. w&m: Thomas Haynes Bayly (1797-1839). SI; SIC #215; PSI; PSIS; Baring-Gould 1895 VI:92; Beadle's N° 10; McCaskey v3; *Good Old Songs* I:19; *Heart Songs* 435; H.K. Johnson 3; Wier 1918, 283; etc. Very widely anthologized. The air and chorus seem to have inspired the chantey "Goodbye, Fare Ye Well" (q.v.).

357. **THE LONG, LONG WEARY DAY**
Poole, ship *Minnesota*, 1868-72. (5/7)
German parlor song "Den lichen langen tag," published in America circa 1856 as a "Swabian folk song"; m: possibly traditional, w: acsribed to Philipp Jacob Düringer. SI; Dichter & Larrabee #384; Beadle's N° 8; Ditson 31; *Heart Songs* 502; McCaskey v2.

358. **THE LOW-BACKED CAR** (Frank 1985, #d53)
When first I saw sweet Peggy it was on a market day. Piper, ship *Europa*, 1868-70. (4/10)
w: Samuel Lover (1797-1868) to the traditional Irish air *The Jolly Ploughboy*. SI; Dichter #1510; Century 34; Ditson 32; Beadle's N° 4; Dime Melodist; Rosenberg #855; McCaskey v4; *Good Old Songs* II:160; Healy 1955, 37, 132; *Heart Songs* 442; H.K. Johnson 404; Page 66; Wier 1918, 286.

359. **MAGGIE BY MY SIDE** (Foster) (Frank 1985, #25)
(A) *The land of my home is flitting flitting from my view.* Smith, bark *Roscius*, 1861. (3/4 + cho./4)
(B) *ditto.* George M. Jones, Albert F. Handy and George E. Sanborn, bark *Waverly*, 1859-63. (3/4 + cho./4)
(C) *Land of my home is flitting flitting from my view.* John S. Coquin, 1860's-'70s. (3/4 + cho./3)
w&m: Stephen Collins Foster, 1852. SI; PSI; Dichter #156; Rosenberg #866; Whittlesey & Sonneck 31. Beadle's N° 7; *Heart Songs* 135; R. Jackson 1974, 59, 176; Wier 1918, 307. Not in Taylor & Howard.

360. **THE MAID OF LLANGOLLEN.** (Frank 1985 #132)
Though lonely my cot and poor be my estate. Theodore D. Bartley, ship *California*, 1851-54 ("The Maid of Langolen") (3/4).
"The beauties of the vale of Llangollen are celebrated in both prose and verse" (Rees, vol. 22, "Llangollen," n.p.). This rare piece, set in a market town in North Wales, "on the banks of the Dee," is usually regarded as a Welsh folksong, but an American sheet music edition (Philadephia: George Willig, n.d., circa 1817-53) proclaims that it was "Sung by Mr. Pearman" and "Composed by Ja[me]s Clarke." SI lists only McCaskey, v3 (III:55). "Maid of Llanwellyn" (Am. Singer 7) is a different song.

361. **MARCHING THROUGH GEORGIA** (Frank 1985, #d54)
(A) *Bring the good old bugle boys, sing the good old song.* Piper, ship *Europa*, 1868-70. (5/4 + cho./4)
(B) *Bring out the good old bugle.* Keith, circa 1865-71. (4/4 + cho./4)
Civil War song, 1865. w&m: Henry Clay Work (1832-1884) "In Honor of Maj. Gen. [William T.] Sherman's Famous March 'from Atlanta to the Sea'" (from the sheet music). SI; Dichter & Larrabee #912; Dichter & Shapiro 116; Beadle's N° 17; Lawrence 423; *Heart Songs* 310; Wier 1918, 292.

362. **THE MARINER'S GRAVE (I)**
I remember the night was stormy and wet. Mills, bark *Aurora* of Westport, 1856-59. (6/4)
Unidentified parlor song.

363. **THE MARINER'S GRAVE (II)**
I remember 'twas down by a darksome dale. Keith, circa 1865-71. (6/4)
Landlubber's parlor-song rendition of death at sea, typical of the genre; authorship and tune not identified, not found elsewhere. Possibly a variant of the preceding.

364. **MARSEILLES HYMN** [Lines from the...] (Frank 1985, #d55)
O liberty can man resign thee. Piper, ship *Europa*, 1868-70. (15 lines in English translation)
French national anthem, dating from the French Revolution of 1789, attributed C.J. Rouget de Lisle (died 1830). Often issued in America in a variety of translations, the first of which, in 1789, accompanied the French text. Often parodied in English, perhaps especially by the Confederacy (e.g., see F. Moore, 30, 216, etc.). SI; Fitz-Gerald 40-54; Am. Songster 237; Amateur; Beadle's N° 1; Grigg's 257; New Song Book 52; Wier 1918, 316; etc.

365. **MARY BLANE**
I once did love a pretty girl. Wood, bark *Andrews*, 1866-67. (3/4 + cho./4)
Anonymous minstrel song. SI; SIS; Wier 1918, 311. The tune served for a political song in the 1884 presidential campaign, a lampoon of James G. Blaine by Ben Warren, entitled "Mary Blaine" (Irwin Silber, *Songs America Voted By,* Harrisburg, Pa: Stackpole, 1971, p. 128).

366. MARY'S WAITING AT THE WINDOW
Years have passed since last we parted. John S. Coquin, 1860's-'70s. (3/8 + cho./4)
w&m: Will[iam] S[hakespeare] Hays (1837-1907). Century 35; Ditson 33.

367. MASSA HAD A YELLOW GAL [The Gal from the South] (Frank 1985, #d57)
(A) *Old massa had a yeller gal he brought her back from the South.* Piper, ship *Europa*, 1868-70. (4/4 + cho./4)
(B) *ditto.* Same source as A. (4/4 + cho./4)
Anonymous minstrel song with alleged roots in African-American song. PSI; Brown Coll. 3&5:#406; Scarborough, *On the Trail of Negro Folk-Songs*, 66; N.I. White, *American Negro Folk Songs*, traces extensive early publishing history, 152.

368 THE MIDNIGHT HOUR ['Tis Midnight Hour] (Frank 1985, #d58)
(A) *Tis midnight hour the moon shines bright.* Piper, ship *Europa*, 1868-70. (2/8)
(B) *ditto.* George Edgar Mills, bark *Aurora*, 1858. (2/8)
(C) *ditto.* William H. Keith, circa 1865-71. (2/8)
Anonymous American parlor song "by an Amateur" (Philadelphia: W.R. Bayley, 1843; Boston: Geo. P. Reed & Co., 1846; etc.). Helen K. Johnson (perhaps erroneously) supposes the melody to be "old English." SI; Dichter #226, #1275; Rosenberg #901; Beadle's N° 5; McCaskey v6; *Good Old Songs* I:78; *Heart Songs* 293; H.K. Johnson 263.

369. THE MILLER'S SONG
Don't you remember sweet Lily Dell. Merrill, bark *Janus* and schooner *Eothen*, 1875-78 (3/4).
Sentimental song, possibly original, in the parlor-song mode.

370. THE MISSIONARY HYMN [The State of the Heathen; From Greenland's Icy Mountains] (Frank 1985, #38)
From Greenland's icy mountains. Bartley, ship *California*, 1854. (4/8)
Hymn in 7s & 8s meter. w: Bishop Reginald Heber (English, 1782-1826); m: Lowell Mason (American, 1792-1872), circa 1829. SI; PSI; Dichter & Shapiro 143; Brown & Butterworth 178. Bradbury, *The Jubilee;* McCaskey v2; *Heart Songs* 201; *Seamen's Hymns and Devotional Assistant,* #551; Stowe, *Ocean Melodies,* n.p. See also "The Appeal."

371. THE MISTLETOE BOUGH (Frank 1985, #83)
(A) *The mistletoe hung in the castle hall.* Bryant, ship *Elizabeth*, 1847-51. (4/9)
(B) *ditto.* Bartley, ship *California*, 1851-54. (4/9)
(C) *ditto.* Piper, ship *Europa*, 1868-70.
Maudlin English parlor song. w: Thomas Haynes Bayly (1797-1839); m: Sir Henry Rowley Bishop (1786-1855). SI; PSI; PSIS; H.K. Johnson 229; *Good Old Songs* I:20; mentioned in tradition, Gardner 481; Randolph #802, IV:323; *Singer's Gem* 176.

372. MOLLY BAWN [Fair Molly]
O Molly bawn why leave me fuming. Donahue, ship *Atlantic*, 1850-53 (2/8).
Parlor song. w&m: Samuel Lover (Irish, 1797-1868) circa 1840; sung by Michael William Balfe in the operetta *Il Paddy Whack in Italia* (Dichter). SI; SI2; Beadle's N° 4; Mackay 400; Page; *Songs of Ireland* 1890. The title monopolized upon a folk ballad of the same name, ubiquitous in Irish tradition, concerning the young namesake, who is mistaken for a swan and shot by her lover)

373. MOLLY MILES—PARODY ON "ANNIE LISLE"
Down on my nightly pillow. Coquin, 1860's-'70s. (4/8 + cho./4)
Not found. "Annie Lisle" by H.S. Thompson, 1857 (SI; SI2; etc.); the melody was used for the Cornell University anthem "Far Above Cayuga's Waters" (Dichter & Shapiro 139).

374. MOTHER WOULD COMFORT ME
Wounded and sorrowful, far from my home. Keith, circa 1865-71. (3/8 + cho./4 + 12 lines spoken intro.)
Civil War-era sentimental song by Charles Carroll Sawyer (1833-1890), son of a Mystic, Connecticut sea captain and shipbuilder; published in 1863. Dichter & Larrabee #915; Beadle's N° 10.

375. MY HEART'S IN THE HIGHLANDS (Burns)
My heart is in the highlands. Beden, ships *Massachusetts* and *South America*, 1851-55. (n/a)
Poem by Robert Burns (1759-1796), sung to the Scottish traditional air "The Musket Salute." SI; SI2; SIC; PSI; Dichter #1812.

376. MY MOTHER DEAR (Frank 1985, #76)
(A) *There was a place in child hood.* Wicks, bark *John Dawson*, 1853-58. (4/6)
(B) *There was a place in childhood.* Inscribed (later) in the journal of John Marble, ship *America* of Hudson, 1839-41. (3/6)
Sentimental song, 1845. w&m: Samuel Lover (1797-1868). SI; Beadle's N° 2; McCaskey v3; Mackay 399; *Singer's Gem* 107; Wier 1918, 299.

377. MY NEIGHBOR'S WIFE
(A) *We are taught to love - from childhood years.* Keith, circa 1865-71. (5/8)
(B) *We are taught to love; from childhood's early years.* Coquin, 1860's-'70s. (5/8)
Sentimental parlor song of forlorn love, coveting thy neighbor's wife. Not found elsewhere.

378. MY OLD KENTUCKY HOME, GOOD NIGHT [The Old Kentucky Home] (Foster) (Frank 1985, #d60)
The sun shines bright in my old Kentucky home. Piper, ship *Europa*, 1868-70. (3/8 + cho./4)
w&m: Stephen Collins Foster, 1853. SI; Dichter #621, #1628; Dichter & Larrabee #454, #1084; Dichter & Shapiro 93; Whittlesey & Sonneck 35; Beadle's N° 7; *Heart Songs* 162; R. Jackson 1974, 67; H.K. Johnson 64; Kieser 112; *Minstrel Songs* 174; Taylor & Howard; Wier 1918, 320; etc.

379. **NEW ENGLAND (I)** [New England, New England, My Home O'er the Sea]
   New England oh New England / My birth place & my home. Colton, bark *Tenedos*, 1840-43 (30 lines). "Feb Second 1846 James S. Colton / B.B. French." Log #930

Sentimental song, circa 1841; w: Anna M. Wells; m: I.T. Stoddard. SI2; Dichter & Shapiro 148; Rosenberg #1002; Beadle's N° 2; *Good Old Songs* I:42; Wier 1918, 336.

380. **NEW ENGLAND (II)**
   Oh why from my own native land did I part. Anonymous scribe, signed "Scraps, Odd-thoughts & Tag Ends of a Rope Hauler," ship *Warren* of Warren, 1832. (5/4)

381. **NO ONE TO LOVE** [Why No One to Love]
   No one to love, none to caress. Keith, circa 1865-71. (3/6)

Sentimental parlor-song; w: A.H.G. Richardson; m: arranged by William B. Harvey. "'Why no one to love'…was issued under the erroneous title 'No one to love.' This edition is described by Whittlesey and Sonneck, page 36. A song by the same title, 'No one to love,' was incorrectly attributed to [Stephen Collins] Foster" (Dichter, p. 99). SI; SI2; Dichter & Shapiro; Beadle's N° 9; *Good Old Songs* II:92; *Heart Songs* 464; *Home Songs*; Wier 1918, 328.

382. **THE OCEAN BURIAL**
(A) *Oh bury me not in the deep deep sea.* Bartley, ship *California*, 1851-54. (6/8)
(B) *Bury me not in the deep deep sea.* Piper, ship *Europa*, 1868-70. (3/8)
(C) *O bury me not in the deep deep sea.* Coquin, circa 1867-75. (5/8)

American sacred parlor song. w: Rev. Edward H. Chapin (1814-1880), published in the *Southern Literary Messenger,* 1839. m: George Nelson Allen (1812-1877), circa 1850-54. PSI; Dichter & Shapiro 148; Beadle's N° 5; Belden 387; Cox #55; Doerflinger 162; Fowke & Johnston 92; Frank 1985 #34; Linscott 245; W.O. & H.S. Perkins, *The Nightingale,* Boston, 1860, 204; Sharp 1932 #169. Belden's attribution of the text to a Captain William H. Saunders is almost certainly erroneous as such but may point to an incident or personality that inspired the poem. Laws lists it among "Ballad-Like Pieces" (Laws I:278). It was popularized by the singing of Ossian Dodge and inspired a western parody, "The Dying Cowboy" ("Bury Me Not On the Lone Prairie"), which Belden attributes to one H. Clemens of Deadwood, South Dakota, in 1872.

383. **OFT IN THE STILLY NIGHT** (Moore)
   Oft, in the stilly night. Keith, circa 1865-71. (2/8 + cho./1)

From *Moore's National Melodies;* w: Thomas Moore (Irish, 1779-1852); m: Sir John Andrew Stevenson (Scottish, 1760?-1833); sheet musicx published by 1815. SI; SI2; Dichter #1291; Beadle's N° 5; Beadle's Dime Melodist 13; McCaskey v1; *Good Old Songs* I:6; *Heart Songs* 91; H.K. Johnson 32; Molloy 106; Moore, *Irish Melodies;* Page 80; Wier 1918, 376.

384. **O GIVE ME A HOME BY THE SEA**
   O give me a home by the sea. Poole, ship *Minnesota* of New York, 1868-72. (3/10)

Parlor song w&m by E.A. Hosmer, 1853 (*not* E.S. Hosmer [1862-1945], as reported in SIC!). SI: SIC; Dichter & Shapiro 148; *Heart Songs* 340.

385. **OH! LEMUEL** (Foster) (Frank 1985, #d61)
   O Lemuel my lark, O Lemuel my beau. Piper, ship *Europa*, 1868-70. (3/4 + cho./4)

w&m: Stephen C. Foster, 1850. SI; Dichter & Larrabee #1085; Whittlesey & Sonneck 38; Taylor & Howard; Wier 1918, 353.

386. **OH! WILLIE WE HAVE MISSED YOU** [Willie We Have Missed You] (Foster) (Frank 1985, #d62)
(A) *O Willie is it you dear safe safe at home.* Piper, ship *Europa*, 1868-70. (3/6 + cho./2)
(B) ditto. Mills, bark *Aurora*, 1859. (3/6 + cho./2)

w&m: Stephen Collins Foster, 1854. SI; Dichter & Larrabee #732; Whittlesey & Sonneck 63; *Heart Songs* 74; Kieser 24; Spaeth 1927, 19; Taylor & Howard; Wier 1918, 500.

387. **THE OLD ARM CHAIR** (Frank 1985, #d63)
(A) *I love it I love it, and who shall dare.* Marble family copybook. (4/8)
(B) ditto. Marble family papers (second copy). (4/8)

English parlor song. w: Eliza Cook (English, 1818-1889), 1837. m: Henry Russell (1812-1900), circa 1837. American sheet music illustrated by Fitz Hugh Lane was published in Boston by Oakes & Swan, 1840. SI; SIC #3125; PSI; Rosenberg #1057; Beadle's N° 5; Brown Coll. 3&5: #668; Dichter & Larrabee #493; McCaskey v3; *Good Old Songs* I:154; *Heart Songs* 270; H.K. Johnson 20; Levy; Miller's 41; Wier 1918, 367.

388. **OLD BOB RIDLEY** (Frank 1985, #d64)
   O white folks I'll sing you a ditty. Piper, ship *Europa*, 1868-70. (3/4)

Minstrel song by Charles A. White (1830-1892), circa 1855. SI; Dichter & Larrabee #1200; Beadle's N° 1; *Minstrel Songs* 122; Wier 1929, 122.

389. **THE OLD CABIN HOME** [My Own Cabin Home] (Frank 1985, #74)
(A) *I am going to leave you now far away to leave.* Jones & Handy, bark *Waverly*, 1859-63. (7/4 + cho./4)
(B) *I am going far away to leave you now.* Piper, ship *Europa*, 1868-70. (3/4 + cho./4)
(C) ditto. Keith, circa 1865-71. (3/6 + cho./4)

Parlor song. w&m: Robert Treat Paine, Jr. (1773-1811); popularized on its posthumous reissue in 1857. SI; SIC #8473; PSI; Dichter & Shapiro 148; Rosenberg #309?, #1060; Beadle's N° 15; *Heart Songs* 457; *Minstrel Songs* 202; Wier 1918, 371.

390. **OLD DOG TRAY** (Foster) (Frank 1985, #d65)
   (A) *The morn of life is past and evening comes at last.* Marble family copybook. (3/7 + cho./1)
   (B   ditto. Tinkham, transcribed between voyages, "March 10, 1855." (3/4 + cho./4)
w&m: Stephen Collins Foster (1824-1864), 1853; "Sung by Christy's Minstrels." *Tray* was commonly used as a dog's name by 18th- and 19th-century lyricists: e.g., see "The Irish Harper and His Dog Tray" by Thomas Campbell (1777-1844), circa 1801 (*Universal* I:93); "The Old Shepherd's Dog" by John Wolcott (1738-1819) (*Universal* II:187); "The Blind Beggar and His Dog Tray" by "Anderson," to the air *Contented I Am* (Universal II:256); "The Happy Farmer," unattributed (Universal III:219); and "Pat and His Dog Tray" (q.v., #398). SI; SIC #1128; PSI; PSIS; Dichter #182; Dichter & Larrabee #494, #1202; Rosenberg #1064; Whittlesey & Sonneck 39f; Beadle's N° 1; R. Jackson 1974, 96; H.K. Johnson 4; *Minstrel Songs* 192; Wier 1918, 370.

391. **THE OLD HOUSE AT HOME**
   There's a low green cottage. (Cho: *The old house at home.*) Mills, bark *Aurora*, 1856-59. (5/4 + cho./4)
Two American parlor songs of this name were no doubt inspired by Irish poet Thomas Haynes Bayly's earlier set of lyrics with this title, one attributed to Isaac Baker Woodbury (1819-1858) (McCaskey v3); and the other by Edward James Loder (McCaskey v8), of which the whaleman's text is evidently a variant or adaptation.

392. **THE OLD MOUNTAIN TREE** (Frank 1985, #75)
   (A) *The home we loved by the bounding deep.* Davis, bark *Midas*, 1861-65. (3/8)
   (B) ditto. Piper, ship *Europa*, 1868-70. (2/8)
Obscure parlor song, circa late 1850s. w&m: James G. Clark. "Oh! the home we loved by the bounding deep" in W.O. Perkins, *The Golden Robin*, 1868. (3/8)Century 39; Ditson 40; Dichter & Larrabee #501; Beadle's N° 6; Perkins, *Golden Robin*, 82.

393. **ON LEAVING HOME** (Frank 1985, #78)
   A kiss, a smile, a sigh, a tear. Piper, ship *Europa*, 1868-70. (2/6)
Farewell song. Not identified; not found elsewhere; air unknown.

394. **ON THIS COLD FLINTY ROCK** (Frank 1985, #d66)
   On this cold flinty rock I will lay down my head. Papers of Eleanor and Jason L. Braley.
Parlor song attributed to John Braham [né Abraham] (1774?-1856), English tenor. *Songster's Repository* (1811), 14 [John Hay Library, Brown University]; *Singer's Gem* (1845), 40; Universal I:83.

395. **THE ORPHAN BOY** [The Orphan Boy's Tale] (Frank 1985, #d67)
   Stay, lady, stay, for mercy's sake. Piper, ship *Europa*, 1868-70. (4/8 + 3 lines)
Parlor song by Amelia [née Alderson] Opie (1769-1853) relating the sad tale of a young boy orphaned by his father's death under Nelson in the Battle of the Nile (August 1798). Lyrics in Bryant II:248; the tune not found, but see Rosenberg #1115.

396. **OUR BEAUTIFUL FLAG** (Frank 1985, #d68)
   Our beautiful flag it is now that we see. Piper, ship *Europa*, 1868-70. (6/4 + cho./4)
Not found. The whaleman's marginal notation reads, "Composed in the year 1862," and the (perhaps identifying) chorus begins, *O be true, O be true / True to the beautiful flag so free.*

397. **PADDLE YOUR OWN CANOE**
   I left my love and sacred home. Titled "I'll paddle my own canoe," In Poole, ship *Minnesota*, 1868-72. (4/4 + cho./4)
Parlor song, w: Henry Robert ["Harry"] Clifton, m: M. Hobson. SI; PSI; Beadle's N° 6 ("I'll paddle my own canoe"); Beadle's N° 16; McCaskey v3; *Heart Songs* 286; *Naval Songs* 22.

398. **PAT AND HIS DOG TRAY** (Frank 1985, #d69)
   (A) *On the green banks of the Shannon when Shelah was nigh.* Piper, ship *Europa*, 1868-70. (6/4)
   (B) ditto. From the same source (second copy). (6/8)
Though it begins like a ballad with an Irish setting, it becomes a sentimental parlor song with wistful memories of long ago, about a boy and his dog, long since departed this mortal coil. Not found elsewhere; tune unknown. See "Old Dog Tray" (above).

399. **THE PILOT** [Fear Not, But Trust in Providence]
   Oh, Pilot, 'tis a fearful night. Coquin, 1860's-'70s. (3/8)
w: Sidney Nelson; m: Thomas Haynes Bayly (1797-1839). SI; Baring-Gould, *English Minstrelsie*; Beadle's N° 7; Bruce 333; McCaskey v3; Hatton & Faning III:36; H.K. Johnson 190; Wier 1918, 388; etc.

400. **THE POWER OF WEALTH**
   Sweet Nelly was a merry sprite. Mills, bark *Aurora*, 1857. (9/4)
Unidentified; not found elsewhere; perhaps original lyrics by the diarist.

401. **PUT ME IN MY LITTLE BED**
   O Birdie I am tired now. Coquin, 1860's-'70s. (3/8 + cho./4)
w&m: C.A. White, circa 1870. Dichter & Shapiro 149; Beadle's N° 29; Davenport 68.

402. **THE QUILTING PARTY** [I Was Seeing Nellie Home; When I Saw Sweet Nellie Home]
   In the sky the bright stars glittered. Keith, circa 1865-71. (2 texts, each 3/8 + cho./4)
Sentimental song, circa 1856; w: Frances Kyle, m: John Fletcher. SI; SI2; Dichter & Shapiro 153; Chamberlain & Harrington; Beadle's N° 2; *Good Old Songs* II:90; *Heart Songs* 403; Wier 1918, 392; Wier 1929, 119.

403. **THE RED, WHITE AND BLUE** [Columbia, the Gem of the Ocean] (Frank 1985, #d70)
(A) *Columbia the gem of the ocean.* Piper, ship *Europa*, 1868-70. (3/8)
(B) *Columbia the gem of the ocean.* Keith, circa 1865-71. (3/8)
American patriotic anthem. w&m: Thomas A. Becket, Sr., for the actor David T. Shaw; first published as "Columbia, the Land of the Brave" (1843), then as "Columbia, the Gem of the Ocean" (1844), then as "The Red, White and Blue" (1861), by which title it enjoyed new popularity as a Civil War song and appears in the shipboard MS. SI; Dichter & Larrabee #1241; Dichter & Shapiro (72) give a catalogue of its early publishing history; likewise Lawrence (300), who incorrectly attributes the song to Shaw (see SI); Beadle's N° 1; McCaskey v1; *Good Old Songs* I:145; *Heart Songs* 469; Wier 1918, 406; etc.

404. **REQUIEM ON THE DEATH OF A MARINER** (Frank 1985, #35)
Mentioned by George Jones, bark *Waverly*, on the occasion of a burial at sea: "Tues. 23rd [April 1863]…we committed his body to the deep, after which the Captain made a short prayer and finished the services by singing a hymn entitled Requiem on the Death of a Mariner."
American hymn, 1849. w: "by Mr. B.S. Hall, on the death of Mr. George O. Bates, of Springfield, Mass., who perished at sea, Jan. 26, 1849. His ship was run into in the night, and most of the crew died from exposure" (Stowe). m: George Kiallmark, originally composed for "Araby's Daughter" (q.v., #238), a poem by Thomas Moore in *Lalla Rookh*.. Text, beginning *O! cold is the night wind,* in Phineas Stowe, ed., *Ocean Melodies and Seamen's Companion,* Boston, 1852 . Johnson 307; Stowe 175.

405. **REST, LILLA, REST**
They have smoothed down the locks of her soft golden hair. Keith, circa 1865-71. (3/4 + cho./2)
Sentimental song; not found elsewhere; perhaps related to "Rest, Darling, Rest" by E.C. Ilsey (Century 42; Ditson 44).

406. **THE RING MY MOTHER WORE**
The world has many terasures rare. Keith, circa 1865-71. (4/8)
Sentimental song, 1860; w: Louis Dela; m: Mary Cinn. Dichter #200; Beadle's N° 12.

407. **RING, RING THE BANJO** (Foster)
This life is never wrong. Mills, ship *James Loper*, 1860. Text "copied from Fran[cos] R. Scott, Jr." (5/8 + cho./4)
Parody or adaptation of the 1851 song "Ring de Banjo" by Stephen Collins Foster (SI; SI2; SIC; Beadle's N° 7; R. Jackson 1974, 110; Wier 1918, 396; Wier 1929, 208; etc.)

408. **ROCK ME TO SLEEP, MOTHER**
Backward, turn backward (3/8 + cho./4)
Sentimental song, circa 1860; w: variously attributed to E.A. Allen or Florence Percy; m: Ernest Leslie ("the accepted melodic setting that attained tremendous popularity"—Dichter & Shapiro 150). SI; SI2; Dichter #201f; Dichter & Larrabee #545, #775; Beadle's N° 8; McCaskey v4; *Good Old Songs* II:120; *Heart Songs* 432; *Home Songs*; Wier 1918, 404.

409. **ROSA LEE** (Frank 1985, #d71)
When I lived in Tennessee. Piper, ship *Europa*, 1868-70. (4/6 + cho./2)
Anonymous minstrel song, 1847; sung by the Ethiopian Serenaders and Christie's Minstrels. SI; Dichter #1654, #1655; Dichter & Larrabee #1063; Dichter & Shapiro 150; Beadle's N° 3; *Heart Songs* 450; *Minstrel Songs* 67; Wier 1918, 399.

410. **ROSALIE, THE PRAIRIE FLOWER** [Rosalie; The Prairie Flower] (Frank 1985, #d72)
On the distant prairie where the heather wild. Piper, ship *Europa*, 1868-70. (3/4 + cho./4)
Minstrel song, 1855. w&m: George Frederick Root (1820-1896), using the pseudonym Wurzel. SI, where the only citation is F.S. Knowlton, *Songs of Other Days* (Boston: Oliver Ditson, 1922); Dichter & Shapiro 150. Not to be confused with "Rosalie" by Launce Knight (*Heart Songs* 446; Wier 1918, 394) or "Rosa Lee" (q.v. above).

411. **THE ROSE OF ALLANDALE**
The Morn Was fair the skies Were/was Clear. Beden, ships *Massachusetts* and *South America*, 1851-55. (4/8: 2 texts)
Scottish song, w: Charles Jefferys, m: Sidney Nelson. American sheet-music published circa 1832. SI; SI2; SIC; PSI; Dichter #1144; Beadle's N° 5; McCaskey v1; *Good Old Songs* I:73; Huntington 1964, 257; H.K. Johnson 379; Wier 1918, 401.

412. **THE SAILOR'S GRAVE** (Frank 1985, #33)
A Bark was far far from land. Smith, bark *Roscius*, 1858-61.
Sentimental song. w: Eliza Cook (British, 1818-1889). m: Edward A. Hopkins, an obscure setting composed specifically for the U.S. Navy (1845); John C. Baker (1847), with which melody Cook's words were transformed "into a folk-song" (Colcord, 161). SI; PSI; Dichter #1861; Doerflinger 161; Wier 1918, 441. Hugill errs in claiming 1859 as the year of publication (*Songs of the Sea,* 55). Fowke (1981, 47) errs in claiming that the phrase "starry flag" is indigenous, as the British context was only later altered to reflect American patriotism. It was also published anonymously in *The Sailor's Magazine,* 23: 2 (Oct 1850), p. 56.

413. **SAVE THE SAILOR** (Frank 1985, #37)
The sailors home is on the wave. Gallup, bark *South America*, 1855-59. (2/4)
Anonymous American hymn in Common Meter, circa 1850, no particular air assigned. Stowe, *Ocean Melodies,* 1852/1866, p. 87.

414. **SHELLS OF OCEAN** [Shells of the Ocean] (Frank 1985, #d73)
¶ *One summer's eve in pensive though[t] I wandered on the sea girt shore.* Piper, ship *Europa*, 1868-70. (2/8)
¶ Title entered (but no text given) by William H. Keith, circa 1865-71.
English parlor song. w: J.W. Lake; m: John W. Cherry [or C.W. Cherry]. SI; Beadle's N° 1; McCaskey v2; *Good Old Songs* II:16; Morrison 204; Morrison & Murray 228. Compare Randolph #84, I:341 (4 versions from tradition).

415. **SHIP OF FAITH**
    Thou to sail on, oh! ship of faith. Coquin, bark *Pacific*, 1860's-'70s. (5/4)
Original hymn lyrics by whaleman/merchant seaman John S. Coquin.

416. **SILVER MOON** [Roll On, Silver Moon] (Frank 1985, #113)
    (A) *As I strayed from my cot at the close of the day.* Jones & Handy, bark *Waverly*, 1859-63. (5/ 4 + cho./4)
    (B) *ditto.* Piper, ship *Europa*, 1868-70. (5/4 + cho./4)
    (C) *ditto.* Keith, circa 1865-71. (5/4 + cho./4)
Parlor song: the allegedly "traditional English" words are usually unattributed but may have been written or revised by Joseph M. Turner (b. 1818), an American entrepreneur credited with having combined the lyrics with the tune by Charles Sloman, famous English music-hall performer (sheet music: Firth & Pond, New York, 1847). SI, SIC #3781; PSI; Dichter & Shapiro 150; Beadle's N° 5; McCaskey v2; *Good Old Songs* I:151; Hugill 180; Huntington 1964, 233; H.K. Johnson 347; Randolph #800, IV:319.

417. **THE SLAVE'S DREAM** [The Slave's Appeal] (Frank 1985, #d74)
    (A) *I had a dream a happy dream.* Mills, bark *Aurora*, 1856-59. (3/8)
    (B) *ditto.* Piper, ship *Europa*, 1868-70. (2/8 + last stanza repeats)
Anonymous minstrel song on an abolitionist theme. Wier 1929, 58.

418. **SLEIGHING SONG** (Frank 1985, #d75)
    O see each prancer pricks his ears. Piper, ship *Europa*, 1868-70. (12 lines). Not identified; air unknown.

419. **SLIDING DOWN THE CELLAR DOOR (A PARODY ON "SWINGING IN THE LANE")**
    How oft we talk of childhood joys. Poole, ship *Minnesota*, 1868-72. (4/8) "Sliding on the Cellar Door (A Parody on 'Swinging In The Lane')"
Beadle's N° 27. See "Swinging in the Lane."

420. **SOME ONE TO LOVE**
    Some one to love in this wide world of sorrow. Keith, circa 1865-71. (2/12)
Parlor song by J. R. Thomas. Beadle's Dime Melodist 11.

421. **THE SOUND OF THE SEA** (Frank 1985, #41)
    Thou art sounding on thou mighty sea. George Marble, ship *Le Baron* of Rochester, 1837-39.
Hymn in Common Meter. w: Felicia Dorothea [née Brown] Hemans (1783-1835). m: by —Nichols. Hemans, *Poetical Works*, 377; Stowe 16.

422. **THE STAR OF GLENGARRY** (Frank 1985, #d76)
    O the red moon is up over the moss covered mountain. Piper, ship *Europa*, 1868-70. (2/10)
English parlor song. w: Eliza Cook (1818-1889). m: Nathan James Sporle. SI; McCaskey v7; *Good Old Songs* II:24.

423. **STAR OF THE EVENING** [Beautiful Star] (Frank 1985, #d2)
    Beautiful star in Heaven so bright. Piper, ship *Europa*, 1868-70. (3/3 + cho.)
American parlor song. w&m: James M. Sayles (also listed as S.M. Sayles), 1855. SI; *Heart Songs* 68; *Good Old Songs* I:124.

424. **THE STAR SPANGLED BANNER** (Frank 1985, #49)
    (A) *O say, can you see by the dawn's early light.* Ritchie, ships *Israel, Herald,* and *Massachusetts*, 1843-47. (4/8)
    (B) *ditto.* Bryant, Jr., ship *Elizabeth*, 1847-51. (4/8)
    (D) *ditto.* Piper, ship *Europa*, 1868-70. (4/8)
American patriotic song, later adopted as the national anthem (1931). w: Francis Scott Key (1779-1843); m: air to the English convivial song *Anacreon in Heaven*, attributed to John Stafford Smith (1750-1836) or Samuel Arnold (1740-1803). Setting in B.F. Baker, *Excelsior Song Book*, 1860. SI; SIC #8021; PSI; PSIS; Dichter #1924-1951; Dichter & Shapiro 34-38; Fitz Gerald 97-100; Howard 124; Lawrence 205; Sonneck, 1909, 7-42; Sonneck, 1914, passim; etc. Extremely widely anthologized.

425. **SWINGING IN THE LANE**
    How oft we talked of childhood days. Poole, ship *Minnesota*, 1868-72. (4/8)
Parlor song; Beadle's N° 15. PSI lists only Vance #871, from tradition. See "Sliding on the Cellar Door (A Parody on 'Swinging in the Lane')."

426. **THE SWORD OF BUNKER HILL** (Frank 1985, #d77)
    He laid upon his dying bed his eyes was growing dim. Davis, bark *Midas*, 1861-65. (3/8)
Sentimental American patriotic parlor song of circa 1855, occasionally found in tradition. w: William Ross Wallace (1819-1881); m: Bernard Covert. SI; PSI; Dichter & Larrabee #603, #1295; Beadle's N° 1; Flanders 1953, 224; *Heart Songs* 316; H.K. Johnson 552; Wier 1918, 435.

427. **TAKE ME HOME TO DIE** (I) [The Last Request] (Frank 1985, #d78)
    (A) *This land is very bright, mother.* Marble family copybook. (8/4)
    (B) *ditto.* Keith, circa 1865-71. (8/4)
Parlor song, in full "Take Me Home to Die; or The Last Request," 1850. w: unknown; m: Isaac Baker Woodbury (1819-1858). Dichter #222; Beadle's N° 7. Possibly the basis for the Civil War song by J.A. Butterfield, "The Soldier's Request; or Take Me Home to Die" (q.v. below).

428. TAKE ME HOME TO DIE (II) [The Soldier's Request; or Take Me Home to Die]
Heaven alone can tell the anguish. Coquin, 1860's-'70s. "Take Me Home to Die" (3/8)
Civil War song by James Austin Butterfield, 1863 (Dichter #322); see the preceding.

429. TAXATION OF AMERICA
While I relate my story. Reynolds, ship *Janus*, 1842-44. Political song, not identified.

430. TELL MY MOTHER I DIE HAPPY
Keith, circa 1865-71.
Sentimental song of the Civil War, "The last words of Lieut. Crosby, who was killed in his battery at Salem Hights [sic] in the fight of Sunday evening, May second, 1863" (sheet music); w: C.A. Vosburgh; m: J. Burns. Dichter #331; Dichter & Larrabee #774; Beadle's Nº 10.

431. TENTING ON THE OLD CAMP GROUND [We're Tenting Tonight] (Frank 1985, #d79)
We're tenting to night on the old camp ground. Papers of Eleanor and Jason L. Braley (4/4 + cho./8)
Union song of the Civil War. w&m: Walter Kittredge (1834-1905). Some authorities claim 1862 as the date of publication but Dichter & Shapiro give 1864 (117). SI; SIC #1904; PSI; PSIS; Beadle's Nº 15; McCaskey v6; *Good Old Songs* II:27; *Heart Songs* 28; H.K. Johnson 524; Wier 1918, 487.

432. THEN I WARN ALL YOU DARKIES NOT TO LOVE HER (Frank 1985, #d80)
When I lived away down in old Virginny. Piper, ship *Europa*, 1868-70. (3/8 + cho./5 + recitation)
Minstrel song of unrequited love. Not identified.

433. THERE'S A SIGH IN THE HEART
There's a sigh in the heart. Keith, circa 1865-71. (4/4 + cho./1)
Sentimental song by Ann Fricker. SI; McCaskey v8.

434. THOU HAST LEARNED TO LOVE ANOTHER (Frank 1985, #d81)
Thou has learn't to love another. George Jones, bark *Waverly*, 1863. (3/8)
American parlor song: originally published anonymously (circa 1845-49) but later (by 1852) the music was attributed to Charles F. Slade. SI; PSI; Dichter & Larrabee #874; Dichter & Shapiro 87; Belden 211; *Good Old Songs* I:61; Huntington 1964, 249 (2 texts from incorrectly identified vessels).

435. 'TIS PAST MIDNIGHT
I wonder why he comes not home. Keith, circa 1865-71. (1/12 + 2/9)
Sentimental song attributed to F. Clemence (Century 49; Ditson 54).

436. 'TIS SAID THAT ABSENCE CONQUERS LOVE (Frank 1985, #d82)
(A) *'Tis said that absence conquers love.* Marble family copybook. (4/8)
(B) *ditto.* Marble family copybook (second copy). (4/8)
Parlor song. w: Frederick William Thomas (1808-1866), circa 1830. m: E. Thomas. Text A was evidently copied from the sheet music or some other text with a musical score. *Singer's Gem* 145.

437. TO GREECE WE GIVE OUR SHINING BLADES [The Sky Is Bright] (Moore) (Frank 1985, #54)
The sky is bright, the breeze is fair. Elizabeth Marble, Fall River: inscribed after the fact in the journal of John Marble, ship *America* of Hudson, N.Y., 1839-40. (2/4 + cho./3)
Byronesque sympathy for the Greek revolution. w: Thomas Moore (Irish, 1779-1852), from his *Evenings in Greece* (1826-32); m: Sir Henry Rowley Bishop (1786-1855). SI; H.K. Johnson 515; J.F. Waller, ed., *Moore's Works,* 498 (text only).

438. TRUTH OR ABSENCE [Truth In Absence] (Frank 1985, #d83)
I think of thee at early morn. Gallup, bark *South America*, 1857-59. (3/8)
English parlor song not often encountered in America. w: Henry Brandreth; m: Edmund B. Harper. SI; Century 49; Ditson 55 ("Truth in Absence"); Hatton & Faning III:104. Not to be confused with the better known song of this title by Franz Abt.

439. TWENTY YEARS AGO (Frank 1985, #d84)
(A) *I have wandered to the village Tom I have sat beneath the tree.* Piper, ship *Europa*, 1868-70. (7/8)
(B) *I've wandered through the village, Tom.* Poole, ship *Minnesota*, 1868-72. (9/4)
American parlor song. w: variously attributed to Frances Huston, William Willing, and others. m: William Willing. SI; Beadle's Nº 1; Brown Coll. 3&5: #233; *Good Old Songs* I:45; *Heart Songs* 280. Published anonymously as "Forty Years Ago" in *Heart Throbs* (74) and Randolph (#869, IV:392). Not to be confused with several other songs of the same name: by George P. Morris and Austin Phillips, 1841 (Dichter #1563); Gustave Blessner, 1851 (Dichter #229); G.J. Chester and Scott Gatty (*Richardson's Collection of Popular Music*, 1881); by C. Kinkel and/or E. Langlotz (Century 49).

440 UNDER THE WILLOW SHE'S SLEEPING (Foster)
(A) Under the willow she's laid with care. Keith, circa 1865-71. (4/4 + cho./4)
(B) ditto. Poole, ship Minnesota, 1868-72.
w&m: Stephen Collins Foster, 1860. SI; SI2; Whittlesey & Sonneck 56; Beadle's Nº 7; McCaskey v7; Wier 1918, 486; Wier 1929, 192.

441. **THE VACANT CHAIR** [We Shall Meet But We Shall Miss Him]
 I am dying, comrades, dying. Keith, circa 1865-71. (3/8 + cho./4)
Sentimental song, 1861; w: Henry S. Washburn; m: George Frederick Root (1820-1895). SI; Dichter #337f; Dichter & Larrabee #931; Beadle's N° 12; McCaskey v3; Heart Songs 32; Home Songs; Wier 1918, 483.

442. **THE VICTIM** (Frank 1985, #d85)
 Hand me the bowl, ye jovial band. Piper, ship *Europa*, 1868-70. (7/8)
Anonymous temperance song in which "the victim" (of addiction to drink), at the moment of his painful epiphany, succumbs to his weakness, reverts to the bottle to "seek relief," and promptly dies. Mentioned by Ewing, who cites Phineas Stowe, Melodies for the Temperance Band: A Collection of Hymns and Songs (Boston: Nathaniel Noyes, 1856), 16; not found elsewhere.

443. **THE VILLAGE BORN BEAUTY** (Frank 1985, #121)
 Yon star breasted villain to yonder cot bound. Kirwin, bark *William Gifford*, 1872-73. (9/4)
English parlor song. w: W. Upton m: air for The High-Mettled Racer, a comparatively obscure sporting song by Charles Dibdin (1745-1814), from his comic opera Liberty Hall (London, 1785). While "The Village Born Beauty" is altogether quite rare and was seldom if ever printed since it was anthologized in the Universal Songster circa 1825, comparison of the two known whalemen's texts (Frank 1985, #121; Huntington 299) reveals a multitude of transformations that can only have resulted from a life in tradition. Universal I:356; Huntington 1964, 299. Tune: Hogarth I:161; Hatton & Faning II:4.

444. **WAIT FOR THE WAGON** (Frank 1985, #d86)
 Will you come with me sweet Phillis. Piper, ship *Europa*, 1868-70. (2/4)
American minstrel song, 1851. Usually attributed to R. Bishop Buckley; some early editions credit the words to John R. Thomas (1829-1896) and the music to George P. Knauff. SI; Dichter #231, #232; Dichter & Larrabee #660; Dichter & Shapiro 153; Century 50; Rosenberg #1463; Pearsall 100; Beadle's N° 1; McCaskey v6; Huntington 1964, 285; H.K. Johnson 429; Randolph #563, III:375; Wier 1918, 513. Note the Confederate Army parody "The Southern Wagon" (Dichter & Shapiro 124).

445. **THE WATCHER** (Frank 1985, #d87)
 The night was dark and fearful. Piper, ship *Europa*, 1868-70. (4/12)
Gothic American parlor song. w: Mrs. Sarah Josepha [née Buell] Hale (1833-1879); m: William Lardner. SI Beadle's N° 5; McCaskey v4; *Good Old Songs* I:60.

446. **WE COME, WE COME** (Frank 1985, #81)
 We come—we come in joy to greet you. Mills, bark *Mary Frances*, 1856. (4/8)
Variant of the minstrelsy piece "We come again with song to greet you," w: Marshall S. Pike; m: L.V.H. Crosby. Sheet music C. Bradlee & Co., Boston, 1846. Miller 22.

447. **WE HAVE MET AND WE HAVE PARTED** [We Have Met, Loved, and Parted] (Frank 1985, #d88)
 We have met and we have parted. Papers of Elizabeth Marble. (frag. 8 lines)
American parlor song. w: Elmer Ruan Coates; m: R.A. Eastburn (pseudonym of Septimus Winner, 1827-1902). SI; PSI; Brown Coll. 2&4:#155; *Good Old Songs* II:126.

448. **WE MISS THEE AT HOME** [Yes, We Miss Thee at Home]
(A) *We miss the[e] at home, yes we miss thee.* Mills, bark *Aurora*, 1856-59. (4/8)
(B) *Yes we miss thee at home yes we miss thee.* Hughson, bark *Java*, 1857-60. "Yes, We Miss The[e] at Home" (3/8)
¶ Title entered (but no text given) by Keith, circa 1865-71.
Parlor song. This is promoted as "an answer to the favorite ballad 'Do They Miss Me at Home'" [#277] has w&m by Charlie Converse (Boston: Oliver Ditson, 1853); Beadle's N° 3. The original song (w: Caroline Atherton [née Briggs] Mason; m: Sidney Martin Grannis) appeared in 1852; there is also "Do They Think of Me at Home?" [#278] (w: J.E. Carpenter; m: C.W. Glover), original date of publication unknown, which was followed by "Yes, We Think of Thee at Home," arranged and likely composed by E.C. Ilsey (Century 54).

449. **WHAT AILS THIS HEART O' MINE**
 What ails this heart of mine. Beden, ships *Massachusetts* and *South America*, 1851-55. (fragment)
Scottish song, w: Susanna Blamire, m: traditional air "My dearie, an' thou dee."

450. **WHAT IS HOME WITHOUT A MOTHER?** (Frank 1985, #d89)
¶ *What is home without a mother.* Marble family copybook. (3/8)
¶ Mentioned by Piper, ship *Europa*, 1868-70.
¶ Title entered (but no text given) by Keith, circa 1865-71.
American parlor song, 1854. w&m: Alice Hawthorne [a pseudonym of Septimus Winner, 1827-1902]. SI; SIC #4054; Dichter & Larrabee #683, #770; Dichter & Shapiro 153; Beadle's N° 2, 40; McCaskey v2; *Good Old Songs* I:156; Wier 1918, 518. A song entitled "What Is Home Without a Father?," w&m by Louis S.D. Rees, was also published in 1854 (Century 51).

451. **WHAT NORA SAID. REPLY TO NORA O'NEAL.**
 Is it lonely ye are then without me? Poole, ship *Minnesota*, 1868-72. (3/8 + cho./4)
"What Norah Said. Reply to Norah O'Neal." American parlor song by W.F. Wellman (Century 51; Ditson 58), construed as the sequel to the parlor song "Nora O'Neal" by Will S. Hays, 1866 (Dichter & Shapiro 148); Beadle's N° 22.

452. WHEN OTHER FRIENDS ARE ROUND THEE
When other friends are round thee. Keith, circa 1865-71. (2/8)
Sentimental song; w: George P. Morris (1802-1864); m: by "C.R.W." SI; SIC; McCaskey v3; H.K. Johnson 305; Wier 1918, 520.

453. WHEN YOU AND I WERE YOUNG, MAGGIE
I wandered today to the hill Maggie. Coquin, 1860's-'70s. (3/8 + cho./4)
w: George M. Johnson; m: James Austin Butterfield; SI; *Good Old Songs* II:147; *Heart Songs* 478; *Home Songs*; Wier 1918, 504; Wier 1929, 40.

454. WHIP-POOR-WILL (I)
The sun has descended beneath the green wave. Reynolds, ship *Janus*, 1842-44; possibly inscribed after the fact, circa 1850s. Not identified (see SI).

455. WHIPPOORWILL (II) [The Whip-poor-will Song]
O meet me when daylight is fading. Poole, ship *Minnesota*, 1868-72. (12 lines)
Parlor song, w&m: Harrison Millard, circa 1865. SI2; Dichter #250; Rosenberg #1530; *Good Old Songs* II:115.

456. WIDOW IN THE COTTAGE BY THE SEA
Just one year ago tonight love. Keith, circa 1865-71. (3/4 + cho./4)
Sentimental song by Charles Albert White (1832-1892). SI2; Dichter & Larrabee #775; Dichter & Shapiro 154; *Good Old Songs* II:87; Howe's 100.

457. WIDOW MACHREE (Frank 1985, #d90)
O widow Machree it is no wonder you frown. Piper, ship *Europa*, 1868-70. (5/9)
w&m: Samuel Lover (1797-1868). SI; Beadle's N° 4; Beadle's Dime Melodist 46; H.K. Johnson 412; Page 118; Wier 1918, 508.

458. [YANKEE DOODLE] The Country Lovers
A merry tale I will rehearse. Gifford, brig *Elizabeth*, 1837-38 (49/4 + cho./4).
Unascribed, to the tune and with the chorus of "Yankee Doodle" [#171].

459. YOU ARE THINKING OF ME, DARLING
You are thinking of me, darling. Keith, circa 1865-71. (7/8 or 8/8). Parlor song; not found.

460. YOU'LL REMEMBER ME [Then You'll Remember Me] (Moore)
(A) *When other lips and other hearts.* Hughson, bark *Java*, 1857-60. (3/8)
(B) ditto. Keith, circa 1865-71. (2 texts, 2 different titles, each 2/8 + cho./1)
(C) ditto. Coquin, 1860's-'70s. (2/8)
Words by Thomas Moore (Irish, 1779-1852), to the Irish air "Were I a Clerk"; there is also a setting by Michael William Balfe (1808-1870). SI2.

References

Abbreviations for Principal Bibliographical and Taxonomic Reference Works Cited

For other, general citations, refer to the Bibliography

Am. Sailor	*American Sailor's Songster (The)*. Philadelphia, New York, and Boston: Fisher & Brother. n.d. [circa 1848].
Beadle's	*Beadle's Dime Song Book,* 34 vols. (*N° 1* through *N° 34*), New York: Irwin P. Beadle; Boston: John J. Dyer & Co.; New York and Buffalo: Irwin R. Beadle; etc., 1859-76.
Bronson	Bronson, Bertrand Harris. *Traditional Tunes of the Child Ballads,* 4 vols., Princeton University Press, 1959-72.
Century	Century Musical Association. *Members' Catalogue: Sheet Music, Folios and Musical Works....* Philadelphia and Chicago: Century Musical Association. n.d. [circa 1894.]
Child	Child, Francis James. 1882-98. *The English and Scottish Popular Ballads.* 5 vols. Boston: Houghton Mifflin. (Repr., 3 vols., New York: Oxford University Press; repr., New York: Cooper Square, 1962; repr., 5 vols., New York: Dover, 1965.)
JFSS	White, E.A.; and Margaret Dean-Smith, eds. *An Index of English Songs contributed to the Journal of the Folk Song Society, 1899-1931; and its continuation, the Journal of the English Folk Dance and Song Society, to 1950.* London: The English Folk Dance and Song Society, 1951.
Laws #A-I	Laws, G. Malcolm. *Native American Balladry.* Publications of the American Folklore Society Bibliographical Series, Vol. 1, "Revised Edition." Philadelphia, 1964.
Laws #J-Q	Laws, G. Malcolm. *American Balladry from British Broadsides.* Publications of the American Folklore Society Bibliographical and Special Series, Vol. 8. Philadelphia, 1957.
O'Neill	O'Neill, Captain Francis. *O'Neill's Music of Ireland.* (*The Music of Ireland* [1903] and *The Dance Music of Ireland* [1907].) Bronx: Daniel Michael Collins. n.d.
PI	*Poetry Index.* William F. Bernhardt, ed/. *Granger's Index to Poetry,* 4th ed. New York: Columbia University Press, [1962] 1964.
PSI	*Popular Song Index* by Patricia Pate Havlice. Metuchen: Scarecrow, 1975.
PSIS	*Popular Song Index—First, Second,* and *Third Supplements*], 3 vols., by Patricia Pate Havlice. Metuchen. N.J.: Scarecrow, 1978, 1984, and 1989.
SI	*Song Index... and Supplement.* Sears, Minnie Earl. 2 vols. in 1. [Hamden, Connecticut]: Shoe String. 1966. (Reissue of H.W. Wilson Co., [New York,] 1926 and 1934.)
SIC	*Songs In Collections* by Desiree de Charms and Pearl F. Breed. Detroit: Information Coordinators, 1966.

References for the Individual Songs

1. **Black-Eyed Susan** [Dark-Eyed Susan]: SI; SIC #2120; PSI; Rosenberg #102; Amateur; Am. Sailor 141; Baker & Miall 175 (notes); Baring-Gould 1895 II:76; Calliope, 408; Devine 20; Chappell II:640; Creighton 1961, 90; Duncan I:258; Forecastle 60; Forget Me Not 131; Frank 1985 #1; Grigg's 107; Hullah #43; Luce 160; Mackay 63; Miller's 70; Naval Songs 60; Skylark 161; Universal I:361. Laws cites only Creighton & Senior, 132.

2. **Tom Bowling** [Poor Tom]: SI; SIC #834; PSI; PSIS. Am. Musical Miscellany 31; Am. Sailor 140; Baker & Miall 223 (Dibdin biographical sketch, 143; note, 226); Forecastle 59; Frank 1985 #6; Grigg's; Heart Songs 236; Hogarth I:176, I:208, I:240, I:245; Hullah #81; Johnson 163; Luce 79; Mackay 90; Minstrelsy of England 94; Naval & Patriotic 151; Naval Songs 18; Shay 1948, 96. Dana, *Two Years Before the Mast* (1840); Melville, *White-Jacket* (1850); Nordhoff (1857); W.M. Davis (1874), who quotes the last 4 lines of the first stanza to illustrate the character of his shipmate "Old Ben" Coffin.

3. **Bay of Biscay O**: SI; Am. Sailor 84; Baker & Miall 214; Baring-Gould 1895 I:111; Creighton 1933, #152; Frank 1985 #2; Grigg's 109; Griggs 1900, 168; Hullah #88; Johnson 175; Luce 174; Mackay 107; Miller's 146; *Minstrelsy of England,* 246; Naval & Patriotic 171; New Song Book 15; Universal I:227; Wier 1918, 62. Dana, *Two Years Before the Mast* (1840), Ch. 29; Melville, *White-Jacket* (1850), 9.

4. **The Storm** [Cease, Rude Boreas]: SI; PSI. Am. Musical Miscellany 52; Baring-Gould 1894, v4; Hatton & Faning 2:40; Hullah #92; Huntington 70; Johnson 120; Luce 70 (whose version is evidently transcribed from a broadside or sheet music and is erroneously attributed to the poet William Falconer, 1732-1769); Mackay 118; Naval Songs 73. For provenance and publishing history of the tune, see Kidson 1900, 12f; and Moffat & Kidson 1901, 184.

5. **Henry Martin** [Salt Sea] (Child #250): SI; SIC #4631 A&B; PSI; PSIS; JFSS; Rosenberg #533. Child #250; Bronson IV:24-46 (50 versions); Cox #26; Eddy #24; Farnsworth & Sharp 10; Flanders 1932, 72; Frank 1998 #3; Karpeles #22 (3); Kidson 1891, 30f (2); Mackenzie #13; Sharp 1916, #1. Not in any of the standard sea-chantey-and-sailor-song collections.

6. **The *Bold Trinity*** [The *Sweet Trinity*; The *Golden Vanity*; etc.] (Child #286): SI; PSI; PSIS; SIC #4617 A-H; Child #286; Rosenberg #1361 A&B. Ashton 1891, 221; Baring-Gould et al., *Songs of the West*; Belden 97; Broadwood 182; Bronson III: 501 (selections from over 100 specimens); Brown Coll. 2&4:#47; Buck; Cazden 1982 #67; Colcord 154; Cox #32; Creighton 1933, #10; Davis & Tozer #15; Duncan 1905 v2; Flanders 1960-65, IV:188 (39 texts and fragments, 21 tunes); Flanders 1932, 230; Fowke 1965, #4 and #61; Frank 1985 #142; Frank 1998 #8; Gardner #83; Greenleaf #19; Harlow 1962, 35; Hugill 62 (3 versions); Masefield 147 (3 texts); Moffat & Kidson; Randolph #38, I:195 (5 versions); *Scottish Students' Song Book*; Sharp 1932, #41 (11 versions); Sharp 1916, #14; L.A. Smith ("The Spanish Canoe");Vaughan Williams 46; Warner #104. "Louisiana Lowlands": see "The Monitor and the Merrimac" [#57]; Waite 58; compare Flanders 1960-65, IV:188-263, especially version P.

7. **High Barbary** [The Coast of Barbary] Child #285; Laws #K-33): SI; JFSS; Child #285. Am. Sailor 85; Ashton 1891, 42; Baker & Miall 72; Bronson IV:306-311; Brown #118; Colcord 153; Farnesworth & Sharp #10; Firth 1908, xxi, 23, 342; Flanders 1960 III:176-187 (7 versions); Frank 1985 #141; Frank 1998 #6; Frank 2000a, 25; Harlow 1962, 161; Hugill 491 (3 chanteys); Luce 77; Naval Songs 16; Neeser; Sharp 1916 #12; Sharp 1932 v1; Shay 1948, 91; Trident; Warner #142; Whall 85.

8. **Spanish Ladies** [Farewell and Adieu]: SI; Baker & Miall 33; Baring-Gould 1895 III:56; Chappell II:736; Frank 1985 #143; Hugill 384; Joyce 283; Mackenzie #97 (extensive bibliography); Palmer 1985 #54; Sharp 1916 #89; Shay 1948, 136; L.A. Smith 45; Whall 15. Correspondents Ingram, Laughton, "A. M.," and Perrin, in *Mariners' Mirror*, 5:5 (Nov 1919), 160; 6:2 (Feb 1920), 60; 7:1 (Jan 1921), 61; 7:10 (Oct 1921), 318; 7:12 (Dec 1921), 356; 9 (1923), 2-10, 46f, 48-55, 66-74, 78-83, 108f, 147f, 180-183, 202-208. Frederick Marryatt, *Poor Jack*, Ch. 17; *The Sea King*, Ch. 15; John Masefield, *A Sailor's Garland*, 180; *Sea Life in Nelson's Time* (cited by Ingram, 7:1, 61); Herman Melville, *Moby-Dick*, Ch. 40; *White-Jacket*, Ch. 74.

9. **The Girl I Left Behind Me**: (1) "I'm lonesome since I crossed the hill": SI; SI2; SIC; PSI; PSI-1; PSI-2; Baring Gould 1894; *Beadle's N° 3;* Buck, *Oxford Song Book;* Chappell, *Ballad Lit. & Popular Music;* Chappell 1893, II:187; Fife 1969, #62; McCaskey v2; Hatton & Faning I;101; Meek; Hullah, 76; Luce, 63 (erroneously attributed to Lover); *Naval Songs* (1874), 67; Wier 1918, 164. (2) "The dames of Fr_dre wild and free" (words by Thomas Davis): SI; SI2; SIC; PSI; Dolph, 507; Fitz-Gerald, 360; Hatton & Malloy, 148; Molloy, 148; O'Reilly, 520; Shay 1948, 202; Spaeth 1926, 16. (3) "The hour was sad I left the maid" (words by Samuel Lover): SI2; PSI; Dolph, 506 (parody); *Good Old Songs*, I:130*; Songs of Ireland* 1890, n.p. (4) "As slow our ship her foamy track" (words by Thomas Moore): SIC. (5) "Come all ye handsome, comely maids": O Lochlainn 1939, #18 ("Moore, Davis, P.D. Joyce and others have written songs to this air"). (6) "I struck the trail in 'seventy-two": PSI. (7) "Oh swing that gal, that pretty little gal" (American square-dance version): PSI; PSI-1 ("*Darling Nellie Gray* and *The Girl I left Behind Me* are two square dances which originated in New York State... [and] became established throughout southern New England" [Tolman & Page, 78]). (8) [unspecified]: Rosenberg #449.

10. **The Lily of Lake Champlain**: Frank 1985 #88; Frank 1995, 7; Huntington MS, 533; Naval Songs, 77 (but not in Luce). See also Schrader 1982.

11. **The Norfolk Girls**: PSI; Frank 1985 #58; Luce 184; Naval Songs 13; Shay 1948, 172.

12. **My Dream**: Not found elsewhere.

13. **My Wife—A Song**: The tune may be "The Indian's Lament" ["The Indian Hunter's Prayer"; "White Man, Let Me Go;" etc.], first line "Let me go to my home in the far distant west," w&m by Isaac Baker Woodbury (1819-1858) [#333]: two texts were recovered from the Marble family; another from the journal of Native American whaleman Sylvanus C. Fullmoon of Long Island, ship *Nimrod* of New Bedford, 1842-45; a fourth from the Braley family; a fifth from William H. Keith's journal, 1865-71; two others reported by Huntington, 180. Most anthologies fail to attribute it; but see Howard, 148. SIC; PSI; Century 22; Beadle's N° 3; Brown III, #270; Frank 1985 #66; Huntington 1964, 180 (2 texts; erroneous tune, in confusion with #331); Thompson #76, p. 172. Fowke & Johnston (33) call it "White Man, Let Me Go" and state erroneously, "It does not seem to have appeared in any published collection, and the Library of Congress has no information about it." Also: Dichter & Shapiro 75; Rosenberg #656-659.

14. **Lines to Mary**: Colcord 163; Frank 1985 #176. The partial inspiration may be a nautical love-poem (or fragment) of ten lines beginning, "'Twas night, and nothing but the wild expanse / Of ocean, deep and dismal, now appeared... ," quoted in an anonymous book of naval fiction of circa 1801, *The Post-Captain; or The Wooden Walls Well Manned* ("Fourth American, from the fifth London Edition," New York: Joseph M'Cleland, 1828), where it is ascribed to "Skeene" (not identified).

15. **The Carpenter and the Maid**: Not found elsewhere.

16. **The Milking Maid**: Not found elsewhere.

17. **Frozen Limb**: Miller, 77.

18. **Can Ladies Be Compared to Man?** Not found elsewhere.

19. **The Lowlands of Holland**: SI; PSI; PSIS. Ashton 167; Bronson II:418-427; Bronson 1976, 237; Flanders 1953, 113; Frank 1985 #106; Frank 1995, 6; Healy 1967 #42; Masefield 259; O Lochlainn 1965 7a; Palmer 1973 #9 (quite credibly claims the 1620s to be the date of origin); Sharp 1932, I #26; Sharp 1916 #23; Shay 1948, 45. For an adaptation more truly indigenous to the whale fishery, see "The Nantucket Mother and Daughter," #20.

20. **The Nantucket Mother and Daughter**: Frank 1985 #175. See "The Lowlands of Holland," #19.

21. **The Banks of the Schuylkill**: PSI lists only Randolph (#769, IV:281); also: *Banner Songster, American Series N° 2* (New York: Beadle, 1865); *Forget Me Not* (text repr. in Jackson, 153). "The Girl Volunteer" / "Johnny's Must Fight" / "Cruel War": PSI; PSI-1; Belden 180; Brown 317; Laws #O-33; Randolph #245.

22. **West's Farewell**: Not found elsewhere.

23. **The British Man-of-War / The Yankee Man-of-War**: PSI; Belden 379; Frank 1985 #101; Kidson 1891, 102; JFSS 7:9. Belden dates "Yankee Man-of-War" to the Civil War, a view consistent with the chronology of the whalemen's texts here and two others gleaned from whaling MSS (Huntington 1964, 108); also with allusions to Jefferson Davis in Cazden 1982 #13; however, the Charles Magnus song-sheet cited as Dichter & Larrabee #763 is likely somewhat earlier. "The Fenian Men o' War" (e.g., in Galvin) is an Irish adaptation. Not to be confused with "The Gallant Yankee Ship" ("The Yankee Man-of-War") (e.g., *Naval Songs* 24).

24. **The Captain Calls All Hands**: PSI (lists only Huntington 1964 99); Huntington MS, 241. For "Our Captain Calls" and "Our Captain Cries," Kennedy cites JAFL 35:375f; JFSS 1901, no. 3, p. 131; JFSS 1906, no. 8, p. 202; Frank Purslow, *The Constant Lovers,* London, 1972. For "The Blacksmith" and other citations, see: Kennedy 1975 #146; Vaughan Williams, 22.

25. **Farewell, Charming Nancy** (Laws #K-14): Brown 342; Healy 1967 #8; O Lochlainn 1965 #22 ("This ballad also appears as 'Adieu, lovely Mary'"); Scarborough 372, 476; Sharp 1916 #30. See #54 (below); Frank 1985 #100. Steve Gardham cites a printing by J. Deacon of London in 1685 entitled "The Seaman's Doleful Farewell, or The Greenwich Lover's Mournful Departure" (Pepys, Vol. 4, p. 186; Roxburghe Ballads, Vol. 8, p. 780).

26. **Adieu, Sweet Lovely Nancy**: Copper 244; Frank 1985 #100; Karpeles 1934 (2 versions); Palmer 1973 #1 (after Copper). Browne, *Etchings,* 1846, 18.

27. **My Mary Ann** [Mary Ann]: SI; SIC; PSI; PSIS; Dichter & Larrabee #1416; Rosenberg #882; Fowke & Johnston 142; Heart Songs 246; Wier 1918, 315. For a detailed provenance and sources, see Cazden 1982 #44, pp 172ff.

28. **Outward Bound**: Frank 1985 #172. Additional source: New Bedford Port Society outward-bound crew lists.

29. **The Sailor Boy's Farewell**: Naval Songs 47; Luce 189.

30. **The Ship Is Ready**: Frank 1985 #99. Sheet music, [New York]: n.p. / Samuel Ackerman, 1838.

31. **Caledonia** [Jamie Raeburn's Farewell]: PSI; Bikel, 132; Ford [1889] 1904, 243; Greig 1914, XXXVI; Meredith & Anderson, 85 and 245; Ord 1930, 357; Wannan 170 (after Russel Ward et al., *Songs from the Bush,* 1957).

32. **Jolly Sailors Bold** [Sailors' Come-All-Ye]: Am. Singer 163 (fine early text); Am. Vocalist 163; Ashton 223 ("Neptune's Raging Fury," circa 1635); Colcord 137, 138; Frank 1985 #164; Frank 1995, 6; Harlow 216, 219, 231 (3 versions); Huntington 1964, 68; Mackenzie #95; Masefield 182 (navy version); Palmer 1973 #29 (navy version). See also "The Joviall Cobler" in Duncan I:51; Simpson 768. Baring-Gould 1895 (VIII:92) documents the publishing history of the precursor, "To All You Ladies Now On Land" (1686).

33. **Boston** ['Twas on the Twenty-First of May]: Frank 1985 #150; Frank 2000a, 26f; Whall 148 (source of Colcord 168, Harlow 155, Trident 66). See Frank 1985b, "'Boston': Two 'New' Texts of an Old Favorite Sea Song," *American Neptune,* 45:3, 175-80. MacEdward Leach has it as "There She Goes" and the Gardiner Collection has it as "From Sweet Dundee." Concerning "Bow, Wow, Wow," see: Chappell I:717; Duncan, vol. I, "The Barking Barber"; Kennedy #354; Universal Songster, passim.

34. **Captain Avery**: Firth (131ff) transcribed his text from a broadside in the Pepys collection; he ties the narrative to the record of "facts set forth at the trial of six of Every's crew in 1696" (347f); "The numerous variants in the later version are merely corruptions and not worth noting" (346). Frank 1998 #12. Concerning broadsides, Steve Gardham notes: "…There are plenty, the longest having 13 double stanzas. There is a full oral version in the Hammond Gardiner collection (VWML) published in 'The Foggy Dew', Purslow, 1974. There is also an exhaustive study of the history of the ballad in *Folk Music Journal,* 7:1 (1995), pp. 5-26, by Joel H. Baer" (private communication, December 2010).

35. **The *Brooklyn***: As noted in the main text.

36. **The *Dreadnought*** (Laws #D-13): SI; Ashton ("The Fancy Frigate") 229; Colcord 170; Creighton 1961, 140 (variant); Doerflinger 126f, 133; Frank 1985 #148; Harlow 101; Hugill 462 (5 versions); Luce 67; Naval Songs 67; Shay 1948, 102; Palmer 1986 #144 (notes on tunes); Trident 72; Whall (1910 et seq., "La *Pique*"; not in 1963 ed.). Concerning vessel and captain, see: Albion 1938; Cutler 1961, ; and Samuel Samuels, *From Forecastle to Cabin,* 1887.

37. **Eighteen Hundred Forty-Nine**: Not found elsewhere.

38. **Unmooring** [The Boatswain's Call]: : SI; Frank 1985 #144; Luce 64; Whall 23.

39. **The Loss of the *Ramillies*** (Laws #K-1): PSI; Doerflinger 143, 354; Frank 1985 #149; Mackenzie #85; Palmer 1973 #17; Palmer 1986 #47.

40. **Prince Edward's Isle**: Frank 1985 #151.

41. **Homeward Bound**: Conway 20; Huntington 1964, 321; Frank 1985 #26.

42. **We'll Soon Be There**: Frank 1985 #178; Miller 27.

43. **Sweet America**: Frank 1985 #177; Huntington MS 35.

44. **The Sailor's Alphabet**: SI; Rosenberg #1235; Brown Coll. 3&5:#229; Creighton 1933 #98 (2 versions); Doerflinger 344 (mentioned only, with citations); Frank 1985 #155; Harlow 52; Hugill 456 (2 versions); Palmer 1986 #107 (Sussex). "The Lumberman's Alphabet": Creighton 1933 #98; Doerflinger 207, 344; Flanders 1953, 112; Frank 1985 #155; Gardner #102; Linscott 1939, 253; Manny & Wilson #82. See also: Palmer 1986 #142; Universal II:14; Warner #183. Tune (additional citations): Chappell II: 677; Luce 52; Manny & Wilson #82, suggesting affinities with certain airs for "Lord Randall" (Child #122; q.v. Bronson I: 210, #53 & #54); Simpson 140 and 172-176, where he presents four versions and a detailed discussion, including the relationship to ballad operas, broadsides, and the ballad "King John and the Bishop" (Child #45). The widely known children's songs of the family "A is for apple so rosy and red… " are related to this genre.

45. **Goodbye, Fare Ye Well**: Bone 117; Colcord 113; Davis & Tozer #9; Doerflinger 87 (3 versions); Harlow 119 (version with a charming extra refrain added to the chorus); Hugill 120-130 (4 texts in English, 2 in Norwegian, 2 in French); Shay 1948, 85; C.F. Smith 77; Terry I:6; Whall 9.

46. **Heave Away** [We're All Bound to Go]: Colcord 93; Doerflinger 62 (2 versions); Farnsworth & Sharp 109; Harlow 14 (2 texts); Hugill 303 (3 versions, extensive notes); Shay 1948, 73; Terry I:28; Whall 53.

47. **Reuben Ranzo**: Bone 55; Colcord 70; Davis & Tozer #20; Doerflinger 23 (2 versions); Farnsworth & Sharp; Frank 2000a, 21f; Harlow 89; Hugill 240 (2 versions, extensive notes); Shay 1948, 50; C.F. Smith 46; Terry I:46; Whall 63. Further notes in Frank 1985, pp. 156-161.

48. **Old Horse**: PSI; PSI-1; Frank 1985, 48-56; Hugill, 553-557. "Old Horse" ("Salt Horse"; "Sailor's Grace"): Davis & Tozer #46; Harlow 69; Hugill 556 (2 versions); see also Whall 136. "Poor Old Man" ("Dead Horse" halyard chantey): Bone 49; Colcord 63; Davis & Tozer #47; Doerflinger 14; Farnsworth & Sharp 107; Harlow 68; Hugill 553; Shay 1948, 26; Terry I:48; Whall 135. Also: Linscott 1962, 142; Flanders & Olney 226.

49. **Homeward Bound and Outward Bound**: SI; Frank 1985 #145; Frank 2000a, 18; Harlow 137; Hugill 541; Kidson 1891, 107; Luce 179; Palmer 1986 #88; Shay 1948, 147; Whall 5. Steve Gardham notes frequent printings: "It appeared on English broadsides under 'Homeward Bound' and 'Outward Bound' titles as well as the combined title, all from [the] mid 19th century. The docks mentioned in the first lines vary from Liverpool to Blackwall to St. Catherine's. Looking at the Nottingham printed version I'd say it likely originated as a theatrical production in the late 18th century" (private communication, Dec. 2010).

50. **Homeward Bound** (II): Frank 1985 #146; Hugill 542. See the preceding, of which "Homeward Bound" is a variant.

51. **Paul Jones's Victory** (Laws #A-4): SI; SIC; PSI; PSIS; JFSS; Laws #A-4 (q.v., notes); Rosenberg #1130; Cazden 1982 #8; Firth 259; Luce 44; Mackenzie #78; Naval Songs 48; Neeser 26; Warner 349.

52. **The *Constitution* and the *Guerriere*** (Laws #A-6): SI; Am. Sailor 152; Baker & Miall 117; Colcord 130; Cox #60; Firth 309, 361; Forecastle 29; Frank 1985 #50; Harlow 184; Lawrence 195; Luce 42; Naval & Patriotic 39; Naval Songs 50; Trident; Whall 43; also Palmer 1985 #85; William M. Davis, *Nimrod of the Sea*, 1874, 336. Another song entitled "The Constitution and the Guerrière," written by L.M. Sargent to the air *Ye Mariners of England* and published in the *Boston Gazette*, was sung at a public victory dinner at Faneuil Hall, Boston, on 5 Sept. 1812 (*Songster's Companion*, 1815, 297; reprinted with notes in Gray, 144).

53. **Columbia's Ships**: Frank 1985 #51. See "Rolling Down to Old Mohee" [#143].

54. **The Sinking of the *Commodore***: Not found elsewhere.

55. **The Hills of Chilia**: Frank 1985 #55.

56. **The *Somers***: *New York Herald*, 11 May 1843; *Melville Society Extracts*, vol. 115.

57. **The *Monitor* and the *Merrimac***: Rosenberg #897; Cazden 1982 #16; Creighton 1933, 131; Frank 1985 #59. See: Doerflinger 111, 326; Warner #11; "Maggie Mac" (Creighton 1933, 283); "Larry Marr" (Hugill, 59); "Virginia Lowlands" (Hugill 59); "In the Louisiana Lowlands" (*Minstrel Songs*, 72).

58. **Lee's Invasion of Maryland**: Frank 1985 #60. No other text of "Lee's Invasion of Maryland" has been found. Glass gives the original (22) and "A Northern Reply" (24), drawn on lines similar to "Lee's Invasion" and is attributed to Septimus Winner (1827-1902). "Maryland, My Maryland": SI; Dichter #1525, also 308, 328, 496; Dichter & Larrabee (numerous citations); Dichter & Shapiro 113; Ewer, 250f; Colonial Dames, 126; Crawford, 21; R. Jackson 1976, 130; McCaskey v5; Whall 141.

59. ***Florida*'s Crew** [The *Florida*'s Cruise]: Townley 1989, pp. 2f, 21; F. Moore 1889, n.p. For a serviceable overview of the *Florida*'s career, see Edward Boykin, *Sea Devil of the Confederacy: The story of the* Florida *and her captain, John Newland Maffitt* (New York: Funk & Wagnalls, 1959).

60. **Navy Song** [We Ride Head to Wind]: Frank 1985 #61.

61. **Bonaparte Crossing the Alps**: Sheet music: Baltimore: F.D. Benteen, c1839-51; Boston: Oliver Ditson, c1844-57; New York: Wm. Hall & Son, circa 1848-58. *The Singer's Companion*, New York, [1854] 1855, 187; Frank 1985 #42; Kennedy 1954, p. 7. "Bonaparte Crossing the Rhine" (O'Neill #1824): Sheet music: New York: E. Riley, c1819-31; Firth & Hall, c1832-48; Wm. Hall & Son, c1848-58; Philadelphia: Geo. Willig, c1819-53; Boston: C.H. Keith, c1834-46; Boston: G.P. Reed, c1839-49. Collins 343 (march); Krassen 207 (hornpipe). Also: "Bonaparte's Advance" (O'Neill #1788; Collins 335); "Bonaparte's Retreat" (O'Neill #1789; Collins 335; Krassen 221; Roche II:33, III:65); "Bonaparte's Defeat" (O'Neill #1710; Collins 318; Krassen 200); "Bonaparte's March" (Roche II: 17); "Napoleon Hornpipe" (1000 FT 103; Dichter #262-268); and see #62 below.

62. **Bonaparte on the Isle of St. Helena**: PSI; Belden 146; Brown Coll. 2&4:#146; Flanders & Brown, 111f; Forget Me Not 205; Frank 1985 #45; Greenleaf #83; Huntington 1964, 205 (2 texts); Sharp 1916 #173 (II: 245); Warner #143. Not to be confused with the hornpipe "Bonaparte's Defeat" (O'Neill #1710; Collins 138; Krassen 200).

63. **Bonny Bunch of Roses O** (Laws #J-5): SI; Creighton 1933 #68; Forget Me Not 222; Frank 1985 #48; Greenleaf #84; Huntington 1964, 207; Mackenzie #72; O Lochlainn #16; Warner, 50. Not to be confused with the chantey "Bunch of Roses" (Hugill, 364).

64. **The Drummer Boy of Waterloo** (Laws #J-1): Cox #82; Creighton 1933 #70; Eddy #58; Forget Me Not 202; Frank 1985 #44; Randolph #82, I:338; other citations listed by Laws and Cox. "The Death of Sir John Moore": Universal III:189. "The Burial of Sir John Moore": SI; Am. Singer 105; Cazden 1982 #10; Frank 1985 #43; Grigg's 270; Johnson 560; Miller's 102; Singer's Gem 132; Universal II:241. "The Orphan Boy": Bryant II:248; Rosenberg #1115.

65. **Napoleon's Dream** [Bonaparte's Dream]: Am. Songster 222; Frank 1985 #46; Huntington 1964, 215. Century (37) also lists "Napoleon's Dream," composed by one S. Nelson, not found, possibly unrelated. See "My Dream" [#12]. Steve Gardham remarks that "It was widely printed on English broadsides, and English oral versions with tunes were published" in Roy Palmer,

ed., *Folk Songs Collected by Ralph Vaughan Williams* (London: J.M. Dent 1983), p. 100; and Karl Dallas, *The Cruel Wars: Soldiers' Songs from Agincourt to Ulster* (London: Wolfe, n.d.), p. 135;

66. **The Green Linnet** (O'Neill #1262): Barry 66; Frank 1985 #47; Huntington 1964, 211; JAFS 67:129; JFSS 7:151. O'Neill #1262; Collins 237; Joyce #372; Krassen 107. Also: Breatnac, *Songs of the Gael* (Dublin: Browne & Nolan Ltd., 1915, p. 314; JFSS, 28:151; Peacock, 2:458.

67. **Lady Franklin's Lament** (Laws #K-9): PSI; Colcord 157; Creighton 1961, 145 (one of the few versions sung to an air not "The Cropy Boy"); Creighton 1971 #97; Doerflinger 145. 147, 342; Frank 1985 #153; Greenleaf #151; Huntington & Herrmann, 103; Palmer 1983, 23; Palmer 1985 #112; *Greig-Duncan* (Shuldham-Shaw), 1:34f. Tune (additional citations): Broadwood & Maitland, 74 and 180; O Lochlainn 1939 #56. Neatby, *The Search for Franklin,* provides a comprehensive history of the expedition and rescue parties; Beattie & Geiger, *Frozen In Time,* present an interesting hypothesis addressing the causes of the Franklin debacle; Pierre Berton, *The Arctic Grail,* provides a scathing critique of the entire British approach to polar conquest.

68. **The Sailor Bride's Lament** (Laws #K-10): Rosenberg #1233 A-J; Brown Coll. 2&4:#112; Cox #113B; Eddy #34; Flanders 1931, 231; Frank 1985 #102; Randolph #762, IV:268; Wolf #2051.

69. **The Sailor Boy** [My Love Willie] (Laws #K-12): SI; PSI; PSIS; Rosenberg #347, #1233, #1362. Ashton 178; Belden 186; Broadwood 74; Brown Coll. 2&4: #104; Cox #10 (9 versions); Creighton 1933 #44; Eddy #33 (6 versions); Frank 1985 #104; Gardner #25; Heart Songs 67; Huntington 1964, 272 (a garbled transcription of text A above, poorly transcribed from the Kendall Whaling Museum); Joyce; Karpeles #43; O Lochlainn 1939 #56; Palmer 1986 #71; Randolph #68, I:296 (5 versions); Sharp 1916 #72; Sharp 1932 #106 (12 versions); Vaughan Williams 94 and 123.

70. **Mary's Dream** (Laws #K-20): SI; PSI; PSIS; Am. Musical Miscellany 195; Bryant I:280; Cox #147; Creighton 1971, #165; Davidson 66, 126; Eddy #83; Frank 1985 #107; Gleadhill 28; Grigg's 168; Huntington 1964, 246; Lyric Gems 182; Miller's 256; Songster's Companion 256; Universal III:213 (2 texts attributed to John Lowe); Whitelaw 151. "There is a version in the Scottish dialect probably by Alan Cunningham, which has often been erroneously regarded as the original" (Cox 435). Davidson II:66 erroneously attributes the poetry to Alexander Lowe.

71. **The Maid on the Shore** (Laws #K-27): Belden 107; Cazden 1982 #75; Creighton 1961, 41; Creighton 1971, #49; Frank 1985 #90; Greenleaf #28; Huntington 1964, 136; Karpeles #28; Mackenzie #19. Compare textual elements of "High Barbary" [#7].

72. **Green Beds** [Young Johnny] (Laws #K-36): Type I (as described by Laws): Eddy #32; Mackenzie #93B; Sharp 1932, #58. Type II (as in Piper's MS): Frank 1985 #116; Frank 1995, 12; Mackenzie #93A and #93C (extensive notes). See also: Rosenberg #498; JFSS; "A Comical Dialogue Between an Honest Sailor and a Deluding Lady" (Ashton 1891, 135; also noted by Laws); Belden 160; Brown Coll. 2&4:#108; Cox #124; Warner #49. "Jackson" (Sandburg 430; also noted by Laws) is a Mexican War adaptation or parody of Type I.

73. **The Sailor and the Country Girl** (Laws #K-38): SI; SIC #4746. Cox #123; Creighton & Senior 6; Davis & Tozer #39 (a distant relation, at best); Doerflinger 294; Flanders & Brown 151; Fowke 1965, 8; Frank 1985 #117; Hugill 461; Karpeles #62; Sharp 1916, #45; Sharp 1932, #687; Vaughan Williams #92. If not the same song as "The Sailor from Dover," closely related to it. Ashton, leaf 48a, is a broadside not cited by Laws. See "The Maiden's Pride Punished" (#74), a related ballad.

74. **The Maiden's Pride Punished**: Frank 1985 #118.

75. **Bright Phoebe**: Cazden 1958, 87; Cazden 1982 #70; Creighton 1961, 96 (N.B.), 97 (N.S.); Huntington 1964, 119.

76. **Tarry Trousers** [The Mother and Daughter]: Laws I:264; Belden 266; Frank 1985 #97; Frank 1995, 7; Greenleaf #31; Huntington 1964, 96 (2 versions); Palmer 1973 #2; Sharp 1932, #133. See "The Nantucket Mother and Daughter" [#20].

77. **Early, Early in the Spring** (Laws #M-1): SI (lists only Sharp); Rosenberg #347; Ashton 1891, 159; Belden 163; Cox #111; Creighton 1961, 98; Creighton & Senior 154; Frank 1985 #96; Hughes IV:13; Logan 28; Randolph I:333; Sharp 1932, II:151ff (5 versions).

78. **William and Harriet** (Laws #M-7): Laws sites several broadsides; Cox #104 (corrupt text lacking a tune).

79. **The Banks of Sweet Dundee** (Laws #M-25): PSI; SIC #7425; JFSS; Rosenberg #63. Belden 137; Broadwood & Maitland 116; Brown Coll. 2&4:#323; Cazden 1982 #50; Cox #119; Creighton 1961, 38; Creighton & Senior 128; Eddy #54; Gardner #69; Greig 1911 #66; Kidson 1891, 54 and 173; Mackenzie #23; Randolph #62, I:275; Sharp 1932, I:399 #67 (3).

80. **The Bold Soldier** (Laws #M-27): SI; SIC #7642; PSI; PSIS. Belden 103; Bronson I #7 (24 versions transcribed from other sources; extensive bibliography); Brown Coll. 2&4:#86; Cazden 1982, #183; Cox #117; Creighton 1933, #112; Eddy #3; Flanders & Olney I:131-149; Flanders & Brown, 232; Frank 1985 #94; Gardner #156; Sharp 1932, #51 (I:1334). Also: Child #7, #8; Hindley VI:229; Bronson III #7; David M. Greene, JAF, v70, 221-230 (cited by Flanders & Olney).

81. **Vilikins and His Dinah** (Laws #M-31b): SI; JFSS; Dichter #461f, #462; Dichter & Larrabee #965, #1063; Rosenberg #1457; Century 50. Beadle's Nº 3; Belden 147; Brown Coll. 2&4:#204; Cox #105; Creighton 1933 #18; Flanders & Brown, 48; Frank 1985 #93; Gardner # 162B; Linscott 401; Randolph #80, I: 331; Spaeth 1926, 59. See "William and Diana" (e.g., Creighton 1933 #17); and for sample adaptations of the air in Irish tradition, see O Lochlainn 1939 , #1 and #50.

82. **The Constant Farmer's Son** (Laws #M-33): SI; JFSS; Broadwood 1908, 28; Cazden 1982 #47; Creighton 1961, 118; Creighton 1971, #38; Creighton & Senior 141; Frank 1985 #92; Mackenzie #26.

83. **Edwin in the Lowlands Low** (Laws #M-34): JFSS; Rosenberg #352; Belden 127; Brown Coll. 2&4:#79; Cox #106; Creighton & Senior 220; Flanders & Brown, 106; Frank 1985 #91; Gardiner 38; Gardner #12; Mackenzie 92; Randolph #140, II:59 (3 versions); Sharp 1932, #56 (11 versions); Warner #56 (a New Hampshire version with the title interestingly corrupted to the landlubberly "Ploughboy of the Lowlands").

84. **Jack Munroe** (Laws #N-7): SI; PSI; Am. Sailor 172; Am. Songster 53; Belden 171; Creighton 1961, 139, 143 (2 versions); Eddy #35 (4); Frank 1985 #98; Gardner #59; Sharp 1932, #65 (20).

85. **The Silk Merchant's Daughter** (Laws #N-10): PSI; JFSS; Rosenberg #1284; Cox #99; Doerflinger 296; Frank 1985 #152; Gardner 176; Greenleaf #25; Huntington MS 280 (garbled); Palmer 1985 #61; Randolph #43, I:222; Sharp 1932 #64 (4 versions).

86. **The Handsome Cabin Boy** (Laws #N-13): PSI; PSIS; Gardner #163.

87. **The Noble Duke** (Laws #N-15): Thomas 1931, 76; Baring-Gould & Sheppard, 87; Huntington & Herrmann, 33.

88. **The Prince of Morocco** (Laws #N-18): Frank 1985 #95; Warner #61 (qqv. for additional citations).

89. **The Dark-Eyed Sailor** (Laws #N-35): SI ("variant of 'The Irish Girl'"); PSI; PSIS; JFSS. Am. Songster 147; Ashton 1891, 204; Cox #319; Creighton 1933, 29; Creighton 1961, 96, 97; Doerflinger 300; Fowke 1965, #3; Frank 1985 #122; Gardner #57; Greenleaf #36; Healy 1967, #4 (air); Huntington 1964, 120; Karpeles #55; Mackenzie #64; Manny & Wilson #65; O Loch lainn 1939 #5; Palmer 1979a #108; Scarborough 267; Vaughan Williams 104; Whall 27. Doerflinger notes variant, derivative, and parody texts, and cites Barry's notion that the air "was influenced by John Leveridge's air for John Gay's song, 'Black-Eyed Susan'" (#1). Palmer 1973 #24, Joyce #331, and others also use the "Dark-Eyed Sailor" air for "The Sailor Boy" ("My Love Willie") [#69]. Compare "Bright Phoebe" [#75] and Huntington's text from the same source as his "Dark Eyed Sailor."

90. **The Mantle So Green** (Laws #N-38): SI; PSI; PSIS; Belden 151; Cazden 1982 #24; Creighton 1933, #79; Gardner #56; Greenleaf #87 (2); Huntington 1964, 122; P.W. Joyce #325; O Lochlainn 1939, #7; Ord 155; Randolph I:371 #94. See also "Waterloo" (Mackenzie #69), which Mackenzie believes to be from the same source. Possibly also related to "The Gown of Green" (Kidson 1891, 62) and perhaps influenced by it, but definitely not the same ballad as both meter and narrative differ; as Kidson remarks, "The old English songs have frequent allusions to wearing the 'green gown,' just as in the same manner the Scotch ones speak of the loss of the snood, and of the 'bonny broom'" (Kidson 1891, 61). Not to be confused with "William Riley" [#103, q.v.], but see Cazden's notion of "Riley Songs" (Cazden 1982, passim).

91. **The Pride of Glencoe** (Laws #N-39): PSI; PSIS; JFSS. Cazden 1982 #25; Creighton 1961, 60; Creighton 1971, #35; Fowke 1981, 67; Frank 1985 #128; Gardner #87; Greenleaf #86; Huntington 1964, 113 (2 texts); Karpeles #56; Mackenzie #68; Manny & Wilson (note) 243; Randolph #126, I:435.

92. **Cuper's Garden** [Cobit's Garden]: SI; SIC; Chappell 1855 II:728; Frank 1995, 2; Hatton & Faning 2:128; Hullah #71; Huntington 1964, 90, 92; Moffat & Kidson; Kidson 1926.

93. **The Lass of Mohee** (Laws #H-8): SI; SIC #7787 A&B; PSI; PSIS; JFSS ("Indian Lass"); Rosenberg #807 A-G. Brown Coll. 2 & 4: #110; Carey 1971, 115; Colcord 199; Cox #116; Creighton 1933 #51; Eckstrom & Smith 233; Flanders 1931, 146; Frank 1985 #123 (2 texts); Huntington 1964, 148 (2 texts); Huntington MS 69 (3 texts); JAF 25:16, 35:408; Kidson 1891, 110f (2 versions of "Indian Lass"); Mackenzie #57, #58; Randolph #63, I:280; Shay 1948, 195; Smithyman 1970, 64-70.

94. **The Jacket of Blue**: SI; PSI; Ford 1901, II:1; Ford 1901, I:1f; Ford 1904, 212 and 214; Frank 1985 #124; Huntington 1964, 275; JFSS (1931) 191; JFSS (1931) 191; Kidson 1891, 118. Related to "The Jacket So Blue" (Cazden 1982, #43), a soldier variant. Not the same song as the "Jacket of Blue" in Joyce, which is a version of "The Sailor Boy" ("My Love Willie") [#69].

95. **Ellen the Fair** (Laws #O-5): Forget Me Not (Philadelphia), 24; Forget Me Not (New York), 141; Huntington MS, 323; Mackenzie #41. Not the same as the English parlor song "Fair Ellen" (Davidson II:381); nor "Fair Ellen" ("Fair Ellender") (PSI, PSI-1, PSI-2), which is a form of "Lord Thomas and Fair Eleanor" (Child #73) and which may have "inspired" the comparatively simplistic "Ellen the Fair" and "Fair Ellen." See also *The English Musical Repository* [*Crosby's English Musical Repository*], Edinburgh, 1811, p. 229.

96. **The Sailor and the Shepherdess** (Laws #O-8): Creighton 1971 #37; Frank 1985 #89; Mackenzie #53.

97. **The Jolly Sailor**: DeMarsan broadsides, New York, circa 1860s; Frank 1985 #126.

98. **The Sailor's Return**: As noted in the main text.

99. **Green Mossy Banks of the Lea** (Laws #O-15): PSI; JFSS (distinguishes between "Green Mossy Banks of the Lea" and "American Stranger"); likewise Cazden 1982 #31; Creighton 1933 #77; Frank 1985 #125 (complete text of B); Gardner #70; Mackenzie #47; O Lochlainn 1965 #98.

100. **The Bold Fisherman** (Laws #O-24): SI; JFSS; Broadwood & Maitland 110; Creighton & Senior 113; Flanders & Olney, 218; Frank 1985 #129; Sharp 1916 (quoting Broadwood, Sharp makes a case for the origins of the ballad in medieval romance; reiterated by Laws).

101. **The Jolly Roving Tar** (Laws #O-27): Creighton & Senior 178; Creighton 1971, #12; Frank 1985 #103. Not to be confused with Warner #71 (q.v.).

102. **The Bold Privateer** (Laws #O-32): SI2; PSI; Rosenberg #119; Beadle's N° 1; Kidson 1891, 101. "Der Bold Privateer" is a German dialect spoof in E. Byron Christy and William E. Christy, *Christy's New Songster and Black Joker* (New York: Dick & Fitzgerald, 1868).

103. **William Riley**: Compare Laws #M-9 and Laws #M-10. Leach, 308; Creighton 1961, 5 ("The Swan").

104. **Jemmy on the Sea**: Frank 1985 #130. Related to "Greeen Grow the Rushes," from which it borrows heavily, but the descent and provenance are unclear.

105. **The Sailor and the Tailor** (Laws #P-4): Creighton & Senior, 167; Sharp 1916, #73 ("The Watchet Sailor").

106. **The Pride of Kildare** (Laws #P-6): PSI; JFSS; Creighton 1971, #48; Frank 1985 #119; Huntington 1964, 131 (2 texts); Manny & Wilson #88; O Lochlainn 1965, #83.

107. **The Rakish Young Fellow**: Frank 1985 #127. Not found elsewhere. Compare "The Nightingale": SI; PSI; PSIS; SIC; Laws #P-14; Belden 239; Eddy #103; Flanders & Olney, 164 ("The Banks of Low Lea"); Sharp 1932 #145 (5 versions).

108. **Mary of the Wild Moor** (Laws #P-21): SI; Century 35; Rosenberg #887 A-F. Beadle's N° 2; Belden 207; Brown Coll. 2&4:#78; Cox #148; Eddy #88; Frank 1985 #d56; Kidson 1891, 77; McCaskey v7; Good Old Songs II:82; Johnson 303; Mackenzie #61; Randolph #72, I:311 (3 versions); Sandburg 466.

109. **Caroline of Edinburgh Town** (Laws #P-27): SI; PSI; Rosenberg #170. Brown Coll. 2 &4:#124; Cox #122; Creighton 1961, 99; Eddy #59; Forget Me Not 175 (whence the illustration); Frank 1985 #120; Gardner #13; Huntington 1964, 137; Linscott 183; Mackenzie #28; Randolph #50; Sharp 1932, #69.

110. **Oxford City** (Laws #P-30): PSI; JFSS; Rosenberg #1126; Flanders & Brown 92; Gardner 75; Vaughan Williams 83.

111. **Jack Robinson**: Am. Sailor 155; Ashton 1891, 270; Davidson II:252; Forecastle 101; Frank 1985 #114; Masefield 190. See "Dark-Eyed Sailor" [#89] and "Pride of Glencoe" [#91] for examples of the love-token songs of reunion; and "Green Beds" [#72] for an example of a sailor's encounter with a landlady, of both of which genres "Jack Robinson" is in part a lampoon.

112. **All Around The Room** [Ellen Taylor]: Frank 1985 #87; Frank 1995, 13; Williams 1923, 173. See also Ashton 1888, 173; Ewen, 12; McCaskey, v8. Steve Gardham remarks, "My notes give both tyhis and 'All Around My Hat' which is closely related as circa 1834" (private communication, December 2010).

113. **Charming Jane Louisa**: Frank 1985 #115; Frank 1995, 18; Wolf #285. See "New York Girls" ("Can't You Dance the Polka?"): Colcord 108; Davis & Tozer 12; Doerflinger 58; Frank 1995, 15; Harlow 37; Hugill 369-374; Whall 47; and "Peter Street" ("Jack All Alone"; "The Shirt and the Apron"): Laws #K-42; Frank 1995, 13; Greenleaf 222; Hugill 376; Kennedy 187.

114. **The Cove Wot Spouts**: Frank 1985 #d15; Frank 1995, 17; *Greig-Duncan* (Shuldham-Shaw), vol. 3; Holloway & Black, 2:16. According to Steve Gardham, "'The Cove Wot Spouts' under this title was printed by the *Glasgow Poet's Box* in 1857. Here the designated tune is 'The Cove Wot Sings.'" "The Cove Wot Sings" had been printed in *The Westminster Review* in1839 and by the *Glasgow Poet's Box* in 1852, with the tune named as "He was the boy that could do it." On broadsides by Catnach (London) and Keys (Devonport) the tune named as "The Devil and Little Mike," which was widely printed, to be sung to the tune "Got 'em" (Steve Gardham, private communication, December 2010). See #115.

115. **I Am One of the Boys** [One of the Boys]: Frank 1985 #d37; Frank 1995, 16; Jackson 57. See "Sailors Ashore" [#116].

116. **Sailors Ashore**: Frank 1985 #147; Frank 1995, 6.

117. **He Is Only Gone Home with a Friend**: Not found elsewhere.

118. **Jayne's Hair Tonic** [Dr. Jayne's Hair Tonic]: Frank 1985 #134.

119. **Come Landlord Fill the Flowing Bowl**: SI; Frank 1985 #d48; Heart Songs 141; Johnson 455; Wier 1918, 274.

120. **Lannigan's Ball** [Lanigan's Ball]: SI; Frank 1985 #d47; Spaeth II:222; O Lochlainn 1939 #52. Double jig: O'Neill #858: Collins 159, Krassen 34, Roche I:45.

121. **The Wild Rover**: Dichter #1355; Rosenberg #1547; Creighton 1933 #65; Forget Me Not 54; Frank 1985 #d91; Clancy & Makem 154.

122. **The Cobbler**: Tune: Chappell, 1855, I:277; Hulla #26. Also: Cox, 491; Huntington & Herrmann, 40; Kennedy, 432; Sharp 1932, 2:75;. Demonstrably unrelated to the Irish folksong "The Cobbler" (Graeme 116).

123. **Dick Turpin's Bonny Black Bess** (Laws #L-9): Fife #7; Frank 1985 #68; Gardner #130; Mackenzie #126; Peters 189. Extensive biographical notes in Logan, 115-118; Kennedy, 736; Mackenzie, 313. For bibliographies of other Turpin songs, see Laws #L-8 and Kennedy #336.

124. **Dick Turpin and the Lawyer** (Laws #L-10): Duncan II:36; Mackenzie #125; Moffat & Kidson 1900, 160; Palmer 1979b #19; Williams, 100. See Laws #L-8, II:169f.

125. **Johnny Sands** (Laws #Q-3): SI; SI2; PSI; PSI1; Dichter #410; Belden 237; Good Old Songs v2, 221; Heart Songs 42; Howe's; McCaskey v2; Randolph #754 (IV:246).

126. **The Farmer's Boy** (Laws #Q-30): SI; SIC #4596 A&B; PSI. Amateur 74; Baring-Gould 1895 I:58; Beadle's N° 2; Beadle's N° 4; Belden 272; Broadwood & Maitland 134; Creighton & Senior 158; Flanders 1932, 118; Frank 1985 #135; noted in Gardner 479; Good Old Songs I:150; Huntington 1964, 216; Kennedy 247; Kidson 1891, 63 and 174; Randolph #118, I:425.

127. **Doran's Ass**: "Doran's Ass": O Lochlainn 1939 #84; Poetry Index; Ward 7. "Finnigan's Wake" has been widely anthologized as a song and as a tune. "The Spanish Lady": Loesberg I:33. "Clare's Dragoon's": Calthorpe 61; Nation 288f.

128. **Limerick Races**: Beadle's Half-Dime Singer's Library N° 13 (1878); Healy 1965 #23; mentioned Pulling, 174f.

129. **The Pearl of the Sea**: Frank 1985 #62. Not the same as the parlor song "Isle of Beauty" in *Beadle's N° 3*.

130. **Et Tu Bruce**: Frank 1985 #136 (q.v. for a discussion of 19th-century political lampoon songs; also Lawrence, 285).

131. **There's Changes in the Mill**: Not found elsewhere.

132. **Go Down Moses** [Let My People Go]: SI; SIC #8279; PSI; PSIS; etc. Frank 1985 #139.; Marsh 1880, #19; Taylor 1882, #86; extensive historical notes in Epstein, 243ff. James Weldon Johnson and Rosamund Johnson (*Book of American Spirituals,* 68) present a credible case for its folkloric origins; reiterated by J.W. Work, *American Negro Songs,* 165. Lomax & Lomax (*Folk Song USA,* 386) further posit that it was fashioned in honor of Harriet Tubman by passengers of the Underground Railroad: "Legend has it that they made their great song, 'Go Down Moses,' about her. It was sung by the Negro regiments of the Civil War" (Ibid, 342). But were this actually the case, one might reasonably expect that it would have turned up in W.F. Allen

et al., *Slave Songs in the United States* (where many of the sources are the various Civil War regiments); or that notes to that effect might appear in at least one of the early anthologies where the song does appear, such as Marsh or Taylor. However, evidence of any direct connection with the Civil War or the antebellum South is conspicuously absent, and there is no record of it in any of the major field collections or classic scholarly studies of African-American folksong (W.F. Allen et al., *Slave Songs of the United States* [1867]; Bernard Katz, *The Social Implications of Early Negro Music in the United States* [1969]; Howard W. Odum and Guy B. Johnson, *The Negro and His Songs* [1925]; Lydia Parrish, *Slave Songs of the Georgia Sea Islands* [1942]; Dorothy Scarborough, *On the Trail of Negro Folk-Songs* [1925]; Newlan I. White, *American Negro Folk-Songs* [1928]; etc.)

133. **The Parson's Narrative**: Frank 1985 #140.

134. **The Greenland Whale Fishery** (Laws #K-21): SI; SIC #9491;PSI;PSIS;JFSS. Ashton 1891,242;Belden 104;Cazden 1982 #95; Colcord 151;Frank 1985 #156;Greig 1914, 86; Huntington 1964, 9, 11; Huntington 1966 #4; Karpeles #42; Palmer 1985, #72; Shay 1948, 122; Vaughan Williams 50; Whall 71.

135. **Arctic Whaling Song**: Greig 1914, 85 ("The most popular of all our whaling songs"); McCarty #133; Ord, 317.

136. **The Coast of Peru** (Laws #D-26): SI (lists only Colcord); PSI (lists only Huntington 1964). Colcord 194; Doerflinger 191; Frank 1985 #157; Harlow 222; Huntington 1964, 2.

137. **Diego's Bold Shores**: PSI; Colcord 196; Frank 1985 #158; Harlow 213 (no tune); Huntington 1964, 30. Huntington MS 22 cites a partial text printed in the 1920s in *The Reynolds Leaflet* claims that the air is "In the Shade of the Old Apple Tree."

138. **There She Blows** [The Wounded Whale]: SI (lists only Colcord); PSI (lists only Huntington 1964,); Colcord 189; Frank 1985 #159; Huntington 1964, 23-27 (2 texts). Tune (additional citations): Gleadhill 238; Heart Songs 440; Johnson 499; Lawrence, 188f; McCaskey v2; Wier 1918, 190.

139. **Blow Ye Winds** ['Tis Advertised In Boston]: SI; Colcord 191; Frank 1985 #160, A-B; Harlow 130, 211 (2 variant tunes, 3 texts); Hugill 219-223 (3 texts, notes); Huntington 1964, 42; Palmer 1985, #118; Shay 1948, 126; Whall 21.

140. **The Bold Harpooner** [Captain Bunker]: Frank 1985 #161; Frank 1985c, 4-7; Greig 1914, 85; Lloyd 1967, n.p.; Ord, 312; Melville 1851, "Extracts" and Ch. 40; after Browne, *Etchings of a Whaling Cruise,* 77. S.M. Frank, Stuart Gillespie, and Ellen Cohn, *Sea Chanteys and Forecastle Songs from Mystic Seaport* (LP recording, New York: Folkways, 1978, #FSS 37300), combines Melville's text with portions of Lloyd's text and tune; Jeff Warner sings (and recorded for the National Film and Sound Archive of Australia at Canberra in 1988) a similar reconstruction.

141. **The Wonderful Whale** [Jack and the Whale]: Frank 1985 #180; Am. Sailor, 175. Steve Gardham cites broadsides by Walker opf Durham and G. Smeaton of London, noting that the alyrics are attributed to J.C. Davidson to the tune of "The Great Sea Snake" (text in Ashton 1891, 266). "The Wonderful Crocodile": Ashton 1888, 147; Flanders & Brown 1932, 168 ("The Rummy Crockodile," collected in Vermont); Broadwood & Maitland 184, tune from tradition in Dorset.

142. **How to Catch a Whale**: Frank 1985 #182. See "The Wonderful Whale" [#141].

143. **Rolling Down to Old Mohee**: PSI; Colcord 97; Frank 1985 #163; Harlow 228, 243; Hugill, *Songs of the Sea,* 120; Huntington 1964, 27; Lloyd 1967, n.p. Tune: Am. Musical Miscellany 109; Chappell II: 666; Dearmer, n.p.; Duncan 1905, I:134; Hullah #42; Hymnal #101; Brown Coll. 2&4:#54; Luce 30 (uses the "Budgeon" air for "The Merman"); see also Broad wood & Maitland 68 and 102. See "Columbia's Ships" [#53] and "The Lass of Mohee" [#93].

144. **No Ke Ano Ahiahi** [Hawaiian Song]: Frank 1985 #165; Frank 2001 #144. Gabby Pahinui and the Sons of Hawaii, liner notes for the LP recordings *Folk Music of Hawaii* (Honolulu: Panini, n.d., #24209) and *Gabby Band Vol. II* (Honolulu: Panini, n.d., #PS 1008); *The Musicians* (liner-notes for the LP recording *Sons of Hawaii,* Honolulu: Island Heritage Panini, 1971, #KN 1001). Other citations refer to private communications from Amy K. Stillman, Harvard University and the Peabody Museum of Salem, Mass., 23 Aug. 1984; and Elizabeth Tatar and Patience W. Bacon, Bishop Museum, Honolulu, 10 Dec. 1984.

145. **One Year in a Blubber Hunter**: Frank 1985 #168. "Limejuice Ship": Hugill 58. "The Old Ship of Zion": SI; Marsh #29; Allen #125; Odum & Johnson 117; N.I. White #34.

146. **The *Aurora*'s Whaling Song**: Not found elsewhere.

147. **The Schooner *Varnum Hill***: Frank 1985 #167; Miller 163-167; Frank, "A Canç ã o da Escuna *Varnum H. Hill,"* in Joã o Afonso, ed., *Livro dos Baleias* (in press at Lisbon, Portugal). Regarding the tunes, "Lisbon" (e.g., Ralph Vaughan Williams, *The Penguin Book of English Folk Songs,* p. 58) so closely resembles "The Banks of the Nile" as to be corollary forms of the same ballad in both major and minor-modal settings (compare Belden 178, Creighton 1961, 147; Palmer 1973, #3; Sharp 1932, #121 [3 versions]; for notes see Laws #N-8 and N-9, and especially Mackenzie #35). See also Vaughan Williams 58; and "One Year In a Blubber Hunter," #145.

148. **Stanzas from the *Mermaid***: Frank 1985 #160, C-D.

149. **On a Passage to the Crozet Islands**: Not found elsewhere.

150. **Cape Horn**: Not found elsewhere.

151. **Address to Young Sailors**: Not found elsewhere.

152. **The Lay System**: Not found elsewhere.

153. **Landsmen One and All**: Not found elsewhere.

154. **The Whaleman's Lament**: Huntington 1964, 15.

155. **I and Betty Martin**: Frank 1985 #173. "My Eye and Betty Martin" ("Hey, Betty Martin"): SI; SIC #7762; PSI; PSIS; Am. Songster 92; Dime Song Book N° 2, 37; Dolph 437. Variant "Milly Martin": Buckley 23.

156. **Indian Ocean Whaling Song**: Frank 1985 #171. See "I and Betty Martin" [#155] and "Bowhead Whaling Song" [#157].

157. **Bowhead Whaling Song**: Frank 1985 #170. See "Indian Ocean Whaling Song" [#156] and "The Whaleman's Lament" [#154].

158. **All the Whales Are Wild and Ugly** [Song… to Captain S. D. Oliver]: Frank 1985 #174; Frank 2000a, 28; Miller 133.

159. **A Song of the Hatteras Whale**: Not found elsewhere.

160. **I Was Once a Sailor Lad**: Huntington 1964, 66.

161. **A Voyage on New Holland**: Frank 1985 #184; quoted, Frank 1995, 11.

162. **Song Composed aboard the Bark *Kathleen***: Frank 1985 #185.

163. **Fisher's Hornpipe** (O'Neill #1575, 1576): O'Neill #1575 and #1576; Dichter #1390; Carpenter 1889, 92; Collins 292; Frank 1985 #186; Frank 2000b, #1; Krassen 168; 1000 FT, 95; Linscott 76. Dance figures: Carpenter 92; Linscott 76; 1000 FT, 95; Tolman & Page 120.

164. **The White Cockade** (O'Neill #1803): O'Neill #1803; Collins 338; Frank 1985 #187; Frank 2000b, #2; Linscott 117, 120; Tolman & Page 114. Ballad "The White Cockade" ("The Summer Morning"; "The Soldier's Farewell"): SIC #7203; Baring-Gould; Copper 282; Farmer #27; Kidson 1891, 114. See #87.

165. **Zip Coon** [Turkey in the Straw]: SI; SIC #7893; Dichter #1672, # 1673; Dichter & Shapiro 53; Ewer, 468; Rosenberg #1604; Brown Coll. 3&5:#94; Damon #20; Frank 1985 #188; Frank 2000b, #3; Jackson 261; Linscott 83, 101; Spaeth I:18. "The texts vary widely and constantly" (Damon, n.p.). Sheet music: G. Willig, Jr., Baltimore, circa 1834; J.L. Hewitt & Co., New York, circa 1834; Firth & Hall, New York, circa 1834-37 (all of these and several others "as sung by Mr. G.W. Dixon"); also Thomas Birch, New York, 1834, "as sung by all the celebrated comic singers" (Harris Coll., Brown Univ.): compare citations in Damon, Jackson, and Spaeth. Dance figures in Tolman & Page: "French Four" (92); "Wild Goose Chase" (93); "Devil's Dream" (112).

166. **Rory O'More** (O'Neill #856): O'Neill #856; Accordion Music 86; Collins 159; Frank 1985 #189; Frank 2000b, #4; Krassen 34; 1000 FT, 62; Tolman & Page 104. For the song by Samuel Lover, see: SI; SIC #2195; Beadle's Dime Songbook N° 2; Johnson 415; Wier 1918, 436.

167. **Oh, Dear, What Can the Matter Be?** SI; SIC #4708; Brown Coll. 3&5:#122; Chappell 1855 II:732; Creighton 1971 #85; Frank 1985 #190; Frank 2000b, #5; Heart Songs 140; McCaskey v1; Wier 1918, 363.

168. **Harvest Home Waltz**: Frank 1985 #191; Frank 2000b, #6. "Harvest Home" (song): Hullah 31; Chappell, II:597. "Harvest Home" (hornpipe): O'Neill #1603; Collins 297; Krassen 207. "The Joys of Harvest Home" (waltz): Dichter #952.

169. **Soldier's Joy** (O'Neill #1642): O'Neill #1642; Collins 305; Frank 1985 #192; Frank 2000b, #7; Krassen 183; Linscott 109, 341 (2 versions); Roche II:12; 1000 FT, 24. Dance figures in Linscott 110; Tolman & Page 148; 1000 FT, 24.

170. **Pop! Goes the Weasel**: SI; SIC #4735; Dichter #1651; Dichter & Shapiro 149. Carpenter 1889, 97 (dance figure, 22); Frank 1985 #193; Frank 2000b, #8; Huntington 1966 #21; Jackson 176; Linscott 107; Randolph #556, III:368; Tolman & Page 94; 1000 FT, 24.

171. **Yankee Doodle**: SI; SIC #8150; Dichter & Shapiro, passim; Sonneck 1909, 79-156; Sonneck & Upton, 479f; Frank 1985 #194; Frank 2000b, #9; mentioned in Melville's "The Fiddler." Nason (18-29) colorfully extols its virtues and follows its course through parodies and spinoffs; Fitz-Gerald (108-116) presents a detailed history; but Sonneck's skeptical notes are classic. Lawrence (32ff) discusses the provenance of the air and presents a wide variety of variants and applications, especially in the broadside literature.

172. **Russian Waltz**: Frank 1985 #195; 2000b, #10; *Universal*, I:263; also Dichter #926. A waltz named "La Russe" by Frederick Bold, with dance instructions by W.F. Mittmann (Carpenter 1889, 186), is an unlikely candidate for the missing piece.

173. **The Poor Old Slave**: SI; Dichter & Shapiro 149; Frank 1985 #196; Frank 2000b, #11; Wier 1918, 388.

174. **Nelly Gray** [Darling Nelly Gray]: SI; SIS #1515; Dichter & Shapiro 142; Ewer, 81; Rosenberg #269; Frank 1985 #197; Frank 2000b, #12; Good Old Songs II:50; Heart Songs 116; Kieser 64; Wier 1918, 112; Tolman & Page 62, 71, 78. Not to be confused with the much older comic ballad by Thomas Hood, "Faithess Nelly Gray," which is said to contain "more puns than any poem of similar length in the language" (G.B. Smith I:220).

175. **Nelly Bly** (Foster): SI; SIC #122; Ewer, 281; Frank 1985 #198; Frank 2000b, #13; Wier 1918, 328; etc. Whittlesey & Sonneck; Jackson 77; Taylor & Howard 71.

176. **Augusta's Favorite**: SI; SIC #4874; De Ville, n.p.; Frank 1985 #199; Frank 2000b, #14; Kastner, 172-186, presents a comprehensive history. There is another tune for "Twinkle, Twinkle, Little Star" in Perkins, *The Nightingale*, 1860, 150; see also Brown Coll. 3&5:#674.

177. **Oh! Susanna** [Susanna] (Foster): SI; SIC; Whittlesey & Sonneck; Dichter & Shapiro 94; Ewer, 291. Brown Coll. 3&5: #408; Colcord 169; Frank 1985 #200; Frank 2000a, 24; Frank 2000b, #15; Good Old Songs II:73; Heart Songs 172; Hugill 116-117; Jackson 89; McCaskey v7; Shay 1948, 114; Taylor & Howard 31; Wier 1918, 365; etc.

178. **Fanny Elssler Leaving New Orleans**: Frank 1985 #201; Frank 2000b, #16; Ivor Guest, *Fanny Elssler*, 1970, 167; *Negro Singer's Own Book*, n.p.

179. **Off She Goes** (O'Neill #914): O'Neill #914; Collins 170; Frank 1985 #202; Frank 2000b, #17; Krassen 41; 1000 FT, 58. Concerning chantey applications, see, e.g., Hugill 7, *Landsman Hay*, concerning HMS *Culloden*, 1804.

180. **Old Leather Breeches** (O'Neill #167, 763): SIC #7774; Rosenberg #775; Clancy 1964, 47; Frank 1985 #203; Frank 2000b, #18; O'Neill #167, #763. "Nell Flaherty's Drake": Behan #66; Collins 29, 142; Healy II #31; O Lochlainn #67A; Ward #30.

181. **Home, Sweet Home**: SI; SIC #308; Dichter & Shapiro 39; Ewewr, 149f; Fitz-Gerald 1-11, presents an interesting history; Baring-Gould 1895 II:30; Frank 1985 #204; Frank 2000b, #19; Grigg's; Griggs 1900, 172; Good Old Songs I:3; Jackson 80; Kieser 232; Luce 135; New Song Book 34; Singer's Gem 136; Turner 140.

182. **Old Folks at Home** [Swanee River] (Foster): SI; SIC #1129; Ewer, 293f; Whittlesey & Sonneck; Frank 1985 #205; Frank 2000b, #20; Good Old Songs I:10; Jackson 10, 178; Taylor & Howard 87.

183. **The Heart that Can Feel for Another**: Frank 1985 #10; Universal I:18; see also Universal I:382.

184. **Bounding Billows**: SI; Dichter #2013 (song collection), 98; Frank 1985 #108; Johnson 345; McCaskey v2.

185. **Lashed to the Helm**: SI; *Beadle's Pocket Songster N° 5;* Baring-Gould 1895, II:81.

186. **Saturday Night at Sea** [The Sailor Boy]: Huntington 1964, 65.

187. **The Minute Gun at Sea**: SI; Am. Sailor 180; Am. Songster 18; Beadle's N° 5; Bryant II:586; Forecastle 212; Frank 1985 #11; Grigg's 94; Johnson 122; Luce 208; Mackay 108; Naval & Patriotic 54; New Song Book 29; Shower of Pearls 21.

188. **Steady She Goes**: Am. Sailor 154; Forecastle 70; Frank 1985 #52; Universal I:308.

189. **True Yankee Sailor** [True British Sailor]: Am. Sailor 188; Am. Singer 79; Barnes 90; Forecastle 150; Frank 1985 #53; Luce 120; McCarty #152; Naval & Patriotic 19; Singer's Gem ("Harry Bluff") 197; Universal II:219. See "The True British Tar," written by —Collins (Universal II:37); and an American parody, "Charley Stewart," published by McCarty (#183) in 1842.

190. **The White Squall**: SI; Baker & Miall 205; Barnes 58; Bryant II:588 (also includes the Thackeray poem); Century 82; Frank 1985 #29; Johnson 115; Luce 108.

191. **The Sailor's Consolation** [Barney Buntline]: SI; SIC #9422; PSIS; Am. Musical Miscellany 137; Frank 1985 #28; Huntington 1964, 68 (variant air, source not identified, authenticity not established); Johnson 114; Luce 190; McCaskey v8; Moffat 1904, 89; Naval Songs 124; Wier 1918, 43. See also "Billy, Let's Thank Providence that You and I are Sailors": Universal I:161, unascribed, sung to the air *Bow, Wow, Wow;* and Am. Songster 245. Farmer #86 has another tune, apparently the editor's own composition (repr. Griggs 1900, 148). For the air "Bow, wow, wow," see *Singer's Companion,* 174.

192. **A Wet Sheet and a Flowing Sea**: SI; SIC #9490; PSI; Dichter #1864. Am. Sailor 159; Bruce 297; Forecastle 40; Frank 1985 #12; Huntington 1964, 49 (2 texts); Johnson 138; Luce 202; McCaskey v5; Miller's 174; Naval Songs 57; Singer's Gem 6; Wier 1918, 510. Several editions of sheet music in the collections of the John Hay Library, Brown University; and the Peabody Essex Museum, Salem, Mass. Mentioned by Ely, *There She Blows,* xxvi and 108. See Frank 1998 #45.

193. **The Sea** [The Sea, the Sea, the Open Sea]: SI; Bryant I:583; Forecastle 104; Frank 1985 #14; Huntington 1964, 63; Johnson 109 (extensive notes); Luce 212; McCaskey v8; Miller's 26; New Song Book 7; Singer's Gem 123. *Sailor's Magazine,* 11:13 (New York: American Seamen's Friend Society, July 1841, 352). Hugill: private communications, 1975-91. Not the same song as SIC #2228.

194. **The Sailor Boy's Last Dream**: Rosenberg #1234; Century 43; Bruce 293; Bryant II:567; Forecastle 114; Forget Me Not 48; Frank 1985 #30; Songster's Companion 280; Universal I:144.

195. **Over the Mountain Wave**: SI; Frank 1985 #27; Johnson & White 72; Levermore #78; McCaskey v2.

196. **Poor Bessy** [The Parting]: SI; Dichter #1857; Frank 1985 #110; Luce 107. *Sailor's Magazine,* 10:14 (June 1842), 320.

197. **The Fisher's Wife** [The Fisherman]: Dichter #1180; Frank 1985 #105 (where the sheet music had not been located).

198. **A Life on the Ocean Wave**: SI; SIC #3123; Dichter & Shapiro 56; Ewer, 224; Fitz-Gerald 185; Forecastle 103; Frank 1995 #13; Good Old Songs I:38; Heart Songs 431; Huntington 1964, 87 (2 texts); Johnson 130; Luce 68; McCaskey v3; Naval Songs 20; Singer's Gem 45; Wier 1918, 260. Turner presents notes and precursors (101, 296); Am. Songster (227) gives a song based on this, to the same air. Mentioned by Ely, *There She Blows* (1844-47/1971), xxvi, 108. See Frank 1998 #44, "Life of the Bold Buccaneer."

199. **The Sailor Boy's Carol**: Sheet music, Parker & Ditson, Boston, 1841; Oliver Ditson, Boston, 1841 and 1842. Frank 1985 #16; Johnson & White 76.

200. **The Soldier's Tear**: SI; PSI; PSIS; Heart Songs 474; Johnson 504; McCaskey v3; Mackay 177; Miller's 227 (lists sheet music: Willis & Co., London, n.d.); Singer's Gem 175; Turner 74; Wier 1918, 427. See "The Sailor's Tear."

201. **The Sailor's Tear**: Rosenberg #1236; Am. Sailor 162; Forecastle 74; Frank 1985 #57.

202. **Hurrah for the Sea** [A Home on the Mountain Wave]: Am. Sailor 137; Am. Songster 224; Forecastle 52; Frank 1985 #17; Harlow 214; Johnson & White 24. *The Knickerbocker* (Feb. 1841), cited in *The Sailor's Magazine,* 11:13 (New York, July 1841), 352.

203. **Away, Away o'er the Boundless Deep** [The Buccaneer's Bride]: Dichter & Shapiro 157; Frank 1985 #15; Huntington MS, 2 texts (reported as ship *Hillman* 1854 and bark *Pacific* 1870).

204. **I'm Afloat, I'm Afloat** [The Rover of the Sea]: SI; PSI-2; Dichter #1807; Rosenberg #4 (?); Wolf #1014; *Accordion Music,* 215; Baring-Gould 1895, I:94; Frank 1985 #69; Frank 1998 #32; Huntington 1964, 80 (corrupt; no tune); Luce, 72; McCaskey, v8; *Miller's,* 202; *Naval Songs* (1883), 26; *Sheet Anchor,* Vol. 2, N° 7; Boston, 6 April 1844, p. 51; Wolf #1014. The lyrics were reprinted from the *New Haven Fountain* in *Sheet Anchor* (2:7; Boston, 6 April 1844; p. 51), a Christian-temperance magazine for seamen.

205. **The Pirate of the Isles**: PSI; Frank 1985 #70; Frank 1998 #88; Harlow 172; Huntington 1964, 74; Luce 66. See also "The Robbers of the Glen" [#206]. For "The Demon of the Sea," by the same author, to the tune of "The Brave Old Oak" by E.J. Loder, see Frank 1998 #36.

206. **The Robbers of the Glen**: Frank 1985 #71; Frank 1998 #60. Steve Gardham cites broadsides by Such (London), H. Paul (London), and Cadman (Manchester).

207. **Pirates' Chorus** (Balfe): SI; PSI; Wolf #120, #1887. Am. Sailor's Songster 235; Frank 1998 #33; Heart Songs 237; McCaskey v4. The University of Nebraska song "The Scarlet and Cream" is sung to Balfe's "Pirates' Chorus" (SI2: T.W. Allen, *Intercollegiate Song Book,* 1927; B.B. & H.B. Kennedy, *Varsity Songs,* 1931). Not to be confused with "Pirates' Chorus" by Alexandre Charles Lecocq, from *Giroflé-Girofla* (first line: "Parmi les choses delicates," i.e, "Ha! ha! the neatest and completest").

208. **The Life of a Tar**: Am. Sailor 158; Forecastle 69; Frank 1985 #23.

209. **Our Way Across the Sea**: SI; Century 56; Frank 1985 #24; Grigg's 166; McCaskey v5; Leslie 160; Singer's Gem 49.

210. **Jamie's on the Stormy Sea**: SI; SIC #7726; PSI; Rosenberg #990. Bruce 321; Bryant II:574; Frank 1985 #111; Good Old Songs II:69; Heart Songs 189; Huntington 1964, 252; Johnson 159; McCaskey v6; Wier 1918, 231.

211. **Willie's on the Dark Blue Sea**: Beadle's Dime Song Book N° 2, 7; Frank 1985 #112; Huntington 1964, 234; JAF 52:27. Huntington MS reports texts in journals of the whalers *Three Brothers* and *Hillman* (both 1851), and cites The Book of Popular Songs (Philadelphia: Evans, 1860), 22; L.O. Emerson, *The Golden Wreath* (Boston: Ditson, 1857), 52; and Carrie B. Groover, *A Heritage of Songs* (Bethel: Gould Academy, n.d.; repr. Norwood: Norwood Eds., 1973), 146. Sheet music for "The Mariner Boy, written and composed by H.S. Thompson, Author of… Willie's on the Dark Blue Sea" (Boston: Oliver Ditson, 1854), is in the Peabody Essex Museum.

212. **Good News from Home**: Dichter & Shapiro 225; Beadle's Dime Song Book N° 2, 38; Frank 1985 #80; Kieser 162; Luce 205.

213. **The Signal to Engage**: Forecastle 38; Frank 1985 #3; Hogarth I:62, I:73-81.

214. **Poor Jack**: SI; Am. Musical Miscellany 58; Forecastle 118; Frank 1985 #4; Hogarth I:176, I-183-89; Johnson 178; Luce 186; Mackay 95; Naval Songs 98; Universal I:131. Parody "Poor Jack" by John Collins (1742-1808), Universal II:165.

215. **Saturday Night at Sea**: Baring-Gould 1895 I:102; Frank 1985 #5; Hogarth I:176, 210, 226. Not the same song as Trident 23 or Luce 23.

216. **Who Cares?** Forecastle 160; Frank 1985 #7; Hogarth I:xxxiii, II:69-72; Universal I:13.

217. **Nature and Nancy**: Frank 1985 #8; Hogarth I: xxxiii, II:226, 235.

218. **The Lass that Loves A Sailor**: SI; Am. Sailor 139; Baker & Miall 141; Beadle's N° 5; Forecastle 58; Frank 1985 #9; Hogarth, I:171; Hullah # 75; Johnson 10; Luce 211. See Moseley 1982.

219. **The Sailor**: Not found elsewhere.

220. **How Cheery Are the Mariners**: As noted in the main text.

221. **On New Year's Day**: Not found elsewhere.

222. **The Sailor Is a Wanderer Free**: Not found elsewhere.

223. **O Think of the Sailor**: Not found elsewhere.

224. **We're Bounding o'er the Dark Blue Sea**: Not found elsewhere.

225. **The Sailor on the Ocean Wide**: Frank 1985 #21; Huntington MS, 149 (attributed to the wrong voyage and year, and provides a tune not original to the lyrics).

226. **The Mariner's Song** [Gaily We Go]: Not found elsewhere.

227. **A Seaman's Life**: Steve Gardham mentions that there were numerous London printings..

228. **Farewell to the Arctic**: Not found elsewhere.

229. **The King of the Southern Sea**: Frank 1985 #162; Frank, "'The King of the Southern Sea' and 'Captain Bunker': Two Songs in *Moby-Dick,*" Melville Society Extracts, 63 (Sept 1985), 4-7; Melville, *Moby-Dick,* "Extracts"; Murphy, *Logbook for Grace,* 1947, 92; *Sailor's Magazine,* 9:12 (May 1840), 288; *Sailor's Magazine,* 16:4 (Dec 1843), 129.

230. **The Sailor Boy's Dream**: Frank 1985 #181; Frank 1988, passim.

231. **Wood and Black-Skin**: Frank 1985 #183; Frank, "'Wood and Black-Skin': The Peripatetic Whaling Wiles of R.G.N. Swift, Songwriter, and the Greatest Whaling Poem Ever Composed," Ninth Annual Music of the Sea Symposium, Mystic Seaport, Mystic, Conn., 11 June 1988 [Kendall Whaling Museum archive; G.W. Blunt White Library archive, Mystic Seaport].

232. **The Homebound Whaleman**: Not found elsewhere than the three editions of sheet music.

Bibliography

I. Primary Sources

Abbé, William Alanson. Bark *Atkins Adams* of Fairhaven, 1858-59. NBWM #454.
Anonymous. "Scraps, Odd-thoughts & Tag Ends of a Rope Hauler." Commonplace book kept aboard the ship *Warren* of Warren, William Mayhew, master, 1832. KNB #A-299.
Anonymous copy-sheet, n.d., circa mid 19th Century. KNB manuscripts archive.
Anonymous papers of the bark *Mars* of New Bedford, George W. Allen, master, 1869-73. KNB manuscripts archive.
Anonymous journal, three voyages of the bark *Mermaid* of New Bedford, James Henry Sherman, master, 1883-90. KNB #142.
Atherton, Charles D. Homeward-bound journal, bark *Oak* of Nantucket, 1867-69. KNB #571 (quoted by special permission).
Bartley, Theodore D. Ship *California* of New Bedford, 1851-54. KNB #509.
Beden, Cornelius H. Ship *Massachusetts* of New Bedford, 1851-53; ship *South America* of New Bedford, 1855. KNB #660.
Bennett, Austin C. Bark *Sunbeam* of New Bedford, 1886-90. KNB #619.
Bennett, Thomas. Ship *Condor* of New Bedford, 1839-40; second mate, ship *William Baker* of Warren, 1840-41. KNB #479.
Braley, Jason L. Third mate, ship *Stephania* of New Bedford, 1847-49; second mate, 1849-50; first mate, bark *Louisa* of New Bedford, 1851-53; master, ship *William Badger* of New Bedford, 1853. KNB #130.
Braley, Samuel Tripp. Master, ship *Arab* of Fairhaven, 1849-52. KNB #255.
Bryant, Thomas R., Jr. Ship *Elizabeth* of New Bedford, 1847-51. KNB #77.
Bunker, Samuel. Master, ship *Alexander* of Nantucket, 1824-27. KNB #821.
Cahoon, Stephen, Jr. Ship *Polly* of Gloucester, 1794-95. KNB #821.
Chaplain, James L. Master, ship *Josephine* of New Bedford, 1859-62. KNB #122.
Chappell, Daniel A. Cooper, ship *Benjamin Tucker* of New Bedford, 1849-51. KNB #30.
Chase, Elijah Pitts. Ship *Navigator* of Nantucket, 1845-49. KNB #154.
Cleveland, George Snow. Second mate, ship *Charles* of New Bedford, 1837-39. KNB #339.
Coffin, Benjamin A. Bark *Catalpa* of New Bedford, 1856-57; ship *James Loper* of Nantucket, 1857-60 [Nicholson Collection, Providence Public Library, Providence, R.I.].
Collins, Edward Willson. Entries dated 1829 in the journal of Silas Collins, brig *By Chance* of Dartmouth, 1826-27. KNB #35.
_____. Ship *Condor* of New Bedford, 1832-33 and 1833-34. KNB #54 and #35.
_____. Master, ship *Midas* of Fairhaven, 1844-45. KNB #884.
_____. Miscellaneous papers, circa 1825-45.
Collins, Silas. Brig *By Chance* of Dartmouth, 1825-26 and 1826-27. KNB #35.
Colton, James S. Bark *Tenedos* of New London, 1840-42. KNB #930.
Coquin, John S. Bark *Pacific* of New Bedford, 1867-68; various merchant voyages out of Boston, circa 1869-73. KNB #827.
Davis, William H. Bark *Midas* of New Bedford, 1861-65. KNB #146.
Dexter, Rodolphus W. Master, ship *Chili* of New Bedford, 1843-45; ship *Israel,* 1846-47. KNB #703 and #304.
Donahue, James. Ship *Atlantic* of Nantucket, 1850-53. KNB #934 (see William Gillaspia).
Eayrs, Joseph H. Boatsteerer, bark *Gratitude* of New Bedford, 1841-45. KNB #
Evans, Charles A. (contributor—see Daniel A. Chapel)
Fisher, Holmes C. (contributor—see George W. Piper)
Fisher, Nathan C. First mate, bark *Ocean* of Sandwich, 1856-57. KNB #451.
Freeman, Benjamin A. Bark *Sea Queen* of Westport, 1851-55. KNB #923.
Fullmoon, Sylvanus C. Ship *Nimrod* of New Bedford, 1842-45. KNB #933.
Gallup, Benjamin Franklin, Jr. Green hand, bark *South America* of New Bedford, 1855-59. KNB #555.
Gibson, Henry. (contributor—see William Keith)
Gifford, George H. Brig *Elizabeth* of Westport, 1837-38. KNB #595.
Gifford, William. Third mate, ship *Benjamin Cummings* of New Bedford, 1854-59. NBWM #235.
Gillaspia, William. Ship *Atlantic* of Nantucket, 1846-49 and 1850-53. KNB #934 (see James Donahue).
Gilman, B. J. Ship *Mary* of New Bedford, 1844-47. KNB #745.
Gor[h]am, Joseph R. (contributor—see George A. Gould)
Gould, George A. Ship *Columbia* of Nantucket, 1841-45. KNB #213.
Greene, Samuel, Jr. First mate and relief master, ship *Flora* of New London, 1835-36; master, ship *Neptune* of New London, 1839-40 and 1844. KNB #612.
Halstead, Israel T. Fourth mate, ship *Mount Vernon* of New Bedford, 1843-46. KNB #214.
Handy, Albert F. Bark *Waverly* of New Bedford, 1859-63 (collaborated with G. M. Jones and G. E. Sanborn). KNB #535.
Himes, Randall. Second mate, bark *Emma* of New Bedford, 1847-48. KNB #498.
Hopkins, Stephen O. Ship *Rosalie* of Warren, 1843-44; bark *Perseverance* of Newport, 1849. KNB #532.
Howland, George Washington. Bark *Pioneer* of New Bedford, 1875-77. KNB #217.
Hughson, Robert Nathaniel. Bark *Java* of New Bedford, 1857-60. KNB #674.
Hutchins, James W. Ship *Florida* of New Bedford, 1843-46 [collection of the New Bedford (Mass.) Free Public Library].
_____. Notations in an anonymous journal of the ship *Florida* of New Bedford, 1843-46. NBWM.
Jenney, Jephtha, Jr. Ship *Hercules* of New Bedford, 1828-30. NBWM #580.
Johnson, William E. (alias Edward Cendyrlin). Deposition #57200, Bureau of Pensions, Pittsburgh, Pa., 11 Feb. 1910.
Jones, George M. Bark *Waverly* of New Bedford, 1859-63 (collaborated with A. F. Handy and G. E. Sanborn). KNB #535.
Jones, John. Steward, ship *Eliza Adams* of New Bedford, 1852. KNB #319.
Keith, William H. Whaling schooners *William Martin* of Boston and *Edith May* of Wellfleet, circa 1865-69; coastwise merchant cruises, including schooner *Cora Nash* of Boston, circa 1871. KNB #797.

Kellogg, Burr R.S. Merchant ship *Horatio* of New Bedford, homeward bound from Canton to New York, 1844 [quoted courtesy of Edward J. Lefkowicz, Providence, R.I.].

Keyser, William F. Bark *Midas* of New Bedford, 1861-65. KNB #871.

Kirby, Nicholas Jr. First mate, merchant ship *Olive Branch* of Boston, 1850-52. KNB ancillary collections.

Kirwin, Edward J. Bark *William Gifford* of New Bedford, 1872-73. KNB #452C.

Lepetit, Eugene A. Ship *Josephine* of New Bedford, 1859-62. KNB #123.

McCleave, Edward. Master, ship *Roscoe* of New Bedford, 1847-51. KNB #910.

McInnis, Emma [Mrs. John McInnis]. Bark *Josephine* of San Francisco, 1891-92. KNB #253.

Marble, Elizabeth Church [Mrs. John C. Marble]. Miscellaneous papers circa 1845-85, including bark *Kathleen* of New Bedford, 1857-60; and bark *Awashonks* of New Bedford, 1860-61.

Marble [Marbel], George D. Brig *Le Barron* of Rochester, 1837-38; boatsteerer, bark *Roscoe* of New Bedford, 1839-42; [second mate, ship *Caroline* of New Bedford, 1842-46; first mate, bark *Octavia* of New Bedford, 1846-48]; master, ship *Helen Augusta* of Newport, 1854-56; first mate, bark *Kathleen* of New Bedford, 1857-60; first mate, [bark *Awashonks* of New Bedford, 1860-61]. KNB #489 and 492 (see John C. Marble).

Marble, John. Green hand, ship *Java* of New Bedford, 1832-33; seaman, boatsteerer, and junior mate, ship *William Wirt* of Fairhaven and ship *America* of Hudson, 1833-41; mate, brig *Pilgrim* of Somerset, 1842-43; master, brig *Leonidas* of New Bedford, 1843-45; ship *Gold Hunter* of Fall River, 1846-49; bark *A. Houghton* of Fall River, 1853-56; bark *Kathleen* of New Bedford, 1857-60; bark *Awashonks* of New Bedford, 1860-61. KNB #490-494, 458, 516, and 618.

Marble, John G. and Lydia. (contributors—see Stephen O. Hopkins and Lemuel C. Richmond, Jr.)

Martin, John F. Ship *Lucy Ann* of Wilmington, Delaware, 1841-44. KNB #434.

Merrill, Frederick. Bark *Janus* of New Bedford, 1875-76; schooner *Eothen* of New York to Hudson Bay, 1878. KNB #972.

Mills, George Edgar. Fourth mate, ship *Java* of New Bedford, 1854-55; third mate, ship *Leonidas* of New Bedford, 1855-56; second mate, bark *Mary Frances* of Warren, 1856; third mate, bark *Aurora* of Westport, 1856-59; third mate, ship *James Loper* of Nantucket, 1859-60. KNB #392 and 632.

Nickerson, Solomon P. Schooner *Varnum H. Hill* of Provincetown, 1863-65. KNB #199.

Norton, Jemeriah C. First mate, ship *Swift* of New Bedford, 1849-52. KNB #349.

Pettey, Henry Tripp. Bark *Mary Ann* of New Bedford, 1853-55; bark *Chili* of New Bedford, 1856-59. KNB #815.

Phillips, Harvey R.C. Ship *Gladiator* of New Bedford, 1853. KNB #812.

Piper, George Wilbur. Ship *Europa* of Edgartown, 1868-70. KNB #A-194.

Poole, William H. Ship *Minnesota* of New York, 1868-72. KNB #751.

Prescott, G.H. Ship *Ocean* of New Haven, 1860-61; bark *Belle* of Fairhaven, 1861-62. KNB #756.

Reed, Israel. Bark *Black Eagle* of New Bedford, 1860-61. KNB #34.

Reynolds, Richard C. Boatsteerer, ship *Janus* of New Bedford, 1842-44.; subsequent voyages into the mid 1850s. KNB #732.

Richmond, Lemuel C., Jr. Carpenter, ship *Perseverance* of Newport, 1849; drayman, San Francisco, circa 1851. KNB #532 (see Stephen O. Hopkins; John G. and Lydia Marble).

Ritchie, Daniel Kimball. Second mate, ship *Israel* of New Bedford, 1843-45; inmate, "The Fort" Prison, Honolulu, 1845; second mate, ship *Herald* of New Bedford, 1845-47; second mate, ship *Massachusetts* of New Bedford, 1847. KNB #478.

Robbins, Charles H. Manuscript papers, 1837-97, including extracts from several voyages. KNB #631.

Rogers, Benjamin Franklin. (contributor—see Solomon P. Nickerson)

Russell, Frederick H. (contributor—see G. W. Howland)

Sanborn, George E. Bark *Waverly* of New Bedford, 1859-63 (collaborator of G. M. Jones and A. F. Handy). KNB #535.

Sears, E. C. Memoirs, essays, and sketch-books, 3 vols., cirfca 1885-1935. KNB #

Smith, Frederick Howland. Boy and seaman, ship *Lydia* of Fairhaven, 1854-58; boatsteerer, bark *Roscius* of New Bedford, 1858-61; 18th Regiment of Massachusetts Volunteers, U.S. Army, 1862-64; third mate, bark *Herald* of New Bedford, 1865-66; second mate, bark *Herald* of New Bedford, 1866-69. KNB #101 and 99.

Smith, Freeman A. Seaman, schooner *Varnum H. Hill* of Provincetown, 1857-58.

Stanton, James E. Boy, ship *Emily Morgan* of New Bedford, 1837-38. KNB #267.

Sullivan, John C. Manuscript in the papers of Elizabeth C. Marble (q.v.), bark *Kathleen* of New Bedford, 1857-60.

Swain, Charles B. Bark *Cachalot* of New Bedford, 1857-59. KNB #697.

Swift, Rupert G.N. Ship *Contest* of New Bedford, 1866-68 and 1868-70. KNB #234.

Tallman, Joseph Robinson. Ship *Coral* of New Bedford, 1846-49; and ship *Swift* of New Bedford, 1849-52. KNB #538.

Taylor, Samuel. Ship *Samuel Robertson,* schooner *Oxford,* and bark *Arab* of Fairhaven, 1858-60. KNB #956.

Tinkham, Daniel L. Bark *Samuel and Thomas* of Mattapoisett, 1852; brig *March* of Mattapoisett, 1855-56. KNB #959.

Tray, Martha Ann. (contributor—see George A. Gould)

Tripp, William H. Photograph #T-986 (schooner *John R. Manta,* 1911). Tripp Collection, KNB #T-986

Tuck, Joseph Washington. Mate, brig *E. Nickerson* of Provincetown, 1850-52; mate, bark *F. Buchinia* of Provincetown, 1852-53; master, *F. Buchinia,* 1857-58.

West, Benjamin L. Ship *Leonidas* of Fairhaven, 1843-46. KNB #624.

Whalon, Jonathan. Master, ship *Henry Kneeland* of New Bedford, 1854-56. KNB #725.

Wicks, Asaph S. Bark *John Dawson* of New Bedford, 1855-58. KNB #523.

Wood, Horace. Bark *Andrews* of New Bedford, 1866-67. KNB #1025

Worth, George P. (contributor—see William Keith).

Worth, William, 2d. Master, ship *Howard* of Nantucket, 1835-38. KNB #729

Wright, Dean C. Boatsteerer, ship *Benjamin Rush* of Warren, 1841-45. KNB #A-145.

II. Secondary Sources and References

Abraham, Roger D. 1974. *Deep the Water, Shallow the Shore.* Austin: University of Texas Press.
Afonso, Jo_ao. 1998. *Mar de Baleias e de Baleeiros.* Angra do Heroí smo (Portugal): Regional da Cultura.
Albion, Robert Greenhalgh. 1938. *Square-Riggers on Schedule.* Princeton: Princeton University Press.
_____. 1939. *The Rise of New York Port.* New York: Scribners'.
Allen, William Francis; Charles Pickar Ware; and Lucy McKim Garrison. 1867. *Slave Songs of the United States.* New York: A. Simpson & Co.
Amateur's Song Book (The): Part First. 1843. Boston: Elias Howe, Jr.
American Musical Miscellany. [1798.] [Northampton, Mass.] Repr., New York: DeCapo Press. 1972.
American Naval and Patriotic Songster. 1831. Baltimore: William Sewell.
American Sailor's Songster (The). Philadelphia, New York, and Boston: Fisher & Brother. n.d [circa 1848].
American Singer's Own Book (The). [*The New American Singer's Own Book.*]. 1841. Philadelphia: M. Kelly.
American Songster (The): A Collection of Songs as Sung in the Iron Days of '76. Philadelphia: Fischer & Brother, n.d. [c.1835].
American Vocalist (The). 1856. New York: Richard Marsh.
Anderson, Charles Roberts. 1939. *Melville in the South Seas.* New York: Columbia University Press.
Ashley, Clifford W. 1926 and 1938. *The Yankee Whaler.* Garden City: Halcyon.
Ashton, John. 1888. *Modern Street Ballads.* London: Chatto & Windus. (Repr., New York: Benjamin Blom, 1968.)
_____. 1891. *Real Sailor Songs.* Unpaginated. London: Leadenhall. (Repr., paginated version ed. by A.L. Lloyd, New York: Benjamin Blom, 1972.)
Baker, B. F. 1860. *Excelsior Song Book.* Boston: Chase, Nicholls & Hill.
Baker, Richard; and Anthony Miall. 1982. *Everyman's Book of Sea Songs.* London: J.M. Dent & Son.
Barbeau, Marius. 1952. "All Hands Aboard Scrimshawing." *The American Neptune,* XII:2 (April 1952); repr., Salem, Mass.: Peabody Museum of Salem, 1966.
Baring-Gould, Rev. S[abine]. 1895. *English Minstrelsie.* 8 vols. Edinburgh: T.C. & E.C. Jack, Grange Publications.
_____, et al. 1905. *Songs of the West.* London: Methuen.
_____; and Cecil J. Sharp. [1906.] *English Folk-Songs for Schools.* London: J. Curwen & Sons.
_____; and H. Fleetwood Sheppard. 1895. *A Garland of Country Song.* London: Methuen & Co.
Barnaby, K. C. [1970] 1973. *Some Ship Disasters and Their Causes.* South Brunswick: A.S. Barnes.
Barnes, James. 1898. *Ships and Sailors, Being a Collection of Songs of the Sea by the Men Who Sail It.* New York: Frederick A. Stokes Co.
Barnhart, Clarence D., et al. 1954. *The New Century Cyclopedia of Names.* 3 vols. New York: Appleton-Century-Crofts.
Barry, Phillips; Fannie H. Eckstorm; and Mary W. Smyth. 1929. *British Ballads from Maine: The Development of Popular Songs with Texts and Airs.* New Haven: Yale University Press.
Baughman, James P. 1972. *The Mallorys of Mystic.* Middletown: Wesleyan University Press; Mystic: Marine Historical Assoc.
Beadle's Dime Melodist. 1859. New York: Irwin P. Beadle.
Beadle's Dime Song Book. 1859-76. 34 vols. [*N° 1* through *N° 34*]. New York: Irwin P. Beadle; Boston: John J. Dyer & Co.; New York and Buffalo: Irwin R. Beadle; etc. (see Johannsen III:55-58).
Beatty, Owen; and John Geiger. 1987. *Frozen in Time: Unlocking the Secrets of the Franklin Expedition.* New York: Dutton.
Beck, Horace P. 1972. *Folklore and the Sea.* Middletown: Wesleyan University Press; and Mystic: Marine Historical Assoc.
Behan, Dominic. 1973. *Ireland Sings.* London: Music Sales, Inc.
Belden, H.M. 1940. *Ballads and Songs Collected by the Missouri Folklore Society.* (The University of Missouri Studies, 15:1 [January 1, 1940].) Columbia: University of Missouri.
_____; and Arthur Palmer Hudson, eds. 1952a. *The Frank C. Brown Collection of North Carolina Folklore, Volume II: Folk Ballads from North Carolina.* Durham, N.C.: Duke University Press.
_____, eds. 1952b. *The Frank C. Brown Collection of North Carolina Folklore, Volume III: Folk Songs from North Carolina.* Durham, N.C.: Duke University Press.
Bikel, Theodore. 1960. *Folksongs and Footnotes.* New York: Meridian.
Bockstoce, John R. 1977. *Steam Whaling in the Western Arctic.* With contributions by William A. Baker and Charles F. Batchelder. New Bedford: Old Dartmouth Historical Society.
_____. 1986. *Whales, Ice, and Men: The History of Whaling in the Western Arctic.* Seattle & London: University of Washington Press.
Bolster, W. Jeffrey. 1997. *Black Jacks: African American Seamen in the Age of Sail.* Cambridge: Harvard University Press.
Bone, David. 1931. *Capstan Bars.* Edinburgh: Porpoise Press (1931); New York: Harcourt, Brace & Co. (1932).
Bradbury, W. B. 1859. *The Alpine Glee Singer.* New York: Mark H. Newman.
Brink, Carol. 1947. *Harps in the Wind: The Story of the Singing Hutchinsons.* New York: Macmillan.
Broadwood, Lucy E. 1908. *English Traditional Songs and Carols.* London: Boosey & Co. (Repr., Wakefield: EP Publishing; Totowa: Rowman & Littlefield, 1974.)
_____; and J.A. Fuller Maitland. 1891. *English County Songs.* London: Leadenhall.
Bronson, Bertrand Harris. 1959-72. *Traditional Tunes of the Child Ballads.* 4 vols. Princeton: Princeton University Press.
_____. 1976. *The Singing Tradition of Child's Popular Ballads.* Princeton: Princeton University Press.
Brown, Theron; and Hezekiah Butterworth. 1906. *The Story of the Hymns and Tunes.* New York: American Tract Society.
[Brown Collection.] *The Frank C. Brown Collection of North Carolina Folklore.* 7 vols., ed. Newton Ivey White et al. Durham, N.C.: Duke University Press. [Individual volumes edited by H.M. Belden et al., and Jan Philip Schinhan. qq.v.]
Browne, J. Ross. 1846. *Etchings of a Whaling Cruise.* New York: Harper & Brothers. (Repr. ed. by John Seelye, Cambridge: The Belknap Press of Harvard University Press, 1968.)
Bruce, Charles. 1874. *Poems, Songs and Ballads of the Sea.* Edinburgh: William P. Nimmo.

Bryant, William Cullen, ed. 1877. *A New Library of Poetry and Song.* 2 vols. New York: Ford's, Howard & Hulbert.
Buck, P.C.; and Thomas Wood. [1927.] *The Oxford Song Book.* 2 vols. London: Oxford University Press.
Buckley, Frederick. 1863. *Buckley's Seranaders Songs [N° 1].* Boston: G.D. Russell.
Bullen, Frank T.; and W. F. Arnold. 1914. *Songs of Sea Labour.* London: Swan & Co.
Burns, Walter Noble. 1913. *A Year With a Whaler.* New York: Outing Publishing.
Calliope: or, The Musical Miscellany. A Select Collection of the Most Approved English, Scots, and Irish Songs, Set to Music. 1788. London: C. Elliot & T. Kay.
Calthorpe, Nancy. 1974. *The Calthorpe Collection: Songs and airs arranged for the voice and Irish harp.* Dublin: Waltons Piano & Musical Instrument Galleries.
Campbell, George Duncan. 1977. "The Sailor's Home." *The American Neptune,* 37:3 (July 1977), 174-7.
Carey, George G. 1971. *Maryland Folk Legends and Folk Songs.* Cambridge, Md.: Tidewater.
_____. 1976. *A Sailor's Songbag.* Amherst: University of Massachusetts Press.
Carpenter, Lucien O. 1889. *J.W. Pepper's Universal Dancing Master, Prompter's Call-Book, and Violinist's Guide.* Philadelphia and Chicago: J.W. Pepper.
Cazden, Norman. 1958. *The Abelard Folk Song Book.* New York: Abelard Schuman.
_____. 1982. *Folk Songs of the Catskills.* 2 vols. Albany: State University of New York Press.
Century Musical Association. *Members' Catalogue: Sheet Music, Folios and Musical Works....* Philadelphia and Chicago: Century Musical Association. n.d. [circa 1894.]
Champion of the Seas Times (The). 1952. Mystic: Marine Historical Association.
Chappell, William. [1855.] *Popular Music of the Olden Time; a Collection of Ancient Songs, Ballads, and Dance Tunes, Illustrative of the National Music of England.* 2 vols. London: Cramer, Beale & Chappell. n.d. [1855-59.] (Repr., 2 vols, New York: Dover, 1965.)
_____. 1893. *Old English Popular Music: A New Edition....* Ed. E. Ellis Wooldridge; containing Frank Kidson's "Supplement to Chappel's [sic] Traditional Tunes." [London, (1840) 1893.] (Repr., New York: Jack Brussel, 1961.)
Chase, Owen. 1963. *Narrative of the ... Shipwreck of the Whaleship Essex [1821].* Gloucester, Mass.: Peter Smith.
Child, Francis James. 1858. *English and Scottish Ballads.* 8 vols. Boston: Houghton, Mifflin & Co.
_____. 1882-98. *The English and Scottish Popular Ballads.* 5 vols. Boston: Houghton Mifflin. (Repr., 3 vols., New York: Cooper Square, 1962; repr., 5 vols., New York: Dover, 1965.)
Christ-Janer, Albert; Charles W. Hughes; and Carleton Sprage Smith. 1980. *American Hymns Old and New.* New York: Columbia University Press.
Christy, E. P. 1853. *Christy's Plantation Melodies.* 3 vols. Baltimore: Fisher & Brother.
Clancy Brothers and Tommy Makem. 1964. *The Clancy Brothers and Tommy Makem Song Book.* New York: Oak.
Clark, A. Howard. 1882. "The Whale Fishery." *Miscellaneous Documents of the United States Senate 1881-1882.* Washington.
Clark, Andrew. 1907. *The Shirburn Ballads 1585-1616.* Oxford: Clarendon.
Cohn, Ellen R. 1982. "Shipboard Music: A Report from American Whaling Journals." *Essays in Arts & Sciences,* 10:2 (March), 187-96.
Colcord, Joanna C. 1938. *Songs of the American Sailormen.* New York: W.W. Norton. (Revised and expanded ed. of *Roll and Go: Songs of American Sailormen,* Indianapolis: Bobbs-Merrill, 1924.)
_____. 1945. *Sea Language Comes Ashore.* New York: Cornell Maritime Press.
Collier, John Payne, ed. 1947. *A Book of Roxburghe Ballads.* London: Longman, Brown, Green, and Longmans.
Colonial Dames of America. 1925. *American War Songs.* Philadelphia: National Committee for the Preservation of Existing Records of the National Society of Colonial Dames of America.
Conway, Laurence Alexander. 1981. "Poetry of Nantucket Whalemen: A Reflection of Melville's American Myth." Unpublished bachelor's thesis, Brown University.
Cooper, James Fenimore. 1844. "Review of the Proceedings of the Naval Court Martial," in *Proceedings of the Naval Court Martial in the Case of Alexander Slidell Mackenzie,* New York, pp. 263-344.
Copper, Bob. [1971] 1972. *A Song for Every Season.* London: William Heinemann, Ltd.
Cox, John Harrington. 1925. *Folk Songs of the South.* Cambridge: Harvard University Press.
Crawford, Richard. 1977. *The Civil War Song Book.* New York: Dover.
Creighton, Helen. 1933. *Songs and Ballads from Nova Scotia.* Toronto and Vancouver: J.M. Dent & Son. (Repr., New York: Dover, 1977).
_____. 1961. *Maritime Folk Songs.* Toronto: Ryerson.
_____. 1971. *Folksongs from Southern New Brunswick.* (Publications in Folk Culture N° 1.) Ottawa: National Museums.
_____; and Doreen H. Senior. 1950. *Traditional Songs from Nova Scotia.* Toronto: Ryerson.
Cushing, Helen Grant. 1936. *Children's Song Index.* New York: H.W. Wilson Co.
Cutler, Carl C. 1930. *Greyhounds of the Sea.* Annapolis: U.S. Naval Institute.
_____. 1961. *Queens of the Western Ocean.* Annapolis: U.S. Naval Institute.
Damon, S. Foster. 1936. *Series of Old American Songs Reproduced in Facsimile from Original or Early Editions in the Harris Collection of American Poetry and Plays, Brown University.* Providence: Brown University Library.
Dana, Richard Henry, Jr. 1840. *Two Years Before the Mast.* New York: Harper Bros. (Repr. ed. by Thomas Philbrick, Hammondsworth: Penguin, [1981] 1986.)
_____. 1841. *The Seamen's Friend.* Boston; et seq.
Davenport, A. 1888. *Heart Songs.* Boston: White, Smith & Co.
Davids, C. A.; and B. H. Albers. 1980. *Wat lijt den zedeman al Vendreit: Het Nederlandse zeemansleid in de zeiltijd 1600-1900.* The Hague: Martinus Nijhoff.
Davidson's Universal Melodist. 1848. 2 vols. London: G.H. Davidson.
Davis, Arthur Kyle, Jr. 1929. *Traditional Ballads of Virginia.* Cambridge: Harvard University Press.

_____. 1960. *More Traditional Ballads of Virginia.* Chapel Hill: University of North Carolina Press.
Davis, Frederick J.; and Ferris Tozer. [1887.] *Sailor Songs or "Chanties."* London: Boosey & Co. n.d.
Davis, Hugh M. 1979. "The American Seamen's Friend Society and the American Sailor." *The American Neptune,* 39:1 (January), 45ff.
Davis, William M. 1874. *Nimrod of the Sea; or, The American Whaleman.* New York: Harper & Bros.
Davison, Archibald T.; and Thomas Whitney Surette. 1922. *140 Folk-Songs, with Piano Accompaniment.* Concord Series, N° 7. Boston: E.C. Schirmer Music Co. [1921].
de Charms, Desiree; and Pearl F. Breed. 1966. *Songs In Collections.* Detroit: Information Coordinators.
De Ville, Paul. 1905. *The Concertina and How to Play It.* New York: Carl Fisher.
Dean-Smith, Margaret. 1954. *A Guide to English Folk Song Collections 1822-1852.* Liverpool: The University Press of Liverpool, in association with The English Folk Dance & Song Society.
Dearman, Percy, et al. [1928] 1964. *The Oxford Book of Carols.* Oxford: Oxford University Press.
[Dibdin, Charles.] 1799. *A Collection of Songs ... of Mr. Dibdin ... To Which Are Added ... American Patriotic Songs.* Philadelphia: H.P. Rice.
Dibdin, Thomas. 1841. *Songs, Naval and Nautical, of the Late Charles Dibdin.* London: John Murray.
_____. [1841] 1860. *Songs of the Late Charles Dibdin.* London: Henry G. Bohn. 3rd ed.
Dichter, Harry. 1947. *Handbook of American Sheet Music.* "First Annual Issue." Philadelphia: Harry Dichter.
_____; and Bernice Larrabee. 1953. *Handbook of American Sheet Music. Second Series.* Philadelphia: Harry Dichter.
_____; and Eliott Shapiro. 1941. *Early American Sheet Music; Its Lure and Its Lore,* New York: R.R. Bowker. (Repr. as *Handbook of Early Sheet Music, 1768-1889,* New York: Dover, 1977.)
Doerflinger, William Main. 1972. *Songs of the Sailor and Lumberman.* New York: Macmillan. (Revised and expanded ed. of *Shantymen and Shantyboys: Songs of the Sailor and Lumberman,* New York: Macmillan, 1951).
Dreamer, Percy, et al., eds. [1928]. *The Oxford Book of Carols.* Oxford: Oxford University Press. (Repr., 1964.)
Duncan, Edmondstoune, ed. [1905]. *The Minstrelsy of England.* 3 vols. London: Augener. n.d.
_____, ed. 1927. *Lyrics from the Old Song Books.* New York: Harcourt, Brace & Co.
Eckstrom, Fanny; and Mary Winslow Smith. 1927. *Minstrelsy of Maine.* Boston and New York: Houghton Mifflin.
Eddy, Mary O. 1939. *Ballads and Songs from Ohio.* New York: J.J. Augustin.
Elton's Songs and Melodies for the Multitudes. New York: T.W. Strong; Boston: C.W. Cottrell. n.d.
Ely, Ben Ezra Stiles. [1849.] *There She Blows: Narrative of a whaling voyage in the Indian and South Atlantic Oceans* [Philadelphia]. (Repr. ed. by Curtis Dahl, Middletown: Wesleyan University Press, 1971.)
Emrich, Duncan B.M. *American Sea Songs and Shanties.* Washington: Library of Congress. n.d. (Liner notes for LP recording #AAFSL27, 2 vols., n.d.)
Epstein, Dena J. 1977. *Sinful Tunes and Spirituals: Black Folk Music to the Civil War.* Urbana: University of Illinois Press.
Ewen, David, ed. 1966. *American Popular Songs: From the Revolutionary War to the Present.* New York: Random House.
Ewing, George W. 1977. *The Well-Tempered Lyre: Songs & Verse of the Temperance Movement.* Dallas: Southern Methodist University Press.
Farmer, John. 1896. *Scarlet and Blue; or, Songs for Soldiers and Sailors.* London: Cassell.
Farnsworth, Charles H.; and Cecil J. Sharp. [1916]. *Folk-Songs, Chanteys and Singing Games.* New York: H.W. Gray; London: Novello. n.d.
Ferguson, Edith P., ed. 1984. *The 1860 Federal Census[:] Provincetown, Barnstable County, Massachusetts.* Bowie, Md.: Heritage Books.
Fife, Austin E. and Alta S. 1982. *Cowboy and Western Songs, A Comprehensive Anthology.* New York: Bramhill. [1969].
Firth, C. H. 1908. *Naval Songs and Ballads.* London: Navy Records Society.
Fitz-Gerald, S. J. Adair. 1898 and 1906. *Stories of Famous Songs.* London: John Nimmo; and Philadelphia: J.B. Lippincott.
Flanders, Helen Hartness. 1960. *Ancient Ballads Traditionally Sung in New England.* 4 vols. Philadelphia: University of Pennsylvania Press.
_____; Elizabeth Flanders Ballard; George Brown; and Phillips Barry. 1939. *The New Green Mountain Songster: Traditional Folk Songs of Vermont.* New Haven: Yale University Press.
_____; and George Brown. 1931. *Vermont Folk-Songs and Ballads.* Brattleboro: Stephen Day.
_____; and Marguerite Olney. 1953. *Ballads Migrant in New England.* New York: Farrar, Straus & Young.
Flood, W.H. Gratton. [1905.] *A History of Irish Music.* (Repr., New York and Washington: Prager, 1977.)
Ford, Robert. [1889-91.] *Vagabond Songs and Ballads of Scotland.* (Repr., Paisley: Alexander Gardner, 1904).
Forecastle Songster (The). 1847. New York: Nafis & Cornish.
Forecastle Songster (The). 1850. New York: Nafis & Cornish.
Forget Me Not Songster (The); Containing A Choice Collection of Old Ballad Songs, as sung by our Grandmothers... . Boston: G.W. Cottrell, n.d. [circa 1829]. [Virtually identical with the ensuing (q.v.) up to page 194, thereafter significantly different.]
Forget Me Not Songster (The); Containing A Choice Collection of Old Ballad Songs, as sung by our Grandmothers... . New York: Richard Marsh (374 Pearl St), n.d. [circa 1829].
Forster, Honore. 1985. *The South Sea Whaler: An Annotated Bibliography of published historical, literary and art material relating to whaling in the Pacific Ocean in the nineteenth century.* Sharon, Mass.: Kendall Whaling Museum; Fairhaven, Mass.: Edward. J. Lefkowicz.
_____. 1991. *More South Sea Whaling: A Supplement to The South Sea Whaler.* Canberra: Australian National Univ.
Fowke, Edith. 1965. *Traditional Singers and Songs of Ontario.* Hatboro: Folklore Associates; Don Mills: Burns & MacEachern.
_____. [1973] 1981. *The Penguin Book of Canadian Folk Songs.* Hammondsworth, Msx.: Penguin.
_____. 1981. *Sea Songs and Ballads from Nineteenth-Century Nova Scotia.* New York and Philadelphia: Folklorica.
_____; and Richard Johnston. 1954. *Folk Songs of Canada.* Waterloo: Waterloo Music.

Frank, Stuart M. 1977. "The Seamen's Friend." *The Log of Mystic Seaport,* 29:2 (July), 52-8.

_____. 1978a. *Sea Chanteys and Forecastle Songs.* (Liner notes for Folkways LP #37300, *Sea Chanteys and Forecastle Songs at Mystic Seaport.*) New York: Folkways.

_____. 1978b. *Sea Chanteys and Sailors' Songs: A Guide for Teachers.* Richmond: Henrico County Public Schools and the Math & Science Center. (Revised eds. 1981-94.)

_____. 1980a. "Songs of the Sea, San Francisco, 1979." (Liner notes for Folkways # 37315, *Songs of the Sea: National Maritime Museum Festival of the Sea, San Francisco,* New York: Folkways, 1980.)

_____, ed. 1980b. *Songs of the Sea: The National Maritime Museum Festival of the Sea, San Francisco, 1979.* LP recording, with Stan Hugill, U. Utah Phillips, Bob Webb, Morrigan, etc. Folkways FSS 37315, New York.

_____. 1982. "Musical Instruments on Shipboard in the Western Arctic Whale Fishery." William Gilkerson and John R. Bockstoce, *American Whalers in the Western Arctic* (Fairhaven, Mass.: Edward J. Lefkowicz, Inc.).

_____. 1984. "Concertina Round the Horn." *Concertina & Squeezebox,* 2:2 (Spring), 10-18.

_____. 1985. *Ballads and Songs of the Whale-Hunters, 1825-1895; from Manuscripts in the Kendall Whaling Museum.* 2 vols. Unpublished Ph.D. Thesis, Brown University.

_____. 1985a. "'Cheer'ly Man': Chanteying in Omoo and Moby-Dick." *New England Quarterly,* 58:1 (March), 68-82.

_____. 1985b. "'Boston': Two 'New' Texts of an Old Favorite Sea Song." *The American Neptune,* 45:3 (Summer), 175-180.

_____. 1985c. "'The King of the Southern Sea' and 'Captain Bunker': Two Songs in *Moby-Dick*." *Melville Society Extracts,* 63 (September), 4-7.

_____. 1987. "'Poor Jack': A Dibdin Song in *Billy Budd*." *Melville Society Extracts,* 69 (February), 6-8.

_____. 1988. "'Wood and Black-Skin': The Peripatetic Whaling Wiles of R.G.N. Swift, Songwriter, and the Greatest Whaling Poem Ever Composed." Ninth Annual Music of the Sea Symposium, Mystic Seaport, Mystic, Conn., 11 June.

_____. 1989. "'Unequal Cross-Lights': Melville's Pictures and the Aesthetics of a Sometime Whaleman." *The Log of Mystic Seaport,* 41:2 (Summer), 45-55.

_____. 1991a. *Dictionary of Scrimshaw Artists.* Mystic: Mystic Seaport Museum.

_____. 1991b. *Meditations from Steerage: The Journals of Dean C. Wright, Boatsteerer, 1841-44; and John Jones, Steward, 1852.* Kendall Whaling Museum Monograph Series N° 7.

_____. 1995. *Oooh, You New York Girls! The Urban Pastorale in Ballads and Songs about Sailors Ashore in the Big City.* The 1995 Vaughan Evans Memorial Lecture. Kendall Whaling Museum Monograph Series N° 9. Sharon, Mass.: The Kendall Whaling Museum; Perth, Western Australia: The Australian Association for Maritime History. 1996.

_____. 1998a. *The Book of Pirate Songs.* Sharon, Mass.: The Kendall Whaling Museum.

_____. 1998b. *More Scrimshaw Artists.* Mystic, Conn.: Mystic Seaport Museum.

_____. 1998c. "The *Somers*: A Newly-Discovered Ballad Text of 1842 from a Contemporaneous Whaleman's Journal." Melville Society Extracts, 115 (Dec, 1998), pp. 1-7

_____. 1998c. "A Canção da Escuna Varnum H. Hill," in Joã o Afonso, ed., *Mar de Baleias e de Baleeiros* (q.v.).

_____. 2000a. *Sea Chanteys and Sailors' Songs: An Introduction for Singers and Performers, and a Guide for Teachers and Group Leaders..* Kendall Whaling Museum Monograph Series N° 11.

_____. 2000b. *"Musick on the Brain": Frederick Howland Smith's Shipboard Tunes, 1854-1869.* Kendall Whaling Museum Monograph Series N° 12.

_____. 2002a. "'I'm One of the B'hoys': A Song about New York Firefighters in the Age of Sail." *Seaport* (South Street Seaport Museum), 37:2-3, special World Trade Center 9/11 issue, Spring/Summer 2002, pp 34-41.

_____. 2002b. "'No Ke Ano Ahiahi': A 'Lost' Hawaiian Narrative Ballad." *Mains'l Haul: A Journal; of Pacific Maritime History* (Maritime Museum of San Diego), 38:3, Summer 2002, pp 22-27.

_____. 2004. "Classic American Whaling Songs." *Maritime Life and Traditions.* Part I, Vol. 23 (London, Summer 2004), pp. 48-67; Part II, Vol. 26 (London, Spring 2005), pp. 16-33.

_____. 2005. "Sea Chanteys." *Encyclopedia of New England,* Burt Feintuch and David H. Watters, eds. New Haven: Yale University Press.

_____. 2007. "Ballads and Chanteys." *Encyclopedia of Maritime History,* John B. Hattendorf, ed. New York: Oxford University Press.

Franklin Songster (The). [No information. Title and half-title missing from the copy consulted. Edited by C.H.S., circa 1835.]

Freud, Sigmund. *Civilization and Its Discontents.* (Repr., New York: W.W. Norton, 1962.)

Frothingham, Charles. 1924. *Songs of the Sea and Sailors's Chanteys.* Boston: Houghton Mifflin.

Gallup, Darwin C.; and Josephine Middleton Peck. 1966. *Gallup Genealogy.* [n.c.:] Gallup Family Association.

Galvin, Patrick. *Irish Songs of the Resistance.* New York: Folklore Press. n.d.

Gardner, Elizabeth; and Geraldine Jencks Chickering. 1939. *Ballads and Songs of Southern Michigan.* Ann Arbor: University of Michigan Press. (Repr., Hatboro: Folklore Associates, 1967.)

Gibbon, J. Murray. 1949. *Canadian Folk Songs.* London: J.M. Dent. [1927].

Gilkerson, William; and John R. Bockstoce, 1982. *American Whalers in the Western Arctic* (Fairhaven, Mass.: Edward J. Lefkowicz, Inc.).

Gilpin, Sidney. 1866. *The Songs and Ballads of Cumberland.* London: George Routledge & Son; Edinburgh: John Menzies; Carlisle: George Coward.

Gleadhill, T. S. 1880. *Kyle's Scottish Lyric Gems.* Glasgow: Joseph Ferrie.

Golden Book of Favorite Songs (The). 1923. [n.c.:] Hall & McCreary. [1915].

Good Old Songs We Used to Sing. 1887-95. Compiled by J.H.C. 2 vols. Boston: Oliver Ditson.

Graeme, Joy, ed. 1971. *Irish Song Book ... The Clancy Brothers and Tommy Makem.* New York: Collier

Gray, Roland Palmer. 1924. *Songs and Ballads of the Maine Lumberjacks, with Other Songs from Maine.* Cambridge: Harvard University Press.

Greig, Gavin. [1907.] *Folk-Song in Buchan.* [Buchan:] Buchan Field-Club, 1906-07.

_____. 1914. *Folk-Song of the North-East.* Peterhead: Buchan Observer.
_____. 1925. *Last Leaves of Traditional Ballads and Ballad Airs.* Alexander Keith, ed. Aberdeen: The Buchan Club.
_____. 1963. *Folk-Song in Buchan and Folk-Song of the North-East.* Hatboro, Pa.: Folklore Associates. (Repr. from Gavin 1907 and Gavin 1914.)
Greenleaf, Elizabeth Bristol; and Grace Yarrow Mansfield. 1933. *Ballads and Songs from Newfoundland.* Cambridge: Harvard University Press.
Grigg's Southern and Western Songster. 1832. Philadelphia: J. Grigg. (Repr. severally to 1850.) [1826].
Griggs, Herbert. 1900. *The Beacon Song Collection Number Two.* New York: Silver, Burdett & Co.
Grinnell, George Byrd. 1901. "Natives of the Alaska Coast Region." John Burroughs, John Muir, and George Byrd Grinnell, eds., *Alaska* [The Harriman Alaska Expedition], 2 vols. (New York: Doubleday, Page & Co.).
Guest, Ivor. 1970. *Fanny Elssler.* Middletown: Wesleyan University Press.
Harlow, Frederick Pease. 1928. *The Making of a Sailor.* Salem: Marine Research Society.
_____. 1962. *Chanteying Aboard American Ships.* Barre: Barre Gazette [Barre Press].
Hart, James D. 1941. *The Oxford Companion to American Literature.* London, New York, Toronto: Oxford University Press.
Hartwig, G. 1875. *The Polar and Tropical Worlds.* Springfield: A.C. Nichols.
Haskins, C. W. 1890. *The Argonauts of California.* New York: Fords, Howard & Hulbert.
Hatton, J. L.; and Eton Faning. *The Songs of England.* 3 vols. London: Boosey. n.d.
_____; and J. L. Molloy. *Songs of Ireland.* London: Boosey. n.d.
Havlice, Patricia Pate. 1975. *Popular Song Index.* Metuchen: Scarecrow.
_____. 1978. *Popular Song Index: First Supplement.* Metuchen: Scarecrow.
_____. 1984. *Popular Song Index: Second Supplement.* Metuchen: Scarecrow.
Hayes, John D.; and John B. Hattendorf, eds. 1975. *The Writings of Stephen B. Luce.* Newport: Naval War College.
Hayet, Admiral Armand. [1942] 1974. *Chansons de marins.* Paris: Tutti.
_____. 1969. *Chansons de la voile "sans voiles."* St. Malo, n.p.
Hayford, Harrison, ed. 1959. *The Somers Mutiny Affair.* Englewood Cliffs: Prentice-Hall.
Healey, James C. 1952. *Fo'c'sle and Glory Hole.* New York: Merchant Marine Publ.
Healy, James N. 1965. *Ballads from the Pubs of Ireland.* 3rd Ed. Cork: Mercier. (Also 3rd ed., 1968.)
_____. 1967. *Irish Ballads and Songs of the Sea.* Cork: Mercier.
_____. [1962] 1976. *The Second Book of Irish Ballads.* Cork: Mercier.
Heart Songs Dear to the American People. 1909. Boston: Chapple Publishing; New York: World Syndicate.
Heart Throbs. 1905-11. 2 vols. New York: World Syndicate.
Hegarty, Reginald B. 1959. *Returns of Whaling Vessels Sailing from American Ports: A Continuation of Alexander Starbuck's "History of the American Whale Fishery" 1876-1928.* New Bedford: Old Dartmouth Historical Society.
_____. 1964. *Addendum to "Starbuck" and "Whaling Masters." New Bedford Customs District.* New Bedford: New Bedford Free Public Library.
Hemans, Mrs. [Felicia Dorothea Brown]. *The Poetical Works of Mrs. Hemans.* London: Frederick Warne & Co. n.d.
Hindley, Charles, ed. 1873-74. *The Roxburghe Ballads.* 2 vols. London: Reeves & Turner.
Hohman, Elmo P. 1928. *The American Whaleman.* New York: Longmans, Green. (Repr., Clifton: Augustus M. Kelley, 1972.)
_____. 1952. *Seamen Ashore.* New Haven: Yale University Press.
_____. 1954. *American Merchant Seamen.* Hamden: Shoestring.
Hogarth, George, ed. 1847. *The Songs of Charles Dibdin.* Fifth Ed. 2 vols. London: G.H. Davidson. [1842].
Holdcamp, Forrest R. 1968. *List of American Flag Merchant Vessels that Received Certificates of Enrollment or Registry at the Port of New York, 1789-1867.* 2 vols., Washington: National Archives.
Holloway, John; and Joan Black, eds. 1979. *Later English Broadside Ballads, Vol. 2.* London: Routledge & Kegan Paul.
Horn, David. 1977. *The Literature of American Music in Books and Folk Music Collections.* Metuchen: Scarecrow.
Howard, John Tasker. 1958. *Our American Music.* New York: Thomas Y. Crowell. [1929].
Howe's 100 Comic Songs. 1869. Boston: Elias Howe.
Hughes, Herbert. [1909.] *Irish County Songs.* 4 vols. London: Boosey & Co.
Hugill, Stan. 1961. *Shanties from the Seven Seas.* London: Routledge & Kegan Paul; New York: E.P. Dutton. (Repr. 1980; abridged repr. with into. by Stuart M. Frank, Mystic, Conn.: Mystic Seaport Museum, 1994.)
_____. 1969a. *Sailortown.* London: Routledge & Kegan Paul.
_____. 1969b. *Shanties and Sailors' Songs.* London: Herbert Jenkins; New York: Prager.
_____. 1977. *Songs of the Sea.* New York: McGraw-Hill.
Hullah, John. 1866. *The Song Book.* Philadelphia: T.B. Lippincott; London: Macmillan.
Humphries, Charles; and William C. Smith. 1954. *Music Publishing in the British Isles from the earliest times to the middle of the nineteenth century: A Dictionary of engravers, printers, publishers and music sellers... .* London: Cassell & Co.
Huntington, Gale. 1964. *Songs the Whalemen Sang.* Barre: Barre Gazette [Barre Press]. (Repr., New York: Dover, 1970.)
_____. 1966. *Folksongs of Martha's Vineyard.* (Northeast Folklore, Vol. III.) Orono: Northeast Folklore Society.
_____. MS: "The Gam: More Songs the Whalemen Sang." Unpublished manuscript, circa 1980, in the Kendall Whaling Museum archive.
_____; and Lani Herrmann. *Sam Henry's Songs of the People.* Athens, Georgia: University of Georgia Press.
Hutchins, John J.B. 1968. *The American Maritime Industries and Public Policy, 1789-1914.* New York: Russell & Russell.
Hymnal of the Protestant Episcopal Church. 1961. New York: Church Pension Fund. [1940].
Ingram, F. K. ["Spanish Ladies."] *Mariners' Mirror,* 7:1 (January 1921), p. 61.
Irving, Pierre M. 1864. *The Life and Letters of Washington Irving.* New York: n.p.
Jackson, George Sturdevant. 1933. *Early Songs of Uncle Sam.* Boston: Bruce Humphries.
Jackson, Gordon. 1978. *The British Whaling Trade.* London: A.C. Black; Hamden: Shoestring.
Jackson, Richard. 1974. *Stephen Foster Song Book.* New York: Dover.

_____. 1976. *Popular Songs of Nineteenth-Century America.* New York: Dover.
Johannsen, Albert. 1962. *The House of Beadle and Adams and Its Dime and Nickel Novels.* 3 vols. Norman: University of Oklahoma Press.
Johnson, A.N.; and Jason White. 1848. *The Young Minstrel.* Boston: George P. Reed.
Johnson, Helen Kendrick. 1881. *Our Familiar Songs and Those Who Made Them.* New York: Henry Holt & Co. [1881, 1889, 1909]. (Repr. 1909 ed., as part of the series *Popular Culture in America 1800-1925,* New York: Arno, 1974.)
Johnson, James Weldon; and Rosamund Johnson.. 1925. *The Book of American Negro Spirituals.* New York: Viking.
Joyce, P. W. 1909. *Old Irish Folk Music and Songs.* London: Longmans, Green & Co.
Karpeles, Maud. 1970. *Folk Songs from Newfoundland.* Hamden: Archon.
Kastner, Joseph. 1983. "Everyone Knows Her Rhyme, But Who Remembers Jane?" *Smithsonian,* 17:7 (October), 172-186.
Katz, Bernard. 1969. *The Social Implications of Early Negro Music in the United States.* New York: Arnor Press and The New York Times.
Keith & Prowse. *Accordion Music. Observation and Instruction for the Perfect Accordion with Semi-Tones.* London: Keith & Prowse. n.d.
Kennedy, Peter. 1975. *Folksongs of Britain and Ireland.* New York: Schirmer.
Kidson, Frank. 1888. *Celebrated Yorkshire Musicians.* Series in the *Yorkshire Weekly Post,* 28 Jan. 1888 - 28 Dec. 1889.
_____. 1890. *Old Airs and Songs: Melodies Once Popular in Yorkshire.* Series of articles in the *Yorkshire Weekly Post,* 4 Jan. - 28 June 1890.
_____. 1891. *Traditional Tunes.* Oxford: Tophouse & Son. (Repr. as "Supplement to Chappel's [sic] Traditional Tunes," in William Chappell, *Old English Popular Music: A New Edition...,* edited by E. Ellis Wooldridge, London, n.d. [1893], [Section III]; the latter repr. New York: Jack Brussel, 1961.)
_____. 1893. "Supplement to Chappel's [sic] Traditional Tunes," in William Chappell, 1893 [q.v.].
_____. n.d. *A Garland of English Folk Songs,* London: Ascherberg Hopwood & Crew, n.d.
_____. [1900.] *British Music Publishers, Printers, and Engravers: London, Provincial, Scottish, and Irish. From Queen Elizabeth's Reign to George the Fourth's.* (Repr., New York: Benjamin Blom, 1967.)
_____; and Martin Shaw. [1913.] *Songs of Britain.* London: Boosey & Co., n.d.
Kimball, Carol W. 1984. *The Poquonnock Bridge Story.* [Groton, Conn.]: Groton Public Library.
Kipling, Rudyard. "The Last Chanty." *The Seven Seas.* [London, 1896.] New York: D. Appleton. 1903.
Kjellströ m, Birgit. 1976. *Dragspel.* Stockholm: Sohlmans Forlag.
Knowles, Frederick Lawrence. 1905. *The Golden Treasury of American Songs and Lyrics.* Boston: L.C. Page & Co.
Knowlton, F. S. 1922. *Songs of Other Days.* Boston: Oliver Ditson.
Krassen, Miles. 1976. *O'Neill's Music of Ireland.* New York: Oak.
Krebiel, Henry Edward. 1914. *Afro-American Folksongs.* 3rd ed. New York: G. Schirmer.
Langley, Harold D. 1967. *Social Reform in the United States Navy, 1789-1862.* Urbanna: University of Illinois Press.
Laughton, L. G. Carr. 1920. ["Spanish Ladies."] *Mariners' Mirror,* 6:2 (Feb. 1920), 60.
_____. 1921. "H.M. Brigantine 'Dispatch' 1692-1712." *Mariners' Mirror,* 7:12 (Dec. 1921), p. 356.
_____. 1923. "Shanteying and Shanties" (2 parts). *Mariners' Mirror,* 9 (1923), 48-55, 66-74.
Lawrence, Vera Brodsky. 1975. *Music for Patriots, Politicians and Presidents.* New York: Macmillan.
Laws, G. Malcolm. 1957. *American Balladry from British Broadsides.* Publications of the American Folklore Society Bibliographical and Special Series, Vol. VIII. Philadelphia.
_____. [1950] 1964. *Native American Balladry.* (Publications of the American Folklore Society Bibliographical Series, Vol. I, "Revised Edition.") Philadelphia: American Folklore Society.
Leach, MacEdward. 1965. *Folk Ballads & Songs of the Lower Labrador Coast.* Ottawa: National Museum of Canada Bulletin N° 201, Anthropological Series N° 68.
Leavitt, Rev. Joshua, ed. [1830]. *The Seamen's Devotional Assistant and Mariners' Hymns.* New York: American Seamen's Friend Society. 1830 et seq.
Leisy, James. 1974. *The Good Times Song Book.* Nashville: Abingdon.
Leslie, C. E. 1888. *The Cyclone of Song.* Chicago: Chicago Music.
Levermore, Charles H. 1898. *The Abridged Academy Song Book, for Use in Schools and Colleges.* Boston: Ginn & Co. [1895].
Levy,Lester S. 1971. *Flashers of Merriment: A Century of Humorous Songs in America.* Norman:University of Oklahoma Press.
Leyda, Jay, ed. 1969. *The Melville Log.* Revised ed. 2 vols. New York: Gordian.
Lingenfelter, Richard E.; Richard A. Dwyer; and David Cohen. 1968. *Songs of the American West.* Berkeley and Los Angeles: University of California Press.
Linscott, Eloise Hubbard. 1939. *Folk Songs of Old New England.* New York: Macmillan. (Repr., Hamden: Archon/Shoe String, 1962.)
Little, Elizabeth A. 1994. "The Female Sailor on the *Christopher Mitchell:* Fact and Fantasy." *The American Neptune,* 54:4 (Fall), 252-258.
Lloyd, A. L. 1967. *Leviathan! Ballads and Songs of the Whaling Trade.* London: Topic. (Liner notes for Topic LP #12T174.)
Loesberg, John. 1981. *Folksongs and Ballads Popular in Ireland.* 3 vols. Cork: Ossian.
Logan, W.H. 1869. *Peddlar's Pack of Ballads and Songs.* Edinburgh: William Paterson.
Lomax, Alan. 1960. Folk Songs of North America. Garden City: Doubleday.
_____. 1968. *Folk Song Style and Culture.* Washington: American Association for the Advancement of Science, N° 88.
Lomax, John A. and Alan. 1938. *Cowboy Songs and Other Frontier Ballads.* New York: Macmillan.
_____; and Alan. 1968. *American Ballads and Folk Songs.* New York: Macmillan. [1934].
_____; and Alan. 1947. *Folk Song U.S.A.* New York: Duell, Sloan & Pearce.
Longfellow, Henry Wadsworth. "The Cumberland" (poem). James Barnes, Op. cit., p. 94.
Luce, Rear Admiral S[tephen] B. [1889]. *Navy Songs.* New York: W.A. Pond & Co. [1889, 1902, 1905].
Lund, Judith Navas. 1997. *Burials and Burial Places in the Town of Dartmouth, Massachusetts.* Dartmouth, Mass.: Dartmouth

Cemetery Commission and Dartmouth Historical Commission.

_____. 2000. *Whaling Masters.* Gloucester, Mass.: Ten Pound Island Books; New Bedford: New Bedford Whaling Museum; Sharon: The Kendall Whaling Museum.

Lynn, Frank. 1961. *Songs for Swingin' Housemothers.* San Francisco: Chandler.

Lyric Gems of Scotland. Glasgow: John Cameron. n.d.

M., A. ["Spanish Ladies."] *Mariners' Mirror,* 5:5 (November 1919), p. 160.

McCarthy, Tony. 1972. *Bawdy British Folk Songs.* London: Wolfe.

McCarthy, William. 1842. *[American National Song Book:] Songs, Odes, and Other Poems, on National Subjects... Part Second—Naval.* Philadelphia: William. McCarthy.

McCaskey, J. P., ed. 1881-91. *Franklin Square Song Collection.* 8 vols. New York: Harper.

McCullough, Ian (illustrator). 1992. *A Little Irish Songbook.* San Francisco: Chronicle Books.

McFarland, Philip. 1985. *Sea Dangers: The Affair of the Somers.* New York: Schoken.

Mackay, Charles. *One Thousand & One Gems of Song.* London: George Routledge & Sons, n.d.

_____, ed. [1877.] *The Songs of Scotland.* London: Boosey & Co., n.d.

Mackenzie, Alexander Slidell. 1843. *Case of the Somers Mutiny: Defense of Alexander Slidell Mackenzie, commander of the U.S. Brig Somers, before the court martial held at the Navy yard, Brooklyn, New York.* New York: Tribune Office.

Mackenzie, W. Roy. 1928. *Ballads and Sea Songs from Nova Scotia.* Cambridge: Harvard University Press. (Repr., Hatboro: Folklore Associates, 1963.)

Maddy, Joseph E.; and W. Otto Meissner. 1942. *All-American Song Book.* New York: Robbins Music Corp.

Malloy, Mary. 1983. "'Storm Along: An American Sea Anthology': A Manuscript by Joanna Carver Colcord in the Collection of the Peabody Museum." Stuart M. Frank, ed., *Proceedings, Fourth Annual Symposium on Traditional Music of the Sea* (Mystic: Mystic Seaport Museum), n.p.

_____. 1998. *"Boston Men" on the Northwest Coast: The American Maritime Fur Trade.* Kingston, Ontario and Fairbanks, Alaska: Limestone Press (University of Alaska Press).

Manny, Louise; and James Reginald Wilson. 1976. *Songs of Mirimichi.* Fredericton: Brunswick Press. [1968].

Marcuse, Sybil. 1975. *A Survey of Musical Instruments.* New York: Harper & Row.

Markham, Clements R. [1875.] *The Arctic Navy List; or A Century of Arctic & Antarctic Officers, 1773-1873.* Repr., Portsmouth: Royal Navy Museum, 1992.

Marryat, Captain F[rederick]. 1840. *Poor Jack.* London: n.p.

_____. 1852. *Complete Works.* New York: Richard Marsh.

_____. 1898. *The Sea King.* [London, circa 1840.] New York: F.M. Lupton.

Marsh, J. B. T. [1880]. *The Story of the Jubilee Singers with Their Songs.* Boston: Houghton, Osgood & Co., [1880] 1882.

Martin, Kenneth R. 1983. *Whalemen's Paintings and Drawings: Selections from the Kendall Whaling Museum Collection.* Sharon: The Kendall Whaling Museum; Newark: Univ. of Delaware Press; London and Toronto: Associated Univ. Press.

Masefield, John. 1906. *A Sailor's Garland.* New York: Macmillan.

Mayhew, Henry. 1851. *London Street-Folk.* (Volumes 1 and 2 of Henry Mayhew, *London Labour and the London Poor,* 4 vols., London: Charles Griffin & Co., 1851-64.)

Maynard's New Concertina Tutor and Budget of Popular Songs. London: R. Maynard. n.d.

Mead, John Halstead. 1973. *Sea Shanties and Fo'c'sle Songs, 1768-1906, in the G.W. Blunt White Library at Mystic Seaport.* Ph.D. thesis, University of Kentucky.

Meek, Bill, ed. 1978. *The Land of Libertie: Songs of the Irish in America.* Skerries (Ireland): Gilbert Dalton Ltd.

Meloney, William Brown. 1927. *The Chantey Man Sings.* New York: privately printed.

Melville, Herman. *Billy Budd.* Edited by Milton R. Stern. (The Library of Literature, John Henry Raleigh and Ian Watt, gen. eds.; Charles Feidelson, et al., eds.) Indianapolis: Bobbs-Merrill. 1975.

_____. *Billy Budd, Benito Cereno, and The Enchanted Islands.* Carl Van Doren, ed. New York: Readers Club. 1942.

_____. *Collected Writings.* Harrison Hayford, Herschel Parker, and G. Thomas Tanselle, eds. Evanston: Northwestern University Press and Newberry Library: Vol. I: *Typee* [1846], 1968. Vol. II: *Omoo* [1847], 1968. Vol. IV: *Redburn* [1849], 1969. Vol. V: *White-Jacket* [1850], 1970. Vol. VI: *Moby-Dick* [1851], 1988.

_____. *Four Short Novels.* New York: Bantam. [1959] 1971.

_____. *Moby-Dick.* [1851.] Edited by Harrison Hayford and Herschel Parker. New York: W. W. Norton, 1967.

_____. *Selected Tales and Poems.* Edited by Richard Chase. New York: Holt, Rinehart & Winston. [1950] 1968.

Meredith, John; and Hugh Anderson. 1985. *Folk Songs of Australia and the Men and Women Who Sang Them.* Kensington, N.S.W.: New South Wales University Press. [1967].

_____; Roger Covell; and Patricia Brown. 1987. *Folk Songs of Australia... Volume 2.* Kensington, N.S.W.: New South Wales University Press.

Miller, Pamela A. 1979. *And the Whale Is Ours: Creative Writing of American Whalemen.* Sharon: The Kendall Whaling Museum; Boston: David R. Godine.

Miller's New British Songster.... 1853. Edinburgh: J.M. Miller.

Minstrel Songs Old and New. 1882. Boston: Oliver Ditson & Co.

Moffat, Alfred. 1904. *The Humorous Song Folio.* London and Glasgow: Bayley & Ferguson; Boston: Oliver Ditson & Co.

_____; and Frank Kidson. 1901. *The Minstrelsy of England.* London and Glasgow: Bayley & Ferguson.

Molloy, J. L. [1873.] *The Songs of Ireland.* London: Boosey & Co. n.d.

Monaghan, Jay. 1951. *The Great Rascal: The Life and Adventures of Ned Buntline.* New York: Bonanza Books.

Moore, Ethel and Chauncey O. 1964. *Ballads and Folk Songs of the Southwest.* Norman: University of Oklahoma Press.

Moore, Frank. 1889. *The Civil War in Song and Story.* New York: P.F. Collier.

Moore, Thomas. 1852. *Moore's Irish Melodies.* Boston: Oliver Ditson & Co.

Morris, Alton C. 1950. *Folksongs of Florida.* Gainesville: University of Florida Press.

Morris, George P., ed. 1841. *American Melodies.* New York: Linen & Fennell.

Morrison, D. H. 1882. *Treasury of Song.* Philadelphia: Hubbard.
Morrison, D. H.; and Myron C. Whitney.. 1891. *New Treasury of Song.* Providence: W.W. Thompson & Co.
Moseley, Caroline. 1982. "'The Lass that Loves a Sailor': Images of Women in Songs of the Sea." Seventh Annual Whaling History Symposium, The Kendall Whaling Museum, October 1982. KNB archive.
Motherwell, William. 1827. *Minstrelsy: Ancient and Modern, with an historical introduction and notes.* Glasgow: John Wylie.
Nason, Rev. Elias. 1869. *A Monogram on Our National Song.* Albany: Joel Munsell.
Nation (Writers of *The Nation*). 1845. *The Spirit of the Nation: Ballads and Songs by the Writers of "The Nation.," with Original and Ancient Music.* Dublin: James Duffy. (Repr. Wilmington, Del.: Michael Glazier, Inc., 1981.)
Naval Songs. 1883. New York: Wm. Firth & Co.
Neatby, Leslie H. 1970. *The Search for Franklin.* New York: Walker & Co.
Neeser, Robert W., ed. 1938. *American Naval Songs & Ballads.* New Haven: Yale University Press.
Negro Singer's Own Book (The). Philadelphia and New York: Turner & Fisher, n.d. [circa 1845].
Neuberg, Victor. 1983. *The Popular Press Companion to Popular Literature.* Bowling Green [Ohio] State University Press.
New Song Book, Containing a Choice Collection of the Most Popular Songs, Glees, Choruses. Extravaganzas, &c. 1851. Hartford: S. Andrus & Son.
Nichols, Charles H. 1969. *Many Thousand Gone.* Bloomington: Indiana University Press.
Nicol, John. 1936. *The Life & Adventures of John Nicol, Mariner.* Alexander Laing, ed. New York & Toronto: Farrar & Rinehart.
Noble, G.C. *The Most Popular Plantation Songs.* [circa 1911]
[Nordhoff, Charles.] *The Boy's Own Sea Stories, Being the Adventures of a Sailor in the Navy, the Merchant Service, and On a Whaling Cruise. Narrated by Himself.* (The Family Gift Series.) London: Ward. Lock, & Co., n.d. [circa 1857].
_____. 1850. *The Merchant Vessel.* New York: Dodd, Mead.
_____. 1857. *Nine Years a Sailor.* Cincinnati: Moon, Wilstack, Keys & Co.
Odum, Howard W.; and Guy B. Johnson. 1925. *The Negro and His Songs.* Chapel Hill: University of North Carolina Press.
["An Old Salt."] 1876. "Whaling in the Crozets." Oliver Optic et al., *The Great Bonanza ... of Adventure and Discovery* (Boston: Lee & Shepard; New York: Lee, Shepard & Dillingham).
O'Keefe, Daniel D; and James N. Healy. 1979. *The First Book of Irish Ballads.* Cork: Mercier. [1955].
Olmsted, Francis Allyn. 1841. *Incidents of a Whaling Voyage.* New York: D. Appleton. (Repr., New York: Bell, 1969.)
O Lochlainn, Colm. 1939. *Irish Street Ballads.* Dublin: Sign of the Three Candles. (Repr., London: Pan, 1978.)
_____. 1965. *More Irish Street Ballads.* Dublin: Sign of the Three Candles. (Repr., London: Pan, 1978.)
One Thousand Fiddle Tunes. [1940]. Chicago: M.M. Cole. 1967.
O'Neill, Captain Francis. *O'Neill's Music of Ireland.* (*The Music of Ireland* [1903] and *The Dance Music of Ireland* [1907].) Bronx: Daniel Michael Collins. n.d.
_____. 1910. *Irish Folk Music, A Fascinating Hobby.* (Repr. Darby, Pa.: Norwood Editions, 1973.)
Ord, John. 1930. *The Bothy Songs and Ballads.* Paisley: Alexander Gardner.
O'Reilly, John Boyle. 1889. *The Poetry and Song of Ireland.* 2nd ed. New York: Gay Bros.
Page, N.C. 1907. *Irish Songs.* Boston: Oliver Ditson.
Palgrave, Francis T. 1906. *The Golden Treasury of Songs and Lyrics.* New York: Macmillan.
Palmer, Roy, ed. 1973. *The Valiant Sailor.* Cambridge: Cambridge University Press.
_____. 1979a. *A Ballad History of England,* London: B.T. Batsford Ltd.
_____, ed. 1979b. *Everyman's Book of English Country Songs.* London: J.M. Dent & Son. (Reissued as *English Country Songbook,* London and New York: Omnibus, 1986.)
_____, ed. 1986. *The Oxford Book of Sea Songs.* Oxford and New York: Oxford University Press.
Partridge, Eric. *A Dictionary of Slang and Unconventional English from the Fifteenth Century to the Present Day.* New York: Macmillan. 5th ed., 1961; 8th ed., edited by Paul Beale, 1984.
Paskman, Dailey; and Sigmund Spaeth. 1928. *Gentlemen, Be Seated.* Garden City: Doubleday, Doran & Co.
Peacock, Kenneth. 1965. *Songs of the Newfoundland Outports.* 3 vols. Ottawa: National Museum.
Pearsall, Ronald. 1972. *Victorian Sheet Music Covers.* Newton Abbot: David & Charles.
Perkins, W. O. 1868. *The Golden Robin.* Boston: Oliver Ditson & Co.
Perkins, W.O. and H.S. 1860. *The Nightingale.* Boston: Oliver Ditson & Co.
Perrin, W. G. 1823. "Notes on the Development of Bands in the Royal Navy" (8 parts). *Mariners' Mirror,* 9 (1923), pp. 2-10, 46-7, 78-83, 108-9, 147-8, 180-3, 202-8.
_____. 1921. ["Spanish Ladies."] *Mariners' Mirror,* 7:10 (October 1921), p. 318.
Peters, Harry B., ed. 1977. *Folk Songs Out of Wisconsin.* Madison: State Historical Society of Wisconsin.
Popular National Songster (The) ... 1845. Philadelphia: John B. Perry.
Post, Irving. 1987. "'My God, Captain, he's a... a Woman!': Hunting whales as George Weldon during the Civil War, Georgiana Leonard fooled them all." Sunday Standard-Times Magazine (New Bedford, Mass.), 18 Jan, 10-12.
Pulling, Christopher. 1952. *They Were Singing, and what they sang about.* London: George G. Harrap & Co.
Quid (The); or Tales of My Messmates. 1832. London: W. Strange.
Randolph, Vance. 1946-1950. *Ozark Folk Songs.* 4 vols. Columbia: Missouri State Historical Society.
Rees, Abraham, ed. *The Cyclopedia; or Universal Dictionary of Arts, Sciences, and Literature.* 41 vols. Philadelphia: Samuel F. Bradford and Murray, Fairman & Co. n.d [circa 1806-1820].
[Reese, William.] [1995.] *Special List: Music.* Bookseller's catalogue. New Haven: William Reese Co., n.d.
Rinder, Frank. *Naval Songs, and Other Songs and Ballads of Sea Life.* London: Walter Scott, Ltd. n.d [circa 1895].
Robbins, Charles H. 1899. *The Gam: Being a Group of Whaling Stories.* (Salem, Mass.: Newton & Gauss, 1913.)
Roche, Francis. 1912-27. *The Roche Collection of Traditional Irish Music.* 3 vols. (Repr., 3 vols. in 1; Cork: Ossian, 1982.).
Rosenberg, Bruce A. 1969. *The Folksongs of Virginia: A Checklist of the WPA Holdings, Alderman Library, University of Virginia.* Charlottesville: The University Press of Virginia.
Rushbook, Frank. 1961. *Fire Aboard.* New York: Simmons-Boardman.

Russell, W. Clark. 1883. *Sailors' Language.* London: Sampson Low, Marston, Searl & Rivington.
Sandburg, Carl. 1927. *The American Songbag.* New York: Harcourt, Brace & Co.
Sanger, William W., M.D. 1899. *The History of Prostitution: Its Extent, Causes and Effects Througout the World.* New York: Medical Publishing Co.
Scammon, Charles M. 1874. *The Marine Mammals of the North-western Coast of North America, Described and Illustrated: Together with an account of the American Whale Fishery.* San Francisco: John H. Carmany & Co.; New York: G.P. Putnam's Sons. (Repr., New York: Dover, 1968.)
Scarborough, Dorothy. 1925. *On the Trail of Negro Folk-Songs.* Cambridge: Harvard University Press.
_____. 1937. *A Song Catcher in the Southern Mountains: American Songs of British Ancestry.* New York: Columbia University Press.
Schinhan, Jan Philip, ed. 1957. *The Frank C. Brown Collection of North Carolina Folklore, Volume IV :The Music of the Ballads.* Durham, N.C.: Duke University Press.
_____, ed. 1962. *The Frank C. Brown Collection of North Carolina Folklore, Volume V :The Music of the Songs.* Durham, N.C.: Duke University Press.
Schnapper, Edith B., ed. 1957. *The British Union Catalogue of Early Music Printed before the year 1801: A Record of the holdings of over one hundred libraries throughout the British Isles.* 2 vols. London: Butterworth's Scientific Publications.
Schrader, Arthur F. 1982. "The Meandering Banks of the Dee." *New York Folklore,* 8:1-2 (Summer), 65-84.
Scottish Student's Song Book. [1891.] London and Glasgow: Bayley & Ferguson.
Seamen's Hymns and Devotional Assistant. 1859. New York: American Seamen's Friend Society.
Sears, Minnie Earl. 1966. *Song Index... and Supplement.* [Hamden]: Shoe String. (Repr. of H.W. Wilson Co., 1926 & 1934.)
Sharp, Cecil J. 1908-12. *Folk Songs of England.* 5 vols. London: Novello.
_____. 1914. *English Folk Chanteys.* London: Simpkin, Marshall / Schott.
_____. 1916. *One Hundred English Folksongs.* Boston: Oliver Ditson & Co. (Repr., New York: Dover, 1967.)
_____. 1932. *English Folk-Songs from the Southern Appalachians.* Edited by Maud Karpeles. 2 vols. London: Oxford University Press.
_____; & C.L. Marson. 1904-09. *Folk Songs from Somerset.* 5 vols. London: Novello.
Shay, Frank. 1927. *My Pious Friends and Drunken Companions.* New York: Macaulay Co. (Repr. New York: Dover, 1961.)
_____. 1928. *More Pious Friends and Drunken Companions.* New York: Macaulay Co. (Repr. New York: Dover, 1961.)
_____. 1936. *The Pious Friends and Drunken Companions.* New York: Macaulay Co. (Consolidated repr. of the 2 vols.)
_____. 1948. *American Sea Songs and Chanteys from the Days of Iron Men and Wooden Ships.* New York: W.W. Norton. (Revised and expanded from *Iron Men and Wooden Ships,* New York: Doubleday, Page & Co., 1924.)
Shower of Pearls (The): A Collection of the Most Beautiful Duets.... 1858. Boston: Oliver Ditson & Co.
Shuldham-Shaw, Patrick; Emily B. Lyle, and Peter A. Hall, eds., *The Greig-Duncan Folk Song Collection*, 8 Vols., Aberdeen: Aberdeen UP, 1987), vol. 3, #563.
Simpson, Claude M. 1966. *The British Broadside Ballad and Its Music.* New Brunswick: Rutgers University Press.
Singer's Companion (The). 1855. New York: Stringer & Townsend.
Singer's Gem (The). 1845. Philadelphia and New York: Turner & Fisher.
Smith, Benjamin E., ed. 1897. *Century Cyclopedia of Names* (*Century Dictionary,* Vol. 19). New York: Century, [1889; 1894].
Smith, C. Fox. 1927. *A Book of Shanties.* London: Methuen & Co.
Smith, George Barnett. 1881. *Illustrated British Ballads, Old and New.* 2 vols. London: Cassell, Petter, Galpin & Co.
Smith, Laura Alexandrine. 1888. *Music of the Waters.* London: Kegan Paul, Trench. (Repr., Detroit: Singing Tree, 1969.)
Smithyman, Kendrick. 1970. "Little Mohee." *New York Folklore Quarterly,* 25:4 (March), 64-70.
Songs of Ireland. 1890. Boston: Oliver Ditson.
Songster's Companion (The). 1815. Brattleboro: [n.p.]
Sonneck, Oscar G.T. 1909. *Report on "The Star Spangled Banner," "Hail Columbia," "America" and "Yankee Doodle."* Washington: Government Printing Office. (Repr., New York: Dover, 1972.)
_____. 1914. *"The Star Spangled Banner".* Washington: Library of Congress.
_____; and William Treat Upton. 1945. *A Bibliography of Early Secular American Music (18th Century).* Washington: Library of Congress.
Spaeth, Sigmund. 1926. *Reed 'em and Weep.* Garden City: Doubleday, Page.
_____. 1927. *Weep Some More, My Lady.* Garden City: Doubleday, Page.
Speaight, George, ed. 1975. *Bawdy Songs of the Early Music Hall.* Newton Abbot: David & Charles.
Spears, John R. 1908. *The Story of the New England Whalers.* New York: Macmillan.
Spinazze, Libera Martina. 1975. *Libera Martina Spinazze's Index to "The Argonauts of California [Charles Warren Haskins, compiler]."* New Orleans: Polyanthos.
Starbuck, Alexander. 1878. *History of the American Whale Fishery, from Its Earliest Inception to the Year 1876.* (Report of the U.S. Commission on Fish and Fisheries, Part IV, Washington, D.C., 1878.) Repr. 2 vols., preface by Stuart C. Sherman, New York: Argosy, 1964. Repr. 1 vol., Secaucus, N.J.: Crown, 1989.
Sternval, Sigurd. 1935. *Så ng Under Segel.* Stockholm: Bonniers Forlag.
Stimpson, George. 1946. *A Book About a Thousand Things.* New York and London: Harper & Bros.
Stowe, Phineas. *Ocean Melodies and Seamen's Companion.* Boston: Phineas Stowe. Fourth ed., 1852; twelfth ed., 1859.
Straus, Robert. 1950. *Medical Care for Seamen: The Origin of Public Medical Services in the United States.* New Haven: Yale University Press.
[Sturgis, William.] 1844. *The Cruise of the "Somers"; Illustrative of the Despotism of the Quarter Duck... with an Appendix Containing Three Letters by William Sturgis.* 3rd ed. New York [July 1844].
[Sumner, Charles.] 1844. "The Mutiny of the *Somers,*" *The North American Review,* 57 (July), 195-241.

Tawa, Nicholas E. 1980. *Sweet Songs for Gentle Americans: The Parlor Song in America, 1790-1860.* Bowling Green, Ohio: Bowling Green University Popular Press.
Taylor, Deems; John Tasker Howard; et al., eds. 1946. *A Treasury of Stephen Foster.* New York: Random House.
Taylor, Rev. Marshall W. 1888. *A Collection of Revival Hymns and Plantation Melodies.* Cincinnati: Marshall W. Taylor & W.C. Echols. [1882].
Taylor, Nathaniel W. [1929.] Life on a Whaler: Narrative of a Whaling Voyage from New London, Connecticut, August 18, 1851, to June 4, 1854. Howard Palmer, ed. New London: The New London County Historical Society.
Teghmeier, K. *Alte Seemansleider und Shanties.* Hamburg: Hauswedell. n.d.
Terry, Richard Runciman. 1921. *The Shanty Book.* 2 vols. London: J. Curwen.
Thomas, Jean. 1931. *Devil's Ditties: Being Stories of the Kentucky Mountain People with the Songs they Sing.* Chicago: W.W. Hatfield.
_____. 1939. *Ballad Makin' in the Mountains of Kentucky.* New York: Henry Holt & Co.
Thompson, Harold W. 1958. *A Pioneer Songster: Texts from the Stevens-Douglas Manuscript of Western New York, 1841-1856.* Ithaca, N.Y.: Cornell University Press.
[Thomson, G., ed.] 1802. *Select Collection of Original Scottish Airs.* 3 vols. London: T. Preston; Edinburgh: G. Thomson.
Tinsley, Jim Bob. 1981. *He Was Singin' This Song.* Orlando: University Presses of Florida.
Toll, Robert C. 1974. *Blacking Up: The Minstrel Show in Nineteenth-Century America.* London: Oxford University Press.
Tolman, Beth; and Ralph Page. 1937. *The Country Dance Book.* (The Country Series, [n.v.].) Guilford: Countryman Press.
Townley, John. 1989. "Music in the Confederate Navy." 10th Annual Symposium on Traditional Music of the Sea, Mystic Seaport Museum, 10 June.
_____. 1983. "The Songs of Charles Dibdin." Stuart M. Frank, ed., *Proceedings, Fourth Annual Symposium on Traditional Music of the Sea* (Mystic: Mystic Seaport Museum).
Trident Society. 1939. *The Book of Navy Songs.* Garden City: Doubleday, Page & Co.; Annapolis: U.S. Naval Institute. [1926].
Turner, Michael R. 1973. *The Parlor Song Book.* New York: Viking.
Tuttle, Charles R. 1885. *Our North Land.* Toronto: Robinson.
Universal Songster; or Museum of Mirth (The). 3 vols. London: George Routledge & Sons. n.d.
Van de Water, Frederic F. 1954. *The Captain Called It Mutiny.* New York: Ives Washburn.
Vaughan, Richard. 1984. "Whalers North of Melville Bay, 1818-1913." Ninth Annual Whaling Symposium, The Kendall Whaling Museum, 21 Oct. 1984 [KNB audiovisual archive].
Vaughan Williams, Ralph; and A.L. Lloyd. 1959. *The Penguin Book of English Folk-Songs.* Hammondsworth: Penguin.
Verrill, A. Hyatt. 1923. *The Real Story of the Whaler.* New York: D. Appleton. [1916].
Waite, Henry Russell. 1876. *Carmina Collegensa.* Boston: Oliver Ditson & Co. [1868].
Waller, J. F., ed. *Moore's Works.* London: William MacKenzie. n.d.
Walser, Robert J. 1982. *Sea Shanties and Sailors' Songs: A Preliminary Guide to Recordings in the Archive of Folk Culture.* Washington: Library of Congress.
Walton's New Treasury of Irish Songs and Ballads. 1966. 2 vols. Dublin: Walton's, Ltd.
Wannan, Bill. 1966. *The Heather in the South: Lore, Literature, and Balladry of the Scots in Australia.* Melbourne: Lansdowne.
Ward, John J. 1947. *Ward's Collection of Irish Comic Songs.* Chicago: Ward Music.
Warner, Anne. 1984. *Traditional American Folk Songs from the Anne & Frank Warner Collection.* Syracuse University Press.
Webb, Robert Lloyd. 1988. *On the Northwest: Commercial Whaling in the Pacific Northwest.* Vancouver: University of British Columbia Press.
Webster, George Sidney. 1936. *The American Seamen's Friend Society.* New York: American Seamen's Friend Society.
Webster's Biographical Dictionary. [1943]. Springfield, Mass.: Merriam, 1974.
Weibust, Knut. 1969. *Deep Sea Sailors.* Hardlingar: Nordiska Museets.
Whall, W. B. 1910 and 1927. *Sea Songs and Shanties.* Glasgow: Brown, Son & Ferguson.
White, B. F.; and E. J. King. 1860. *The Sacred Harp.* Philadelphia: S. Collins.
White, Newlan I. 1928. *American Negro Folk-Songs.* Cambridge: Harvard University Press.
White Star Journal (The). 1951. Mystic: Marine Historical Association.
Whitelaw, Alexander. 1875. *The Book of Scottish Song.* London: Blackie & Son.
Whittlesey, Walter R.; and Oscar G. Sonneck. 1915. *Catalogue of First Editions of Stephen C. Foster (1826-1864).* Washington: Library of Congress.
Whittier, John Greenleaf, ed. 1876. *Songs of Three Centuries.* Boston: James R. Osgood & Co.
Who's Who in New England. 1908. New York: Marquis.
Wier, Albert E., ed. 1909. *Songs that Will Live Forever.* New York: North American Music.
_____, ed. 1918. *The Book of a Thousand Songs.* New York: World Syndicate, 1918; Mumil, 1922.
_____, ed. 1929. *Songs of the Sunny South.* New York: Appleton, Century.
Wilbur, Curtis D.; and Dudley W. Knox, eds. 1927. *Official Records of the Union and Confederate Navies of the War of the Rebellion.* Several series in multiple vols. Washington: Navy Department.
Williams, Alfred. 1923. *Folk-Songs of the Upper Thames.* London: Duckworth & Co.
Williams, James H. 1959. *Blow the Man Down! A Yankee Seaman's Adventures Under Sail.* William F. Kuehl, ed. New York: E.P. Dutton.
Wilson, H. Lane. 1927. *Old English Melodies.* London: Boosey & Hawkes. [1899].
Wolf, Edwin, 2nd. 1963. *American Song Sheets, Slip Ballads, and Poetical Broadsides 1850-1870: A Catalogue of the Collection of the Library Company of Philadelphia.* Philadelphia: The Library Company of Philadelphia.
Wood, Thomas. 1927. *The Oxford Song Book.* 2 vols. London: Oxford University Press.
Work, John W. 1940. *American Negro Songs.* New York: Howell, Soskin & Co.

III. Informants

Andersen, Carl.† Retired sailor; senior rigger at Mystic Seaport Museum in the 1970s. Native of Denmark; until his retirement in the 1950s served before the mast and as sailmaker, rigger, and boatswain in square-riggers, later as an Able Seaman in steam.

Cohn, Ellen R. Editor, The Papers of Benjamin Franklin, Yale University. Native of New York, graduate of Wesleyan University, studied Scottish song with Jean Redpath, teacher of traditional song and dance for several societies and organizations.

Doerflinger, William Main.† Editor at E.P. Dutton in New York City; avocational music historian specializing in sea songs he collected from retirees at Sailors' Snug Harbor on Staten Island, N.Y.; author of *Shantymen and Shantyboys: Songs of the Sailor and Lumberman,* revised and expanded as *Songs of the Sailor and Lumberman.*

Evans, Vaughan.† Maritime historian. Born in England; served in the Royal Navy in World War II; afterwards employed at Lloyd's of London; co-founder of the Thames Shiplovers' Society; emigrated to Australia; co-founder and founding Secretary of the Australian Association for Maritime History; editor, *The Great Circle;* Medal of the Order of Australia 1988.

Herman, Mark.† Mamaroneck, New York. Collected and performed folk songs as a premedical student at Columbia University until his premature death.

Hugill, Stan.† "The last chanteyman on a British square-rigger." Raised in a nautical family in England; to sea in sail at an early age; served in steam and as a POW during World War II; diploma, London University Institute of Asian Languages; boatswain, Outward Bound sailing school, Aberdovey, Wales; author *Sailortown* and several seminal books on chanteys.

Huntington, Gale.† Folksong collector on Marthas Vineyard, originally from Florida; chronicler of Tilton Family song traditions on Marthas Vineyard, author-compiler of the flawed but useful *Songs the Whalemen Sang* and an unpublished sequel.

Killen, Louis. Folksinger. Native of Gateshead-on-Tyne, County Durham, England; heir to family singing traditions expanded through persistent contact with leading singers and folklorists, notably Bob Copper, A.L. Lloyd, Ewan MacColl, and Stan Hugill.

Kotta, Robert.† Curator of Education, Kendall Whaling Museum. San Francisco native of Irish, Italian, and Mexican ancestry; graduate Evergreen State College and Munson Institute of American Maritime Studies; folksinger and recording artist.

Lomax, Alan.† Folklorist. Son and collaborator of John Lomax; former archivist, Library of Congress; faculty, Hunter College; author/editor of numerous folksong articles and anthologies.

Malloy, Mary. Professor of Humanities, Sea Education Association, Woods Hole, Mass.; museum studies faculty, Harvard Universaity Raised in Spokane, Washington; B.A. in music, University of Washington; graduate, Munson Institute of American Maritime Studies; M.A., Boston College; M.A., Ph.D., Brown University; author of books, articles, exhibitions on the history of the maritime fur trade, Joanna Colcord, Herman Melville, whaling, and African Americans at sea.

Phillips, U. Utah. Folksinger from Spokane, Washington, specializing in American occupational and labor songs.

Ramsey, Buck.† Retired cowboy from Amarillo, Texas. Singer, poet, musician, raconteur; authority on cowboy songs and range ballads (Buffalo Bill Historical Center, Cody, Wyoming; Cowboy Hall of Fame, Oklahoma City; University of Texas, Austin; Western Music Association).

Stillman, Amy Ku'uleialoha. Anthropologist specializing in Native Hawaiian song; she was a Ph.D. candidate at Harvard and an Associate of the Peabody Museum of Salem, Mass., when consulted in 1984, and is currently Associate Professor of Music and American Culture at the University of Michigan.

Swiderski, Richard M. Professor of Anthropology, Bridgewater State College, Bridgewater, Mass. B.A., Princeton University; Ph.D., University of Chicago; specialist in magical songs of the sea, pirate songs, shipwreck songs.

Terkel, Studs.† American labor historian and media commentator in Chicago, specialist in labor practices and occupational mores.

Townley, John. Folksinger, astrologer, and editor, New York City and White Stone, Virginia. Former member of the sea chantey ensemble X Seamen's Institute; specialist in sea songs and ballads of the Confederacy and shipwreck songs.

Veldkamp, Albert. Master mariner and Schelde River harbor pilot in Vlissingen, Zeeland, The Netherlands; former first mate of the Dutch floating-factory whaleships *Willem Barentz* and *Willem Barentz* (II); captain of R/V *Plancius* on Arctic archaeological expeditions; organizer and director of the Scheldt harbor pilots' choir, Schelde Loodsenkoor

Warner, Jeff. Folksinger, folksong historian. Son of folksong collectors Frank and Anne Warner; raised on Long Island, N.Y., graduate of Duke University; perpetuated Warner family traditions as collector, performer, teacher, and editor; past President of the American Folk Song and Dance Society; editor, *Traditional American Folk Songs from the Anne & Frank Warner Collection.*

Webb, Robert Lloyd. Folksinger, folksong historian, performer. Former Research Associate, Kendall Whaling Museum; former Curator, Maine Maritime Museum. Native of Culver City, California; graduate of the California State University at Northridge; author of *On the Northwest* and numerous articles about whaling, folk songs, and musical instruments.

---

† Deceased

Glossary of Technical Terms

Able Bodied Seaman (A.B.S.) or **Able Seaman**: the highest rating of the common sailor of foremast hand. The navy, the merchant service, and the whale fishery depended upon their skill and experience in working and maintaining the ship, manning the boats, and training green hands,. See *Green Hand, Ordinary Seaman,* and *Boatheader.*

Air: informally, any singable tune or melody; formally, especially in Scottish and Irish tradition, a tune or melody specifically intended to be sung with words.

Articles (**Ship's Articles**): the official document that a sailor signs in engaging his services for a voyage. In the whale fishery it is commonly referred to as the Whalemen's Shipping List. If a recruit could not sign his own name (comparatively rare among native-born Americans; see *Journal*), he could "make his mark" before witnesses. The articles customarily identified the man by name, age, citizenship, place of residence, and station (rank); they might also specify physical features and birthplace, in the manner of a passport or *Seaman's Protection Paper* (q.v.).

Ballad: Without endeavoring to enter into or take a prejudicial position on the perpetual controversy surrounding this term, it is utilized here in its broadest traditional context, as a song that "tells a story." Almost since the era of Samuel Pepys, the celebrated diarist and Admiralty administrator who collected printed broadsides in 17th-century England, scholars have debated the definition, genesis, and dissemination of ballads in the British Isles and abroad. While the intricacies of such discussion may enlighten the studies of folklore, literature, and philology, they pertain only marginally to the exposition and exegesis of the ballads and ballad-like materials in this anthology. With respect to any controversial aspects of ballads, the songs in this anthology may be regarded as providing raw materials and additional data for further scrutiny by ballad specialists, rather than as positing any particular theory or hypothesis about the origins and cultural significance of balladry itself. See *Broadside Ballad.*

Broadside Ballad: a ballad (q.v.) of which the origins or provenance were (or are thought to have been, or have the appearance of having been) in print, typically in the form of so-called ballad-sheets, called *broadsides* from their having been printed on one side of a page. The medium was by no means limited to songs and ballads but included prose compositions, topical prose, and partisan polemic—like the ballads, often tending toward the sensational and lurid, the newsworthy and ephemeral. The genre refers to the means of printing and distribution more than to the contents, which were begged, borrowed, purchased, stolen, or written for the occasion, with or without accurate acknowledgement of the source; hence the quality varies considerably. In Tudor England, broadsides were set in a blackletter typeface and were frequently illustrated with woodcut vignettes; the latter were as often as not generic, interchangeable, and frequently recycled, often incongruously. In later times the typeface changed, but the manner of hackneyed and haphazard authorship, cheap printing, and hawking the products on urban street corners did not. Some of the earlier pieces, from Elizabethan times to the Restoration, are thought to be coeval with or descended directly from the canon of *English and Scottish Popular Ballads* established by Francis James Child (1882-98) and, in fact, provided Child some of his most fertile source materials. The latter-day broadside ballads are a related but distinct phenomenon, as described and classified by G. Malcolm Laws in *American Balladry from British Broadsides* (1957) and *Native American Balladry* (1964). Dating roughly from the last quarter of the 18th century, through the great colonial wars and the Napoleonic era, to the middle decades of the 19th century, they evolved contemporaneously with the Industrial Revolution in Britain and America. The literary (as opposed to folkloric) and even mercenary origins, comparatively late vintage, and commercial circulation of these ballads has stigmatized them as degraded and of lesser cultural and artistic value than the Child canon; however, the line between the two castes is perhaps not so clearly demarcated as Child's followers might have supposed; and, in any case, rather than the hoary ballads of Child's canon, it was the latter-day broadside ballads—with all their independent richness of sensational drama and hackneyed poetry—that captured the hearts of the common working people, especially sailors, from the late 18th century to the third quarter of the 19th.

Boatheader: In strict parlance anterior to the 1820s or so, the term usually referred specifically to the first mate of a whaling vessel, who was second in command of the ship and chief of manning and maintaining the whaleboats. By the third or fourth decade of the 19th century the term had come to refer to the officer in charge of each boat, i.e., any of the three or four mates. Thus, each whaleboat was manned by five men: a *boatheader* (the officer in charge); a *boatsteerer* (the harpooner, a petty officer second in command); and four *oarsmen* or *hands,* optimally including at least one *Able Bodied Seaman,* an *Ordinary Seaman* or two, and a *green hand* or two (see the various ratings). In the late 19th century the original meaning was informally revived in some vessels whaling in the Western Arctic;

Boatsteerer: the technically correct term for the *harpooner* or *harpooneer,* a petty officer upon whose judgment and skill wielding a harpoon the success of the hunt largely depended.

Gam: a term originating in the whale fishery, referring to a meeting of two or more vessels at sea, often including a visit by one captain and a boat's crew — or even virtually an entire ship's company — on board the other ship. It was a social occasion usually much welcomed by sailors, characterized by an exchange of news, mail, books, and, among the captains, intelligence about the whaling grounds and prospects for the hunt. By extension, it became nautical lingo for any casual chat; "to have a yarn." The grammar is flexible: such a meeting is a *gam*, sailors or ships can be said to *gam* or to *have a gam*, and thus to engage in *gamming*. As a verb, *to gam* can be either transitive ("we gammed the *Kathleen* for about three hours") or intransitive ("we gammed for about three hours").

Green Hand: a *greenhorn* or first-time sailor. See *Boatheader*.

Harpooner (harpooneer): see *Boatsteerer*.

Idlers: members of a whaleship's company whose specific functions are not sailorly, such as the cook, the steward, often the cooper, the carpenter, and, on some ships, the blacksmith, the sailmaker, and the ship's boy ("cabin boy"). These men did not customarily stand regular watches along with the rest of the crew, and stayed on board when the boats were lowered after whales: they were thus said to be *idle* when the "real" work of the ship was underway.

Journal: the private record of a voyage, typically kept in the form of daily entries, often in emulation of the official logbook (q.v.). Native-born American sailors in the 19th century were, on average, more literate and better schooled than is commonly supposed, and certainly more so than their British and immigrant counterparts. In fact, perhaps owing to the early introduction of compulsory education in New England and New York, a native-born *green hand* (q.v.) who could not sign *articles* (q.v.) and read at a common-school level was a rarity in the whale fishery and even in the New England merchant service. Especially on the whaling grounds, where there was ample after-hours leisure for private pursuits, and where the extreme youth of the crew (who typically ranged from early teen-age to around thirty) was combined with the Yankee work-ethic to make good and get ahead. Thus, the impetus to learn how to keep a proper journal (and thus apprentice in the art of keeping an official logbook), and the inclination to record the voyage in words—and to illustrate the experience with drawings, scrimshaw, poetry, and song—were strong. Soon after coming aboard a green hand could be inculcated in a shipboard culture devoted to literary and artistic pursuits of this kind.. It was therefore commonplace for there to be several men on board keeping regular journals, including the captain, officers, and crewmen of all ranks and stations. Occasionally, foreign-born sailors serving on Yankee ships kept journals in their native languages, most typically Portuguese or French. In all of these it was not uncommon for seamen to transcribe the words to songs and poems learned along the way, or to use their journals to write down their own original reflections in verse as well as in prose.

Logbook: the official record of a voyage as mandated by admiralty law, with legal standing as such in any lawsuit, consular action, or evidentiary proceeding that may ensue. Keeping the log was nominally the responsibility of the master (captain); aboard whalers it was often delegated to the chief mate; on merchantmen it was often the collaborative responsibility of master and supercargo (commercial supervisor and owners' representative); in the naval and merchant services generally, several of the officers might be involved. Standard data recorded included day-by-day accounts of the weather, the vessel's course and position (expressed as latitude and longitude), disposition of sails and rigging, vessels sighted (i.e., passed at a distance), vessels "spoken" (i.e., encountered and information exchanged), land sighted, landfalls made, ports visited, liberties granted ashore, provisions or cargoes taken on, provisions broken out, cargoes lost or sold, changes in personnel, and any unusual or noteworthy occurrences, such as altercations or transgressions among the crew, punishments, commendations, illness, and death. See *Journal*.

Melody: a singable tune or air (qq.v.).

Ordinary Seaman (O.S.): the journeyman rank of common sailor, generally achieved after a voyage or two; midway between *green hand* and *Able Bodied Seaman* (qq.v.). See *Boatheader*.

Protection Paper / Seaman's Protection Paper (Passport): In order to protect the citizenship of sailors from the new Republic calling at foreign ports, and to guard against British boarding parties claiming sovereignty, Congress in 1789 passed an act stipulating that each American sailor must carry a Protection Paper identifying him by name, age, birthplace or residence, and physical characteristics. These documents, issued by customs district authorities in various ports, are today invaluable sources of biographical, statistical, and demographic information.

Tune: informally, any melody or air; formally, especially in traditional music, a musical composition intended to be played for dancing or singing. As Francis James Child provided a canon of traditional English and Scottish popular ballads, and G. Malcolm Laws described a taxonomy of *broadside ballads* (q.v.) in North America, there are also canons and taxonomies of traditional tunes and airs, such as Captain Francis O'Neill's collection of Irish tunes and analogous collections of Scottish and American fiddle tunes and dance tunes.

Index of Songwriters, Lyricists, and Composers

The majority of the words and music are anonymous and undated. Known songwriters are listed alphabetically. The numbers refer to song numbers rather than to pages. Names in italics are whaleman- or sailor-lyricists (including wives and families of the mariners), as opposed to professional or vocational songwriters.

Arne, Thomas, 143
Ashley, George H., 37
Baker, Benjamin A., 114, 115
Baker, George A., 190
Balfe, Michael William, 207
Bayley, F.W.H., 201
Bayly, Thomas Haynes, 200
Bickerstaffe, Isaac, 143
Bishop, Henry Rowley, 138, 181
Bricher, Thomas, 202, 232
Bryant, Dan, 165
Bryant, Neil, 120
Carey, Hattie, 58
Chadwick, Matthew A., 28
Cherry, Andrew, 3
Coffin, Benjamin A., 154
Cook, Eliza, 203
Colman, George, 191
Cornwall, Barry, 190, 193
Covert, Bernard, 210
Cunningham, Allan, 192
Davy, John, 3, 191
Dibdin, Charles, 2, 213, 214, 215, 216, 217, 218
Dimond, William, 194
Dixon, George Washington, 165
Drake, Joseph Rodman, 203
Farrell, Bob, 165
Foster, Stephen Collins, 158, 175, 177, 182
Fox, H., 142
Gavan, Mr., 120
Gay, John, 1
Gallup, Franklin, 145, 224
Gilmore, Patrick Scarsfield, 212
Gorham, Joseph R., 42
Gould, Hannah Flagg, 30
Griffith, G.W.H., 173
H—, J—, 205, 206
Hanby, Benjamin Russell, 174
Hansell, John, 112
Hayward, H.W.D., 29
Hodson, George Alexander, 196
Hook, James, 185
Horton, D.P., 29
Howland, George W., 17
Hudson, Thomas, 111
Hughson, Robert N., 228
Hutchings, James W., 160
Johns, Captain, R.M., 190
King, Matthew Peter, 187
Kirby, Nicholas, Jr., 223
Knight, Joseph Philip, 197
Lawler, Mr., 141
Lee, George Alexander, 121, 200, 201, 209
Leveridge, Richard, 1
Lover, Samuel, 166
Lowe, John, 70
Lunt, George, 195
Meade, R.W., Sr., USN, 29
Merrill, Frederick, 35
Mills, George Edgar, 18, 132, 146, 158, 170
Moir, David Macbeth, 210
Morton, Thomas, 188
Neukomm, Sigismund von, 193
Osborne, John, 135
Parke, William Thomas, 183
Parry, John, 81, 161, 162
Pastor, Tony, 120
Payne, John Howard, 181
Pitt, William, R.N., 191
Pocock, Isaac, 189, 196
Power, Thomas, 199
Procter, Bryan Waller, 190, 193
Randall, James Ryder, 58
Reynolds, Richard C., 149, 150, 151, 152, 153, 221
Richter, Moritz, 30
Robinson, Mary Darby, 184
Rockwell, H.W., 202
Rogers, Benjamin F., 147
Russell, Frederick H., 17
Russell, Henry, 198, 204
Sanderson, James, 138
Sargent, Epes, 198
Sears, E.C., 60
Sharpe, R.S., 187
Shaw, Oliver, 30
Short, Bob, 15
Shuckburgh, Richard, 171
Sinclair, John, 125
Smith, Frederick Howland, 225
Spicer, William F., USN, 11
Stevens, George Alexander, 4
Stockwell, H.W., 202
Sullivan, John C., 161
Swain, Charles B., 12, 13, 174
Swift, R.G.N., 133, 230, 231
Thompson, H.S., 211
Turner, Joseph W., 108
Tyte, M., 27
Upton, W., 183
Vanlentine, John, 112
Waller, Sidney, 200, 201
Warde, W., 142
West, Benjamin L., 22
Wetmore, W.J., M.D., 202
White, Edward L., 195
White, John M., 204
Wiesenthal, T.V., M.D., 203
Williams, Barney, 27
Woodbury, Isaac Baker, 13, 194
Wooley, James H., 68

Index of Titles, Alternate Titles, First Lines, and Tunes

Listed alphabetically, excluding Appendices 5 and 6, where the songs are already inventoried alphabetically by title. Numbers refer to song numbers rather than page numbers.

Ah! Vous Derai-je, Maman, 176
All Around My Hat, 112
All around the room I waltzed with Ellen Taylor, 112
All hands on deck the boatswain he cries, 38
All in the Downs, 1
All the Whales Are Wild and Ugly, 158
The Alphabet Song, 44
The Alpine Horn, 199
An American frigate from Baltimore came, 51
The American Stranger, 99
Andrew Bardeen, 5
Arctic Whaling Song, 135
As Dick Turpin was riding o'er yon moor, 124
As down by yonder valley I happened for to stray, 23
As I walk'd forth one fine summer's morning, 103
As I walked out one May morning,, down by the river side, 100
As I walked out one evening all along by the ocean side, 89
As I walked out one evening of late, 91
As I walked out one fair days morning, 76
As I walked out one fine summer's morning, 76
As I walked out one May morning, down by the sea side… , 98
As I walked out one May morning down by the river side, 100
As I walked out one May morning my fortune for to seek, 107
As I was a roving and rambling for pleasure one day, 93
As I was a walking on South Street so wide, 162
As I was a walking one evening of late, 91
As I was out walking for pleasure one day, 93
As I was out walking one morning in May, 90
Augusta's Favorite, 176
The *Aurora*'s Whaling Song, 146
Away, Away o'er the Boundless Deep, 203
Away! Away We Bound o'er the Deep, 203
Away down upon the Swaney River, 182
The Baffled Knight, 139

The Banks of Dundee, 79
The Banks of Glencoe, 91
The Banks of Newfoundland, 36
The Banks of the Schuylkill, 21
The Banks of Sweet Dundee, 79
Barbary, 7
Bark *Kathleen,* 161, 162
Bark *Ohio* Outward Bound, 28
Bark *Roscius* Outward Bound, 28
Barney Buntline, 191
Bay of Biscay O, 3, 191
Behold the stately merchant ship, 219
Beidh Rí l Againn, 13
Beig Rinnce Againn, 13
Believe Me, Dearest Susan, 14
Betty Martin, 155
Black-Eyed Susan, 1
The Blacksmith, 24
Blow on, blow on, wild gale, 232
Blow Ye Winds, 139
The Boat Song, 138
The Boatswain's Alphabet, 44
The Boatswain's Call, 38
A Bold Brave Crew, 202
A bold brave crew on an ocean blue, 202
The Bold Fisherman, 100
The Bold Harpooner, 140
The Bold Privateer, 102
The Bold Soldier, 80
The *Bold Trinity,* 6
Bonaparte Crossing the Alps, 61
Bonaparte Crossing the Rhine, 61
Bonaparte on the Isle of St. Helena, 62
Bonaparte's Dream, 65
Boney he is gone from the wars of all fighting, 62
Boney's Defeat, 62
The Bonnet of Blue, 94
The Bonnie Ship the *Diamond,* 140
Bonny Bunch of Roses O, 63
The Bonny Scotch Lad, 96
Boston, 33
The Bosun's Alphabet, 44
Both young men and damsels that to love belong, 85
Bounding Billows, Cease Your Motion, 182
Bowhead Whaling Song, 157
Bright Phoebe, 75
Brightly the morning sun, 28
Brighton Camp, 9
The British Man-of-War, 23
The Brooklyn, 35
The Broom of Cowden Knowes, 160
The Buccaneer's Bride, 202
The Budgeon it is a delicate Trade, 143
By the border of the ocean one morning, 63
By the town of Ashthoir lived one Johnny Lanagen, 120
Caledonia, 31

Can Ladies Be Compared to Man?, 18
Cape Horn, 150
Captain Avery, 34
Captain Bunker, 140
The Captain Calls All Hands, 24
The Captain's Wife, 157
Caroline of Edinburgh Town, 109
The Carpenter and the Maid, 15
The Castaways, 85
Cease, Rude Boreas, 4
Charming Jane Louisa, 113
Cheer Up, My Lively Lads, 139
The Coast of High Barbary, 7
The Coast of Peru, 136
The Cobbler, 122
The Cobbler's Jig, 122
Cobit's Garden, 92
College Hornpipe, 111
Columbia's Ships, 53
Come all my jolly sailors, who ever you be, 152
Come all that's bald and all that's gray, 118
Come all ye young and jolly lads, come listen to my song, 145
Come all you bold Americans wherever you may be, 157
Come all you bold seamen that's bound round Cape Horn, 136
Come all you bold whalemen that plow the rough main, 161
Come all you fellows that has doubled Cape Horn, 136
Come all you gay young people and listen to my song, 84
Come all you jovial mariner men that ploughs the raging main, 32
Come all you jovial whalemen that leave your native home, 43
Come all you nice young girls, O if you did but know, 32
Come all you pretty fair maids that sports on Cupid's plain, 87
Come all you young and seamen bold, 67
Come all you young seamen with courage so bold, 34
Come all young maidens attend unto my rhyme, 109
Come and Listen to My Ditty, 4
Come lads and listen to me, 156
Come landlord fill the flowing bowl, 119
Come listen all ye sailors bold, 65
Come now, brother sailors, a warning take, 151
Come now my good fellows all, 39
Come ye lovely come ye fair one, 73
Coming Home from the Wake, 16
The Constant Farmer's Son, 82
The Constant Lovers, 85
The *Constitution* and the *Guerriere,* 52

The Cove Wot Spouts, 114
Covent Garden, 92
The Crocodile, 141, 142
Cuper's Garden, 92
Cupid's Garden, 92
Curiosity bore a young native of Erin, 66
The Dark-Eyed Sailor, 89
Dark-Eyed Susan, 1
Darling Nelly Gray, 174
Dear is the white rolling surges commotion, 129
Deep Blue Sea, 211
The Derby Ram, 139
The *Diamond,* 140
Dick Turpin, 124
Dick Turpin and the Lawyer, 124
Dick Turpin's Bonny Black Bess, 123
Diego's Bold Shores, 137
Doran's Ass, 127
Down by one murmuring river side, 69
Down by yonder ocean so carelessly I did stray, 23
The Down-East Maid, 75
A down in cobit's garden with pleasure I did go, 92
Dr Jayne's Hair Tonic, 118
A Dream, 19
A Dream of Napoleon, 65
The *Dreadnought,* 36
Dribbles of Brandy, 120
Drops of Brandy, 120
The Drummer Boy of Waterloo, 64
Early, Early in the Spring, 77
Early One Morning, 17
Edwin in the Lowlands Low, 83
Eighteen Hundred Forty-Nine, 37
Ellen Taylor, 112
Ellen the Fair, 95
Ere the twilight bat was flitting, 210
Erin's Green Shore, 90
Et Tu Bruce, 130
Ever be happy and light as thou art, 207
Fain Waterloo, 90
Fair Edith if you will be mine, 74
Fair Ellen one morn from her cottage had strayed, 95
The Fair Maid by the Sea Shore, 71
The Fair Maid's Lamentations, 104
Fair Phoebe and Her Dark-Eyed Sailor, 89
Famed Waterloo, 90
Fanny Elssler Leaving New Orleans, 178
Fanny, is you gwyne up de riber, 178
Far, far to the Arctic Ocean, 158
The far distant West, 13
Fare thee well! the ship is ready, 30
Fare Ye Well, 45
Fare you well and adieu to ye Spanish Ladies, 8

Fare you well my dearest dear since I must leave you, 24
Fare you well my own true love, 27
Farewell and Adieu, 8
Farewell, Charming Nancy, 25
Farewell Mother; Taylor calls me, 22
Farewell, My Dearest Nancy, 26
Farewell my own Mary Ann, 27
Farewell to father, blessed hulk, 29
Farewell to the Arctic, 228
The Farmer's Boy, 126
Father and I went down to camp, 171
The Female Cabin Boy, 86
The Female Smuggler, 88
Fine Time o' Day, 178
Finnigan's Wake, 127
The Fisherman, 197
Fisher's Hornpipe, 163
The Fisher's Wife, 197
The Flash Frigate, 36
The Flash Packet, 36
Florida's Crew, 59
The *Florida's* Cruise, 59
For the evening there is love, 144
Franklin's Crew, 67
From the West Indies Docks I bid adieu, 49
Frozen Limb, 17
Fuller and Warren, 53
Gaily we go o'er the salt blue sea, 226
The Galway Races, 128
Get Up Jack, Let John Sit Down, 49
The Girl I Left Behind Me, 9
The Girls Around Cape Horn, 35
Go Down Moses, 132
Go patter to lubbers and swabs, do you see, 214
Gold Rush Voyage Song, 37
The *Golden Vanity*, 6
The *Golden Willow Tree*, 6
Good News from Home, 212
Goodbye, Fare Ye Well, 45
The Great Meat Pie, 141, 142
Green Beds, 72
The Green Linnet, 66
The Green Mossy Banks of the Lea, 99
The *Green Willow Tree*, 6
The Greenland Whale Fishery, 134
Grog Time o' Day, 178
Gum Tree Canoe, 59
Hail to the Chief, 138
The Handsome Cabin Boy, 86
Harriet and Young William, 78
Harry Bluff when a boy left his friends and his home, 189
Harvest Home, 168
Harvest Home Waltz, 168
Has a love of adventure and a promise of gold, 137
Hawaiian Song, 144
He jumped into the boat as it lay upon the strand, 201

He Ploughed in the Lowlands Low, 83
He stood upon the hill to take a last fond look, 200
The Heart that Can Feel for Another, 183
Hearts of Gold, 32
Heave Away, 46
Henry Martin, 5
Here, a sheer hulk, lies poor Tom Bowling, 2
He Is Only Gone Home with a Friend, 117
He Only Gone with a Friend, 117
Hey, Betty Martin, 155
High Barbary, 7
The Hills of Chilia, 55
The Hills of Glenochry, 138
Home fare thee well the ocean storm is o'er, 209
A Home on the Mountain Wave, 202, 211
Home, Sweet Home, 181
The Homebound Whaleman, 232
Homeward Bound, 38, 41, 45, 49, 50
Homeward Bound and Outward Bound, 40, 49
How Cheery Are the Mariners, 220
How to Catch a Whale, 142
Hurrah for the Sea, 202
Hurrah! Hurrah! were homeward bound, 42
Hurrah my boys do you hear the news, 50
Hurrah my lads get under weigh, 38
Hushaby Benjamin, let the wind blow, 130
I am a cobbler brave, 122
I am going for to sing a song a song what happened the other night, 114
I Am One of the Boys, 115
I and Betty Martin, 155
I built my love a goodly ship, 19
I can no longer stop on shore, 134
I command a band a sturdy band, 205
I dreamed once a dream, a dream of home, 12
I dreamed that my love was sailing, 19
I have a ship in the North Countries, 6
I have been a wild rover these dozen long years, 121
I was born in a city, which I left with a free good will, 55
I Was Once a Sailor Lad, 160
If lubberly landsmen to gratitude strangers, 216
I'll tell you of a soldier who lately came from sea, 80
I'm a simple Irish lad, 128
I'm Afloat, I'm Afloat, 204

I'm lonesome since I crossed the hills, 9
In Chatham lived a merchant, 84
In eighteen-hundred forty-nine, 37
In London fair city it's known very well, 105
In New Bedford I got on a lark, 155
In Oxford city there lived a fair one, 110
In Scotland city there lived three brothers, 5
In slumber of midnight the sailor boy lay, 194
In storm when clouds obscure the sky, 185
In the city of London a rich merchant did dwell, 78
In the Louisiana Lowlands, 57
In the month of October on the twenty-second day, 149
The Indian Lass, 93
Indian Ocean Whaling Song, 156
The Indian's Lament, 13
The Island of St. Helena, 62
It happened on a certain day, 39
It is just one year ago today, that I remember well, 173
It is night and o'er the dark expanse, 14
It is of a pretty female, as you shall understand, 86
It is of a young sailor boy of courage stout and bold, 88
It oft times has been told that the British seamen bold, 52
It was down in yonder meadow where fearlessly did stray, 23
It was early, early all in the spring, 69
It was early, early in the spring, 77
It was early spring and the year was young, 68
It was in the pleasant month of May when the hills and fields were flowery, 113
It was of a rich nobleman's daughter, beautiful I am told, 79
It was of a shepherdess a feeding of her flock, 96
It was on a dark and stormy night, 54
It was on the briny ocean in a whaleship I did go, 154
It was the 14th of April, I remember well the day, 147
It was through the streets of Boston so carelessly I did stray, 101
It's Advertised in Boston, 139
It's of a comely young lady fair, 89
It's of a pretty fair maid, as you shall shortly hear, 79
Jack and the Whale, 141
Jack Munroe, 84
Jack Robinson, 111

Jack Steadfast and I were both messmates at sea, 183
Jack Tar, 73
Jack Went A-Sailing, 84
The Jacket of Blue, 94
Jamie's on the Stormy Sea, 210
Jayne's Hair Tonic, 118
The Jealous Young Man, 110
Jemmy on the Sea, 104
Jimmy and Nancy, 25Johnny Sands, 125
John Reilly, 194
Johnny the Sailor, 72
Johnny's Gone a Sailing, 84
Johnny's So Long at the Fair, 167
The Jolly Miller, 143
The Jolly Roving Tar, 101
The Jolly Sailor, 97
Jolly Sailors Bold, 32
Josephine's Lament, 66
The Joviall Cobbler, 32
The King of the Southern Sea, 229
Kingsfold, 53
The Knight and the Shepherd's Daughter, 96
The Lady and the Dragoon, 80
Lady Franklin's Lament, 67
A lady lived in London town, 97
The Lady of Greenwich, 97
The Lady of Lake Champlain, 10
The Lady of the Lake, 10
Landlord Fill the Flowing Bowl, 119
Landsmen One and All, 153
Lanigan's Ball, 120
Lashed to the Helm, 185
The Lass of Mohee, 93
The Lass that Loves a Sailor, 218
The Lay System, 152
Lazarus, 53
Leather Breeches, 180
Lee's Invasion of Maryland, 58
Let me go to my home, 13
Let My People Go, 132
Let swabs with their vows, their palaver, and lies, 217
The Life of a Tar, 208
A Life on the Ocean Wave, 198
The Lily of Lake Champlain, 10
The Lily of the Lake, 10
The Limejuice Ship, 145
Limerick Races, 128
Lines to Mary, 14
List, Ye Landsmen, 4
Listowel, 61
Little Mohee, 93
The Liverpool Landlady, 72
Lo as the sun from its ocean bed springing, 138
The Loss of the *Ramillies*, 39
Loud roared the dreadful thunder, 3
Louisiana Lowlands, 57
Low as the sun from its ocean bed rises, 138
The Lowlands of Holland, 19
MacDonald, 91

MacDonald's Return to Glencoe, 91
The Maid of Llangollen, 9
The Maid on the Shore, 71
The Maiden's Pride Punished, 74
The Maid's Lamentation for the Loss of Her True Love, 19
A man whose name was Johnny Sands, 125
The Mantle So Green, 90
The Mariner's Dream, 194
The Mariner's Song, 192, 226
Mary Ann, 27
The Mary Jane of Sunderland is under our lee, 140
Mary o' the Dee, 70
Mary of the Wild Moor, 108
Mary over the Wild Moor, 108
Maryland, My Maryland, 58
Mary's Dream, 70
Matrimony (lyrics to "Pop! Goes the Weasel"), 170
The Merchant's Daughter, 82
Mid pleasures and palaces, 181
The Milking Maid, 16
The Minute Gun at Sea, 187
The *Monitor* and the *Merrimac*, 57
The moon had climbed the highest hill, 70
The moon on the ocean was dimmed by a ripple, 218
The Mother and Daughter, 76
The Mother 's Daughter, 76
Murmuring Side, 69
My boy he was a sailor, he sailed away to sea, 46
My Boy Willie, 69
My Dream, 12
My Eye and Betty Martin, 155
My Jamie's on the Stormy Sea, 210
My Little Mohee, 93
My Love Nell, 53
My Love Willie, 69
My Lover's on the Stormy Sea, 210
My Mary Ann, 27
My name is David Williams, in Glasgow I was born, 31
My Wife, 13
The Nantucket Mother and Daughter, 20
Nantucket Song, 140
Nantucket Whaling Song, 32
Napoleon Crossing the Alps, 61
Napoleon in Exile, 62
Napoleon's Dream, 65
Nature and Nancy, 217
Navy Song, 60
Neath the shady forest trees by the silent river side, 174
Nell Flaherty's Drake, 180
Nelly Bly, 175
Nelly Gray, 174
The New York Trader, 37
No Ke Ano Ahiahi, 144
The Noble Duke, 87

The Norfolk Girls, 11
Now We Steer Our Course for Home, 41
O come all my young Seamen, who ever you be, 153
Oh, Dear, What Can the Matter Be?, 167
O I'm come for to go for to sing a song, 142
O Johnny was no sailor, 47
Oh my dearest Molly you and I must part, 102
O now we have doubled Cape Horn my boys, 150
O Rare Turpin, Hero, 124
Oh she was a milking maid so gay, 16
Oh! Susanna, 177
O the very first voyage I went to sea, 33
Oh! the whale is free, of the boundless sea, 229
O Think of the Sailor, 223
Off She Goes, 179
Old Folks at Home, 159, 182
Old Horse, 48
Old horse, old horse, what brought you here, 48
Old Leather Breeches, 180
The Old *Ramillies*, 39
Old Zip Coon, 165
On a Monday took shipping on tuesday set sail, 85
On Board of a Man-of-War, 23
On a Passage to the Crozet Islands, 149
On New Year's Day, 221
On the banks of the Schuylkill, 21
Once more we are waved by the Northern gale, 143
Once more with a favoring northern breeze, 143
One cold and frosty evening, 17
One day while sleeping, the other side of land, 230
One night came on a hurricane, 191
One night off Mobile the Yanks thought they knew, 59
One night sad and languid I went to my bed, 65
One night sad and languish'd I went to my bed, 65
One night when the winds they blew cold, 108
One of the Boys, 115
One Paddy Doyle lived in Killarney, 127
One Year in a Blubber Hunter, 145
Original Whaleman's Song, 137
Our Captain Cried, 24
Our orders came this morning, 20
Our topsail's reefed, 11
Our Way Across the Sea, 209
Outward Bound, 28
Outward Bound and Homeward Bound, 49, 50

Over the Mountain Wave, 195
Oxford City, 110
The Parson's Narrative, 133
The Parting, 196
Parting Moments, 26
Paul Jones's Victory, 51
The Pearl of the Sea, 129
The perils and dangers of the voyage are past, 111
Le Petit Tambour, 192
Phoebe, 75
Phoebe and Her Dark-Eyed Sailor, 89
The Pirate of the Isle, 205
Pirates' Chorus, 206
The Plains of Waterloo, 31
Poor Bessy was a sailors bride, 196
Poor Jack, 214
Poor Old Horse, 48
Poor Old Man, 48
The Poor Old Slave, 173
A poor sexton woman were longing to see, 117
Poor Tom, 2
Pop! Goes the Weasel, 170
Pretty Mohee, 93
Pretty Susan, 106
Pretty Susan, the Pride of Kildare, 106
The Pride of Glencoe, 91
The Pride of Kildare, 106
Prince Edward's Isle, 40
The Prince of Morocco, 88
The Pyeman's Trip to Bagshot Health Camp, 141, 142
The Rakish Young Fellow, 107
The *Ramillies*, 39
The Rare Old Whale, 227
The Rebel hordes by thousands came, 58
Red Haired Mary, 127
Red, White and Red, 59
Reuben Ranzo, 47
The Rich Merchant, 78
The Robbers of the Glen, 206
Rock-a-bye, Baby, 130
Rolling Down to Old Mohee, 143
Rory O'More, 166
Rounding the Horn, 35
The Rover of the Sea, 204
Rover Song, 204
Russian Waltz, 172
The Sailor, 218
The Sailor and His Bride, 68
The Sailor and the Country Girl, 73
The Sailor and the Shepherdess, 96
The Sailor and the Tailor, 105
The Sailor Boy, 69, 100, 186
The Sailor Boy's Bride, 68
The Sailor Boy's Carol, 199
The Sailor Boy's Dream, 194, 230
The Sailor Boy's Farewell, 29
The Sailor Boy's Last Dream, 194
The Sailor Boy's Trick, 88
The Sailor Bride's Lament, 68
The Sailor Deceived, 77

The Sailor Is a Wanderer Free, 222
The sailor loves a gallant ship, 186
The Sailor on the Ocean Wide, 225
Sailor Song, 202
The Sailor's Alphabet, 44
Sailors Ashore, 116
The Sailor's Bride, 68
Sailors' Come-All-Ye, 32
The Sailor's Consolation, 191
A Sailor's Dream, 67
The Sailor's Epitaph, 2
The Sailor's Farewell, 26
The Sailor's Grace, 48
A Sailor's Life, 69
The Sailor's Return, 98
The Sailor's Song, 32, 33, 116, 192
The Sailor's Tear, 201
A Sailor's Trade, 69
A sailors trade is a roving life, 69
A sailor's trade is a weary life, 69
Salt Horse, 48
Salt Sea, 5
Saturday Night at Sea, 186, 215
The Saucy Sailor, 73
The Saucy Sailor Boy, 73
The Schooner *Varnum Hill*, 147
The Sea, 193
The Sea Captain, 71
The Sea, the Sea, the Open Sea, 193
The sea was bright and the bark rode well, 190
The Sea Witch, 202
A seaman's life is the life I love, 227
She wanders by the ocean, 197
The Shepherdess, 96
The Ship Is Ready, 30
The Ship *Rambolee* [*Ramillies*], 39
A ship's crew of sailors as you now shall hear, 94
The ships from young Columbia's shore, 53
The Signal to Engage, 213
The Silk Merchant's Daughter, 85
The Sinking of the *Commodore*, 54
Sir John Franklin, 67
So be cheerful, my lads, let your hearts never fail, 140
Soldier's Joy, 169
The Soldier's Tear, 200
The *Somers*, 56
Song Composed aboard the Bark *Kathleen*, 162
A Song Concerning Love, 24
A Song of the Sea, 202
Song... to Captain S D Oliver, 158
Spanish Ladies, 8
The Spanish Lady, 127
A Sperm Whaling Song, 138
Stand stranger stand your jewels give me, 206
The Standing Toast, 218
Stanzas from the *Mermaid*, 148
The Star of the County Down, 53
Steady She Goes, 188

Steele, S.S., 59
The Storm, 4
A story, a story, a story of one, 72
The sun had gone down behind yon hill, 126
Swanee River, 182
Sweet America, 43
Sweet Home, 181
The sweet scented flowers from natures gay bowers, 115
The Sweet *Trinity*, 6
Sweet William, 69
Sweet William's Farewell... , 1
The Tarry Sailor, 73
Tarry Trousers, 76
The Test of Love, 85
There is a bark, a gallant bark, which lies in Boston Bay, 35
There is a flash packet, a packet of fame, 36
There is a flashy packet ship, and a ship of great fame, 36
There is as pretty a landscape as ever you did see, 10
There She Blows, 138
There was a farmer's daughter, so beautiful I'm told, 79
There was a girl in Warren town, 15
There was a rich merchant in London did dwell, 81
There was a rich old farmer near London town did dwell, 82
There was a young maiden all crossed in love, 71
There was two lofty ships I would have you understand, 7
There were three brothers, 5
There's a low green valley on the old Kentucky shore, 174
There's Changes in the Mill, 131
There's joy upon the sparklin' sea, 199
There's need of all the patience that to us all was given, 131
They advertised in Boston, New York, and Buffalo, 139
They sailed away in a schooner, you know, 133
This is the beginning of the year, 221
Though lonely my cot and poor be my estate, 9
The Three Brothers, 5
The Thresher and the Squire, 53
'Tis advertised in Boston, New York, and Buffalo, 139
'Tis of a comely young lady fair, 89
To an ebbing tide, all sail apeak, 159
To St. Catherine's Docks we will bid adieu, 49
Tom-Big-Bee River, 59
Tom Bowling, 2
The True British Sailor, 189

The True Yankee Sailor, 189
Turkey in the Straw, 165
Turpin and His Bonny Black Bess, 123
Turpin and the Lawyer, 124
Turpin's Valour, 124
'Twas a bright summers morning as I roved along, 104
'Twas down in Cupid's [Cuper's; Cobit's] Garden, 92
'Twas early in the month of May, 75
'Twas in eighteen hundred forty one, 134
'Twas in the storm on Albion's coast, 187
'Twas in the year 1848, 40
'Twas just one year ago to day, that I remember well, 173
'Twas on a certain day, 39
'Twas on the twenty-first of May, 33
'Twas Saturday night, the twinkling stars, 215
Twinkle, Twinkle, Little Star, 176
Two fine ships from England did sail, 7
Undaunted Mary, 79
Unmooring, 38
Vilikins and His Dinah, 81, 161, 162
A Voyage on New Holland, 161
The Watchet Sailor, 105
We are bound for the land of the glorious and brave, 228
We are home ward bound, we cannot stay, 45
We came round Cape Horn, boys, to capture sperm whales, 146
We can no longer stay on shore, 134
We ride head to wind, 60
The Wealthy Merchant, 84
Welcome, Brother Debtor, 4
We'll Soon Be There, 42
We're All Bound to Go, 46
We're Bounding o'er the Dark Blue Sea, 224
West's Farewell, 22
A Wet Sheet and a Flowing Sea, 192
Whale Song, 229
The whale was off at a furious pace, 231
The Whaleman's Lament, 154
Whalemen's Song, 128
The Whalemen's Wives, 32
The Whalers' Song, 135
Whaling Song, 135, 136, 137, 138, 140, 155, 156, 157
What Can the Matter Be? 167
When battle roused each warlike band, 64
When first from sea I landed, 106
When first I arrived in this country, 99

When first in this country I landed, 99
When fortune's blind goddess forsook my abode, 123
When Israel was in Egypt's land, 132
When spring returns with western gales, 135
The White Cockade, 87, 164
White Man, Let Me Go, 13
The White Squall, 190
Who Cares?, 216
Widow's Daughter, 76
The Wild Rover, 121
William and Harriet, 78
William O'Reilly, 90
William O'Riley, 90
William Riley, 103
William the Sailor, 104
William's Farewell..., 1
Willie's on the Dark Blue Sea, 211
A wish to thee dearest from over the sea, 13
The wished for day at last has come, 41
The Wonderful Crocodile, 141, 142
The Wonderful Whale, 141, 142
Wonders, or The Whale, 141
Wood and Black-Skin, 231
Woodland Mary, 64
The world gets wiser every day, 18
The Wounded Whale, 138
The Wreck Off Scilly, 32
Yankee Doodle, 171
The Yankee Man-of-War, 23
The Yankee tar no danger knows, 188
Ye gentlemen of England, 3
Ye tars of Columbia come listen to my song, 57
Yes I was once a sailor lad, 160
You seamen bold that have withstood, 67
Young Edmon Bold, 83
Young Edwin, 83
Young Johnny, 72
The Young Prince of Spain, 88
The Young Sailor Boy, 80, 88
Zip Coon, 165

Right: Scrimshaw corset busk engraved anonymously on sperm whale panbone (jawbone) by the whaleman-artist known only as the Banknote Engraver, circa the 1830s. Kendall Collection, New Bedford Whaling Museum.

AUTHOR'S VITA

Stuart M. Frank is Senior Curator of the New Bedford Whaling Museum in New Bedford, Massachusetts, the Founder and Director of the Scrimshaw Forensics Laboratory®, and Director Emeritus of the Kendall Institute and Kendall Whaling Museum. He originated the Sea Music program and annual Music of the Sea Symposium at Mystic Seaport and is the author of *Herman Melville's Picture Gallery, Dictionary of Scrimshaw Artists, More Scrimshaw Artists, The Book of Pirate Songs, Sea Chanteys and Sailors' Songs: An Introduction for Singers and Performers and Guide for Teachers, Songs of the Polly 1795,* and numerous articles and monographs about nautical art, history, literature, and music, as well as forthcoming catalogues of Dutch Old Master paintings and scrimshaw in the New Bedford Whaling Museum, and the forthcoming books *Scrimshaw and Provenance* and *"The Wealth of Seven Shores": Japanese Woodblock Prints of Whales and Whaling*. A native of New York City, he holds a B.A. from Wesleyan University, an M.A.R. from Yale University, diplomas from the Munson Institute of Maritime Studies, and an M.A. and Ph.D. in American Civilization from Brown University, where his dissertation was *Ballads and Songs of the Whale-Hunters 1825-1895*. Dr. Frank has been Research Associate at Mystic Seaport, Artist-in-Residence and Scholar-in-Residence at the Virginia Museum of Fine Arts, President of the Council of American Maritime Museums, served on the Secretary of the Interior's Advisory Committee on Maritime Heritage, the executive board of the International Congress of Maritime Museums and the editorial boards of the *International Journal of Maritime History* and *The American Neptune*; he was awarded the John Lyman Prize for his *Dictionary of Scrimshaw Artists*, and has been an American Friends of Canada Fellow, Australian Bicentennial Fellow, Lowell Lecturer in Boston, Vaughan Evans Memorial Lecturer in Western Australia, and a Visiting Fellow at the Prins Hendrik Maritime Museum in Rotterdam and the Nederlands Scheepvaartmuseum in Amsterdam. With his wife, Dr. Mary Malloy, he has performed traditional sea songs, cowboy songs, and occupational music across the USA, Canada, Europe, Australia, and Japan.

www.ingramcontent.com/pod-product-compliance
Lightning Source LLC
Chambersburg PA
CBHW080719300426
44114CB00019B/2429